People, Politics & Government

Political Science: A Canadian Perspective

Third Edition

James John Guy

PRENTICE HALL CANADA INC.
SCARBOROUGH, ONTARIO

To my wife Patti, my daughter Katha, and my son Trevor

Copyright 1995 Prentice-Hall Canada Inc.,
Scarborough, Ontario

Prentice-Hall, Inc., Englewood Cliffs, New Jersey
Prentice-Hall International (UK) Limited, London
Prentice-Hall of Australia, Pty. Limited, Sydney
Prentice-Hall Hispanoamericana, S.A., Mexico City
Prentice-Hall of India Private Limited, New Delhi
Prentice-Hall of Japan, Inc., Tokyo
Simon & Schuster Asia Private Limited, Singapore
Editora Prentice-Hall do Brasil, Ltda., Rio de Janeiro

Canadian Cataloguing in Publication Data
Guy, James John, 1943–
      People, politics & government : political science :
a Canadian perspective

3rd ed.
ISBN 0-13-206350-6

1. Political science. 2. Canada – Politics and government. I. Title.

JA66.G88 1994   jC813'.54   C94-931300-9
PZ7.I22Ei 1995

Printed and bound in Canada

1 2 3 4 5   99 98 97 96 95

CREDITS

Title page: Denis Drever, National Capital Commission
Ch. 1:   Buston/Canapress
Ch. 2:   Julio Etchart/Reportage
Ch. 3:   Canapress
Ch. 4:   Hanson/Canapress
Ch. 5:   Ministry of Citizenship and Immigration
Ch. 6:   Embassy of Ireland
Ch. 7:   National Archives
Ch. 8:   Revenue Canada
Ch. 9:   Supreme Court of Canada
Ch. 10: Canapress
Ch. 11: McKenna/Canapress
Ch. 12: Canapress
Ch. 13: Hanson/Canapress
Ch. 14: Keith Gosse/*St. John's Evening Telegram*
Ch. 15: Canapress
Ch. 16: Virginia Boyd for CPAR

p. 114: Brian Gable, *Globe and Mail*
p. 340: Brian Gable, *Globe and Mail*
p. 430: Cameron Cardow, *Regina Leader-Post*
p. 491: Mike Constable
p. 557: Bob Krieger, *The Province,* Vancouver

Editor: Jane A. Clark
Design and Typesetting: Goodness Graphics
Illustrations: Goodness Graphics
Production Co-ordinator: Stephanie Cox

Cover design: Richard Peachey, Goodness Graphics
Cover sculpture: "Totem," by Doug DeLind

For information on this or related Prentice-Hall titles,
please contact:
Pat Ferrier, Acquisitions Editor
Dawn du Quesnay, Developmental Editor

CONTENTS

Preface xv
Acknowledgements xviii

1 *What is Politics?*

2
What is Political Science?

3
Contemporary Political Ideologies

4

Nations, States, Rank, and Power

5
Government

6
Executives

7

Legislatures

8

The Administration of Government

9

Law and the Judiciary

10
Constitutions and Constitutionalism

11
Political Parties and Pressure Groups

12

Elections and Electoral Systems

13

The International System

14

International Law

15

Diplomacy

16

Toward the Next Millennium:
The Challenges

Appendix A

The Canadian Charter of Rights and Freedoms 595

Appendix B

Index

Tables

Figures

Preface

The publication of the third edition of *People, Politics, & Government, Political Science: A Canadian Perspective* testifies to the very positive response this book has received from the Canadian academic community. So many professors and students at universities and colleges in every province have been generous in accepting the first two editions of this book. Their many searching questions, helpful suggestions, and encouraging comments have led me to write this third edition, which I know readers will find very different from its predecessors.

As with the first two editions, the purpose of this textbook is to help Canadians begin to study political science in its focus on the world of politics and government. It is written in simple language in order to make the facts plain and the ideas clear. It offers a basic framework for learning about politics and governments at home and abroad; like a box of tools, it is to be used rather than exhibited. Beyond that, I wanted to show the student that political science is a discipline with both a history and a contemporary vitality, and that it is especially relevant for Canadians. Through the extensive use of Canadian examples and through a focus on Canadian political processes and issues, the original goal remains to make political science come alive for the reader. The fundamental objective, as in previous editions, is still to make the text a tool students will use to help them understand their place in a rapidly changing national and international society.

There is no better experience than revising a political science textbook to remind one of the astonishing pace of change that has taken place since 1990 within Canada and the international arena. While the challenges are considerable, such a writing enterprise must take into account not only the landmark transformations in Canada, but also those transpiring in the rest of the world that ultimately affect everyone here.

The changing forces that now affect Canadians in this dynamic international community make political science and understanding politics more important than ever. As we rush towards the beginning of the twenty-first century, the emergence of a new global economy, the impact of technology and communications, and the sweeping changes affecting all of Canada's governments bring new challenges and new issues into our daily lives.

In 1990, the unravelling of Europe's greatest communist empire progressed at lightning speed, leading to the dramatic extinction of the Soviet Union and some of its East-European allies. These momentous events put an abrupt end to the bipolar Cold War period. We saw the destruction of the Berlin Wall, and within months, the reunification of Germany. In the Middle East, Canada, the United States, and other forces in an international coalition fought a short but decisive war against Iraq in the Persian Gulf. As the Cold War fades from our collective memories, the Middle East remains a tinderbox, and the dangerous cross-currents of conflict and antagonism in the area could once again draw Canadians into the brush fires of world politics.

The drive for democracy in much of the

world, the prominence of a dynamic group of successful economies in Asia and the Pacific Rim, the intractable poverty of Africa, and the prospect of ecological collapse are challenging the world we have come to know. The world's agenda, once dominated by security issues, is now crowded and confused, with economic, ecological, and human rights issues occupying a much more central place.

At home, the Free Trade Agreement (FTA) and the North American Free Trade Agreement (NAFTA) placed Canadian managers and workers in a complex sea of continental economics. The old paradigms of economic production and distribution had shifted the sands under everyone's job. The changing political complexion of the provinces began to reflect the ambivalent moods of everyone in the country. And in the aftermath of the failed Meech Lake and Charlottetown Accords, the massive debt burdens of the federal and provincial governments, the unprecedented unemployment levels, and the need to reconcile native land claims, Canadians began to assess with much uncertainty the future of their beleaguered political system. In the face of angry and determined separatists in Québec, many public doubts have been expressed about whether Canada can still be the federation it struggles to be in the twenty-first century. Thus, this new edition of the book shows that Canada's political system — like most others — is under pressure from within, that its ability to cope with the problems it faces is being questioned by many individuals and groups in our society.

All of these swift currents and shifts in political power are charted in this revised edition. Most of the organizational format of the earlier editions of this book has been retained

by the universal acclamation of the adopters. But this third edition has been thoroughly and extensively revised not only to reflect the most recent kaleidoscopic events, but to focus as well on the broader trends and newer interpretations of the Canadian political system. The goal is not just to update its contents but to make it an even better book — introducing clarity, if it is lacking, and expanding the coverage of subjects that have become more politically relevant, or of more interest to the discipline, in the past few years.

Many new features and topics are incorporated into this edition. Changes have been made in all chapters with new as well as updated tables, charts, and figures. Every paragraph has been improved in some manner; either in style, content, or both. Among the changes are the addition of new sections that present, among others, such topics as the New Europe, the global economy, the new arms race, the challenge of AIDS, the GATT and NAFTA, and the sources of ideologies. A new **Appendix** for political science students has been added that features the work of political scientists and an explanation of research methodology. There are also several new **Profiles,** including those of a political scientist, UN Ambassador, and Supreme Court justice. The latest election results in Canada, the U.S., and other significant states are presented, along with updated events and statistics. The new edition contains special analysis of constitutional change and impasse in Canada. The book covers significant new Supreme Court of Canada decisions dealing with abortion, euthanasia, and many other important Charter issues.

As in previous editions, the book offers the essential "nuts and bolts" about the various systems of government from a comparative perspective. But we also want our students to understand why and sometimes how these important features have evolved, their impact on government and individuals, and why some are controversial and worth investigating.

In revising this book for a third edition, I set three goals. First, I believe that a textbook should be lively and stimulating to read, so I have attempted to re-write the text to be as clear and readable as possible for the uninitiated student, without sacrificing scholarship or content. Second, I have attempted to place Canadian politics and government in the context of global affairs by using the comparative political science approach. Canada is not a political island in the world of international politics. Students must see the influences of all the other forces in the international system on their country and on their lives. Thus, the comparative nature of the text is a vital teaching and learning tool. Third, I have attempted to show our students that politics and government are the products of themselves, reflecting how they think and behave in the complex political network that is called Canada. At the same time, the book emphasizes the importance of each person to the quality of Canadian government and politics.

Improvements to the design and pedagogy of the text enhance its attractiveness for students and adopters alike. The book's authoritative cover design gives it new appeal. The typeface has been changed to make the book more attractive as well as more readable, and the elegant new design of the chapter openers, text, and special features increase the "user-friendliness" of this edition. Many figures and charts incorporate interesting and appealing graphics that effectively present the data. The use of less formal headings and many new subheadings throughout the book adds much to the physical appeal of learning about political science. In addition, new headings on the top of every right-hand page facilitate the location of a particular section by indicating the major topic being covered on that page; the headings on the left provide the chapter number and title. **Chapter Objectives** at the beginning of each chapter inform users of what information that chapter provides and in what order it appears. Each chapter includes a **Glossary** of relevant terms presented in alphabetical order for ease of use. The expanded glossaries also feature a number of useful terms that may not be specific to political science, which are featured in special "call-outs" – boxes appearing in the text adjacent to each of these terms. Some concepts also are highlighted within each chapter in the section heads and subheads, which have been designed to outline a particular argument and to aid students in reviewing the material. **References** are updated and new **Suggested Readings,** appearing at the end of each chapter, will direct students to complementary sources of information that will enrich and expand upon the concepts covered. Finally, the **Index** has been completely revised and honed, with the addition of many new subject headings and cross-references to help readers trace the different aspects of terms.

All of these improvements have been designed to present the information as effectively as possible and to do the job of engaging the interests of prospective political scientists as they explore this relevant, vital, and fascinating field.

Acknowledgements

So many wonderful people contributed to the publication of this third edition. At the University College of Cape Breton, my special gratitude goes to our new president, Dr. Jackie Scott, who made possible the sabbatical that provided me with the block of time to write the book. Drs. Bill Clemens and Robert Morgan enabled me to successfully complete much of the research. Dean David White kept me abreast of the latest computer programs so that my work could be submitted in state-of-the-art fashion to the publisher. My dear colleague Dr. Mohini Gupta again read the manuscript in its entirety and gave much knowledgeable advice and encouragement. Two new colleagues, Drs. David Johnson and Brian Howe, made extensive comments and offered many new ideas concerning improvements to the book and its content.

Our head librarian, Penny Marshall, was magically able to find the most obscure research items on very short notice, and another skilful librarian, Mary Dobson, traced the answers to many editorial questions in the final stages of production. A special thank-you goes to Carol Ann Sheppard for all her work on the bibliography and end notes. Ainslie White answered my computer questions and did many of the initial computer graphics for the book's charts and figures. Sandy McNabb and Evo Dipeiro tackled many of my picky questions and helped me to secure interviews with Ambassadors Chrétien and Frechette. My thanks, too, to Margaret Macleod for typing sections of the manuscript, and to Brian Doue for helping to make sure that it arrived safely at the publisher's.

In Maxwell Macmillan's College Division, Frank Burns expressed his persistent confidence in the new edition, and furnished the human resources necessary to produce it, while Eileen Mathewson kept our adopters well informed on its progress.

We were fortunate to have the book reviewed by four eminent Canadian political scientists, who deserve an added thanks: Dr. John H. Redekop of Wilfrid Laurier University, Dr. Jene M. Porter of the University of Saskatchewan, Dr. T. J. Derksen of Red River Community College, and Dr. Elliot Tepper of Carleton University. Their thoughtful comments and criticisms resulted in many improvements to the manuscript.

A special favour assigned the resourceful assistance of Jane Clark as the project's editor. She guided the book through all of its phases: the reviewing, editing, artwork, design, and production. Without her many personal and professional skills, not the least of which was her abundant sense of humour, this writing task would have been much more difficult. My warmest thanks are also extended to Liba Berry for her excellent copy-editing and proofreading. I marvelled at her hawk-eyed precision and perceptive observations.

The attractive cover and design features are the creative enterprise of Richard Peachey and Christine Higdon of Goodness Graphics, whose work was skilfully co-ordinated by Stephanie Cox. And finally, the mighty research energies of Shannon Berseth were unleashed in the final hours before publication to track down the very latest available statistics.

Finally, thanks to my wife Patti, who continued to apply her psychiatric counselling skills to an incurable client — me!

People, Politics & Government

ONE

What is Politics?

Chapter Objectives

After reading this chapter, you will be able to:

- define the concept of politics and relate it to government
- think about politics as something personal as well as public
- understand politics as a product of culture, values, human conflict, and co-operation
- recognize how politics varies around the world
- identify the roles politics play in nation-building
- understand how we learn about politics, as children, adolescents, and adults
- recognize the agents of political learning in society
- differentiate how we learn political information from how we express our political opinions
- present the properties of political opinions and learn how they can be measured
- think about whether our political opinions really influence governments and other groups in the political system

What is Politics?

All of us have some idea of what politics is. Headlines abound with political information from different societies around the world: "Canada's National Debt Could Reach A Trillion By 2000"; "AIDS Virus Threatens Global Depopulation"; "China – The Next Super-power." Today's headlines make very clear the complex political relationships that take place in all societies. Every society is an organized community of individuals and groups who aspire to achieve a distinctive social order and survival. **Politics** is the means by which they create and strive to maintain this order.

Many political scientists and political activists have defined politics in an attempt to provide an understanding of the political world. David Easton sees politics as a "process by which values are **authoritatively** allocated in society."[1] Harold Lasswell referred to politics simply as "who gets what, when and how."[2] Lenin, the great Bolshevik revolutionary, saw politics as "who does what to whom,"[3] and Mao Tse Tung, China's greatest communist leader, defined it as "bloodless war."[4] Chancellor Bismarck of Prussia asserted that politics was the art of getting things done. He defined politics as "the doctrine of the possible, the attainable."[5]

In all of this there is much room for disagreement. The world does not consist of a political reality that everyone sees in exactly the same way. This is because politics is highly complex social behaviour driven by different ways of thinking, living, and governing ourselves. Many political scientists try to understand politics using Aristotle's premise that we are basically political animals – not just from force of habit but because otherwise we could not survive. Politics is central to how human beings relate to one another and adapt to the world around them.

On a *social level*, this includes the most fundamental and enduring forces that influence the political and governmental system: the family structure, the ways people conduct themselves, what goods and services they produce, the social movements and structures they create, and the outstanding cultural characteristics in the population. The *political level* includes the political culture, political opinion, political parties, interest and pressure groups, and the mass media. The *governmental level* includes the constitutional rules of the game, the institutions, and the officials that have the formal legal responsibilities for making public policy (figure 1.1).

In Canada, politics is seen as both an **institutional** and **behavioural** phenomenon. For example, Professor John Redekop defines it this way:

"Politics, then, refers to all activity whose main purpose is one or more of the following: to reshape or influence governmental structures or processes; to influence or replace governmental office-holders; to influence the formation of public policies; to influence the implementation of public policies; to generate public awareness of, and response to,

> ■ ■ **authoritative:** the characteristic of a person, group, institution, or government which makes legitimate either in reality or in appearance the acts and commands exercised in its name. ■ ■

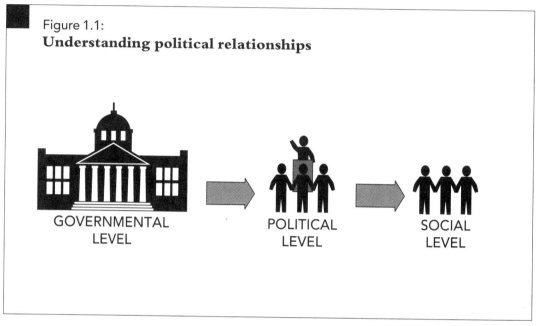

Figure 1.1:
Understanding political relationships

GOVERNMENTAL
LEVEL

POLITICAL
LEVEL

SOCIAL
LEVEL

governmental institutions, processes, personnel and policies; or to gain a place of influence or power within government."[6]

Institutions are excellent places to start looking for politics, but we should be prepared to discover political elements at other levels of human interaction. Politics is a recognizable characteristic of people acting towards, responding to, and influencing one another in the public milieu. It may manifest itself as group demands for more money, order, or justice in a society. One person may feel that voting for a particular party or candidate in an election will bring job security and a higher standard of living. Another will complain that there is too much government intervention in society and will support a party that advocates reducing bureaucratic regulation. A women's organization might pressure a provincial government to censor pornographic materials in sex shops, and organized labour may lobby cabinet ministers to create more jobs.

These actions are examples of traditional political behaviour. But less traditional activities are just as political in their social effect as are voting, supporting a party, or lobbying: for example, boycotting companies that pollute the environment; crossing or not crossing picket lines; or joining a group of citizens that takes legal action against a company using dangerous chemicals to spray forests near populated areas. All of these activities involve people in the political structures of their society. Political activities of these kinds are inextricably linked to the pursuit and balance of private and social interests.

Politics as Behaviour

Some social scientists have pointed out that politics is a natural result of people interacting with their environment.[7] A number of important theoretical studies have identified the two primary dimensions of political behaviour as the psychological and the social.

Psychological Basis

From the psychological perspective, political behaviour appears as thought, perception, judgement, attitudes, and beliefs. The psychological basis of politics is also seen in the constructs of personality, expectations, and motivations that explain individual and group responses to environmental stimuli. For example, some studies point out that leaders are more likely to possess certain personality characteristics to a higher degree than do followers.[8] Leaders are found to demonstrate a higher rate of energy output, alertness, originality, personal motivation, self-confidence, decisiveness, knowledge, and fluency of speech than do followers. The psychological dimension of politics underlies how we package and sell issues and candidates. In most countries, modern election-campaign strategies apply advanced propaganda and entertainment techniques to gather crowds for rallies and to influence voter behaviour. Images and issues can be carefully crafted to appeal to the widest possible range of voters. The psychological manipulation of voter preferences today is built into the campaign strategies of most candidates for public office.

Social Basis

The social basis of politics is found in actions such as voting, protesting, campaigning, lobbying, and caucusing. In the broadest social sense, behaviour with political consequence may be observed in any institutional or behavioural setting. It is often revealed as ag-gression, co-operation, compromise, negotiation, posturing, decisiveness, assertiveness, dominance, and virtually any human strategy that leads to decisions that have social impact. In short, political behaviour is both the essence and form of politics.

What better place to witness these two dimensions of political behaviour than at leadership conventions? Not only are the candidates for the leadership of political parties presenting their ideas in formal speeches to the delegates who attend, but many other examples of political behaviour are also evident. At such events enthusiasm is high and the opening ceremonies become contests to see which camp has the strongest lungs. There are not only vocal battles for attention: posters, banners, and placards bounce up and down in eager hands, balloons float through the arena, and hats and T-shirts sporting different alliances weave through the convention hall.

Much of the wheeling and dealing for the votes of the delegates goes on during the convention festivities. Some of the best political sideshows take place around the activities of these conventions. When the delegates arrive, the candidates are waiting with all of the paraphernalia that has become so much a part of selecting political leaders in Canada. Hotel lobbies fill with booths plastered with pictures of the candidates. Campaign buttons appear everywhere and there seems to be an endless flow of food, beer, and liquor. Bars open early and close late. The methods may vary from political party to political party, but the candidates' goals remain the same: to get and keep each delegate's vote. At all leadership conventions candidates woo delegates with food, fireworks, music, and giant screens flashing well-known faces. In some instances, teary-eyed orators, lavishing praise, introduce their candidates with appeals to the emotions of the delegates. Campaign strategists make sure that support for their candidates appears on placards at every corner of the convention floor. Whom candidates talk to, look at, and walk toward all become psychologically dynamic gestures in the process of selecting a political leader.

For the candidates themselves, image, win-ability, and what pundits call "the sizzle factor" supersede the issues raised and the policies debated by the party intelligentsia. The ultimate test that demonstrates the leadership qualities of a candidate is the test of his or her individual character. Character shows itself as the respect candidates display towards the delegates and the coolness and grace they display under fire.

For candidates, the pressures of politics are enormous. They have just completed exhausting campaign tours around the country. They have invested themselves, their time, and their money. As tension builds on the floor of the convention hall, their emotions become quite raw. At the Conservative Leadership Convention in 1993, the first ballot gave Kim Campbell 48 percent of the vote, compared with 39 percent for second-place Jean Charest. Etched in the minds of television viewers is the moment following this announcement, when leadership candidate James Edwards stunned the convention by walking across the floor to Kim Campbell. Charest's organizers were thunderstruck: we saw Charest sag; we saw his people sag. No one exaggerated the stress and intensities of the emotions involved. When all was said and done, issues were of secondary importance. Most of the undecided delegates seemed drawn to the gleam and sparkle of the candidate they thought looked like a Canadian prime minister.

Party conventions are ideal places to witness the psychological and social determinants of political behaviour, because we can see how the environment sets the stage for political action and that politics as a form of behaviour cuts across many levels of social conduct. Imitation, frivolity, faddism, mimicry, and emotion are as fundamental to political behaviour as are decision-making, elections, authority, and consensus.

Politics as Culture

The Elements of Political Culture

We could think of a **political culture** as the accumulation of beliefs, customs, expectations, attitudes, traditions, skills, symbols, and values in a given political system (figure 1.2). All these components are products of a society's political experience from its remote and recent past. They are inputs into the political environment of a society in its quest to survive and to maintain social order. Because every society has a unique past, every political culture is unique, and many nation-states (such as Canada and the United States) even experience different political subcultures flourishing within them. Although a great variety of political cultures exist throughout the international system, each reflecting distinctive qualities, certain components are found in all of the ways of conducting politics:

■ *Political customs* are conventional and accepted practices that may be recognized as a functional part of the political system and may be reinforced through the legal actions

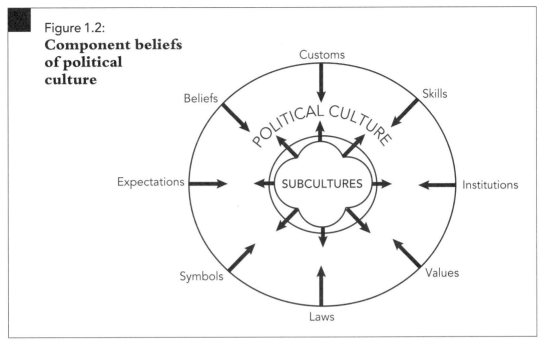

Figure 1.2:
**Component beliefs
of political
culture**

of the state, e.g., when a cabinet minister resigns because of inappropriate behaviour or because he or she cannot subscribe to the policies of the government.

■ *Political beliefs* are deeply held convictions about political reality that are based on one or more fundamental assumptions about human behaviour, e.g., that humans are basically selfish and governments should legislate and enforce the sharing of resources in a complex society.

■ *Political expectations* are assertions about what people believe ought to happen in the political world, e.g., that governments should not engage in **patronage**.

■ *Political symbols* are entities that represent something else, e.g., the maple leaf is a symbol of Canada.

■ *Political attitudes* are learned predispositions that relate to political issues, events, personalities, and institutions in either a favourable or unfavourable manner and usually in a consistent or characteristic way.

■ *Political values* are attitudes and standards of judgement about what things are important, desirable, and right, e.g., most Canadians consider it desirable and proper for people to pursue their own goals and interests as individuals under the law.

■ *Political traditions* are customs made legitimate by long and continued practice, e.g., the tradition of appointing Canadians to the post of governor general began in 1952, when another tradition began, that of alternating the appointment of English-speaking and French-speaking Canadians to that office.

- *Political skills* consist of the application of knowledge, procedures, strategies, and tactics for achieving desired social goals, e.g., lobbying, negotiating.

Political Cultures Differ

There are many different political cultures. In each one, people share similar ideals, similar procedures of government, and similar patterns of political behaviour that are learned and passed on from generation to generation. We are all very much part of our own political culture and we identify with it to distinguish ourselves from other political cultures.

Gabriel Almond was the first political scientist to bring to our attention the link between political behaviour and the wider phenomenon of transmitting political knowledge from the past into the present. For Almond, "every political system is embedded in a particular pattern of orientations to political action."[9] Once established, a political system tends informally to generate its own support mechanisms within a society. These usually take the form of certain norms and values that are regarded as virtues and recognized by succeeding generations of political actors. For example, candidates to Canada's Parliament have learned that legislators must be loyal to their party positions – because the survival of the parliamentary system requires it. But south of the border, different values are adopted by novice members of Congress. In the United States, the expectation is that representatives will usually act independently, and will advance the interests of their constituency before those of the party.

Samuel Beer and Adam Ulam theorized that a political culture transmits to people "how government ought to be conducted and what it should try to do."[10] The all-encompassing nature of culture is what prompts people to expect certain qualities and values in political behaviour and to behave politically the way they do. For example, in Canada and in the United States, most people believe that their constitution, as the basic law of the land, will last indefinitely and be amended only from time to time. But in the 20 Latin American republics, where there have been more than 200 written constitutions since 1810, people have come to expect that constitutions can be whimsically abandoned by any government that gains power. This is in line with what Sidney Verba contends about political culture: that it is a "system of beliefs about patterns of political interaction and political institutions."[11]

The Qualities of Political Culture

We can identify three general qualities of political culture. First, there is widespread awareness of the rules and structures of the political system. Canadians are generally conscious of the presence of Parliament and how it operates as a political and law-making institution. The formal and informal political relationships of politicians are generally understood and centre around this institution in most cases, most of the time. Second, politics and the political system are widely accepted. Not only are people committed to the *roles* and *functions* of political institutions, but they usually comply with the laws and regulations the system produces. Compliance is the invisible glue of any political system; without it, the political and social fabric of nation-states would fall apart. In Canada, most people believe that Parliament is a legitimate government institution: People respect its procedures and generally comply with the laws it generates.

Sometimes politicians violate the cultural expectations of a political system: In 1993, Québec Progressive Conservative MP Maurice Tremblay was fined $12,000 because he gave office expense money to a number of his constituents to pay for trips to Acapulco. And in 1994, Toronto Liberal MP Jag Bhaduria was forced to leave the Liberal caucus after he had severely threatened Toronto school board authorities and later falsely claimed he held a law degree.

Finally, the third element of a political culture is the expectation of certain behaviour within the political system. People are sensitive to the growth and size of government as an encroachment on their lives. They hold government accountable for its actions and deem certain behaviour appropriate or inappropriate for political actors.

Because of size and ethnic composition, many nation-states contain more than one political culture. Usually in multi-ethnic and multinational states (which contain a number of linguistic and ethnic minorities), there are distinctive regional political cultures or political subcultures that constitute the political system. A regional political culture has been defined as "a set of values, beliefs, and attitudes which residents of a region share and which, to a great or lesser extent, differentiate them from the residents of other regions."[12]

Many Political Cultures

Steven Ullman observes that while a homogeneous political culture is detectable across a wide range of Canadian political behaviour, regional political cultures can also be identified. In some instances, political cultures appear along provincial boundaries, as well as in regions that may consist of one or more provinces. One soon discovers that a Cape Breton coal miner, a Montreal taxi driver, a Saskatchewan wheat farmer, an Alberta oil executive, and a student at the University of Victoria do not share the same political values and beliefs about Canada's political destiny.

In the Canadian political culture, a majority of people hold in common certain fundamental attitudes and beliefs regarding the role of Parliament, the ethical behaviour of politicians and bureaucrats, and the legitimacy of national legislation and certain governmental programs, such as unemployment insurance and medicare. But one would also find basic differences in the attitudes and values of Albertans and Maritimers over the extent to which provincial and federal governments should be actively engaged in the economy. Richard Simeon and David Elkins have explained the presence of regional subcultures in Canada by pointing to the many differences in the historical and economic development of various parts of Canada.[13] Indeed, Canada is divided by its economics and politics and united perhaps only by its media and a national communications system.

All political cultures, whether national or regional, nurture symbols with which people identify. A *political symbol* is a meaningful object that represents some shared value or goal of a community of people. Thus the Canadian flag, which is a rectangular, multi-coloured piece of cloth, represents "the true North strong and free," democracy, justice, and other values. Canadians have come to make a psychological association between the flag as an object and the values it represents.

The significance of the flag is much greater than its physical appearance. Similarly, the House of Commons, which is little more than an ornate building on a large lawn, has come to stand for the majesty, prestige, and authority of Canadian government and politics. All Canadians understand that the House of Commons is a shorthand reference for their national law-making institution. Everyone makes the association between the terms and their meaning; everyone shares the symbol as part of the political culture. Symbols direct our political actions and provide cultural expectations for our behaviour and preferences; they bind us as a group and unite our loyalties.

Another aspect of political culture is the *political style* of a society. Every political system develops its own characteristic style of politics that reflects its people's historical experiences, traditions, and values. We have in Canada a highly competitive, open political system that invites the voluntary participation of people who want pragmatic solutions to social problems. Domestically, Canada has achieved a high degree of bargaining, compromise, and negotiation in the area of interprovincial and federal politics. The intensities of political competition are high at all levels of the Canadian political system.[14] This has made politics in Canada a healthy exercise for both the citizen and the professional politician.

South of the Rio Grande exists an exciting world of unique political cultures. Here we discover the politics of *continualismo, imposición,* and *personalismo.* **Continualismo** has been widely practised throughout Latin America. It is a strategy to keep an executive or junta in office beyond the terms and limits set by the constitution. The methods usually involve changing the constitution so as to le-

gitimize the continuation of an individual or group of individuals in power. By changing the constitution of Nicaragua, Anastasio Somoza Sr., who took office in 1937, extended his term of office in l939, and served to 1948; he then returned to office in 1950 and served until his assassination in 1956. In Argentina, Juan Perón changed a 100-year-old constitutional provision against re-election and won re-election in 1951.

Imposición is similar in style to continualismo, but involves tampering with the election process rather than the constitution. A government may rig the election, restrict party competition, ban certain parties, or control the media during the campaign. From 1964 until it withdrew from politics in 1985, the military government in Brazil had imposed an artificial two-party system on voters and guaranteed the success of a military president by controlling the electoral college.

Another Latin American political style is found in the phenomenon of **personalismo.** Politicians project strong features of their personalities to attract popular support. People are encouraged to show allegiance and loyalty to a political leader because of his or her personal charisma and mystique rather than to the institutions of government or the rules of the political system. The attractiveness of a leader's personality is the primary means for mobilizing mass support and centralizing political authority in the hands of one person. José María Velasco Ibarra, the five-time president of Ecuador over a thirty-eight-year period beginning in 1933, was so sure of his ability to gain public support from the force of his personality that he was quoted as saying, "Give me a balcony anywhere in the world and I will get elected."

It is necessary to know that politics as culture is an important way of understanding the uniqueness of every political system. Our political culture is a looking glass through which we observe and judge other political cultures. We must constantly be aware of how our own values affect our political evaluations of the other people who make up the international system. We must learn that our views of national unity, honesty in government, regular and peaceful succession of political leadership, and economic growth are not shared by all people. We must also learn that elements of Canada's political culture may be inconsistent with one another and not shared equally among all social groups.

Politics as Values

The Power of Strong Beliefs

Sociologists tell us that all societies are made up of groups that share certain values. Within groups, values are widely believed to be desirable for their own sake and are used as standards to judge the behaviour of others. Values reveal themselves as human preferences and priorities, as beliefs about duty, about right and wrong, and about what ought to be done in certain situations. Seymour Lipset found that Canadians tend to value authority more than do Americans.[15] For him, Canadians are more law-abiding and more inclined to recognize the authority of the police than are Americans. By comparison, Americans value personal freedom so highly, they tend to resist regulations and are more likely to feel hostile to authority figures.

Political values are shared beliefs that provide standards for judging human thought and action. They may be viewed as pressures that motivate social behaviour within a political culture. Politics results from the interplay of values among individuals and groups pursuing different goals for their own benefit. Within every society or among societies, politics is the **process** of competition and co-operation by which values gain priority.

These priority values are authoritatively allocated by the political system in order to legitimize their binding effect on the lives of the majority of people. One value that has become an integral part of the fabric of Canadian society is political *equality*. Because of this, various groups have fought for the authoritative allocation of equal treatment in Canada. For example, by the 1990s, Canadian women had celebrated over 70 years of being recognized as "persons" under the British North American Act. In 1920, Judge Emily Murphy, Nellie McClung, and three other women from Alberta successfully took legal action that affirmed that Canadian women should not be classed with "lunatics and children" as people who were not responsible for their actions. Similarly, the federal government granted Canadian native peoples full citizenship only in 1960. It was 1967 before a Supreme Court order struck down the prohibition that natives were not legally entitled to drink alcohol. And in 1989, the Canadian Human Rights Commission ordered the Armed Forces to open all combat roles to women. The point is that a belief in equality held by a majority of Canadians does not mean that this standard has been applied in practice to all groups in Canada.

Values in a society provide people with a way of judging whether they are satisfied or dissatisfied with the distribution of social rewards that flow from community expectations.

Politics is the process that settles claims people make on their political system so that they feel part of the same set of shared social values.

We can identify a number of important values that generate politics and that are pursued by people in most societies. In varying degrees, people make demands on the institutions of society and thus engage in political behaviour in pursuit of these values.

Politics and the Pursuit of Power

Lord Acton made the now-famous remark that "Power tends to corrupt, and absolute power corrupts absolutely." Power is the currency of all political behaviour and it weaves its way into every area of human interaction. People want to experience power and are fascinated by those who appear to be in positions of influence. They have a natural curiosity about the political impact of people like K.C. Irving and Ken Thomson, two of Canada's seven known billionaires, or about the methods and tactics used by cabinet ministers in managing the Canadian government.

In Canada, power and political institutions are intimately related. As a value, however, Canadians prefer to think of power not in coercive terms but rather as authority that is granted by consent. In other words, rulers must be recognized as having the right to control the behaviour of other people.

Power and authority do not come from personal characteristics or from the office held, but are often vested in persons whom Canadians have traditionally considered rightful leaders. However, the real basis of institutional power in Canada is derived from legal and procedural authority. This authority is granted by the position; it is not in the person.

The rights, privileges, obligations, and power come with the office. When an individual leaves that office, the next person to occupy it is granted the same rights and obligations.

When in an office of power, a person is expected to behave in accordance with certain values and standards of conduct. In 1994, Intergovernmental Affairs Minister Marcel Masse was forced to apologize to the House of Commons for his inappropriate use of the costly Challenger Jet, which he used (at an estimated cost of $173,000) to travel to two U.S. speaking engagements. He was reported to have violated the rigorous new standards set by Prime Minister Jean Chrétien for public office-holders and government officials.

At first glance, power appears to be only an institutional or governmental phenomenon. However, in reality, power is more properly understood as a relationship among individuals, groups, and societies. In this regard Robert Dahl sees power as "the capacity to change the probability of outcomes,"[16] and Karl Deutsch sees it as "the ability to make things happen that would not have happened otherwise."[17] For both men, power involves access to a position of regulation and control where decisions can be made concerning the thoughts, feelings, and behaviour of others and oneself. All people desire to expand their capacity to gain and share power and they demand these opportunities from their political system.

Politics and the Pursuit of Wealth

Wealth has been a political issue since the dawn of time. It enables people to satisfy their material needs, individually and collectively, in society. But invariably wealth leads to the exercise of political power. The political nature of wealth has always revolved around its possession, use, and distribution in a society. All political systems are sharply affected by the internal divisions of income and wealth. Wealthy economies like those of Canada and Europe have more equitable income distributions than poorer countries such as Tanzania and Mexico. The association of **industrialization** and wealth has been significant historically and tends to be significant today. The global inequalities of wealth seen in most pre-industrial societies are the primary causes of the political instability of many developing states. It is a reason often used to explain the susceptibility of poorer societies to radical ideologies and egalitarian political movements.

> ■ ■ **poverty line:** an amount of money determined by the government to be the least amount required to meet the cost of living (accommodation, food, clothes, transportation, etc.) in the economy. ■ ■

By 1990, Canada's net worth was just over two trillion dollars – nearly $100,000 for each Canadian if the country were liquidated and the wealth divided equally among its 27 million people. This national balance sheet calculated by Statistics Canada includes tangible assets – houses, durable consumer goods, business and government buildings and equipment, land, and money owed to individuals, businesses, and governments – totalling $4.6 trillion. When financial liabilities amounting to $2.6 trillion are subtracted from tangible assets, our net worth is $2.0 trillion. Collectively, Canadians may be very wealthy; however, many individuals never share in the affluence of the economy.

In Canada, wealth is a widely valued commodity but is usually accompanied by attendant poverty. One out of every 12 Canadians lives on welfare and one in six children grows up in a poor family. The rate of poverty among children was reported as 17.4 percent in 1990 (figure 1.3). Yet the levels of welfare payments paid to families with children designated as "poor" that have been established in *all* provinces are below the **poverty line**. The Anti-Poverty Association estimated that over five million Canadians were living below the federal government's poverty line in 1993. In 1992, Statistics Canada reported that about four million Canadians were below that line, at $15,175 for a single person and $26,146 for a family of three. Yet with a per capita gross domestic product (GDP) in excess of $15,700, Canada's middle class ranks as one of the most affluent in the world.

In Canada, the distribution of poverty is not random but tends to be concentrated among certain racial minorities, aboriginal peoples, female-headed households, and children. The proportion of Canadian families living in poverty and suffering homelessness has increased significantly since 1980. There is also considerably more poverty in Canada than in other democratic states with developed capitalist economies (figure 1.3). Among the richest economies in the world, Australia and the United States are the only two states reporting higher levels of poverty than Canada. Germany, Sweden, and Norway have been much more successful in reducing the incidence of poverty within their general populations. The tendency towards increased poverty among a growing number of groups is politically important because Canadians have come to expect a steady improvement in how well they live.

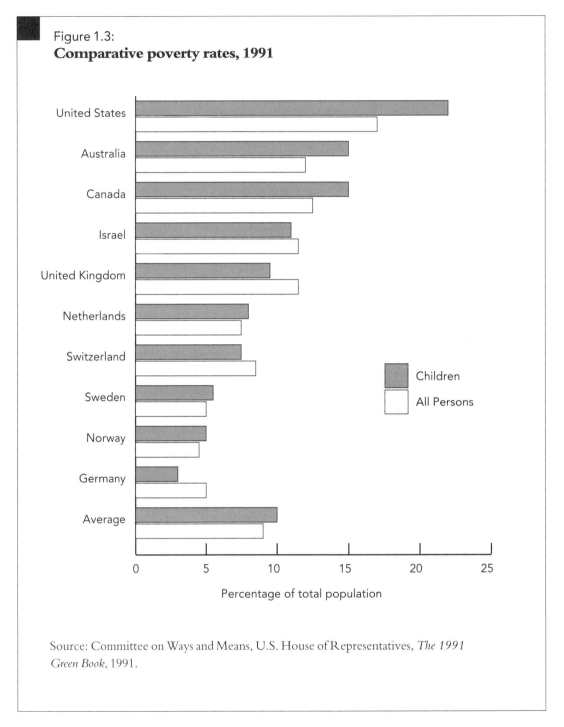

Figure 1.3:
Comparative poverty rates, 1991

Percentage of total population

Source: Committee on Ways and Means, U.S. House of Representatives, *The 1991
Green Book*, 1991.

Yet, as Canada has moved into the advanced stages of industrialization and technological innovation, its collective wealth has noticeably increased. Leo Johnson has observed that while Canada's wealth and living standards have generally improved, the middle and upper strata of income-earners do proportionately better than lower-income groups.[18] The rich are getting richer and the poor are getting poorer. Yet, in spite of greater inequality, most Canadians still believe that economic mobility is possible and they do not see themselves eternally tied to their present situations by fate or political design. Wealth remains an important political and social value in Canada.

The Politics of Health

Some of Canada's great wealth is used to purchase health and well-being. Even though most of the health and welfare services are within the constitutional jurisdiction of the provinces, the largest department of the federal government is Health and Welfare Canada, which spends approximately 40 percent of the annual government budget. Canadians, through their federal government, have made considerable efforts to improve public health. At present, a newborn Canadian female has about an 81-year life expectancy, and a male has about a 75-year life expectancy. This contrasts with states such as Nepal and Afghanistan, where life expectancy for both males and females is well below the age of 50.

Canadians take their health very seriously, as evidenced by the role the federal government has played in health services since the passage of the Federal Medical Care Act in 1966. By the 1990s, nearly ten percent of Canada's GDP was being spent on health-care services. This is primarily the result of political decisions. There is a widely held value that access to good health care is in the national interest and that individuals should not be left vulnerable to the high costs of medical services. Notwithstanding severe budgetary stresses, Canada ranks with Sweden, Switzerland, the Netherlands, Germany, and Britain for its exceptionally well-developed arrangements for health care in the community, including care of the elderly and the handicapped. In this decade, Canada's aging baby boomers have placed upward pressures on health-care costs already, forcing politicians to consider new policy directions for care of the aged. According to Statistics Canada, the number of Canadians 65 and older is likely to double in the next 50 years, and the number of those over 85 will increase twice as fast.

Politics and the Need to Learn

In most states, governments assume a major role in education, especially of their young people, although many states now also have special programs for adult education. Because education requires great social investment to pay for teachers, professors, researchers, administrators, libraries, schools, colleges and universities, there is a politics of education. What budget priorities should governments assign to education? Who should assume most of the costs?

In industrial societies, education is one of the main means of upward mobility. While there are still great differences between rich economies and poor economies, education stands out as a primary value in all societies. Levels of literacy among people 15 years of age and older range from one percent in Gabon to 99 percent in Canada and the United States.[19] Similar contrasts are found with respect to university and college students. The number of university students per 1000 population ranges from 0.2 in Ethiopia and Malawi, to 43 and 46 for Canada and the United States, respectively.

Despite the popular expectation that equality of educational opportunity exists in Canada, wealth and social class are still significant factors in determining access to university. Educational opportunities vary provincially. A person from Alberta, British Columbia, or Ontario is more likely to acquire a university education than someone from the Atlantic provinces or Quebec. This ensures continued social differences across the country. Native Canadians, in particular, tend not to acquire a university education. Fewer than one percent of aboriginal people attend university, compared with 14.5 percent of the population aged 18 to 24.

Education is a global political value because it is closely related to what people can learn and what they produce in their societies. It is an important political resource because those who possess it improve their own welfare and make demands on the political system. Yet, despite the importance of education, poor national economies have great difficulty making strides in this area. It is difficult for a developing economy to spend the required amount of its GDP on education because that means sacrifices elsewhere.

Politics and Employment

Work and employment are the basis of all cultures. It is no wonder that work should be so highly prized as a political value in society.

Employment links a person to a network of socially rewarding interactions. People gain self-worth from what they do. Without work people feel disenfranchised from their social and political systems. In short, they become alienated.

At the peak of recession unemployment levels in 1993, 1,586,000 Canadians, or about 13.0 percent of the labour force, could not find jobs, the highest rate since World War II (figure 1.4). Because of general public concern, unemployment was recognized by the federal government as the major socioeconomic problem in Canada, ranking higher than inflation and interest rates as a national priority.

Work and skill have been seriously affected by national policy in Canada since 1966. At that time the Canadian government consolidated its manpower policy to co-ordinate labour market developments and immigration. Canada Manpower Centres were established to provide services to individuals seeking a job. Employment counsellors were hired to make placement referrals, and allowances were taken out of general taxation to administer training. As a consequence, the Canadian government has assumed many responsibilities in relation to matters of job placement, income support, and mobility grants. Today, Canada Employment Centres try to match workers to jobs by funnelling information from employers to prospective employees. Occupational mobility and the maintenance of skills in the marketplace have necessarily been elevated to the highest level of political concern in a country as large and as complex as Canada. Because politics and government policies are now seen as being largely responsible for Canada's job market,

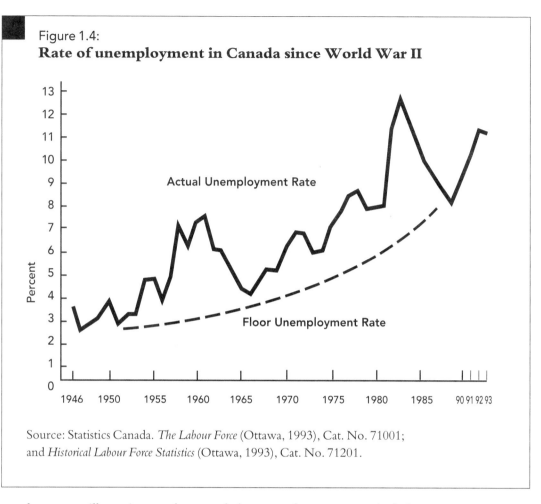

Figure 1.4:
Rate of unemployment in Canada since World War II

Source: Statistics Canada. *The Labour Force* (Ottawa, 1993), Cat. No. 71001;
and *Historical Labour Force Statistics* (Ottawa, 1993), Cat. No. 71201.

employment will continue to be regarded as an important political value.

The Politics of Justice

Justice and righteousness are passionately and universally pursued in the international community. General principles of international law focus on justice and equity in global affairs. Since World War II, the idea that individuals and states can commit "crimes against humanity" demonstrates the need to apply principles of justice everywhere in the world. All legal and court systems in their own ways attempt to portray a "justice" of some kind. However, all justice and legal systems are imperfect; some fail completely by the standards of other systems. In Canada, the Marshall Inquiry painfully retraced the circumstances that led to the wrongful conviction of a young Micmac Indian, Donald Marshall, who served 11 years in prison for a murder he did not commit. The inquiry's recommendations focused on the failures and prejudices of a justice system reputed to be one of the best in the international community.

Throughout the world, different perceptions of justice and morality are held. In all societies there is a politics of justice, because the ways governments operate their legal and court systems are an integral part of their social value system. It might appear that the rules they apply are universal but the distribution and application of justice varies from one political culture to another.

The difficulty we have in establishing this dominant political value is that there is not just one justice but many. Justice and morality cluster, compete, and conflict. Most debates about justice are not debates between right and wrong but between rights and rights — and this makes their resolution endlessly complicated.

Politics and Human Respect

The rights and freedoms people demand from their communities are based on the need for human respect. People expect their governments to respect their needs and demands. The right to privacy, freedom of speech, freedom of religion, and freedom of assembly are some of the many rights through which people derive respect and dignity in their political and governing system.

Some of the highest honours bestowed on human beings are conferred by governments in respect of their accomplishments and qualities. In Canada, the governor general grants orders, declarations, and medals as the highest marks of merit achieved by Canadians. For example, the Order of Canada recognizes excellence in many important fields of human endeavour.

The need for respect surfaces in areas of international relations, as well. Debtor militancy among the economies of the Third World is a message to the banking systems of the wealthy nation-states that they should respect the impoverished economies of the developing world. At the Olympics, where respect is literally put to the test, politics transcends the spirit of the games when states count their medals as tallies of national strength. And the separatist and independence movement in Québec is in large part driven by the demand that its sovereign aspirations to become an independent French-speaking republic be respected.

Respect for the territorial integrity of states and the principle of non-intervention have become most important in the international law of the twentieth century. The charters of the United Nations, Organization of American States, and the Organization of African Unity make frequent references to these norms of international behaviour.

The need for respect may often appear hidden behind rhetoric and human aggression. Terrorist groups, unions, interest groups, and governments are all social and political manifestations of this powerful value in politics.

Politics and Human Security

As a political value, security is usually defined in military terms, whereby the power of armed forces is regarded as a deterrent to external and internal attack. However, many states now recognize that real security is not exemplified by military strength alone, but also by the ability of a society to satisfy basic human needs. While these needs may include the prevention of war, they also include adequate food, health care, shelter, a healthy and safe community environment, and respect for human rights.

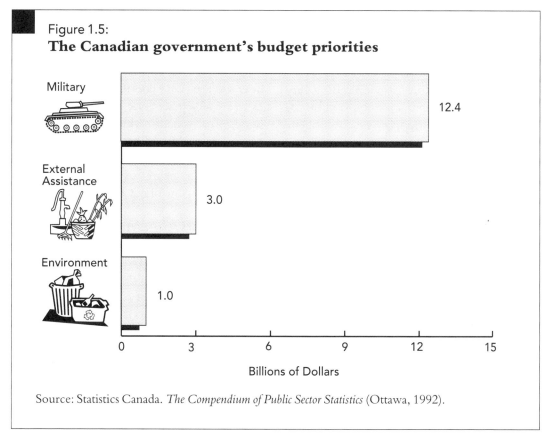

Figure 1.5:
The Canadian government's budget priorities

Military — 12.4

External Assistance — 3.0

Environment — 1.0

Billions of Dollars

Source: Statistics Canada. *The Compendium of Public Sector Statistics* (Ottawa, 1992).

Increasingly, people in all parts of the world are asking if they can be "secure" when poverty is widespread and permanent, when economic prosperity requires the destruction of the environment, when criminal violence is epidemic, and when racism and discrimination are commonplace and, in many states, institutionalized, as in Canada's federal Department of Indian Affairs and Northern Development.

The problems that threaten security are both military and non-military, both global and domestic. Real security cannot be ensured by military means alone. Yet, in most nation-states, including Canada, defence policy still tends to dominate security policy. Most governments exaggerate the military element in matters of security, thus causing other security needs to be shortchanged. In political terms, the overemphasis on military security blinds societies to the fact that personal security is not necessarily threatened by the possibility of external military attack.

Can governments continue to spend billions on military equipment and personnel when security means so much more? Can Canada afford to spend billions annually on military technology and administration? Is global war still a serious threat? It is true that the Cold War is over but the arsenals and stockpiles of that war still exist. But many other threats face the international community, such as global poverty and environmental destruction. These are at least as real as the threat of war. Millions of people die every year due to basic deprivations of food, housing, or medical attention, or as a result of environmental problems. And, even though the threat of a nuclear holocaust has diminished, the collapse of the global environment would be at least as disastrous as global nuclear war.

Canada spends over $12 billion annually on its Department of National Defence (DND). In 1990, it spent 12 times more on the military than on the environment, and over four times more on the military than on external assistance to developing economies (figure 1.5). In 1992, Canada spent almost ten times more on its air defence systems ($305 million) than it contributed to the United Nations ($33.4 million). Canada's annual spending on munitions and arms alone – $325 million – could pay for the immunization of 30 million children worldwide. And the entire cost of the proposed United Nations Action Plan to halt global desertification could be paid with just half of Canada's military budget.

However, on the domestic front, Canada's government is one of a minority that spends more on social programs as a percentage of Gross National Product (GNP), than on the military. But many ask to what extent military spending cuts into resources available for matters of domestic security, such as health and education, crime prevention, justice administration, legal aid, and police services.

Increasingly, people and governments are realizing that security may be much more than a military issue. As security is a political value, many societies recognize that the chief threat to human security is the way we organize our political and economic systems, and how we treat one another and the environment in which we live. Many now feel that none of us is secure while injustice, oppression, and deprivation exist. None of us is secure while the global environment is at risk. None of us is secure while states arm themselves in the name of security.

Politics and Affection

At first glance, love and affection seem distant from politics. But upon closer examination we can see how the need for human affection touches every level of society, including the political system. For Plato and Aristotle, people and politics are part of a cosmic order built for the perfection of human beings as they relate to one another in society. Politics must establish the framework within which love is possible, even though it cannot specify exactly how it shall be sought.

Although it can always be shown that politics does much to destroy goodwill among human beings, there is also much evidence that political behaviour fosters friendship and co-operation. Each day governments extend courtesies to one another through cultural, diplomatic, and scientific exchanges. For example, at certain times Canada has given immature bald eagles from Cape Breton to the United States Fish and Wildlife Service so as to re-establish the U.S. eagle population. And as an act of gratitude toward the City of Boston, which was the first community to come to the rescue of the citizens of Halifax after the Halifax explosion in December 1917, the province of Nova Scotia each year gives Bostonians a large spruce Christmas tree, ceremoniously lit by the premier. Similarly, the CANADARM was a gift of the Canadian government to the U.S. space shuttle program. As well, the United Nations sponsors national and international programs aimed at improving cultural co-operation and international friendship among states.

Hundreds of treaties of friendship and mutual aid are signed by governments each year. In fact, the greatest proportion of interactions and transactions among the states of our international system each day are amicable. Never before in history have so many international organizations been established for peaceful and friendly purposes.

At the national level, many governments are genuinely concerned about generating friendly relations among citizens. In Canada, a number of federal government departments, such as Communications Canada, work to foster such an environment. They represent the political values of Canadians to co-operate and collaborate with one another. They reflect the idea that friendship, love, and affection can be encouraged within formal institutional settings in addition to the personal and social contexts where we assume these values will exist. If we look closely, we can see that politics often does succeed in fostering the growth of affection among people.

Politics as Conflicting Interests

The Issue of Abortion

Some issues, more than others, can dramatize the role of politics in the process of harmonizing individual and group interests. When the Supreme Court of Canada made its historic decision in January 1988 to strike down the 1969 abortion law as unconstitutional, it triggered a flurry of competing interests across the country. The 200-page judgement placed the issue right back into the political arena, reopening emotionally heated debates on abortion at all levels of Canadian society. Almost immediately, pro-choice and pro-life groups organized demonstrations (even to the point of arrest and conviction for criminal contempt and public mischief), initiated face-to-face lobbying with parliamentarians, and conducted national education campaigns to draw support to their respective positions. The Campaign Life Coalition, which opposes therapeutic abortion and claims a membership of 200,000, urges its members to support anti-abortion MPs. They also campaign against prominent pro-choice supporters, and invite internationally acclaimed pro-life advocates such as Mother Teresa to address groups in Ottawa. The Canadian Abortion Rights Action League, which claims a much smaller membership, encourages its members to support pro-choice candidates.

Each individual contemplating an abortion was also challenged by the Supreme Court decision. For Dr. Henry Morgantaler, the decision was the culmination of almost two decades of legal defiance, during which time he had performed an estimated 20,000 abortions. For politicians, the decision created agonizing deliberation. Abortion is an issue most politicians want to avoid: It cuts across party lines, divides party members, and can cost traditional party support. Party strategies of compromise and equivocation on the abortion issue break down under the pressures of translating religious and philosophical beliefs into public policy. To balance the rights of the unborn and the rights of the mother creates an issue with no middle ground.

Under the 1969 abortion law, which created the now defunct Section 251 of the Criminal Code, an abortion was lawful only when a properly constituted hospital committee certified that the continuation of the pregnancy would be likely to endanger the life or health of the mother. All five of the judges who comprised the majority position in the Supreme Court's decision in the Morgantaler case found that the committee procedure was contrary to Section 7 of the Charter of Rights and Freedoms, which guarantees "the right to life, liberty and security of person." To the government, this meant that no new legislation with similar administrative practices would be acceptable. Government strategists knew that any new law to restrict abortion could be ruled by the courts to be in open contradiction of the Charter. One province – Nova Scotia – outlawed free-standing abortion clinics by making it illegal to perform abortions anywhere other than government-approved hospitals. But the Supreme Court of Canada ruled that Nova Scotia's action violated the Charter.

In the summer of 1988, the federal government proposed a compromise motion, subject to a free vote to establish a general policy that would guide the Cabinet in drafting legislation to replace the abortion law. The motion, which called for relatively easy access early in pregnancy with tougher restrictions coming later, was defeated 147:76 by a coalition of anti-abortion Tories, pro-choice New Democrats, and Liberals who favoured compromise but rejected the partic-

ular plan offered by the government. The tortuous Commons debate continued into the early hours of the morning throughout a week of bitter deliberation, leaving the government with no clear guidance on what policy to pursue. One of the five defeated amendments to the motion brought all 23 women present in the House at the time together in strong opposition. This non-partisan female force of unity scuttled the anti-abortion motion which would have banned abortions except when two doctors decide the life of the mother is threatened.

After all was said and done during the free vote, the government did not venture to stake out a formal position that might alienate half the voters in the country or its deeply divided Tory caucus. As the likelihood of an election increased dramatically in the late summer of 1988, Canadians were left to wait and see without any law on abortion. It remained a matter between a woman and her doctor, without any guidance from government. Growing national sentiment on the issue suggested that any proposed law would be a compromise to allow early abortion as a condition of prohibiting late abortion. Based on a 1988 Decima poll, one in ten Canadians opposes abortion under any circumstances while about one-third favour abortion on demand. Of the rest, 60 percent approve of abortion under special circumstances. Pro-choice supporters feel that women do not need a law to help them make decisions on abortion.

But the abortion controversy remained unresolved as the Mulroney government prepared for a fall election. In the interim, former Manitoba cabinet minister Joseph Borowski, a vocal anti-abortionist, appealed to the

Supreme Court of Canada to overturn a 1987 Saskatchewan Court of Appeal decision that rejected Borowski's claim to grant the fetus the right to life, liberty, and security of person. But the Supreme Court reserved decision on the appeal because Canada no longer has an abortion law. And in March 1989, the Supreme Court refused to decide the issue of whether the fetus has constitutional rights, stating that it would not deal with the question in the absence of an abortion law. But in 1991, the Supreme Court reaffirmed the position that a fetus cannot be considered a person by upholding a British Columbia Court of Appeal decision that found that an unborn child is not a person and cannot be considered a person until it has completely left its mother's body. By so deciding, the High Court rejected the argument that the term "person" and "human being" are not equivalent terms in the Criminal Code.

In 1989, the Law Reform Commission of Canada recommended amendments to the Criminal Code that would balance the interests of the mother and the fetus. Mothers' rights would weigh more heavily for the first 22 weeks, after which the fetus can usually survive outside the womb. Abortions would be permitted before then if a woman and her doctor felt her physical or mental health were threatened. After 22 weeks, a second medical opinion would be required and abortion would be allowed only if there were a threat to the woman's life or a serious threat to her physical health. An abortion would be permitted at any time if the fetus is found to have a lethal defect. Mental or physical handicap is in itself not a reason to permit abortion under the recommendations of the Law Reform Commission.

By 1990, it was feared in Ottawa that without a new federal law on abortion, provincial governments would come under pressure to pass their own laws or to find other ways to impede the practice of abortion within their jurisdictions. The federal government moved to fill the legislative vacuum that had existed since 1988 with its Bill C-43, which would have returned abortion to the Criminal Code. Under the new bill, a doctor could have been sentenced to two years in prison for performing an abortion if the pregnancy did not threaten the woman's physical, mental, or psychological health. Medical groups lobbied hard against its passage because it could incriminate doctors. Pro-choice groups argued that many women would be at least nominal criminals to whom an exception had to apply. And pro-life advocates pointed out the bill would be unlikely to reduce abortions and lacked legal recognition for the fetus. The end of Bill C-43 could not have been more symbolically significant had the vote been rigged. The controversial bill was defeated in dramatic fashion with a politically stunning 43:43 Senate vote. Under Senate rules, a tie vote defeats a Commons bill.

Thus, Canada's foremost governmental institutions, Parliament and the Supreme Court, could not, or would not, provide a decisive solution on this issue. In this regard, politics is a process between and within communities whereby divergent groups co-operate or clash in order to satisfy their basic needs. The political process forced the federal government once again to consider the difficult task of framing new abortion legislation.

Table 1.1:
Urban population as a percentage of total population, 1970–2000

	1970	1980	1990	2000
World total	37.4	41.2	45.2	50.1
Developed regions	66.2	71.9	77.0	81.4
Underdeveloped regions	25.0	29.8	35.0	40.8
Canada and U.S.	74.2	78.8	82.9	86.4
Europe	64.7	69.6	74.3	78.7
Oceania	70.2	73.1	75.8	78.2
Latin America	56.9	63.8	69.7	74.8
East Asia	28.5	32.9	37.7	43.2
Africa	21.9	27.1	32.5	37.7
South Asia	21.1	25.0	29.6	35.0

Source: *Demographic Yearbook 1990* (New York: United Nations, 1990).

Politics as Nation-Building

Modern societies are not born; they are built. And politics plays a major role in their construction. The economic and social base of any society requires political direction. At various levels, politics constructs the building blocks of national development – the **infrastructure** of a community. In the broadest sense, the infrastructure consists of systems of transportation, communication, education, power grids, the industrial and technological base, and the political system itself. These all form the structural components of a political economy.

In the same way that a house is constructed from various building materials, in different patterns and designs, rapidly or slowly, according to the will and power of its builders, so a nation-state develops from its resources, according to different plans, quickly or gradually, from the will and skills of its citizens.

The political system organizes, plans, and directs policies towards its developmental goals. Public policies are intimately related to nation-building at all levels of government. Public policies can make us richer or poorer, happy or angry, live or die. Public policy is what a government *does* as well as what public officials sometimes choose not to do. In the most fundamental ways, societies survive and

Table 1.2:
General municipal services

Locally financed	Cost-shared
Fire protection	Public education
Planning and maintenance	Transportation
Refuse collection and disposal	Health
Municipal libraries	Public housing
Police	Hospitals and medical care
Water supply	Public welfare
Parks and recreation	Pollution control

change on the basis of whatever governments choose to do or not to do. Government policies on municipal services, education, health, welfare, agriculture, business, defence, and relations with other states are all part of the nation-building process.

Local Government and National Development

Political science research has only recently begun to discover the important role that cities and towns play in national development. The political decisions and actions of local governments transform the landscape of a country. They plan and regulate local construction and land use and provide important services like utilities and transportation.

By the year 2000, most of the world's population will live in cities (table 1.1). At that time, the gradual shift of political and economic power to urban centres will be irreversible, making cities the primary centres of human development and important deci-

sion-making units of most political systems. In 1950, there were 76 cities in the world with a population over one million; the United Nations projects that by the end of the century there will be 440 such cities, 284 of them in the developing world. Already the physical expansion of the corporate limits of cities has created overwhelming human problems and added many jurisdictional questions to the national and subnational legislatures of most states. As cities and towns have grown, so have public demands for increased responsibilities and services, which in some cities, such as Mexico City and São Paulo, are in response to unmanageable and ungovernable social conditions.

The result is that the division of powers and responsibilities between national governments and local governments carries momentous significance for the politics of development. Usually the cost of administrating public services goes beyond the financial capacities of cities, so other levels of government share costs or completely finance the administration of services (table 1.2). National governments are increasingly dependent on cities as economic and social centres of development. Thus, municipal problems have become national problems and municipal successes have become national successes.

In Canada, over 4000 municipalities and countless boards, commissions, and other local bodies contribute to the growth and development of Canadian society. But their contributions have not been without recurrent financial problems and a general public attitude that local government should be primarily concerned with administration and efficient service delivery, but not with politics.[20] Canadians have not linked urban growth with national development and have been reluctant to give greater autonomy to local governments. Under Section 92 of the Constitution Act, 1867, the provinces were granted full responsibility for municipal institutions and, thus, local governments have remained what a federation of Canadian municipalities calls "puppets on a shoestring."[21]

In spite of the fact that in the 1990s over 80 percent of all Canadians live and work in cities and receive most essential services from their municipal governments, local administrations remain the most neglected and least regarded of all three levels of government. In the years ahead public opinion may reverse its sentiments about the role of local governments in Canada's national development and draw closer to Sir Ernest Simon's view that "the City Council's services mean the difference between savagery and civilization."[22]

Subnational Governments and National Development

In geographically large states, nation-building requires the co-operation of two or more levels of government, each with its own special jurisdictions, political institutions, and popular support. In Canada, provinces have special powers reserved for them in the Constitution Act, 1867, listed under Section 92. In addition to ten provincial political systems, Canada has two large territories that together make up 40 percent of the entire area of the country and yet hold only 0.2 percent of Canada's population. The Yukon Territory is governed by a commissioner as head of government and for an elected legislative body called the Yukon Legislative Assembly. The Northwest Territories – the largest region within Canada – is governed by an appointed commissioner and a council made up of 24 elected members.

The Constitution Act, 1867, enumerated 15 classes of subjects that have given provinces exclusive and substantive law-making powers and elevated them to economic instruments of nation-building. The provinces have responsibility for local governments, jurisdiction over education, control of provincial crown lands, natural resources, and the provincial administration of justice. They also have concurrent powers with the federal government in agriculture and immigration. Historically, the politics of federal and provincial relations have included the transfer of additional spending powers to the provinces, particularly under successive Liberal governments since 1968. The federal government spends billions annually in the areas of health, welfare, and post-secondary education, but allows provinces to administer

Table 1.3:
Provincial gross domestic product, 1992

	$ Billions
British Columbia	$86,571,000
Alberta	73,744,000
Saskatchewan	19,837,000
Manitoba	23,751,000
Ontario	275,421,000
Québec	158,296,000
New Brunswick	13,910,000
Nova Scotia	18,004,000
Prince Edward Island	2,126,000
Newfoundland	9,368,000
Yukon and Northwest Territories	3,156,000
Total (gross domestic product)	$684,184,000

Source: Statistics Canada, *Provincial Economic Accounts*, (13-213P)
Annual Estimates 1988-92, 1992.

and influence the policy direction of these programs.

Any account of the contribution of the provinces and territories to nation-building should include some remarks about their economic importance in the Canadian economy (table 1.3). Each province of Canada generates a gross provincial product that is a constituent part of the gross domestic product, which is the total value of all goods and services produced within national boundaries. For example, British Columbia offers a primary product and resource economy to Canada. The United States, the United King-dom, and the Pacific Rim economies are the main importers of fish, pulp and paper, primary metals, and manufactured goods produced in British Columbia. Table 1.3 shows that British Columbia contributed $86,571 billion to Canada's GDP of $684,184 billion in 1992.

All of the provinces are key political and governing units within the federal system, and as such, they contribute to Canada's economic development as an independent nation-state in the international community. How provincial governments manage their economies, their deficits, and their cumulative debts

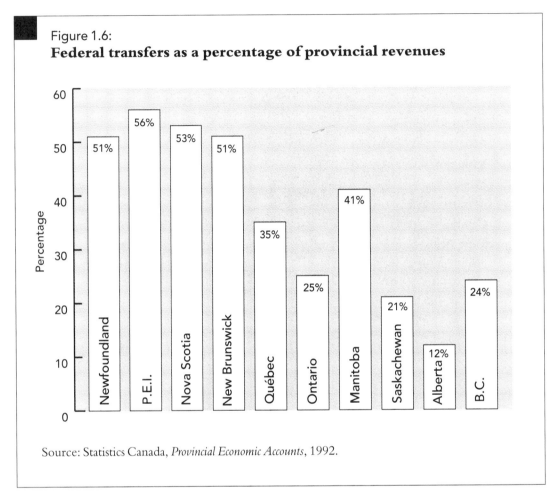

Figure 1.6:
Federal transfers as a percentage of provincial revenues

Source: Statistics Canada, *Provincial Economic Accounts*, 1992.

affects the economic integrity of the country. No one province can divorce itself from the overall economic viability of the Canadian economy.

Together the provinces constitute just 60 percent of the area of Canada. But sprawling across the top of the Western hemisphere are the Northwest Territories and the Yukon. They encompass an area nearly one-and-a-quarter times the size of India with a population of only about 70,000 people. These territories are just beginning to attract

Canada's business pioneers in the areas of mining, hydrocarbon exploration, and oil exploration and refining. In 1992, they generated $3.15 billion of Canada's gross national product.

National Governments

The ultimate instruments of nation-building are held by national governments. They are the final arbiters of politics and legitimate decision-making in most states. National governments control the overall capacity of a political and economic system to affect every level of society.

From the perspective of public policy, nation-building in Canada has had an important regional dimension that is far-reaching for all three levels of government, but in particular for the federal government. Since the 1950s, new federal policies and programs have been introduced in rapid succession. In the mid-1950s, "rural adjustment" programs were followed by a policy focus in the 1960s on "growth centres," which in turn led to more comprehensive regional federal-provincial development strategies under the General Development Agreement approach of the 1970s, and the Economic and Regional Development Agreement in the 1980s. Billions of dollars have shifted from the national treasury through federal transfer payments to adjust and diminish regional economic differences in Canada. Because the pace of development has been very uneven in Canada due to the country's great size, distribution of population, and regional resource endowments, the federal government transfers payments to provincial governments in an effort to equalize the benefits of development across the country (figure 1.6). The heavy reliance of the four provinces of Atlantic Canada on transfer payments – as shown in figure 1.6 by the contributive percentages these payments comprise of their provincial revenues – is indicative of the severity of regional disparities in eastern Canada.

Ever since it was elevated to the level of public policy in Canada, regional development has been politically driven. Indeed, the federal structure of Canada's governing system tends to reinforce the focus of public policy on regionalism and regional solutions to

economic development. Yet, the concept has never been adequately defined either in economic or political terms. Some economists even reject the idea that "region" is a valid concept for economic policy analysis. They hold that economic development can only be directed at people, as opposed to places or regions. In short, regional development means different things to different people, but appears to have been politically instituted in intergovernmental affairs in Canada.

Lucian Pye noted the centrality and importance of politics in the process of nation-building.[23] His position is that without a developed political and governing system, national development will falter. For him, the quality of politics determines the capacity of a governing system to execute public policy effectively and efficiently in the best interests of the nation-state. National governments establish a set of complex political and economic structures in order to achieve desired national goals: these may include energy self-sufficiency, economic independence, universal medical services, or economic prosperity. For example, Canadian governments have created Crown corporations to facilitate the process of nation-building and province-building in areas of the economy in which the private sector cannot or will not assume the cost and risks of development. Even though some public corporations have been privatized under recent governments, such economic institutions still number about 400, making major contributions in such fields as coal, steel, oil, gas, forestry, potash, ferry services, and manufacturing ventures.

In Canada, the job of nation-building has always been initiated, controlled, and directed by the federal government. The Constitution

Act, 1867, granted the federal government the nation-building powers it needed to expand the role of the state directly and indirectly into the lives of individuals and groups, and into the jurisdictions of other levels of government. It is important to note that the division of powers outlined in our constitution clearly gives most powers to the federal Parliament, establishing it as the dominant decision-making authority in Canada. The "peace, order and good government" clause of the 1867 constitution grants **residual power** to the federal Parliament, giving it the necessary legal basis to involve itself in areas of jurisdiction not specifically assigned to the provinces. Historically, this constitutional legitimacy, when combined with federal spending and taxing power, has provided the federal government with the means for expanding the national state apparatus to build Canada.

The size of the government sector has grown steadily since Confederation and rapidly since World War II. Total government spending as a percentage of gross national expenditures (the total output of the economy) grew from 23.7 percent in 1947 to over 42 percent in 1992. The number of federal government portfolios grew from 19 in 1947 to 40 by 1984. However, Kim Campbell's ministry was reduced to 25 in an attempt to downsize the Cabinet and control the cost of the federal government. The number of departments was reduced from 32 to 23. Eight departments were redesigned, three received new mandates, and 15 were merged or broken up. All departments were stream-

■ ■ **residual power:** jurisdictions or powers that are not specifically enumerated in a constitution delegated to a specific government, or that cannot be implied from powers that are delegated to a recognized government. ■ ■

lined. After his election victory in 1993, Jean Chrétien continued the practice, appointing an even smaller Cabinet of 24. Notwithstanding a leaner federal Cabinet in allocating the resources of the people, much of the never-ending politics of nation-building in Canada is in the hands of the national government.

Debt and Nation-Building

In the 1990s, the politics of nation-building is conditioned by the debts governments have incurred to administer the affairs of state, manage their economies, and invest in their futures. Whether governments administer their affairs efficiently determines overall economic performance and their ability to overcome **national debt**. The way governments borrow, as well as the ways they spend, raise revenues, and deliver their services substantially contributes to their nation-building ability. All of this may be complicated by corruption in government, inefficiency and mismanagement, and the politics involved in how governments tax their populations. Most national economies have incurred severe national debt and recurring **budget deficits** in recent decades. Growing deficits mean that governments must pay higher interest costs to cover them. Many politicians and economists believe that continuing large deficits threaten the long-term health of the economy. Such circumstances restrict the ability of governments to develop their societies. Uncontrolled national debt reduces or eliminates a government's ability to spend money on education, systems of transportation and

Table 1.4:
Debt to gross domestic product ratio, selected economies, 1992

National Economy	Debt/GDP ratio (%)
Burundi	87
Ethiopia	80
Canada	85
Guyana	800
Italy	91
Morocco	84
Mozambique	409
Poland	80
United States	97
Zaïre	117

Source: World Bank, *Report 1992;* Statistics Canada, *Compendium of Public Sector Statistics*, 1992.

communication, health care, and research and development.

When the level of national debt begins to threaten the growth of the gross domestic product, the economy can no longer pay for its social and business programs. By the 1990s, many nation-states had amassed national debts almost equal to or greater than their gross domestic product (table 1.4). The public sector debt ratio includes the sum total of national, provincial, municipal, and government agency debt.[24] The indebtedness of Ottawa and all the provinces amounts to about 85 percent of Canada's gross domestic product ($684 billion in 1992).

An unfavourable debt to GDP ratio endangers national economic growth because in order to pay off loans, governments have to use funds that could otherwise be reinvested in the national economy.[25] Canada's growing debt equals almost all of the economic activity going on in the economy as measured by the GDP during one year. Economies that are heavily indebted in this way experience a serious hemorrhaging of the financial resources that they desperately need for social and economic development.

Nation-building is a complex process involving many levels of government combined with the productivity and political will of people. How each level of government operates, and spends and raises money is vital to the fate of the political system. Politics is a powerful force that people often use to steer a social system in the directions they feel will best build their national futures.

Learning About Politics

Political Socialization

Political socialization is the process of learning about politics. It is the master concept used by political scientists to account for the ways in which the content of a political culture is transmitted to new generations. In various ways, every society teaches its members the political values, traditions, norms, and duties that it deems desirable and acceptable. All individuals experience the subtle pressures that entice them to **internalize** their society's norms. Even though individuals in democracies may be dissatisfied with their political leadership, they have learned to accept elections – rather than riots or insurgencies – as the best route to political change. In totalitarian societies, individuals learn that only one political party has the undisputed right to interpret and implement political goals without dissent or competition from individuals or groups. In societies undergoing violent change, people will internalize the use of violence as a necessary and acceptable means of political and governmental change. Death and destruction in Sarajevo, the bodies of soldiers everywhere, the death by sniper-fire of innocent children and civilians have all left a permanent imprint in the minds of Serbs and Croats that politics and violence are part of the same process.

Political science sees political socialization as both a *process* and a *goal*. As a process, political socialization has been defined by David Easton and Jack Dennis as "those developmental processes through which persons acquire political orientations."[26] For Roberta Sigel, "political socialization refers to the learning process by which the political norms and behaviours acceptable to an ongoing political system are transmitted from generation to generation."[27]

The goal and effect of political socialization in some political cultures is to mould a child or adult to a prescribed set of conventions in which people are usually not treated as active innovators and modifiers of their own political learning. Following the successful Cuban revolution, children were housed, socialized, and educated by state organizations. Adult political values were shaped by organizations like the Committees for the Defence of the Revolution (CDR), which still induct people into Cuba's revolutionary political culture.

Political socialization may be incidental to other life experiences, or it may be as deliberate as a state-monitored program of indoctrination. As a general rule, democratic political systems provide a subtle environment in which political information is transmitted in a casual manner. In most non-democratic states, however, political information may be organized and engineered to ensure that what people learn is approved by the regime.

Profile of the Political Self

Much more research is anticipated on what psychological processes are involved in early political socialization because so little is known about it. It is very difficult to get into the heads of children as they acquire the initial political stimuli in their lives. Many political scientists who have specialized in this area have based their theories on observations of their own children or on observations of relatively small numbers of randomly selected children. However, their work has been extremely important in helping us to understand how children first learn about politics.

At the outset we should avoid making the false assumption that early socialization engenders indelible lifestyles, especially with regard to political behaviour. Adult character is highly malleable and continues to be well into old age. Nevertheless, it is useful for us to focus on early or primary political socialization as an attribute of the child's development of "self." Each person's self-development is unique and may not follow the expected stages of human growth from child to adult. Some children may be more politically aware than their parents, even though the opposite is normally true. While research observations can be made about political learning in children, adolescents, and adults, understanding the "political person" in all of us requires a knowledge of our "self" and its general learning experiences.

The American sociologist Charles Horton Cooley saw the self as a looking glass in the process of socialization, political or otherwise.[28] Our political behaviour is a reflection of how we see ourselves in a complex world. Self-image determines our general interest in politics and affects our political identities. We learn political behaviour that satisfies the needs of our self as we pass through various levels of human development.

Political socialization is a lifelong process intimately tied to self-definition. The foundations of political behaviour are laid in childhood. Political socialization begins as children interact first with their parents and later with peers, teachers, and other adults. It also occurs as we are exposed to messages from radio, television, and other mass media. Beyond these, political socialization is linked to the preservation of political culture, because the process of absorbing political values and inculcating them in new members is accomplished by teaching and learning. Each political system tries to teach new members, especially children, what its accepted behaviours, norms, and values are. The goal is to condition the self-defining individual to accept the means society uses to achieve social order. If political socialization is effective, new members adopt supportive attitudes toward office-holders, political procedures, institutions, and the ways policy decisions distribute rewards and punishments.

■ ■ **internalize:** to accept and adopt a society's norms as part of one's personality and notion of self. ■ ■

How Children Learn About Politics

David Easton and Robert Hess found that even though children do not develop a political vocabulary until the ages of 11 or 12, many basic political attitudes and values have been firmly established by the time the child begins elementary school. James Chowning Davies discovered that before schooling starts, a child's familiarity with power is well at work within the framework of the family.[29] Later, in school, children learn that there are *public* forces in their lives. Government policy dictates that they be in school, that they get immunized against disease, that public property does not belong to them, and that there are many rules and regulations that should be respected in the outside world.

In spite of the apparent regulatory nature of the political world, Easton and Dennis point out that the North American child "learns to like the government before [he/she] really knows what it is."[30] Early in their lives, children naturally develop favourable feelings towards the symbolic and ceremonial character of the state and government. The flag, the national anthem, emblems, the military, and the head of state are all presented as special representations of the majesty of the state and country.

This is particularly true for most Canadian youth. One study of 6000 Canadian children found that students from grades four to eight held high levels of affection for the Queen, the governor general, and the prime minister.[31] **Party identification** also tended to increase from grades four to eight, with some changes in affection noted toward the prime minister. Ronald Landes discovered that Canadian children possess more knowledge about leaders than about institutions and processes.[32] The low-to-moderate levels of political awareness in children suggests the variable importance of politics in their growth. Formal politics, its institutions, and its actors are not central factors in a child's personal development. However, the underlying current of political behaviour such as competition, co-operation, compromise, power, and manipulation are learned during childhood and with experience are linked to later adolescent and adult political behaviour.

Adolescents and Political Learning

Adolescents learn political lessons more explicitly. Social Science, History, and Political Science classes deal with the structure of Canadian government, bringing issues of democracy, freedom, and equality to the attention of students.

During adolescence people become increasingly aware of the existence of authority outside the family and school. Adolescents become familiar with institutions of authority such as the courts, Parliament, and municipal government. At this stage, the individual begins to express independent political views and to distinguish parental influences from general social ones. Adolescence is a period of biological maturation and change, and the formation of social and political attitudes are also part of this development.

Politicization may become highly personalized during adolescence. It may reveal itself as **political cynicism**, **political efficacy**, **apathy**, or **political participation**. During adolescence, individuals demonstrate different capacities for learning political information and reflect different levels of maturity with respect to opinion formation and expression.

By the time they reach their twenties, most Canadians have a reasonably well-formed set of basic values, a sense of belonging to a political party, some policy preferences, and some evaluations of government performance.

Learning About Politics as an Adult

Because of the widespread belief that politics is the domain of adults, much more is known about adult political socialization than about that of children and adolescents. Adult socialization refers to changes in learning and attitudes that take place after the adolescent years. Because adult political socialization is a continuous experience, we should avoid the assumption that young people are usually more liberal and that aging leads to political conservatism. Roberta Sigel and Marilyn Hoskin noted that adults change political attitudes regularly throughout their lives in response to issues that affect self-interest.[33] A person who at 35 held politically conservative views on social and economic assistance may, at age sixty-five, show strong support for government-sponsored programs.

Changes in adult values and behaviour from those of childhood and adolescence may be due more to changes in personal roles than to age. Between the idealized state of adulthood and the reality of life as a parent, spouse, and breadwinner, there is sometimes quite a difference. Adults quickly learn that their political and economic freedoms are only relative. As people establish homes and families, they begin to worry about property, taxes, school for their children, protection against crime, and such things as garbage collection. Politically they must make trade-offs between the independence they longed for as adolescents and the social and economic responsibilities life places upon them. Most important of all, they learn that there is still much to learn politically at all stages of adulthood.

Taking on a new job or profession, moving to a different community, or experiencing upward or downward social mobility relate more directly to changing political attitudes and behaviour than does age. These kinds of changes in our lives can affect our political behaviour and alter our socio-political belief system. In effect, our values and beliefs learned in childhood may no longer be adequate or relevant to us as adults who are experiencing such role changes.

Under some government regimes, adults may experience a political *re-socialization* — one that is forced upon the individual by a government agency such as the secret service or the military, or by a government with different ideological positions that has come to power. The term *"brainwashing"* is used to describe an attempt to change attitudes or ideologies against a person's will. Brainwashing is a translation of an expression used by the People's Republic of China for purifying the mind of any political beliefs in the old order that existed before the Chinese revolution. With this extreme form of political socialization, the old, mistaken ideas are washed away and the "right" political values are put in place. Both re-socialization and brainwashing are abrupt, peremptory methods of adult political learning. Under democratic governments such as Canada's, adult political socialization is a gradual life experience, resulting from a person's change in roles.

Because we are describing political socialization as a process of attitudinal behavioural change and not as the result of specific age categories in adult life, it is important to study the social context of political socialization. What are the environmental agents of socialization? How do they influence the way we learn about politics?

Agents of Political Learning

The agents of political socialization most frequently identified by political scientists have been the family, school, peers, the media, and the political system. By *agents* we mean those social institutions and experiences that condition, indirectly influence, or directly determine the development of a person's political

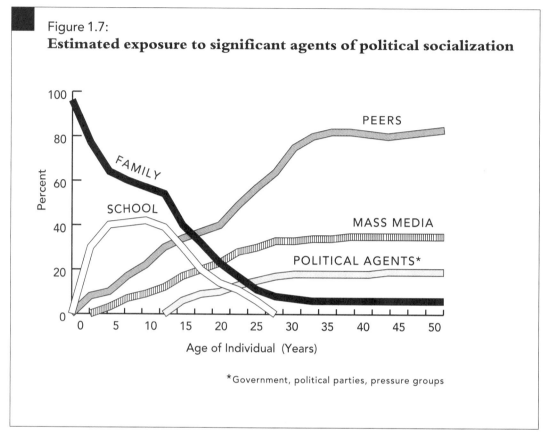

Figure 1.7:
Estimated exposure to significant agents of political socialization

PEERS

FAMILY

SCHOOL

MASS MEDIA

POLITICAL AGENTS*

Age of Individual (Years)

Percent

*Government, political parties, pressure groups

views and actions. The politicization of an individual is affected not only by exposure to the most common agents of socialization, but also by the degree to which the agents themselves are politicized. Accordingly, a person whose parents have little interest in politics is less likely to acquire political knowledge than one whose parents are highly active and motivated politically. The greater the exposure a person has to politically charged agents of socialization, the greater the likelihood that those values will be assimilated and internalized.

Figure 1.7 shows the approximate exposure of an individual to five of the most familiar agents of socialization. In Canada, as in most other places, people learn the norms and expectations of their community from their parents, from teachers at school, from their friends and associates, and through TV, radio, and the print media, as well as from political parties and government agencies. These are the primary sources of political information for most people. They help to shape our attitudes, values, and political behaviour throughout our lives. In figure 1.7, the age of a person – from birth to age 50 – is represented on the horizontal line. The vertical line shows exposure as the percentage of interactions people experience with the agents that have a significant socializing effect on them.

The Family

Most children get their first ideas about government and politics from their parents and siblings. Very early, by the age of five or six, they learn that they are Canadians, living in a state that has a queen and a governor general. They begin to hear about the existence of a government headed by a prime minister who travels all over the country.

Families share their opinions directly with children, who may adopt these opinions. In effect, parents say or do things that children imitate. The family as a social institution places its members in a network of social and economic relationships that influence how children see the world as well as how the world sees them.

Even though the family is neither instituted nor designed as an agent for transmitting political values, it is considered by many scholars to be the most important source of political learning. In our society, the child's exposure to family influences remains high until late adolescence, when other agents of socialization begin to attract as much or more attention. But the family may intentionally or unintentionally influence a person's predispositions toward authority, party identification, and general political norms and behaviour throughout a great part of a person's life. Because most of our early personal development takes place at home, we can understand why the family contributes so much to the profile of our political self.

The School

Canadian children spend a substantial portion of their time in a school setting. For many, attendance at a university prolongs this exposure into early adulthood. Because of their constant influence in the formative years of life, schools rival parents as agents of teaching important values and norms in a community. Because most schools in Canada are tax-supported public institutions that determine teaching standards and follow standardized curriculum guidelines, they inadvertently serve to transmit socially and politically approved values. Schools usually promote positive orientations toward the political and economic system and introduce students to the rituals and symbols of the political process. Teachers, whose credentials are normally set by provincial governments, also transmit political skills and values over and above those in the curriculum. The schools, the teachers, and the curricula constitute a learning culture through which we all must pass.

Peer Groups

Figure 1.7 shows that as the family influence wanes, there is increased contact with peers. **Peer groups** are normally formed among individuals who share common backgrounds, outlooks, and values. In Canadian society, peer groups occupy an important position for influencing adult socialization in all matters – including politics. For most of us, peers affect us before we enter school. With peers, we are first introduced to the value of equality – being equal among equals. We learn to share, compete, co-operate, compromise, and manipulate those in equal standing to ourselves. We also learn about leadership and the unwritten rules of being recruited and accepted by a group. In adult life, peer groups become the most significant agents of political socialization, particularly when politics is important to the group itself. Because of the personal nature of most peer-group relationships, they apply subtle pressure on individuals by communicating political values and encouraging certain standards of political conduct.

The Mass Media

Another source of political socialization cannot be ignored: the mass media. The impact of the media on children and adults has been the focus of increased government and scholarly attention in recent years. In Canada, the mass media have played a major role in politicizing the population. Most newspapers and magazines are highly political in content and coverage. Radio and television are universal media that link Canada's ten million square kilometres by providing coverage of politics, economics, and cultural happenings across the country.

The mass media enlighten us about public policy, how well policies are working, who are the best political leaders, what alternative leaders and policies might be considered, and what effects they have. The media also act as a vehicle for the government, political parties, and interest groups that want to communicate their positions to the people, educating and persuading, or even manipulating their opinions.

The media act as *independent* agents of political socialization, bypassing parents, the education system, and peers. Canadians spend 50 percent more time (about 25 hours per week) watching television than on any other leisure activity. The electronic media (television, followed by newspapers, radio, and magazines) are considered the most influential and believable of all media sources. Television especially plays a central role in the formation and change of political orientations among Canadians by structuring their attitudes about

politics and the information on which these attitudes are based.

Political Agents: Government, Parties, and Pressure Groups

The political system is filled with numerous competing groups – the government, political parties, interest groups – that have a vested interest in educating the public. Political events do not always speak for themselves; often they are explained to the public by the interest groups or political parties that have a political axe to grind. As such, they bring particular biases or points of view to bear in transmitting information about politics to the general public. Political leaders' interpretations of what is going on can also have significant effects on public perceptions.

Government does far more today than it did during the early years after Confederation. As the federal and provincial governments have taken on more responsibilities over the years, it is natural for politicians and bureaucrats to want to explain and defend to the public the role of these governments. Governments spend millions each year trying to tell Canadians about the positive consequences of what they do. Governments want us to know that they are improving the economy, that they are creating jobs, and that they are managing public affairs competently. In this way, they are teaching us about politics and government from their perspective. Today they play a major role in the general process of political socialization.

For many people, it is rational and sensible not to spend much time on politics. Political parties can greatly simplify matters for these voters. Often people will choose a political party as a shortcut or substitute for interpreting issues and events they may not fully comprehend. Competition among political parties can also increase public awareness of, and interest in, candidates and issues. Party competition attracts attention and gets people involved.

Although interest groups differ in size, goals, budgets, and scope of interest, they are intensely involved in educating the public about their concerns. Interest groups perform certain functions in Canada's political system that cannot be performed as well through the conventional structures of government. As groups dedicated to informing their members about questions of public interest, they are important agents of political learning.

Expressing Political Opinions

When we express our attitudes about politics and government, we are participating in an important form of political behaviour. We are influencing others by what we say and we are being influenced by what they say. Every political opinion is learned and is an indication of how much we have learned about politics. Usually, political opinions express our political values in day-to-day terms. They indicate how people feel about their representatives, their institutions, their national goals. Political opinions reflect upon our ideology, our values, our conduct, and our expectations. To be sure, many opinions lead to no action, but most political opinions imply that political behaviour will follow. It is because of this expected linkage between opinion and action that democratic theorists lay such great emphasis on the role played by **public opinion** in political affairs.

We can trace the appreciation of the importance of public opinion from the earliest writings of political philosophers to the present day. Although Greek and Roman philosophers described it as "mass opinion," they quickly identified its importance to the world of politics. Among modern political theorists, Jean-Jacques Rousseau was the first to make use of its present meaning by employing the phrase "l'opinion publique" in regard to his notion of "general will."[34] Since the eighteenth century, public opinion has been courted by politicians, condemned by philosophers, catered to by business and governments, feared by military leaders, and analyzed by statisticians. Public opinion is perceived to have such power that British Columbia prohibits the publication of public-opinion polls during election campaigns, and federal members of Parliament have introduced bills in the House of Commons to do the same in federal elections.

The passion for expressing opinions is universal. Scholars, newspapers, and television journalists, politicians, interest groups, government agencies, and most citizens are all willing to generate or try to fathom Canadian public opinion. Political scientists are interested in the formation and expression of opinions to the extent that they influence and change public policy. By observing the role of public opinion in the formation of public decisions, we heighten our understanding of some of the factors that affect government actions. We learn if there is congruity between public policy and public preferences.

What is a Political Opinion?

All opinions amount to expressions of attitudes and beliefs. In our society, opinions constitute an expression of personal and group power. We build and destroy governments with opinions. In our legal system, opinions judge the behaviour of individuals and corporations. They represent the anticipations of people and reinforce or change the most fundamental beliefs of society. They operate as forceful and dynamic *social messages* representing any collection of individual opinions that are expressed.

In everyday discourse, public opinion refers to general public attitudes toward everything from athletics to the zodiac. But political opinions specifically relate to all matters of government and political affairs. So, as students of politics, we should consider V.O. Key's definition of public opinion as "those opinions held by private persons which governments find it prudent to heed."[35] For purposes of political analysis, public opinions become significant when they link the opinions of people to political action and government attention. They reflect how people interpret their political culture and the extent to which political socialization is succeeding or failing.

Is There Only One Public?

Often, people make the incorrect assumption that there is only one "public" when referring to political opinion. This interpretation of public opinion is often misleading; there are very few issues in a society that concern the entire public. We assume that "the people" really is one enormous individual with a single opinion, quite probably one that agrees with our own. For analytic purposes, however, it is important to be careful with aggregate references to "Canadians" or "Americans," keeping in mind the wide range of views that individual members of a given segment of the public may hold on most questions. It is true that for issues of widespread impact such as war, inflation, unemployment, capital punishment, and universal medicare, the general public will voice related opinions that are measurable as a national response. But only on a relatively small number of issues does a public respond organically. It is much more accurate to hold that there are many publics with special interests in issues of a local nature. For example, most Manitobans are unlikely to be concerned about the state of the fishery in British Columbia. Unless it affects them directly, the issues of the fishery would constitute a quite distant reality. Analysts have concluded therefore that only *special publics* that are immediately affected by a particular event are likely to hold informed opinions on the matter. In fact, all across Canada there are many special publics holding intense and directed opinions, as distinct from the *general public* that holds opinions on everything.

Properties of Political Opinions

Political opinions have several distinctive characteristics. First, they have *content*. They are about something with political consequence – candidates, issues, or economic and social conditions. Second, they have *direction*, i.e., an opinion is not a simple statement about an alleged fact: it indicates or implies a value preference. A Canadian's opinion about the Organization of American States (OAS), for example, can express approval or disapproval of the organization, as well as his or her understanding of what the OAS is and does. The direction of an opinion informs us whether the public response is positive, negative, or indifferent. Third, opinions have _intensity,_ i.e., an emotional characteristic of public opinion that tells us how committed people are to the position they have taken. In May 1980, intense clusters of Québec opinion polarized in an approximate 60/40 percent distribution on the issue of self-determination. Intensity not only involves the "extremeness" of an opinion, but also the extent to which the issue is salient to a person, i.e., how much he or she really cares about it. On the question of Canada's membership in the OAS, very few Canadians hold intense opinions. More significant is that the intensity of opinions held by a small group of people who constitute a "special" public opposed to membership can influence a foreign-policy decision affecting most people, the large majority of whom are generally unconcerned. In the case of Québec, the results of the referendum indicated the intensity of the conflict in that province. While appearing to be a victory for federalists, the referendum also served to dramatize how severely public opinion had polarized in Québec.

The intensity of opinions is of great importance to government decision-makers. If people hold opinions of low intensity on an issue, governments may decide to proceed with a particular policy direction that is not very popular. Or intensity may reflect a strong consensus compelling a government to act or not to act in a particular policy direction. In Canada, governments spend millions of dollars each year on public-opinion surveys to test how people will react to policy initiatives. Between July 1992 and October 1993, just

prior to the federal election, various departments of the federal government commissioned over 222 public-opinion surveys. Likewise, all provincial governments are frequent users of opinion polls to measure the direction and intensity of public reactions to their policies.

The _stability_ of public opinion is another characteristic of particular interest to governments. Stability is the degree to which the direction and intensity of an opinion remain the same over time. Some people may adhere to a particular viewpoint for decades, while others shift positions frequently. People also vary greatly in the consistency of their opinions. A Canadian may believe that government spending should be increased, but if he or she also wants taxes reduced, we would regard the opinion as inconsistent. Changes in opinion may require a modification of policies and programs by governments. The stability and volatility of public opinion are important measures for government decision-makers and a constant challenge to political leadership.

Measuring Public Opinion

Nearly two centuries ago, the great French social theorist Alex de Tocqueville argued that a society is a democratic one when elected officials pay attention to their electorates. When governors do not know what the people really want, it is impossible for them to be responsible. However, finding out what the public thought about particular issues took a great deal of effort. Before the 1930s, governments, historians, and political observers had to guess at public opinion by analyzing the contents of newspaper stories, political speeches, voting returns,

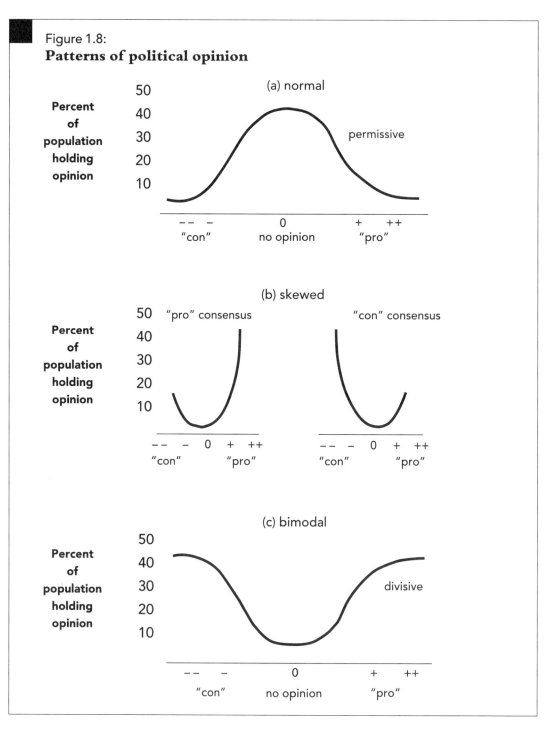

Figure 1.8:
Patterns of political opinion

and travellers' diaries. The founding fathers in both Canada and the United States felt that they could tap into public opinion by implementing *representation by population* in the legislative structures of each country. They thought that attitudes and actions in the legislatures would reflect public opinion on a wide variety of issues. However, after much experience with these legislative structures of government, it became evident that bills passed by a majority of elected representatives do not necessarily reflect the opinions of a majority of citizens.

Random Sampling

In the nineteenth century, newspapers and magazines often enlivened their coverage of politics by conducting **straw polls** or mail surveys of their readers. The difficulty in relying on the results of these polls was that the method of **sampling** was not **random**. Not until the 1930s were efficient new scientific surveys and sampling techniques pioneered by George Gallup, Elmo Roper, and Archibald Crossley, all of whom had developed modern polling methods in American advertising and marketing research. The first scientifically measured public-opinion poll in Canada was conducted during the Second World War. The "little" Gallup poll was based on the theory that a sample of individuals selected by chance from a population will be "representative" of the entire population, so that a few thousand interviews, representative of the total population would be far more effective in reflecting public opinion than millions of ballots collected in a biased or haphazard fashion. This means that the traits of *individuals* in a sample — their attitudes, beliefs, political

■ ■ **random:** the quality of occurring by chance, or in no predictable fashion. ■ ■

characteristics, and so on — will reflect the traits of the *entire* population. Sampling theory does not posit that the sample will exactly match the population, only that it will reflect the population within some predictable degree of accuracy.

Three factors condition the degree of accuracy on the sample. One is that the *sample must be taken randomly,* such that each individual in the population has the same chance of being selected. In Canada, direct random sampling is complicated, given the size and dispersion of the population. Instead, pollsters first divide the country into geographical areas, then randomly choose areas, and eventually sample individuals who live in those areas. The second factor that affects the accuracy of sampling is *the amount of variation in the population.* It is important to stratify the sample so that the same variations in the population — i.e. linguistic, racial, sex, etc. — are reflected in the sample. Finally, *the size of the sample* also affects the accuracy. The larger the sample, the more accurately it will reflect the population. For example, a sample of four hundred individuals will predict accurately to a population within six percentage points (plus or minus), 95 percent of the time. Most national samples, such as the Gallup or Reid polls, are accurate within two and a half to four percentage points, 19 times out of 20.

The results of public-opinion polls are often displayed in charts like those in figure 1.8, which depicts three idealized patterns of distribution — normal, skewed, and bimodal. Two basic elements that contribute to the shape of the opinion distribution are the percentage of the population that holds the opinion (vertical axis) and the direction and intensity of the opinion (− − to ++, horizontal axis). Different patterns of public opinion affect the options open to policy-makers. Opinions that are normally distributed permit government policies to range on either side of the centrist position (note the portion of the population with no opinion or weak opinion that clusters around the centre). Thus, pattern (a) is *permissive* because leaders may act freely without fear of much public reaction. The patterns in (b) are skewed to the pro side or con side of an issue and represent the *consensus* pattern of opinion. In these patterns the options open to leaders are more limited because most people have made up their minds and hold an opinion on one side of the issue. It would be politically perilous for government to ignore such a consensus of opinion, pro or con. The pattern of public opinion in (c) is conflictive and *divisive*. In such a bimodal distribution, opinions divide almost evenly over an issue. Bimodal distributions of opinion have the greatest potential to generate political conflict, especially if people on both sides feel intensely about the issue.

Do Polls Influence Us?

The problems of accurately measuring something as complex as public opinion has stimulated public doubts about the role of polling in a democracy. Do polls simply measure public sentiments from time to time? Do they influence political behaviour when they are widely published or released during election campaigns? There is growing academic suspicion that the predictive value of polls influences undecided voters, politicians, and governments, encourages or discourages volunteer campaign workers, and positively or negatively affects the fund-raising efforts of political parties. Increasingly, observers are noting that elections are poll-inspired and election campaigns are poll-driven. But if polls do have extensive persuasive effect, people are not willing to admit that they do. Pollsters in a Globe-Environics survey tested respondents after the Canadian federal election in 1988 and found that only 13 percent admitted public-opinion polls influenced their voting decision. Of the rest, 85 per cent stated that they were *not* influenced and two per cent refused to answer. Another "poll on polls" conducted by Gallup found almost the same results, with most voters saying they were not influenced by published polls.

There are three kinds of polling organizations: 1) professional organizations that conduct public-opinion surveys and marketing research for both political and non-political clients, such as Gallup and Harris; 2) political pollsters who usually work for a candidate or a political party, such as Decima for the Conservatives and Goldfarb for the Liberals; and 3) media pollsters: survey research conducted by the electronic or print media, for example, CBC or CTV. In the 1979 and 1980 federal election campaigns, only a handful of national polls were conducted by professional polling companies and TV networks. By 1984, the federal election inspired 11 independent national polls. During the 1993 election campaign, 34 independent national polls were completed, an average of five polls a week — the most polling ever conducted during any Canadian election.

Governments and politicians are interested in polls, and increasingly conduct their own polling not only to find out whether they are winning or losing but also to learn if

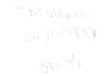

they are popular or unpopular with certain groups. Learning which groups are not supportive enables governments and politicians to make special appeals in that direction.

Because public attitudes are often unstable or uninformed, critics of Canadian political opinion argue that we are too easily manipulated into thinking one way or another by polls. During election campaigns people learn that political parties and their candidates are "sold," not unlike cars or toothpaste. What does it mean if government or the media can deliberately manipulate our political attitudes?

References

1. David Easton, *A Framework for Political Analysis* (Englewood Cliffs, N.J.: Prentice-Hall, 1965), 50; Alan Ball, *Modern Politics and Government* (London: Macmillan Education Limited, 1988), 3-15.

2. As Harold D. Lasswell so aptly put it in the title of his book, *Politics: Who Gets What, When, and How* (New York: McGraw-Hill, 1936).

3. V.I. Lenin, "Left Wing Communism: An Infantile Disorder," in *Selected Works* (New York: International Publishers, 1943).

4. Quoted in Stuart Schram, *The Political Thought of Mao Tse Tung* (New York: Frederick A. Praeger, 1969), 287.

5. Hugh Percy Jones, *Dictionary of Foreign Phrases and Classical Quotations* (Edinburgh: John Grant, 1923).

6. John Redekop, "Canadian Political Institutions" in John Redekop *Approaches to Canadian Politics* (Scarborough, ON: Prentice-Hall Canada Inc., 1983), 149

7. Harold D. Lasswell and A. Kaplan, *Power and Society: A Framework for Political Inquiry* (New Haven: Yale University Press, 1950), 4-6; J.C. Davies, *Human Nature in Politics* (New York: Wiley, 1963), Ch. 1.

8. E.P. Hollander, "Leadership and Power" in G. Lindzey & E. Aronson, eds., *The Handbook of Social Psychology* (New York: Random House, 1985; and M.C. Rush and J.E. Russell, "Leader prototypes and prototype-contingent consensus in leader behavior descriptions." *Journal of Experimental Psychology* (24), 88-104.

9. Gabriel Almond, "Comparative Political Systems," *Journal of Politics XVIII* (1965): 396.

10. Samuel Beer and Adam Ulam, *Patterns of Government* (New York: Random House, 1958), 12.

11. Sidney Verba, "Conclusion: Comparative Political Culture," in Lucian W. Pye and Sidney Verba, eds., *Political Culture and Political Development* (Princeton: Princeton University Press, 1965), 515.

12. Stephen Ullman, "Regional Political Cultures in Canada: A Theoretical and Conceptual Introduction," in Richard Schultz, Orest Kruhlak, and John Terry, eds., *The Canadian Political Process* (Toronto: Holt, Rinehart and Winston of Canada, Ltd., 1979), 7.

13. Richard Simeon and David Elkins, "Regional Political Cultures in Canada," *Canadian Journal of Political Science VII*, no.3 (September 1974): 397; and Roger Gibbins, *Regionalism: Territorial Politics in Canada and the United States*, (Toronto: Butterworths, 1982).

14. See J.A.A. Lovink, "Is Canadian Politics Too Competitive?" *Canadian Journal of Political Science VI*, no. 3 (Sept. 1973).

15. Seymore Martin Lipset, "Historical traditions and national characteristics: a comparative analysis of Canada and the United States," *Canadian Journal of Sociology* II (2), 133-155.

16. Robert Dahl, *Modern Political Analysis* (Englewood Cliffs, NJ: Prentice-Hall, 1965), 50.

17. Karl Deutsch, *Politics and Government, How People Decide Their Fate* (Boston: Houghton Mifflin Company, 1980), 26.

18. Leo A. Johnson, "Precapitalist Economic Formations and the Capitalist Labour Market in Canada, 1911-71," in James E. Curtis and William G. Scott, eds., *Social Stratification: Canada*, 2nd ed. (Scarborough: Prentice-Hall Canada Inc., 1979), 143.

19. UNESCO, *Statistical Yearbook, 1992* (Paris: UNESCO, 1992).

20. Jack Laxton, "City Politics in Canada" in Michael Whittington and Glen Williams, *Canadian Politics in the 1990s,* 3d ed., (Scarborough, ON.: Nelson Canada, 1990), 401-422.

21. Canadian Federation of Mayors and Municipalities, "Puppets on a Shoestring: The Effects on Municipal Governments of Canada's System of Public Finance," (Ottawa, April 28, 1976).

22. Quoted in K.G. Crawford, *Canadian Municipal Government* (Toronto: University of Toronto Press, 1954), 4.

23. Lucian Pye, *Politics, Personality and Nation-Building* (New Haven, CT: Yale University Press, 1963), 1-14.

24. H. Richard Hird, *Working With Economics* (Toronto: Maxwell Macmillan Canada, Inc., 1992), 127-128.

25. Manfred Borchert and Rolf Schinke, eds. *International Indebtedness* (London: Routledge, 1990).

26. David Easton and Jack Dennis, *Children in the Political System* (New York: McGraw-Hill, 1969),7; See also Robert Coles, *The Political Life of Children* (Boston: The Atlantic Monthly Press, 1986).

27. Roberta Sigel, "Assumptions about the Learning of Political Values," *Annals of the American Academy of Social and Political Science* 361 (1985):1; M. Jennings and R. Niemi, *Generations and Politics* (Princeton, NJ: Princeton University Press, 1981).

28. See Charles Horton Cooley, *Human Nature and Social Order* (New York: Schocken, 1964); As applicable to Canadians, see David V.J. Bell, "Political Culture in Canada" in Michael S. Whittington and Glen Williams, eds., *Canadian Politics in the 1990s* (Scarborough, ON: Nelson Canada, 1990), 137-157.

29. James Chowning Davies, "Political Socialization: From Womb to Children," in Stanley Renshon, ed., *Handbook of Political Socialization* (New York: Free Press 1977), 142-147.

30. David Easton and Jack Dennis, "The Child's Image of Government," *The Annals of the American Academy of Political and Social Science* 361 (1965): 56.

31. The principals in the survey were T.G. Carroll of Brock University, Donald Higgins of St. Mary's University, and Michael Whittington of Carleton University. The findings of this study are summarized in Richard Van Loon and Michael Whittington, *The Canadian Political System Environment, Structure, and Process* (Toronto: McGraw-Hill Ryerson Ltd., 1981), 120.

32. Ronald Landes, "The Use of Role Theory in Political Socialization Research: A Review, Critique and Modest Proposal," *International Journal of Comparative Sociology* 17, nos. 1-2 (March-June 1976): 59-72.

33. Roberta Sigel and Marilyn Hoskin, "Perspectives on Adult Political Socialization - Areas of Research," in Allen Renshon, ed., *Handbook of Political Socialization: Theory and Research* (New York: Free Press, 1977), 267.

34. Quoted in Paul Palmer, "The Concept of Public Opinion in Political Theory," in Paul Palmer, *Essays in History and Political Theory in Honor of Charles H. McIlwain* (Cambridge, MA: Harvard University Press, 1936).

35. V.O. Key, *Public Opinion and American Democracy* (New York: Alfred A. Knopf, 1961), 14.

Suggested Readings

Gabriel Almond, *Comparative Politics: A Theoretical Framework* (New York: HarperCollins College Publishers, 1993).

Janine Brodie, Shelley Gavigan, and Jane Jenson, *The Politics of Abortion* (Toronto: Oxford University Press, 1992).

William Gamson, *Talking Politics* (New York: Cambridge University Press, 1992).

John Harrigan, *Political Change in the Metropolis* (New York: HarperCollins College Publishers, 1993).

Ronald Pynn, *American Politics: Changing Expectations* (Madison, WI: W.C. Brown Communications Inc., 1993).

John Rothgeb, *Defining Power: Influence and Force in the Contemporary International System* (New York: St. Martin's Press, 1993).

Mark Sproule-Jones, *Governments at Work* (Toronto: University of Toronto Press, 1993).

Bernard Susser, *Approaches to the Study of Politics* (Toronto: Maxwell Macmillan Canada, 1992).

Jill Vickers et. al., *Politics as if* University of Toronto Press, 19

Howard Wiarda, *Introduction to Comp* (New York: Wadsworth, 1993).

Glossary

authoritative: The characteristic of a person, group, institution, or government which makes legitimate either in reality or in appearance the acts and commands exercised in its name.

behavioural: Any human activity, ranging from internal psychological responses (as in thought, perception, judgement, and opinion), to overt and observable and physical actions.

budget deficit: The amount by which government expenditures exceed its receipts during some specified period of time, usually one year.

continualismo: The practice of many Latin American chief executives to extend their terms in office beyond the limits set by constitutions or political promises.

imposición: The practice in many Latin American states of pre-selecting a candidate and manipulating the political process to ensure that candidate's election.

industrialization: The process by which a society comes to be characterized by an economic system and a mode of social life based on machinery and the factory system of production.

infrastructure: The social and political substructure of a community that includes the institutions, laws, economy, communication, transportation, and education systems.

institutional: Established patterns of human behaviour consisting of structured economic, political, or social interaction within a framework of common goals and values.

institutional role: Consists of those actions, behaviours, and outputs typically performed by a political or legal body, in accordance with the prescriptions of a constitution, set of by-laws, or rules and regulations endorsed by state authority.

internalize: To adopt a society's norms as part of one's personality and notion of self.

national debt: The federal government's total indebtedness at a moment in time, mostly the result of previous deficits.

party identification: The sense of psychological attachment or positive state of mind a voter has for a party, which is not the same thing as voting for a party in any given election.

patronage: A system by which those in government provide jobs and other social amenities to friends, relatives, and supporters.

: sim-

', so-

the

ɔm

insti-

ess

Women Mattered (Toronto:
3).

rative Politics

GLOSSARY

based on the attitude that perceived benefits in political participation are less than the anticipated costs of lost time or income.

political culture: All the learned behaviour, beliefs, customs, and institutions a people use to do politics.

political cynicism: Expressed feelings of doubt, distrust, and sarcasm aimed at the competence, credibility, and honesty of people in government and politics.

political efficacy: The belief that one's participation in politics has some impact on political outcomes and government decisions.

political participation: Actions of private citizens by which they seek to influence or support government and politics.

political socialization: The ways in which we learn about the world of politics and government, as well as the people and institutions that teach us many of the political beliefs we adopt, and the ways in which we transmit our political values to others.

political system: All interrelated institutions, practices, and traditions that enable a society to make authoritative, binding, and coercive decisions extending to all its members.

political values: Those beliefs, goals, and standards that a society professes and tries to achieve.

politicization: The transformation of an activity that apparently has no political connotations into one that fulfills political ends.

poverty line: An amount of money determined by the government to be the least amount required to meet the cost of living (accommodation, food, clothes, transportation, etc.) in the economy.

process: Any rational sequence of related actions or operations leading to a desired goal or result.

public opinion: The expressed views of people about anything that concerns a society; for example, its politics, economy, or cultural interests.

random: The quality of occurring by chance, or in no predictable fashion.

residual power: Jurisdictions or powers that are not specifically enumerated in a constitution delegated to a specific government, or that cannot be implied from powers that are delegated to a recognized government.

sampling: The selection of part of a population or universe of members of any class of things that might be studied.

straw poll: A general canvass of political opinion in certain sections of an electorate prior to an election, designed to discover voters' views about candidates and public issues.

TWO

What is Political Science?

Chapter Objectives

After reading this chapter, you will be able to:

- trace the development of political science through the ages

- differentiate among the ways of approaching political inquiry

- understand the distinctive character of Canadian political science

- recognize how other fields of knowledge can help us learn about politics and government

- examine the presence of political science in the international community

What is Political Science?

Each day Canadians are bombarded with information from the media about political events occurring at home and around the world that evoke curiosity and spark our interest. On the radio we hear that the United States accuses Canada of "dumping" steel into its market. In the newspaper we read that many federal government departments still continue to waste and mismanage public monies in spite of the auditor general's long-standing struggle to make Ottawa more accountable for its spending decisions. On television we watch a documentary on the economic unification of Europe. We analyze this data, draw our own conclusions from it, and decide to act or not to act as a result of our evaluations. This constant barrage of information may leave us feeling overloaded and somehow threatened by the apparent complexities of the political world. But, like untutored music-lovers who discover after some instruction that they can understand music, we too can acquire an appreciation of politics and government.

An understanding of politics is not a gift; it is an achievement. Learning to cope with the vast amounts of political information that come to us every day is a matter of training. We need to place this data in proper perspective by imposing some organization and structure on the flow of world events. First we must be motivated to learn about the political personalities and decisions that affect our lives. Then we must apply a **methodology** to our process of learning that will pro-

■ ■ **methodology:** the process of gathering, measuring, analyzing, and evaluating knowledge within a particular discipline. ■ ■

vide a system for receiving new information. With such a methodology in place, the information we receive becomes a contribution to our growing body of knowledge about politics and government, rather than a hodge-podge of seemingly unrelated events.

Learning how to study politics and government teaches us to think like political scientists. Their field, the study of **political behaviour** and **political ideologies**, is expansive and requires a great deal of instruction, experience, and reading to master. Political scientists want to know how people *behave* with regard to matters of politics and government. The facts, concepts, and perspectives in this course are largely the product of decades of work by thousands of political scientists all over the world.

Like you, political scientists want to learn about politics in a meaningful way. Over the years they have built a recognized academic discipline designed to discover the purpose and significance of all political behaviour. Nothing in politics just happens; events can be explained if a **systematic approach** to information is used. An introductory text in political science has the dual function of showing the student what information is politically relevant, and how to organize this information in a coherent way.

One of the important tasks of political science is to study in an orderly way how politics affects the lives of people. People and their needs are both the causes and objectives of politics. People's needs, values, beliefs, and their share of material possessions are the stuff of politics. For this reason, a knowledge of politics brings us closer to a knowledge of ourselves. Whether we are aware of it or not, each of us has a political dimension. Nothing occurs in politics that in some way does not relate to our private attitudes and behaviour.

None of our institutions (such as parliaments, congresses, and political parties) or processes (such as legislation, administration, and revolution) exist apart from the political ideas and behaviour of people.[1] When we look at political phenomena from this perspective, we see the world of politics not only as an institutional mosaic, but as groups of people interacting with one another because of different personal preferences and expectations. It is in this context that we can define political science as the study of people as individuals or groups who are engaged in political behaviour of all kinds – including the ways they think about politics, the political, legal and governmental institutions they create, and the relations they develop in the international system.

From the earliest times, political scientists have studied **normative** questions, questions about how people should behave in the world of politics and government. These students of politics ask such questions as: What is "justice"? How can we achieve it? What is good government? Who should lead us in our society? What should the individual's relationship with government be? Everyone has a stake in these kinds of questions because we all want society, acting through government, to resolve problems and make life much better. To know what "better" is, we have to think about ourselves and others in a normative way.

■ PROFILE
OF A POLITICAL SCIENTIST
Dr. Leo Panitch

Dr. Leo Panitch is a distinguished political scientist and teacher of politics and government. Professor Panitch began his political science studies at the University of Manitoba. He completed his Ph.D. at the London School of Economics and Political Science. His scholarly and professional activities include writing books and articles, editing books and journals, giving papers at conferences, doing media commentaries, and assessing research projects submitted by other political scientists to Canadian research councils and journals.

He teaches graduate and undergraduate political science courses at York University in Toronto. He especially enjoys teaching introductory courses. His regard for his students has moulded his approach for conveying information in a language and within a frame of reference that undergraduates can appreciate.

The Origins of Political Science

In one sense, the study of politics is as ancient as recorded history. In another sense, "political science" is a product of the twentieth century. Political science as a modern academic discipline took a considerable time to grow before the characteristics fundamental to a bona fide social science were present. It should be noted that there are many conceptions of what political science is, based on the many different ways one can view political reality.

Philosophers have been writing about politics for thousands of years. Some of them, notably Plato and Aristotle, made contributions to the study of politics that are still relevant and debated today. However, political science as such did not exist until this century, and was not generally included among the social sciences until 50 years ago. As this section will explain, most of the evolution of political science has occurred gradually over the centuries. In fact, you are about to trace the emergence of a very old discipline.

The Early Political Scientists

The Greeks

We can trace the beginnings of the study of government and politics to the Greeks of over 2400 years ago. The Greeks used the word "idiot" to refer to anyone who had no interest in politics. They took politics so seriously that they studied it as the "queen of the sciences." To them, the study of government was **architechtonic**, i.e., a highly organized and

Dr. Panitch believes that politics affects us all, and we can affect politics.

Professor Panitch came to York University in 1984 from Carleton University, where he had established an international reputation as one of Canada's foremost political economists. From 1989 to 1994 he was Chair of York's Department of Political Science. He is the author and editor of numerous books and articles, including *The Canadian State* (1977) and *Working Class Politics in Crisis* (1986), *The Assault on Trade Union Freedoms: From Wage Controls to Social Contract* (1993), and *A Different Kind of State?* (1993). He was attracted to York because of the diversity of its academic programs and the multicultural character of its student body.

Panitch on Political Science

Dr. Panitch sees politics as something that manifests itself in human behaviour, and the world of political ideas as a natural function of all institutions. He says, "The study of politics is not just the study of parliaments or bureaucracies or even a broader study of the most powerful decision-makers in all spheres of society. It must be a study as well of the social forces "from below." Some will say that is the proper field of sociology, especially insofar as the activities of those below, even if they influence the decision-makers, do not have enough power "to change the system." But this is an impoverished view of political science.

There is another important dimension to political science, of course, which precisely has to do with "changing the system"; which is not just about analyzing what the state and ruling class do, criticizing it on this basis, or even coming forward on the basis of this structured approach to building a society and its political institutions.

The enduring contribution of the Greeks to political science lies in the way they thought about politics. They saw it as a natural form of human behaviour. They tried to discover the form of political society that would best enable human nature to flourish and achieve its highest expression of reason. We know the Greeks did not apply the same methods used by modern social scientists who seek to detect regularities in political behaviour from which to generalize about society. But they did possess a "social science attitude" through which they applied independent objective reasoning to the Hellenic world of politics.[2] In fact, the word "politics" itself is derived from the Greek word for city–state, πολισ (*polis*). To the Greeks, the **polis** was the centre of the political universe.

Plato (427–347 B.C.) is credited with writing the first major utopian study, widely regarded as a classic in political science. In *The Republic*, he displays the critical attitude that is necessary for the proper study of government and prescribes reforms and models for politics as actually practised. He elevated the study of politics to an independent academic enterprise when he founded an academy near Athens. It is widely believed to have been the first school of political science and law.

Plato's student, Aristotle (384–322 B.C.), used systematic reasoning and critical inquiry in the *Politics* to conclude that "man is by nature a political animal." Aristotle held that all people are politicians even though those in public office appear to be more political than others.

Political scientists usually think of Aristotle as the father of modern political philoso-

analysis with "public policy" proposals for enabling the state to manage the system better. Rather, this other dimension of political science is about developing analyses of the processes and strategies involved in changing the system from one based on class competition, exploitation, and conflict to a different system based on the elimination of classes and the development of as fully a democratic, egalitarian, and co-operative society as possible.

Here we begin to raise larger questions about what "science" is really all about. We can see, in this sense, the importance of a political science that is trying to know more than how to uncover how the power elites rule the world, but which also has an understanding that the majority subjected to that rule also has power capacities, and is trying to discover how those capacities might be enhanced: not just to criticize the elites or ruling classes, not just to influence their decisions through struggles "from below," but to "transcend" the present system of power relations entirely. This is less a matter of constructing utopian visions of a "good society" than of discovering the means whereby the subordinate classes have increased their power historically and of trying to discover further and better means.

Political science has a role to play in demonstrating that most people are not just passive recipients of someone else's power, that they currently exercise some power even if just in relation to the greater power of the dominant classes. It could have a larger and more creative role to play in discovering the limits to the ways in which subordinate classes have organized so far, and by trying to think through and offer advice on how to phy and political science. When he established the Lyceum in about 335 B.C., he employed special research assistants to compile information for political analysis. In fact, the Lyceum was dedicated to the scientific study of politics, using principles of knowledge from every known field of study. As far as we know from his work at the Lyceum, Aristotle was the first to recognize the **eclectic** nature of political inquiry and to encourage it in an institutional setting. We must credit Aristotle with nurturing the genesis of a modern political science, even though many other conditions had to evolve before it could become the modern scholarly enterprise of today.

We can see that the Greeks viewed politics as an activity that is observable, classifiable, and understandable. Even in ancient times, it was clear to them that the serious study of politics was the only way to reform the weaknesses of a political system and to preserve the strengths of a civilization.

The Romans

Roman political thought made two special contributions to the study of government. The Romans focused their political inquiry on the study of law and on *public administration*. Knowledge of the law was an important stepping-stone to many appointed positions of government in the Roman Empire. The successes of the empire were due mainly to the Roman genius for the universal application of law and the imperial government administration.

Cicero (106-43 B.C.) took the lead in studying and writing about Roman government and politics. His two major works, *The Republic* and *The Laws,* provide us with a clear analysis of how the Roman political system

organize for a fundamental challenge to the powers that be.

This will, above all, be a matter of discovering the kind of political organizations that enhance the intellectual capacities of working people themselves so that they can become leaders and educators in their own communities and develop their capacities to run their society and state in a fully democratic manner. To be a political scientist, in this conception, is to be someone who is oriented to discovering how to help those who have the potential power to change the system to realize that they have that potential – and then actually to act upon that potential. Philosophers, a great social scientist once said, have always tried to understand the world, but the point of this understanding, he appropriately insisted, was to change it."

fused *ius civile* (civil law), *ius gentium* (law of man), and *ius naturale* (natural law). Indeed, he was the only outstanding Roman of his time who took an objective interest in law and public administration as aspects of a unique governmental system that aspired to rule the world. Without Cicero, the study of politics for the advancement of knowledge under the Roman Empire would not have taken place.

The Medieval Period

The medieval period lasted roughly from the fall of Rome in the fifth century to the Renaissance in the fourteenth. The astonishing growth of Christianity during this period turned the minds of the great writers from the general study of political affairs to theological and ecclesiastical concerns. In the words of William Dunning, "the Middle Age was unpolitical."[3]

The most notable writers were Augustine (354-430), John of Salisbury (1120-1180), Thomas Aquinas (1226-1274), and Marsiglio of Padua (1275-1343). While they wrote to influence governments and rulers, they did so as dutiful sons of the Church and with the main goal of positing theological doctrine. Thus, the attitude of the Church toward society and the state became the subject of extensive controversy.

Augustine's great book, *The City of God*, was inspired by his shock at the sacking of the "Eternal City" of Rome in 410; it was his attempt to explain such a devastating occurrence. In this book, Augustine posited two cities – the city of God and the city of man. He proposed that peace, harmony, and justice are found in the city of God, whose citizens are motivated by the love of God. The citizens of the city of man are motivated by love of self and this city is, therefore, imperfect and doomed to end. Although Augustine was speaking primarily of two spiritual states, the city of God could also be identified with the Church, and the city of man with the Roman Empire.

John of Salisbury posited the supremacy of ecclesiastical over temporal power. He held that a monarch must rule in conformity with Church principles or risk being overthrown. Thomas Aquinas, the "Angelic Doctor," saw himself as primarily a theologian rather than a political philosopher. Although agreeing with Aristotle that the purpose of the state is to direct a person to virtuous living, Aquinas held that human virtue was only attainable through the knowledge of God. For him, the state was theologically oriented. Marsiglio of Padua is widely considered to be the bridge between the medieval period and the Renais-

sance. As a practising physician, his scientific outlook made him skeptical about the dogmatic character of much of medieval thought. Marsiglio broke with the Middle Ages by rejecting the supremacy of theology over politics. His use of common sense, objective observation, and critical analysis made him a modern thinker with whom contemporary social scientists can identify. He introduced a **secular** approach to a predominantly religious framework of thinking about the world.

Because the Christian church so dominated intellectual and social life in the Middle Ages, existing political thought centred on moral questions of "ought" (dogma) rather than scientific questions of "is" (facts). But during the high Middle Ages, a new institution emerged that would profoundly affect intellectual life in Europe and the world to the present day. This was the revival of the university, which ranks as the most enduring medieval contribution to modernity. The rise of universities spawned the growth of a class of intellectuals committed to original and independent thought – all necessary for the evolution of a modern discipline dedicated to the study of government and politics.

The Renaissance

The Renaissance was a period of transition from the medieval to the "modern" world. Modern political science begins here: A new world was being born, one founded on nationalism, the power of human reason, and the emergence of the nation-state.

During the Renaissance, Europe witnessed a growing national consciousness and political centralization, developed an urban economy based on organized commerce and capitalism, and saw ever-greater secular control of thought and culture. People appreciated and even glorified the secular world, secular learning, and purely human pursuits as ends in themselves, separate from church influence. Between the fourteenth and sixteenth centuries, intellectuals shook off the religious and institutional restrictions of medieval life to rediscover worldly things and a new place for the individual in a changing society.

The dawn of the Renaissance is identified with the writings of Dante Alighieri (1265-1321). Dante's work ushered in a revolutionary period of changing social values and a revival of interest in learning about Greece and Rome. Dante's most important political work, *De Monarchia*, contributed to political thought by stressing the need for monarchical world government, and by arguing that the pope and the emperor derive their authority directly and independently from God. Modern political science is indebted to Dante for his practical analysis of the instruments for the peaceful settlement of disputes between states. In *De Monarchia,* Dante envisioned a world order supported by global institutions that would legislate, arbitrate, and adjudicate peace.

Perhaps the best-known Renaissance thinker, whose works revived the national, secular, and scientific spirit that had lain dormant since the Greeks, is Niccolo Machiavelli (1469-1527). If the most important discovery of the Renaissance was man, the most important discovery of Machiavelli was political man. Of Machiavelli, the seventeenth-century philosopher Francis Bacon wrote: "We are much beholden to Machiavelli and others that wrote what men do and not what they ought to do."[4] Machiavelli asserted that the true guide to the science of politics was realism, and that all human behaviour must be observed for what *is*, not for what it *should be*.

In *The Prince* and later in *The Discourses on the First Ten Books of Titius Livius*, Machiavelli pointed out that when human beings occupy positions of power, ethics and morality tend to become lower priorities. For this reason, Machiavelli is labelled as if he invented assassination, corruption, and political expediency. But he never advocated immorality for its own sake; rather, his **amoral** views reflected a scientific objectivity in the study of human political behaviour. As a modern student of politics, Machiavelli replaced the "ideal" with the "actual." By doing so, he offered the first rigorous analysis of **power politics** in understandable language.

The Reformation

During the Reformation, politics once again became a subject dear to the hearts of theologians. A religious movement swept through Europe in the sixteenth century, challenging the authority of the Roman Catholic Church and leading to the rise of Lutheranism, Calvinism, and the Protestant churches. Appalled by the corruption of the Church and by its abuse of political power, reformers like Martin Luther (1483-1546) claimed that salvation was achieved through the faith of the individual Christian and not through the practices of the Church. Luther also weakened the Church's political authority by claiming that political leaders had power over the Church. Luther received much support from German princes who were resentful of the political power of the pope, who to them was an Italian ruler. John Calvin (1509-1564) was converted to the ideas of the Reformation, but he went much further than Luther. Calvin was determined to establish God's "Holy Commonwealth" on earth, and he established a **theocracy** in Geneva, which he himself ruled with great strictness. Both Luther and Calvin saw themselves as free critics of the political and social order. The study of politics became a popular intellectual concern at this time, with the rapid spread of the printing presses in over 250 European cities. This dramatically increased the output of political information, so necessary for the development of modern political science.

Jean Bodin (1530-1596), a political theorist who wrote prolifically for a conservative group known as the "Politiques," coined the term "sciences politiques" (political science). For him, political science was concerned with the study of sovereignty, the functions of government, and all institutions that make law. Even though this was a much more restricted definition of what is today regarded as political science, it was an important step in the evolution of the discipline. The emergence of politically independent states provided students of politics with materials for comparative political studies. This stimulated a scholarly curiosity about the various forms and functions of government and about the political behaviour of executives and legislators. The study of politics had become a self-conscious activity. Already the core of political inquiry was recognizable and distinguishable from other fields of study.

The Age of Reason

The late seventeenth century, known as the Age of Reason, nourished a belief in the positive consequences of the free and unprejudiced use of the human intellect. This liberation of thought extended especially to political questions. People everywhere asserted their own ideas on the rights of individuals and the responsibilities of governments. The most outstanding political writers of the time considered such issues as the dispersion of powers in government, and in whom the supreme authority of the state should rest. Access to political information was almost limitless. Controversial political ideas were circulated in books, periodicals, and newspapers. Never before in European history had so many people shown so much interest in politics.

Thomas Hobbes (1588-1679) advocated absolute government to control human behaviour, based on a special social contract binding upon all citizens that was designed to protect them from the ruthlessness of their own selfish human natures. Hobbes is an important part of the philosophical tradition of political science. He employed the *deductive method* of reasoning, whereby his assumptions about human nature were used as premises for building an appropriate political system.

His contemporary, John Locke (1632-1704), used the same method of reasoning as Hobbes, but Locke held a much more optimistic view of human nature. He felt that government should be limited, accountable, and changeable to give people the freedom to be themselves rather than to protect them from themselves. The text of the United States Declaration of Independence is a purely Lockean document. But the spirit of Locke's *Two Treatises of Civil Government* (1690) can also be found in Part I of Canada's Charter of Rights and Freedoms, where the inalienable rights of individuals are listed (Sections 1-31). Political science is indebted to Locke for his advocacy of freedom of speech and inquiry.

Without such freedom, an independent social science dedicated to the open discussion and critical analysis of government and all forms of political behaviour could never have flourished.

Charles de Secondat, Baron de Montesquieu (1689-1755), argued for a separation of powers among the executive, legislative, and judicial branches of government so that no one branch could ever dominate the political system. His revolutionary framework of government was later incorporated into the Constitution of the United States as well as the constitutions of most Latin American states.

The Enlightenment

The Enlightenment was an intellectual groundswell in support of reform and change in eighteenth-century European society. The writers and critics who forged this new social attitude came to be known as the "philosophes." The names Voltaire, Diderot, Rousseau, Hume, and Kant are but a few associated with those intellectuals who wanted to reform thought, society, and government for the sake of human liberty. Their demands for freedom shaped the constitutions and institutions of every modern democratic state.

With the Industrial Revolution (beginning in the mid-18th century) came a new era of revolutionary thought and events, including the American Revolution (1776) and the French Revolution (1789). This new age of revolution unleashed two complementary developments that advanced the growth of the social sciences. The first was the evolution of a widespread trust and belief that science and its exacting methods of inquiry would lead to the most reliable understanding of human behaviour; second, the specialization of human skills and knowledge associated with the rapid growth of towns and cities, which was an incentive for people to choose a professional career in the study of social and political affairs.

Many of the intellectual responses to the Industrial Revolution were attempts to build an alliance of scientific methods and human knowledge. The British **utilitarians** attempted to quantify political reform by advancing the scientific principle of utility – the greatest good for the greatest number. Jeremy Bentham (1748-1832), James Mill (1773-1836), John Stuart Mill (1805-1873), and Sir Edwin Chadwick (1800-1890) all proclaimed a *rational*, scientific approach to political and economic affairs so that no single group would receive privileged consideration. This new attitude toward the study of political matters led to a greater use of the *empirical method*, i.e., learning that came from actual experience, through the senses, and that was subject to scientific testing for verification.

Karl Marx and his collaborator Friedrich Engels attempted to apply science to international politics and world history. They presented their "scientific" philosophy of history to explain the development of humankind as a dialectic of class struggles leading to new social orders – from feudalism to capitalism and from socialism to communism (*The Communist Manifesto*, 1848). Marx's "scientific" method for discovering socio-political truth had its pitfalls when measured by twentieth-century standards. But his determination to derive an exacting method of studying political economy contributed to the birth of a real science of politics. Not long after his death in 1883, the most concentrated effort to apply scientific methods to political inquiry would take place in the United States.

Modern Political Science

Political Science in the United States

The emergence of modern political science and its establishment as an independent self-conscious discipline is intimately tied to the growth of universities in the United States.[5] By 1875, British, French, and German scholarly influences in political studies had reached the United States, expressing themselves in the formation of university programs especially designed to train people in political science.

In June 1880, Columbia University (then called Columbia College) established its School of Political Science, headed by John W. Burgess. Within a few years, the school launched the *Political Science Quarterly,* which quickly gained world recognition for the quality of its publications and continues to maintain its reputation today. At Johns Hopkins University, Herbert Baxter Adams developed a program of advanced training and research in history and political science in 1876, followed by the establishment of the Johns Hopkins Historical and Political Science Association in 1887. From the experience of these two universities, the teaching of political science as a unique academic discipline spread rapidly to the leading academic centres of the United States.

Impressed by the achievements of the natural sciences, the first generation of American political scientists began to encourage the research of new knowledge using scientific methods that had already proved their po-

tency in such fields as biology, mathematics, and physics. The gradual "Americanization" of political science brought with it a commitment to use the most modern approaches in studying politics and to distinguish the analysis of political behaviour from the total social environment. But we should not neglect the role of a small group of "realists" who were critical of the formalistic character of political inquiry during this period and who urged students of politics to focus on the "facts" to find out how government really works. Their influence encouraged researchers to study what the political system *is* rather than what it *should be.*

The American Political Science Association (APSA) was born in 1903 in a period of intellectual ferment and political reform that came to be known as "progressivism." In the opening years of the twentieth century, progressives were concerned about whether science and technology could help the United States remain an industrial giant with the same democratic ideals inherited from the past. Many of the original 214 members of APSA were progressives who wanted their colleagues to engage in scientific study of the organization and function of the state. As the first modern organization of its kind, APSA was the single most decisive factor that determined the professional status of political science. Almost immediately, political science gained international respect as a distinct academic pursuit.

The *American Political Science Review* (*APSR*) began to publish in 1906 and attracted manuscripts from around the globe. It became the model journal of political science and was followed in 1907 by the *American Journal of International Law* and the *Academy of*

Political Science Proceedings in 1910. Decade by decade the number of journals increased to reflect the multiple interests and the newer methods of studying political science. By the 1990s, there were nearly 200 political science journals published in the United States alone.

While the drive to Americanize political science characterized the first decades after the creation of APSA, European influences continued to hold their ground as departments of political science spread across the United States. The continental influence was sustained by the migration of European-trained political scientists, some of whom would complete their studies and begin new careers in the United States. Many of the émigrés were gifted scholars. They, along with U.S.-born and trained practitioners, have been instrumental in developing the two master approaches to the generic study of politics in the twentieth century – the traditional and behavioural approaches.

The Proven Ways of the Past

Despite the drive toward **scientism** in the interwar years, European influences ensured that the traditional approach to political science was firmly embedded in the United States. It should be noted that traditionalism was not identified as a conscious, coherent movement in political science until after World War II. The term "traditionalist" was invented by a small group of American researchers who advocated scientific approaches to the study of politics and who wanted to stigmatize their academic opponents. In spite of this, what is now referred to as traditionalism remains important; without it, the modern study of politics would not have achieved its present status as a credible social science.

Traditionalism in American political science embraces a wide variety of European approaches to political inquiry. Practitioners of political and social philosophy believe that a knowledge of classical political literature is essential for prescribing moral choices in the modern world. Like their European colleagues, they are political counsellors who offer general advice to the rulers and the ruled.

Traditionalists see themselves as practical observers rather than scientists. This is not to suggest that they are anti-science, but to them, politics is an *art* that resists study by scientific methods. All political systems have information that is scientifically and technologically inaccessible, i.e., that cannot be measured with precision and certainty. Policy questions relating to ethics, fairness, and justice readily lend themselves to traditional approaches of investigating political phenomena. On these kinds of issues, traditionalists see no need to separate facts from values; they recognize an intrinsic relationship between human political behaviour and morality. Thus, for the traditionalist, politics are best understood through informed judgement derived from careful study and observation, often by suggesting what ought to be done in order to perfect or improve a situation.

Let us outline the main components of the traditional approach that became so prevalent during the interwar years, and continues today as a widely accepted practice in the international political-science community:

- **Methodology**: The general goals of traditional political analysis are to *describe* and *explain* what one observes in the world of politics and government. The orderly understanding of politics proceeds from descriptive questions of "what" to explanatory questions of "why." A description of facts is explained through the personal talents and informed judgement of the observer, who applies his or her creative imagination to the task at hand. Quantitative methods are rarely applied because traditionalists doubt whether human political behaviour can be scientifically measured.

■ **Historical analysis**: Historical methods are used for political research. The researcher collects information and evaluations of a particular subject by using primary sources, such as public documents, to develop a chronology of events or ideas that leads to a conclusion.

■ **Institutional analysis**: Analysis focuses on the structures and functions of political *institutions* through careful observation. The researcher presupposes that all significant politics take place in institutional settings. The analyst accumulates facts using official government documents and records as source materials. The study of institutions provides answers to questions of authority, power, and legitimacy.

■ **Legal analysis**: Formal legal terms, practices, and institutions in a political system are studied. This usually involves the analysis of charters, constitutions, the process of lawmaking, and interpretation. After studying these, the analyst prescribes legal and political reforms to improve the political and government system.

■ **Philosophical analysis**: The deductive method of reasoning is used to analyze normative questions. The analyst recommends political rules, values, and institutional needs from general premises about human nature and human behaviour. On the basis of the philosophical approach, traditionalists prescribe normative solutions to political problems. In their view, no political inquiry into social problems can remain neutral or completely free of normative judgements or prescriptions. The results may appear as a set of convictions that map out an interpretation of the political world so as to reform the fabric of society.

■ **Careerism**: There is a belief among traditionalists that political science should be used to prepare people for government service in public administration and diplomacy, teaching political science, political leadership, and service to international organizations. Political science has special responsibilities in public affairs to provide instruction in democratic principles of government, in addition to training political researchers and teachers.

The Scientific Pathway

Traditional political science did not remain unchallenged for long. The scientific intent of the founders of APSA began to appear frequently in the works of political scientists of the day. This new generation of political scientists were the first in a long line of American practitioners who would aspire to a greater degree of precision in the analysis of political phenomena by using the skills of science and by integrating concepts that were applied in other social sciences such as sociology and psychology.

As a point of fact, the term "behaviouralism" was recognized as part of a larger scientific movement occurring simultaneously in *all* of the social sciences, now referred to as the behavioural sciences. For political scientists, behaviouralism emphasized the systematic understanding of all identifiable manifestations of political behaviour. But it also meant the application of rigorous scientific and statistical methods to standardize testing and to attempt **value-free** inquiry of the world of politics.

The rise of behaviouralism in political science was aided by major advances in survey and polling techniques and the use of computers to store and process information in all areas of human activity. This stimulated an information revolution in the mass production of scientifically generated data, particularly in the social sciences. After World War II, a growing number of American political scientists regarded behaviouralism as the only acceptable approach to valid generalizations about political life.

Since that time, American behaviouralists have claimed considerable success in assembling theoretical hypotheses in political science. They have postulated that a science is as applicable to human political behaviour as it is to all other forms of animal behaviour. To them, science can help explain, predict, and construct **generalizations** about the political world. Many behaviouralists believe in remaining neutral with respect to prescribing morals and values for a society. These are questions of concern for politicians and electorates. For the behaviouralist, the role of political science is primarily to gather and analyze facts as rigorously and objectively as possible.

By letting the facts fall where they may, the analyst surrenders the moral implications of the data to other people. The following is an outline of the components of behaviouralism:

■ **Approach**: The primary focus of political analysis is on actual observable behaviour of individuals and groups rather than just on institutions where equally relevant political behaviour may be overlooked. The analyst seeks to discover patterns and regularities of behaviour that can be expressed as verifiable generalizations.

■ **Methodology**: The scientific method of inquiry is used to generate data for analytical purposes. The method involves essentially four steps:
1. organization and collection of information;
2. classification of **variables**;
3. formation of **hypotheses** on the interrelationship of variables;
4. testing of hypotheses.

■ **Eclecticism**: Political science developed as an eclectic discipline that integrates relevant findings from related natural and social sciences into a body of political knowledge. By working closely with other social sciences, political science contributes to a bank of testable knowledge leading to **models** of human political behaviour.

■ **Goal**: A body of empirical generalizations is assembled that states the relationships among variables for the purposes of explanation and prediction. This knowledge is recorded as logically related sets of hypotheses that, when tested, provide answers to political questions of cause and effect. Behaviouralism is capable of constructing theories out of research from pure science, e.g., knowledge of politics for its own sake; or from applied science, e.g., knowledge of politics for the immediate application to society's problems.

■ **Professionalism**: Behaviouralist political scientists strive to conduct value-free inquiry. Practitioners avoid mixing their moral standards, ethics, and personal preferences with the design and conclusions of research projects.

Behaviouralism spread rapidly across the United States after World War II, reaching its peak in the 1960s. The behavioural movement aspired to establish political science as a social-science discipline, meeting all the criteria by which any behavioural science is judged. There is no question that behaviouralism has had a permanent effect on the basic values and objectives of political science.

But as behaviouralism matured, it soon became obvious that the emphasis on methodology had sacrificed relevance for exactitude. Widespread frustration with the behaviourial obsession with being "scientific" led to significant numbers of political scientists abandoning this approach to political inquiry. This group of predominantly younger political scientists called upon the American Political Science Association to recognize the limitations of scientific detachment. They encouraged APSA to redirect its energies toward a post-behavioural synthesis of methodology with relevant policy considerations and political reform.

A Plea for Relevance

Post-behaviouralism called for a literal re-vision, or viewing again, of the aims of political science.[6] The practice of a post-behavioural political science has proved to be a healthy reassessment of basic goals and values within the discipline. The essence of the post-behavioural revolution is that political science has a *public* purpose. Not only must it strive to understand the political processes scientifically, but it must deliberately attempt to address the most urgent political problems of the contemporary world in an active and relevant way.

The credo of post-behavioural political science asks its practitioners to commit themselves to making this a better world. Thus, the object of contemporary political research should be to apply the precision of scientific inquiry to improve political systems. Post-behaviouralists confront pertinent issues at every level of society by advocating political action and reform for problems of the environment, domestic violence, education, health and welfare, sexual equality, and unemployment, to name but a few. The possession of expert political knowledge and the skills to gather it in exacting ways places special social responsibilities on the political scientist to act in the service of society.

For some, like Michael Haas and Henry Kariel, not to act on this knowledge is "immoral."[7] In making the connection between having the knowledge and using it as a social obligation, post-behaviouralists belong to a tradition inherited from the Greeks and continued through to the establishment of modern political science.

Other implications flow from this post-behavioural shift to implement a relevant political science. First, political scientists must be able to communicate with the victims of society, not just the elites in government, business, academia, and the military. Practitioners must aim their expertise at all of society, not just at privileged segments. Second, the choice of research projects is crucial and must reflect an immediate concern for the struggles of the day. The call to respond to the most pressing political issues facing societies leads to the making of a political profession. Post-behaviouralists acknowledge that no group in society is spared the effects of political crisis and therefore no group can afford to remain aloof. Universities as well as professional associations cannot stand on the sidelines of the political turmoil they want to study.

Post-behaviouralism has resulted in a healthy cynicism about our ways of discovering political truth – a skepticism that rejects the idea of postponing burning issues in times of stress until a sufficient body of systematic theory grows out of the extensive analysis of lesser matters. The components of post-behaviouralism are:

■ **Approach**: Political science is a composite of both traditional and scientific political knowledge. One task of the political scientist is to apply a varied approach that combines the use of precise measurement and prescriptive analysis. The practitioner makes value judgements based on information derived from scientific inquiry.

■ **Methodology**: A great variety of methods can be used to evaluate political problems effectively. Methodology can no longer be treated as a restricted preserve of the scientist who wants precise knowledge. To the post-behavioural political scientist, methodology is concerned not only with technique but also with broader questions of values such as justice and morality.

■ **Scope**: Political science has a public dimen-sion that imposes professional responsibilities and moral obligations upon practitioners. The responsibilities flow from the fact that political scientists are privy to a large body of accumulated knowledge that may be used to train new professionals and to help people understand and change their political world. The moral obligations require political scientists to direct their special skills to the public good.

■ **Policy engineering**: Political scientists should focus their insights on problems of political organization and behaviour, with the object of improving society. This is a professional orientation that combines values and goals, not always scientifically derived, to prescribe practical ways of reforming an imperfect society.

It is in the contexts of traditionalism, behaviouralism, and post-behaviouralism that we can best appreciate the development of political science in the United States.[8] These three approaches have advanced the organization and respectability of political science as a modern social science everywhere in the world. They represent the broadest and most comprehensive efforts on the part of American practitioners to learn about the complexities of politics.

Political Science in Canada

Prior to the twentieth century, political science scarcely existed as a subject in Canadian colleges. Political studies first appear in 1877 at Queen's University, then at the University of Toronto in 1888, where a professorship of Political Economy and Constitutional History was established. In its infancy in Canada, political science was assumed to be a natural part of economics, history, and philosophy. There was still some reluctance to lend an air of academic respectability to politics, let alone to recognize political science as an independent academic pursuit.

McGill University established its Department of Economics and Political Science in 1901, and shortly thereafter the internationally acclaimed Stephen Leacock became chairman, a position he held from 1908 to 1936. The spread of separate political-science departments occurred in a halting, hesitant way from the turn of the century until the 1950s. The University of Saskatchewan established its department in 1910, but many of Canada's universities, like McGill, only offered courses in political studies as adjuncts to other departments, such as economics, history, and philosophy. Thus, the organization of political instruction and the development of political research grew very slowly. In fact, as late as 1958, Canada had only produced an academic core of political scientists totalling 33.[9] But despite its meagre size, the determination of this small, highly competent group of political scientists enabled the discipline to reach a self-consciousness of a different character from that of the powerful branch across the border.

From the beginning, Canadian political scientists, even those who would have accepted the label "scientist," were much less concerned with the need to define the scope and methodology of their discipline than were their U.S. colleagues. Early Canadian practitioners were much more flexible in adopting traditional approaches from Europe and were more tolerant of disciplinary developments.[10] W.J. Ashley, the British academic who first headed the department at the University of Toronto, laid the foundations for an eclectic political science by calling for the study of all important values, ideas, and subjects related to politics.

The Canadian Political Science Association (CPSA)

When the Canadian Political Science Association (CPSA) was formed in 1913, its first president, Adam Shortt, presided over political science as well as economics, sociology, and anthropology. This small but diversified association of professionals attracted members from many fields: administrators, journalists, lawyers, and politicians. And, unlike its American counterpart, the CPSA was organized to develop the study of politics by simply "studying political problems," not with a mission to marry science to political inquiry. Upon its establishment, the CPSA gave recognition to political science as a pluralistic discipline: no one methodology design was implied or intended.

On the eve of World War I, Canadian political science was not of a clear and single mind with respect to the orientation the discipline should embrace. Its differentiation from other disciplines was far from complete, the emergence of a Canadian contingent of political scientists was still to follow, and the struggle for separate departments of political science would not begin for another 40 years. The establishment of the CPSA was a tremendous step forward, and was decisive in determining much of what would happen to political science in future decades. But the outbreak of the war would slow its progress until 1929-30, when the CPSA revived its annual meetings and began to encourage a healthy pluralism in adopting approaches to political affairs.

The formation of an autonomous, domestic, university-based political science began in Canada after World War I.[11] At this time, a small number of able and influential political scientists established their presence not only by writing but also by teaching at Canadian universities. The contribution of these early practitioners to Canadian political science has been to provide a substantive bloc of reputable works, such that it is impossible to imagine what the present contours of the discipline might have been were it not for their efforts.

In 1935, the *Canadian Journal of Economics and Political Science* (*CJEPS*) became solidly established as the central publishing organ of the CPSA. At this time, political scientists shared the journal with economists, and it provided extensive coverage in both fields. For many years, the combined journal was able to accommodate the critical writings of both disciplines. But eventually the *CJEPS* was unable to provide the necessary exposure for the many specializations emerging in the study of political affairs. However, during its existence it furnished a national forum of communication for Canada's sparse population of political scientists and helped disseminate professional political analysis to a small but attentive public. By 1968, a sufficient number of scholarly manuscripts were reaching the editorial desks of the *CJEPS* to warrant a separate journal, the *Canadian Journal of Political Science*.

The Spread of Political Science Departments

During the interwar period, political science in Canada gradually became academically es-

tablished. Usually, it was first introduced at the university level simply as a subject of study. In piecemeal fashion, political science gradually spread across the country and appeared as an independent academic discipline under separate departments: at the University of British Columbia in 1920, Acadia University in 1927, University of Ottawa in 1936, and the Université Laval in 1939.

Following World War II, a number of important works were published focusing on Canadian government, especially its "political" aspects: H. McD. Clokie, *Canadian Government and Politics* (1944); J.A. Carry, *Democratic Government and Politics* (1946); and R.M. Dawson, *The Government of Canada* (1947). These distinguished works by Canadians were instrumental in encouraging colleges and universities to recognize political science as a legitimate academic field of study of Canada.

The establishment of separate departments of political science proceeded swiftly in the late 1950s and 1960s. From 1958 to 1969, over 30 institutions either separated political science from other departments or established new departments. The number of political scientists teaching at Canadian universities grew from 33 in 1958 to over 500 in 1970.[12] Yet, between 1960 and 1970, when faculty positions grew by 475, only 27 doctorates were awarded in Canada to political scientists. This led to the widespread recruitment of qualified non-Canadian political scientists, many of whom were drawn from the United States. They brought with them various tenets and methodologies – mostly of American political science. By 1970, nearly half of the more than 500 political-science professors in Canada were foreign-born. And although some had become naturalized Canadians, only 63 percent of the total number were Canadian citizens.

In the minds of some, this represented a threat to the national distinctiveness of the discipline. Many expressed fears that as the job market tightened, Canadian political scientists would not be able to find jobs. But because the majority of important departmental decisions still rested in the hands of Canadian political scientists at the associate- and full-professor levels, these fears proved groundless, if indeed they were ever well-founded. The situation eventually corrected itself; by 1981, over 80 percent of newly appointed political scientists were Canadian citizens.

A Distinctive Canadian Political Science

There is no denying that American political science has played a major part in the history of Canadian political science. But while the discipline in Canada has been strongly influenced by the moods and values of American political science, it has not been overwhelmed by them. Canadian political scientists have remained masters in their own house, combining and preserving the generalist influences from Europe with the trend-setting behavioural and post-behavioural influences from the United States.

During its short history, Canadian political science has nurtured its own identity and has earned the respect of the international political-science community. Its healthy self-image is reflected in the current focus on Canadian institutional and behavioural studies. Of the more than 1400 professional political scientists in Canada, nearly 50 percent regularly conduct research into the study of

Canadian problems. About 40 percent of practitioners have research interests in foreign and cross-national politics, while the general field of international relations attracts about ten percent of Canada's political scientists.[13] This represents a vigorous dispersion of professional interest in both domestic and external affairs. Many practitioners have advised successive governments in Canada at all levels.

Canadian political science also owes a large debt to francophone influences. Because of its varied Canadian and European heritage, francophone political science has enriched the quality of political research in Canada by its eclectic approach to the discipline.

In 1978, the Société québécoise de science politique (SQSP), formerly founded in 1964 as the Société canadienne de science politique, was a successful attempt to function autonomously from the CPSA. With its own journal, *Politique*, established in 1982, and a membership of about 300, the SQSP offers an interdisciplinary character to political research. Beyond a doubt, political science in Québec has successfully asserted its claim as a recognized academic pursuit.[14] In addition to the many universities in Québec, the Colleges d'enseignment général et professionnel (CEGEPS) have departments of political science.

It is obvious that the academic presence of political science is complete in Canada. The establishment of a firm organizational basis for political-science research has also been achieved. By the 1990s, Canada could rely upon an impressive entourage of its own experts to conduct independent political research into national and international affairs. As keen observers of the second-largest governing community in the world, Canadian political scientists have first-hand access to their country as a laboratory on federalism, parliamentary government, and a diverse multicultural and linguistic political society.

The Subject Areas of Canadian Political Science

1. **Canadian Politics and Government** focuses on political behaviour in Canada. It involves the study of input agencies and forces (interest groups, political parties, and public opinion), the election process, as well as the activities of the output agencies (Parliament, the judiciary and the Supreme Court).

2. **Comparative Government and Politics** denotes, by and large, the comparative study of several political systems, such as the major democratic and communist countries, or countries within a bloc, such as the comparative study of democratic societies, the communist states, or developing economies.

3. **International Politics and Relations** is the study of transnational politics. It has two major related components: international politics (the study of relations between countries), and international and regional organizations and international law.

4. **Political Theory** serves as a kind of underpinning for all political science study. It deals with major concepts, ideas, and values. Throughout the ages, major political theorists have asked the question, What constitutes a good government and how can it be established? Political theory speculates about "what ought to be" rather than "what is."

5. **Public Administration** deals with the administration and enforcement of public policies at all levels of government, with some focus on the bureaucracy, its organization, and personnel.

6. **Public Law** is the sub-discipline that focuses on the judicial process and, particularly, on the making and the enforcement of laws in the public realm.

7. **Public Policy** embraces all the laws, regulations, and rules made by the output agencies (i.e., legislature, executive, and judiciary) of a polity. It constitutes the total authoritative output of a political system.

8. **Municipal Government and Politics**, as the title implies, deals with the political activities and agencies closest to home, those on the local and state level.

Allied Fields of Study

Political behaviour does not occur in a vacuum. It is a highly complex aspect of general social behaviour. It often appears as aggression, co-operation, institutionalization, negotiation, organization, and revolution. Because of the inclusive nature of politics, political scientists cannot approach the study of politics in a narrow fashion. They must draw from many other fields of knowledge that, in their own way, help to explain human behaviour. For this reason, political science is truly an eclectic discipline. Even though political scientists collaborate with those working within many other fields of study, the study of political science still retains its own character. It is not philosophy, although philosophy is inherent in its nature; it is not history, sociology, or economics, although it embodies something of all of these. In fact, there are at least eight specialized fields of study from which political scientists now frequently gather relevant information to construct theories about political behaviour. A thumbnail sketch of each of these fields will help you understand the eclectic nature of political science.

Anthropology

Anthropology has elements of both a social and a natural science. Briefly put, it is the study of humankind in its earliest and pre-industrial forms, using the insights of archaeology, biology, cultural history, and physiology.

Political science has drawn on the findings of political anthropology to learn about the political behaviour of ancient peoples. For example, accumulated data from anthropological and archaeological sources have contradicted the assumptions of political theorists such as Hobbes, Locke, and Rousseau. These thinkers held the view that human beings entered into a **social contract** for protection and survival, and that this prepared the way for the creation of democratic and non-democratic forms of government. Anthropologists have informed us that a social contract like the one assumed by early political theorists was never a consideration of pre-literate peoples. Anthropology gives the student of politics insight into a great variety of political systems, from the earliest examples of human political cultures to the present.

Economics

Economics – widely recognized as the most highly developed social science – studies human behaviour as it is manifested in the production, distribution, and use of goods and services. In Canada, approximately 42 percent of our GNP is spent by governments

at all levels – federal, provincial, and municipal. As governments have taken a greater role in making decisions that affect our lives, so too have politics increasingly encroached upon the distribution of goods and services. In today's world, the problems of inflation, recession, unemployment, and economic growth are as much related to political behaviour as they are to economic behaviour. Governments now run businesses, promote industries, intervene in the operation of the marketplace, and redistribute wealth. For these reasons, the disciplines of economics and political science have drawn closer in recent years.

One of strongest areas of interest to political scientists is international economics. An understanding of this important field is essential for analyzing international relations. Newspapers abound with stories about international monetary crises, the need for a new international economic order (NIEO), economic integration, and global trade. International economics provides the political scientist with the necessary analytical tools for evaluating the role of government policies on exchange rates, interest rates, commodity prices, the balance of payments, and many other factors in a world composed of interdependent national economies.

Geography

Geography is the study of the relationships that human beings have with their natural environment – the social as well as the spatial and physical aspects of the environment. Geographers are interested in ecological problems created by industrialization and urbanization as well as in the whole range of economic behaviour resulting from our use of land, water, and other natural resources.

In Canada, politics is intrinsically bound to geographic factors; regionalism is as much a political as a geographical fact of life. The Maritimes, Prairies, and British Columbia are geographically remote from one another, yet they share a common alienation from the centre of political power in Ottawa. Canada's geographical divisions have not always been conducive to political unity, making Canada an entity constantly at war with its own geography.

The term "geopolitics" is often used to describe the character and structure of the international political system. No state is made up of institutions alone. States are territorial units that often develop relations with other states based on geographical proximity, collective security, and regional economic integration.

History

History, as most of us are aware, is the study of the past. Historians have provided political scientists with a chronological framework for understanding past political ideas and events. While it is true that political scientists are usually more interested in current problems, the contemporary world of politics can only be understood by the chronological organization of information generated by historians. For example, the development of multiculturalism in Canada has been well documented by Canadian historians. From this documentation, political scientists have been able to place the multi-ethnic character of Canada in political perspective. In the late nineteenth century, Canada's population was not as diversified as it is today.

One hundred years later, people of British origin accounted for 59 percent of the population, 30 percent were French, and only 11 percent was made up of people of other nationalities.

Since the 1940s, Canada has become a country of wide population diversity, with over 26 percent of the population belonging to neither of the two founding European peoples. Political scientists have noted the effects of multiculturalism on Canadian elections, campaigning, political parties, pressure groups, and intergovernmental relations. Some political scientists have adopted the historical approach to politics as their primary research methodology. Others have used it to enrich their scientific methods of political inquiry.

Philosophy

Philosophy is the branch of inquiry concerned with the world of ideas, knowledge, and being. Philosophy has provided modern political science with a rich tradition of writers whose works constitute the subfield of political inquiry known as political philosophy. Political philosophy, which is part and parcel of political science as a discipline, considers questions of social and economic values, political reality, and intellectual approaches to political analysis.

Historically, political philosophy has been associated with normative theory. The philosopher is concerned with political values, moral judgements, and ethical and metaphysical questions – with what "ought" to be our social and political goals. These issues are

■ ■ **normative theory:** philosophical positions promoting a subjective preference for certain standards of human conduct in the realm of politics. ■ ■

difficult to test scientifically because concepts such as justice, happiness, and freedom resist measurement, and the philosopher will not hesitate to use logic, intuition, speculation, and personal conviction to describe or explain political reality.

In contrast, the scientific method usually dictates that scholars focus their attention on testing hypotheses, that they avoid value judgements, and that they shun intuition as a reliable source of truth. Thus, political philosophy retains an important role in modern political science by daring to tread where science fears to go. Political philosophers can speculate and dream without the constraints of a rigorous scientific methodology. This encourages the development of creativity, which is so necessary in a social science that is often asked to measure the immeasurable.

Psychology

Psychology is the study of the behaviour of individuals and groups. Because of its advanced experimental and scientific methodologies, psychology has earned the reputation of an advanced social science.

It is in the field of social psychology, however, that psychology comes closest to political science. Social psychologists have answered many questions on how a person's attitudes, beliefs, and general personality traits are keys to understanding his or her social behaviour. The political psychologist is interested in how we develop our political selves from childhood to adulthood. Psychological research has contributed to our understanding of the personality characteristics of leaders, personality dynamics in voting behaviour, and the psychological factors behind political conflict.

Because political behaviour is so much influenced by personality, we are inclined to ask how expectations, motivations, and perceptions affect our political system. Are there distinct personality types drawn to the House of Commons? Are politicians driven by the genuine wish to help people, or is their altruism a disguise for selfish career goals? Although personality is not always a prime factor in explaining political behaviour, it cannot be ignored. Indeed, the more that politics is studied as a behavioural phenomenon, the greater the tendency to call on psychology for insights.

Finally, political scientists have learned much from psychologists' use of interviews, questionnaires, and survey techniques. Increasingly, political researchers are generating their own data to test hypotheses by using these methods of social research. Because of this, the application of psychological-testing approaches to the world of politics has gained recognition from political scientists all over the world.

Sociology

No other social science has as much affinity to political science as does sociology. Sociologists study social relationships as they manifest themselves in human group experiences. Because sociology is concerned with the comprehensive study of group behaviour, it is of special interest to political science. In almost all instances, groups are the basis of political behaviour. That politics is a group process can be seen in the behaviour of political parties, interest groups, legislative bodies, and public bureaucracies. To the political sociologist, the state is but one of many groups interacting in a society. This pluralistic approach to politics posits that power is shared among a multiplicity of groups that are competitive with the state.

The label "political sociology" refers to the sociology of politics. Political sociologists identify politics as cultural phenomena: the way we "do" politics is a reflection of the way we do other things in a particular social setting. Political sociology is concerned with the social foundations of political power, the effects of group conflict on political institutions, and the many social variables affecting political action. In Canada, political sociologists might consider whether Canadian society is pluralistic by questioning if various groups compete for political and economic power. If competition is found not to exist or to be weak, then they would want to know whether there is actually a coalition of groups unified as an elite who shape government policies to meet their demands.

As political scientists penetrate every level of society in search of answers to political problems, the distinction between sociologists who study politics and political scientists who adopt a sociological approach to politics has virtually disappeared.

Social Work

There is a continuing disagreement among social scientists about whether social work is actually a social science. There is no question that as a practice, social work is a service profession that intervenes to help clients obtain their entitlement in a changing social and political system. But in Canada, professors of social work and field workers also conduct research into social and political problems in order to build a theoretical knowledge base for social-work practice. This research and the information it generates can be particularly useful for political scientists.

It is strange that many political scientists have only recently discovered the contributions of social-work research to their field, because obviously the social-work profession is a front-line observer of the failures and weaknesses in our political system. Social workers address the problems of child neglect, domestic violence, drug abuse, violations of human rights, women's rights, native rights, and the effects of unemployment on the lives of people. From the research conducted by those within the social-work profession, political scientists have become increasingly aware that stress can be politically generated, and can have widespread social ramifications such as suicide, depression, and social disintegration. Often, in contrast to political scientists, social workers have been leaders in prescribing legislative and structural reforms at the political level. As political scientists seek to build a more relevant social science that can improve society, there is renewed concern for a value-centred discipline capable of political action. In this regard, social work may be to political science what engineering is to physics.

Statistics

When states first began to collect information about their citizens, these numbers were appropriately called "statistics." Today, the discipline of statistics, with its methods for collecting, presenting, analyzing, and interpreting data, has gained momentum in its applications to many fields of knowledge. Social-science practitioners in such fields as anthropology, economics, political science, psychology, and sociology are all expected to have a minimum of what is called statistical literacy. In fact, it is virtually impossible to become professional in any of these fields without having learned to gather and interpret statistics for analytical purposes.

A knowledge of statistical methods enables political scientists to form hypotheses for testing, to gather population samples from which to infer the probability of outcomes, to interpret the many charts, graphs, and tables that describe the political world, and to confidently plot patterns and trends of political behaviour. The political-science profession has become increasingly competent with the use of statistical techniques in research. Today, practitioners collect their information for analysis with statistical tools.

Computers have greatly simplified calculations used in statistical analysis. Software packages contain computer programs that perform particular types of statistical analysis, and a large number have been written for users at many levels of expertise. These packages now permit the user to apply a wide variety of statistical techniques to the same data using only a few keystrokes.

Political Science in the International Community

In 1949, the United Nations Educational, Scientific, and Cultural Organization (UNESCO) co-ordinated the establishment of the International Political Science Association (IPSA).[15] As of 1990, 37 national political-science associations were listed as collective members of IPSA, along with 500 individual memberships. The association has been active in promoting the development of political

science in the international community. It publishes the *International Political Science Review, International Political Science Abstracts,* and the *International Bibliography of Political Science.* In 1973, Montreal hosted the first IPSA World Congress to be held outside of Europe. Professor Jean LaPonce of the University of British Columbia became its first Canadian president.

Political scientists in democratic states tend to engage in open criticism of national and international issues. Each national association of political scientists bears the stamp of its own unique political culture, traditions, and ideologies. British political scientists have tended to remain loyal to the traditional historical and philosophical approaches. Only since the mid-1970s has behaviouralism had significant impact in Britain. However, post-behavioural sentiments have steadily penetrated the methodologies of British political science. Since World War II, many Italian political scientists have focused on the factors that led to fascism before and during that war. In Sweden, the traditional orientation of political science is used to trace the development of Swedish political institutions from the Middle Ages to the present. In Germany, political science reflects a conservative concern with constitutional and administrative law, the integration of the political culture of citizens of the former German Democratic Republic (GDR), as well as a cautious surveillance of democratic and anti-democratic thought. Throughout the democratic states of Europe, the reconstructive pressures of post-behaviouralism have influenced both research and teaching. But there is a very real sense that an understanding of the political world can still be achieved without the widespread application of scientific methodology, with its need to build models or theories.

Political science in "authoritarian" states tends not to be open or critical, at least as a visible legitimate discipline. In Argentina and Brazil (even under new governments), political scientists are cautious and sensitive to government censorship and political repression. In other states, such as Guatemala and El Salvador, social scientists are closely watched and their politics are constantly scrutinized by government officials, sometimes with dangerous consequences.

In the remaining "totalitarian" states, the development of political science as an autonomous and independent discipline has been slow. It has been typical for governments in these states to monitor political criticism very carefully and to require those who engage in the social sciences to conform to the ideological line of the totalitarian system. Chinese and Cuban political analysts tend to support the political and economic system they study.

Political science has had a long and honourable history. For centuries, its practitioners have been analyzing basic questions about the politics of people in society. What is justice? What forms of government are best? Are rulers accountable? When and why must people obey? These are ancient issues, yet they engage us at every turn in our modern world. The great writers of the past — Plato, Aristotle, Machiavelli, Augustine, Hobbes, Locke, and Rousseau — can still inform us on these matters, even today.

Pre-scientific thinking about political behaviour and governmental institutions was characteristically devoted to describing what should be, rather than to studying what is. Early political theory was concerned with re-designing society according to the philosopher's own favoured system of conduct rather than with carefully observing how a polity actually operates.

Not until the first decades of the twentieth century did most political theorists seek to discipline their theorizing and subdue their concerns for political reform with rigorous methods for systematically observing the society around them. These modern political scientists were far from being the first students of political behaviour, but they were the first to adopt an empirical perspective and scientific method in such studies. Many of them learned that modern methodologies could be directed toward the questions of political and social reform that had been posed by earlier students of politics. Today, all political scientists share with their ancestors the basic premise that the serious study of politics is crucial to the survival of humankind.

References

1. Heinz Eulau, *The Behavioral Persuasion in Politics* (New York: Random House, 1963), 3.

2. S. Sidney Ulmer, *Introductory Readings in Political Behaviour* (Chicago: Rand McNally and Company, 1961), 74.

3. William Dunning, *A History of Political Theories* (London: Macmillan and Co. Ltd., 1923), 131.

4. Francis Bacon, *The Advancement of Learning, Book II,* complied by F. G. Selby, (London: Macmillan and Co. Ltd., 1895), 116.

5. See Lawrence Vesey, *The Emergence of the American University* (Chicago: University of Chicago Press, 1965); and Anna Haddow, *Political Science in American Colleges and Universities,* 1636-1900 (New York: Appleton-Century, 1939).

6. Louis Cantori, "Post-Behavioral Political Science and the Study of Comparative Politics" in Louis Cantori and Andrew Ziegler Jr., *Comparative Politics in the Post-Behavioral Era* (Boulder, CO: Lynne Rienner Publishers, 1988), 417-426.

7. Michael Haas and Henry Kariel, eds., *Approaches to the Study of Political Science* (Scranton, PA: Chandler Publishing Company, 1970), 525.

8. William M.J. MacKenzie, *The Study of Political Science Today* (London: MacMillan, 1971), 32.

9. G.H. Thorburn, *Political Science in Canada: Graduate Studies and Research* (Ottawa: A Study for the Healy Commission, 1975), 79; see also Ian Drummond, *Political Economy at the University of Toronto: A History of the Department* (Toronto: University of Toronto Press, 1983).

10. Michael Stein, John Trent, and André Donneur, "Political Science in Canada in the 1980s: Achievement and Challenge, " (paper delivered at the Congress of the International Political Science Association, Rio de Janeiro, August 9-14, 1982), 1; see also John Trent and Michael Stein, "The Interaction of the State and Political Science in Canada: A Preliminary Mapping" (paper presented at the XIVth World Congress of the International Political Science Association, Washington, D.C.: 1988), 1-34.

11. Alan Cairns, "Political Science in Canada and the Americanization Issue," *Canadian Journal of Political Science* VIII, no. 2 (June 1975): 193-195.

12. N.H.W. Hull, "The 1971 Survey of the Profession," *Canadian Journal of Political Science* VI, no. 1 (March 1973): 89-120.

13. Stein, Trent, and Donneur, "Political Science in Canada in the 1980s: Achievement and Challenge," 37; see also John Trent and Michael Stein, "The Interaction of the State and Political Science in Canada: A Preliminary Mapping"(paper presented at the XIVth World Congress of the International Political Science Association, Aug 28 - Sept 1, 1988).

14. See Raymond Aron, "Reflexions sur la politique et la science politique française" in *Revue française de Science Politique* 5 (1), 1985 : 55:22; Leon Dion, "Politique et Science Politique" *Canadian Journal of Political Science,* VIII, (3): 367-380.

15. See UNESCO publication 426, *Contemporary Political Science* (Paris: UNESCO, 1950).

Suggested Readings

David Easton et. al., *The Development of Political Science* (New York: Routledge, 1991).

Donald Fisher, *The Social Sciences in Canada* (Waterloo, ON: Wilfrid Laurier Press, 1991).

David Held, *Political Theory Today.* (Stanford, CA: Stanford University Press, 1991).

Jarol Manheim and Richard Rich, *Empirical Political Analysis* (New York: Longman Publishing Company, 1991).

Louise White, *Political Analysis: Technique and Practice* (New York: Wadsworth, 1990).

Herbert Winter, *Political Science and Theory* (New York: HarperCollins College Publishers, 1992).

Glossary

amoral: Behaviour that reflects an indifference to morality.

architechtonic: In the language of Aristotle, this term refers to the master art that prescribes the content of all other arts, occupations, and skills of life.

eclectic: In political science, an approach to knowledge that draws information from other disciplines by selecting and combining the appropriate methods and conclusions for political research.

generalization: A statement about a class or categories of things or events.

hypothesis: Any tentative statement that describes or explains the relationship between or among variables.

methodology: The process of gathering, measuring, analyzing, and evaluating knowledge within a particular discipline.

model: A set of assumptions a researcher accepts as true that influences the perception of that which is being observed.

normative: That which pertains to value judgements or standards as to the way things *should* be.

normative theory: Philosophical positions promoting a subjective preference for certain standards of human conduct in the realm of politics.

polis: Usually refers to the Greek city-state which exercised independent jurisdiction over a small population and permitted citizens to participate in the decision-making process of the community.

political behaviour: Human responses to the world of politics in the forms of perceptions, attitudes, beliefs, thoughts, and values, as well as overt actions such as campaigning, corruption, protesting, and voting.

political ideologies: The ideas, values, beliefs, and generalized systems of thought that influence our political behaviour and institutions of government.

power politics: The description derived from the German *Machtpolitik*, and *Realpolitik*, which hold that the world of politics is essentially conducted among groups with power.

scientism: The belief that scientific method is applicable to all human problems and that it will generate the only possible solution to them.

secular: A term referring to those political and social philosophies that advocate the separation of worldly things from religious and sacred interests.

social contract: A theory of popular sovereignty based on the notion that humans had originally consented to a binding social agreement.

systematic approach: An approach to the study of political knowledge that treats politics and government as a set of human interactions occurring within a larger social and international environment.

theocracy: A term coined by the Jewish historian Josephus who described government as embodied in the Torah, where divine laws are treated as civil obligations, but, as commonly used, the term came to mean government by priests.

utilitarians: Those who in the 19th century advocated the concept of utility as the foundation of morals or the Greatest Happiness Principle, which posited that actions are right in proportion as they tend to promote happiness, wrong as they produce its opposite.

value-free: The predisposition of a social scientist to pursue research objectives without the intrusion of personal opinions and values, which might otherwise distort conclusions.

variable: Any characteristic or property of something that contains two or more values that change in degree and help explain a particular event or phenomenon.

THREE

Contemporary Political Ideologies

Recent RCMP graduates in Regina

Chapter Objectives

After reading this chapter, you will be able to:

- understand what roles political ideologies play in our lives

- identify and describe ideologies by type

- ponder how we learn our political ideologies and how they affect our behaviour

- unpack the components of ideologies and describe each of them carefully with an eye to comparing what they mean in each ideology

- examine the goals of ideologies in various political and governing systems

- describe the outstanding features of democratic ideologies

- analyze the qualities of non-democratic ideologies with a focus on Marxism

- examine the content of other ideologies such as nationalism, anarchism, fascism, and feminism

- consider how movements and ideologies are connected

- discuss the relevance of ideologies in Canada and in other political systems

What is an Ideology?

During the Enlightenment, the French philosopher Antoine Destutt de Tracy coined the word *"idéologie"* to mean the "science of ideas"; the study of the origins, evolution, and nature of ideas. Many philosophers of the time (the *philosophes*) believed that the application of human reason to society could reveal laws in human relationships that would unfold into detectable patterns of belief systems, which in turn would set ideals, ends, and purposes for communities to pursue.[1] Until the Enlightenment, ideologies were primarily religious – the world was perceived and explained in terms that linked political and economic beliefs with religious ones, for example those of Buddhism, Calvinism, Catholicism, Islam, and Shintoism. The writers and critics who forged the "enlightened" ideas of the eighteenth century felt that the future of humankind lay not so much in the blind adherence to divine commandments but rather in the application of **human reason** to economic, social, and political challenges.

The term "ideology" enjoyed good standing until the nineteenth century, when Napoleon began to call his political enemies "ideologues" because they advocated liberal ideals and held utopian and anti-religious views. As a result, a negative connotation became attached to the word, a connotation that continues to this day in some countries of the world, depending on how the term is used. To many Americans and Canadians, ideology is to politics what superstition is to religion. In societies founded on philosophical **pragmatism** and freedom, where individual choices determine leadership, programs of action, and

reforms, people distrust the intellectual and emotional commitment required to sustain what in their minds is an ideology. They see ideologies as abstract, utopian systems of ideas that demand of believers a blind and uncritical allegiance to fixed ways of thinking.

To so view ideology serves no useful purpose to scholarship or understanding because, in varying degrees, all societies are ideological. An **ideology** is a value system through which we perceive, explain, and accept the world. Ideologies give us a total view of things and claim to supply answers to all questions. Karl Deutsch holds that ideologies are like maps in that they outline "a simplified image of the real world."[2]

To some degree, consciously or unconsciously, all people are **ideologues** in that they map out their interpretation of the real world and its significance to their world. Robert Dahl emphasized this fact when he said, "Prior to politics, beneath it, enveloping it, restricting it, conditioning it...is ideology."[3]

Contemporary ideologies, such as anarchism, capitalism, conservatism, communism, and socialism, contain mainly socio-economic elements that dominate the beliefs people adopt and the biases they reflect. Ultimately, these systems condition people's political behaviour. *Political ideology* may be defined as a "belief system that explains and justifies a preferred political order for society, either existing or proposed, and offers a strategy (processes, institutional arrangements, programs) for its attainment."[4] Robert E. Lane classified a number of important functions of political ideologies.[5] They are summarized as follows:

■ Ideologies present a simplified "cause and effect" interpretation of a complex world.

■ Ideologies integrate a theory of **human nature** with life's basic economic, social, and political values.

■ Ideologies appear normative and moral in tone and content and aspire to perfect our behaviour.

■ Ideologies draw their philosophical premises from constitutions, declarations, manifestos, and writings.

■ Ideologies constitute a broad belief system and advocate reforms in the basic fabric and structures of society.

■ Ideologies address fundamental questions about leadership, recruitment, political succession, and electoral behaviour.

■ Ideologies have the effect of persuading and **propagandizing** people who learn not to be influenced by opposing views.

Because ideologies are value-laden belief systems, they often come into conflict and competition: thus, conservatism vs. liberalism, capitalism vs. socialism, and nationalism vs. internationalism. Some political cultures appear more ideologically based than others. But whether an ideology is prominent, as in China or Cuba, or subtle, as in Canada or Australia, there is an ideological base to all political cultures.

We should at this point distinguish political ideology from other forms of political thought, such as *political philosophy* and *political theory*. Political philosophy is a detached and often solitary "search for the principles of the good state and the good society."[6] The political philosopher asks fundamental questions about the nature of political society and often prescribes moral and **ethical** solutions for what "ought" to be a better polity. Political theory attempts to formulate generalizations that can be tested and verified by analyzing related variables that explain a particular political phenomenon. Where the political philosopher is **rational** and deductive, the theorist is empirical and **descriptive** of what *is* rather than what *ought to be*. The words of Carl Friedrich help us to further clarify the distinctions we have just made:

"Ideologies are action-related systems of ideas. They typically contain a strategy for their realization, and their essential function is to unite organizations which are built around them. It is confusing and fails to provide the opportunity for political analysis, to call any system of ideas an ideology, such as the philosophy of Aristotle or the theology of the Old Testament. Such systems of ideas *may* provide the *basis* for an ideology, but only after being related to action in a specific sense and for a specific situation. Ideologies are sets of ideas related to the existing political and social order and intended either to change it or defend it...what makes them (ideas) "ideology" is their function in the body politic."[7]

The action-related character of ideologies to which Friedrich refers is significant. History confirms that ideologies energize people, capture their imaginations, and motivate them to dismantle old orders or construct new ones. Ideologies tend to inspire organizational behaviour, which always reflects itself at the political level. The ideological message is mobilized and carried by political **elites**, political parties, insurgent groups, pressure groups, education systems, and the media.

Once in place, an ideology is culturally transmitted through families, peer groups, the media and other agents of political socialization. In the final analysis, societies exercise political power on the basis of their ideological perspective.

Types of Ideologies

Political ideologies can be distinguished broadly as *dominant ideologies* and *counter-ideologies*. Dominant ideologies generally prescribe and support existing social and political arrangements while counter-ideologies rally the forces of change in society.

Dominant ideologies

Dominant ideologies are the prevailing mindsets that assert themselves in the social and governing system. For example, the institution of private property and capitalism dominate Canada's economy and its political organization. In the context of a socialist state, however, public ownership and the collective means of production prevail in the economy and are protected by the political system.

Ideologies can be dominant in two ways. First, they are dominant when most people accept and articulate them. Second, they can be dominant because the most powerful people in society support them, even though the majority or significant numbers of people may not accept the ideologies. Many believe that aboriginal peoples lost their title and rights to territorial sovereignty when large migrations of Europeans settled in North America. They hold that aboriginal peoples should assimilate into the Euro-Canadian culture, accepting Canadian laws and other social prescriptions as their own. The dominant characteristics of this ideology are embedded in the Indian Act,

and in the treatment of native peoples by Canadian authorities when they made their claims on Canada's governing system.

Other prevailing ideological prescriptions include sexism and ageism, which justify the unequal treatment of people based on their gender or age. The Supreme Court of Canada ruled that mandatory retirement at age sixty-five is not discriminatory and that women cannot claim child-care costs as business expenses. These kinds of ideas can circulate within the context of democratic ideology, even though it preaches the lofty values of equality and justice for all. The same ideas may also circulate within the ideologies of communism and socialism.

The dominant ideology enables a society to control subordinate groups, such as women, young and old people, and those who adhere to ideologies of socialism, communism, and environmentalism, if they constitute a minority in society.

Counter-ideologies

Counter-ideologies advance reforms and radical change in society. Sometimes the dominant ideologies in one society can be the counter-ideologies in another. In Canada, Marxists and communists compete for the ideological support of those who advance democratic views. Counter-ideologies such as fascism and democracy challenge the fundamental assumptions of dominant ideologies and can eventually supercede them. In the former Soviet Union, the democratic movement swelled to the point of counter-revolution, eventually forcing economic and governmental institutions to radically change.

Counter-ideologies are a response to perceived inequality, which, for one reason or another, is a product of how a society thinks and behaves. Counter-ideologies challenge the status quo and threaten to discredit it so that it loses credibility among adherents. Feminism is a counter-ideology that challenges the practices and assumptions of such dominant ideologies as capitalism, socialism, and democracy. Men and women relate to one another under many different ideological systems. Feminists ask whether there is gender equality in any society, however it may be organized. Feminism politicizes human relations, making equality and human freedom fundamental ideological prescriptions. Thus, questions of human rights and legal rights challenge the dominant belief systems under which we survive as a society.

The competitive interaction among groups that hold dominant and counter-ideologies is one reason that political change takes place in society. For years, leftist counter-ideology in Canada proclaimed that public enterprise should be a tool of public policy to control the ruthless marketplace and to offer services that the private sector failed to provide. Now all political parties in Canada support the need for the presence of certain public enterprises in the Canadian economy. And the "green" counter-ideology, which gained widespread support during the 1980s, calling for concern for the environment, zero-population growth, and recycling of waste products, was to become permanently ingrained in the platforms of political parties across the country. It is out of clashes among proponents of competing ideas, embodied in political parties, interest groups, and social movements, that political and social change occurs.

The Components of Ideologies

Ideologies address fundamental questions about the nature of society and its political character. We can identify some of the most common themes found in modern political ideologies: 1) the disposition of human nature; 2) the role of the individual in society; 3) the role of the state; 4) the sources and limits of political authority; 5) a preferred economic and social order.

These are some of the important elements analysts look for when examining the contents of ideologies.

What is Human Nature?

One theme found in many ideologies addresses the question of human nature. Are human beings born basically good or bad, or does social conditioning determine their character? Is it possible to perfect human nature or is it fundamentally unalterable? Modern attempts to scientifically answer this question have been inconclusive. Convincing evidence falls on all sides of the question and ultimately conclusions tend to be based on our own value preferences.

Whatever view is expressed in the ideology has immediate implications for the economic, political, and social preferences that flow from its belief system. The conservative view generally asserts that human nature is unchangeable and that the purpose of social and political institutions is to control the undesirable tendencies in human behaviour. Belief in the inherent goodness of human nature leads to the corollary that people should not be too closely controlled and directed by government.

At the same time, the belief that people are perfectible can lead to ideological prescriptions of radical social and institutional change as exemplified in Marxism.

Making a choice among the many ideologies open to societies automatically implies the choice of a view of human nature, as well. On the one hand, the democrat regards people as basically rational and trustworthy, neither mired in sin nor dependent on a superior social order for self-fulfillment. On the other hand, the authoritarian sees people as capricious who, without the guidance and control of the party or the state, would have no predictability and direction in their lives. For the authoritarian, emotion is thought to have a more significant role than rational judgement in determining human behaviour.

The Role of the Individual

Through the centuries, political thinkers have wrestled with various questions. Where does the individual fit into the total scheme of things? Does the state and its government serve the interests of individuals or are individuals subservient to the goals of the state? Where do we draw the line on the role of the individual in the political and social system? Many ideologies take into account the social obligations of individuals. They hold that those who live in society are not isolated individuals. Invariably, the way in which people act as individuals affects the opportunities for the self-development of others. And so other questions arise as to whether the state and its associated institutions of government should try to regulate the inevitable conflicts that result from the free thoughts and actions of individuals.

■ ■ social contract: an original agreement among individuals to create an organized political society. ■ ■

To the doctrinaire socialists who adhere closely to the ideology of Marxism, the individual's welfare is subordinate to the welfare of the whole society. To them, the many will benefit most if the interests of individuals are not taken to represent the well-being of everyone. Even modern liberals concede that the greater liberty of one person can be the lesser liberty of another. So the government is understood by contemporary liberals to be the necessary instrument for refereeing, equalizing, and thus maximizing individual freedom. A fundamental tenet of liberalism is the obligation to respect and protect each person's rights and to safeguard them from deprivation by other individuals or groups. One of the prominent ideological conflicts in the contemporary world has contrasted the role of individuals in democratic societies with the collectivist positions expounded in socialist and communist doctrine.

The Role of the State

Ever since political ideas were first debated, the state has been the focus of much ideological controversy. In times past, the state was posited to have derived from the will of God, the fall of man, the **social contract**, the process of natural evolution, the family, and the institution of private property. The controversy continues well beyond the notion of how the state originated, as ideologies also differ sharply on its role in the political and social system. In some ideologies the state appears as a necessary evil or as a target for destruction. Some anarchists, libertarians, and ultra-conservatives see the state as a set of institutions that attracts uncontrollable corruption, impedes economic and social progress, and threatens human liberty. In other ideologies the state represents the highest of human endeavours. Its purpose is viewed as raising civilized standards; its hallmark as justice; and its essence as law, founded on right reason and popular consent. Most modern ideologies, with the exception of some strains of anarchism, believe that humans need a state apparatus of some kind to cope with the many problems of surviving in a competitive international community. The great ideological debates are not presented simplistically in terms of state or no state. Rather they are focused on the degree of state intervention, the scope and character of political authority, and the methods of public administration necessary to achieve the goals of public policy. Included in the ideological treatment of the role of the state are competing views on the functions of government bureaucracies and the nature and scope of **sovereignty,** by which the state can exercise legitimate force to regulate the affairs of its citizens as well as its relations with other states.

In some ideologies the concept "sovereignty" denotes the supreme and final power of the state above and beyond which no other power exists. Others concede that actually there is no such thing as absolute, utterly unqualified state power, and hence no absolute sovereignty. With respect to domestic or internal sovereignty there are wide variations among ideologies as to the whereabouts and scope of sovereign power. Where does sovereignty reside, in the people or in the state? Is sovereignty divisible or indivisible? Who may express sovereignty?

■ ■ **consensus:** a widespread agreement on a particular issue, policy, or course of action by those participating in the making of the decision without a formal verification of the statistical proportion of support. ■ ■

Political Authority

One inevitable component of most modern ideologies is the consideration of the source and scope of political authority. Political authority is usually portrayed as a form of power based upon the recognition it receives from those over whom it is exercised. For some this authority is derived from the consent of the governed, while others point to the source of political authority as the coercive will of the state or of dictators. Democracy and liberalism hold the essence of authority to be subjective, psychological, and moral, i.e., consent flows from within individuals who freely permit others to govern them as a rightful human need. Authority is an influence that is intimately related to legitimacy, the belief of a citizenry that a government has the right to rule and that a citizen ought to obey the rules of that government.

In the ideologies of fascism and Marxism-Leninism, authority is portrayed as something that flows objectively from the coercive arm of the state, government, and party institutions. The hallmark of totalitarian authority is the rigid hierarchy and the rank subordination of followers to the authority of a single or collective leadership. Authority, when attached to the state, is distinguishable more by command than by voluntary acceptance or compromise, more by dogmatic assertion than by **consensus**.

Political authority has relevant meanings common to all ideologies. One is the *credibility* of the political communication itself – be it a law, regulation, decree, or succession of power. It is believed, almost regardless of its content, because it is derived from a source that has the power of force or procedure. A second is that political authority is to be obeyed, not always blindly or uncritically, but because compliance ensures the legitimate performance of the political system. In essence, political authority is a communication between leaders and the led, enabling them to relate to each other in such a way that the political system survives, be it a democracy or dictatorship.

The Economic and Social Order

Ideologies usually address the economic and social conditions that mobilize human beings for productive purposes. How will society organize, protect, and distribute the products of human labour and ingenuity? What social and political institutions should be in place to facilitate the required economic and social order? Who should reap the benefits of economic productivity and its attendant wealth? Aristotle perceptively noted the economic and social basis of politics. Since his analysis, most modern ideologies have reflected the close relationship between the economy and the system of government. Medieval political thinkers, who in most cases were members of the clergy, recognized the obligations of monarchs to protect the economic and social well-being of their subjects. And the revolutions of the seventeenth and eighteenth centuries brought about extensive reviews of how people thought about the nature of production, distribution, ownership, and wealth in society. Changes in the ways we behave and produce goods and services will inevitably induce sweeping changes elsewhere in society. In this regard ideologies try to reconcile a society's values with its political and economic structures.

The Marxists have searched for a more equitable way of organizing society and of ensuring that the satisfaction of individual economic needs does not contradict the fulfillment of social needs. Anarchists, insofar as they are willing to entertain the concept of order at all, insist on the free and spontaneous association of citizens in the economic and social life of society. For most anarchists, the highest social order, and the only moral one, derives from each person's enlightened understanding of why humans are so interdependent in society. For capitalists, the economic and social system works best and the competitive ideal is most likely to be achieved when people are free to decide for themselves what they want and what they are willing to pay for it.

The Goals of Ideologies

Although ideologies differ a great deal in scope and content, they perform similar functions. Most of the time people are not even aware that ideologies influence and condition their social behaviour. But ideological assumptions do consciously or unconsciously justify many of our thoughts and actions. Ideologies make us feel comfortable or uncomfortable about the institutions, leaders, and expectations of the political society we have created. They can divide or unite us. They can move us to act or acquiesce.

Doing it Right

The process whereby ideology gains acceptance for itself in the eyes of those who are influenced by it is one of *legitimation*. For some Marxists, legitimacy is the major function of ideology because it represents the prescribed political institutions and processes in such a way that political obligation seems natural and right.[8]

From an ideological perspective legitimacy is a relative term. What is deemed legitimate by one ideology may not be regarded as legitimate in another. But generally an ideology will advance the belief that a political system is valid and justified and will be recognized as such by those over whom its authority is exercised.

In capitalist societies, **stratification** tends to be widely accepted and even defended – not just by people identified as privileged but often by those in the lower strata, as well. Sociologists sometimes refer to this form of ideological legitimation as *false consciousness* because members of the lower stratum of society often accept the ideology that justifies the system oppressing them. Instead of blaming the system, they attribute their low status to "luck," "fate," "nature," or the "will of God" – factors usually beyond their control. However, when an ideology facilitates *class consciousness* – an objective awareness of the lower stratum's common plight as an oppressed group – they may begin to question the legitimacy of the system or the ideology that sustains the system. The lower stratum may then be attracted to a different ideology, one that justifies their own class interests, and consequently, one that may seem revolutionary to the dominant stratum.

Some analysts note that all governments legitimately operate on "make-believe."[9] The make-believe involves accepting the idea that governors are the servants of the people or

> ■ ■ **stratification:** a system of social inequality based on hierarchical orderings of groups according to their members' share in socially valued rewards. ■ ■

that the people have a voice in government or that everyone is treated equally in society by governments. As they are consumed by the public, these kinds of fictions produce the basis of legitimacy for the governing regime. The fictions are often the basis for the defence of the governing system and are the underlying assumptions of the dominant ideology.

Leadership

One goal almost always articulated in ideologies is leadership. With the exception of anarchism, which is an ideology founded upon the absence of leadership, all ideologies address this phenomenon on the social and political level. Who may lead us? What qualifications should leaders have? How should we choose our leaders? When and how should leadership change? Ideologies often contain specific references to the nature of leadership and how it should shape the collective patterns of society. But while ideologies may prescribe certain desirable leadership characteristics, the personal qualities of a single, highly placed decision-maker may themselves become a factor of power or revolutionary historical change: Castro in Cuba, de Gaulle in France, Tito in the former Yugoslavia, Nehru in India.

From the ideological perspective, leadership is closely related to authority, power, influence, and political succession. Leadership was a central feature of fascist and Nazi ideologies as expressed in their concepts of the leader, *Il Duce,* and in the *Führerprinzip,* whereby the leader embodied the state and for this reason had to be obeyed. With Marxism, leadership was intrinsic to the "dictatorship of the proletariat," which would bring under state control all the means of production, communications, transportation, and commerce. Lenin instituted the leadership of an elite revolutionary party in order to develop revolutionary consciousness among the masses. The party would become the vanguard of the people without necessarily having the support of the people. These patterns of leadership are not compatible with democratic thought. Democracy requires that the system of leadership recruitment be open, that the right and opportunity to seek the leadership not be arbitrarily denied to any individual or category of persons. For democrats, a leader is someone who has legitimately won popular support of other human beings, be it of a majority or of a minority. The procedures of democracy are organized to facilitate a consensual relationship between a leader and followers.

Purpose

One common attribute in the major ideologies is an end, goal, or purpose. Most of these ideologies focus on material abundance as the leading goal or purpose of the political system. Liberalism was the first ideology to articulate this end clearly and to develop the institutions designed to promote material rewards. Conservatism also keeps a watchful eye on national growth and the preservation of wealth. Communism, born much later, focuses on the possibility of overcoming scarcity, showing a passion for accelerating the pace of economic superabundance. This need to accelerate the pace of economic growth and development is also constituent to the indigenous revolutionary ideologies of the less-developed countries. The fascists also have material abundance as a priority, although they apply social and racial restrictions on which citizens would share in the national wealth.

Ideological conceptions of purpose also focus on what governments are expected to do. The idea of "constitutional government" as expressed in the great democratic ideologies posits that government cannot do everything and should be restricted to certain specific social functions. The classical form of liberalism limited these to the preservation of order and property. Modern liberalism has added the concept of "welfare" to the proper role of government, and restricts and constrains the older views of unrestricted individual action. Quite to the contrary, Nazism subjugates the role of government to the state by postulating the idea of the *Volkstadt,* in which there was no distinction between governmental institutions and the will of the state. All political and governmental activity bears immediately on society and all free social activity needs the endorsement of the state. Nazis openly admit to the role of government and party as a "totalitarian" one.

Critique

One important psychodynamic of many ideologies is *criticism*. Karl Mannheim, best known for his development of the sociology of knowledge, saw the significance of differing and opposed positions in ideologies.[10] Mannheim distinguished two kinds of ideological thinking. One is utopian, which is the thinking of reformers who are unhappy with the status quo and want to tear it apart in order to build new institutions and values. The other is in defence of the status quo that is under attack.

Democrats, who strongly believe that criticism is necessary for political systems to function, are themselves the target of severe attacks from opposing ideologies. The very nobility of democracy's goals invites an especially caustic flow of criticism regarding the gap between theory and practice. The heaviest attacks are concentrated on the practice, rather than the ideals, of democracy. Virtually every democratic government in history has permitted and sometimes generated elements of aristocracy and oligarchy. Maurice Duverger defined democracy as government *of* the people by an elite sprung *from* the people.[11] Many democratic legislatures (particularly upper houses) give added weight to age, wealth, conservatism, and social status, resulting in an unacknowledged fusion of democracy with oligarchy and privilege.

> ■ ■ **bourgeoisie:** from the French for town dweller, the term was used by Marx to identify the class of property and production ownership that flourished under capitalism. ■ ■

For Marx, the fundamental contradiction of capitalism was the private ownership of the means of production, founded on the economic principle that the distribution of wealth is based on private and personal effort and advantage: this would inevitably generate a society of immense inequality, causing many men, women, and children to suffer from poverty and want. According to Marx, capitalist ideology justified the use of the institutions of the state and their most characteristic expression – law – as a means of consolidating and perpetuating the socio-economic domination of the **bourgeoisie**.

Prescription

Many ideologies are concerned with the normative implications of political organization and behaviour: the way the state and society should be organized and the way citizens should relate to these prescribed structures and social values. Ideologies make certain assumptions about human behaviour, which are then followed by prescriptions as to which political order best protects or challenges these assumptions. For example, democrats believe that humans achieve most in a society that permits the highest expressions of individual freedom under the law. Governments are therefore to be limited in what they can do and how they can do it. As they are transmitted throughout a society, ideologies are a variable blend of facts, values, and propositions about what is and what ought to be. Each ideology, by means of its own logic and evidence, claims to possess the path to progress and directs its followers to implement its goals.

Anarchists prefer no government and reject the state, contending that individuals must have maximum choice to achieve the highest levels of morality, fulfillment, and perfectibility. They therefore prescribe a society of individuals under no coercion. Nationalists, on the other hand, prescribe a strong government and a competent state so as to unify the national character of a preferred group. The moral corporate personality of the nation is institutionally protected against the whims of individualism or the cultural incursions of other nations. In its extreme, as national socialism, the nation is seen as superior to the individual as well as to all other nations. Liberal democracy commits the state and government to the protection of the individual, while at the same time acknowledging the presence of the community and the nation as the collective expression of individualism.

What ideologies instruct us to do can stir us to act, arousing our commitments to achieve the goals the ideology puts forward. Hardly any period in history or any part of the world has been without groups espousing ideological prescriptions on the way society should be organized. These ideological instructions often include an interpretation of the past, an evaluation of the present, and a vision of the future. They serve as both the foundation and justification of the desired political system and ultimately depend on the passion, the drive, and the methods employed by those who have accepted the ideology.

Democratic Ideologies

Democratic thought is usually traced to the Greeks, although many aboriginal and Indo-American cultures produced democratic governing institutions that predate those in Greece. During the fifth century, the Athenians, in particular, used the term "democracy" to refer to government by the many, as contrasted to government by the few (oligarchy), or by one person (monarchy). In his famous "Funeral Oration," Pericles (495-429 B.C.) declared that "our [Athens'] constitution is named a democracy, because it is in the hands, not of the few, but of the many."[12] The idea that the ultimate political authority lies with, and should flow from, the general public remains central to all modern conceptions of democracy.

The first great European political theorist to consider democracy as a coherent system of thought was Aristotle, the Athenian philosopher who lived from 384 to 322 B.C. Aristotle saw democracy as direct popular government, which he thought would degenerate into mob rule because it lacked institutions capable of ensuring individual liberty and of controlling self-seeking interests. Direct democracy was too unrestrained and unstable, so Aristotle enlarged the concept by combining other elements: popular sovereignty, majority rule, and minority rights, which formed what he called constitutional government or polity. Aristotle's assessment of democracy in the *Politics* had remarkable range and prescience. He believed that what was necessary for constitutional democracy was the presence of a large middle class and a fairly even distribution of property: "It is clear therefore that the political community administered by the middle class is the best...in which the middle class is numerous...it sways the balance and prevents the opposite extremes from coming into existence."[13]

The earliest Greek democracies were city-states. They emphasized the equality of all who qualified as citizens in their right to participate in the life of the community. Participation was widespread, with decisions based on oratory and face-to-face discussion. Citizens took part in such processes as jury trials and lawmaking, but more important than any other political rights was a broad notion of civic spirit. We are indebted to antiquity for the earliest examples of European democracy in theory and practice. But many of the fundamental principles we now accept as generic to the ideology took many more centuries to develop. Indeed, democracy in its first manifestations was quite limited by the elite, who ensured that slaves, women, and outsiders (especially those of different races), were excluded from citizenship.

Since Aristotle, many philosophers contributed to the development of democracy. But the foundations of modern European democratic ideology were fashioned in the seventeenth, eighteenth, and nineteenth centuries. The great thinkers of the time, John Locke, Jean-Jacques Rousseau, Thomas Jefferson, Thomas Paine, Jeremy Bentham, James Mill, John Stuart Mill, and Alexis de Tocqueville all contributed to the present composition of modern democratic ideologies. The great debates over the creation of the best institutional framework for democracy resulted in three fundamentally distinctive ideological orientations: liberalism, conservatism, and socialism.

Liberalism

Liberalism as a discernible ideology in the eighteenth and nineteenth centuries was an outgrowth of an earlier revolt against oligarchic government, one which culminated in the "glorious revolution" of 1688 in England. The bloodless "glorious" revolution, which saw the downfall of James II, established the sovereignty of Parliament over the monarchy, barring it from suspending acts of Parliament and interfering with the courts.

The **Industrial Revolution** stimulated a demand to free the taxpayer from arbitrary and restrictive government action. This demand for freedom of action came primarily from the rising industrial and trading classes and was directed against restrictions imposed by the government (in legislation, common law, and judicial action) upon the freedoms of economic enterprise.

Liberals derived their political ideas from the writers of the Enlightenment, and the so-called "principles of 1789" as embodied in the French Declaration of the Rights of Man and Citizen. The leading thinkers of the eighteenth century believed that human-made laws and institutions were the modern answer to progress. Liberal politicians in Europe wanted to establish a political framework that would permit legal equality, religious toleration, and freedom of the press. Their primary goal was to construct a political structure that would limit the arbitrary powers of monarchical government against the persons and property of individual citizens. They believed that the legitimacy of government was not inherited but rather emanated from the freely given *consent* of the governed. They felt the popular basis of this kind of government should be expressed through elected, representative, and parliamentary bodies. For liberals, free government required that the political executive must be "responsible" to the legislature rather than to the monarch. The British philosopher Leonard Hobhouse listed the key liberal principles that became prominent throughout the evolution of modern liberalism:[14]

■ *Rule of law:* The principle that Liberals fought for – to limit government power by proclaiming the supremacy of law so as to secure the legal equality of all individuals and to protect the rights of people from arbitrary interference by officials.

■ *Responsible government:* The democratic principle that all public officials are accountable to the people and can rule only by their consent.

■ *Civil liberties:* The fundamental principles of any civilized society. At the basis of these lie the freedoms of thought, expression, association, religion, and of the press.

■ *Constitutionalism*: The principle that all social, legal, and political rights should be protected and entrenched by means of a fundamental charter, social contract, or convention that outlines, defines, and limits the exercise of governmental power by law.

■ *Individualism*: The principle that the chief function of government is to foster the well-being of each person and to permit that person to reach self-fulfillment.

■ *Majority rule*: The principle that public decisions are weighted in favour of the greater number of citizens.

■ *Popular sovereignty*: The principle that states that all government and public authority should flow from the people.

■ *International co-operation*: Liberals called for the reduction or elimination of all trade barriers, tariffs, quotas, and other instruments of economic protection in order to expand national economies and foster international interaction.

These ideological prescriptions may seem quite ordinary for us today. But such democratic guarantees existed in none of the major European states in the late seventeenth and eighteenth centuries. The people who espoused these changes in governments tended to be those who were excluded from the existing political processes but whose new wealth and education made them feel that such exclusion was unjustified. Liberals were usually intellectuals or people involved in the rapidly expanding commercial and manufacturing segments of the economy. The existing monarchical and aristocratic regimes often failed to recognize them as newly empowered

groups or to provide for their economic and professional interests. In the chaotic years of eighteenth century Europe, these groups organized for the purpose of winning control of government. They stressed the values of liberty, human dignity, individualism, and advocated political democracy. They sought to establish a constitutional order that would protect civil liberties, limit government, permit political competition, and separate church and state.

The twentieth century has witnessed a further transformation of democratic liberal thought from its earlier forms to an ideology that postulates the "best" society, rooted in individual freedom, social concern, and human dignity. Liberalism abandoned its eighteenth century advocacy of the economic freedoms of laissez-faire capitalism, and by the twentieth century, proposed new roles for democratic government: to manage the economic and social maladjustments of industrialization, to redistribute wealth, and to develop a policy framework for the health, education, and welfare of all citizens.

One outstanding intellectual who helped to develop the rationale to support a greater government role in modern society was John Dewey (1859-1952).[15] This popular American philosopher noted the intimate connection between political democracy and economic well-being in society. For him, the political system should guarantee a dignified life for *all* citizens.

Contemporary liberalism is a loosely knit mosaic of beliefs, practices, theories, and differing pragmatic approaches to solving economic, political, and social problems. Liberals believe that a strong central government is necessary to protect individuals from the inequities of a rapidly changing technological society. For liberals, the growth of government has enhanced, not diminished, individual freedom. They see the role of the state as correcting the injustices of the marketplace, not supplanting it.

Conservatism

The term "conservatism" was coined from the French word *conservateur,* the label given to French writers and statesmen who demanded a return to pre-revolutionary conditions after the fall of Napoleon I. The birth of conservatism is usually associated with the publication of Edmund Burke's *Reflections on the Revolution in France* (1790), which excoriated the French revolutionaries for the arrogance with which they assumed they could alter the natural continuity of history.[16] The defeat of Napoleon and the diplomatic settlement of the Congress of Vienna re-established the conservative social and political order in Europe.

Monarchies, aristocracies, and the established churches made up the main pillars of conservatism. Though these institutions were ancient, the conscious allegiance of the throne, wealth, and altar was new and made them reluctant allies. Conservatives knew they could be toppled by liberal political groups who hated them. They regarded themselves as surrounded by well-organized enemies; they felt permanently on the defensive against the forces of liberalism, nationalism, and popular sovereignty. A sense of alarm felt by European aristocrats, families of long-established wealth, and the clergy encouraged them to organize their own political groups.

Classical Conservatives

Classical conservatism combined the ideological perspectives of Burke and those of other thinkers such as Thomas Hobbes and David Hume. Hobbes had asserted that human nature was essentially selfish, requiring the restraint of coercive governmental power in order to tame the natural tendencies of people to satisfy their needs at the expense of others in society. Conservatives saw this selfishness expressed as social whim, demands for rapid or radical change, and licence for unfettered individual freedoms. David Hume, in his *Treatise of Human Nature* (1740), argued that given the tendency of human reason to reach selfish conclusions, it was necessary for people to be controlled by laws, conventions, and institutions that had proved their social wisdom over time.

Burke presented his conservative views of the world with power and conviction. He held that *humankind* was wise, but that the *individual* was not. Burke confirmed the fundamental conservative distrust of human nature. As individuals, people were basically weak, given to passion and instinct, and generally untrustworthy. Such characteristics required institutional restrictions on human behaviour by law, government authority, and other social constraints on individual freedoms. The role of the state was seen essentially to control people for their own good.

Burke also stressed the *organic* nature of society – the idea that society is an organism to which all people in a community belong. The institutions that have evolved within this organic social system cannot be cut away without endangering the life of that organism, just as removing the internal organs of any living being would destroy that human organism.

Thus, society is not merely a social contract, as the liberals asserted, but an indissoluble and perpetual convention that assigns duties and responsibilities to be carried out from one generation to the next. Individuals are temporary and perishable. But society as an organic expression is a partnership between those who are dead, those who are living, and those yet to be born. As a product of evolution rather than revolution it is much larger and more enduring than any individual. Therefore, the interests of society must transcend individual interests.

In the early part of this century, the British political writer F.J.C. Hearnshaw outlined a classical statement of the principles of conservatism:

■ *Reverence for the past*: Societies accumulate wisdom from their customs and traditions, and respect the accomplishments of their ancestors.

■ *Organic conception of society*: Societies are greater than the sum of their parts and take on a corporate or communal identity and unity.

■ *Constitutional continuity*: Constitutions are indissoluble conventions that carry the proven political norms and practices of the past into the present.

■ *Opposition to revolution*: Conservatives reject radical change because it destroys proven customs and institutions.

■ *Cautious reform*: Change should be evolutionary and carefully deliberated.

■ *The religious basis of the state*: The state has a moral, religious, and sacred character beyond its political and legal personality.

■ *The divine source of legitimate authority*: Political and legal authority is divine in its origin.

■ *The priority of duties over rights*: Conservatives recognize that individuals have civic duties as well as personal rights and are obligated to fulfill them in the interests of the body politic.

■ *Loyalty*: Conservatives demonstrate loyalty to church, family, school, party, institutions, and country.

■ *Common sense and pragmatism*: Conservatives are people of practical action rather than theory; devoted to sound administration rather than prolific legislation.[17]

Modern conservatism is much less the body of coherent beliefs (as outlined by Hearnshaw) than a modern attitude or a state of mind. Conservatives usually want to preserve the status quo or return to a preferred previous state of affairs. In the 1990s, conservatism aspires to trim the size of government, reduce public spending, reform the taxation laws to encourage investments, deregulate business to promote economic growth, and manage the fiscal and monetary sides of the economy.

In other economic matters, conservatives draw upon many of the ideas of nineteenth-century liberalism. Conservatism essentially has become a defence of economic individualism against the growth of the **welfare state**. In its earlier classical manifestations, conservatives were the supporters of strong central government. They believed that only a government of a talented and propertied elite could preserve the sacred rights of humans. As the voting franchise extended to more and more people during the twentieth century, conservatives lost their faith in central government and focused on the rights of property, independent of the state, and rights of individuals to be free of government interference. Thus, contemporary conservatives tend to oppose any increase in the role of the state in the economy and contend that a vibrant and unfettered private sector can best create jobs for the poor, immigrants, and minorities. Welfare programs, conservatives argue, often create a permanent class of the poor who are dependent on the state, and who have little incentive to enter the work force.

On social and cultural issues, conservatives come close to Burke's ideals. They believe that the state should promote virtue and social responsibility, thus improving the moral climate of society. Therefore, they usually oppose abortion, pornography, and many also oppose affirmative rights for groups such as homosexuals. Conservatives challenge the idea of quotas and other affirmative policies: they argue that human rights guarantee equality of treatment, not equality of social results.

■ ■ **utopian socialists:** those who believed that the quality of humanitarianism would produce ideal socialist experiments, the success of which would quickly be perceived by the rest of society, and the models adopted. ■ ■

Democratic Socialism

Socialism is articulated by democratic as well as non-democratic ideologies. Unlike other systems of thought, it has enjoyed political prominence throughout recorded history. It has been adopted in both pre-industrial and modern societies as a rationale for societal planning and social equality. The prominence of socialist thought and practice over time in most parts of the world may have resulted from the very nature of society: men, women,

and children surviving together as families, tribes, villages, cities, and nation-states. All societies have had to make choices regarding the reconciliation of the individual's welfare to the welfare of the whole society. The early socialists lacked any strong following: their doctrines were blurred and were viewed as outlandish by their contemporaries.

The Utopians

Among the first to articulate this social bias was a group of writers called **utopian socialists** by their later critics.[18] Thomas More (1478-1535), Francis Bacon (1561-1621), and Tommaso Campanella (1568-1639) were considered utopians because they were idealists whose ideas were visionary. These utopians looked nostalgically at earlier societies as though they were without selfishness and social antagonisms. They were called socialists because they criticized existing economic systems. One such early socialist pioneer was the French aristocrat, Claude Henri, Count of Saint Simon (1760-1825) who believed that private wealth, property, and enterprise should be socially administered by experts at arm's length from these assets to alleviate poverty and social dislocation. He came to be regarded as the father of the modern welfare state.

The major British contributor to early socialist thought was Robert Owen (1771-1858), a successful cotton manufacturer. Owen held a partnership in a large British cotton factory at New Lanark, Scotland, where he put socialist ideas to practice, organizing the industry so that workers and managers lived together and produced their goods in co-operation. Although his experiment failed in New Harmony, Indiana, Owen contributed to socialist thought by his belief that the practicality of co-operative production under humane working conditions was possible. Charles Fourier (1772-1837), a contemporary of Owen, advocated the construction of morally liberated agrarian communities called *phalanxes* that would permit individuals to perform different tasks to avoid boredom and dullness. Fourier believed that societies would be more productive if social classes and labour specialization were eliminated.

In the latter part of the nineteenth century, the democratic socialists who exerted the most influence were associated with the Fabian Society. Founded in 1884, the Society took its name from Q. Fabius Maximus, the Roman general who defeated Hannibal by waiting a very long time before attacking. By acting out this strategy, the Society advocated a gradual approach to major social reform. Some of its notable members were Sidney (1859-1947) and Beatrice (1858-1943) Webb, H.G. Wells (1866-1946), Graham Wallas (1858-1932), and George Bernard Shaw (1856-1950). They believed that through democracy the great social questions of the day could be addressed. They wanted to replace individualism with state action. In their view, the goals of socialism could be achieved without revolution. This belief was echoed in the work of the German socialist revisionist, Eduard Bernstein (1850-1932), who questioned whether Marx had been correct in his pessimistic appraisal of capitalism and the necessity of revolution. In his *Evolutionary Socialism* (1899), Bernstein pointed to the rising standard of living in Europe and the failure of Marx's predictions to materialize. Revisionists wanted socialist parties to gain control of governments in their respective states, but the socialism to be thus established would be more moderate and limited than the sweeping transformation of society urged by doctrinaire socialists.

Contemporary Socialism

In the twentieth century, democratic socialism is a political and economic ideology that aims to preserve individual freedom in the context of social equality achieved through a centrally planned economy. While a private sector of the economy will continue to exist under socialism, major industries and corporations are owned by the state in the national interest and thus the government is responsible for planning and directing the economy. The state takes ownership of only strategic industries and services, such as railways, airlines, mines, banks, radio, TV, telecommunications, medical services, universities, and important manufacturing enterprises such as chemicals and steel.

Important decisions concerning foreign investments, wages, and prices are placed in the hands of public institutions. The tax system is designed to prevent excessive profits or an undue concentration of wealth. No democratic socialist state aspires to communism. What separates democratic socialists from non-democratic socialists is the latter's acceptance of violent revolution: democratic socialists advance peaceful and constitutional change and want to achieve goals.

But while socialist societies may redistribute wealth more evenly than capitalist ones, they are less efficient at creating wealth in the first place. In socialist economies, decisions are more centralized and not left up to individuals. Because individuals may not own most of the resources, it is difficult for them to decide on the uses of those resources. Economic decisions are made by a group of individuals with official status. Public administrators often determine what goods and services will be produced, their prices, and who will receive them. The twentieth century has provided persuasive evidence that socialist societies are more bureaucratic and less productive than capitalist ones.

The contemporary descendants of evolutionary socialism are the social democratic and labour parties of North America, Western Europe, and Latin America. They have often abandoned the more radical elements of their ideology (for example, nationalization of industry and opposition to capitalism). Where they have gained power, they have pursued policies aimed at creating a welfare state and winning votes – all within the capitalist framework.

Non-democratic Ideologies

Communism

The idea that there should be no private property and that all things should be held in common is an ancient one. In the Biblical book of Genesis, everything comes from God and no one has inherent rights of possession. In Deuteronomy, all debts are automatically cancelled every seven years in the "year of release," according to the ancient Hebrew beliefs of egalitarianism, welfare, and communist norms. In Leviticus, the "year of Jubilee" is described as the time every fifty

years when all the accumulated inequalities of land distribution are eliminated and the land is redistributed equally among Hebrew tribes. Much later, in the sixth century, some Christian monastics repudiated private ownership and called for a return to the ancient principle of equality believed to have been prominent in a "golden age" of communal life. In sixteenth-century Austria – 300 years before Marxism – the Hutterites, a radical religious sect, practised social and economic communism and proclaimed that all human beings should live in communal societies. The utopian socialists wrote of societies organized according to communist principles that were founded among the earliest human communities.

Marxism

The person who had the most profound impact on modern notions of communism was Karl Marx (1818-1883). His socialist philosophy eventually triumphed over most alternative versions of socialism in Europe – even though varying interpretations, criticisms, and revisions of his monumental work continue to the present.[19] As a student at the University of Berlin, Marx immersed himself in Hegelian philosophy, which introduced him to the idea that all phases of human history are the inevitable product of class and ideological conflict. French utopian socialists gave Marx his focus on the ideals of communal life. And the British economists, notably Adam Smith, David Ricardo, and Thomas Malthus – who shared the view that the condition of the working class could not be improved – gave him a pessimistic focus.

In 1844, Marx met Friedrich Engels, another young middle-class German, whose

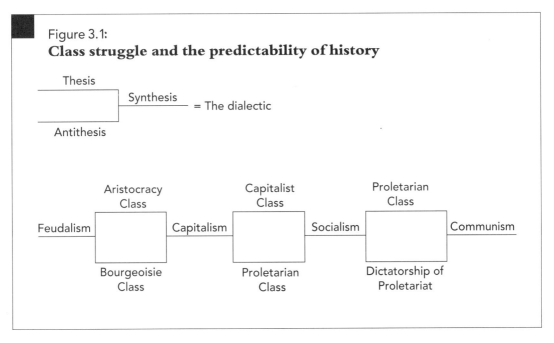

Figure 3.1:
Class struggle and the predictability of history

friendship with Marx led to an intellectual collaboration of enormous ideological consequences. In 1847, they wrote *The Communist Manifesto* for a newly organized secret Communist League. They had adopted the name "communist" because the word was much more emphatically radical than "socialist." Communism called for the outright abolition of private property and required the extensive reorganization of society. A work of less than fifty pages, the *Manifesto* would become the most influential document in modern European history. By the time *Das Kapital* (Vol. 1, 1867) was published, which predicted the disintegration of capitalism, Marxism had emerged as the single most important strand of socialism in Europe.[20]

Under the influence of Hegelian thought, Marx and Engels contended that human history must be understood rationally and as a whole. The basic means of produc-

tion in an economy facilitates the structures, values, and ideas of society. The lesson from history is that the organization of the means of production generates conflict between the classes who own the means of production and those who work for them. History is driven and unfolds by this necessary conflict. Marxian analysis was therefore conditioned by the assumption that the path to socialism was via revolution rather than reform. The era of the utopian community had ended.

The fundamental concepts in communism flow from the theoretical contributions of Marx, Engels, V.I. Lenin, Leon Trotsky, Josef Stalin, Josip Tito, Nikita Khrushchev, Mao Tse Tung, and Mikhail Gorbachev. They include: materialism, historical inevitability, alienation, labour theory of value, class struggle, dictatorship of the proletariat, the revolutionary role of the vanguard party, and imperialism.

The Materialist Conception of History

Marxism begins with the "materialist conception of history," which asserts the human necessity to produce and acquire what we need to live. In order for us to understand the historical significance of materialism, Marx asks us to look at the role of labour, the abundance or lack of raw materials, and the instruments of production available in society. This material basis for the "mode of production" determines the political, moral, legal, and religious **superstructure** of society and is the driving force of societal development from lower to higher stages. That is, the material lives of people determine their ideology and their supporting institutions. Changes in material conditions necessarily bring about changes in the social and political structures of society. Thus, history is the product not of deliberative decisions or ideas, but of material processes and conditions that are identifiable, observable, and predictable.

■ ■ **superstructure:** the legal, political, and social institutions which reflect, express, and consolidate the relations of economic power that flow from the mode of production practised by a society. ■ ■

Historical Inevitability

Marx borrowed another idea from Hegel and others – that history moves in predictable directions. Marx and Engels developed a theory about the movement of history that purports to explain why one economic system (mode of production) would give way to another and why it is possible to predict this movement to the final historical stage of human development, which is communism (figure 3.1). They devoted much of their work to plotting the development of human history from pre-industrial communism through slavery and feudalism to capitalism and socialism.

However, to a large extent, their work was sharply focused on capitalism and its inevitable collapse, not on the future of societies. They believed that capitalism marked a transient stage of historical development destined to disintegrate because its antagonistic classes – capitalist and **proletariat** – will clash, resulting in a victorious workers' revolution.

The identification of the inevitability of historical forces was regarded by Marx and Engels as the "scientific" quality of their analyzes. The scientific study of history was thus the analysis of the way in which human beings respond to material change in their societies and the capacity to predict the consequences of these changes.

Class Struggle

Marx recognized that many social classes had emerged at different times under different modes of production. For example, in pre-industrial Europe, the aristocracy, who owned the land, were the ruling class and the peasants, who tilled it, were the workers. During the industrial period, two classes alone – the bourgeoisie and the proletariat – were the forces that shaped the economic destiny of the period. But for Marx, social classes were more than ranks in a hierarchy; they were the building blocks of society. Social classes arise from the "relations of production" that occur in the economy. Accordingly, the major classes of the modern era were the landowners and capitalists, and the class of wage-earners.

In the course of time, classes become self-aware. They perceive the social and economic characteristics that distinguish them from other groups, some more advantaged, some less so. This class consciousness leads to organization, politicization, and ultimately confrontation between or among groups. Because the state is a prominent component of the superstructure that reflects the ideology of the ruling class, its coercive power is applied against the challenges of the proletarian class. The superstructure consists of the laws, the political and social institutions, and the economic organizations that enforce, produce, and consolidate human relations in society. The superstructure is almost always controlled by the most powerful classes, who manipulate the institutions of government to protect their interests over those of other classes.

> ■ ■ **dialectic:** a concept borrowed from Hegel by Marx which asserts that all societies contain within them the seeds to their own destruction – the struggle of opposites generates social transformation. ■ ■

Out of this situation revolutions are born. Marx saw history as a **dialectic** of revolutionary change (figure 3.1). For him, the dialectic is a process of class conflict and struggle involving social and political contradictions as *thesis* and *antithesis*, producing a conflict out of which a new and higher social order, *synthesis,* emerges. Marx and Engels asserted that class conflict would be resolved in the final proletarian revolution, which would result in the final historical synthesis, communism.

Alienation

The Marxian theory of alienation seeks to explain how individuals living in a capitalist society lose their understanding and control of the world around them, and in the process become something less than full human beings. Under capitalism, the source of alienation is the organization of work. Workers feel dissociated from the process of production because they compete with other workers, receive only a small portion of the value of what they produce, are divided and specialized in what they produce, and do not own the means of production or have much say in how they are used. Marx believed that the capacity to work is a distinctive human characteristic. All other species, he argued, were simply objects in their worldly environment; human beings are the sole subjects in the hierarchy of existence, because they consciously act on and change the environment, shaping their lives, cultures, and personalities in the process. Because workers in a capitalist system have diminished responsibilities and are reduced to a minute part of the work process, they perceive themselves as mere cogs in the production of society. Work becomes an enforced activity, not a creative or satisfying one, essentially because the profit produced by the labour of the worker goes to someone else. Marx did not see capitalism as the original source of alienation, but he believed that under capitalism alienation is maximized.

Labour Theory of Value

Marx witnessed some of the worst manifestations of capitalism while he lived in England. He saw abusive child labour, the vicious competition of workers for low-paying jobs, dangerous and unhealthy working conditions, and ruthless employers who cared very little about the fate of those who worked for them. From his experience he concluded that the majority of men, women, and children suffered from poverty and need. They were the victims of a mode of production that permitted the few who did not do manual labour to enjoy most of the wealth produced by labourers. Thus, from his perspective, the capitalist mode of production extracted *surplus value* from wage-labour to the benefit of the capitalist class. As Marx saw it, the true value of any commodity is derived by computing the labour that was necessary to produce it (labour theory of value). He believed that because capitalists are not labourers, they do not produce value. On the other hand, workers are not compensated for the total value of the goods they produce, and what the capitalist withholds from the worker is surplus value. The surplus value is used to expand capital, a process conditioned by competition. The accumulation of capital generates increasing demands for labour. But at the same time, accumulation leads to the concentration of capital, placing greater amounts of capital in fewer and fewer hands.

Ultimately, the fundamental contradictions of capitalism are linked to the labour theory of value. The natural tendency for capitalists to expand surplus value, or profits, feeds the impoverishment of workers, creates underconsumption, and results in surplus production. In Marx's view, surplus value was a waste of social energy, because the amount of effort workers invest into generating wealth for individual capitalists could be used to benefit society as a whole.

Dictatorship of the Proletariat

According to Marx, after the inevitable revolution, a short period of socialist transition would take place following the collapse of capitalism. The *dictatorship of the proletariat* would be the state under the control of the proletarians – those who defend the gains made during the revolution and guide society through the inequalities and deprivations that would occur during the transformation to communism. By means of its political dominance, the proletariat would be able to bring under its control all the means of production: industry, land, business, communications, transportation, and commerce.

The term "dictatorship" was never fully explained by Marx, although it may have been used rhetorically to add legitimacy to state representation of workers' interests in the period of transition to a socialist economy. The state would be a committee of proletarians making decisions, drafting laws, and taking action on behalf of the proletarian class. Marx argued that the advent of a socialist revolution would mean the disappearance of a class-based state apparatus. For this brief period, the proletariat would be the ruling class that prepares the way for a classless society.

Marxism-Leninism

The Vanguard Party

V.I. Lenin (1870-1924) was a determined, relentless **Bolshevik** revolutionary who studied the strengths and weaknesses of pure Marxist theory as it could apply to a revolution occurring in a backward country such as Russia. He brought his own ideas to Marxist thought, producing what came to be known as Marxism-Leninism. In his work, *What Is to be Done?* (1922), Lenin explained why the autocratic conditions of Russia demanded a unique kind of organization to guide the revolution to fruition. Lenin rejected Marx's concept of a "mass party" composed of workers, because in his view, revolutionary consciousness had not sufficiently developed in the small Russian working class during and after the 1917 revolution. For him, the Russian proletariat was diminutive, disorganized, easily subverted, and without a clear understanding of its revolutionary mission. Only a small elite, made up of people "who make revolutionary activity their profession" could lead the masses with any disciplined determination.

Lenin argued that the socialist revolution was inevitable for Russia only if a small, specially constituted, vanguard party made it so. In fact, one of his theoretical contributions to Marxism was that a socialist revolution can take place in a pre-capitalist society if it is properly planned and engineered. In 1905, Lenin complemented his organizational theory for the party with a program for revolution in Russia. His *Two Tactics of Social Democracy in the Bourgeois-Democratic Revolution* (1905) urged that the socialist revolution unite the Russian proletariat and the peasants under one party organization. Lenin grasped better than any other revolutionary the profound discontent in the Russian countryside, even after the 1917 revolution. He knew that an alliance of workers and peasants in one party would be a formidable revolutionary combination.

Imperialism

In 1916, Lenin published *Imperialism: The Highest Stage of Capitalism,* thereby adding another ideological element to Marxism-Leninism. In his book he elaborated upon Marx's assertion that monopolies are a natural tendency in developed capitalist economies. Lenin stated that monopolies will ensure their further expansion by penetrating and exploiting new markets in foreign economies.

Otherwise, continued exploitation of a domestic market would result in Marx's predicted severe social crisis and, ultimately, economic collapse.

Lenin observed that advanced capitalist economies had temporarily postponed social and economic chaos by entering new markets in the developing economies of the world. New markets absorbed excess production that could not be sold in the domestic economy because of the spreading impoverishment of the masses. Thus, imperialism and colonialism were seen as a consequence of monopoly capitalism. Lenin's observations altered Marxism by linking colonialism with the spread of capitalism in the developing world, and by advancing the possibility that revolutions need not occur necessarily in the most advanced industrialized economies.

Leninism

Lenin escorted Marxism into the twentieth century by applying its will, action, and initiative to a real revolution. Lenin sounded like Marx when he said "the philosophers have *interpreted* the world in various ways; the point however is to *change* it."[21] Until Lenin's revolutionary activism, Marxists believed that the dialectic movement of history was determined by class forces that were beyond the control of any single individual. Lenin's main theoretical contribution to Marxism was to show that voluntarism and political organization can generate socialist revolution independent of any movement of history resulting from a clash of classes. For Lenin, revolution

Figure 3.2:
Significant contributors to Marxism-Leninism

Leon Trotsky
(1879–1940)
Called for permanent revolution on a global scale to defeat the forces of capitalism and establish a world communist commonwealth.

Nikita Khrushchev
(1894–1971)
Attacked the policies of Stalin by denouncing him as a criminal against socialist justice, and adopted a policy of peaceful co-existence in regard to relations with capitalist states, which implied that communism would replace capitalism by peaceful competition rather than war.

Josef Stalin
(1879–1953)
Advocated establishing socialism in one country, the newly formed Soviet Union, by using the ruthless power of the state to serve as a model and base for expanding socialist revolution in other states.

Mao Tse Tung
(1893–1976)
Built the largest independent socialist revolution in the world by establishing an alliance for the permanent *cultural revolution* of workers and peasants, and turned Marxism on its head by saying that the communist revolution could fully precede industrialization. He also advocated the spread of communism by means of guerrilla and conventional war.

Marshal Josip Broz Tito
(1892–1980)
Pursued a national and independent course toward socialism, did not accept the direction and control of the Communist Party of the Soviet Union, and developed in the former Yugoslavia a model of peaceful transition from capitalism to socialism through legislative institutions and working-class parties.

Mikhail Gorbachev
(1930–)
Called for "new thinking," *glasnost* (open criticism) and *perestroika* (restructuring of social and economic institutions) that led to the eventual unravelling of the Soviet Union and threatened the collapse of other communist regimes around the world.

was not necessarily spontaneous or historically inevitable; rather, it could be planned, calculated, and orchestrated by a disciplined, militant party organization.

Another important principle developed by Lenin in his theory of party organization was **democratic centralism**. Under this principle, democratic participation by means of free discussion is permitted for all party members until a decision is taken, at which time no further debate or dissent is tolerated and party members are expected to fully support the decision. Democratic centralism became a fundamental decision-making component in Soviet totalitarianism because it reinforced the control of the party and the government over ideological opposition. The Leninist variant of Marxism was essentially party-centric, proposing: a) a party of professional revolutionaries, b) the democratic dictatorship of the proletariat under the leadership and structure of the party, and c) *partinost*, the notion that advances the party as the repository of ideological truth.

As discussed, Lenin's theory of imperialism altered Marx's position that revolutions will occur only in the advanced capitalist economies. A corollary to Lenin's rationalization of engineered revolutions was his "theory of the weakest link." In it, Lenin held that the greatest possibilities of revolution are not found in capitalist economies but in the weakest links of the capitalist chain, where the proletariat and/or the peasantry was more susceptible to revolutionary rhetoric and mobilization. Russia was portrayed as the weakest link in the chain of European capitalism prior to 1917. Lenin expressed confidence in the ability of Russia to attain socialism.

Many attempts were made to change the direction of Marxism-Leninism after Lenin's death (figure 3.2). Trotsky and Mao wanted world communist revolution in the light of the fundamental principles of Marxism-Leninism. Others (Stalin, Tito, and Khrushchev) took a more nationalist approach to the ideology, calling for it to succeed first within the confines of a national political system and economy, and then to spread by force of example and sometimes by force alone to other receptive political systems. Gorbachev wanted fundamental change of the political and governing structures that had evolved since Lenin, so as to readjust to contemporary conditions and technologies.

The Collapse of Communist Regimes

The 1980s and 1990s saw startling changes in the world of totalitarian socialist regimes. These political and economic systems collapsed in Eastern Europe, and the Soviet Union ceased to exist. However, the disappearance of Soviet power does not mean the subsequent departure of communist ideology.

The Russian Revolution in 1917 was the first phase in the development of the Union of Soviet Socialist Republics (USSR) and the states it came to dominate. With the ascension to power of V.I. Lenin in November of that year, the USSR became the first modern nation-state committed to implementing socialism, and ultimately, communism, within its sphere of influence. Beginning in 1939, the USSR, through negotiation and military action – including brutal invasions of Poland, Hungary, and Czechoslovakia – came to dominate most of Eastern Europe. For nearly half a century, the Soviets imposed and maintained totalitarian rule in these states through repressive government action. Planned economies were linked together by Soviet dominance.

The ideological crisis that led to the collapse of Communist-party domination in Eastern Europe and the Soviet Union resulted in the decline of communism as a global movement. By the 1990s, some states once under communist leadership rejected it in everything but name, while other states rejected even that. But even before the remarkable events in Eastern Europe in 1989, the international communist movement was far from unified. The Eurocommunists of France, Italy, and Spain disagreed on many fundamental ideological positions, but especially opposed the style of implementing Soviet and East-European communism. The Chinese distinguished their communism as peasant-based, and differed even with the Vietnamese, who also proclaimed a peasant-based communist revolution. The Albanians disagreed with most other communist regimes, and the Cubans heralded a neutral and Latin approach to communist ideology.

Many people equate communist ideology with the totalitarian socialism practised in the former closed political societies of the Soviet Union and the East European satellites. But there is a difference. Although communism in theory was supposed to result in the "withering away" of the state, these socialist governments in practice tended toward totalitarianism, controlling both economic and political life through a dominant party organization and an expanding state bureaucracy. A genuine communist system would have relied exclusively on social incentives rather than state repression to stimulate labour and manage social evolution.

Other Ideologies

Nationalism

The roots of nationalism can be traced deep into the past, appearing when England, France, and Spain were transformed from feudal principalities to national monarchies and when their people regarded themselves as "English," "French," and "Spanish" nationals, rather than as Yorkshiremen, Gascons, and Andalusians. Somewhat later, during the Hundred Years' War (1337-1453), England and France drew upon strong feelings of national sentiment to centralize their governments, to build their economies, and to wage war. Much later, in the seventeenth century, the Treaty of Westphalia (1648) nurtured distinctive nation-states, each with its own political, cultural, and religious identity. The emergence of the nation-state unleashed the forces of competitive nationalism in the modern world.

In the following century, writers of the Enlightenment generally championed a cosmopolitan outlook on the world, but the political leaders of the time fashioned a national perspective characterized by autocracy, censorship, and government repression. Napoleon demonstrated the power of nationhood. His toppling of ancient political structures, such as the Holy Roman Empire, demonstrated the need for a new type of political organization in Europe. Nationalism proved to be one of the strongest motivating forces of the nineteenth and twentieth centuries, demonstrating its powerful tendencies to unite millions of people on the one hand and, when desirable, to destroy millions on the other.

German **romantic** writers portrayed nationalism as the glorification of individual cultures. Johann Fichte (1762-1814) challenged the younger generation of Germans to recognize the national duty that historical circumstances had placed on their shoulders. He called for the revival of the German nation so as to receive the gratitude of later generations. Johann Herder (1744-1803) saw human beings and societies as developing organically, like plants, over time. He urged the collection and preservation of distinctive German songs and sayings and seized upon the conception of the *volksgeist,* or national spirit. Perhaps the most important person to develop the ideology of nationalism during the romantic period was G.W.F. Hegel (1170-1831), who recognized that the individuality and worth of separate peoples and cultures working as a national unit constituted one of the few spiritual forces capable of changing world history.

These romantic writers defined *nation* in terms of common language, common history, common customs, and loyalty to a homeland. This cultural nationalism would later become transformed into a political creed that ideologically asserted the unique spirit of belonging together and the corporate nature of the polity. The belief spread rapidly that every people, ethnic group, or nation should constitute a separate political entity and that only when it so existed could the nation be secure in its own unique character.

French nationalism also reflected a romantic and culturally homogeneous character. Writers such as Voltaire, Montesquieu, and Rousseau advanced a cultural nationalism, observing that each people had a language, history, and world view of its own, which must be preserved and perfected. They then passed on to a political nationalism, holding that in order to preserve the national culture, each nation should create a sovereign state. Thus, all persons of the same nationality should embody the same nation-state.

The nineteenth century saw the emergence of the contemporary nation-state, the political consolidation of one or more nations under the jurisdiction and administration of a single state. Prior to this time, the characteristic political organizations were small states comprising fragments of a nation, such as were present in Europe – Hanover, Baden, Sardinia, Tuscany, and the two Sicilies – and the large sprawling empires made up of all sorts of peoples, distantly ruled from above by dynasties, such as the Romanov, Hapsburg, and Ottoman. For many people in the nineteenth century, nationalism, the winning of national unity and independence, and the creation of the nation-state became a kind of secular faith.

At about this time, governments recognized that they could not effectively rule or construct the full powers of a state without enlisting the membership and support of their subjects. The consolidation of the nation-state had some noteworthy phases. In its territorial phase, it meant the union of pre-existing smaller states, and psychologically it meant the construction of new relations between the government and the governed, the inclusion of new strata of the population into political life, and the creation and extension of representative institutions. As an ideology, nationalism came to mean the *will* of a particular nationality or group of nationalities to accept the power of a state to administer its interests, such as with the creation of a new Italy, a new Germany, and a new Canada.

During the nineteenth century, nationalism was not doctrine so much as it was a state of mind, arousing the emotional responses of people when national interests were questioned. In many societies nationalism was fused with conservatism, liberalism, socialism, or republicanism. Within the confines of these ideological parameters, patriots began to call for the preservation of their historic cultures. Intellectuals collected folk tales and ballads, studied languages, and compiled dictionaries of their mother tongues. They encouraged their compatriots to give up "foreign ways" and began the writing of heroic histories. The nineteenth century had generated the ideological prescription that the only legitimate basis for political organization was nationality. The results of this belief were the spread of national independence movements and the consequent development of an international system and community of sovereign nation-states.

Nationalism in the contemporary state system is in many ways similar to and an extension of its nineteenth century predecessor.[22] However, nationalist sentiment has taken on a more doctrinaire form in the present century. The contemporary ideology of nationalism accepts the idea that the human species will naturally form into nations that reflect a particular character. Each nation enjoys the right of self-determination and possesses many legal rights and duties when represented by a state apparatus that is recognized by other states as independent in the international community. Loyalty to the nation is seen to supercede other loyalties. Human freedom and harmony are said to be enhanced by an international system formed on the basis of independent nation-states.

■ ■ **irredentism:** taken from the Italian expression *Italia irredenta* meaning Italy unredeemed, this refers to the desire of the people of a state to annex those contiguous territories of another country that are inhabited by the same linguistic or cultural minorities. ■ ■

Totalitarian Nationalism

In its extreme form during the twentieth century, nationalism manifested itself as the irrational ideologies of fascism and national socialism (Nazism). Latent in German thought in the nineteenth century, nationalism became an obsession. One eminent German historian, Leopold von Ranke (1795-1886), in his work *Latin and Teutonic Peoples,* taught that the Germans had a mission from God to develop a "pure" culture "corresponding to the genius of the nation." Such cultural nationalism was further considered by many philosophers and other intellectual authors who contributed to the development of anti-democratic thought. Friedrich Nietzsche (1844-1900) wrote about the "heroic man," the "superman," the "spineless multitude," and the "slave morality" and influenced the superiority theories of Adolf Hitler. Another German philosopher, Arthur Schopenhauer, who wrote *The World as Will and Idea,* advocated the idea of "subjective truth," which inspired Hitler's use of propaganda to distort reality and engage in psychological warfare.

Even though there are important theoretical differences between Italian fascism and German national socialism, both emphasized the historical importance of building state institutions that united the common cultural identities of the people. These ideologies invariably focused on the nation rather than the individual, and on the superiority of the state over the citizen. There was never the emphasis on individual rights, natural rights, or social contract that had formed the basis of liberal democracy.

In ancient Rome, the *fasces* (a bundle of rods tied to an axe) symbolized the unity of the nation served by an administrative state. In the twentieth century, governments regarded as fascist were intensely nationalistic, **imperialistic**, anti-democratic, anti-Marxist, and anti-Semitic. They expressed a deep pride in their past cultural achievements and a bitterness that – despite a self-proclaimed cultural superiority – the less-cultured nations exercised real political and military power in the world. The fascist and Nazi attitude towards war and the quest for empire was related to cultural glorification and expressions of racial superiority. Benito Mussolini often referred to Italy's *sacro egoismo* as irredentism, the rationale for taking the territory of other states where Italians live. The Nazis likewise called for the union of all Germans to form the "Great Germany" and demanded more *lebensraum* (living space). Those who did not share in the super-patriotism of the period and the resurrected glory of the past were treated as "un-German" or "aliens."

The underlying nationalist ideology of Nazism was racist. Hitler embraced the image of the "Aryan race" as a blond, blue-eyed, and uniquely gifted "master race," which had diluted its genetic heritage by intermarriage with "lesser breeds." The fear of intermarriage with whomever was deemed the bad race became linked with all kinds of sexual fears and phobias. In the Nuremberg Laws (1935) proclaimed by the Nazis, German Jews were denied their citizenship and intermarriage between Germans and Jews was outlawed. Anti-Semitism thus became a fundamental policy of the Nazi government.

Fascist ideology had rejected the political inheritance of the French Revolution and the democratic traditions of liberalism. Sovereignty was vested in the national state. All individuals existed to enhance the power of the state and the nation it represented. The mystical entity of the nation was viewed as an organic body headed by the leader and sustained by unity, force, and discipline. This new philosophy of statecraft drew heavily upon the historic nationalism which it greatly exaggerated. The organic theory postulated the nation as a living organism within which the individual person was but a single cell. Individuals possessed no independent existence, receiving all worth from the nation that nurtured them. Law itself was defined as the will of the nation operating through the institutions of the Nazi state. The new national order was designed to be monolithic. Germany ceased to be a federal state, and old states such as Prussia and Bavaria were abolished so that the historic process of national unification could be finalized.

Canadian Fascism

Three major events in the early 1930s contributed to the birth of right-wing social movements in Canada – the Great Depression, the prairie drought, and the spread of communist ideology. The communists appealed to those who were hungry and the unemployed. They promised to throw off their capitalist masters and assume control of their national destinies.

Fascism emerged within this economic climate in Canada. In 1929, a professional journalist in Montreal, Adrien Arcand, spawned a movement in Québec based on racial nationalism. Calling itself the "Ordre Patriotique des Goglus," and modelled after Italian fascism, the group claimed as many as 50,000 members by February 1930. Even before Hitler came to power, Arcand was a loyal patron of fascist ideology. He shared Hitler's anti-Semitism and he organized boycotts of stores and other businesses owned by Jews. Arcand edited a weekly newspaper in which he publicized his idea that Jews should be expelled. He attacked communism and socialism as did all fascists, but in Canada this won him support among some business owners.

Once Hitler came to power, Arcand's group became even more virulent in its anti-Semitism. His followers wore blue shirts, mimicking the fascists operating in Europe. Other fascist groups, some competing with Arcand's, sprang up, as well. A brownshirt group, the Canadian Nationalist Party, headed by William Whittaker, an ex-British soldier, was operating in Manitoba. This party regularly published anti-Semitic literature. In Ontario, "Swastika Clubs" emerged, comprising gangs of youth who wore swastika insignia and who harassed Jews in public places. In 1939, a National Fascist convention was held in Massey Hall in Toronto, attracting about 2000 participants. Arcand, his group now publicized bilingually as "Le Parti National Social Chrétien/The National Social Christian Party of Canada," wanted to be known as the Canadian *Führer*. Eventually he outdistanced his closest rivals — the black-shirted Canadian Union of Fascists — in competition for dominance.

■ ■ **xenophobia:** an extreme fear of foreigners, sometimes accompanied by a pathological hatred of strangers, which can lead to racism and ethnic cleansing. ■ ■

When the Nazis began their invasions in Europe, Arcand and other fascists were arrested and imprisoned for the duration of the war. Following his release after the war, Arcand continued to produce anti-Semitic literature until he died in 1967.

But the extreme right has never disappeared in Canada. The Ku Klux Klan and other racist groups have used terror, intimidation, and political agitation. Klan agitation has been very successful; in 1929, it contributed to winning amendments to Canada's immigration laws that established quotas for targeted less-preferred immigrants, and it was a force behind the toppling of the Liberal government in Saskatchewan in the same year. Many other groups comprise the racist right in Canada.[23] Neo-Nazi groups have formed in most Canadian cities, finding new support among frustrated and disaffected people. Groups such as Aryan Nations, the Aryan Resistance Movement, The Church of the Creator, The Heritage Front, and Final Solution portray a mixture of xenophobia, white supremacy, and nostalgia for the hegemonic power of Nazi Germany. Neo-Nazis, after years of skulking at the margins of politics in Europe and North America, suddenly feel part of a wider international movement. Most of these groups attempt to enlist young people into their movements by recruiting actively at schools, distributing hate literature, and engaging in violence against gays, Jews, African-Canadians, and natives.

Anarchism

The Greek word *"anarchos"* means without a

leader or chief. Like the Greek cynics, who first developed the doctrines of anarchism, modern anarchists believe that government and the state apparatus are unnecessary for the meaningful arrangement and operation of society. They are essentially optimistic about human nature, believing that the inherent goodness in people alleviates the need for political and organizational constraints on their behaviour. Today, anarchists are not universally agreed on what kind of economic order is desirable. The debate over the economic system currently splits anarchism into two schools. One school believes that only capitalism can be appropriately combined with anarchism, while the other school advocates returning to an agrarian economy based on socialist economic principles. As for social justice, all anarchists advocate that we should live in a society where there is no compulsion of any kind. For them, social justice means the chance to lead the life that best suits each individual.

Because anarchists are philosophically opposed to all forms of political organization, very few anarchist political parties have ever been established. They are anti-political in that they do not believe that the electoral system can bring about real change in society. Because they are against the excesses of organized political power, they have tried to establish a countervailing force at the basic infrastructure of society, e.g., through tenants' associations, daycare and housing associations, and municipal organizations. In Montreal, anarchists work through the Civic party or the Montreal Citizens' Movement to bring about change at the municipal level. Instead of forming political parties, anarchists prefer to project themselves as a movement, advo-

cating and co-ordinating their goals within the organizational framework of established labour, communist, and socialist parties. In Latin American states such as Argentina, Chile, and Mexico, and the European states of France, Germany, and Spain, *anarcho-syndicalism* has appeared in various labour parties. The central element of anarcho-syndicalism is workers' control. These anarchists argue that society should be organized on the basis of the control of each industry by the workers in that industry. Once this occurs, representatives from each industry come together to administer the economic life of the whole country.

In the context of communist and socialist parties, anarchists frequently identify with the theories of Peter Kropotkin, Alexander Berkman, and Herbert Reid.[24] Kropotkin argued that co-operation rather than conflict was a natural law of human nature. He and Herbert Reid believed that the ultimate level of co-operation will only be possible when people are able to do away with coercive institutions. Berkman's contribution to anarchist thought emphasized the need to develop a society without any social coercion. He contended that capitalism created economic inequality and governments perpetuated this inequality with laws that protected those who own the means of production. For many anarchists of the left, capitalism, government, and the law are the roots of all evil. For them, the emphasis of anarchism is on the voluntary association of individuals in a variety of forms, one of which is the society or commune that makes political decisions by consensus.

The vitality of anarchism as an ideology has varied throughout this century. In the

United States and Canada, anarchists helped establish co-operatives and libertarian communities. Because of the popular fears and misunderstandings concerning anarchists at the turn of the century, they were the only group restricted from immigration into the United States because of their political beliefs. Anarchism as a movement appealed to the peasants and labourers in certain parts of Europe, especially Spain. The Confederación National de Trabajo, formed in 1911, had 700,000 members by 1918; by the 1930s, the Federación Anarchista Iberica had over 200,000 members, some of whom wanted to form a syndicalist party.

In the period from the mid-1930s to the 1960s, not much was heard of anarchism in any part of the world. However, by the late 1960s, a growing number of academics began to publish manuscripts on anarchism. Students who rioted in Paris in June, 1968, carried the anarchist banner. By the mid-1970s, the black flag of anarchism was frequently seen in anti-war and disarmament demonstrations in Europe and North America. In spring 1982, the Montreal-based Anarchos was established as a clearing house of information and as a vehicle of public education in the Western hemisphere. Today, in many states, people who actively engaged in the peace movement share anarchist beliefs about the dangers of nuclear war. Anarchists point to the absurdity of nuclear-weapons' competition among organized political systems. They

explain the tensions of global politics in terms of the competitive interaction of states, with organized governments as both the actors and targets of human aggression. Thus, anarchists want to dismantle the sovereign state system and replace it with a global society of autonomous groups that interact for political purposes on bases other than those now subsumed under the concepts "state" and "government." They argue that there is a need to go beyond disarmament. Human beings would still have the knowledge to re-arm after a disarmament. Therefore, there is the need to change institutions to mitigate against the possibility of a new arms' race. Weapons must be dismantled, say the anarchists, and the global arms industry must be abolished.

Ideologies of Development

[handwritten: DEVELOPING SOCIETIES]

The political ideologies that are most popular among the developing nation-states have eclectic roots in the great systems of nationalist, democratic, non-democratic, and socialist thought.[25] Most modern ideologies of development date to the end of World War II, when a large number of European colonies in Asia and Africa began their struggle towards political independence. The republics of Latin America have had a much longer period of independence after the revolutionary insurrections of the early nineteenth century. But the widespread adoption of ideologies of development south of the Rio Grande is also a post-war phenomenon.

To be sure, the origins of modern developmental thought go back to Marx, but never before did his critical observations succeed in crystallizing into so many divergent ideological perspectives as in the latter part of the twentieth century. Many leaders in the developing world often interpret and apply traditional ideologies in novel ways, usually by adding indigenous qualities and characteristics to the phenomenon of political and economic development.

Pragmatism and Development

Practical solutions within the framework of nationalism, socialism, and other ideological prisms are devised as the vehicle for economic and political modernization. Pragmatism is the underlying principle of operation: what is good for a developing society is what works well for it in the light of its own conditions. Hence, leaders in the developing world have taken from the ideological reservoirs of democratic and non-democratic systems that are exemplified everywhere in the world. What works best for them in their own political and economic circumstances is borrowed and blended with indigenous ways of doing politics and government.

The same leaders have felt equally free to reject the ideals of liberalism, capitalism, socialism, and communism if, in their view, the application of such ideas would not work. Thus, an individualist, politically competitive capitalist and market-oriented system might not fit easily into the political environment of some African states. It may be more attractive to leaders of Latin American states, where such ideas conform to the local political culture. But a socialist economic philosophy, articulated by a single dominant party, may be more adaptive to African political systems. In all developing nation-states, political leaders search for a unique blend of ideological solutions to their national development goals.

The most common ideological goals of developing states can be reduced to four: 1) national self-determination; 2) economic development; 3) political and social modernization; 4) self-styled democracy. The ideological component of self-determination postulates the right of a people who consider themselves separate and distinct from others to determine for themselves their economic, political, and social destiny.

In Asia, Africa, and the Caribbean, the drive towards political independence included demands for a new national society based on economic, social, and cultural equality. Characteristically, these states adopt an ideology that prescribes a strong charismatic leader, a single party, a loyal but conspicuous military, and authoritarian methods to achieve national priorities. Economic development demands rapid agricultural, commercial, and industrial improvements led by a strong central government. The ideology calls for a "quick fix" to underdevelopment through land reform, the redistribution of wealth, the nationalization of certain industries, and economic planning.

Political modernization is portrayed as an ongoing process that leads to greater citizen participation, better representative institutions, and a more efficient and egalitarian decision-making system. Social modernization is an aspiration to advance the quality of life by improving the educational infrastructure, the system of transportation, communications, life-expectancy, health-care facilities and employment opportunities. Political democracy is self-styled by means of a powerful executive supported by an acquiescent legislative branch of government. The evolution towards democracy is said to be "guided" or "directed" by an elite party organization or through executive government directives.

Revolutionary Thought: Ideologies or Movements?

The meaning of the word "revolution" has changed considerably since it was first used as a political term in 1648 during the "Glorious Revolution" in England.[26] Initially, a revolution was reactionary: it referred to a revolving return to some pre-established point or some pre-ordained order, i.e., the restoration of the English monarchy in 1660 was therefore a "revolution." In the eighteenth century, as enlightened philosophies flourished, the term "revolution" came to mean progress, moving forward – ideas or actions that could alter history. By the nineteenth century, revolution was equated with liberation and freedom. Marx, for example, argued that the final revolution would end in communism, and would include the elimination of class conflict and the ultimate abolition of the state.

In the twentieth century, the term "revolution" came to incorporate three distinct processes: 1) the destruction of an old regime; 2) a period of chaotic disorder; and 3) the creation of a new social order. Revolution became identified with the most radical and far-reaching kinds of societal change – a sharp break with the past and a change in the basic patterns of life, altering institutions, traditions, and social expectations. As the twentieth century progressed, revolutionary thought expressed itself through many ideologies and movements, such as anarchism, communism, national liberation, and feminism. More than in any previous century, the ideologies of recent times express the interests and goals of major social groups.

The word "movement" suggests collective behaviour that is ideologically inspired, and accompanied by a strong sense of solidarity, idealism, and an emphasis on action. Movements are often a prelude to revolutionary change because they create or resist attitudes, behaviour, and institutions. Political and social movements depend on ideologies to establish their identities as well as to gain public visibility. A movement's ideology serves several functions: it provides direction and self-justification; it offers arguments for use in both attack and defence; and it is a source of inspiration for members. Some movements are shapeless, without leadership or clear goals. Others are more directed and fundamentally more ideological.

There are broad distinctions among contemporary movements:[27] *Value-oriented movements* concentrate on matters of general social and political concern, such as democracy, peace, and nationalism. *Norm-oriented movements* are much narrower; for example, to establish or change a particular social or political practice such as the use of alcohol, birth control, and gun control. A *power-centred movement* uses political muscle to achieve certain ends: examples include the Prohibition movement; movements organized around the abortion issue in Canada; and the civil rights movement in the United States. Power-centred movements sometimes use illegitimate means to meet their goals. A *persuasion-centred movement* uses education, including propaganda, and legitimate political action to advance its cause. This approach is practised by some feminists, pacifists, and environmental

activists. These movements tend to favour gradual change and compromise. *Participation-centred movements* focus on creating a unified group of committed members such as those within utopian communities and many religious sects. *Revolutionary movements* seek fundamental changes in the entire social structure – usually in combination with violent social conflict – to establish a new political and social order.

Canada has given birth to many movements, reflecting a social tendency to political fragmentation and lack of consensus among Canadians. Various groups – farmers, French-speaking Canadians, and women – have at one time or another felt estranged from the mainstream of society. As a result, movements such as the Farmers' Union, the Co-operative Commonwealth Federation, the Social Credit League, the National Action Committee on the Status of Women, and the Parti Québécois have evolved. Canadian social movements vary from being general in nature to being very specific, such as the reform movements which accept the basic structure of society but seek to modify part of it. But because they seek to overthrow the existing social and political order, revolutionary movements are often driven underground, while reform movements appear respectable within society and attempt to gain support by means of discussion and persuasion.

The Front de Libération de Québec (FLQ) was a typical revolutionary movement, trying to alter the social order by force. The Parti Québécois, however, provides a good example of a reform movement that began as an organized collectivity and grew into an institution. While the Parti Québécois addresses the genuine injustices that have been suffered by French Canadians, the FLQ went far beyond that and advocated militant socialism.

Revolutionary Ideologies

Algerian psychiatrist and theorist Frantz Fanon (1925–1961) advocated the creation of revolutionary movements to initiate radical political change in the developing nation-states. While in Algeria, Fanon became a supporter of the revolutionary movement that eventually led to the French withdrawal from the country. He became one of the most widely read anti-colonialists. Fanon's revolutionary ideology rejected the Marxist assertion that the proletariat is necessarily the revolutionary class and opted instead to identify the African peasantry as such. He emphasized the idea of revolutionary action, or **praxis**, such as acts of violence by black peasant "subjects" against white (and black middle-class) colonial "masters." Revolutionary action generates revolutionary consciousness. Fanon believed that the peasant masses would achieve national liberation once the first acts of violence materialized within the newly independent African republics. His advocacy of revolutionary praxis stimulated movements in Algeria, Kenya, Zaïre, and the Portuguese colonies of Angola and Mozambique.

Another revolutionary theorist, Herbert Marcuse, rejected the working class as a group that has revolutionary potential. For Marcuse the possibility for revolutionary change would likely be found in the substratum of a society's outcasts and outsiders, the exploited and the persecuted, the unemployed and the unemployable. Marcuse was essentially a Marxist influenced by Freudian psychology. He developed a notion of political and sexual liberation that he viewed as contrary to the prevailing trend towards repression and exploitation in advanced societies. Marcuse believed that there was a "logic to domination" – people become conditioned to oppression usually by the infusion of carefully planned but limited affluence. Regis Debray, the French philosopher who spent considerable time in Cuba after Fidel Castro came to power, saw revolution not only as containing elements of violence or military action, but also as a process by which the military within the revolution becomes the guerrilla *foco* (focal point) itself, generating theory and providing inspiration to the masses. The guerrilla force is the party in embryo but war is necessary to make the revolution. In fact, the conditions for a successful revolution can be engineered. Debray taught that the Cuban lesson of armed guerrilla warfare should be applied throughout the world of underdeveloped states to win revolutionary struggles. This is as Debray's book title clearly states, a *Revolution in the Revolution*.

These iconoclasts held that a political revolution, as opposed to any other basic transformation of society, aims to overthrow a government and destroy the power of the social groups that support it. The revolutionaries mobilize popular support through direct action, usually involving violence, and demand basic changes in the social order. Ideologically, this has translated into a number of fundamental precepts about revolutionary behaviour:

1) Organized armed forces are vulnerable to popular or trained guerrilla insurrections.
2) Violent action (praxis) can generate ideal conditions for revolution before

they may naturally evolve.

3) The rural setting is better than urban areas for the organization and initiation of violent revolutionary guerrilla warfare.

4) Guerrilla warfare is not decisive in itself. Revolutionary change requires the fundamental alteration of economic, social, and political institutions.

A political revolution should be distinguished from a political revolt or coup d'état, actions which merely replace one set of leaders with another or only change the form of government without affecting the social order.

Feminism: Ideology or Movement?

The political struggle for sexual equality is not new in North America. In 1848, some 300 women and men met at Seneca Falls, New York, to protest the oppression of women. This first manifestation of the "women's movement" had grown out of the demand for social reforms of the 1830s and 1840s, when women were denied the right to speak out publicly against slavery.[28]

By the mid-nineteenth century, the women's movement had faded from view, subsumed within the Victorian cultural ideal of feminine purity and dependency. The movement was revived during the reform-minded Progressive period in the early twentieth century. The Canadian women's movement was influenced by developments in Britain and the United States. The political needs of working women and children were advocated by the National Council of Women, founded in 1893 by Lady Aberdeen,

the British wife of Canada's governor general at that time, The Earl of Aberdeen. Other organizations, such as the Toronto Women's Literary Club and the Women's Christian Temperance Union, demanded the right to vote, a right that was gained in every province between 1916 and 1922 (except Québec, where women could not vote until 1940).[29] In North America and Europe, suffragettes devoted their energies to gaining the right to vote and to establishing greater access for women into the political system. Women won voting rights first in New Zealand in 1893; Australia, Sweden, Norway, and Finland soon followed. In Russia, women participated in socialist/terrorist movements before and after the revolution; a woman led the assassination of the Czar, and many women fought as soldiers for the Bolsheviks. Under totalitarian socialism women seemed to gain greater opportunities, particularly in occupations, than in other countries.

In democratic states, suffragettes made the erroneous assumption that the power of the franchise would bring about changes in the workplace, university, religion, and the family. In fact, gaining the vote made very little difference in the lives of women. The high unemployment levels of the Depression sustained the widely held belief that men should get the few jobs generated in the economy. Not until World War II was this trend reversed. World War II served as a benchmark for opening paid employment opportunities to women. During the war, government propaganda declared that it was women's duty to work in factories and offices to support the war effort. However, after the war, women were encouraged to leave the labour force to assume their traditional role of homemakers so that returning veterans would find employment. Many women liked working outside the home and wanted to continue after the war ended. But peace terminated employment opportunities for most women, closing child-care centres and discontinuing training programs. Throughout the 1950s, the women's movement entered a dormant period, lacking communication and organizational networks to facilitate the spread of its nascent ideology.

The 1960s saw most of the elements of a successful political movement come together: organization, leadership, an enlarging membership, and an ideology focusing a widespread sense of frustration. In Canada, women's organizations, such as the Canadian Federation of University Women, and the Fédération des Femmes de Québec, established a communications system among knowledgeable, politically active women. In the United States, the 1961 President's Commission on the Status of Women led to the establishment of the National Organization for Women (NOW), the chief organization in the older, reform-oriented wing of the American women's movement. In 1963, Betty Friedan's *The Feminine Mystique* linked the oppression of women to cultural variables and began to articulate the ideological basis of the contemporary women's movement in North America. Friedan's book encouraged millions of women to re-examine their social roles in economic and political terms.

By the 1970s, the women's movement had evolved through the norm-oriented "women's rights" form to a value-oriented "women's liberation" form. In Canada, the National Action Committee on the Status of Women, the umbrella organization for most

other contemporary feminist groups, was established in 1972. Feminists began to identify women's inferior position in society with male supremacy in the family and other social and political structures. During this decade, feminism began to win widespread public acceptance and gained new economic and legal advantages for women. Membership in the movement grew dramatically both in Canada and the United States, attracting predominantly white, middle-class and college-educated people who supported programs that would benefit working-class and minority-group women.

At the end of the decade, the women's movement took on the characteristics of a power-centred movement, with detectable conservative, moderate, and radical wings. It also developed an international character in that leaders and organizers in different countries became known to one another and communicated on a regular basis. Most of the countries of the world now have an identifiable women's movement, albeit with diverse ideological, political, and strategic goals.

Just as no single organization can claim to represent the whole movement, no unified political ideology is detectable either. *Liberal feminism*, sometimes called reform or bourgeois feminism because it accepts the structure of the present society, calls upon the political and legal system to re-examine the degree to which individuals enjoy equal opportunities from the perspective of the inherited qualities of sex and race. This current of feminism wants society to remove all the barriers that actively discriminate against women. *Radical feminism*, sometimes called cultural or separatist feminism, points to the biological and psychosocial differences between men and women. It advocates the development of a women-centred culture with alternative lifestyles, and antimilitaristic, non-hierarchical political and social structures based on co-operation. *Socialist feminism,* sometimes called Marxist feminism, identifies capitalism and its social and political super-structures as the systemic reasons for the oppression of women. This perspective posits that women are the proletarians in the gender division of labour and men are the bourgeoisie because they control the means of production. The initial advantage fell to men because of their greater physical strength and women's pregnancies, but the advantage has been maintained by institutionalized norms and values that keep women in an inferior position. The Marxist framework has generally formed the ideological basis of the contemporary feminist movement.

Feminism has focused on certain ideological factors present in most contemporary societies, regardless of their economic and political organizations. One is *patriarchy*.[30] In feminist writings, patriarchy refers to the dominance of social, economic, and political institutions by men. A close correspondence exists between patriarchy and capitalism, in which both the generation and distribution of wealth reflects a male lineage. Historically, the idea that political authority is a male preserve has been the justification for the exclusion of women from access to social power. Both in and out of the family, human societies have been characterized by patriarchal authority whereby males have come to control economic resources, to make consequential decisions, and to have the final say in all matters related to the social good. Patriarchal authority is culturally transmitted and ideologically approved male supremacy.

Culture is the focus of socially mediated information about the role of women in society and male views of femininity.[31] In many cultures, women are expected to be neat, pretty, sexually passive, emotional, understanding, cultured, child-oriented, slightly helpless, dependent and in need of male protection. Culture conditions gender identity by creating stereotypes about men and women as reflected in children's books, the adult print media, television, and the movies. These stereotypes are reinforced by toys, games, and sports that influence the learning of gender identity in school, the workplace, and at home. Culture subtly transmits the ideologies of oppression or liberation in matters of gender identity.

Another focus of feminism is *epistemology*, the theories and methods of perceiving, and thus acquiring, knowledge. Feminists recognize that all knowledge is socially constructed and our perceptions and interpretations of the world are coloured by the society in which we live, as well as by our position within that society. Many feminists believe the dominant ideology (including law, religion, political philosophy, and so on) is essentially sexist and serves the legitimized interests of the male ruling class. In their view, all knowledge is culturally conditioned. Feminists are concerned with the process by which knowledge arises in a particular culture, why it takes the form it does, and how it sustains the various stratifications within society. From the perspective of society, socialization is an important by-product of epistemology because through it, cultural perpetuation and continuity are achieved. In most contemporary societies, sex-role socialization assigns accessory roles to women, as wives, mothers, and employees. Socialization ensures that individuals will develop a social character and will comply with a consensus among the majority of society's members as to the "correct" ways of behaving, thinking, interacting, and responding.

Feminist analysis also takes critical note of history by exposing the actual and interpretative discriminations against women that have prevailed in previous generations. Feminists note as well the male influence in historical interpretation, particularly in social and economic histories, which has tended to reinforce the ideology of subservience characteristic of the role of women in the past. Women have been granted invisible status within the profusion of historical analysis. Having only

recently been given the rights of citizens, women have suffered society's refusal, throughout history, to include them in the public sphere. Feminists call for a reconstruction of historical interpretation to trace the moral and political beliefs about women to deeper metaphysical or even biological sources.

The social and political movement of feminism and the ideologies attached to it have matured rapidly, producing a body of knowledge of significant size. The impact of feminist political thought has enriched the intellectual history of the twentieth century. What remains to be seen is the extent to which the analytical frameworks of feminism can translate into the exercise of political power.

References

1. F. L. Baumer, *Main Currents of Western Thought,* 4th ed. (New Haven, CT: Yale University Press, 1978), 373-376.

2. Karl Deutsch, *Politics and Government: How People Decide their Fate* (Boston: Houghton Mifflin Company, 1980), 9.

3. Robert Dahl, *A Preface to Democratic Theory* (Chicago: University of Chicago Press, 1956), 132.

4. Reo M. Christenson et al., *Ideologies and Modern Politics* (New York: Dodd, Mead & Company, 1971), 5.

5. Robert E. Lane, *Political Ideologies* (New York: Free Press of Glencoe, 1962), 14-15.

6. Andrew Hacker, *Political Theory:Philosophy, Ideology, Science* (New York: Macmillan, 1961), 5.

7. Carl Friedrich, *Man and His Government:An Ethical Theory of Politics* (New York: McGraw-Hill, 1963), 90.

8. John Plamenatz, *Ideology* (New York: Praeger, 1970), 13-15.

9. Edmund Morgan, *Inventing the People: The Rise of Popular Sovereignty in England and America* (New York: W.W. Norton, 1988), 12-19.

10. Karl Mannheim, *Ideology and Utopia,* trans., L. Wirth and E. Shils (New York: Harcourt, Brace Jovanovich, 1936), 36

11. Maurice Duverger: *Political Parties* (New York: John Wiley & Sons, Inc., 1954), 425.

12. See Thucydides. *The History of the Peloponnesian War,* Ed., Sir Richard Livingston (New York: Oxford University Press, 1951), 111-113.

13. *Aristotle in Twenty-Three Volumes, XXI Politics,* trans., H. Rackham, (London: Heinemann, 1977) Book III, 331.

14. Leonard T. Hobhouse, *Liberalism* (New York: Oxford University Press, 1911).

15. John Dewey, "The Future of Liberalism," in *The Journal of Philosophy* (April 25, 1935), 225-230.

16. Rod Preece, "The Political Economy of Edmund Burke," in *Modern Age* 24 (1980), 266-273.

17. F.J.C. Hearnshaw, *Conservatism in England* (London: Macmillan and Co. Ltd., 1933), 22-23; for contrast, see David Green, *The New Conservativism* (New York: St. Martin's Press, 1987).

18. Albert Fried and Ronald Sanders, eds., *Socialist Thought: A Documentary History* (Garden City, N.Y.: Anchor Doubleday, 1964).

19. Alan Gilbert, *Marx's Politics: Communists and Citizens* (Boulder, CO: Lynne Rienner Publishers, 1988).

20. Karl Marx and Friedrich Engels, *The German Ideology* (Moscow: Foreign Languages Publishing House, 1947), see "The Material Basis of Ideology," 247-255; Robert C. Tucker, ed., *The Marx-Engels Reader* (New York: W.W. Norton & Company, 1978), 3-12.

21. Karl Marx, *Selected Works* (New York: International Publishers, no date), 1:473.

22. Anthony Smith, *Theories of Nationalism* (New York: Harper & Row, 1971), 21; Ernest Gellner, *Nations and Nationalism* (London: Cornell University Press, 1983), 1-14.

23. For a short history of racism in Canada, see D.G. Hill and M.Schiff, *Human Rights in Canada: A Focus on Racism,* 2nd ed., (Ottawa: Canadian Labour Congress and Human Rights Research and Education Centre, University of Ottawa, 1986); and B. Singh and Peter Li, *Racial Oppression in Canada* (Toronto: Garamond Press, 1988).

24. Frank Harrison, *The Modern State: An Anarchist Analysis* (Montreal: Black Rose Books, 1983); David Osterfeld, *Freedom, Society, and the State: An Investigation into the Possibility of Society without Government* (Lanham, MD: University Press of America, 1983).

25. Stephen Chilton, *Defining Political Development* (Boulder, CO: Lynne Rienner Publishers, 1987), 1-135; Magnus Blomstrom and Bjorn Hettne, *Development Theory in Transition* (London: Zed Books Limited, 1984), 8-26.

26. Jack Gladstone, "The Comparative and Historical Study of Revolutions," in *Annual Review of Sociology, 1982,* 200; Crane Brinton, *The Anatomy of Revolution* (Englewood Cliffs, N.J.: Prentice-Hall, 1952); and A.S.

Cohan, *Theories of Revolution* (London: Thomas Nelson and Sons, 1975), 162-175.

27. Ralph Turner and Lewis Killian, *Collective Behavior* (Englewood Cliffs, N.J.: Prentice-Hall, 1972), Chapters 16-19.

28. Jo Freeman, "The Origins of the Women's Liberation Movement," in *American Journal of Sociology* 78, no.4 (1973), 792-811; William Chafe, *Women and Equality* (New York: Oxford University Press, 1977), 117-122.

29. Nancy Anderson, Linda Briskin, and Margaret McPhail, *Feminist Organizing for Change: The Contemporary Women's Movement in Canada* (Toronto: Oxford University Press, 1988); Angela Miles, *Feminist Radicalism in the 1980s* (Montreal: Culture Texts, 1985), 1-39.

30. Bonnie Fox, "Conceptualizing 'Patriarchy.'" *Canadian Review of Sociology and Anthropology* 25 (May 2): 163-182; and Monica Boyd, *Canadian Attitudes Towards Women: Thirty Years of Change* (Ottawa: Supply and Services Canada for Labour Canada, 1984).

31. Arlene Tigar McLaren, ed., *Gender and Society* (Toronto: Copp Clark Pitman, 1989), 337-346.

Suggested Readings

Sylvia Bashevkin, *True Patriot Love: The Politics of Canadian Nationalism* (Toronto: Oxford University Press, 1991).

John Dunn, *Democracy: The Unfinished Journey, 508 BC to AD 1993* (London: Oxford University Press, 1992).

William Ebenstein and Alan Ebenstein, *Introduction to Political Thinkers* (Fort Worth, TX: Holt, Rinehart and Winston, Inc., 1992).

Will Kymlicka, *Liberalism, Community, and Culture* (London: Oxford University Press, 1991).

Roy Macridis, *Contemporary Political Ideologies* (New York: HarperCollins Publishers, 1992).

Ruth Roach, Paula Bourne, Marjorie Cohen, and Philinda Masters, *Canadian Women's Issues* (Toronto: James Lorimer & Company Ltd., Publishers, 1993).

Martin Robin, *Shades of Right* (Toronto: University of Toronto Press, 1992).

Lyman Tower Sargent, *Contemporary Political Ideologies: A Reader* (Pacific Grove, CA: Brooks/Cole Publishing, 1990).

Max Skidmore, *Ideologies: Politics in Action* (Fort Worth, TX: Harcourt Brace Jovanovich College Publishers, 1993).

Alan Whitehorn, *Canadian Socialism: Essays on the CCF-NDP* (Don Mills, ON: Oxford University Press, 1992).

Glossary

aristocracy: From the Greek for "rule by the best," by which virtue is the title to power, but which is more commonly described as rule by the privileged, who may enjoy a hereditary status or whose power flows to them by virtue of their class position in society.

Bolshevik: A Russian term that means "majority," and which was used by the supporters of Lenin who organized in 1912 and successfully led the Russian Revolution of 1917.

bourgeoisie: From the French for town dweller, the term was used by Marx to identify the class of property and production ownership that flourished under capitalism.

consensus: A widespread agreement on a particular issue, policy, or course of action by those participating in the making of the decision without a formal verification of the statistical proportion of support.

democratic centralism: A term introduced to the Communist Party of the Soviet Union that permits free discussion on issues within the party, but once a decision is reached, the iron discipline of the party prevails and all must support the decision taken.

descriptive: An analytical skill that involves applying appropriate conceptual labels to people, things, events, and ideas that are observed.

dialectic: A concept borrowed from Hegel by Marx which asserts that all societies contain within them the seeds to their own destruction – the struggle of opposites generates social transformation.

elite: Any select group of individuals enjoying privileged status in a society and often united by certain common ties, interests, or objectives.

ethics: Encompassing rules and codes of morality that describe human goodness and rightness and embody absolute rules upon which humans should pattern their conduct.

human nature: Those psychological and biological qualities universally characteristic of the human species.

human reason: The distinctive human faculty that permits a process of thinking, leading to logical conclusions.

ideologue: Someone who is committed to a particular ideology, who advocates its provisions and defends it against the logic of other ideologies.

ideology: The way of life of a people or group, as reflected in their most fundamental beliefs, their social goals and moral values, and in the way they conduct their politics, government, and economy.

imperialistic: An economic, political, or military strategy by which a state and its people are subordinated to the will of a foreign state.

industrial revolution: A period of productive change beginning in the eighteenth century that employed machinery and steam power to manufacture goods and services in society.

irredentism: Taken from the Italian expression *Italia irredenta,* meaning Italy unredeemed, this refers to the desire of the people of a state to annex those contiguous territories of another country that are inhabited by the same linguistic or cultural minorities.

oligarchy: Taken from the Greek, meaning rule by the few, where power is concentrated and not shared.

polity: A term referring to the political organization of a society, its citizenry, and the institutions and procedures through which the state governs.

pragmatism: A philosophical perspective traceable to the American writers William James and John Dewey who stressed that concepts and actions should be evaluated in terms of their practical consequences and not necessarily according to theoretical rationale.

praxis: A term derived from the Greek for "action" which later came to refer to what people do as against what they think, an active means of shaping historical conditions to one's advantage.

proletariat: As used by Marx, the term referred to a class of labourers characterized as property-less, rootless, poor, and mobile, who have nothing to sell but their labour power.

propagandize: To convey ideas rapidly to many people, usually a large targeted audience by means of symbols, media campaigns, music, and other instruments to arouse strong and emotional reactions for or against some policy, person, idea, or government.

romanticism: The cultural movement that began in eighteenth-century Europe, marking the transformation of intellectual thought from the rational to the intuitive as a means of perceiving and understanding the world. Romantics were fascinated by dreams and hallucinations that suggested a world beyond the empirical.

social contract: An original agreement among individuals to create an organized political society.

sovereignty: The power possessed by the state to make decisions of last resort, decisions that cannot be overridden or reversed by any other human decision-maker or agency.

stratification: A system of social inequality based on hierarchical orderings of groups according to their members' share in socially valued rewards.

superstructure: The legal, political, and social institutions which reflect, express, and consolidate the relations of economic power that flow from the mode of production practised by a society.

utopian: A term coined by Sir Thomas More, derived from the Greek *outopos*, "no place." More emphasized the word *eu*, meaning best, thus suggesting that Utopia was a nonexistent best place in reference to an ideal and harmonious society.

utopian socialists: Those who believed that the quality of humanitarianism would produce ideal socialist experiments, the success of which would quickly be perceived by the rest of society, and the models adopted.

welfare state: Refers to nation-states with elaborate government insurance, public assistance, education and medical programs that are designed to maximize the economic and social welfare of their citizens.

xenophobia: An extreme fear of foreigners, sometimes accompanied by a pathological hatred of strangers, which can lead to racism and ethnic cleansing.

FOUR

Nations, States, Rank, and Power

G-7 leaders

Chapter Objectives

After reading this chapter, you will be able to:

- differentiate the concepts of nation, state, political system, and government

- plot the growth of nation-states in the international community

- define the concept of power and relate it to the behaviour of governments in the international system

- analyze the components of power and apply them to individual political systems

- distinguish the concepts of unitary and federal state

- evaluate the effect of adopting a unitary or federal structure of government on performance and efficiency

- identify the various economic systems

- differentiate the terms "first world," "second world," "third world," etc.

- illustrate what makes a state powerful or not

What is a Nation-State?

Some of the most widespread confusions in our political vocabularies concern the meaning of the terms *nation, state,* and *country.* People may sometimes use these terms interchangeably in casual conversation but, for professional purposes, they should be distinguished. They have somewhat different meanings and require definition for use in political science and international law.

The term "state" refers to a legal/political and administrative entity composed of a governing central authority that makes and enforces laws and is recognized as the primary subject of the international legal system. The Montevideo Convention on the Rights and Duties of States (1933) laid down four criteria that states must possess to qualify as **persons** under international law. The convention declared that a state must have: 1) a permanent population; 2) a defined territory; 3) a government; and 4) a capacity to enter into relations with other states. In the contemporary international system there are over 190 such legal/political entities functioning as states and claiming international legal status. This status entitles them to sign treaties, form alliances, join international organizations, and exchange ambassadors.

One state may be the host of many nations. In contrast to a state, a nation is a **socio-cultural** entity, made up of a group of people who identify with one another ethnically, culturally, and linguistically. A nation may not have a government or a geographically delim-

■ ■ **persons:** legal entities that are subject to international law and have the capacity to enter into binding relations with all concomitant rights and duties. ■ ■

ited territory of its own. But many nations may exist within the political and administrative jurisdiction of a state. Canada is a multi-national entity, with over 58 first nations and millions of Québécois who identify with one another as nationals.

Many scholars refer to the relationship between the state and the nationalities it serves as a *nation-state.*[1] The modern nation-state weaves nationalities together according to a deliberate political design: it determines official languages, creates a uniform system of law, manages a single currency, controls the education system, builds a national bureaucracy to defend and socialize different people and classes, and fosters loyalty to an abstract entity, such as "Canada," "Brazil," or the "United States." Scholars may use the term "state" in referring to the actions of a government or its bureaucracy, and, likewise, international organizations usually call their members "states." In international law, as well, the term frequently used is "states." However, many scholars use the term "nation-state" when they refer to a society in its entirety, as a political, social, and governmental entity.

Today the nation-state is the most effective instrument of social and political integration, as well as the primary vehicle for national modernization. But sometimes nation-states unravel into a multiplicity of smaller governing entities; the most dramatic recent example of this is the Soviet Union, which in 1991 collapsed into 15 independent

Table 4.1:

The new independent nation-states of the former Soviet Union

Armenia

Capital: Levon Ter Petrossian
Population: 3,400,000
Ethnic composition:
Armenians, 90%;
Azerbaijanis, 6%;
Russians, 2.3%;
Kurds,1.7%.

Azerbaijan

Capital: Baku
Population: 7,000,000
Ethnic composition:
Azerbaijanis, 78%;
Russians, 8%;
Armenians, 8%;
Others, 6%.

Belarus

Capital: Minsk
Population: 10,200,000
Ethnic composition:
Byelorussians, 79%;
Russians, 12%;
Others, 9%.

Estonia

Capital: Tallin
Population: 1,500,000
Ethnic composition:
Estonians, 62%;
Russians, 30%;
Others, 8%.

Georgia

Capital: Tiblisi
Population: 5,400,000
Ethnic composition:
Georgians, 69%;
Armenians, 9%;
Russians, 7%;
Others, 15%.

Kazakhstan

Capital: Alma-Ata
Population: 16,000,000
Ethnic composition:
Kazakhs, 36%;
Russians, 41%;
Others, 23%.

Kirghiz

Capital: Frunze
Population: 4,100,000
Ethnic composition:
Kirghiz, 54%;
Russians, 22%;
Uzbeks, 13%;
Others, 11%.

Latvia

Capital: Riga
Population: 2,600,000
Ethnic composition:
Latvians, 52%;
Russians, 34%;
Others, 14%.

Lithuania

Capital: Vilnius
Population: 3,700,000
Ethnic composition:
Lithuanians, 80%;
Russians, 9%;
Others, 11 %.

Moldavia

Capital: Kisiniov
Population: 4,500,000
Ethnic composition:
Moldavians, 64%;
Ukrainians, 14%;
Russians, 13%;
Others, 9%.

Russia

Capital: Moscow
Population: 147,000,000
Ethnic composition:
Russians, 83%;
Tartars, 5%;
Ukrainians, 5%;
Others, 7%.

Tajikistan

Capital: Dushanbe
Population: 5,000,000
Ethnic composition:
Tajiks, 59%;
Uzbeks, 23%;
Russians, 10%;
Tartars, 6%; Others, 6%.

Turkmenia

Capital: Ashjabad
Population: 3,400,000
Ethnic composition:
Turkmens, 68%;
Russians, 13%; Others, 19%.

Ukraine

Capital: Kiev
Population: 52,000,000
Ethnic composition:
Ukrainians, 74%;
Russians, 20%;
Others, 6%.

Uzbekhistan

Capital: Tashkent
Population: 19,000,000
Ethnic composition:
Uzbeks, 69%;
Russians, 11%;
Kirghiz, 5%;
Tajiks, 4%;
Turkmens, 3%; Others, 8%.

Source: *Times Atlas of the World*, 9th ed., (London: Times Books, 1992).

nation-states (table 4.1). Only 195 such nation-states make up the present international system, yet together they host over 1400 nationalities existing in the world.[2]

The term "country" refers to the all-inclusive characteristics of a geographical entity – its physical, material, and socio-economic components. Use of this term is widespread in political-science literature but can sometimes result in confusion if it is not properly clarified. To refer to the country of Ireland requires specific reference either to the six counties of Northern Ireland under Great Britain or to the 26 counties in the south that form the Republic of Ireland. The same problem exists with other divided countries, such as Korea.

The Growth in the Number of Nation-States

By 2000, the modern nation-state system will have existed for only 352 years – less than ten percent of the 5500 years of recorded human history. In 1648, the Peace of Westphalia terminated the Thirty Years' War in Europe, bringing an end to the view of the world as an organized system (the Holy Roman Empire) based on a Christian commonwealth governed by the Pope and the Holy Roman Emperor. We know that states such as England and France predate the Peace of Westphalia as sovereign political units. But at the time of the Peace of Westphalia, the international system was transformed formally and legally into a society of legally equal states, each exercising complete territorial jurisdiction over well-defined boundaries.

With the disintegration of the Holy Roman Empire into autonomous political organizations, the modern nation-state came to dominate the international system as a legal/political entity subject to no higher secular authority. The doctrine of **sovereignty** thus became the first general principle of international law. It asserts that the nation-state is the supreme decision-making power within a geographically delineated frontier and is subject to external authority only by its consent.

A question of sovereignty arose in 1985 when Canada's historic claim to most of the Northwest Passage as territorial waters was challenged by the United States. The U.S. Coast Guard icebreaker *Polar Sea* passed through the arctic waterway without Canada's consent, and proceeded as if the passage was an international strait open to all states. Canada issued a strongly worded statement on the controversial voyage, stating that future use of the Arctic "shall only be on the basis of full respect for Canada's sovereignty." In January of 1988, Canada and the United States signed an agreement on Arctic cooperation, under which U.S. icebreakers are required to receive Canadian permission before entering waters claimed by Canada. However, the agreement avoided the issue of U.S. military vessels entering the waters of the Arctic and the Northwest Passage as if they were international ocean highways open to entry by any nation-state without Canadian consent.

Out of the doctrine of sovereignty emerged the principle of the **legal equality of states**. This establishes that sovereign nation-states enjoy the same rights and duties under international law, regardless of size, population, wealth, or military power. This principle is affirmed in the legal equation of one state, one vote, practised and enjoyed by all nation-states in the international councils of the world.

The proliferation of nation-states was a gradual occurrence from the Peace of Westphalia until the second half of the twentieth century, when the **decolonization** of European empires escalated following World War II. Since 1945, the number of nation-states has tripled from roughly 65 to 195, with most of these newcomers appearing in Africa, but many appearing in Eastern Europe since the disintegration of the Soviet Union (figure 4.1). The processes of decolonization and **devolution** in the post-war period resulted in the independence of some 100 nation-states and over one billion people – all in the span of a single generation. Today, less than one percent of the world's population and territory remain without self-government. The emergence of new nation-states is likely to continue for some time, but at a much slower pace. One very recent addition to the international community is Vanuatu, formerly known as the New Hebrides. From 1906 to 1984, this collection of 80 scattered islands, inhabited by 121,000 people, was jointly ruled by Britain and France in what is called a *condominium*. In the last century, the people of Vanuatu were regarded as bloodthirsty cannibals incapable of self-government in their Pacific environment. Today, Vanuatu is one of the newest of the world's independent nation-states, trying to find its own identity as a now-independent territory after a confusing but colourful history. Another of the world's newest nation-states is Eritrea, which was once part of Ethiopia.

Power and the Nation-State

The preceding chapter considered the interpersonal nature of power as a phenomenon that permeates all human relationships and

that is widely upheld as a value in our personal lives. The nation-state provides us with the most visible manifestations of this phenomenon because it is an organization specifically designed to accumulate, institutionalize, and articulate power in a competitive international system. Indeed, the interactions of nation-states represent the most salient expressions of political power in the world community.

Most analysts of international relations see the power of a nation-state in terms of its capacity to influence other entities in its environment. K.J. Holsti defines power as "the general capacity of a state to control the behavior of other states."[3] Karl Deutsch sees it as "the ability to prevail in conflict and overcome obstacles."[4] For Robert Dahl, "Power is the ability to shift the probability of outcomes."[5] Dahl also sees it as a psychological relationship between those who exercise it and those over whom it is exercised. Each of these definitions is an attempt to explain a highly complex set of power components that cluster together, building the overall capacity and potential of the nation-state. Ray S. Cline constructed a conceptual formula to illustrate the parameters of power at the disposal of a nation-state.[6] He states it as:

$$Pp = (C + E + M) \times (S \times W), \text{ where}$$

$Pp =$ perceived power

$C =$ critical mass: size, location, population, and natural resources

$E =$ economic capability

$M =$ military capability

$S =$ strategic purpose

$W =$ will to pursue national strategy

Perceived power expresses the psychological relationship between those who use

Figure 4.1:

Independent nation-states, 1648–1994

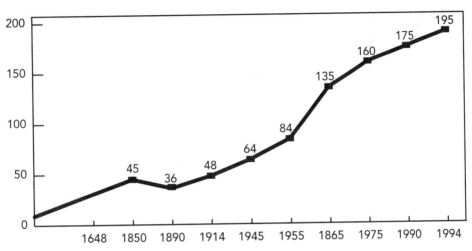

Sources: C.J.H. Hayes, *The Historical Evolution of Modern Nationalism* (New York: Macmillan, 1948); Michael Wallace and David Singer, "Inter-governmental Organization in the Global System, 1815-1964: A Quantitative Description," *International Organization* 24 (Spring, 1970):272; for the period 1965-1985, see John Paxton, ed., *The Statesman's Year Book* (London: Macmillan Press, 1994), various years.

power and those over whom power is exercised. It has both a domestic as well as an international dimension: the power of a nation-state is a product not only of its externally perceived power but also of its own self-perception. One of Prime Minister Trudeau's first foreign-policy statements in 1968 was to disclaim Canada's post-war international status as the smallest of the large powers by repositioning Canada's contemporary role as "the largest of the small powers."[7] Trudeau's perception of Canada's power was a reflection of Canada's internal aspirations to relate its international role to domestic capabilities: "We shall do more good by doing well what we know to be within our resources to do than to pretend either to ourselves or to others that we can do things clearly beyond our national capacity."[8]

The perception of the power of a nation-state can flow from the characteristics of its critical mass, its economic capability, and its military capacity. But these elements alone will not determine the power potential of a nation-state. They must be brought together by the deliberate and planned strategy of decision-makers who formulate foreign policies to use power in their national interest. Thus, strategic purpose coupled with the will to pursue a strategy of power are important considerations in realistically appraising the strength of a nation-state. Let us examine each of these various components of power.

Critical Mass

The tangible elements of national power – **tangible power** – are frequently identified as size, location, population, and natural resources.[9] These elements affect the political conduct of people and are used in association with the study of national strength. Together they constitute the power inventory of a nation-state. They are measurable features that condition rank and status in the international system. We know that physical and human resources may serve to enhance the power status of a nation-state, but they may also function to create major obstacles to development. For example, Japan has earned its reputation as an economic **superpower** in the 1990s, but it is severely circumscribed by population pressure and the lack of raw materials. And Canada, the second-largest country in the world, with a population approaching 30 million, a modern economy, and vast natural resources, can only attain middle ranking in the international community. Both nation-states, for opposite reasons, must overcome obstacles created by their size and the distribution of their populations. In the final analysis, individual elements of national power must be seen in conjunction with other variables, usually of a political, social, and strategic nature.

Size

Political geography informs us that the size of a nation-state – the amount of territorial space it incorporates – presents advantages and disadvantages to a government's ability to enhance its power profile. After all, the total world land mass is limited, and larger states do have greater access than do smaller states to the bulk of resources from which power can be derived. The United States (the fourth-largest) is a superpower blessed with a wide range of raw materials. The abundance of natural resources is a prime requisite for power, perhaps even more important than the capacity to exploit those resources. Countries such as Australia, Brazil, Canada, China, and Mexico are nation-states with great potential for increasing their influence in world affairs based on their size and share of natural resources. While it is true that size alone does not determine national power, it is also true that the U.S., the world's most powerful nation-state, happens to be very large.

With vastness in size come problems of social cohesion, economic disparity, political organization, and national control. Canada is a good example. The physical characteristics of Canada create enormous challenges for achieving political and economic integration. Canada's area is nearly ten million square kilometres. The country spans seven time zones and possesses large natural internal barriers: the Appalachians, the Canadian Shield, the Rocky Mountains, the Great Lakes, and the Arctic desert. These features tend to divide rather than unify its population. In addition, Canada is a composite of six geographic regions: the Atlantic provinces, Québec, Ontario, the Prairies, British Columbia, and the North, each with distinctive physical characteristics that tend to foster both economic and political regionalism. Politically, Canada is at war with its geography. Of the world's federal states, Canada has the most decentralized federal system, with each provincial government possessing significantly wider political powers and jurisdictions in economic, social, and cultural matters than do those in other federations. At the extreme, some provinces have even developed a special role in international affairs, as in the case of Québec. For Canada, sheer size has made its functioning as an independent nation-state a political miracle.

Table 4.2 lists the relative size of the ten largest nation-states in the world. These ten countries control more than half the land surface of the globe. We can see from the table that size is not the most significant criterion upon which to judge the power profile of a nation-state: six of the ten biggest countries of the world are Third and Fourth World nation-states. And in the case of Canada, size creates staggering political and economic problems in terms of national unity and development. Very large states often experience internal divisions due to natural barriers caused by vastness – Australia's central desert and Canada's Rocky Mountain belt exemplify this. Both Canada and Brazil have the problem of diminishing the "empty" aspect of their sparsely populated regions by encouraging population resettlement in these areas. Brazil relocated its capital from Rio de Janeiro to Brasilia, in the heart of the jungle, just for the purpose of encouraging the westward migration of people. The African state of Sudan is vast, extending from Arab Africa into black Africa. The Arab population in the north, which concentrates in the capital of Khartoum, is racially and culturally distinct from the black Africans in the south. Very few nation-states have utilized and exploited the vast spatial characteristics of their terrains in an efficient way. The United States and China have succeeded in populating a large land area

westward across rivers and mountains and then, through their powerful central governments, inculcating a strong sense of national unity among their people.

Location

The location of a nation-state influences its power potentiality in strategic as well as geographic ways. Location determines a state's neighbours, its access to the oceans, its proximity to the world's major trade routes, and its strategic importance in matters of collective security. Therefore, location is politically important to a nation-state for purposes of trade, transportation, defence, and attack. While it is true that the location of a state is permanently fixed geographically, the political ramifications of the space it occupies constantly change as other nation-states evaluate its significance in terms of their national interest. For example, the strategic importance of El Salvador, Guatemala, Honduras, and Panama to the United States have changed over the years because of the presence of the socialist regimes that nurtured relations with other totalitarian states such as China, Cuba, and the former Soviet Union. Since the Eisenhower administration in the late 1950s, the United States assumed a *domino theory* of foreign policy in the Central American region. Such a theory holds that if Marxist states appear in close proximity to one another, other states in the same region are vulnerable to the spread of totalitarian socialism.

Access to oceans and important waterways is another critical factor in determining a state's power. Most of the nation-states of the world are adjacent to seas and oceans. From an economic viewpoint, oceans are highways of commerce linking the world's markets.

Table 4.2:

The world's ten largest countries by area

Country	Area (in sq. km.)	Percentage of World Total
Russia	17,075,000	17.9
Canada	9,976,139	7.3
China	9,596,961	7.1
United States	9,363,123	6.9
Brazil	8,511,965	6.3
Australia	7,686,848	5.7
India	3,287,590	2.4
Argentina	2,766,889	2.0
Sudan	2,505,813	1.8
Algeria	2,381,741	1.8
Subtotal	76,162,069	61.6
World Total	135,830,000	100.0

Source: *The International World Atlas* (Maplewood, NJ: Hammond, Inc. 1993).

They are extensions of the land-based commercial power of a nation-state. Strategically, access to oceans provides states with the military advantages of sea power. Today, sea power is a crucial factor in both conventional and nuclear-war deterrence. The world's foremost sea powers possess the naval capability of massive retaliation from any point on the globe in response to a first strike from an enemy state. During the Persian Gulf war, the United States, Canada, and other coalition forces mounted a massive naval operation off the coasts of Kuwait to launch air strikes at Iraq and to supply ground forces on the mainland.

Not having access to oceans and waterways also affects the power of a state. Because

they do not have easy access to the international marketplace, the 34 independent nation-states of the world that are landlocked have special economic problems (table 4.3). The export/import relations of such economies are dependent upon the national policies of coastal states and are always subject to higher transportation and handling costs. At best, landlocked states must negotiate with coastal states to gain permission to carry on overseas trade without interference or harassment.

In 1921 in Barcelona, a Freedom of Transit Conference was held that produced a convention to encourage signatories to assist landlocked states in the movement of goods to the nearest seaport without levying discriminatory taxes or freight charges against them. In 1965, the United Nations drafted a convention outlining concessions to landlocked states to provide them with customs exemptions, free storage, and free ports of entry. Landlocked states must nevertheless enter into bilateral treaties with coastal states and usually bargain at a disadvantage.

Location has had important political implications for Canada's international role. Canada's geographical position is unusual in that it shares a vast border with only one country and that country happens to be a superpower. The presence of only one powerful land neighbour has been the single most significant factor in the history of Canada's external relations. While historically Canada has used its access to the oceans to escape the influence of the United States on its culture and economy, the North American Free Trade Agreement (NAFTA) has entrenched Canada's international interests in the western hemisphere. Geographically, Canada's location is unique; it is the only mainland country directly connected to three oceans.

The total length of Canada's coastline, bordering on the Atlantic, Pacific, and Arctic oceans, is over 36,000 kilometres, more than twice the circumference of the earth. These three ocean avenues have allowed Canada to diversify its international ties, as well as to enrich its natural resource base. The Atlantic Ocean has maintained Canada's links with Europe, especially with Great Britain and France. The Pacific Ocean has opened ties with Asia and the economies of the **Pacific Rim**. By the early 1970s, Japan had surpassed Great Britain as Canada's second-most-important trading partner after the United States. The Arctic Ocean is vital to Canada both for its vast untapped natural resources as well as for its strategic value in protecting the western hemisphere.

Population

The nation-states of the world vary as much in population as they do in territorial size. Population ranges from the Vatican with a population of about 1000 to China with a population of over 1.3 billion people, or about one-fifth of all humanity. When population is discussed as a global concern, the tendency for analysts is to focus on those nation-states with the largest populations (table 4.4). But it is interesting to note that over 140 of the states of the world contain populations of less than 20 million people. From the perspective of a majority of these states, not enough population is a more central concern in terms of economic growth and development than is overpopulation.

Difficult problems are often faced by large countries with small populations. For example, Canada's total population of about 30 million inhabitants makes up only one-half of one percent of the global population, yet this population has the task of developing nearly ten percent of the world's habitable area. Canadian governments construct highways, railways, communications networks, and participate in a military system that serves the western hemisphere and Europe. Canada's businesses and governments must manage vast natural resources with a population about the same size as that of the state of California. In the development of their capital projects, Canadians must depend heavily on foreign investment, over 80 percent of which flows from the United States. Other nation-states, such as Australia, South Africa,

Table 4.3:
Landlocked states

AFRICA	AMERICA	ASIA	EUROPE
Botswana	Bolivia	Afghanistan	Andorra
Burundi	Paraguay	Bhutan	Austria
Chad		Mongolia	Belarus
Central African Republic		Nepal	Czech Republic
Lesotho			Hungary
Malawi			Kyrgyzstan
Mali			Liechtenstein
Niger			Luxembourg
Rwanda			Macedonia
Swaziland			Slovak Republic
Uganda			Tajikistan
Upper Volta			Switzerland
Zambia			San Marino
Zimbabwe			Vatican City

Source: *The Statesman's Year Book*, 1992-93 (New York: Macmillan Co., 1993)

Argentina, and Peru have similar problems. Even Russia, which has the sixth-largest population in the world, has most of its population clustered west of the Ural Mountains, leaving large expanses of territory unoccupied and undeveloped.

Like the factors of territorial size and location, the size of a nation-state's population is not necessarily an indication of its power. However, the effectiveness of the population, whatever its size, in contributing to the agricultural, industrial, and military capacities of the state in a highly competitive world *is* important. In addition, the size of a population must be analyzed not only with respect to the space it occupies but also with respect to the resources at its disposal and the political and economic organization of the state.

The population of a nation-state is truly a national resource and includes all people capable of contributing usefully to the development of the economy. It is made up of the male and female work force, the young and the elderly, the military, and the bureaucratic

Table 4.4:
Leading nation-states in population, 1993

Nation-State	Population	Percentage of World Total
China	1,308,175,291	19.2
India	861,320,030	13.1
United States	253,880,800	6.5
Indonesia	173,700,010	5.9
Brazil	155,206,400	5.5
Russia	147,000,000	5.4
Japan	125,790,530	5.2
Bangladesh	111,400,000	5.0
Pakistan	110,800,000	5.0
Nigeria	105,355,000	4.7

Source: *World Development Report 1993* (New York: Oxford University Press, 1993).

machinery of the state. The growth, distribution, density, and mobility of a population are factors that must be constantly evaluated to get a clear picture of the potential in a nation-state. For Canada, a population increase can contribute to the productive strength of the country only because the problems of food supply, welfare, education, and other factors are adequately met by the economic system. But for Bangladesh, Ethiopia, and India, population increases are too burdensome for the capabilities of the economy, nullifying the benefits of these human resources. Bangladesh, for example, ranks first in density of population and is 20 times as crowded as the world in general. For some nation-states, a growing population may be a source of power and productivity, but for many their populations are unwanted consumers of limited resources of food, clothing, housing, and education.

Natural Resources

The natural resources of a nation-state generally refer to the resources found on, above, and under the surface of the earth. A country's soil, animal life, forests, vegetation, water, sunshine, climate, and minerals are its natural resources. For example, Canada is the most powerful country in the world in its capacity to generate hydro-electricity. By 1990, Canada's waterways were producing over 75 percent of its electrical power. The lack or abundance of resources like these can be crucial

Table 4.5:
The world's leading producers of the 1990s, select agricultural and mineral products

Country	Leading Agricultural Products	Leading Mineral Products
Australia	barley	bauxite
Brazil	sugar, coffee, cocoa	titanium
Canada	canola	asbestos, nickel, zinc
China	rice, tobacco, cereals	tungsten
India	tea	lignite
Malaysia	palm oil	tin
Mexico	sorghum	silver
Russia	cotton, wheat, coal, oil	platinum, iron ore
South Africa	groundnuts, sunflower seeds	chromium
Ukraine	buckwheat	salt
United States	maize, soya	lead, molybdenum, copper, phosphates natural gas
Zaïre	cassava	cobalt, industrial diamonds

Source: 1993 *CRB Commodity Year Book* (New York: Commodity Research Bureau, 1993); and John Allen, *Student Atlas of World Politics* (Guilford, CT: The Dushkin Publishing Group, Inc., 1994), various charts.

in developing the power potential of a nation-state. For some countries, such as Australia, Canada, the United States, Russia, and Ukraine, nature has provided an extravagant resource endowment (table 4.5), but for others, such as Chad, Ethiopia, and Mali, nature's provisions have not been so generous. For these states, the hope of achieving any measure of self-sufficiency and industrial diversification from an accessible resource base is scant.

Sometimes, however, the sheer will and capacity of a population to industrialize from imported raw materials can propel it to economic superiority: Japan has few locally accessible natural resources. But Japan is an exception. For most of the economies of the world, national power is directly related to the possession of and accessibility to raw

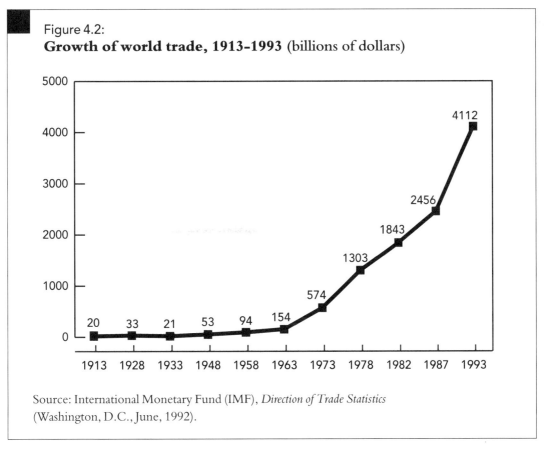

Figure 4.2:
Growth of world trade, 1913–1993 (billions of dollars)

Source: International Monetary Fund (IMF), *Direction of Trade Statistics*
(Washington, D.C., June, 1992).

materials and the capacity to use them to produce food. Without a solid agricultural base and access to raw materials, nation-states cannot develop into prosperous industrial trading economies.

No national economy is completely self-sufficient in respect to foodstuffs or natural resources. **Economic interdependence** is a basic law in the modern international system. The uneven distribution of arable land and raw materials is the primary motivation for national economies to engage in international trade. Never before in human history have nation-states relied so much on one another

to obtain the essentials of life. Since World War II, the growth of world trade in goods and services has greatly expanded: it is estimated that it now totals $4.112 trillion U.S. (4,112 billion) per year (figure 4.2). The material resources of a nation-state, derived from its agricultural and industrial output, help determine its power potential. States use this power to influence the behaviour of other states by either imposing their will on them or by resisting the influence they attempt to exert. Natural resources and the extent to which they are exploited determine the economic power of the state.

Economic Capability:
The Political Dimension

All independent states exercise effective organization and control over their territorial boundaries. The politico-territorial organization of a state is not just the organization of geographical space, but also the foundation of its economic capacity. The way a state divides or centralizes political power and the decision-making functions of government translates into economic advantage or disadvantage. Economic capacity is almost always a product of political organization.

The political system establishes the communications and transportation networks, the arrangements of the land-tenure system, and the application of an overriding structure to enhance human opportunity and exploit natural resources. For example, an efficient communications network is of vital importance for political and economic cohesiveness in a nation-state. In Canada, the federal government has invested heavily in developing a comprehensive network of communications for purposes of national integration. Canada's communications system is technically the most advanced in the world. With the launching of the ANIK satellite series in 1972, Canada became the first state to establish a national telecommunications system based on signals from space. The ANIK satellites presently in orbit can transmit information of the highest broadcast quality to the remotest parts of Canada. The application of this advanced technology in the field of communications is crucial for Canada's national defence, as well as for the maintenance of cultural identity.

The manner in which a nation-state has organized its government, its economy, and its system of defence is an important indication of the internal institutional power of the state and its perceived external power in the political world. The political organization of a nation-state, as distinct from its form of government, is either unitary or federal.

Unitary States

The **unitary state** is the most common type of political organization, accounting for 90 percent of all independent nation-states. A unitary state is one in which all sovereign power resides in the national government: all other units of government are merely its subdivisions.[10] Any delegation of power to regions, districts, or municipalities is largely at the discretion of the national government and may be legally reduced, increased, or removed even if only for reasons of administrative efficiency. In this type of political organization, the national government can impose its decisions on local governments, regardless of the unpopularity of these decisions. This high degree of political centralization is not always intended to foster economic efficiency: rather, it is frequently implemented to facilitate political and social control.

As a general rule, unitary states such as Japan and France enjoy a high level of internal homogeneity and cohesiveness. But some unitary states, such as Spain and South Africa, lack social homogeneity and are geographically large enough to warrant federal systems. In Spain, the existence of four spoken languages –

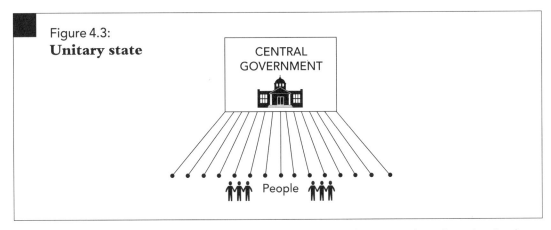

Figure 4.3:
Unitary state

CENTRAL GOVERNMENT

People

Spanish, Portuguese (in Galicia), Basque, and Catalan – serves to divide rather than unify the affairs of state. In 1910, the Union of South Africa joined four provinces – Cape Colony, Transvaal, Natal, and the Orange Free State, each with its own special social characteristics and distinctive physical geography – under a unitary system that continues to exist today. Unitarism has provided both Spain and South Africa with a political structure that maximizes the authoritative power of the central government.

The average unitary state is small and densely populated with one **core area**. There is a direct one-level relationship between the people and their national government (figure 4.3). People are not burdened with the complications and duplications of government services. One central agency designs school curricula, issues licenses and permits, raises taxes, and plans the economy. All governmental units are administrative subdivisions of the same government so that under normal conditions, unitarism has cost-efficient benefits.

■ ■ **core area:** A relatively small portion of a country in which the political power of the entire state is concentrated, often where a nation-state originated. ■ ■

Many former colonial territories have embraced the unitary form of political organization. All of the former French territories adopted the unitary system. Most British-influenced states in Africa – including Kenya, Sierra Leone, and Ghana – are unitary. All Arab states in the Middle East are unitary; the majority of emergent African states also chose this form of political organization. All Central American republics are unitary states, and in South America, Colombia, Ecuador, Peru, Chile, Bolivia, and Paraguay function under unitary systems.

China holds the distinction of being the largest unitary state in the world. The unitary organization of the Chinese government enables the totalitarian regime to maintain direct controls on all regions of the country. Among Southeast Asian states, all are unitary except Malaysia. Again, the European influence has made a strong contribution to the establishment of unitary systems in this part of the world. The unitary system is also popular because of the facility that this system gives to the consolidation

Table 4.6:

Federal states

Name	Date Formed	Number of Units	Area (million sq. km)	Pop. (1993)	Capital City	Type of Federation
Republic of Argentina	1816	24	2.8	33,577,000	Buenos Aries	Centralized
Commonwealth of Australia	1901	6	7.7	18,891,000	Canberra	Matured
Brazil	1889	22	8.5	144,600,000	Brasilia	Centralized
Canada	1867	10	9.9	29,747,000	Ottawa	Conciliatory
Germany	1955	11	2.25	81,345,000	Berlin	Matured
Union of India	1950	21	3.2	781,400,090	New Delhi	Conciliatory
Islamic Federal Republic of Comores	1961	3	0.18	503,000	Moroni	Conciliatory
Islamic Republic of Pakistan	1947	7	0.8 0	114,000,000	Islamabad	Centralized
Malaysia	1963-65	3	0.13	15,557,000	Kuala Lumpur	Conciliatory
Mexico	1824	29	2.0	84,664,000	Mexico City	Matured
Republic of Nigeria	1960	12	0.92	88,600,000	Lagos	Centralized
Confederation of Switzerland	1848	25	0.04	8,331,400	Bern	Conciliatory
United Republic of Tanzania	1964	2 0	0.94	23,453,000	Dar Es Salaam	Centralized
United Arab Emirates	1971	7	0.84	1,327,000	Dubai	Conciliatory
Russia	1991	12	22.4	148,000	Moscow	Centralized
United States of America	1782-87	50	9.3	246,600,800	Washington	Matured
Republic of Venezuela	1830	20	0.91	18,900,600	Caracas	Matured

Source: *The Statesman's Year Book*, 1993-94 (New York: Macmillan Press Co. 1994); United Nations, *Population and Vital Statistics Reports* [quarterly] (New York: Statistical Office, 1993).

of power. A unitary state can exercise full control over all areas of a country without the complications of contested jurisdictions from subnational components (i.e., provinces or states).

Federal States

Federalism is not a common way of organizing governments around the world. Only 17 of the world's nation-states are politically organized as federal systems (table 4.6). Yet, over 50 percent of the world's people live in a federal system. No simple generalization can be made about the size of **federal states**. A mutually interdependent political relationship links a system of national and subnational governments according to legal and constitutional prescriptions. While it is true that a federal structure is especially suitable for large states, it is also true that many unitary states are larger than the federations of Switzerland, Malaysia, or the Islamic Federal Republic of Comores. Geography is but one of the many divisive complications. All federal states have human as well as geographic factors that divide them. The federal structure is amenable to countries occupied by people of widely different ethnic origins, languages, religions, and political cultures. India, which has the world's second-largest population and a federal system of government, has 14 main languages and over 200 secondary ones. Canada has a complicated federal system in which these social differences have regional political expression, in that some peoples see different parts of Canada as a homeland.

The word "federal" finds its origins in the Latin *foederis*, meaning "league." It implies an alliance of a state's diverse internal regions and people. K.W. Robinson says that "federation does not create unity out of diversity; rather, it enables the two to coexist."[11] "Federalism" describes a system of governing in which significant government powers are divided and shared between the central government and smaller subgovernmental units. Neither one completely controls the other; each has room for independent policy-making. The federal arrangement is a political balance of constantly shifting centrifugal and centripetal forces in a country. *Centrifugal* forces move power away from the political centre of a state to the component areas. These forces are many and varied: regional loyalties, different historical experiences, distinct forms of economic specialization, differences of language, culture, and population density, as well as remoteness from the federal capital. In contrast, *centripetal* forces centralize political power and control at the federal level of government. They diminish separatist pressures by diminishing the perception of internal differences, encouraging a loyalty to the nation-state, unifying the economy, and centralizing political decisions.

Table 4.6 is a list of all the federal states in the world. It identifies the formal name of each state, gives its founding date(s), and the number of subnational units federated, as well as its territorial area, current population, and type of federation. In every example of a federated political organization, there exists a constitutional division and sharing of powers among the various levels of government. Simply put, federalism means that more than one unit of government has responsibility for a citizen living in any part of the country (figure 4.4). The subnational units are well defined geographically. They are called states in the United States and Mexico, provinces in

Figure 4.4:
Federal state

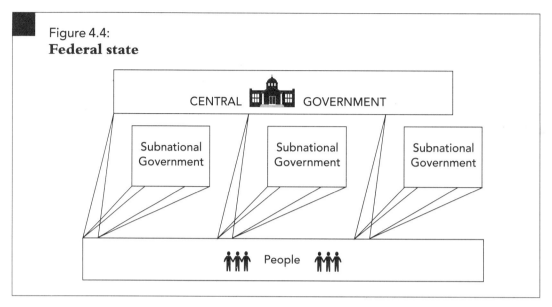

Canada, *Länder* in Germany, cantons in Switzerland, and autonomous provinces in Russia.

There are three types of federations among the 17 nation-states that practise federalism: mature federations, conciliatory federations, and centralized federations. A *mature federation* is one that over time has achieved national, economic, and political integration among people of diverse ethnic origins. In this type of federation, the constituent parts share a mutual interest in the goals of the national government and have a stake in supporting the original divisions of power and jurisdiction. The component parts accept their constitutionally designated autonomy and are willing to yield powers to the federation in order to make viable the larger economic and political unit. Five nation-states fall into this category, with the United States and Australia as prime examples.

Conciliatory federations are characterized by a high degree of constitutionally designated

centralization, but an ongoing process of compromise and negotiation between the national government and the subnational units produces a rough equality of autonomy in matters affecting jurisdictions and the divisions of power. Unlike those in mature federations, the various entities that make up conciliatory federations have retained their own identities, with their own laws, policies, customs, and languages. These federations appear inherently contentious, and perhaps even contradictory as a form of political organization. **Jurisdictional** disputes frequently arise. Constant bickering punctuated by charges of usurpation of power characterize the relationship between the central government and the governments of the lower units. In this type of federalism, no level of government can effectively govern without the cooperation of the other levels. Nevertheless, conciliatory federalism is much more responsive to local and regional needs than a unitary state would be. Six states can be labelled conciliatory: Canada, India, Malaysia, Switzerland, the Islamic Federal Republic of Comores, and the United Arab Emirates. All these federations have required a great deal of compromise and adjustment since they were formed.

Canada's experience illustrates the nature of conciliatory federalism.[12] The Constitution Act, 1867, placed in the domain of the federal government four important powers that enabled centralized government. These powers – the residual power, the declaratory power, and the powers of disallowance and reservation – gave the federal government the sovereign capacity of a unitary state cloaked in the guise of federalism. The *residual power* is enshrined in the "Peace, Order and Good Government of Canada" clause that – in certain circumstances such as those that encouraged the government to invoke the War Measures Act in 1970 and wage-and-price controls in 1975 – permits the federal government to penetrate provincial jurisdictions. The *declaratory power* allows the federal government to displace provincial powers if, in the view of Parliament, such an action is "for the general Advantage of Canada or for the Advantage of Two or more of the Provinces." *Disallowance* is a pre-emptory power of the federal government to void a provincial law within a year of its passage. And finally, *reservation* allows all federally appointed lieutenant-governors to reserve royal assent on a provincial bill, placing the final decision before the federal Cabinet.

Much has changed in Canada's federal character since 1867. At the outset of Canadian federalism, the character of the system was "quasi-federal" because the national government assumed major administrative responsibilities for the bulk of public services. In the period between 1896 and 1914, provinces demanded more power and consultation from the federal government. "Emergency federalism" characterized the war period, when Parliament delegated sweeping authority to Ottawa to levy personal and corporate income taxes, to apply wage-and-price controls, and to prohibit strikes in wartime. This quality of federalism would return just prior to and after the Depression until the end of World War II. But during the 1920s, provincial autonomy grew as a result of revenues drawn from licensing automobiles and taxing gasoline and liquor. The late 1940s and 1950s saw the forces of centralism return to Canadian federalism. What has been called "Father knows best" federalism resulted from the enormous post-war taxing powers of the federal government and its ability to penetrate the administrative purview of the provinces by funding certain shared-cost programs. "Co-operative federalism" began in the 1960s as provincial governments experienced unprecedented demands for expanded services in health, education, welfare, and resource development. Today, all provinces spend over half their budgets in these areas. As well, the rise of nationalism in Québec spawned the concurrent spread of provincial autonomy in the other provinces.

By the 1990s, Canada, with all of the requisites of a highly centralized state, had become the most decentralized federation in the international system. Over the decades, this dramatic change of character was brought about largely by provincial challenges to federal autonomy. Many of these challenges were supported by a number of judicial decisions that ruled on the side of the provinces in jurisdictional disputes with the federal government. In addition, since the 1940s the federal government has been reluctant to use its four autonomous powers against the provinces. As the provinces have gained more ground against the federal government, they have developed a confrontational attitude, tantamount to the role of the opposition parties in the House of Commons. Another major cause of decentralization lies in the changing priorities of Canadian society since the nineteenth century. When the Constitution Act, 1867, was adopted, provincial powers in the areas of education, health, municipalities, and welfare were of minor importance. Today, Canadians no longer consider the role provincial governments play in their lives as secondary to that of the federal government.

Centralized federations include nation-states that have federal constitutions on paper, but in practice are run like highly centralized unitary states. Argentina, Brazil, Russia, Tanzania, Pakistan, and Nigeria are centralized federations. In these states the federal structure really serves the interests of the national government while giving the appearances of decentralized decision-making. There is usually no actual division of powers between the national and subnational governments. Any attempts on the part of the subnational governments to govern autonomously is controlled or prevented entirely by the powers of the national government.

Economic Organization

Political organization is as essential for the economic structure and strength of a nation-state as it is for the administration of political power. A national economy is the organized process of developing markets for natural resources, industrial production, agricultural output, and technological innovation. All nation-states must choose not only how their natural resources should be exploited to meet social needs, but also how to distribute the goods and services produced from them. Essentially, these political decisions determine the economic organization of a nation-state. The economic institutions established within national economies to solve the problems of what commodities to produce, how to produce them, and how to distribute output and income, constitute the economic system.

The kind of production and distribution systems nation-states adopt contribute to their capacity to generate wealth or poverty within their economies. Thus, the world is divided into rich economies and poor economies, some with such extreme internal contrasts that their citizens can live fundamentally different kinds of lives from one another. While the average Canadian enjoys a comfortable home, a car, two television sets, and so on, the average citizen of Bangladesh and Somalia struggles for a living, and may at any time face a sudden national disaster or economic failure that threatens his or her life (figure 4.5).

In rich economies, a high proportion of citizens are able to afford the cost of feeding themselves and of providing for the need for decent shelter, education and transportation. The wealthy economies have achieved a technological sophistication in their communications capabilities, such that people are able to share information in business, education, finance, and government with great ease, efficiency, and speed. One simple illustration is access to a telephone. Today in Canada the telephone is available to almost

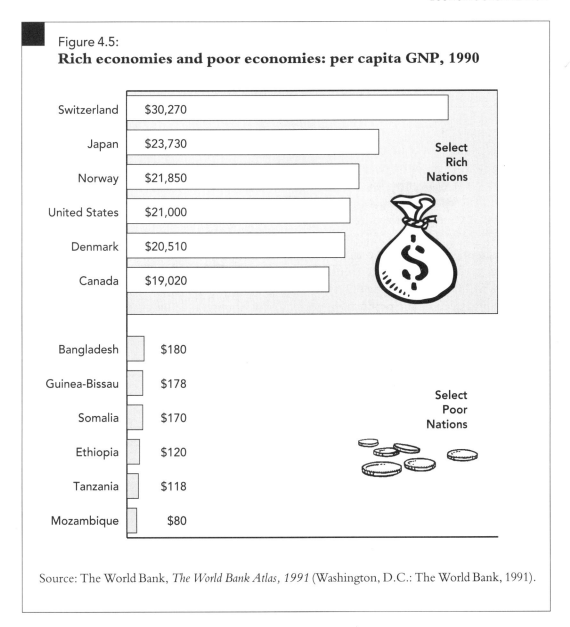

Figure 4.5:
Rich economies and poor economies: per capita GNP, 1990

Switzerland	$30,270
Japan	$23,730
Norway	$21,850
United States	$21,000
Denmark	$20,510
Canada	$19,020

Select Rich Nations

Bangladesh	$180
Guinea-Bissau	$178
Somalia	$170
Ethiopia	$120
Tanzania	$118
Mozambique	$80

Select Poor Nations

Source: The World Bank, *The World Bank Atlas, 1991* (Washington, D.C.: The World Bank, 1991).

everyone. Now, as a portable technology, the telephone is being used for an increasing number of communications purposes, networking computers and telecommunications systems around the country and the world.

Canadians have about 20 million telephones to service a population of about 30 million people; whereas the combined populations of China, India, Bangladesh, Indonesia, Pakistan, and Nigeria, totalling nearly 2.7 billion people, can afford only 18 million phones among them, less than the number of phones in Canada. This serves to dramatize comparisons only in technology between rich and poor economies, but access to the basic necessities of life such as food and shelter are just as disproportional.

In the world today, three main types of economic systems are distinguishable among nation-states: the *capitalist system,* the *socialist system,* and the *mixed economic system.* The capitalist system is characterized by the widespread practice of private enterprise, by the private ownership of resources, and by a limited amount of government intervention in the economy. Theoretically, in this type of economic organization, the production, pricing, and distribution of goods and services are determined by millions of individuals, each attempting to maximize personal gain. Of course, in the real world, these factors are also determined by large domestic corporations, multinational corporations, and the political actions of other states. A pure capitalist economy does not exist in the international community. Capitalist economies are more or less organized as "free enterprise" environments. In a socialist system, all resources are theoretically owned and controlled by the state for social purposes. In a politically directed economic system, the supply, demand, and prices of goods and services are determined by government policies. In many economies the two systems have merged into a hybrid organization called a mixed economy. In this system, control of the economy is shared by public and private institutions.

The differential performance of these economic systems has produced what many analysts refer to as five worlds of development in the international community. The *First World* includes the industrialized nation-states of Europe, North America, and Asia that have adopted a more or less capitalist, market-oriented economy. Canada, Japan, the United States, the developed economies of Europe, and New Zealand and Australia clearly qualify as members of the First World. These are the rich economies, with economic power that translates into domestic and foreign-policy goals. They control the world's financial and banking institutions and have the power to extend credit to all levels of the international community.

The *Second World* includes all centrally planned economies. The collapse of the Soviet Empire and the centralized communist regimes of Eastern Europe in the late 1980s and early 1990s threw into question the fate of the Marxist-based economic systems. Their numbers quickly dwindled to only a few, whose economies had relied heavily on the presence of other communist economies for preferential trade, investment, and development assistance. Even though totalitarian socialist economies appear to be heading for extinction in the last decade of the twentieth century, the future of centrally planned economies is not dead.[13]

The *Third World* is made up of large numbers of "less-developed countries" (LDCs) that need time and technology to build modern developed economies. The nation-states in this category include the oil-rich states and other resource-rich states, which are widely viewed as potentially wealthy economies if the process of modernization is not interrupted by political instability or severe international recession. They are highly dependent on other economies for trade and investment capital.

Third World economies, such as those of Brazil, Ivory Coast, Mexico, Nigeria, and Venezuela must overcome difficult domestic problems related to rapid urbanization, high concentrations of wealth and land ownership in the hands of the few, low levels of literacy, and galloping inflation and unemployment. Economists are optimistic about the developmental fate of these economies because these countries possess valuable resources, which, if properly organized and managed, can propel them into the First World class of economies.

The *Fourth World* consists of those nation-states that may possess enough raw material resources to build a modern economic *infrastructure*, but lack the capital, foreign investment, and the time it takes to develop their economies. This category includes Benin, India, Kenya, and Sri Lanka. They show low per capita savings and generally poor economic performance.

The *Fifth World* comprises those national economies that are doomed to remain on some kind of international dole. They possess very few easily exploited resources and are unable to grow enough food to feed their starving populations. The most notable in this disparate group of poverty-ridden economies are Chad, Ethiopia, Guinea-Bissau, Mali, Mozambique, and Nepal.

Economic power is both a means and an end to the status of political and international power. At all times, economic considerations influence the power equation of a nation-state. Economic power serves as both a goal and a tool of national power. The use of economic instruments by states for their political ends is called "economic statecraft."[14] One of the goals of economic statecraft is sovereignty, whereby states want to keep control of their economies as a fundamental aspect of their international power status. A second goal is economic prosperity, whereby national economies are able to grow and to compete in the global economy.

In the 1990s, nation-states are reassessing their power potential with a new awareness of the importance of the economic parameters of power. Economic might breeds political power. Rich states have the capacity to save money, to lend it, and to reinvest it in their economies. In such economies, economic growth enhances the standard of living, permitting better employment, education, and health benefits. Economic strength also enables rich nation-states to control their destinies in a competitive international system. They are in the strongest position to influence international trade and **monetary policy** so that it works in their favour. Finally, the industrialized nation-states are best able to carve out a sizable role for themselves in international affairs in terms of aid and investment. Industrialized economies can also convert their economic assets into military and political ones.

Military Power

Force, or more often the threat of force, play prominent roles in international relations. Many of the states of the world use their military as an expression of national power. The ability to project military prowess beyond national boundaries is viewed by some analysts as a key indication of power among states.

It is tempting to assume that the possession of nuclear or conventional weapons is the most significant factor in the power equation of a nation-state. But a paradox emerges in a world of militarily credible states. Those states that have vast military strength cannot always exercise it as an effective instrument of national policy. Modern international law rejects inter-state violence as a means of settling disputes, except in cases of self-defence or collective international peacekeeping operations.[15] With increasing frequency, the international community engages the military power of a coalition of states to force the compliance of recalcitrant states, their leaders, or states that are experiencing civil war. The use of multilateral military power against Iraq (1991), Somalia (1992), Haiti (1993), and the threat of its use in Bosnia-Herzegovina, Croatia, and North Korea (1994) reflects a growing international consensus that military action by groups of states can defend certain nation-states and ethnic minorities against violence.

Although force continues to be used by some states **unilaterally**, such acts are now legally indefensible in the eyes of the international community unless they are conducted in self-defence. As well, modern weapons of mass destruction are themselves not normally a deterrence against their use. Most states believe that nuclear technology will not be used against them, so the capacity of nuclear states to coerce and intimidate other states may not often be greater than it would be in the absence of the nuclear threat.

Some analysts have noted that military power is more a result than a cause of international tensions. The underlying causes of military competition for power among states are widely regarded as economic and social. Historian Paul Kennedy, in his widely acclaimed book *The Rise and Fall of the Great Powers,* suggests that the military power of a state tends to

be based on its relative economic standing in the world.[16] If Kennedy is correct, the rise of the United States as a world military power in this century is entirely logical, given the growth and dominance of its economy.

The 1980s and 1990s have brought startling changes in the global military and economic systems. Communism collapsed in Eastern Europe. The Soviet Union ceased to exist. The disappearance of Soviet power would seem to indicate the emergence of the United States as the world's greatest military power. The Persian Gulf war confirms such a development, at least in the military arena. The ability to send more than 500,000 troops to the Persian Gulf region on short notice reflected the status of the United States as a military "superpower"; that is, a state armed with the necessary military technologies to project its power into any area of the globe.

It may be an oversimplification to argue that military capabilities and the power of a state are synonymous. Political reality today tells us that power is also expressed in terms of trade, aid, economic productivity, and scientific and technological advancement. The extent to which military capability enhances the power of a state is still open to debate. The fact that more states are acquiring advanced weapons gives the impression of a global grab for power. In the 1990s, Argentina, Brazil, Iraq, Iran, Pakistan, South Korea, and Taiwan, among others, are expected to join the expanding "nuclear club." Would Argentina have been a more successful combatant against Great Britain in the Falkland Islands if it had possessed nuclear weapons? Does Pakistan graduate from the Fourth World to the Third World on acquiring a nuclear arsenal? Would nuclear weapons promote Canada from the rank of middle power to that of superpower? The proliferation of sophisticated military technology may make states more *dangerous*, but not necessarily more *powerful*.

In 1993, the governments of the world spent $1.4 trillion U.S. on defence. Many spent their money on military personnel, equipment, and weapons to maintain internal security, not to build reputations of power among the other nation-states in the international arena. It is also noteworthy that a large number of the world's states in Africa and Latin America do not even view their militaries as having an external defence function.[17] They are not threatened by their neighbours nor are they prepared to extend their sovereignty over other peoples. In these states, the military is used primarily to repress the domestic population. In the final analysis, before we can generalize about the relationship between power and military capacity, we must consider the **strategic purpose** of each state's defence.

National Will and Strategic Purpose

The tangible elements of power, i.e., population, geography, and natural resources, remain stagnant without national will and strategic purpose, the intangible elements of power. Together they enable a state to influence and control the behaviour of others. Although *will* is difficult to measure, some analysts rank it as the most important determinant of power.[18] Hans Morgenthau sees it as "the degree of determination with which a nation supports the foreign policies of its government in peace and war."[19] Support may be enthusiastic toward a particular strategy or it may be sluggish and apathetic.

The will of a population and its leadership will often compensate for the lack of some economic and military resources within a nation-state. Recent history abounds with examples of powerful states deferring to seemingly less-powerful states. National will is the force that enabled North Vietnam and the Vietcong to repel the United States, even though the U.S. held superior economic and military strength. In 1980, the determination of Iran paralyzed the efforts of the United States to rescue its diplomatic personnel. National determination is what enabled Fidel Castro to defy the economic and military aggressions of the United States and many of its allies in the western hemisphere. In the 1980s, Afghan guerrillas confirmed the worst fears among Soviet military strategists that a protracted exchange of force would demonstrate the vulnerability of the former USSR to an insurgency. And sheer determination may have been the fatalistic momentum behind Saddam Hussein's defiance of near-global condemnation for his adventurism in Kuwait.

However, national will can also temper leadership to refrain from exercising the full economic and military powers at its disposal. During the Vietnam War, the political and military establishment in the United States

strategic purpose: the capacity of a state to utilize location, natural and human resources, military strength, economic advantages, and other political or social variables for the purpose of enhancing its perceived power among other states.

153

favoured using more military might against Vietnam. But by 1975, the groundswell of Americans' disgust with the war discouraged the U.S. government from continuing its combat commitment to South Vietnam and Cambodia.

In Canada, a public conservative on military matters has kept a watchful eye on the development and direction of Canadian foreign policy. Canadians have been a major source of restraint on their political leaders in carving out a distinctive role for Canada in international affairs. In recent years they have encouraged their foreign-policy makers to pursue goals more in tune with Canada's national capabilities.

Canada emerged from World War II with the enhanced status of "a minor great power."[20] Post-war politicians seized the opportunity to project Canada as a second principal Western power. As a chief participant in the creation of the United Nations, the North Atlantic Treaty Organization (NATO), the North American Defence Agreement (NORAD), and as an intermediary in Commonwealth disputes, Canada stood as a rising power with a global perspective in international politics.

This pattern of **internationalism** in Canadian foreign policy did not change until Pierre Elliot Trudeau shifted public opinion in favour of a more hemispheric and continental focus for Canada. Under Trudeau, Canada developed a foreign policy that saw itself primarily as an independent North American nation-state, capable of exercising a responsible role in managing global order. As Peyton Lyon noted, Canada had taken "a giant step in the direction of continental isolationism…One that will be much cheaper, and more sharply focused on national interests."[21]

In the 1970s, Canadians insisted on a counterbalance to the extremes of superpower diplomacy by encouraging a set of policies that would build Canada's reputation as a peace-keeper state in East-West relations. Even beyond the Cold War era, Canada has projected this image very well. Canada is widely regarded as a peacemaker, a powerful negotiator, and an advocate of parliamentary diplomacy.

Viewed generally as an equal among participants, Canada's acclaimed negotiating skills have sustained the momentum of the annual **Group of Seven (G-7)** meetings around the world. At Cancun in 1981, Canada led the cause of the LDCs by advancing the "North-South dialogue." The dialogue revolves around such issues as the formation of cartels (international trading blocs), the role of multinational corporations in the developing world, loans to developing economies, and foreign aid. As a major economy in the international system, Canada is part of an informal international economic directorate made up of seven of the most economically powerful nation-states in the world (Canada, France, Germany, Great Britain, Italy, Japan, and the United States). The strategic issues that directly affect Canada as one of the G-7 are jobs, trade, international investment, and the regulation of currencies in the global economy.

A calculation of the critical elements of power as it is perceived and used by analysts such as Cline in international politics have placed Canada as high as fourth and seldom below tenth as the most powerful nation-state in the world. Yet, Canadians have consistently rejected the military road to power, favouring economic strength and diplomatic skills as the most desirable indicators of rank and status. The meteoric rise in the importance of national resources in the 1980s and 1990s – especially food, fuel, and water – has provided Canada with the opportunity of becoming a principal power in continental politics.

What conclusions can we draw about state actors from the various parameters of power discussed in this chapter? All states are structurally designed to accumulate and articulate power in various ways. As the main currency of international politics, power is the capacity of an actor to change the behaviour of other actors. Some states express their influence in economic ways, through trade, aid, and investment. Others use their political skills in bilateral and multilateral negotiations to gain important concessions from the international system. A number resort to military strategy and force to exercise power. However, most states combine their economic, political, and military capacities for the purpose of persuading or coercing the other states with which they interact.

Sometimes expected conclusions about power are confounded. The Vatican, an independent state of 104 acres, with fewer than 1000 people, and no military or natural resources, exercises powerful influence in every corner of the world. This example shows that size, location, population, resources, and military preparedness are significant in some situations and meaningless in others.

For the analyst, this leads to frequent failures of power predictions in international affairs. In many cases, intuitive notions of power are as relevant as the systematic empirical study of power relations. Even in Cline's equation for measuring national power, the elements of strategic purpose and the will to pursue national strategy are immeasurable. But his analytical design is flexible enough to incorporate the intangible elements of power as variables that can change the power formula. It enables the researcher to challenge the classical assumptions that size and military capability are decisive determinants of national power.

But in focusing only on the domain of power within a state, the Cline framework cannot consider the complete array of factors in the international environment. States are no longer the only significant organizations: multinational corporations, terrorist groups, and non-governmental organizations (NGOs) must also be taken into account as important components in the international power structure.

In subsequent chapters, we will analyze how these other actors affect the behaviour of states. We will observe that power is dispersed among non-state actors that also share in the international power equation. We will learn that the state-centric model of the global political system has become obsolete and that the presence of non-state actors cannot be ignored.

References

1. Leonard Tivey, *The Nation-State* (New York: St. Martin's Press Inc., 1981), 13-39; Paul Brass, *Ethnicity and Nationalism* (Newbury Park, CA: Sage Publications, 1992); James Kellas, *The Politics of Nationalism and Ethnicity* (New York: St. Martin's Press, 1991).

2. See *Encyclopedia of World Cultures,* Vols 1-4 (Boston, MA: G.K Hall & Co., 1991); Joyce Mass, George Wilson, *Peoples of the World* (Detroit, MI: Gale Research Inc., 1992); George Peter Murdock, *Atlas of World Cultures* (Pittsburgh, PA: University of Pittsburgh Press, 1981).

3. K.J. Holsti, *International Politics, A Framework for Analysis* (Englewood Cliffs, NJ: Prentice-Hall, Inc., 1988), 141.

4. Karl Deutsch, "On the Concepts of Politics and Power," in *Journal of International Affairs* 21 (1967): 334.

5. Robert Dahl, "The Concept of Power," in *Behavioural Science* 2 (July 1957): 201-215.

6. Ray S. Cline, *World Power Trends and U.S. Foreign Policy for the 1980s* (Boulder, CO: Westview Press, 1980), 113; Ray S. Cline, *The Power of Nations in the 1990s: A Strategic Assessment* (Lantham, MD: University Press of America, 1993).

7. Quoted in Kim Richard Nossal, *The Politics of Canadian Foreign Policy* (Scarborough, ON: Prentice-Hall Canada Inc., 1985), 12.

8. Office of the Prime Minister, Press Release, May 29, 1968.

9. John Rourke, *International Politics on the World Stage* (Guilford, CT: The Dushkin Publishing Company, 1993), 234-239.

10. Gabriel Almond, G. Bingham Powell, Jr., and Robert Mundt, *Comparative Politics* (New York: HarperCollins College Publishers, 1993), 135-137.

11. K. W. Robinson, "Sixty Years of Federation in Australia," in *Georgia Review* 50 (Jan 1961):2

12. D.V. Smiley, *The Federal Condition in Canada* (Toronto:McGraw-Hill Ryerson, 1987), 87-90; Garth Stevenson, *Unfulfilled Union* (Toronto: Gage, 1989); R.O. Olling and M.W. Westmacott, eds.,

Perspectives on Canadian Federalism (Scarborough, ON: Prentice-Hall Canada Inc., 1988).

13. Anthony Arblaster, "The death of socialism – again." in *Political Quarterly*, (62, 1991), 41-45.

14. David Baldwin, *Economic Statecraft* (Princeton, NJ: Princeton University Press, 1985).

15. Harlan Cleveland, "Re-thinking international governance: Coalition politics in an unruly world," in *The Futurist* (May-June, 1991): 20-27; Lea Brilmayer, *Justifying International Acts* (Ithaca, NY: Cornell University Press, 1989); David Weisbrodt, "Humanitarian law in armed conflict: The role of international nongovernmental organizations," in *Journal of Peace Research* (24, 1987): 297-306.

16. Paul Kennedy, *The Rise and Fall of the Great Powers* (New York: Random House, 1988).

17. Paul Zagorski, *Democracy vs. National Security: Civil-Military Relations in Latin America* (Boulder, CO.: Lynne Rienner Publishers, 1992).

18. Cline, *World Power Trends*, 143, Michael Sullivan, *Power in International Relations* (Columbia, SC: University of South Carolina Press, 1990); Richard Merritt and L. Zinnes, "Alternative Indexes of National Power" in Richard Stroll and Michael Ward, eds., *Power and World Politics* (Boulder, CO: Lynne Rienner Publishers, 1989), 11-28.

19. Hans Morgenthau, *Politics Among Nations: The Struggle for Power and Peace* (New York: Alfred A. Knopf, Inc., 1973), 135.

20. Peter C. Dobell, *Canada's Search for New Roles: Foreign Policy in the Trudeau Era* (London: Oxford University Press, 1972), 1; Michael Tucker, *Canadian Foreign Policy: Contemporary Issues and Themes* (Toronto: McGraw-Hill Ryerson Ltd., 1980), 10-12; J.L. Granatstein, *Canadian Foreign Policy: Historical Readings* (Mississauga, ON: Copp Clark Pitman, 1986).

21. Quoted by Peter Dobell, "A Review of a Review," in *Journal of Canadian Studies* 5, (May 1970), 34.

Suggested Readings

John Allen, *Student Atlas of World Politics* (Guilford, CT: The Dushkin Publishing Company, 1994).

David Conklin, *Comparative Economic Systems* (New York: Cambridge University Press, 1991).

Augie Flerass and Jean Elliot, *The Nations Within Aboriginal-State Relations in Canada, the United States, and New Zealand* (Don Mills, ON: Oxford University Press, 1992).

Ricardo Grinspun and Maxwell Cameron, *The Political Economy of North American Free Trade* (Montreal, PQ: McGill-Queen's University Press, 1993).

Mary Hawkesworth and Maurice Kogan, *Encyclopedia of Government and Politics* (New York: Routledge, 1992).

Michael Howlett and David Laycock, *The Puzzles of Power* (Mississauga, ON: Copp Clark Pittman Ltd., 1994).

Charles Reynolds, *The World of States* (Brookfield, VT: Edward Elgar Publishing Company, 1993).

François Rocher and Miriam Smith, *New Trends in Canadian Federalism* (Peterborough, ON: Broadview Press, 1994).

John Rothgeb, Jr., *Defining Power: Influence and Force in the Contemporary International System* (Scarborough, ON: Nelson Canada, 1993).

Garth Stevenson, *Federalism in Canada* (Markam, ON: McClelland & Stewart, 1990).

Glossary

autonomous: The freedom of political systems and subsystems to manage their own affairs without external interference.

core area: A relatively small portion of a country in which the political power of the entire state is concentrated, often where a nation-state originated.

decolonization: The forces of national self-determination that led to the rapid dwindling of empire and the birth of new, independent nation-states.

devolution: The transfer or transition of sovereignty to other governing units, sometimes within a federal state from the national government to the subnational governments and sometimes to a new separate and independent government.

economic interdependence: The degree to which the economic performance of a nation-state is dependent on the international economy to generate growth and employment.

extinction (state): When a previously independent state relinquishes its legal personality voluntarily, or by merging with another state, or by forcible annexation of conquest.

federal state: A system of government, such as exists in Canada, in which powers are divided and/or shared among a national government and subnational governments, such as provinces.

Group of Seven (G-7): Annual summit meetings of leading industrial states to develop and synchronize economic policies in the capitalist international economic system. Participating states are Canada, France, Japan, Italy, United Kingdom, United States, and Germany. Russia was admitted to political discussions in 1994, but will not sit as a full participant until the Russian economy strengthens and is competitive with the other seven.

industrialized economy: An economy that relies primarily on mechanized production for its subsistence.

internationalism: The idea that political activity should define its objectives not in terms of the constitution, history, or geographical boundaries of any particular state but in terms of the global community of states.

jurisdiction: The recognized right of a state to exercise control over people, property, territory, and events within a given geographical area.

legal equality of states: A fundamental principle of international law that asserts the legal equality of all independent governing entities in the international system.

monetary policy: Embraces all measures intended to affect the growth, utilization, efficiency, and diversification of the financial system, especially measures intended to encourage the growth of savings in the form of financial assets, to develop money and capital markets, and to allocate credit between different economic sectors.

Pacific Rim: A group of countries identified for purposes of trade and other international relations by their proximity to the Pacific Ocean. They include Australia, China, Hong Kong, Indonesia, Japan, Malaysia, New Zealand, Philippines, Singapore, South Korea, Taiwan, and Thailand.

persons: Legal entities that are subject to international law and have the capacity to enter into binding relations with all concomitant rights and duties.

secede: The voluntary withdrawal of a state, nation, or subnational government from some federation of which it forms a part.

sociocultural: Those groups that tend to define

themselves – through their norms, values, language and behaviours – as a distinctive nation. Such groups may measure other nations against their own sociocultural characteristics.

sovereignty: The most essential characteristic of a state, involving governmental independence, autonomous political and legal decision-making, and the power to consent to binding treaties under international law.

strategic: The capacity of a state to utilize location, natural and human resources, military strength, economic advantages and other political or social variables for the purpose of enhancing its perceived power among other states.

superpower: The perceived status assigned to nation-states by virtue of their size, population, industrial-technological capacities, and military prowess that enables them to exercise influence throughout the entire international system.

tangible power: Those obvious elements of power that are relatively easy to observe and measure, such as the size of a country, its military, and its weapons arsenal.

totalitarian: The systematic political and social control by a government or party organization potentially over every facet of private and public life by means of technology.

unilateral: Term for a state that depends completely on its own resources for national security and the advancement of its interests.

unitary state: A centralized government in which local or subnational governments exercise only those powers given or assigned to them by the national government.

FIVE

Government

New Canadians take the Oath of Citizenship

Chapter Objectives

After reading this chapter, you will be able to:

- define and classify governments

- profile the parliamentary form of government

- outline the characteristics of the presidential form of government

- compare the similarities and differences in both forms of government

- discuss the significance of an emerging United States of Europe

- describe the components of supranational government as it is represented in the European Union (EU)

- understand the fundamental elements of dictatorship

- distinguish between authoritarian and totalitarian dictatorships

- evaluate the advantages and disadvantages of different forms of government

What is Government?

Anthropologists tell us that about 30,000 years ago human beings began to organize into societies. These first human communities attempted to regulate human behaviour with respect to food gathering, family life, and protection from predatory animals. The social system may have been informal, folk-sustained, uncentralized, and non-institutional – but it did contain a *social government. Political government,* the centralized system that maintains an institutionalized system of order within a society large or small, first appeared only about 10,000 years ago when the first civilizations developed in Asia Minor and northern Mesopotamia. As people gradually concentrated in cities, social controls were needed to maintain order in a more complex organizational system. Government by political elites and by detailed **legal codes** was developed to maintain control over these populations.

The word "govern" is derived from Middle English *governen* and the Old French *governor.* The Latin *gubernare* (to direct, steer) is taken from the Greek *Kubernan* (to steer, govern). The Greeks combined the notions of steering and government in the concept of *kubernetes,* the word for "steersman" or "helmsman" of a ship (a person who governs a ship by operating the rudder). The image of "the ship of state" appears in the writings of many political writers, especially in those of Plato and Aristotle.

The American political scientist Karl Deutsch adapted the modern concept of cybernetics (the science of communication and control) to the study of government. For Deutsch, "steering depends on a country's *intake* of information through its "receptors" from the outside world (such as embassies abroad or statistical offices at home), the recall of other information from *memory* (including memories about where one wants to go), the transmission of commands for action to "effectors," and the *feedback* of information from the outside world about the results of the action taken."[1]

Modern governments are elaborate networks for transmitting and receiving information. Governments gather and store information on attitudes and events occurring in their domestic and external environments. In Canada, all three levels of government process information on every aspect of Canadian life. Municipal governments monitor where we build and renovate our homes for tax purposes. Health and Welfare Canada informs us that "most Canadians don't smoke" based on research it conducts on drug addiction across the country. For 1993, Revenue Canada tells us that in terms of income assessed, West Vancouver, B.C., is Canada's wealthiest city while Montréal Nord, Québec, is the poorest. The Department of Foreign Affairs knows that all of the states in the western hemisphere are positive about Canada's role in the Organization of American States (OAS). Such knowledge can be the basis for creating or changing public policy.

The idea of government as "helmsman" affords us the opportunity to distinguish this concept from the concepts of state and politics. Many people erroneously consider the state to be synonymous with government and politics. The *state,* the most formal of political organizations, is one of the hallmarks of civilization.

Inherent in the concept of the state is the idea of a sovereign and permanent bureaucracy that functions to administer the public affairs of its citizens as well as relations with other states. As we have already noted, states are primary legal units in the international community **recognized** as such because they have a population, occupy a defined territory, and have an effective government capable of entering into binding agreements with other states.

The international rights and obligations of a state are not affected by a change of government. New governments are bound by the provisions of treaties signed by previous governments, unless they can negotiate different terms with the other signing parties. A *government* is an organized group of people who – for a time – constitute the political executive, which controls the administrative machinery of a state by allocating authoritative decisions and steering the political system in the direction of specific policy goals.

Governments are *political*; they rise and fall, while states are *bureaucratic* and more enduring. *Politics* is influential behaviour that leads to the making of public decisions, either within or outside the institutional frameworks of government. All political behaviour has an impact on the community. Thus, the activities of a group of women who wish to start a community crisis centre for sexual assault victims are as political as the decisions of politicians to fund the project at various levels of government. While there is a tendency for us to identify politics

■ ■ **civilization:** a term that covers the stages of human development made possible by a type of complex society that has achieved an organized and efficient agriculture, and an improved and progressive condition of people living under an organized government with political structures that perform beyond the family or clan. ■ ■

with government, we should be aware that many, if not most, political decisions are made outside government. For example, a political decision is made outside government when a community-based group decides to combat abuse by establishing, without government assistance, a shelter for abused family members . *Politics is the articulation and, when possible, the harmonization of conflicting values and preferences, while government is the institutionalized process of allocating and distributing values as binding decisions on people.*

In a nation-state of nearly 30 million diverse people, living and interacting in various regions, from various ethnic and racial backgrounds, conflict in Canada's social system is unavoidable. Politics is an inescapable process that serves to harmonize conflict in human affairs. Government is the set of organizations within which much of that process takes place. But why government? What is its purpose? For political philosophers such as John Locke and Jean-Jacques Rousseau, government is essential to **civilization**. To government falls the task of ensuring human protection, decency, and restraint. "Taxes," wrote American Justice Oliver Wendell Holmes (1902- 1932), "are what we pay for civilized society." The English philosopher Thomas Hobbes wrote that in the absence of government, life among individuals would be "solitary, poor, nasty, brutish, and short."

Throughout history philosophers have theorized that government in varying degrees is essential to protect people from one an-

Table 5.1:
Aristotle's typology of government

Ideal Form	Number of Rulers	Degenerate Form
Kingship	Rule of one	Tyranny
Aristocracy	Rule of the few	Oligarchy
Polity	Rule of the majority	Democracy

other, by force if necessary. If people kill or assault one another or steal from each other, government must intervene to protect society. If it does not, civilization is simply not possible. People could not enjoy the fundamental pleasures of life – a walk in the park, a hockey game, a concert – if their physical well-being were constantly threatened by others whose violent acts could go unhindered or unpunished. Although anarchists would disagree, government is essential to non-violent human liberty.

Every political-science student quickly learns that governments differ in many ways: in size, ideology, degree of centralization, openness, legitimacy, effectiveness, and the degree and kind of political participation by individuals and groups outside the centre of authority. Correspondingly, there are various ways in which governments may be classified by structure and character, from democratic to authoritarian and totalitarian, open to closed, leftist to rightist.

Traditional Classifications of Government

The earliest and most famous classifications of government were developed by the Greeks.

Although they were rudimentary by today's research standards, the Greek **typologies** were the first serious attempts to build a systematic body of knowledge about existing governmental structures and institutions. The Greek historian Herodotus grouped all governments into monarchies (government by one), aristocracies (government by elites), and democracies (government by all).

Nearly a century later, Aristotle revised the typology to include six types of government (table 5.1). He made the distinction between genuine forms of government (in which the ruling authority governs according to constitutional guidelines based upon the "common good" (the good common to all) and the degenerate forms (in which the ruling authority uses the powers of government for selfish gain). Thus, as rulers depart from constitutional guidelines, kings become tyrants, aristocrats become cliquish oligarchs, and democrats become selfish **demogogues**. An oligarchy, for example, which is oriented around wealth, is not directed to achieve the common good, therefore it may be classified as a degenerate form of government.

Throughout history, many political theorists have constructed typologies for classifying various systems of government. Classical comparisons were essentially normative in that they pertained to value judgements on how to perfect human behaviour, and prescriptive in that they asserted the preferred means of achieving desired social goals. Plato and Aristotle compared and described governments in order to discover their "ideal form." Plato was primarily interested in studying these ideal forms of government. His typology was designed to prescribe the best form of government without necessarily referring to a real situation. Aristotle, on the other hand, rejected Plato's forms and described forms of government that actually existed, while passing normative and prescriptive judgements on them.

In the fifteenth century, Machiavelli saw advantages in the **republican** form of government and urged political expediency for governing executives (princes) to unify states. Later, Thomas Hobbes, in his *Leviathan*, recommended an absolute monarchy as the preferred form of government to contain the destructive tendencies of people in society. In contrast to Hobbes, John Locke concluded that the sovereign trust can safely reside in the people and is revocable from government if its leaders and institutions should become absolutist and arbitrary. Thus, his comparative choice strongly favoured a constitutional democracy, holding governments constantly responsible to popular scrutiny.

By the eighteenth century, theorists focused on reforming political institutions rather than advancing hypothetical forms of government. Montesquieu compared monarchical and parliamentary institutions, advocating a separation of powers among the executive, legislative, and judicial branches of government. James Madison and others in the *Federalist Papers* incorporated this experimental model of government in the United States Constitution of 1787.

The comparative study of political institutions grew steadily during the nineteenth century. Theorists assumed that the British and American models of government were the best. Other governing systems were measured by comparison with these two models. In Europe, the political order seemed to stand still. For nineteenth-century students of comparative government, the **empires** were in their heaven: all was right with the world. But not for long.

One of the most renowned critics of traditional governmental systems in Europe was Karl Marx. For Marx, various types of government were the products of class struggle, where the dominant class came to control the political institutions by virtue of its economic strength. But Marx's influence as a political analyst was posthumous. With the exception of Latin America, the break-up of Europe's large empires and the consequent explosion in the number of new states and their governments was a twentieth-century phenomenon.

Other critics of the traditional typologies identified with Marx's elitist assumptions about class and group power. Two Italians, Gaetano Mosca (1858-1941), the political theorist and politician, and Vilfredo Pareto

> ■ ■ **empire:** A term that originally referred to territory governed by emperors, but that now refers to large areas of land and peoples conquered or coerced by a foreign power. ■ ■

Table 5.2:
Citizen expectations of government performance

	Democratic	Authoritarian	Totalitarian
durability	+	/	+
accountability	+	—	/
political competition	+	/	—
adaptability	+	—	—
civil order	+	X	X
legitimacy	+	/	+
human rights	+	—	—
rule of law	+	/	X
political violence	—	X	/

High: +   Relatively High: X   Relatively low: /   Low: —

Source: Adapted from Roy Macridis, *Modern Political Systems* (Boston: Little, Brown and Company, 1986).

(1848-1923), seriously challenged the principle of majority rule in democratic governments and posited the hypothesis that small minorities control the reins of government.[2] From their viewpoint, the important analytical focus was not the formal processes of government institutions, but the sociology of government, i.e., how is an elite recruited and over whom does it exercise its power?

Comparing Governments Today

The field of comparative government is based on the assumption that students of government can better understand how societies are ruled if they compare political cultures and institutions across national boundaries. Analysts learn by making comparisons, by distinguishing similarities and differences, by measuring performances, and by contrasting the succession and durability of government systems. Political scientists examine the broader contexts of modern governments as they appear in democratic, authoritarian, and totalitarian forms. The special qualities and features of each governmental system can be measured against the background of problems that are common to all governments.

In the present world, all governments look for solutions to many of the same problems, each according to that society's peculiar way of doing politics. Even though all governments are different from one another, they share an attempt by the few (i.e., a cabinet government) to control the many. As a result, these elite groups of governors usually have more in common with one another than with their own citizens. In taking a comparative perspective, we learn that governmental institutions are the products of those behavioural patterns by which people seek order and stability. No government can be understood without giving principal consideration to that fact.

Since the turn of the century, the comparative study of government has undergone many changes. The emergence of political science as an academic discipline influenced the nature and scope of political inquiry into the dynamics of government. Comparative studies were broadened to include the whole world, not just Western governments, and focused on the gap between the rich and poor economies. The imprint of behaviouralism on political science shifted the concentration of study towards politically relevant social behaviour and the environmental process of government. Analysts began to construct a political sociology of government. David Truman advanced the proposition that governments were an outgrowth of group competition and interaction.[3] Truman's group theory encouraged political researchers to look behind the institutional façade of government to discover the social variables of political power. In emphasizing the sociological basis of government, group theorists had penetrated a vital area of political knowledge, laying the foundations for the more sophisticated concepts of political culture and political modernization.

The concept of *political culture* (a term developed by political scientists Gabriel Almond and Sidney Verba) opened new vistas for learning about the evolution of modern governments.[4] Political culture can be simply defined as the way citizens orient themselves to politics and government. Drawing heavily on the insights of psychology and sociology, political scientists were able to isolate the particular actions, attitudes, values, and skills that culturally determine the persistence and maintenance of certain types of governmental systems (table 5.2). They called attention to the fact that the cultural environments of governments differ in countries of varied historical experience, even though their political systems are described as democratic, authoritarian, or totalitarian. Almond and Verba found that if there is general popular acceptance and expectation of democracy, the government will probably be democratic. Similarly, if people have come to accept and expect authoritarian institutions, there will probably be repression and tyranny.

A range of similarities may exist among political cultures that generate similar types of government, even though the political and governing institutions appear to be quite different. Canada and the United States are two similar political cultures that have produced markedly different democratic institutions. In many ways, Canadians are more like Americans than any other people one might select for comparison. Both countries span a continent with all of the diversity of territory, settlement, and development that this implies. Both are sociologically similar, occupied by Aboriginal peoples and settled by immigrants from abroad, with histories deeply rooted in Anglo-Saxon, European, Asian, and African

Figure 5.1:
Continuum of selected states with democratic, authoritarian, and totalitarian characteristics: A hypothetical dispersion

Democracy	Authoritarianism	Totalitarianism
• accountability • constitutionalism • human rights, civil liberties • majority rule, minority rights • individualism • political competition • rule of law • popular sovereignty	• dictatorial decision making • restricted pluralism • personalistic ideology • controlled political competition • militarism • directed economy • limited political participation	• official ideology • a single elite-directed mass party • secret police • state-controlled media • state control of weapons • command economy • restricted pluralism

strong ◄──► weak   weak ◄──► strong   weak ◄──► strong

Canada   Argentina   Cuba
                Mexico   Rwanda   China

☛ Where would you place the following nation-states along this continuum? Australia, Albania, Brazil, Costa Rica, Croatia, El Salvador, France, Germany, Great Britain, Guatemala, Honduras, Hungary, India, Israel, Kenya, Latvia, Pakistan, Paraguay, Poland, Russia, Switzerland, Turkey, Ukraine, United States, Venezuela, Zambia.

traditions. Many other national attributes that underscore their likeness would lead one to expect very similar systems of government. Yet Canadians borrowed heavily from the British system of parliamentary and cabinet government, whereas Americans chose a different path in 1787, adopting a republican form of government with a novel presidential/congressional scheme.

Political scientist Allan Kornberg addressed himself to the comparison of political practices in Canada and the United States.[5] His analysis led him to the conclusion that while there are striking similarities in the political cultures and folkways in each country, divergent political practices can be explained as a different response to the different forms of democratic institutions. The governing institutions of both states, through the process of political socialization, instill certain expectations and behaviour patterns in their citizenry. Canada and the United States both achieve democracy, but through uniquely different institutional forms.

Classifying Governments

For political scientists, the tasks of classifying governments is a challenging one. Clearly, the notion of political culture has been a valuable tool for understanding the similarities and differences among systems of government. Political culture sensitizes us to the distinctive character of each government as a particular type of political system. Its overall value has been to encourage us to look beyond traditional labels to the patterns of belief, culture, and behaviour that shape and support each government. The basic message derived from the analysis of political culture has been that every government is unique. This has made it difficult for political scientists to assemble typologies that can be used to neatly classify governments into "either/or" categories. For example, to say that Canada and Mexico are democracies can be as much of an oversimplification as to say that El Salvador and Peru have authoritarian systems. More accurately, their political cultures have constructed political systems of varying degrees of democracy and authoritarianism. Canadians enjoy more elections, more party competition, and a greater amount of government accountability than do Mexicans. Some governments are more democratic than others, just as some are more coercive than others.

Instead of thinking of governments in a compartmentalized fashion, we should consider a continuum of governments running from democracy to totalitarianism, as represented in figure 5.1. A continuum is analytically more sophisticated than a typology because it permits the analyst to distribute governments according to a range of perceived criteria detected in the political culture. Thus, if due process of law or party competitiveness are found to be stronger in one democratic state than in another, the former would appear closer to the generic type. Though each observer may choose to scatter states along the continuum somewhat differently, the figure presented here will serve to magnify the variations within and between forms of government.

The improper identification of governments is a common occurrence in the media, as well as among those who conduct national or international affairs. In a world of nearly 200 nation-states, it is not surprising that significantly different ways of governing do exist. It is important for us to realize that while it is possible to classify governments under general categories, every governing system is unique.

Democratic Forms of Government

The word "democracy" comes to us from the Greek *democratia*: *demos* for people and *kratia* for government. Throughout the history of governments, democracies were not always viewed in such high regard. Even the Greeks, who invented the concept, believed that democracy could only work in small communities where all of the citizens could directly participate in the making of public decisions. They feared that otherwise, democracies would eventually degenerate into unrestrained mob rule.

Until the nineteenth century, there was continuing distrust in the ability of ordinary people to make rational decisions about complex social matters. In fact, the Athenian model of direct democracy has been a rare occurrence in history (e.g., the Athenian general assembly, the North American town meeting, and the Israeli **kibbutz**). In recent times, an ambivalent Winston Churchill said that "democracy is the worst form of government...except for all the others." This remark captures the mixed feelings prevalent about democracy.

Despite widespread skepticism, democracy is what Bernard Crick describes as "the most promiscuous word in the world of public affairs."[6] Even Libya's Khadafy applied the term in a rather unique adaptation to his country: "Democracy – it has been construed to be a Greek word, but originally it is an Arabic word from two parts – *demo*, which in Arabic means the continuation, and *cracy*, the chair. And, therefore, the continuation of the people on the chairs of power is democracy."[7] Almost every state in the international system claims a democratic form of government with all of the trappings: a constitution, elections, and the appearance of popular sovereignty. Yet even though many states in Latin America and Europe appear to be moving in the direction of democratic government, in the 1990s we actually live in a sea of non-democratic governments. Canada is one of a minority of states that closely corresponds to the modern qualities of a liberal democratic system; three-

fifths of humankind live under some form of dictatorship, most under authoritarian regimes, and the rest under the few remaining totalitarian governments, especially China's, with its more than one billion citizens.

Because only a minority of the world's states host credible liberal democratic systems, it is necessary to examine the basic characteristics of this form of government. All democratic systems exhibit the following attributes, although the institutions and procedures for their implementation tend to vary from state to state:

■ *accountability* of all public officials, directly and indirectly, by constitutional limitations, fair elections, and public opinion;

■ *constitutionalism*, whereby the scope of government authority is limited in a written or unwritten constitution that can be tested in an independent judiciary;

■ *human rights* and *civil liberties* protected by a constitution or government legislation to guarantee freedoms and safeguard against the arbitrary abuse of legitimate power;

■ *a doctrine of individualism* that relegates government to the service and protection of each person, so that individuals can realize their full capabilities;

■ *majority rule and minority rights* that govern the decision-making apparatus in the political system, permitting consensus to override dissent but giving the minority the right to challenge the majority;

■ *political competition* flowing from the principle

Figure 5.2:
Basic institutions of Canadian government

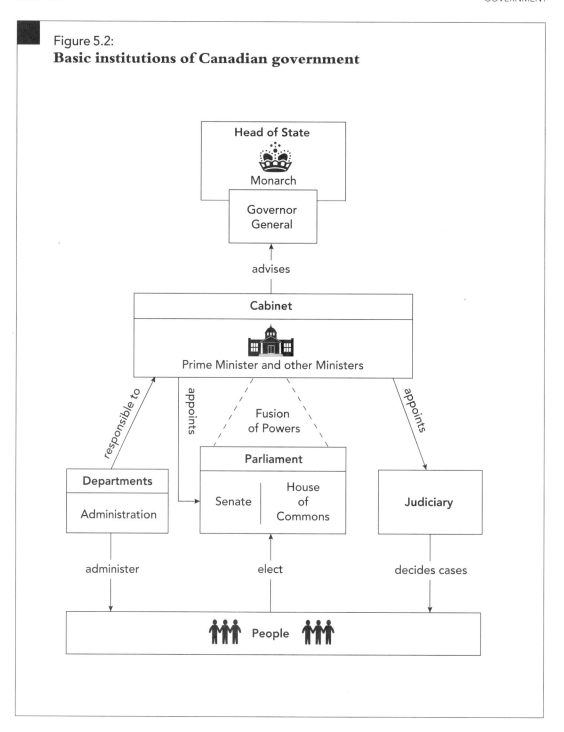

of **pluralism** that allows individuals and groups to compete for political power;

- *popular sovereignty* demonstrating the basic democratic principle that people directly or indirectly are the ultimate source of political authority; and

- *rule of law*, which proclaims the legal equality of all individuals and the supremacy of law over unlimited personal and bureaucratic power.

Two types of democratic government have evolved in the Western world and are prevalent today. One is the parliamentary form of government (also referred to as cabinet government), modelled after the British system. The other is the presidential form of government, modelled after the American system. Both are general political frameworks into which power, authority, and democratic values are allocated by different institutions. Some states such as France, Finland, and Portugal, combine some of the characteristics of a presidential system with those of a parliamentary system. In practice, the institutions that make democracies what they are include an executive and legislative branch of government, an independent judiciary, a bureaucracy, and competitive political parties.

Parliamentary Government

Among the democratic states, the most widely practised form of government is the parliamentary system, which places sovereignty (the legitimate right to govern) in parliament. A parliament is a legislative body usually comprising two houses of assembly. The Canadian Parliament consists of the Queen and her Canadian representative, the House of Commons, and the Senate (as shown in figure 5.2). In addition to Canada, the parliamentary form of government appears in states where monarchies have become constitutional democracies, for example, some members of the Commonwealth and Scandinavia; but it also appears in other countries, such as France, Germany, and Italy.

The Parliamentary Executive

The parliamentary executive comprises a *head of state* (monarch or president) and a *head of government*, usually called a prime minister (chancellor in Germany), who is nominally selected and sworn into office by the head of state. The prime minister or head of government in turn chooses the cabinet, which is collectively responsible to parliament. The cabinet is the most visible and central executive committee of government in the whole parliamentary system. It guides, directs, and virtually drives the process of parliamentary government. In terms of policy and lawmaking, the cabinet is the government. The supremacy of parliament is premised on the assumption that a government should be formed from among elected members of parliament (MPs), even though in Canada, senators are sometimes appointed to cabinet. The executive is thus *fused to* the legislative branch of government that collectively embodies the sovereignty of the people. Unlike other forms of government, the executive in the parliamentary system is dependent for both its authority and tenure in office on maintaining the confidence of the parliament.

Thus, in Canada, the word "government" has two basic meanings. In a narrow legal sense the government is essentially the prime minister and cabinet, who have been appointed by the governor general to administer or govern the country. The Cabinet determines priorities and policies, ensures their implementation, and presents government legislation to Parliament for approval. This narrow sense of government also includes the federal government departments that assist in developing, complementing, and administering the government's policies. The word "government" is also used to describe the range of institutions and even the philosophies that make up our "system of government." Canada's system of government is a constitutional monarchy and parliamentary democracy.

Fusion of Powers

In Canada, the essential fusion of the executive and legislative branches of government is accompanied by the belief that parliament is supreme and legitimate. Canadian political culture dictates that sovereignty resides in Parliament; laws cannot be made or amended, taxes cannot be raised or monies borrowed unless formal parliamentary approval is granted. But in Canada as well as in some other parliamentary systems, both the prime minister and the Cabinet, known collectively as the government, have differentiated themselves more and more from Parliament, placing them in a strong position to control policy and legislation. The government usually enjoys majority support in the House of Commons, the only popularly elected house in the Canadian Parliament. The continuous support of the majority party assures the legislative confidence of Parliament and is regularly demonstrated when the government submits its programs and policies for approval.

However, it is not always a *majority government* that is formed. Occasionally *minority governments* are formed in the House of Commons and provincial legislatures. Such was the case in June 1979, when Prime Minister Joe Clark's new government captured only 136 seats (six short of a majority), becoming Canada's eighth minority government in 60 years. The defeat of the Clark government came, after only six months in office, on a **non-confidence motion** that fatally attacked the Tory budget. Minority governments are vulnerable to the whims of partisan politics in the House of Commons. In these circumstances the Cabinet tends to be much more responsible to Parliament in order to maintain the necessary support to sustain the government. In the period from 1972 to 1974, a minority Trudeau government successfully wooed the New Democratic Party into supporting it by adjusting its legislation and by being more consultative with the **opposition**. In 1988, Manitobans elected a minority Conservative government led by Gary Filmon. When he called the provincial legislature into session, Filmon had some difficulty producing legislation that won the support of both his twenty rurally based right-wing members in the Conservative caucus and the powerful Liberal opposition.

The Opposition

Because majority governments have so much control over the direction and passage of legislation, the continuing supremacy of parliament falls squarely on the shoulders of the opposition. Given the desired tendency of the Canadian parliamentary system to develop strong executive authority based on a cohesive party majority, it follows that the opposition has a crucial role to play in the democratic process. The role of the opposition is to criticize government, its behaviour, and the administration of its policies, as well as to endorse or offer alternatives to those policies.

On rare occasions, Canadian elections have produced no elected opposition. In the election of 1987, a rejuvenated Liberal party in New Brunswick, led by Frank McKenna, won all of the 58 seats in the provincial legislature – an electoral accomplishment seen only once before in Canadian history when, in 1935, the P.E.I. Liberals took all 30 seats under Premier Wallace Lea. Single-party legislatures challenge the assumptions of parliamentary democracy, which rest upon the presence of an elected opposition to provide legitimate checks on the actions of government. In a single-party government, the role of the opposition can fall upon **backbenchers**, who may use legislative rules and procedures to question or criticize ministers. In addition, many expect the media, acting as an extra-legislative opposition, to play a key role in scrutinizing government initiatives. Some rely on the vigorous opposition of defeated parties and interest groups outside the legislature to generally raise the dust and keep a close watch on government business. But in the final analysis, only an opposition present in the legislature can effectively represent the interests of those who did not vote for the government.

Inside legislatures, opposition parties "tailgate" governments by forming a **shadow cabinet.** In 1993, Liberal opposition leader

> ■ ■ **non-confidence motion:** when a legislative assembly passes a vote of non-confidence in government (i.e., the Cabinet), the prime minister and the cabinet must resign and request the dissolution of parliament. ■ ■

Jean Chrétien assigned one critic for each of the 23 ministers in the Kim Campbell government. The shadow cabinet is expected to recommend new policies or changes to existing policies, and to work vigorously to criticize the government.

Many of the strengths and weaknesses of the parliamentary system are determined by the quality of the opposition. An obstructionist opposition prevents the government from getting on with the business of running the country in an efficient way, thus interfering with the spirit of parliamentarianism. Sometimes, in the collective mind of the opposition, delaying the passage of a **bill** is a patriotic act. Such were the sentiments of the opposition Conservative members of parliament who walked out of the House of Commons in March 1982, allowing the **division** bells to ring for two weeks, and forcing a government compromise on the energy security bill. On rare occasions, opposition parties find themselves in complete agreement with the government, allowing a piece of legislation to pass without a whimper. In October 1987, a bill to increase legislative salaries and pay raises to MPs for extra duties whizzed through the House with the blessing of all three parties.

In Canada, the rules and procedures of the House of Commons permit the opposition to "oppose" the government by the technique of **filibuster**, by which every member of the opposition speaks as long as the rules allow during each stage of the debate. Such a strategy can effectively delay, if not prevent, the passage of government legislation.

The opposition frequently uses the threat of filibuster to gain concessions from the government on the content of legislation before the House. The rules give the government an ace-in-hand by providing for **closure**, whereby the government, by means of the Speaker's ruling, limits the tenure of debate to not more than ten sitting days of Parliament. The Conservative government invoked closure three times after it introduced its free-trade legislation in December 1988. Since 1969, a change in the **Standing Orders** of the House of Commons has substantially strengthened the ability of a government to control the length of debate. For example, Standing Order (SO) 75(c) allows the government to unilaterally limit debate at each stage in the passage of a bill. The severe competition for time in Parliament usually leads to deals between the government and the opposition parties. Hence, it is rare for parliamentarians to resort to the extreme tactics of filibuster and closure, as it tends to turn public opinion against the protagonist.

The basic tenet governing parliamentary practice is *accountability*: the ultimate responsibility of all public officials is to the people. In the parliamentary mould, two competing principles are in a constant state of tension. One is that because the government represents the majority of seats in the House of Commons, it should design and implement policies in their interests. The other is that the opposition represents the concerns of those who do not identify with the elected majority and whose rights and interests should also be protected.

■ ■ **standing orders:** established rules and procedures of Parliament, each house having its own, which from time to time may be altered or suspended. ■ ■

General Audit Function

In the Canadian parliamentary system, accountability is facilitated by what Richard Van Loon and Michael Whittington call the "general audit function."[8] These are rules and procedures that allow members of parliament to publicly scrutinize and criticize the government record. Party cohesion and discipline guarantee that most of the watchdog functions of Parliament are conducted by opposition parties. But government backbenchers may also avail themselves of the same procedures to question and criticize their government's performance. Sometimes government backbenchers will publicly question and criticize their government's policies.

The process of general auditing is witnessed in a number of parliamentary debates and procedures. Standing Order 38(1) of the House of Commons requires a debate on the "Address in Reply to the **Speech from the Throne**." The Throne Speech Debate continues for eight days and usually elicits everything from expressions of undaunted support from the government of the House, to pessimistic appraisals of government intentions from the members of the opposition. The Throne Speech Debate gives backbenchers the opportunity to bring to public attention the most salient issues in their constituencies, as well as to criticize or applaud the government.

Another important general audit function of the Canadian Parliament is seen in the 25 supply days allocated to the opposition (five days in the fall, seven days before March 31, and 13 days before the end of June). These "opposition days" are intended to give members of parliament time to criticize the spending policy of the government. The opposition chooses the topics for debate and their motions enjoy precedence over government business. Each speaker is recognized for 20 minutes during which time government business (ways and means) is discussed. The opposition always uses its allocated days to expose cases of wasteful government spending, mismanagement, and wrong-doing.

The most widely observed parliamentary debate is the Budget Debate, which follows the Budget Speech. Parliamentary accountability is at its height at this time, preceeded only by another sacred tradition of British cabinet government – *pre-budget secrecy*. In order to prevent anyone from profiting from inside knowledge, the budget is traditionally kept top secret until the finance minister reads the speech in the House of Commons. The premature release of information contained in a budget would pre-empt the privilege of parliament as the only legitimate forum to hear first-hand the financial and monetary direction the country will take over a designated period of time. In 1989, the release of Finance Minister Michael Wilson's fifth budget was precipitated by an unprecedented leak, when details were broadcast on the Global television network the night before the budget was scheduled to be tabled in the House of Commons. The entire budget had been leaked by an employee of the Department of Finance.

According to the customs of parliamentary accountability, a minister of finance would resign when there is a serious breach of budget secrecy. In the case of the budget leak that occurred under Finance Minister Michael Wilson, the government maintained that because the leak came about as a result of the employee's illegal act of releasing a cabinet document to the press, the event was not a breach of budget secrecy, and that therefore, Wilson should not have to resign. He did not.

The country watches attentively as the minister of finance brings down the budget by tabling the government's Ways and Means motions. The Budget Debate begins with the minister's speech and lasts for six days, during which time members of parliament speak to the ways and means proposals contained in the budget. The debate is an occasion for the opposition parties to raise issues of national significance, such as economic policy, unemployment, and tax policy.

Another important dimension of parliamentary accountability in Canada is the Question Period. Standing Order 39(5) sets aside 40 minutes a day, while the House is sitting, for MPs to ask the government "questions on matters of urgency." Opposition members seize the opportunity to embarrass ministers by confronting them with intrusive questions about their actions, words, and policies. If not satisfied with the minister's reply, a member will call for a supplementary question in order to clarify an evasive answer. These televised exchanges are often quite humorous as members banter and heckle each other across the floor of the House.

Sometimes MPs simply require information from the government. Such questions are written and placed on the **Order Paper**. The answers to both the written and oral questions are printed verbatim in **Hansard**.

As a final recourse of action for a member who feels a question was not fully answered, a member can serve notice that the matter will again be raised "on the adjournment" of the

Figure 5.3:
Basic institutions of American government

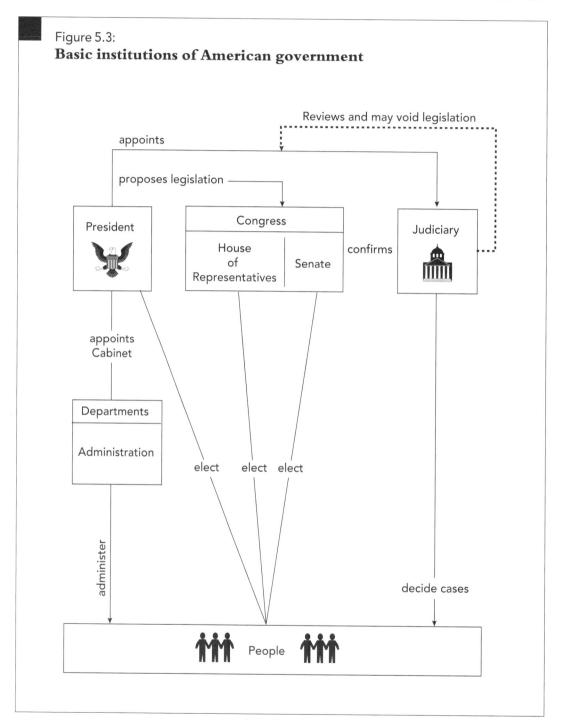

House. Questions raised on the adjournment are debated at the end of the daily sitting period when a member with a question can speak for seven minutes and other members have three minutes in which to make comments. These adjournment debates are yet another example of parliamentary accountability.

The operation of parliament is thus at once facilitated and constrained by party divisions and party organization. Yet, despite the ambiguous role that parliament performs in our political system and the diversity of views about how it might be reformed, there is no shortage of men and women who wish to become MPs. Indeed, it could be argued that the effectiveness of parliament depends less on its internal procedures than on the quality of the MPs.

Finally, the evidence concerning the adaptability of parliamentary government in states outside the Western mould is not yet conclusive. Most of the new African and Asian nation-states, which were once under British control, have tended to adopt the parliamentary form of government without the monarchy. The most successful application of this form of government by a non-Western state has been in Japan.

Presidential Government

"Presidentialism" and "presidential democracy" are two terms frequently used by political scientists to describe a form of government in which the executive is institutionally separated from the legislature. The oldest working presidential form of government is the United States'.[10] American government has played a model role for many other political systems, especially those operating in Latin America, where varieties of this model are more common than in Europe or Asia (figure 5.3). However, fidelity to the constitutional dictates of presidential democracy is another question. In many states of Central and South America, presidentialism is a façade for an authoritarian dictatorship. In these systems, the president dominates all institutions of government and is above the law.

In all presidential democracies, however, the unique feature of government is the strict adherence to the constitutional proclamation of the **separation of powers**.

Separation of Powers

According to the Constitution of the United States, "all legislative powers herein granted shall be vested in a **Congress**" (article 1), "the executive Power shall be vested in a President" (article 11), and the "judicial power... shall be vested in one Supreme Court, and in such inferior Courts as the Congress may from time to time ordain and establish" (article 111).

The principle of separation of powers has two functional dimensions. First is the **separation of personnel**, whereby no person may hold office in more than one of the three branches of government at the same time. Thus, unlike the practice in the parliamentary form of government, the executive cannot simultaneously hold a seat in the legislature. If a U.S. senator is elected president or is appointed to the Supreme Court, he or she must resign the Senate seat. Second is the system of **checks and balances**. Under this system, powers are shared by the three branches of government so that no one branch comes to dominate the governmental apparatus. In effect, all three branches share executive power.

The executive power of the president to **veto** a bill by returning it to Congress can be overridden by a two-thirds vote in the House of Representatives and the Senate. Article 1, section 7 of the U.S. Constitution also provides for a "**pocket veto.**" If a president neither signs nor vetoes a bill within ten days of its passage by Congress, the bill becomes law without his signature unless Congress adjourns within ten days. President Franklin D. Roosevelt holds the record for the most vetoes (625) of which 263 were pocket vetoes and 9 were overridden. The Supreme Court can also exercise such power by declaring an Act of Congress unconstitutional and blocking the actions of the executive branch. Thus, executing, lawmaking, and judging are divided and shared by all three branches of government.

■■ **veto:** the U.S. president may reject, and thus "veto" any bill or joint resolution passed by Congress, with the exception of proposed amendments to the U.S. Constitution. ■■

The President

To understand the distinguishing characteristics of presidential democracy, it is necessary to identify the principal features of the presidential type of government. In political systems such as the United States, Mexico, and Venezuela, the president represents the majesty and pageantry of the state. The president is both the *ceremonial* head of state as well as the *political* head of government. As the ceremonial or titular head of state, the president is analogous to a monarch. He or she is the only symbolic representative of all of the people. As the political head of government, the president is responsible for supervising the national bureaucracy, executing legislative decisions, and enforcing court orders.

In presidential systems, the constitution specifies a fixed term for the president, who is usually directly elected. In the United States, as a matter of form, the president is indirectly elected by an electoral college. But, in fact, the election of the president is the result of a popular vote, and most voters so perceive it. In France, the president is directly elected for a seven-year term and is eligible for a second term. In the U.S., the fixed term of an independently elected executive means that the president cannot dissolve the legislature and call a general election as in the parliamentary system of government. But in France, where the constitution is a presidential and parliamentary blend, the president can dissolve the legislature at any time and call for an election. The U.S. president cannot be legally removed from office during the fixed four-year term except through the legal process of **impeachment** and conviction. In France, no impeachment procedures exist, but the president can be tried by a special tribunal for acts of treason or for acts contrary to the Criminal Code.

The presidential form of government seems to focus primarily on the executive branch. But in actual fact, it is a multi-dimensional form of government based on balancing the competitive forces among executive, legislative, and judicial institutions. Under this arrangement, the executive institutions carry out the decisions of the two other branches of government; the legislative institutions deliberate and decide on making general laws; and the judicial institutions apply these laws to particular cases.

In the presidential system, the general

audit function is a product of political competition among institutions. The elaborate machinery of lawmaking is meant to ensure that laws are formulated carefully and that the bulk of the population – as well as major interest groups – perceive the laws passed as legitimate.

Supranational Government

The United States of Europe

Few people would have imagined at the close of World War II that in the 1990s a United States of Europe was forming as a *supranational* political system – what many see as the new superpower of the twenty-first century.[11] It is a community of nation-states, seeking to eliminate borders and trade barriers and to unite its members through the use of one currency and a common foreign and defence policy. As a government it uniquely combines elements of parliamentary and presidential organization with a powerful bureaucracy.

The genesis of a United States of Europe took place in 1951, with the formation of the European Coal and Steel Community (ECSC). The concept was that European wars had their origin in economic rivalry. To substitute peace for war, it was necessary to substitute economic co-operation for economic rivalry. The European Community (EC) started this way simply because coal and steel were the sinews of war and because former enemies found more and more interests to share. The six founding nation-states of the ECSC – Belgium, France, Germany, Italy, Luxembourg, and the Netherlands – were the major powers in Western Europe that agreed to gradually eliminate duties, quotas, and the price discriminations in coal and steel. From

that simple idea, the ECSC deepened economic integration by creating the European Economic Community (EEC) in 1957, and by 1967, emerged as the European Community. By 1973, the six founding members were joined by Ireland, Britain, and Denmark. In 1981, Greece joined the EC, and in 1986, the membership reached 12 with the entry of Portugal and Spain.

With the entry into force of the Maastricht Treaty in November 1993, the European Union – EU – became the umbrella term for the institutions of the EC. The EU of the twenty-first century could encompass as many as 25 member states with 16 languages spoken among them. For example, in 1994, Austria, Finland, Norway, and Sweden made formal application to the EU for membership by January 1, 1995, and initiated referenda on the issue within their own political systems. The granting of formal membership requires ratification by the EU.

The dream that began with Charlemagne and that has been shared by Kant, Rousseau, Victor Hugo, and Garabaldi, among others – the dream of a United Europe – is close to being fulfilled. The new Europe of the 1990s is a community of 340 million people who share a new flag, a government in Brussels, a Court in Luxembourg, and a Parliament in Strasbourg. It is a Europe that aspires to be a world power, filling the vacuum created by the collapse of the Soviet empire, being whole as its manifest destiny. But for now the road to Europe's manifest destiny takes the more pedestrian route of the *single market*.

Europe's Governing Institutions

It was inevitable that the visionaries of a new supranational governing system for Europe

Figure 5.4:
EU: Decision-making process

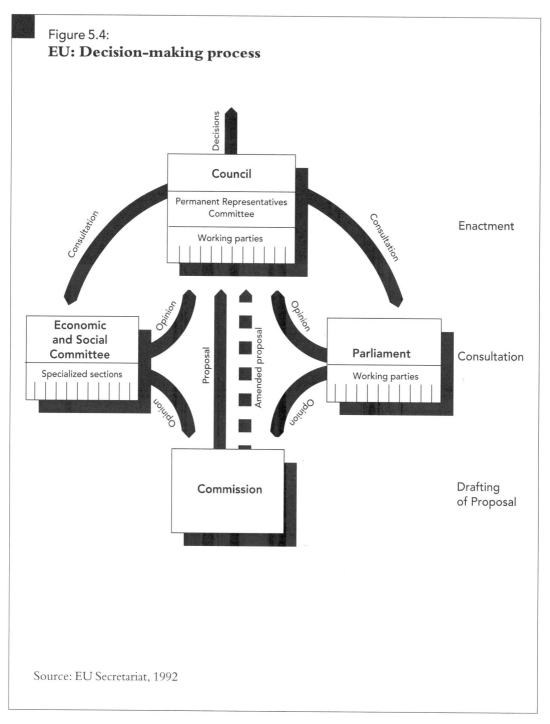

Source: EU Secretariat, 1992

would collide with the advocates of nationalism and national sovereignty. How could a United States of Europe spring from the traditional forces of national pride and patriotism? The signing of the Single European Act (SEA) of 1987 reflected a determination to deepen European integration by unifying the economic and monetary policies of the EU's member states and weakening the remaining forces of nationalism. Further amendments to the SEA were agreed to in the Maastricht Treaty. The treaty included a Central Bank and a single currency, the European Currency Unit (ECU) by 1999, and a planned Social Charter that would prevent companies from shopping around Europe for the lowest wage rates.

The major governing institutions of the EU are the Council of Ministers, the European Council, the European Commission, the European Parliament, and the European Court of Justice (figure 5.4). All these bodies derive their financial resources directly from a 1.4 percent levy on the yield of each member state's Value Added Tax (VAT), the major indirect tax, as well as from customs duties, agricultural levies, and duties on industrial imports.

Council of Ministers

Based in Brussels, the Council of Ministers is the autonomous decision-making body of the EC. The Council is composed of the foreign ministers of each member state and represents *national* as opposed to *community* interests. It acts on proposals made by the European Commission after these proposals have been scrutinized by the European Parliament. The Council has the power to amend or reject proposals made by the Commission. In effect,

all of the decisions of the Eurocrats have to be approved by the Council. Certain decisions require the unanimous support of the Council; for example, whether to admit new member states. On most other matters, voting is by qualified majority, by which a measure must obtain 70 percent of the Council's support to pass.

In practice, much of the day-to-day work of the Council of Ministers is carried out by civil servants appointed by member states, and by working groups organized by the Council. Since the adoption of the SEA, specialized councils, such as the Agriculture Council, meet to discuss problems related to their interests.

The European Council

The European Council, or Summit, is composed of the heads of member governments, usually a prime minister for most nation-states, a president for France. The Council meets at least once every six months and is presided over by the head of government who is currently president of the Council of Ministers. The purpose of the European Council is to provide a forum at the highest level to reconcile policy differences. The European Council has launched such key initiatives as the European Monetary System (EMS) in the late 1970s, and the principle of political union in 1990. When fundamental policy conflicts threaten to split the EU – for example, the pace of political, economic, and monetary integration in the 1990s – the European Council is the arena of last resort in which these policy conflicts are addressed and influential recommendations (with no formal constitutional status with the EU) are offered.

Figure 5.5:
European Parliament

Members meet in political groups
regardless of nationality

Parliament is presided over by a president
assisted by 12 vice-presidents

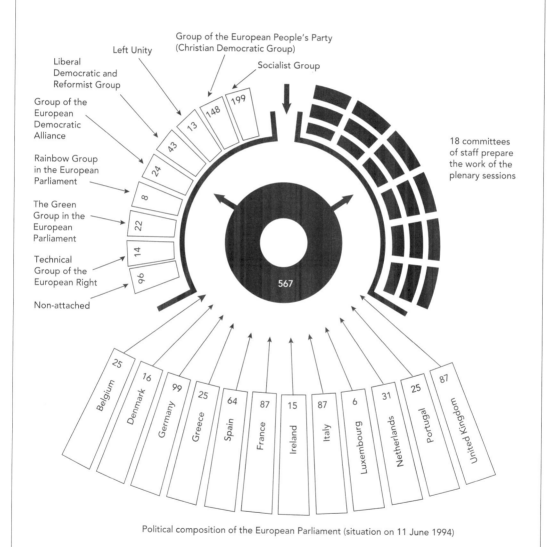

Group of the European People's Party
(Christian Democratic Group)

Left Unity

Socialist Group

Liberal
Democratic and
Reformist Group

Group of the
European
Democratic
Alliance

Rainbow Group
in the European
Parliament

The Green
Group in the
European
Parliament

Technical
Group of the
European Right

Non-attached

13

148

199

43

24

8

22

14

96

567

18 committees
of staff prepare
the work of the
plenary sessions

Belgium 25
Denmark 16
Germany 99
Greece 25
Spain 64
France 87
Ireland 15
Italy 87
Luxembourg 6
Netherlands 31
Portugal 25
United Kingdom 87

Political composition of the European Parliament (situation on 11 June 1994)

Source: EU Secretariat, 1992

European Commission

The European Commission is a special embodiment of the EU, with an existence distinct from the member states and governments. Located in Brussels, it consists of 17 commissioners, appointed by the member states for four-year terms, two each from Germany, Italy, Britain, France, and Spain, and one each from the remaining seven member states. The Commission serves as the executive of the EU, overseeing and implementing policy. It manages a large bureaucracy, with over 15,000 "Eurocrats" who are employed by the Commission in Belgium, Luxembourg, and other EU locations. As the nerve centre of the new Europe, the Commission functions independently of any member state in the interests of the European Union as a whole, and implements the treaties the EU members ratify. It has the authority to initiate EU policies, and generally has the sole right to propose legislation to the European Parliament (EP).

It is here in the new International Congress Centre in Brussels that the Eurocrats draw the blueprints for further integration and make rules affecting everything from taxes to making beer to making sure that German toasters work when they are plugged in in France. All of this bureaucracy is intended to serve the interests of a new Europe, where trade barriers have come down and the free flow of people, goods, and capital is a routine occurrence. In all, thousands of industrial and manufacturing standards are implemented in the 12 member states. This means Eurocrats must work overtime, deciding everything from the length of condoms to the maximum noise level of lawnmowers.

The Eurocrats are the elite, the clergy of the new Europe, who spend much time with the many lobbyists who approach them for political favours. The drive toward the single market has produced another kind of competition – competition for the Eurocrat's ear. EU officials are the ones who are drafting the rules for this new single market, so it is not surprising that most of the lobbying associated with the European Union is centred in Brussels. Nearly 1000 multinational companies now have an office in Brussels – twice the number of companies in Washington, D.C. In all, there is about one lobbyist for every five bureaucrats. The Eurocrats have become the high priests of European integration, accountable to no one but themselves.

The Commission issues directives that aspire to achieve the objectives of the policies decided on by the Council of Ministers. These directives address an endless array of matters. They can prohibit member governments from subsidizing their own farmers, veto mergers of companies on the grounds that they will reduce competition in Europe, and ban the sale of food and drugs that have been deemed unsafe.

The Commission exercises considerable influence as the powerful bureaucratic component of European government. It sees its mandate as accelerating the pace of European integration, sometimes against the expressed national interests of member states. It can take members of the European Communities to the European Court of Justice should they breach treaties or renege on their responsibilities to the supranational organization.

European Parliament

The European Parliament (EP) has both a legislative and an advisory role. The Parliament is the only directly elected EU institution in Strasbourg. There are 567 members of the European Parliament (MEPs), elected to fixed five-year terms by elections held on the same date in each member state. They are grouped by political affiliation, not national affiliation. Party representation in the European Parliament consists of Socialists, European People's Party (Christian Democrats), Liberal Democratic and Reform Group, European Democratic Alliance, the European Right, The Rainbow Group, Left Unity, and Independents (figure 5.5).

The EP's main functions are to debate, question, and formally register advisory opinions on proposals made by the Commission. The European Commission and the Council of Ministers are not bound by these opinions, but no legislation can be enacted without the EP first officially issuing its opinion. The EP has the power to dismiss the entire Commission but not individual commissioners. This extraordinary measure has only been initiated once (in 1977) but was not carried out.

The EP may comment both on the European Commission proposals and on the common position reached by a qualified majority in the Council of Ministers. The Parliament may consider a wide range of legislative matters, from the marketing of plums and bananas to the tariff barriers placed on non-members. It has the right to reject the budget of the EU as a whole, and it has the last word on amendments to the budget. The EP is the watchdog over the workings of treaties, such as the Lome Convention, signed between the EU and other states, as well as treaties signed among members, such as the Maastricht Treaty and the Treaty of Rome.

European Court of Justice

The European Court of Justice (ECJ) sits in Luxembourg with 13 justices and six advocates-general appointed by agreement of the member states for six-year terms. It should not be confused with the European Court of Justice on Human Rights (ECJHR) at Strasbourg. In the broadest sense, the ECJ is an international court empowered to interpret EU treaties and to settle disputes that arise among the institutions of the EU, between individuals, enterprises, and member states. About one-third of its new cases are requests for preliminary rulings submitted by national courts. Its decisions are binding on member states, national courts and parliaments, all EU institutions, enterprises, and individuals. The rulings of the European Court have empowered EU law, granting it precedence over national law when the two are in conflict.

Any member state, EU institution, corporation, or individual may appeal to the court for the enforcement of EU laws or treaty rights. In effect, the decisions of the court tend to influence EU policy. Basically, the ECJ may declare an act or behaviour of any member state illegal if it violates the EU or subsequent European law. The court has ruled, for example, that the principle of equal pay as provided in Article 19 of the Treaty of Rome applies to women in any member state, notwithstanding how national laws may or may not protect women in the economy. Such a ruling has been extended by the EU to affect gender-equality policies, job training, employment, and treatment in matters of social security in all member economies.

Until 1989, the ECJ was the sole judicial organ of the EU. In 1989, a new court called the European Court of First Instance was established for the purpose of adjudicating special matters. In these cases the ECJ acts as a court of appeal.

The European Court has been an important instrument for the advancement of supranational policies in Europe. It is the government body that settles the disputes that will inevitably arise between those who believe in national sovereignty and the EU ideals of integration.

Authoritarian Dictatorship

Authoritarian regimes are familiar phenomena to political scientists.[12] The similarities of authoritarian and totalitarian dictatorship are well known, but as we shall see, the two systems of government are quite different from one another. Today, many of the nation-states of the world are governed by authoritarian regimes or dictatorships.

Authoritarianism is a system of government principally characterized by **autocratic decision-making, restricted pluralism, and limited public participation**. Just as democracy is an outgrowth of a society attached to values of open government, pluralism, and political party competition, so is authoritarianism a product of unique historical variants within a political culture. That pattern reveals itself historically as a tendency to concentrate all political power in the hands of a few, to distrust democratic institutions, and to expect **political succession** to take place as a violent and unstable event. This contrasts with democracies, wherein free elections usually enable the peaceful transition of power.

Four types of authoritarian governments manifest themselves in the international system.

Tyrannies are governments dominated by an absolute civilian or military rulership which arbitrarily exercises political power in a highly repressive and often *personalistic* fashion. Governments in contemporary Guatemala, El Salvador, and Uganda are some examples. Dynastic regimes are monarchies wherein members of the royal family exercise absolute political powers ascribed by religious law, custom, and inheritance. Examples of these are Saudi Arabia, Bahrain, and the Sultanate of Brunei. Military regimes are governments in which the executive, legislative, judicial, and administrative institutions are controlled by members of the armed forces. A multitude of African examples exist in states such as Guinea-Bissau and Sierra Leone. Single-party regimes are governments instituted with the support of only one political party or a coalition of parties that dominates the electoral system often exclusively, but sometimes tolerating weak opposition parties. States such as Kenya, Iraq, Syria, and Tanzania provide examples of this type of regime.

The chief characteristics of the authoritarian type of government are:

■ Dictators are often **charismatic**, elitist, and personalistic. They exercise political power in personalized and subjective ways rather than according to the rules of democratic governing institutions, where the rule of law supersedes the rule of the rulers.

■ **Personalism** is an effective means of attracting mass support and centralizing government power. People are encouraged to identify with the leader rather than institutions or the ideals of a formal governmental system.

■ Authoritarian dictators do not promote an official, undisputed ideology that prescribes a national or international mission for their government. If an ideology exists, it reflects their personal world view and frequently reflects short-range, pragmatic considerations.

■ A plurality of interest groups may exist with the permission or tolerance of the dictators but these groups are licensed or closely monitored by the government. If they support the regime, their activities go unhindered, but if they oppose the government, they are usually harassed or repressed.

■ The political party system may appear to be competitive but is always dominated by one political party, the *government* party. Opposition party competition is sometimes legal, provided it remains weak and divided.

■ A pretence to constitutional law based on liberal democratic norms masks authoritarian operating structures. Authoritarian regimes practise a type of legalism that embraces law and regulation but its purpose is to control people, not to limit government.

■ The economy is "directed" to the problem of securing economic development and modernization. But authoritarian governments generally do not attempt to control every aspect of human economic activity. Free enterprise, free markets, and other components of laissez-faire principles are permitted in the economy.

■ Authoritarian regimes usually have a strong military component that from time to time intervenes in the political process. The military in an authoritarian state makes itself felt in ways ranging from holding a veto over the actions of a civilian government, to directly intervening in the political process, to instituting a military regime.

■ The government limits and controls popular participation in the system. Political mobilization is encouraged by the government only for support of its economic and political policies. Contemporary authoritarian systems, particularly one-party dominant states, permit the symbolic involvement of citizens through elections, referendums, and plebescites.

Civilian Dictatorships

To a greater or lesser degree, all authoritarian governments are dictatorial. Dictatorship may manifest itself in a number of different civilian and military forms. *Caesarism* is the kind of dictatorship in which the leader enjoys absolute power by virtue of control over the military. The military is the coercive arm of the civilian dictator. It can be summoned to neutralize political enemies, as well as to repress dissidents in the population. Thus, most civilian dictators court the loyalty of the military by catering to its materialistic needs, such as regular pay raises, fringe benefits, overseas travel, and access to state-of-the-art equipment and hardware.

The caesaristic dictator often has the support of the masses, a modern political machine, and a program combining personal charisma with a socio-economic plan of action for modernization. Many people, including the dictator, regard the dictatorship as the only salvation for the country.

Caudillismo – from the Spanish word *caudillo,* meaning man on horseback – is a type of dictatorship that has been a principle feature of Latin American politics since the nineteenth century. The strong-arm style of rule is based on the force of personality (*personalismo*) of the *caudillo*, not on an ideology as a program of action. The *caudillo* comes to power on the back of a personal mystique, using charm and effective oratory to capture the support of the people. By appealing to the forces of nationalism and high ideals, the *caudillo* gains mass appeal.

However, behind this popular façade is almost always a repressive dictatorship that uses the loyalty and physical power of the military to maximize personal gain and effectively control opposition. Political rights and liberties are often suspended: restrictions are placed on the activities of political parties and interest groups; and newspapers are monitored or bridled. Elections become an event of the past or the future and the authority of the judiciary is curtailed. Whatever opposition exists is kept weak so as not to seriously challenge the political strengths of the *caudillo*. Some of the most infamous Latin American dictators who have led authoritarian regimes in the twentieth century have been Anastasio Somoza and his son Anastasio Somoza Debrayle in Nicaragua, François Duvalier and his son Jean Claude ("Baby Doc") Duvalier in Haiti, and Raphael Trujillo in the Dominican Republic.

Military Dictatorships

Militarism – the intrusion of the armed forces into the political life of a country – is a salient feature of authoritarian governments all over the world. Since 1945, over two-thirds of the states of Africa, Asia, the Middle East, and Latin America have experienced varying degrees of military government.[13] Cycles of military intervention alternating with civilian rule are a typical pattern within authoritarian states, especially in Haiti, El Salvador, and Guatemala. In such systems, the armed forces are likely to step in during periods of political and economic crisis. In many cases, any circumstance that threatens the status quo is enough to bring the military running from the barracks. In the post-war period, the armed forces in Latin American states were inclined to attribute their political intrusions to the threat of communism. But often the rationale for military intervention is civilian corruption or government mismanagement. One reason that is openly admitted to by military officers is adventurism. Soldiers have guns, tanks, and planes – the most persuasive tools for acquiring the ultimate power of the state. By engaging a **cuartelazo**, which is a military coup d'état against a military government, militarism is perpetuated.

By definition, military regimes are those in which the armed forces have seized power by a coup d'état, and have taken command of the highest positions of government. A military council, or **junta,** is usually formed to control all executive and legislative functions. Many military governments create mixed military/civilian executives to enhance the legitimacy of the regime. Civilians are almost always included in the cabinet and high bureaucratic positions as advisers in the formation of government policies. But their presence and influence is largely at the sufferance of the military governors.

> ■ ■ **junta:** The Spanish word for a council, which usually describes a group of military officers who collectively exercise the powers of the government. ■ ■

From the beginning of their tenure in power, the military portray themselves as responsible and patriotic officers who are temporarily forced to take the reins of government away from incompetent civilians or a previous inept military regime. Ostensibly, their goals include altering the system of government to rid it of excessive, corrupt, and inefficient partisan politics. Often, intrusive actions are taken to protect a corrupt military leader, such as Panama's president, General Manuel Antonio Noriega, who was indicted in Florida on drug-smuggling and money-laundering charges. The 15,000-member Panamanian Defence Forces annulled the elections held in May 1989, when results showed that the opposition had won. And in 1993, Haiti's military rulers refused to allow the return of democratically elected President Jean-Bertrand Aristide, who was deposed in a bloody coup in September, 1991.

Initially, the military are concerned with economic problems they claim resulted from civilian rule: high inflation and unemployment, wasteful government spending, and balance-of-payments deficits. Viewing themselves as "iron surgeons," they often employ drastic economic measures to correct the malaise in the economy. They restrict the supply of money to address inflation and invite foreign investment to reduce unemployment. Cutbacks in social security, medical, and education programs are implemented to reduce public spending. But progressive measures to redistribute wealth and institute land reforms are usually avoided in the military's strategy to reconstruct the economy. The basic contours of the social system are preserved or only mildly altered. Military governments will usually eliminate or extensively limit the political rights of the civilian population. For this reason, and in anticipation of a military coup in Burundi in 1993, the entire Cabinet fled the country, taking refuge in bordering states. Some political parties, newspapers, and trade unions are permitted to operate under the close scrutiny of government authorities. Almost always, the existing leadership of political organization and labour unions are purged and replaced by people acceptable to the regime.

The immediate reasons for limiting political competition and muzzling the media are quite apparent. The military take power to prevent certain changes. They will not provide former rulers and their supporters with the means to challenge them. Because the justification for taking power is to prevent failures in civilian government performance, the military are determined to neutralize the power potential of those responsible for these failures.

If the significance of a particular form of government depends upon the frequency with which it occurs, then the study of military government is paramount. Given the frequency of military interventions in Western as well as non-Western systems, military governments must be viewed as a global political phenomenon. Since 1945, among the twenty Latin American republics, only Costa Rica and Mexico have institutionally neutralized the threat of military intervention. Between 1945 and 1990, close to 60 percent of all Latin American presidents have been military men. During the same period, in nine of the 18 Asian states, military officers carried out successful coups against established governments. By the 1990s, nearly two-thirds of the Middle Eastern and North African states had experienced at least one attempt by the military to seize political power. Algeria, Egypt, Iraq, Libya, the Sudan, and Syria were particularly affected. In the brief independence period of tropical Africa since the 1960s, over half the civilian governments have been overthrown – in Congo/Brazzaville, the Central African Republic, Benin, Ghana, Nigeria, Togo, Uganda, and Burkina Faso.

Research confirms that the most likely aftermath of military government is military government. As authoritarian governments tend to spend more of their gross national product each year on militarization, the greater will be the likelihood of military interventions in their political systems.

Totalitarian Dictatorship

Totalistic Controls

Totalitarianism is a uniquely novel product of the twentieth century, quite distinct from modern authoritarianism and far removed from the autocracies of the past. Under authoritarian dictatorship, average citizens retain a great degree of control over their private lives and usually are not cognizant of the all-pervasive influence of government in society. In contrast, the essential trait of totalitarianism is its claim upon most aspects of a citizen's life to the service of national goals as determined and interpreted by the rulers. In the totalitarian state, the regime's presence is "totalistic," in that no realm of private and social life is completely immune from its control.

The emergence of totalitarianism (since World War I) is attributable to breakthroughs in mass-communication technologies as well as in techniques of social control and manipulation discovered through experimental research in social psychology. By means of these devices, totalitarian states are characterized by a system of government in which one party enjoys a monopoly of political, economic, judicial, and military power. The party has the capacity to penetrate all levels of society, to determine its values, and to direct the lives of individuals towards the achievement of its prescribed ideology.

Big Brother

In 1948, George Orwell alarmed the democratic world with his nightmarish novel *1984*, an icy satire of life under totalitarian rule. Orwell's vision of totalitarian government portrayed a society with the political and technological capacity to remould and transform people according to an official plan. With modern electronic devices, the government of *1984* spies on its citizens: television cameras scan the streets; listening devices monitor private conversations; even private thoughts and actions can be learned by the state. Watched by an ever-present "Big Brother," people are highly controlled by the government. They are subjected to constant censorship and surveillance and indoctrinated in daily "two-minute hate" sessions, directed against a phantom enemy with whom they are endlessly at war. In the end, the hero becomes a mindless robot, believing everything the government tells him to believe, fearing what he is told to fear and hating what he is told to hate.

In hindsight, Orwell's novel was a projected exaggeration of the most menacing and horrific features of totalitarianism. But all totalitarian governments have the institutional and technological capacity to achieve the most repressive forms of social control. In China, the government has ensured the compliance of its citizens by means of torture, harassment, and fear. Often, recalcitrant citizens have been subjected to threats, molestations, questioning, searches, eviction, firing, and imprisonment. Recall the repressive reaction of the Chinese government to the peaceful demonstration led by citizens and students in Tiananmen Square in May, 1989. And in Cuba, the 6000 Committees for the Defence of the Revolution (CDRs) keep close watch on the social and political behaviour of Cubans.

Elements of Totalitarian Dictatorship

One of the most comprehensive analyzes of totalitarianism was conducted by Carl Friedrich and Zbigniew Brzezinski.[14] They identified six essential characteristics of this twentieth-century governmental phenomenon:

■ An official undisputed ideology that encompasses all aspects of human life: history, the economy, and all social and political institutions, as well as one that prescribes an international mission of global conversion or domination.

■ A single, elite-directed mass party, led by a dictator and a core of militants dedicated to realizing the goals of the ideology. Recruitment of party membership is controlled, usually about 15 percent of the population. The organization of the party is linked to the formal institutions of government and touches every level of society.

■ A secret policy apparatus that uses modern communications technology and psychological methods to ensure mass allegiance to party ideology.

■ The monopolized control of the mass media in order to indoctrinate the masses in the official ideology. The media function as organs of mass propaganda to educate citizens as to the goals of the state.

■ The state monopoly of weapons control to prevent the possible armed resistance of dissidents.

■ A centrally controlled "command economy" in which most means of production and consumption are owned and planned by the state according to ideological prescriptions.

Models of Totalitarian Dictatorship

Two models of totalitarianism have appeared in the twentieth century: right-wing totalitarianism and left-wing totalitarianism. Italian fascism and German national socialism are the two generic examples of right-wing totalitarianism. But fascism and Nazism were not uniquely Italian and German experiences.[15] Both were outgrowths of an ideological movement that swept Europe in the period between the two world wars. Right-wing totalitarianism first appeared in Italy, where by 1922 Benito Mussolini had gained complete control of the Chamber of Deputies. By 1933, in Germany, the National Socialists, under the iron grip of Adolf Hitler, were the only legal party. Germany and Italy aided Francisco Franco and his Falangist Party in Spain and inspired Juan Perón in his successful quest for power in Argentina.

These totalitarian governments of the

right reflected remarkable similarities with totalitarian communism. They had a high degree of centralized governmental decision-making. A single party monitored, controlled, and infiltrated government at all levels with a prescribed ideological mission. The party was elitist and claimed to be the vanguard of the people. Leadership tended to be absolute, charismatic, and personalistic. The scope of secret police actions was comprehensive, arbitrary, and unaccountable except only to the highest party leaders. Fascism proclaimed a romantic ideology of mythic consensus, homogeneity, and personal comfort in conforming to social roles. Human dignity was to be achieved by the integration of individuals into an all-encompassing corporate moral order, represented by the fascist state. But none of the fascist regimes revolutionized their societies; rather, they built a powerful governmental apparatus for social control and expected individuals to glorify the goals of the state.

Totalitarianism of the left is the more revolutionary of the two models. In China and Cuba, this form of government has fundamentally changed all levels of society so that previous social and political structures are no longer recognizable. Upon assuming power, these governments take immediate action to collectivize almost every facet of private property and to bring it under state control. In China, the land-tenure system was restructured into a system of collective and state farms, permitting only a minimum amount of private ownership of land. In Cuba, although about 25 percent of the land under communist rule is privately farmed because state management is impractical, private growers are usually told what to grow and most of their produce is sold by state-managed food stores. Non-democratic socialist states nationalize the means of production in their industrial and commercial sectors. This has usually been extended to individual entrepreneurs, artisans, street vendors, taxi drivers, and other small commercial services. But some governments are encouraging economic innovation by permitting the spread of private enterprise in these sectors. Today in China, it is possible to purchase a computer or a modern sound system from private businesses throughout the country.

In all societies that try to regulate almost everything, **black economies** and **black markets** (second economies) have come to play a large part in the economic structure of the country. Economies that are centrally planned by their governments are not able to accommodate the natural everyday forces of supply and demand that inevitably accrue in all societies. In the past, many people under communist regimes have resorted to illegal sources to procure goods and services needed from day to day. Black-market capitalism grew spontaneously in all totalitarian socialist states at least in part because of the absence of privately motivated market mechanisms based on profit.

The absence of an official acceptance of the profit principle in such systems created far-reaching consequences for labour as well as for managers. Under the few remaining communist command economies, productivity remains low in comparison to the leading market economies. Historically, unions remained under the control of the party, which placed pressures on workers to meet or exceed the targets of government planners. The unions exercised the will of the party and the government and thus were unable to initiate reforms in a stagnant economic system. In carrying out the directives of the government and party, unions contributed to the litany of economic problems that include shortages of food and consumer goods, and the overproduction of unwanted consumer products.

This chapter has provided a survey of governmental regimes within the threefold typology of democratic, authoritarian, and totalitarian governments. The overall evaluation of the performance of any of these types of government requires us to ask whether they promote human dignity. To what extent is human well-being enhanced by the presence of the regime? Do people feel they can participate in the decisions of the system?

Are the rights of individuals respected by the government and its officials? Does the government respond to the most necessary demands of its citizens? What about the functional performance of a government? How well does it manage the natural and human resources under its jurisdiction? Does it use its capacity to generate good for all of its citizens most of the time?

In the following chapters we will learn that governments are multi-dimensional, usually comprising four branches: the executive, legislative, bureaucratic, and judicial. Each can be compared as a separate part of a political system, and each must be understood as a constituent element of the whole polity.

References

1. Karl W. Deutsch, Jorge Dominguez, and Hugh Heclo, *Comparative Government: Politics of Industrialized and Developing Nations* (Boston: Houghton Mifflin Company, 1981), 13.

2. See James H. Meisel, *Pareto & Mosca* (Englewood Cliffs, NJ: Prentice Hall, 1965), 57-62, and 141-60.

3. David Truman, *The Governmental Process* (New York: Knopf, 1951); see also Jeffrey Berry, *The Interest Group Society* (Boston: Little, Brown and Company, 1984).

4. Gabriel Almond and Sydney Verba, *The Civic Culture Revisited* (Boston: Little, Brown and Company, 1980).

5. Allan Kornberg "Caucus and Cohesion in Canadian Parliamentary Parties," *American Political Science Review* LX (March 1966): 83-92

6. Bernard Crick, *In Defence of Politics* (London: Weidenfeld and Nicolson, 1964), 56.

7. See Patrick Watson and Benjamin Barber, *The Struggle for Democracy* (Toronto: Lester & Orpen Dennys Ltd., 1988), 79.

8. Richard Van Loon and Michael Whittington, *The Canadian Political System, Environment, Structure, and Process* (Toronto: McGraw-Hill Ryerson Ltd., 1981), 630-636.

9. See C.E.S Franks, "Question Period and Debate in the House" in Paul Fox, *Politics: Canada*, 7th ed. (Toronto: McGraw-Hill Ryerson, 1991).

10. Lewis Lipsitz and David Speak, *American Democracy* (New York: St. Martin's Press, 1993).

11. See Leon Hurwitz and Christian Lequesne, eds., *The State of the European Community: Policies, Institutions and Debates in the Transition Years* (Boulder, CO: Lynne Rienner Publishers, 1991); and Alan Cafruny and Glenda Rosenthal, *The State of the European Community, Vol.2: The Maastricht Debates and Beyond* (Boulder, CO: Lynne Rienner Publishers, 1993).

12. See Anton Bebler and Jim Seroka, eds., *Contemporary Political Systems: Classifications and Typologies* (Boulder, CO: Lynne Rienner Publishers, 1990).

13. See Herbert Tillema and John Van Wigen, "Law and Power in Military Intervention," *International Studies Quarterly* 26 (June 1982), 220-250; and Berth Duner, *Military Intervention in Civil Wars: the 1970s* (Aldershot, Hampshire: Gower, 1985); and Eric Nordlinger, *Soldiers in Politics: Military Coups and Governments* (Englewood Cliffs, NJ: Prentice-Hall Inc.,1977).

14. Carl J. Friedrich and Zbigniew Brzezinski, *Totalitarian Dictatorship and Autocracy* (New York: Praeger Publishers, 1956), 9-10; and Boris Kagarlitsky, *The Thinking Reed: Intellectuals and the Soviet Union from 1917 to the Present,* translated by Brian Pearce (New York: Routledge, 1989).

15. Roy Macridis, *Contemporary Political Ideologies* (New York: HarperCollins College Publishers, 1992), 159-186; and Ernst Nolte, *Three Faces of Fascism* (New York: Holt, Rinehart and Winston, Inc., 1966), 3-10.

Suggested Readings

Michael Burgess and Alain-G. Gagnon, *Comparative Federalism and Federation* (Toronto: University of Toronto Press, 1993).

Joseph Camilleri and Jim Falk, *The End of Sovereignty? The Politics of a Shrinking and Fragmented World* (Brookfield, VT: Edward Elgar Publishing Company, 1993).

Michael Curtis, *Introduction to Comparative Government* (New York: HarperCollins College Publishers, 1993).

Gabriel Almond, G. Bingham Powell Jr., and Robert Mundt, *Comparative Politics A Theoretical Framework* (New York: HarperCollins College Publishers, 1993).

Mark Sproule-Jones, *Governments at Work* (Toronto: University of Toronto Press, 1993).

David Judge, *The Parliamentary State* (Newbury Park, CA: Sage Publications, Inc., 1993).

Roy Macridis, *Introduction to Comparative Politics: Regimes and Change* (New York: HarperCollins College Publishers, 1993).

Robert Pinkney, *Democracy in the Third World* (Boulder, CO: Lynne Rienner Publishers, 1993).

Ernest Wistrich, *After 1992: The United States of Europe* (New York: Routledge, 1991).

Peter Woll, *American Government* (New York: HarperCollins College Publishers, 1993).

Glossary

autocratic: The quality of absolute power invested in a single ruler who exercises authority without being accountable to any person or institution.

backbenchers: All of the members of the legislature in the British model of parliament who are not members of the Cabinet or leaders of the opposition parties.

bill: A proposal placed before an assembly that must pass through various stages of scrutiny before becoming law.

black economy: Economic activity that is not recorded in the national income accounts, although it does involve the actual production of goods and services. It is carried out either by barter or for cash that is not declared as income for taxation purposes.

black market: An illegal market created when the demand for a commodity which is controlled and rationed by the state exceeds the legal supply, such that people are willing to pay a much higher price than the controlled price to obtain greater amounts of the commodity.

budget speech: The speech made when the Minister of Finance completes estimates for a financial year.

charisma: An extraordinary set of aptitudes that enables a person to lead and inspire others without the necessity of having formal authority.

checks and balances: The political ideal embodied in the separation of powers, whereby each branch of government serves to limit or check on the powers of the other branches.

civilization: A term that covers the stages of human development made possible by a type of complex society that has achieved an organized and efficient agriculture, and an improved and progressive condition of people living under an organized government with political structures that perform beyond the family or clan.

closure: A device used by the governing party to end debate in the House of Commons and to force a vote.

Congress: The legislative branch of government of the United States federal government, authorized by Article 1 of the Constitution, which creates two houses, the House of Representatives and the Senate.

coup d'état: A sudden political or military action, frequently initiated by people possessing some authority, to overthrow an existing government by force.

cuartelazo: A barracks revolt, used to refer to a military coup d'état.

demagogue: A political leader who takes advantage of social and political unrest by making emotional and prejudiced appeals to the general population for political gain.

division: The process of formal voting in a legislative assembly, committee, or political convention.

empire: A term that originally referred to territory governed by emperors, but that now refers to large areas of land and peoples conquered or coerced by a foreign power.

filibuster: A time-consuming tactic used by legislators to prevent the passage of a proposed bill or amendment by taking as long as possible to delay a piece of legislation.

Hansard: An official record of the daily proceedings of the Canadian House of Commons and the Senate, which is edited, translated, and printed in English and French. Hansard is the name of the printer in England who began preparing reports of parliamentary debates in the eighteenth century.

impeachment: The power of the U.S. Congress to indict a president, or members of the Cabinet and judiciary, by a single majority vote in the House of Representatives, followed by a trial in the Senate, where a two-thirds vote of members present can convict and remove the president from office.

junta: The Spanish word for a council, which usually describes a group of military officers who collectively exercise the powers of the government.

kibbutz: A collective farm in modern Israel.

legal codes: A collection and consolidation of existing statutes and common laws.

militarism: The influence and sometimes predominance of the armed forces in the political and governing life of a nation-state, by holding a veto over a civilian government, intervening in its affairs, or establishing a military government.

non-confidence motion: When a legislative assembly passes a vote of non-confidence in government (ie., the Cabinet), the prime minister and the cabinet must resign and request the dissolution of parliament.

opposition: Members of parliament who do not belong to the government party.

order paper: The daily agenda for the House of Commons.

personalism: A characteristic of governing whereby the personality of the ruler dominates the institutions, structures, and constitutional prescriptions in a political system.

pluralism: The existence of diverse social forces, such as political parties, political action groups, labour unions, social and religious groups, and service clubs.

pocket veto: The U.S. president may refuse to sign a bill passed by Congress within a ten-day period before adjournment.

political succession: The designated constitutional or extra-constitutional methods used to fill vacated offices of government, and to transfer political power within a nation-state.

recognition: An official act, such as the the exchange of ambassadors, that acknowledges the existence of a government and indicates a willingness to engage in formal relations with it in good faith.

republican government: A theory of government held by the founders of the United States that government must be based on popular consent, be limited in its power, protected against the majority, with no monarchical or hereditary institutions.

separation of powers: A major principle of American government whereby governing power is distributed among three branches of government – the legislative, the executive, and the judicial. The separation of lawmaking, the execution of law, law enforcement, and law interpretation is designed to prevent the tyranny of any one branch.

separation of personnel: The officials of each branch of government are selected or elected by different procedures, have different terms of office, are independent of one another and may not retain office in more than one branch of government at the same time.

shadow cabinet: A group of opposition legislators specifically assigned to observe and criticize cabinet ministers.

Speech from the Throne: The traditional opening ceremony for each session of Parliament that outlines the proposals of the prime minister and the Cabinet, and is read by the governor general or the Queen.

standing orders: Established rules and procedures of Parliament, each house having its own, which from time to time may be altered or suspended.

state recognition: The process by which a political and administrative entity becomes an international "person" under international law and is accepted by existing states as a new member of the global community with all legal rights, privileges, and responsibilities.

typology: The systematic classification and grouping of phenomena by class or type.

veto: The U.S. president may reject, and thus "veto" any bill or joint resolution passed by Congress, with the exception of proposed amendments to the U.S. Constitution.

Ways and Means (motions): These are government motions introduced before Parliament imposes a new tax, increases the rate of an existing tax, or extends a tax to include people not already paying tax; the motions also include many of the financial instruments needed to implement a budget in Canada.

SIX

Executives

Mary Robinson, president of the Republic of Ireland

Chapter Objectives

After reading this chapter, you will be able to:

- identify and describe the executive branch of government

- list the resources available to executives in the exercise of their official duties and functions

- describe the general functions of executives

- classify executives

- differentiate and explain the qualities of the parliamentary executive

- outline and describe the components of Canada's ceremonial and political executive

- outline and describe the components of the executive branch of government in the United States

- compare the parliamentary and presidential executives

- profile the executive elements of dictatorship

- describe the characteristics of the executive branch of government in totalitarian regimes

The Powerful Resources of Executives

Of all of the branches of government, the executive is the oldest and the most widely adopted institution. Archaeological evidence in the Middle East indicates that the institution of **kingship** was already well established over 5000 years ago.[1] From the very beginning of human experience with organized structures of government, the executive has been the focal point of political power and effective decision-making. Even today, in the mind of the public, the executive is synonymous with government. Every political system has an executive in which leadership is concentrated in the hands of a single individual or a small elite group. Whether in democratic or non-democratic political systems, executive power is inevitable. In this modern world of few democracies and many **autocracies**, executives have come to be the major and sometimes the sole actors in every organized system of government. This can be explained by the fact that all political executives have access to a wide range of available political resources, usually inaccessible to other branches of government.

■ ■ **kingship:** a society with its political power concentrated in a hereditary king or monarch who rules in the name or guise of the gods or in the tradition of royalty. ■ ■

The Power of Information

One important political resource available to executives is information. Because executives are primary decision-makers, they are privy to classified information flowing from within the country, as well as internationally, from other governments. They know how well or how badly things are going before most of us do. For this reason, executives tend to know much more than either assemblies or judiciaries about what is going on in government. Executives can control, to a great extent, what other participants in government get to know because they generate considerable information themselves and can act in secrecy.

In Canada, the Cabinet exercises extensive control of government information with the assistance of the **Prime Minister's Office (PMO)**, the **Privy Council Office (PCO)** and the **Treasury Board**. Sometimes called the "gatekeepers," these three bodies advise the prime minister and the Cabinet on the advisability and financial feasibility of pursuing a given policy.[2] All administrative and security information is filtered through these offices to the prime minister and the Cabinet. At this level, information is carefully guarded; even backbenchers on the government side of the House must wait for access to information in secret caucus and remain silent according to the written and unwritten rules of party discipline.

In the United States, the president and his appointed Cabinet draw and control vital information from four sources: the **Executive Office of the President (EOP),** the **National Security Council (NSC),** the **Office of Management and Budget (OMB),** and the **Council of Economic Advisors (CEA).** The doctrine of *executive privilege* allows a president to guard secrets in matters of national security, internal bureaucratic discipline, and individual privacy. Even executive decisions can be made within the bounds of secrecy and are accountable only through the works of congressional investigation, journalism, and judicial testimony.

In non-democratic states, executives enjoy a vast amount of information control because they usually are not accountable to a legislature, the media, or the people. They participate in the formation of policy, by which information may be deliberately kept secret, or may be released at the convenience of the state. Befitting Kim Il-Sung's obsession with secrecy, in 1994 North Korean officials waited a full 34 hours before disclosing the death of their "Great Leader." In many nondemocratic states, executives acquire direct or indirect control of the communication facilities and have the coercive powers to destroy all rival centres of information and communication. Usually, military **intelligence** is the major clearing house for political information in a non-democratic state, though this may also be the case in democratic states.

The Power of Organization

A second political resource readily available to the executive branch of government is organization. All executives are surrounded by some form of civil or military bureaucracy, as well as a political party organization.

In Canada, the prime minister and the Cabinet enjoy a virtual monopoly of power over the organization of government. Canada's political executive has instant access to an army of bureaucratic expertise from which to draft and legislate policy. Not only do the PMO and PCO provide essential ex-

pertise for executive decision-making, but the entire public service is also at the disposal of the prime minister and the Cabinet. The political executive can draw upon ministerial staffs, the party structure, and the government caucus for information and advice on policy initiatives.

In the United States, the White House staff is only a small part of the presidential establishment, but it links the president with the vast organizational machinery of American government.[3] Under the numerous agencies of the EOP, NSC, OMB, and CEA, over three million executive-branch employees serve the president. Every year those executive agencies bring forward their new proposals for legislation, both to improve the handling of existing programs and to innovate with new ones. Unlike the Canadian executive, which is fused to the legislative process and thus to the entire bureaucracy of government, the U.S. Congress is a genuinely independent government body, with a separate bureaucracy of its own to serve it. Because the American executive leadership and the congressional bureaucracy do not necessarily work in concert, there is always tension between the president and the other organizations of government.

In autocratic states, executives have much more direct control over the various organizations of government. In the absence of a competitive and accountable political system, non-democratic executives have distinct organizational advantages over their democratic counterparts. The ministries and bureaucracies are implementing agencies, or simply function as legitimators of policy after the decisions have already been reached by the executive.

The Power of Rightful Authority

Another important political resource available to executives is *legitimacy*: the exercise of political authority in a way that is perceived as rightful and is accepted by the members of the political community. One test of legitimacy is the degree of coercion the executive must use against people to achieve acceptance and obedience. As a general rule, the more coercion, the less legitimacy.

No executive can claim to rule on the basis of force alone; such an approach allows equal legitimacy to any dissenting groups or opposing movements. In democratic political systems, executives have legitimacy because they adhere to constitutional principles and follow standard procedures when establishing policy. Judgements about the wisdom or morality of a particular executive decision may vary, but legitimacy goes unquestioned. For example, in Canada, the Cabinet's strategy for reducing unemployment, the national deficit, and debt may leave much to be desired, but most Canadians would still consider as legitimate the budgetary laws passed for dealing with these problems under the current rules. In the U.S., President Ford's decision to pardon former president Nixon for any crimes committed while in office was generally accepted as the legitimate exercise of presidential power, even though most Americans disputed the wisdom, merit, and morality of Ford's action.

Even in dictatorial regimes, executive institutions are protected from the adverse consequences of unpopularity by the appearance of legitimacy. In these types of political systems, legitimacy attaches to executive institutions because people sense that they are firmly established and here to stay. The legitimacy of the executive is not based merely on coercion but is instilled quite early in the lives of civilians through the processes of political indoctrination and socialization. Especially in totalitarian regimes, children are taught early to trust and respect political authority, often symbolized by executives. In these political systems, authoritarian patterns of the family and schools serve to reinforce the legitimacy of the political executive as an institution.

In authoritarian regimes, dictatorial executives have decisive control over government but choose not to control a wide range of social and private behaviour. Thus, executive legitimacy is frequently based on the personal charisma of the leader in the absence of an official ideology to legitimize executive power. Popular support is the predominant source of legitimacy in the modern authoritarian executive; without it even a monopoly of political violence will not prevent a change of power at the top. Legitimacy enables the authoritarian executive to play the largest and most important role in the exercise of political authority. Not only does it permit the executive branch to dominate the process of executing rules, but it allows the executive to exercise an ever-enlarging share in the process of rule-making and rule adjudication, usually exercised by the legislature and judiciary.

Economic Power

Economic power is another major resource often favouring the executive branch of government. Because of their dominance in the structure of government, executives appropriate to themselves a vast share of the economic resources of their country. These resources are available to them through their position in government, the powers of taxation and confiscation, and may also be derived out of the profits of state enterprises. Between 1988 and 1993, former Prime Minister Brian Mulroney's riding of Charlevoix received 327 federal contracts worth over $5 million. In addition, instruments of control, i.e., regulation and nationalization, are available to executives to obtain the financing for their policies or to eliminate the rival centres of economic power in the country.

In Canada's political executive, the Cabinet wields enormous economic power.[4] It is through the Cabinet that revenues are raised, finances managed, and policies planned and legislated within the confines of the budgetary process of government. The Financial Administration Act is the legislation that gives the Cabinet full control of the budgetary process. The Treasury Board, a statutory committee of Cabinet, oversees the economic power of the Canadian government. It advises the Priorities and Planning Committee of the Cabinet about the financial feasibility of government goals. The Department of Finance Canada is the revenue-raising organ of the Canadian executive. Its authority extends over all aspects of the taxation system, and it co-ordinates its efforts with the Cabinet committees directly responsible for the making of public revenue policy.

In the United States, the economic policy of the national government receives its most overt expression in the executive budget. Every year the president makes thousands of decisions to spend or not to spend money on particular projects. Those include dams, environmental programs, urban-renewal projects, highways, airports, university facilities, and numerous other public works. Increasingly, presidential discretion has played a greater

role in deciding where and when a particular project will be implemented. Different presidents have different attitudes about the extent to which political considerations should dictate decisions concerning federal expenditures. Nevertheless, even the most conservative administration will recognize that funding for some categories of projects can be allocated in accordance with political considerations favourable to the executive. Because members of the House of Representatives and the Senate are always eager to obtain federal projects for their constituents, the White House can use this executive economic power – which in some cases is at the sole discretion of the executive branch – to lure favourable votes in Congress.

In authoritarian states, the economic powers of the executive are often corrupted. It is not uncommon to find the highest public officials with their hands deep in the national till, taking public property including land, money, and lucrative concessions through criminal as well as legal activities. In 1992, the International Monetary Fund disclosed that Zambia's former president, Kenneth Kuanda, had stashed billions away in foreign banks. In Latin America, many dictators have taken advantage of their economic powers to amass great personal wealth. Former president of Panama General Manuel Antonio Noriega received millions in kickbacks for the role he played in the illegal cocaine trade throughout the western hemisphere. After he was overthrown in 1955, Juan Perón of Argentina took an estimated $700 million U.S. with which to live luxuriously in Spain. Both Fulgencio Batista of Cuba and Perez Jimenez of Venezuela personally accumulated $250 million U.S. while in office. In Nicaragua, the

Table 6.1:
Types of executives

State	Head of State	Head of Government
Canada	Monarch	Prime Minister
France	President	President
United Kingdom	Monarch	Prime Minister
United States	President	President
Federal Republic of Germany	President	Chancellor
Russia	President	Prime Minister

Somozas came to control over one-fifth of the economy, amassing a family fortune approaching $1 billion U.S. No source of easy money was overlooked. Besides helping himself to a large proportion of funds in the national treasury, Anastasio Somoza Debayle extracted large-scale profits from the funds and supplies sent from abroad after the earthquake that devastated Nicaragua in 1972.

Totalitarian executives exercise economic powers largely through party channels and the state apparatus. In communist regimes, the single most-powerful individual is not a government official but rather the general secretary of the Communist party. The ideological priorities of the highest party officials determine the direction of economic planning and investment in the economy. In political systems such as these, the executive can mobilize the entire resources of the country to achieve its economic goals. These executives wield the decision-making capacity to improve the standard of living and the material well-being of their citizens.

What Executives Do

Even though political styles and organizational structures differ remarkably across the international system, the functions of executive leaders do lend themselves to generalization. In all cases, executive conduct is a product of the political culture; the roles and functions of modern executives are determined by the ways people think about and do politics.

The Role of Symbol and Ceremony

All of the symbolism and ceremony in the executive branch of government is centred on the **head of state**. In Canada, the pomp and circumstance surrounding the formal delivery of the Speech from the Throne rivals the regal splendour of British imperial majesty. The appearance of the president of the United States before a joint session of Congress to deliver the State of the Union Address has the magnificence of a Hollywood spectacular. In most systems of government there is a separation of personnel within the executive into the roles of head of state and head of government (see table 6.1).

There are a number of advantages to having the separation of the head of state and the head of government. For many states it is important to have some office (and the person who occupies it) independent of the deeply enmeshed political battles of government. The head of state transcends the brush-fires of partisan politics and can foster both unity and continuity within the nation-state. In Canada and Great Britain, the reigning monarch or the official representative of the reigning monarch is the living symbol of the state and acts independently in the interests of the community as a whole. The head of state opens Parliament and attends public functions at which the majesty of the state is to be given symbolic or ceremonial representation. When there is an election, or when a government falls, the head of state formally appoints the political executive. In this way the head of state is the transmitter of legitimacy and the personification of the state.

Heads of state like those in Britain, Canada, the Netherlands, and Norway who are seemingly only figureheads, subject to overriding powers of the political executive, often exercise considerable de facto executive power and influence. For example, when there is doubt about who leads a majority party following an election, or when no party commands a majority, the head of state can decide who should be prime minister-designate. In Canada this power ensures that Canadians always have a prime minister, even if it is used to deny a request to dissolve Parliament and initiate an election. This situation occurred in 1925, when Canada's governor general, Lord Byng, refused to grant Prime Minister Mackenzie King a dissolution of Parliament. Instead, he called upon the Leader of the Opposition, Arthur Meighen, to form a new government, because Meighen's Conservatives had gained enough support from former King supporters to permit him to appoint a cabinet.

In political systems in which the ceremonial and political executive are the same person, as in the United States, there is always the risk that the president will use symbolic authority to enhance political power or that involvement in politics will hamper the unifying and ceremonial functions of the executive. In the United States this dual role of the president in the affairs of state *and* government has given the presidency almost continuous media exposure and thus preeminent power among competing political institutions.[5] However, this power can be checked and/or balanced by Congress by means of its ability to override the president on matters of legislation and to scrutinize and check presidential initiatives in the areas of foreign policy and judicial appointments.

Providing Leadership

The executive has evolved to become the locus of leadership in all modern political systems. It is where political power gravitates, concentrates, and disseminates through the various levels of government. The leadership qualities of those entrusted with the destiny of a state can activate every factor of power and extract inordinate advantages from limited resources. There is no question that a society's success or failure, indeed its very survival, depends in large part on the quality and competence of the executive leadership it is able to attract.

In fact, the ability of a single highly placed decision-maker to mobilize other human resources is itself a factor of power. No political leader can do the job alone. Thousands of other people must be included in the process of leadership if the resources of a state are to be used to maximum capacity. The role of the political executive in recruiting other human talent is therefore paramount. Presidents and prime ministers have extensive appointive powers, not just to fill a cabinet, politburo, or judiciary, but to place key personnel in the bureaucratic machinery of the state.

In times of peace or war, the political executive must effectively lead the people and the institutions that constitute a state. In the nuclear age, the role of leadership is particularly crucial because world leaders carry the heavy burden of maintaining international peace, or at least of avoiding nuclear war. Executives in states that possess nuclear weapons hold the fate of all of humankind in their hands: they have the final responsibility for using weapons of global destruction. Ultimately, their decisions reach far beyond their national constituencies.

Even in the realm of domestic economic problems, political leadership has global implications. Executives who do not manage their economies well threaten the security of the international economy. Leaders in states such as Brazil and Mexico can destabilize the economies of the developed world by failing to manage their huge public debts. Similarly, leaders in Canada and the United States can make matters worse for the debt-strapped developing economies by sustaining heavy deficits, thus contributing to huge interest rates that compound the indebtedness of the underdeveloped world.

Making Policy

Executives are the nerve centres of modern government decision-making. Ever since the beginning of organized government, making and enforcing binding rules has been the preserve of the executive branch of government. For centuries, executive political structures functioned without legislatures for making laws.[6]

Not surprisingly, the modern executive is the most important structure of policy-making in all governments around the world. Public policy may be defined in a variety of ways, but it is generally the result of whatever executives choose to do or not to do with the resources available to them. Financing AIDS research, reducing or raising taxes, increasing defence spending, or launching a bill to establish a centre to deal with substance abuse, are all examples of public policies. Nowadays the executive initiates new policies and programs and, depending on the division of powers between the executive and the legislature, has a substantial role in their adoption. Under any system, whether democratic or non-democratic, the executive oversees the implementation of its policies with the assistance of an army of professional administrators.

Often it is only the political executive that can adequately communicate with the general public on questions of public policy. By means of press conferences, statements, speeches in parliament, and frequent exposure on radio and television, the political executive has many opportunities to communicate important information to the public about domestic and foreign-policy issues. These kinds of communications are an advantage to executives seeking public support for their policies and programs.

Supervising the Bureaucrats

Every executive is responsible for implementing legislative decisions and enforcing **court orders**. To fulfill this role, political leaders must supervise the bureaucratic machinery at the national level. In many states, the national bureaucracy is an immense, complicated organization. In the U.S. political system, the national bureaucracy is a multi-layered system of organizations, criss-crossed between the executive and legislative branches of government. The president of the United States has his own administration, separate from Congress, which itself controls a vast bureaucratic machine. In Canada, the federal bureaucracy comes under the supervision of the Cabinet, which manages the various departments of government, boards, commissions, and crown corporations. Here the administration of government is a *fusion* of executive and legislative functions, unlike the *separate* administrations operating in the United States.

In the final analysis, the role of the executive and its administrative bureaucracy is to apply laws, to make sure that the programs of government are put into action, and to enforce statutes. Of course, the executive also initiates programs, as when the minister of finance announces a tax reform or when the prime minister and the minister of foreign affairs embark on new foreign-policy directions for Canada.

Diplomatic and Military Functions

Diplomacy and defence have remained primary responsibilities of the executive branch of government throughout history. Both diplomatic and military matters have always been intrinsically tied to the security of the state, thus requiring the decisiveness and se-crecy of executive decision-making. Diplomats are appointed representatives of the head of state and are, by custom and convention, personifications of the sovereign authority of the executive wherever they are accredited. All diplomats take their directives from, and are responsible to, the political executive. The principal executive powers in the area of diplomacy are those of (a) sending and receiving diplomats, (b) recognizing new governments and establishing or withdrawing diplomatic relations, (c) determining and implementing foreign policy, and (d) negotiating treaties and agreements through normal diplomatic channels and at the summit level. In fact, in most states, tradition, constitutional interpretation, and decree have established the head of government as the sovereign power in foreign affairs, making this person the chief diplomat. In Canada, depending on the importance of a particular foreign-policy matter, either the prime minister or the minister of state for foreign affairs fulfills such a role.

In all states where there is a military, the control of the armed forces is an exclusive function of the executive. In some states, the military accepts a distinctly subordinate position to the civilian chief executive, whether president, prime minister, party chairman, or monarch. In other states, there is virtually no distinction between the highest-ranking members of the military and the executive branch of government. On matters of internal security or foreign involvements, the executive can summon the legitimate physical force of the military to protect the interests of the state.

Canada's Department of National Defence is one example of armed forces under civilian control. At the top of the organizational scheme of Canada's armed forces is the minister of defence, who is chairperson of the Defence Council, which meets once a week with its mixed staff of civilian and military advisors. The minister must answer to Parliament for everything involved in the operation of Canada's defence and peacekeeping forces. That means being prepared to investigate the conduct of Canadian peacekeeping troops, as in Somalia in 1993, where Canadians were charged with the beating death of a Somali citizen. Or it involves defending the purchase of military helicopters in the face of cutbacks in social programs. In the United States, the president acts as as commander-in-chief of the armed forces. The U.S. Constitution vests in the president extensive military powers for preserving internal order and defending the country against external aggression. To these ends, the president may decree partial or total mobilization of the armed forces to cope with a serious internal or external threat.

Judicial Functions

In the judicial realm, many political executives have assumed or have had conferred upon them extensive authority. Usually in accordance with the constitution, the executive is required to oversee the general administration of justice and to guarantee its impartiality and fairness to all citizens. That is why one of the most important judicial functions of the executive is the power to appoint judges. The chief executive is charged with enforcing the law by ensuring that judicial decisions are carried out. Executives are responsible for the operation of the courts and must make sure that the judges selected comport themselves with dignity and that their official conduct reflects their national responsibilities.

Among the important judicial powers, an executive is usually authorized to grant **pardons** and **reprieves**, both as a means of preventing possible judicial malpractice and in the spirit of justice and mercy. Another executive judicial power is the granting of **amnesty** – a blanket pardon extended to large groups, usually political offenders and conscientious objectors. Less than 24 hours after taking the oath of office, President Jimmy Carter granted an amnesty to the U.S. military deserters of the Vietnam War.

In some states, a blanket executive amnesty for illegal immigrants has been a useful tool. It allows governments to grant a large number of people a swift change of status, thus avoiding costly and lengthy proceedings, and addresses the problem of illegals filtering into the economy. Since World War II, Canada has offered seven partial immigration amnesties, allowing, in effect, more than 140,000 people, who would not have qualified as refugees, to jump to the head of the immigration lines.

Classifying Executives

We will focus on four classifications of the executive branch as the most salient aspect of modern government. Executives in the principal modern states may be classified under these four types, corresponding to the governmental systems discussed in the last chapter: parliamentary and presidential executives as they appear in democratic, authoritarian, and totalitarian systems of government. Within these classifications, the methods of selection, tenure in office, and public accountability of executives vary enormously. But these broad generalizations enable us to recognize the important differences among the various types of executives in the world.

The Parliamentary Executive

The parliamentary executive is the most widely adopted form of democratic leadership. It is used by most of the world's political democracies: Australia, Austria, Belgium, Canada, Denmark, Finland, Germany, Iceland, India, Ireland, Israel, Italy, Japan, Luxembourg, Netherlands, New Zealand, Norway, Sweden, and the United Kingdom.

In these states, the executive is divided into two parts: a head of state and a head of government. The main political function of the head of state is to appoint the head of government, usually the party leader who wins a national election. The powers of the head of state are essentially formal, although many governments entrust this person with the authority to protect and defend the political system. The head of government is the more important politically. Whether called prime minister, premier, or chancellor, he or she is the leader of the majority party in the parliament or a person able to form a coalition that will sustain the *confidence of the House.* The political executive chooses the cabinet, which is a collective body politically responsible to the parliament. Theoretically, parliament is supreme over the executive. But no matter what constitutional documents may say about their fusion of powers or legislative supremacy, the executive is de facto the essence of government and the embodiment of authority. The legislature may have critical functions, but its position is always defined by its relationship to the executive.

The Executive in Canada

The Constitution Act, 1867 (Section 9) affirms that executive authority is vested in the Queen and exercised by her appointed representatives, the governor general and the lieutenant governors. In 1947, the legitimizing authority of the Queen was delegated to the governor general, but it was not effective until 1977. However, in practice, the governor general usually plays only a passive executive role by following the advice of the prime minister and the Cabinet. In actual fact, the governor general is acquiescing to the will of the Canadian electorate when they give one party a majority of seats in the House of Commons.

Governor General

Under the Canadian Constitution, the governor general has the right to be consulted, to advise, and even to warn the political executive if they abuse their powers. Considerable differences of opinion may be found concerning the advantages of the Crown as a formal appendage to executive government in Canada. But a brief summary of the duties of the governor general indicates the significance of the office as both a formal and effective part of Parliament: (a) The governor general summons, **prorogues**, and **dissolves** Parliament; (b) the governor general appoints the prime minister and the Cabinet and swears them into office; (c) the governor general signs all bills, conferring **royal assent** before they become law; (d) the governor general must be advised of and signs all **orders-in-council** issued by the Cabinet; (e) the governor general signs a *Letter of Credence,* which serves to introduce Canadian ambassadors, and accepts similar credentials of ambassadors and high commissioners appointed to Canada. As the personification of the Crown, the governor general is above all political affiliations and is in a position to represent and speak for Canada at home and abroad.

Notwithstanding the legal supremacy of the formal executive over the political executive in Canada's Constitution, the office of governor general has essentially become symbolic and ceremonial by custom and convention. Although the monarch may do so from time to time, the governor general usually delivers the Speech from the Throne at the opening of each session of Parliament. As the representative of the head of state, the governor general accepts the credentials of diplomats, entertains other heads of state and political executives, bestows honours and awards on Canadians, and generally embodies the majesty of the Canadian state. Hence, this person is a symbol of the unity and continuity of Canadians.

The **Letters Patent** of 1947 provides for the replacement of the governor general should this person die, become incapacitated, or be absent from the country for a period of more than one month. The replacement is the chief justice of the Supreme Court of Canada, and if that post is vacant, the senior *puisne* (lower-rank) justice is appointed as the administrator of Canada, assumes all of the formal executive powers, and serves until the governor general can return to office.

While the position of governor general is the oldest continuous institution in Canada,

■ ■ **crown:** reference to the composite character of sovereign power in a monarchy and a symbol of the institutions of state as with crown law, crown lands, crown courts, crown office, crown debts, etc. ■ ■

reflecting Canada's evolution from colony to independent nation-state, Canadians have been appointed to the office only since 1952. By 1990, of the 23 governors general, only six had been Canadians. History has shown that the importance of the office largely depends on the personal dynamism and esteem of the incumbent.

The office of governor general has never had the full support of Canadians.[7] One reason for this is a lack of public awareness of the significance and role of the **Crown** as a functional institution in the Canadian political system. A poll conducted by Data Laboratories Research Consultants found that 42.5 percent of Canadians identified the prime minister as head of state.[8] Some 14.3 percent named the governor general as head of state, and 36.7 percent recognized the Queen as head of state. Another reason is the reluctance of many French-speaking people in Québec and other parts of Canada to identify with the symbolism of the British Crown.

Queen's Privy Council

Another feature of Canada's formal executive is the Queen's Privy Council (Section 11, Constitution Act, 1867). Originally a private advisory body to royalty, privy to the secrets of the Crown, the Privy Council evolved to become the legal precursor of the modern-day Cabinet. The Cabinet is not mentioned in the Constitution and thus has no legal existence whatsoever apart from the fact that it forms a committee of the Privy Council. In order to transfer constitutional legality from the formal executive to the political executive in Canada, members of the Cabinet are sworn into office as members of the Privy Council. So the government of Canada is a committee of the Queen's Privy Council. Accordingly, Cabinet decisions are issued as "orders in council." The Privy Council has survived as the formal machinery through which the prerogative powers of the sovereign are exercised.

The Privy Council is made up of all present and former Cabinet members, regardless of party affiliation, and other persons appointed by the governor general on the recommendation of the prime minister. People appointed to the Queen's Privy Council in Canada serve for life. Members include people of distinction such as the Duke of Edinburgh, the Prince of Wales, and even a British prime minister. Hence, we find that in the 1990s there are over 100 members of the Privy Council, yet the Cabinet ranges in size from only 20 to 40 people. Even though former Cabinet ministers remain Privy councillors for life, by constitutional custom they may not advise the government of the day. The full Privy Council meets rarely, usually to honour a visit by the Queen or other members of the Royal Family in the Privy Council Chamber in the East Block of the Parliament Buildings.

Canada's Political Executive

The political executive in Canada consists of both parliamentary and bureaucratic components. Within the framework of Parliament, the executive is the prime minister and the Cabinet who are elected to *govern* the coun-try; these people are responsible and accountable to Parliament and the Canadian public. They are assisted by the Prime Minister's Office (PMO) and the Privy Council Office (PCO), which serve both to advise and administer the affairs of government at the highest levels.

The Prime Minister

The focus of leadership and political power in Canada culminates in the prime minister and the Cabinet, which derives its legality and legitimacy through the House of Commons and by constitutional convention and custom. The prime minister is uniquely powerful because of his **prerogative** to call an election, to gain public visibility, to instruct the formal executive, to lead a political party, to form a government, and to build a federal consensus among the premiers.[10]

The authority to advise the dissolution of the House of Commons at any time is an important strategic power enjoyed by the prime minister. The political careers of all members of parliament are challenged by an election. Consequently, the timing of an election is crucial. Usually, the prime minister will go to the polls when the government party enjoys a safe margin of popularity over the opposition parties. Sometimes what appears to be a propitious decision to call an election turns against the prime minister, and members of the prime minister's party bear the brunt of bad judgement. Such was the fate of the Liberals in Canada, for example, when John Turner decided to call a snap election in the summer of 1984. The Liberals were enjoying an 11-percent lead in popularity over the Conservatives, but won only 40 seats in that election, down from 147 in 1980. And John

Turner earned the dubious distinction of serving the second-shortest term in office as prime minister after Sir Charles Tupper, who governed for only 69 days in 1896. At other times, a prime minister has very little option concerning when to call the election, either because the government has been defeated or because the five-year limit on Parliament has come due. Such was the case for Kim Campbell when she called the election that led to the dramatic defeat of her government in October 1993 as the five-year Parliament was ending.

■ ■ **prerogative:** an exclusive right inherent within an office or position that may be constitutional or may have developed out of custom and tradition. ■ ■

Another dimension of executive power flows from the fact that the prime minister tends to dominate public perceptions of national politics. In Canada, everything about a prime minister seems to be a source of fascination to the mass media – what the PM has for breakfast and dinner, how the PM spends leisure time, what the PM's spouse does, the prime minister's tastes in decorating 24 Sussex Drive, and what pets the prime minister might have. This extremely high level of visibility can be an important and powerful political resource. But by the same token, the singular visibility of the prime minister so dominates public perceptions of the political world that every action – casual or official – occupies a crucial place in the emotions of the public. This high visibility and role of political leader means that the PM is held accountable when things go wrong, regardless of any actual responsibility for them. By the same token, the prime minister will sometimes take credit for events when it is not deserved.

Usually, however, the prestige of the office can be used by the prime minister in a highly personalized way to gain political advantage. Standing at the centre of Canadian politics, the prime minister can steal the show from most political opponents by capturing the lion's share of news and other media coverage. No matter how narrow the electoral margin that brought the government to power, the prime minister will find that many Canadians approve of what is done simply because the prime minister does it.

One of the most distinguishing features of prime ministerial power is the unique relationship this person has with the formal executive. The prime minister is the sole link between the formal and political executives. *Only* the prime minister can advise and instruct the governor general to prorogue and dissolve Parliament. It is the prime minister who formally recommends those who are appointed to the Privy Council and the Senate. It is also the prime minster who connects the Cabinet, and indeed, Parliament, with the governor general. Thus, on the initiative of the prime minister, constitutional legitimacy is transferred from the formal executive to the political executive.

The power of the prime minister is also enhanced by the fact of leading a political party, usually one with a majority of seats in the House of Commons. Because the prime minister is seen by the governing party as the architect of electoral victory, i.e., the person who tied the party to the reins of political power in Canada, the PM is usually in an impregnable position within the party. As a rule, the rank and file are highly supportive of a successful leader.

The party caucus can be a much more critical body because it consists of some of the prime minister's rivals for office. But by virtue of his or her powers to appoint party faithfuls to rewarding positions in the public and diplomatic service, as well as to the bench, the prime minister is able to command the loyalty of the caucus. In addition to the Cabinet, the heads of crown corporations, deputy ministers, and other key mandarins in the public service are among more than 4000 Canadians appointed under the authority of the prime minister. The people surrounding the prime minister are among the most influential on Parliament Hill, and their ranks always include friends and advisers who helped during the election campaign. In the House of Commons, party discipline places the prime minister at the apex of the apparatus of government. As government leader, the prime minister has control over the political futures of the party's elected members. The prime minister can fire recalcitrant members who are serving as parliamentary secretaries or refuse to assign them to committees. Others who oppose the prime minister or violate the norms and expectations of the party face the possibility that their nomination papers will not be signed in the next federal election.

The possibility of transforming **backbenchers** into ministers and vice versa is a continuing asset of the prime minister in the process of encouraging undisputed party loyalty and support. In addition, the Senate has long been treated by the prime minister as a place to put political workhorses out to pasture. The great majority of Canadian senators have their posts because – and only because – of prior loyalty to the prime minister.

Cabinet-Making

We have yet to account in full measure for the conventional prerogatives of the prime minister. Nothing demonstrates the strength in the office of the chief political executive so forcefully as the power to form a government by appointing a cabinet. As an organization in its own right, the Cabinet is the executive council of the Canadian government, the key decision-making forum for initiating laws and policies, raising and spending public monies, and acting as a source of advice to the prime minister pondering major decisions.

The prime minister chooses who will enter the Cabinet, how large a body it will be, and the extent to which individual cabinet ministers will exert influence on the direction of public policy in Canada. It has been said that the prime minister is the first among equals (*primus inter pares*) in relations with his Cabinet colleagues. But no Canadian Cabinet has ever operated as a body of individuals equal in power.

Many factors affect the prime minister in determining the size and composition of the Cabinet. One is the mood of the country and within the PM's party about whether the government, as presently constituted, is too big or too small. Since John A. Macdonald's first 13-member Cabinet in 1867, Canada had, by the 1990s, evolved one of the largest cabinets among the democratic states of the world. Since the 1970s, the wholesale growth of governmental responsibilities prompted the enlargement of the Cabinet. Trudeau's largest Cabinet had 37 ministers, nine more than the largest convened under Pearson. Under John Turner, the size of the Cabinet was reduced to 29, the same number of ministers as in the short-lived Clark government.

But the largest Cabinet in Canadian history was assembled by Brian Mulroney in 1984; it totalled 40, including the prime minister, selected from among 210 Tory MPs. After the 1988 federal election, Mulroney's Cabinet consisted of 39, including the prime minister, drawn from 169 Progressive Conservative MPs. Kim Campbell, who pledged to reduce the size and temper of government, reduced the size of her Cabinet to 25 ministers. Jean Chrétien formed his Cabinet of 23 ministers following the federal election of October 1993.

Another factor of major importance for the prime minister when forming the Cabinet is the principle of *representation*. Today, the general political parameters a prime minister must follow in striking a cabinet roster cut across economic, geographic, gender, linguistic, political, and social criteria. In some cases, the choices for representation with major portfolios are well signalled. There is always the difficulty of forming a truly national government. This means that, to the extent it is possible, every province or region should be allocated at least one cabinet minister. When this is not possible because representatives have not been elected to the governing party's caucus from every province, the prime minister sometimes appoints senators to the Cabinet to represent these provinces, or gives a minister from a neighbouring province special ministerial assignments in a province with no government representation.

To complicate the job of making a representative government along provincial and regional parameters, every effort must be made by the prime minister to include people who represent the business community, native Canadians, women, representatives from a variety of religious groups, and those of French and other non-English origins. John A. Macdonald once said: "Like any cabinet-maker, I do the best I can with the lumber you furnish me."

The Cabinet must be representative of women, who make up over fifty percent of Canada's population. In 1984, Mulroney named a record six women to his first Cabinet from the 28 elected nation-wide, doubling the previous record of three. However, these six women comprised only 15 percent of the Cabinet. Prior to these appointments, only eight women had ever sat around a Canadian Cabinet table. Women were given some tough portfolios, including external relations, energy, mines and resources, and the environment, a signal that when women are elected with the right credentials, they do not have to sit as backbenchers. In 1989, Mulroney's first cabinet shuffle again included only six women, selected from 39 elected to a larger House of Commons. His successor, Kim Campbell, had five women, including herself, in her Cabinet, and Jean Chrétien appointed four women to his Cabinet.

There is also an obvious political or partisan dimension to cabinet-making. The prime minister may place heavy emphasis on loyalty in the selection, drawing on personal memory of early campaign and convention supporters. Leadership candidates at party conventions are often able to win cabinet appointments because of the politics at the party convention, where their supporters and delegates may have been helpful to the victory of the prime minister.

Having appointed the ministers to the Cabinet, as well as to its standing committees, the PM retains a large amount of authority and power over their political destinies. By means of the cabinet shuffle, the PM can promote the most loyal and promising ministers or demote those whose performance is less than satisfactory. Sometimes a prime minister will appoint an *interim cabinet* to finish old parliamentary business before making more permanent appointments. Such was the case with Prime Minister Kim Campbell, who produced an interim cabinet reduced in size from 38 to 25 ministers to complete parliamentary business before the election was called in October 1993. The principle of *cabinet solidarity* ensures that collectively the Cabinet is one with the prime minister and that recalcitrant ministers will either acquiesce to the corporate will of the government or resign.

Traditionally, ministers appointed to the Cabinet were assigned **portfolios** to head a major government department. In fact, only the prime minister and the government leader in the Senate were appointed without portfolios and did not and still do not carry any departmental responsibilities. Today, the only other administrative responsibility of the prime minister is the Privy Council Office.

The Ministries and Ministers of State Act 1970 (revised 1985), places the present designation of cabinet ministers into five categories.[9] The first are the ministers of regular government departments, such as Minister of Finance Canada. The second designation is for ministers who are assigned parliamentary responsibilities without heading a department or ministry, such as House Leader. The third category includes ministers

■ ■ **portfolios:** the office and duties of a cabinet minister who is in charge of a government department. Some portfolios are "senior," such as the ministry of finance, and they co-ordinate their vast responsibilities with a "junior" portfolio, such as the ministry of state for finance. ■ ■

of state who are assigned a junior portfolio, such as junior finance minister. The fourth category is for ministers of state appointed to assist a regular minister, such as the minister of state for science and technology under the Department of Industry, Science and Technology. The last category consists of ministers without a portfolio appointed as undesignated ministers of state who are assigned to assist a minister with a portfolio.

Even among the various ministries, a pecking order exists beneath the prime minister. Historically, the Departments of Finance, Justice, and Foreign Affairs wield much more influence in the inner circles of Cabinet than do Communications or Fisheries and Oceans. The prime minister chairs the plenary Cabinet and its most important Priorities and Planning Committee. As such, he or she is the co-ordinator and arbitrator of the executive decision-making process, in particular in relation to government spending. Priorities and Planning and the Treasury Board exercise the exclusive power to authorize any government spending on new programs or to expand spending on current ones. The powerful co-ordinating position of the prime minister in the Cabinet keeps this person as the political nerve-centre of government. He or she can expand or reduce the size and number of cabinet committees, as did Kim Campbell in 1993 when she decreased the size and number of committees from 11 to five.

No coalition of political forces can match a prime minister's power. Becoming a Canadian prime minister means more than being the country's top politician. Prime ministers inevitably get pushed into becoming keepers of the national conscience. Custom and precedent have vastly multiplied a prime minister's powers to include making major appointments, leading the provinces, and being the final arbiter on the ministerial budgets. As the only person capable of making a government once Canadians have decided who goes to Ottawa, the prime minister must aim above all else to provide the political glue for national unity.

The Prime Minister's Office (PMO)

In Ottawa, the initials PMO are a synonym for power.[11] They refer to the Prime Minister's Office, the partisan political staff that advises, schedules, briefs, represents, and runs errands for the prime minister of Canada. Located in the Langevin Block near the Parliament Buildings, this executive support agency protects and promotes the personal and professional interests of the prime minister. The prime minister has appointed his or her most loyal and trusted advisors to this executive body. On a personal level, they boost the prime minister's ego and shield the PM from enemies and the incursions of the media. Correspondence to the prime minister can reach as much as 300,000 pieces per week. The correspondence unit of the PMO is kept busy receiving, answering, and filing mail.

On matters involving the prime minister's professional role, the staff assists in everything from drafting the Speech from the Throne and other speeches to guiding the prime minister through the maze of political and bureaucratic hurdles confronting executive leadership in Canada. The PMO collaborates with the Privy Council Office to develop a national policy framework, including a public relations strategy for the government. The PMO is therefore a practical policy think-tank charged with an advisory capacity on the political fortunes of the prime minister and his cabinet. On a daily basis the PMO answers the prime minister's mail, schedules his appointments and invitations, and keeps a close watch over the patterns of popularity and unpopularity that affect the political executive.

Thus, the PMO supports the prime minister in carrying out the role demanded of a head of government and of a leader of a political party and member of parliament. Its political staff provide advice on policy development and patronage appointments affecting every area of Canadian government.

The Privy Council Office (PCO)

One executive body formally attached to the Privy Council is the Privy Council Office (PCO).[12] The role of the PCO has evolved from that of a body responsible for dealing with the occasional formalities of the Privy Council to a major policy-advising agency of the federal government. It is a department of government that provides public-service support to the prime minister and the Cabinet. Under the direction of the Clerk of the Privy Council and Secretary to the Cabinet, the PCO helps the Cabinet to facilitate the smooth and effective operation of the Government of Canada.

The Privy Council Office is staffed by career public servants. These are people who are recruited from other government departments and serve in the PCO for a limited period, after which they leave for positions in other departments. This rotational policy brings new expertise into the PCO on a regular basis and enables its staff of over 300 to effectively brief the prime minister, the plenary cabinet, and its sub-committees on the activities of the government and matters of national policy.

By comparison with other government departments, the PCO is a small organization. Its restricted size means that it can provide direct support to the prime minister and the Cabinet, avoiding the duplication of expertise and activities found in other government departments that support ministers in carrying out their portfolio responsibilities.

As the Cabinet secretariat, the PCO sets cabinet agendas, takes minutes at cabinet meetings, and transmits cabinet decisions to the bureaucracy: The PCO arranges the meetings, circulates agendas, distributes documents, provides advice to each chairperson on committees and records cabinet decisions. It works with departments of government to prepare ministerial proposals for the Cabinet to consider and keeps government departments informed about what the Cabinet has decided. The PCO also ensures that Orders in Council and other statutory instruments are promulgated throughout the government.

The Treasury Board

The Treasury Board, like the Cabinet, is formally a committee of the Privy Council, headed by a cabinet minister who is called the President of the Treasury Board. Until 1966, the Board's functions under the jurisdiction of the Department of Finance were to act as an overseer of the budgetary process of government, ensuring that public funds were being spent only on authorized government projects. Today, as a separate government department,

the Treasury Board not only keeps track of current and projected expenditures, but with its large secretariat, it operates as a board of management for the government, providing highly influential advice in both financial management and the overall personnel management of the public service. The financial management of contemporary government priorities and objectives would be chaotic were it not for a central monitoring agency like the Treasury Board. By means of a management system, such as the Policy and Expenditure Management System (PEMS), the Treasury Board can apply controls on the spending demands of federal departments as each ministry tries to gain a greater share of the government budget.

The Presidential Executive

The modern presidential type of chief executive began with the U.S. Constitution of 1787. In spite of its great success in the United States, it has not been as widely embraced as has the parliamentary type of executive. The presidential executive is most commonly found in Latin American states because of their historical links with the American experience. It has also been installed by Liberia and the Philippines, as well as in some of the newer African states like Burundi, Mali, and Nigeria. Sri Lanka adopted the presidential executive in 1978, as did Guyana in 1980. While a growing number of states have adopted this type of executive, many of its advantages have not been widely recognized. The presidential executive establishes a solid and stable centre of power in the executive branch, an advantage particularly appropriate to newer states requiring a strong democratic

Figure 6.1:
The Electoral College: state and district delegations

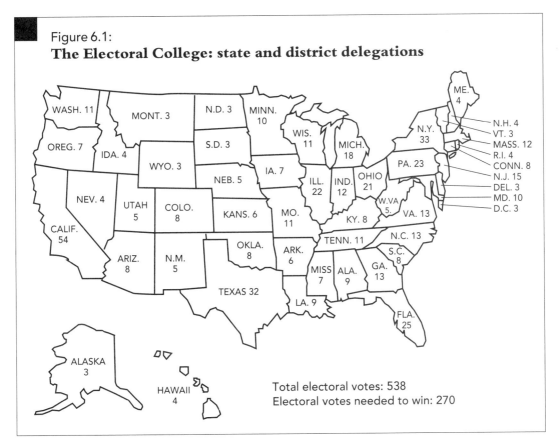

Total electoral votes: 538
Electoral votes needed to win: 270

central government. The presidential system provides that the head of state, who is also the head of government, is elected for a definite term of office. The president has the entire country as a constituency and is independent of the legislative branch of government. The president acts as the official ceremonial head and as leader of the government that proposes, directs, and enforces the state's public policies.

The U.S. President

In the United States, the president is indirectly elected by an electoral college for a fixed term of four years. In the electoral col-

lege, each state has a number of electoral votes equal to the size of its *congressional delegation*, the number of House representatives and Senators: e.g., California 54, New York 33 (figure 6.1). If a presidential candidate wins a *plurality* of votes in a particular state (i.e., one or more votes over any opponent), he or she also wins all of the electoral votes for that state.

Of a total of 538 electoral votes, 270 are required to elect a president.[13] The largest states are hotly contested during a presidential election because they yield the greatest number of electoral votes. Thus, a minimum winning coalition of states needed to secure 270 electoral votes and win the presidency could be California, New York, Pennsylvania, Illinois, Texas, Ohio, Michigan, Florida, New Jersey, Massachusetts, and Wisconsin.

In 1984, Ronald Reagan won 525 electoral votes and his opponent, Walter Mondale, won only the District of Columbia and the state of Minnesota, giving him 13 electoral college votes. In the 1988 presidential election, George Bush did not match the enormous landslide of his predecessor but took 40 states for 426 electoral votes against Michael Dukakis who won only ten states and the District of Columbia for a total of 112 electoral college votes. In 1992, Bill Clinton defeated George Bush by winning 370 electoral votes to Bush's total of 168. Ross Perot, who ran as a third presidential candidate, won no electoral votes.

According to the twenty-second amendment of the U.S. Constitution, adopted in 1951, "no person shall be elected to the office of President more than twice." Once elected, the only legal way a president can be removed from office is through the process of impeachment. By a simple majority vote, the House of Representatives can vote to **impeach** the president as well as other members of the executive. Once this happens, the Senate convenes as a court, chaired by the chief justice of the Supreme Court, to weigh the evidence for and against the president. It takes a two-thirds majority of the Senate to convict the accused. The only president in U.S. history to stand trial before the Senate was Andrew Jackson in 1868. However, the Senate failed to convict him by one vote.

■ ■ **impeach:** the power of the U.S. Congress to remove the president, the vice-president, federal judges, and other federal employees from office if they are convicted for treason, bribery, or other high crimes. ■ ■

To qualify for holding the office, a presidential candidate must be a "natural-born" citizen, at least 35 years of age, and have held residency in the United States for 14 years. If a president is impeached and convicted, dies, resigns, or is incapable of performing the duties of the office, the presidency goes to the vice-president, then, in order of succession, to the Speaker of the House of Representatives, the president *pro tempore* of the Senate, and then to cabinet members.

The U.S. Constitution briefly enumerates the executive authority of the president in general terms: that he "shall take care that the laws be faithfully executed" and that he shall "take an oath to preserve, protect and defend the Constitution." Provision is also made in the Constitution for the president's relations with the other branches of government. From time to time the president must give Congress a report called the "**State of the Union Message,**" and may recommend policies and programs for its consideration. The president is authorized to call special sessions of Congress, and most bills and joint resolutions passed by Congress must be signed by the president. Some exceptions are joint resolutions, which are rarely signed; a president may decide not to sign a bill and it may well die unless the veto can be overridden by a two-thirds vote in each house.

In the United States, the work of the federal executive is conducted by 13 departments and a host of non-cabinet agencies such as the Central Intelligence Agency (CIA) and the Federal Trade Commission (FTC). Each department is headed by a *secretary*, appointed by the president and confirmed by the Senate. Thus, there is a secretary of state, of commerce, of treasury, and so forth. The president, the vice-president, and the secretaries make up the *cabinet* in American government. From election day in November to Inauguration Day on January 20, a president or president elect has about 11 weeks to select a cabinet and form the next administration.

As in Canada, the term "cabinet" does not appear in the Constitution, but any parallels drawn to the Canadian Cabinet, which plays a major leadership role in Canada's political life, would be totally misleading. Nevertheless, all presidents since George Washington have had one. The American cabinet is *not* the executive council of government. Its meetings are infrequent, brief, and often superficial. Most presidents use cabinet meetings to inform their secretaries of new directions in the strategies of the executive and to inform one department what other departments are doing. For actual consultation on policy matters, presidents use hand-chosen advisors. Traditionally, only one or two members of the president's cabinet have a significant advisory function. For the most part, the cabinet is chosen to satisfy different factions in the president's party, i.e., the secretary of labour is usually someone associated with organized labour and the secretary of commerce is a prominent business person.

One expert on the American presidency, Richard Neustadt, has written that "a President is many men or one man wearing many hats."[14] There are several major roles that any president must carry out: head of state, head of government, party leader, chief legislator, commander-in-chief, and chief diplomat.

As the *head of state*, the president is the central figure in the elaborate ceremonial life of the country. The president speaks and acts on behalf of all of the people and is the foremost symbol of the political community. It is the president who greets foreign dignitaries in the name of the United States, makes the annual State of the Union Address, opens a national arts centre, and proclaims National Codfish Day. In so doing, the president shows that he is the personal embodiment of the United States of America.

In sharp tension with his ceremonial role as head of state, the president is also *head of government*. As chief of the executive branch of government, the president controls a vast portion of the federal bureaucracy. Because of the separation of powers, he does not have full control of the permanent civil service, but he does have considerable influence over it. In the United States, the federal civil service consists of over three million people.

In addition to appointing the cabinet, the president appoints approximately 8000 people and through them supervises and directs federal policies in the complicated network of the federal government. These "president's people" link the executive with the other branches of the federal bureaucracy and are crucial appointments for the success of any administration. So important are these appointments to the executive control of government that modern-day presidents establish special personnel-selection teams to search for loyal and qualified individuals. The president guides the operation of government through the cabinet, the White House advisors (also known as the Domestic Council), the Executive Office of the President, and the Office of Management and Budget. The National

Security Council plays a similar role with respect to foreign policy. As head of the government, the president steers the other branches of government in the direction of the administration's policies.

The tensions between the ceremonial and political functions of the president are especially evident in the role of *party leader*. As partisan leader, the president leads one political faction of the country against all others, yet as the head of state, the president must represent and unify all factions. Since the president has such vast powers of appointment and is the leader of a successful political party, it is not surprising that top-level policy-making positions will be offered to members of the president's own party. Party patronage is used to reward those who have been loyal to the president, a loyalty expressed as campaign contributions or other influential support that enable an individual to win the party's presidential nomination, and then the presidency itself.

In addition to job patronage, the party expects its leader to take the lead in raising campaign funds and to endorse and campaign on behalf of party candidates at the national, state, and local levels. Hence, it is always difficult for the American chief executive to appear above politics as the embodiment of the lofty aspirations of the state, yet at the same time to be politically responsible to the party.

Closely associated with the president's role as party leader is that of *chief legislator* – proposing a legislative program and urging Congress to pass it. What is distinctive about the U.S. political system, unlike most parliamentary democratic governments, is that executive leadership and the legislature do not necessarily work in concert. Often, the policy views and political interests of these two independent institutions are not identical. Each year numerous executive agencies come forward with the president's proposals for legislation, both to improve the administration of existing programs and to create new ones. Not all members of the president's party will automatically vote for what is proposed, but the executive program will definitely be a partisan focus for the party's congressional membership.

The president will make use of every available power to influence and gain the support of Congress. All congresspersons are interested in directing the highly desirable patronage appointments of the president to their own political supporters. They know that the **pork barrel** in Washington will contain lucrative federal projects for their constituents. In addition, Congress does take note of the popularity of the president when considering executive requests, although it often ignores such requests. But by appearing on television, a president can gain the support of millions of Americans in a single speech. And when all else fails, the president can exercise the executive veto. Sometimes, this alone is enough to persuade Congress to frame its legislation to the president's liking.

■ ■ **pork barrel:** the public treasury that is drawn on by public officials legislating out of special interests for their constituents or for their own political image. ■ ■

The Military and Diplomatic Power of the President

One constitutional power of the president that has great significance far beyond the national boundaries of the United States is that of *commander-in-chief*. Since 1776, presidents of the United States have involved their country in six "undeclared wars" and in 128 instances – including Lebanon and Grenada in 1983, the Persian Gulf in 1988 and 1992, and Somalia in 1993 – U.S. presidents have ordered the armed forces to take military actions abroad without obtaining prior congressional authorization.

However, the president can only act alone as commander-in-chief for a limited time when military action is initiated. In order to continue military actions abroad, the president requires congressional co-operation to engage the armed forces and use public funds. The Vietnam experience demonstrated that once a president commits U.S. troops into combat, Congress is expected to support the executive decision by providing personnel and funds for the continuation of the military operation.

The War Powers Act of 1973 requires that if a president commits armed forces anywhere without a declaration of war, a written report must be submitted to Congress within 48 hours of any such commitment. Under these circumstances, the armed forces must terminate their mission within 60 days after the president reports to Congress unless Congress (1) declares war; (2) authorizes a continuation of the use of armed forces; or (3) cannot convene because of an armed attack against the United States.

Both tradition and constitutional prescription have established the president as the *chief diplomat*. The Constitution outlines the foreign-policy responsibilities of the president to "make treaties," to "receive ambassadors and other public ministers," and to exercise "the Executive power." But the Constitution requires that treaties need the support of two-thirds of the Senate and that the appointment of diplomats needs the advice and consent of the Senate.

More importantly, the power to declare war is a joint legislative and executive responsibility. The executive power allows a president to enter into an agreement with a foreign executive and bypass treaty procedures that require Senate approval. Executive agreements have been routinely formulated by presidents since World War II in Europe, Asia, and Latin America.

By tradition, the president has acquired many foreign-policy powers. Unlike the Congress, the president is in "continuous session" and international events happen quickly, requiring an immediate executive response. The president is always poised to act, aided by huge intelligence operations and instant contact with a network of embassies and consulates spread throughout the world. The options open to the chief executive with respect to world affairs range from the use of summit diplomacy (when international urgencies demand the president's participation), to the deployment of military forces anywhere on the globe.

Much of the history of the United States – its highest and lowest points – has been written largely as a result of the political behaviour of its presidents. More than other executives, the president of the United States can alter world history. In the words of William Young, "The President of the United States of America is, without question, the most powerful elected executive in the world."[15]

The Authoritarian Executive

The formal constitutional framework for most authoritarian executives today fictitiously appears as a "democratic," "parliamentary," or "presidential" system.[16] What the constitutions may prescribe is one thing but the practice of executive power is sometimes quite another. In all authoritarian states, instead of being constitutionally limited and responsible, the executive so far overshadows the other branches of government that for all practical purposes, the president or prime minister *is* the government. "L'état c'est moi," boasted Louis XIV of France; in all authoritarian states, the executive comes close to being a twentieth-century version of that French monarch.

One of the key characteristics of the authoritarian executive is the dominance of the individual person, often a charismatic leader, in the political and government system. Political power is highly *personalized* (in the interests of the leader) rather than institutionalized (in the interests of the state), often despite constitutional guarantees to the contrary. Other centres of power exist besides the ruler, sometimes acting as a check on the extensive powers of the political executive. Such institutions as the church, the military, economic organizations, the bureaucracy, and political parties are often sources of restraint on arbitrary government. However, the power relations among these groups are manipulated or controlled by the ruler, so that none of them is able to establish an independent position of power or threaten the dominant position of the executive.

The most common form of authoritarian executive today is military rule, already well entrenched in the Latin American region and now appearing increasingly in the newer states of Asia, Africa, and the Middle East. In this type of executive, a military *junta* (or council) collectively exercises executive powers. Juntas are usually made up of three ranking officers of the army, navy, or air force who preside over the executive branch of government following a successful coup d'état.

Regardless of whether the executive appears in the civilian or military mode, the powers of the authoritarian president or prime minister are great – far greater than in most democratic states. In many cases, the executive exercises a broad collection of legislative, administrative, and judicial powers. Included among these many powers is the authority to issue decrees, form a cabinet, make administrative and judicial appointments, declare a state of siege, suspend the constitution, command the military, control finance and public revenues, grant pardons, and intervene in local government.

One very important power of the authoritarian executive is the authority to issue decrees. Decrees are laws issued by the executive rather than passed by the legislature. The decree power gives the executive supraconstitutional legislative authority because decrees have the same legal standing as congressional laws, and give a dictator the powerful option to bypass the legislature or to neutralize the electoral process.

Authoritarian executives cannot run a

national administration single-handedly. Next in importance to the president or prime minister are ministers, who act as chief advisors and oversee the various administrative departments of government. Collectively they constitute the cabinet. In selecting a cabinet, the executive takes into account such human virtues as loyalty, dependability, and competence. But in all authoritarian regimes the main criterion for executive appointment is trustworthiness. The cabinet must be made up of trusted confidants and advisors; the very life of the dictator depends on their loyalty and faithful performance of duty. The chief executive may frequently make changes in the cabinet for reasons of political expediency. Frequent personnel changes have a definite psychological impact on the citizenry, showing them who is unquestionably the boss, thus reinforcing and maintaining the strong centralized power of the chief executive. Often dictators will change the composition of their cabinets as a housecleaning strategy aimed at restoring public confidence and asserting the legitimacy of the government.

Within the framework of authoritarian government, the chief executive has virtually unlimited power to appoint administrative and judicial officials. In the appointment of high officials such as ambassadors, ministers, judges, and ranking officers of the armed forces, many constitutions require that the choice of the chief executive be approved by a senate, or some other body. This approval is more fictitious than real; authoritarian legislatures tend to be weak and ineffective as a check on the leader and instead function as bodies that give unquestioned support to executive initiatives.

Easily one of the most important powers of the authoritarian executive is the authority to proclaim a *state of siege*, also known as the suspension of constitutional guarantees. This emergency power is used when the state is threatened by a foreign invasion or by serious internal disorder. Military governments may declare a state of martial law, which is similar to the state of siege, the main difference being that under the latter the civilian police and regular organs of civilian government continue to function, while under martial law, civilian control is replaced by that of the military. This special emergency power grants extraordinary powers to the president or prime minister and authorizes the executive to take drastic steps that affect all aspects of national life. The president or prime minister can divert a larger portion of the national budget for military purposes and indefinitely suspend the private rights of citizens that may be guaranteed by the constitution. In recent years, martial law has been declared in Algeria, Burma, Guyana, South Korea, and Haiti in order to crush democratic uprisings in each country. And only four weeks before South Africa's history-making democratic elections in April 1994, President de Klerk declared a "state of emergency" in Natal and its apartheid-created homeland KwaZulu, granting authorities unlimited powers to arrest without warrant, to search and seize, to ignore court orders, and to prevent the media from reporting events.

Yet another area in which authoritarian executives enjoy unique powers is internal *intervention*. Intervention is the coercive action undertaken by the national government in the affairs of subnational units, particularly in federal states, as well as in the financial institutions, the judicial system, and the media.

The practice among federal states varies, but intervention can be extensive, such as the replacement of state and provincial governors, legislators, and other officials whom the president deems a challenge to national executive authority and national autonomy. Intervening actions have taken place in such states as Nigeria, Rwanda, Senegal, Guatemala, El Salvador, and Peru, where traditions of autocratic decision-making permit presidents and prime ministers to ruthlessly change political leadership at all levels of government. Authoritarian executives also have very broad powers over the financial institutions of the state. Under this unusual grant of power, a president or prime minister can authorize a new monetary system, reorganize the structure of financial institutions, and modify the banking system. Often, drastic measures are taken by dictators in order to appease foreign bankers and international lending institutions, such as the International Monetary Fund. It is not uncommon in authoritarian states to see the executive interrupt the process of justice, to pack the courts with supportive judges, or to simply ignore the judicial branch of government. Dictatorship almost invariably plays havoc with judicial independence.

Finally, in authoritarian states, the president or prime minister represents a serious threat to the media. In almost all cases, authoritarian executives strongly resist the critical scrutiny of a free press. Restrictions on the freedom of the press are usually imposed by decree, ostensibly under the authority of the constitution. Under Nigeria's sweeping press law, the military has virtual control over all news media operating in the country. According to its provisions, the government is protected from a critical media; even if the truth of allegations is proved, an editor, publisher, or writer can be censured or jailed.

The Totalitarian Executive

The models of the totalitarian executive have been produced historically in fascist and so-called communist states.[17] In today's international system, the fascist model is no longer present and there is a much closer correspondence between dictatorial or "communist" states and totalitarianism, although these states have been dramatically reduced in number since the disintegration of the Soviet empire.

Still, executive power in those remaining communist states is exercised mainly through party channels. The executive authority of the party, which is the distinguishing trait of communist regimes, initiates and co-ordinates the major decision-making and policy directions of the state. The state's bureaucracy is subordinate to the party executive. It is the instrument the political executive uses to enforce and administer party policy through the government ministries.

Many communist states are headed by a collective executive, called a *politburo* or *presidium*, as in Cuba. Some are headed by a *council of state*, as in China. These collective bodies are made up of high-ranking state officials headed by a chairman who sometimes also serves as head of state.

In communist political systems, the party and the state apparatus are constitutionally and organizationally distinct but they overlap in personnel, thus interlocking the power of the communist party with the bureaucracy of the state. This fusion of party and state authority is represented at the highest levels in the politburo, presidium, or council of state.

There is no question that this is the most important executive decision-making organ in totalitarian socialist states. Members of this body are elected by a majority vote of the party's central committee, an unwieldy plenary committee of the party membership. Whatever the degree of executive power, the Communist party in all communist societies controls and co-ordinates government activities; it exercises "sovereign" authority. Thus, the executive organ of the party dominates the executive structure of government and the policy process. However, the formulation of policy, normally the preserve of the cabinet in democratic systems, is really the province of the party elite in communist states.

In many communist states, it is *only* the party and *not* the government that issues directives and administrative orders that have the weight of law. Thus, the basic executive function of the top party leadership is to control a complex and interlocking network of bureaucratic and governmental structures, enabling a small group of people to control society.

This reality illustrates a characteristic tendency of communist political systems to concentrate executive power in the hands of one or a very few dictators. The leader or leaders then often become the embodiment of the state apparatus and the continuing revolution, as has been demonstrated in such executives as Castro in Cuba, Mao Tse Tung in China, Kim Il-Sung in North Korea, Enver Hoxha in Albania, Ho Chi Minh in Vietnam, Tito in the former Yugoslavia, and Robert Mugabe in Zimbabwe. All these people initiated the revolutions that brought communist or socialist totalitarian rule to their states.

One of the important differences between totalitarian and authoritarian dictators is that the former are less inclined to subvert the aims of the party for personal reasons and ambitions. While the "cult of personality" does surface in communist states, political power still tends to be institutionalized more than it is personalized. Many communist ideologues may adulate a particular leader, but their allegiance and loyalty remain with the ideological ideals of state institutions and organizations to achieve goals at some future time.

References

1. David Rodnick, *An Introduction to Man and His Development* (New York: Appleton-Century-Crofts, 1966), 53-64.

2. See Marc Lalonde, "The Changing Role of the Prime Minister's Office," *Canadian Public Administration* 14, no.4 (Winter 1971), 487-537; Robert Adie and Paul Thomas, *Canadian Public Administration* (Scarborough, ON: Prentice-Hall, 1987), 224-227.

3. Edward Greenberg and Benjamin Page, *Struggle for Democracy* (New York: HarperCollins College Publishers, 1993), 430-431.

4. David Smith, "The Federal Cabinet in Canadian Politics" in Michael Whittington and Glen Williams, *Canadian Politics in the 1990s* (Scarborough, ON: Nelson Canada, 1990), 359-379.

5. Milton Cummings Jr., and David Wise, *Democracy Under Pressure* (Fort Worth, TX.: Harcourt Brace Jovanovich College Publishers, 1993), 366-367.

6. Michael Curtis et. al., *Introduction to Comparative Government* (New York: HarperCollins College Publishers, 1993), 1-26.

7. Ronald G. Landes, *The Canadian Polity* (Scarborough, ON: Prentice-Hall Canada Inc., 1987), 95-98.

8. "Canadians think the Queen is just fine," *Weekend Magazine*, (October 2, 1977), 4; see also, "The Queen's Eroding Role," *MacLean's*, (June 15, 1992), 32.

9. Robert Adie and Paul Thomas, *Canadian Public Administration* (Scarborough, ON: Prentice-Hall Canada Inc., 1987), 213-233.

10. Leslie Pal and David Taras, eds., *Prime Ministers and Premiers: Political Leadership and Public Policy in Canada* (Scarborough, ON: Prentice-Hall Canada, 1988).

11. Marc Lalonde, "The Changing Role of the Prime Minister's Office," *Canadian Public Administration* (Winter 1971), 509-537.

12. Gordon Robertson, "The Changing Role of the Privy Council Office," *Canadian Public Administration* (Winter 1971), 487-508; *The Privy Council Office* (Ottawa: PCO, 1991).

13. Theodore Lowi and Benjamin Ginsberg, *American Government* (New York: W.W. Norton & Company, 1993), 248-309.

14. Richard Neustadt, *Presidential Power* (New York: New American Library, 1964), viii.

15. William Young, *Essentials of American Government* (New York: Appleton-Century-Crofts, 1964), 251.

16. Roy Macridis, *Modern Political Regimes* (Boston: Little, Brown and Company, 1986), 212-278.

17. Anton Bebler and Jim Seroka, *Contemporary Political Systems: Classifications and Typologies* (Boulder, CO: Lynne Rienner Publishers, 1990), 270-277.

Suggested Readings

Herman Bakvis, *Regional Ministers: Power and Influence in the Canadian Cabinet* (Toronto: University of Toronto Press, 1991).

C. Campbell and M.J. Wyszomirski, (eds), *Executive Leadership in Anglo-American Systems* (Pittsburgh: University of Pittsburgh Press, 1991).

Stephen Clarkson and Christina McCall, *Trudeau and Our Times*, 2 Vols. (Toronto: McClelland and Stewart, 1990 and 1992).

Mattei Dogan and Dominique Pelassy, *How to Compare Nations* (Chatham, NJ: Chatham House Publishers, 1990).

Jeffry Elliot and Sheikh R. Ali, *The Presidential-Congressional Political Dictionary* (Santa Barbara, CA: *ABC-CLIO*, 1993).

Larry Gerston, *American Government* (New York: Wadsworth, 1993).

David Judge, *The Parliamentary State* (Newbury Park, CA: Sage Publications, Inc., 1993).

John Laschinger and Geoffrey Stevens, *Leaders and Lesser Mortals* (Toronto: Key Porter Books, 1993).

Glossary

amnesty: An executive determination that an entire class of people shall not be prosecuted or will be, because of special circumstances, exempted from the application of the law.

autocracy: A form of government in which power is held by a single person unencumbered by legal or other restraints.

backbencher: An elected member of parliament who does not hold office under the Crown, i.e., is not a cabinet minister.

Council of Economic Advisors (CEA): An executive office agency established in 1946 to analyze the U.S. economy, advise the president on economic programs, and recommend policies for economic growth.

court order: The direction of a court or judge that commands a party to do or not to do something in particular.

crown: Reference to the composite character of sovereign power in a monarchy and a symbol of the institutions of state as with crown law, crown lands, crown courts, crown office, crown debts, etc.

dissolution (of parliament): To terminate a parliamentary term that is followed by a general election.

Executive Office of the President (EOP): The office containing the major staff organizations of the president, such as the White House Office and the Office of Emergency.

intelligence: Information strategically gathered by a government about the capabilities, strengths, weaknesses, and intentions of other states, international organizations, terrorist groups, and others, including corporations and individuals.

impeach: The power of the U.S. Congress to remove the president, the vice-president, federal judges, and other federal employees from office if convicted for treason, bribery, or other high crimes and misdemeanors.

kingship: A society with its political power concentrated in a hereditary king or monarch who rules in the name or guise of the gods or in the tradition of royalty.

Letters Patent: An official document permitting a person or a corporation authority from the government to do some act or exercise some right.

National Security Council (NSC): An executive office agency charged with advising the president on matters related to national security.

Office of Management and Budget (OMB): A federal agency, created in 1970, within the executive office that replaced the Bureau of the Budget which was formed in 1921 to handle the preparation of the annual budget.

orders in council: Laws and decrees passed by the Cabinet without reference to the House of Commons.

pardon: An executive annulment of a penalty already prescribed.

pork barrel: The public treasury that is drawn on by public officials legislating out of special interests for their own constituents or for their own political image.

portfolio: The office and duties of a cabinet minister who is in charge of a government department. Some portfolios are "senior," such as the ministry of finance, and co-ordinate their vast responsibilities along with a "junior" portfolio, such as the ministry of state for finance.

prerogative: An exclusive right inherent within an office or position that may be constitutional or may have developed out of custom and tradition.

Prime Minister's Office (PMO): An executive agency of government that functions as a source of advice to the prime minister on policy matters and matters related to public opinion concerning the government.

Privy Council Office (PCO): An executive government agency to advise on government matters and to communicate and co-ordinate cabinet decisions with relevant officials.

prorogue: To end a parliamentary session that is not followed by a general election.

public policy: The culmination of the whole political system from which governmental actions or inactions are directed at a society's goals, priorities, and problems, based on the human and physical resources available to decision-makers.

reprieve: The executive postponement of the carrying out of a sentence.

royal assent: The final step in the passage of a bill, whereby the Crown accepts and signs it into law.

State of the Union Message(U.S.): The annual presidential message to a joint session of Congress, provided for in Article II, Section 3 of the Constitution, in which the president reports on current problems and proposes his legislative initiatives.

Treasury Board: A statutory committee of cabinet charged with overseeing the budgetary process of government.

SEVEN

Legislatures

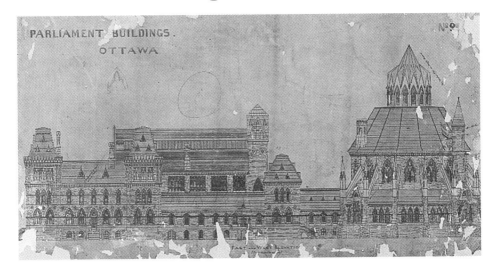

Thomas Fuller's plans for the original Parliament buildings

Chapter Objectives

After reading this chapter, you will be able to:

■ distinguish between the legislative and executive branches of government

■ explain the various features of legislative assemblies, such as size and tenure

■ understand the concepts of fusion of powers and separation of powers

■ distinguish among and explain unicameralism, bicameralism, and tricameralism

■ outline and compare the functions of democratic and non-democratic legislatures

■ describe the features of Canada's legislative assemblies

■ identify and describe the functions of the chief legislative officers of the House of Commons

■ discuss the role of committees in the legislative process

■ distinguish between the legislative functions of the Canadian Senate and the House of Commons

■ recount the process of how a bill becomes law in Canada

■ outline the federal legislative process in the United States

■ compare how bills are passed into law in Canada and the United States

■ describe the functions of legislatures in dictatorships

Assemblies

Compared with the executive branch of government, the legislature is a relatively new creation among political institutions. The only legislature to survive to the present without changing its earliest forms is the British Parliament. Dating back to the eleventh century, the English legislative structure has become the prototype of the modern legislature, inspiring many variations on the parliamentary model, even among authoritarian and totalitarian regimes. When William of Normandy conquered England in 1066, he imposed Norman feudal institutions on his new subjects. These included the *Curia Regis*, an assembly of nobles to advise the king, and the *Curia Regis Magnae*, a large assembly of lesser nobility that met three times annually to counsel and present petitions to the king.

Over time, English kings summoned this Great Council with increased frequency. Made up of knights, burgesses, and members of the clergy, the council met separately from the barons' *Curia Regis* to advise the king and approve taxes for projects that affected their constituencies. Eventually, this body of advisors came to be the House of Commons and the assembly of nobles became the House of Lords. Originally, neither institution was intended to be democratic and autonomous. But by the nineteenth century, the British Parliament came to symbolize modern democracy.

Most modern states have developed a legislative branch of government consisting of bodies of elected or appointed individuals called parliaments, congresses, assemblies, diets, or chambers. A small number of absolute monarchies, such as Oman and Saudi Arabia do not have some kind of legislative assembly. Kuwait suspended its National Assembly in 1986, and is now ruled by an emir, who appoints a prime minister and a cabinet. In all other states, the role and function of the legislature are determined by the type of political system, i.e., whether that system is democratic, authoritarian, or totalitarian. It is significant that despite the character of a regime, nearly all modern nation-states find it necessary to maintain some form of representative assembly either as an effective lawmaking body or as a symbol of government legitimacy. Even in the most repressive regimes, the legislature contributes to the formal proclamation of the law by lending popular endorsement to the lawmaking initiatives of the executive.

Number of Legislative Chambers

Parliamentary bodies can be *unicameral* (one chamber), *bicameral* (two chambers), or *tricameral* (three chambers). Today, unicameral national assemblies outnumber bicameral assemblies by a ratio of three to two.[1] On the eve of World War I, most of the world's political systems had bicameral national assemblies. But as new nation-states emerged, more and more political systems adopted the unicameral form of legislature. The largest number of unicameral legislatures is found in Africa, Asia, Central America, and the Middle East. One-house assemblies can also be found in homogeneous nation-states with democratic traditions, such as Denmark, Finland, and New Zealand. Even in those states with bicameral national assemblies, many of the subnational legislative bodies are unicameral: for example, the Diets (*Ländtage*) of the *Länder* in

Start

Germany, Canada's provincial legislatures, those of the states of India, and that of the state of Nebraska in the United States. In 1994, South Africa's parliament abandoned its tricameral structure and adopted a bicameral legislature consisting of a National Assembly and a Senate.

Democracies and Bicameralism

Approximately two-thirds of all democratic governments have bicameral legislatures.[2] The centre of political power is always located in the "lower house," which tends to have a larger elected membership and shorter terms of office. Examples of such houses are, the Canadian *House of Commons,* the *Assemblée Nationale* of France, the Swiss *Nationalrat,* and the U.S. *House of Representatives.* The second chamber, customarily called the "upper house," usually has the smaller membership, longer tenure, and is selected in different ways. For example, the members of the Canadian Senate are appointed by the governor general on the advice of the prime minister and must retire at age 75. In the United States, senators are elected in state-wide constituencies for six-year terms. In contrast, members of the Austrian Bundesrat are elected by the legislatures of the various *Länder* (lands).

One justification for bicameralism in democratic federal states is that it permits a system of dual representation for the constituent parts of the union. This certainly applies in democracies such as Australia, Germany, Switzerland, and the United States. But in Canada, the traditionally inferior legislative role of the Senate to the House of Commons has diminished its ability to effectively represent regional and provincial interests, as originally intended.

Another asserted advantage of bicameral legislatures is that they prevent the concentrations of legislative power in one assembly and provide a second forum for deliberating legislation. In democracies, a second chamber is considered to be a necessary conservative influence, a place for sober second thought that reduces hasty or impulsive decision-making in a lower house. In the United States, the Senate performs this conservative function with respect to the House of Representatives. But as a deliberative body it also has important checks on the initiatives of the president, with its power to confirm presidential appointments and ratify treaties the president signs.

In some states the second chamber is particularly well suited for advising the lower house, as does Germany's Bundesrat (upper house), whose members are state government members advising the Bundestag (lower house) of ramifications of national legislation on the *Länder.* In Canada, the upper house has considerable legislative powers on paper, and, although it is limited by its non-elective character from conducting any effective legitimate deliberation in the lawmaking process, it has delayed and even killed legislation. Generally, however, the Canadian Senate, as presently mandated, functions as a house of formal reward for party stalwarts who have paid their political dues. Accordingly, as the Canadian Senate demonstrates, the mere presence of a second chamber is no guarantee that bicameralism is functional or even appropriate to fulfill the representative needs of state and country.

But two chambers can be particularly adaptive to multi-ethnic and multinational states because the legislatures provide political representation of these special groups. Some-

Table 7.1:
Size and tenure of national assemblies (selected nation-states)

Nation-State	Legislature(s)	Size	Term
Botswana	National Assembly House of Chiefs	40 8	5 years appointed
Canada	House of Commons Senate	295 104	5 years appointments to age 75
China	National People's Congress	2978	5 years
France	Assemblée Nationale Senate	577 321	5 years 9 years
Indonesia	House of People's Representatives	400	5 years
Japan	House of Representatives	512	4 years
United States	House of Representatives Senate	435 100	2 years 6 years

times an upper chamber is a power concession made to special groups in order to reduce political tensions. Bicameralism can provide actual and symbolic concessions to special groups. In Switzerland, the Council of States provides representation to four linguistic groups: the German, French, Italian, and Romansch.

Why States Choose Unicameralism or Bicameralism

There are no hard or fast rules to explain why a particular state adopts a unicameral, bicameral, or tricameral legislature (such as Croatia's *Sobar*). Legislative structure depends on the traditions, needs, and goals of a political system or regime. Some states, such as Vietnam, have adopted unicameral legislatures for ideological reasons, one being that "the will of the people must be one." In these states, a second chamber is associated with the privilege of the bourgeois capitalist state. In authoritarian regimes, the unicameral legislature facilitates centralized political control and functions as a rubber stamp for the actions and policies of the dictator.

But there can be any number of reasons why it is expedient for a political system to use single or multiple chambers in the legislative process. For reasons of efficiency and the centralization of decision-making, Sweden reduced its bicameral parliament to a single chamber in 1971. Pakistan reverted from unicameralism to bicameralism in 1973, as did

233

Spain in 1977, when its new bicameral parliament, the *Cortes*, was constituted.

Size and Tenure of Assemblies

The size of most legislatures is determined by *constituency* representation as it relates to total population. Some legislatures use a system of *functional representation,* whereby people are represented according to occupations rather than according to where they live. For example, in Ecuador's upper house, senators represent occupational groups in agriculture, commerce, industry, journalism, and labour. Similarly, the 60-member Irish Senate (*Seanad Éireann*) employs functional representation: 11 members are nominated by the prime minister, six are elected by universities, and 43 are elected from special panels of candidates representing the public services and other interests such as the arts, languages, literature, agriculture, banking, labour, and industry. In Indonesia, the 400-member House of Representatives has 300 elected representatives and a functional group composed of 100 representatives who gain their seats from the support of professions, occupations, and the military.

But most legislatures follow the principle of **representation by population**. As a general rule, as population varies so does the representative size of legislatures. In Canada, under federal law, independent three-member commissions in each province redraw constituency boundaries approximately every ten years. Using data from the 1981 census, the size of the House of Commons was increased by 13 seats from 282 to 295 effective July 13, 1988. The new boundaries gave Ontario an increase of four seats to 99, Alberta increased by five seats to 26, and British Columbia increased by four seats to 32. The total number of MPs from each of the remaining provinces and the Yukon and the Northwest Territories remained unchanged. But within each province, the boundaries of many constituencies were redrawn to adapt to population swings while producing ridings with roughly the same number of electors.

Many less-populated states in Africa, Asia, and Latin America have lower houses with fewer than 100 members. For example, the National Assembly of Botswana has 40 members, the House of Representatives in Gambia has 42 members, Gibraltar has only an 18-member House of Assembly, and El Salvador's National Assembly elects just 84 members. Another large group of states such as Austria, Colombia, Mexico, and Venezuela have legislatures with between 100 and 200 members. Canada, with its 295-member House of Commons, falls into a group of states with relatively larger lower houses. The more populous states tend to have lower houses ranging in sizes from 400 to 3000 members: Germany's Bundestag has 662 members, China's National People's Congress has 2978 members, Great Britain's House of Commons has 635 members, Japan's House of Representatives has 512 members, and the United States House of Representatives has 435 members.

Most upper chambers have fewer members than lower houses. Paraguay's Senate has 36 members, Canada's Senate has 104 members, and the Senate of France has 321 members. This is usually because most upper houses exercise regional representation and represent larger constituencies than does the lower house. There are some notable exceptions to the upper house having fewer members than

Table 7.2:
The high cost of Canada's parliaments

Parliaments	Budget/1992	Population	Cost per Capita
House of Commons	$229,350,000	27,023,100	$8.49
Senate	43,489,300	27,023,100	1.61
Newfoundland	6,752,700	571,700	21.91
Prince Edward Island	2,542,100	129,900	29.67
Nova Scotia	7,648,600	897,500	18.62
New Brunswick	6,602,000	725,600	19.20
Québec	76,000,000	6,811,800	21.26
Ontario	129,131,700	9,840,300	23.22
Manitoba	9,749,800	1,092,600	19.02
Saskatchewan	14,435,700	995,300	24.60
Alberta	23,346,717	2,501,400	19.43
British Columbia	24,711,000	3,185,900	17.86
Northwest Territories	9,209,000	54,000	180.64
Yukon	2,196,000	26,500	91.43

Source: Robert Fleming, *Canadian Legislatures, 1992: Issues, Structures and Costs*
(Agincourt, ON: Global Press, 1992), p.70

the lower house. One is the case of the non-elective British House of Lords, which has nearly twice the number of members as the House of Commons. The size of the membership of the British upper house is based on peerages created by the sovereign without limit of number. They are held for life and may or may not be hereditary.

Like size, the length of legislative terms in lower houses varies considerably. The United States House of Representatives has a two-year term; Australia, Mexico, New Zealand, and Western Samoa have legislatures with three-year terms; Canada, Great Britain, France, Ireland, Italy, and South Africa all have five-year legislative terms; a term of six years is found in India, the Philippines, and Sri Lanka.

Many upper chambers differ in tenure from their legislative counterparts because of the divergent systems of representation and the sometimes different ways of selecting representatives for upper houses and lower houses. Members of upper chambers are selected by **appointment**, **indirect election**, or **popular election**. In the United Kingdom and Luxembourg they are appointed for life. In some other states they are appointed by the head of state on the advice of the head of government for limited terms, as in the Bahamas, Canada (to age 75), and Jamaica. Indirect election is conducted in Austria, France, and the Netherlands, for fixed terms. Directly elected upper chambers are found in Australia, Colombia, Italy, the United States, and Mexico.

Problems with Large Legislatures

It is normally more difficult for large legislatures, like those in China, Great Britain, Japan, and the United States, to deliberate complicated issues and to reach a collective decision easily. In most democratic states, even if all other commitments (serving constituents, ceremonial functions, studying community problems, electioneering, and political party work) allowed time enough for legislators to meet and deliberate, no one of them could be reasonably informed about the variety of matters that require legislative action. How, for instance, can a Canadian MP become sufficiently knowledgeable so that he or she can deal in quick succession with legislation on air safety, tariff policy on textiles, immigration quotas, and a fishing treaty with the United States? Most legislative leaders are aware that the larger the legislature and the more complicated the issues, the less likely the legislature as a body will deal effectively with them.

Large legislatures are also very expensive. They require vast sums of taxpayers' money to meet the expenses of individual members'

pensions, of travel to and from their constituencies, staff and research, of renting offices, and buying computer and other technological equipment, the costs of television and other media broadcast expenses, and other housekeeping costs involved in the legislative process.

The Role of Legislative Committees

Larger legislatures delegate the drafting of legislation to small groups of legislative experts. As a way of coping with the complex lawmaking process, many legislatures have established *committee systems*. In Canada, committees of the House of Commons were in place since Confederation but did not function in a efficient way until the 1960s; in the United States, a much longer history of **standing committees** and **subcommittees** have been the response to complex congressional matters.

Today in Canada and the United States, committees and subcommittees conduct a decisive amount of legislative work. Policies are shaped, interest groups heard, and legislation hammered out. Standing committees are the permanent committees that consider bills and conduct hearings and investigations. They constitute the heart of the committee system because they have an ongoing role in the legislative system. They perform the valuable function of division of labour and specialization. No legislator can hope to know the details of hundreds and sometimes thousands of bills introduced in a parliament or congress. They must rely on the expert knowledge that members of committees gather in their consideration of the bills before them. Once a committee has approved a bill, other members of the legislature generally assume that the committee has considered the legislation carefully, applied its expertise, and made the right decision after all is considered.

As a result of using committees to consider bills, legislators specialize in various fields, such as transportation, gun control, the media, health or education. Sometimes they become more knowledgeable in their areas than the public servants who administer the laws. Although committees usually process legislation, they perform other tasks, such as educating the public on important issues by means of hearings and investigations. Finally, many scholars argue that a legislative body should have some forum where members of competing political parties can resolve their differences. Committees serve this purpose; they are natural arenas for political bargaining and legislative compromise.

Functions of Democratic Legislatures

Because legislatures are a product of a unique political culture found in every polity, they differ in organization, power, and structure. Independent legislatures, exemplified by the Congress of the United States, reflect a tradition of institutional competition in the lawmaking process. Some legislatures are weaker than others, such as in Great Britain and Canada, where Parliament is dominated by majority parties that control all cabinet posts. Many legislatures are captive, as in many nondemocratic states, where real power is solely an executive exercise and the legislature serves primarily to legitimize executive decisions. But whether they are democratic or non-democratic institutions, whether they are independent, weak, or captive, legislatures perform similar functions in a political system. They represent people, formulate, initiate, and enact laws, control public finances, check the executive, adjudicate on executive behaviour, and amend constitutions.

Representation

Hanna Pitkin defines representation as "representation, that is, making present of something absent – but not making it literally present. It must be made present indirectly, through an intermediary; it must be made present in some sense, while nevertheless remaining literally absent."[3] That is precisely what a legislature does. It makes present an authorized sample of the population representing all the rest, who must remain absent from the decision-making process of society. In Canada, the average number of constituents each member of parliament represents is about 92,000.

Legislatures are a political compromise between the principles of "perfect" democracy (direct popular participation in the lawmaking process) and the realities of indirect representation in modern complex nation-states. Because there is no way for entire societies to assemble, deliberate, debate, and decide, we compromise our commitment to these principles by instituting representation by which a select group of people meet and decide on the issues of the day, but are ever conscious of the interests and preferences of those who sent them to the meeting.

Many variables come into play as influences on those who represent us (table 7.3). Such characteristics as the size of the legislature affects members' ability to speak on behalf of constituents. Party discipline can cause

Table 7.3:
Some influences on the behaviour of representatives

- Size and tenure of the Legislative Assembly
- Type of electoral system used in elections
- Member's own values and beliefs
- Values and beliefs of constituency voters
- Party discipline
- Other members of the Legislative Assembly
- Members of committees and subcommittees and their staffs
- Member's staff
- The executive branch of government
- Interest groups
- National and subnational party leaders
- The media

a representative to vote as a partisan party member, sometimes at the expense of the wishes of constituents. One important influence on the quality of representation is the electoral system that elects or appoints representatives. Proportional representation permits legislatures to represent on the basis of the percentage of popular support. Thus a party that earns 25 percent of the popular vote can expect to hold approximately 25 percent of the seats in the legislature. In Canada, an electoral system based on plurality permits a candidate to win a seat in the legislature by simply gaining one or more votes than an opponent. If this occurs in many ridings it is possible for our representatives to win a majority of parliamentary seats with less than a majority of popular support.

Representative assemblies have proved to be enormously popular as government decision-making instruments in Canada. In addition to Parliament, we have provincial legislatures, town and city councils, school boards, and various regional boards and commissions. Today about a quarter-million Canadians hold office as elected representatives. In Canada, representative institutions have diffused well beyond formal government. No political ideal, with the possible exception of majority voting, is so deeply a part of Canada's political culture as is the institution of representative assemblies.

In modern democratic legislatures, representation is based on three principles: *authorization*, *accountability*, and *responsibility*. Authorization means that a representative is one who is given the right by a constituency to act on its behalf. Accountability means that representatives are responsible to the people by means of elections, **initiatives**, **referenda**, **petitions**, **recall**, **public-opinion polls**, and **roll-call voting** in legislatures. Responsibility is the way the representative acts. Some argue, as Edmund Burke did, that true responsibility is acting in the best interests of the constituency, regardless of whether **constituents** agree with the actions of the representative. Burke defended a representative's independence of judgement and action. Once elected, the Burkean representative is responsible for the whole interest of the nation and empire, and owes to his or her constituents only good judgement, freely expressed. Others argue that true responsibility means that representatives should act as their constituents want them to act, even if they disagree on personal, professional, and political grounds.

■ ■ **private-member's bill:** a bill introduced by a member of parliament who is not a minister. ■ ■

Making Laws

In most democratic legislatures, the formulation and initiation of policy has become an executive function.[4] Australia, Canada, Great Britain, and other parliamentary systems operate legislatures that *fuse* executive and legislative powers according to the majority principle: the political party or coalition that enjoys the support of a majority of seats in the legislature forms an executive that drafts and initiates legislation. These "government" bills are introduced by a minister. Then, as a body, the legislature debates and enacts government bills into law. As a general rule in parliamentary democracies, any member whether on the government or opposition side may introduce a bill. But the success rate of **private-members' bills** is extremely low because of the urgency of government bills and the power of the executive to mobilize disciplined party support to push their program through the legislature. In fact, for this reason, some states do not permit individual legislators to introduce bills of their own. For example, in the German *Bundestag* (lower house), individual members who want to initiate a bill must form a *fraktion* (a group of at least fifteen members) before the bill can be introduced. This guarantees that there is a group of legislators who are supportive of the bill and that there is the possibility that others can be converted to supporting the proposition.

Increasingly, in the United States, *law initiation* originates in the executive branch, where one of many agencies drafts a proposal and finds a sympathetic legislator to introduce the bill in Congress. But even in the U.S. political system, unless there is widespread support for a proposed bill, the legislation will die 80 to 90 percent of the time. In the 102th Congress (1991), 3589 bills were introduced and only 339 became law.

In the world's two major types of democratic political systems, the parliamentary and presidential, the support and leadership of the executive must accompany the role of the legislature in the enactment of law. The parliamentary system is particularly well suited to executive leadership in the legislature through the prime minister and the cabinet, as the Canadian experience has shown. The presidential system is much more complicated because the president and the cabinet are not present in the congress. But in both systems, the increasing complexities of government have made the legislature dependent on the executive for the initiation and proclamation of the laws. Essentially, the function of the modern democratic legislature is to criticize, examine, amend, adopt and, from time to time, reject legislation and bring down governments.

Control of Public Finances

The power to scrutinize and control public finances varies widely among legislatures. In Canada and the United States, executive budgets are drawn up and submitted to the legislature for approval. In states with an elected cabinet, such as Canada and Switzerland, the budget is approved or rejected in its entirety by the legislature. If it is rejected, the government is defeated, the Cabinet must resign, and Parliament is dissolved. If approved in Canada, the House of Commons has an important *audit function* that guarantees a measure of financial control over the ways the government raises taxes and spends money.[5] The Canadian **auditor general** reports directly to the House of Commons and conducts audits of government spending to assure the legislature that the provisions approved in the budget are implemented faithfully. Unlike other executive officers, the auditor general is an employee of Parliament, *not* of the Cabinet. In France and Germany, the executive has greater power of the purse than does the legislature. The French president can overrule legislative disapproval of the budget by executive order. The German chancellor may also bypass the legislature and authorize expenditures by

■ ■ **auditor general:** the financial watchdog of Parliament, who performs an annual audit of the Public Accounts, prepares an annual report to Parliament on the government's financial management, and releases the report to the general public. ■ ■

executive **prerogative**. In the United States, the president can only veto the entire budget or accept the entire budget. But, the president may refuse to spend the money.

Perhaps the oldest and most enduring function of the legislature is the power to levy taxes. But as with so many other legislative functions, the raising and spending of revenues have shifted primarily from legislative to executive control. Most democratic legislatures now only retain the power to scrutinize and revise budgets proposed by the executive branch. The pressure for higher tax revenues comes largely from the increased cost of government programs – costs of defence and domestic policies. As these programs become more and more costly, the executive is forced to demand new revenues. The legislature is always in a tricky political position – caught between the desire for increased government spending and public resistance to paying the cost through higher taxes.

Checks on the Executive

The universal expansion of executive authority has steadily increased the importance of the legislature to check and supervise the executive branch of government. This is accomplished in a variety of ways. In democratic parliamentary governments, the function of supervision is built into the system by the fusion of the executive in the legislature. Ministers must be members of the legislative body and are responsible to it, as in Australia, Canada, Great Britain, and Ireland. In other states, cabinet ministers are not members of either house but the legislature has the power of approving executive appointments, as in France, the Netherlands, and Norway. In the United States, the Senate must approve executive appointments for ambassadors, the cabinet, and federal judges and other officers.

Many other executive acts may be subject to legislative approval, like the ratification of treaties, the issuing of decrees, and declarations of national emergency. In Canada, there is no constitutional requirement for the parliamentary ratification of treaties. The decision to accede and ratify a treaty is an executive act legitimized by the royal prerogative. Most treaties are simply tabled in the House of Commons. But major multilateral treaties are, by tradition, submitted to Parliament before ratification.

One of the most effective means of controlling the executive is legislative scrutiny. In democratic states, legislators can supervise the policies and activities of executive members by asking questions in oral and written forms. In Canada, Great Britain, and many of the other Commonwealth states, the parliamentary **question period** is an effective device for gaining information about government actions. In other parliamentary systems, the process of **interpellation** is a more pointed method of legislative scrutiny of the executive. In Japan, opposition parties can question, or interpellate, government ministers and their assistants in the various committees drafting legislation before it goes to a full or plenary session of the Japanese Diet. The opposition wants to embarrass, delay, and even shape government-sponsored

> ■ ■ **interpellation:** a procedural action by a legislative member to interrupt the order of the day by filing formal petitions to be acted upon by the legislature or the total electorate in a general election or referendum. ■ ■

legislation. In Belgium, Italy, the Netherlands, and Switzerland, interpellation forces specific questions that are unsatisfactorily answered to debate and formal vote, sometimes resulting in a motion of censure against government. The functions of discussing, criticizing, and reviewing executive initiatives by the legislature constitute an important check on powerful executives.

Judicial Role

Some democratic legislatures have the power to adjudicate the behaviour of executive officials. The Constitution of the United States gives Congress the power to impeach any civil officer of the national government: the House hears the evidence and decides whether to impeach; the Senate sits as the court, with the power to convict on a two-thirds vote of its members. In France, the Assemblée Nationale and the Senate can decide to impeach the president and the ministers of state, but the accused must be tried by the High Court of Justice. In Canada and Great Britain, Parliament does not impeach members of the executive, because the House of Commons has the power to defeat a government whose members have acted illegally or unethically. Most parliamentary systems permit a prime minister to remove a minister from the cabinet who has been found guilty of a crime. But usually the person removed retains a seat in the legislature unless by a unanimous vote he or she is deprived of members' parliamentary privileges.

In Canada, the House of Commons has investigated the activities of MPs to determine if they could hold their seats. For example, in 1890 the House reviewed a previous conviction for forgery and the allegation that an MP's conduct was corrupt on a matter involving the granting of timber permits. And on two occasions, Louis Riel was expelled, once because he failed to obey a House order to appear in his seat, and once for having been judged an outlaw for a felony. The House demonstrated its right to expel an MP when, in 1946, Fred Rose was convicted and sentenced to six years' imprisonment for conspiring to commit offences under the Official Secrets Act. Since then a number of MPs who have been convicted in the courts (for example, Michel Gravel, 1988, Richard Grise, 1989, and Maurice Tremblay, 1992) have resigned before the House could exercise its right to expel a member.

Amending Constitutions

The legislatures in most democratic states have certain powers over the amendment of the national constitution. Because many constitutions were originally drafted by national legislatures, it is appropriate that they are authorized to exercise some role in the process of constitutional reform. In some states, such as Great Britain and New Zealand, constitutional change is primarily a function of the national legislature. In other states, such as Australia, France, and Switzerland, constitutional amendments are proposed by the national legislature, then ratified by voters in a nationwide referendum. In the United States, Congress has the power to propose a constitutional amendment by a two-thirds vote, then the proposed amendment must be ratified by three-quarters of the states in order to be adopted. In Canada, constitutional reform

is a lengthy and complicated process involving five different methods, depending on the nature of the amendment. In three of the methods, the legislative assembly of each province, or of those provinces to which the amendment applies, or the federal Parliament must approve of the proposed constitutional amendment.

In general, legislatures are involved in basically three methods of amending constitutions. One is by the action of the legislature alone, with certain variations in the usual requirements for passing a law. For example, Ecuador requires that a constitutional amendment must be approved by unanimous vote of the total membership. Another method of amendment involves a proposal by the legislature followed by a constitutional convention to ratify the amendment, as employed in Argentina. A third method, practised in most federal states, gives a distinctive role in the amending process to the subnational units – in Canada's case, to the provinces.

Canada's Legislative Assemblies

Canada's bicameral Parliament consists of two houses: the *House of Commons* and the *Senate*. Elected members of the House of Commons are called members of parliament (MPs); members of the Senate are called senators, although technically they are also members of parliament. The Canadian House of Commons is modelled after the British lower house. The country is divided into political constituencies that are roughly equal in population, each sending a representative to Ottawa. Originally, the Senate was modelled

Figure 7.1:
House of Commons chamber

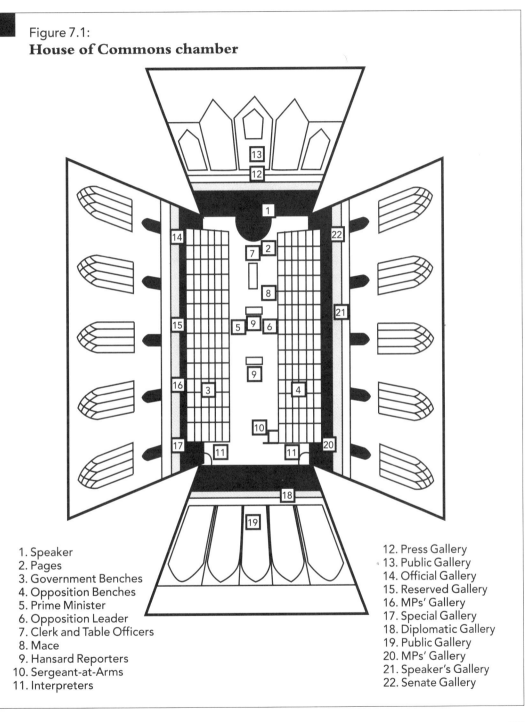

1. Speaker
2. Pages
3. Government Benches
4. Opposition Benches
5. Prime Minister
6. Opposition Leader
7. Clerk and Table Officers
8. Mace
9. Hansard Reporters
10. Sergeant-at-Arms
11. Interpreters

12. Press Gallery
13. Public Gallery
14. Official Gallery
15. Reserved Gallery
16. MPs' Gallery
17. Special Gallery
18. Diplomatic Gallery
19. Public Gallery
20. MPs' Gallery
21. Speaker's Gallery
22. Senate Gallery

after the British House of Lords. But in Britain there is no limit on the membership of the House of Lords: new appointments may be made from any constituency. However, Canada's Constitution Act, 1867, limits the size of the Senate by the principle of equal regional representation, but permits the government under Sections 24, 26, and 28 to add Senators in certain circumstances to a maximum number of 112. The Constitution also stipulates that there must be a session of the Parliament of Canada at least once each year and that the maximum life of a Parliament between elections is five years. Under certain emergency conditions, such as war, this normal tenure can be and has been extended.

The House of Commons

If Parliament is the symbol of political authority in Canada, the House of Commons is where the actualities of this legislative authority are centred. The House of Commons consists of 295 members and is responsible for most of the legislation introduced in Parliament. The House of Commons is a rectangular room divided by a central aisle. The government sits on the Speaker's right and the opposition on the left (figure 7.1). On the government side, about halfway down the aisle, the prime minister sits in the front row and the cabinet ministers sit in the centre seats of the first two rows. The leader of the Official Opposition sits directly opposite the prime minister, surrounded by the senior members of his or her party. Leaders of smaller opposition parties sit farther away from the Speaker. The principal divisions of legislative power do not run between Parliament and Cabinet, but within the House of Commons between the majority party

(which controls the Commons and Cabinet) and the opposition.

The Speaker

These divisions are reflected in the structural composition of the House of Commons, between the government and the members of the opposition, with the Speaker as the presiding officer of the House. On the Speaker's right sits the government, and on the left sits the opposition, an adversarial positioning of political opponents in the legislative framework.

By presiding over the debates and acting as the administrative head of the House of Commons, the Speaker plays a central role in the legislative process. The Speaker is a bilingual member of the House who is elected by that body for the duration of Parliament on the nomination of the prime minister. As the presiding officer of the House of Commons, the Speaker is expected to be **non-partisan** and impartial in applying the rules and procedures and in recognizing members who want to debate. During each sitting of the House, the Speaker rules on time limits for debate, on parliamentary privileges when they are violated, and on motions of adjournment and closure. In case of a tie, the Speaker casts the deciding vote. As the administrative head of the House of Commons, the Speaker is responsible for preparing and defending the internal estimates, which are the costs of staffing and operating the lower house.

Concurrent with the election of the Speaker is the election of a *deputy speaker*. The deputy speaker replaces the Speaker when he or she is absent and acts as the chairperson of the committees of the whole. Like the Speaker, the deputy speaker can be selected from either the government or opposition sides of the House, although the conventional practice is for the government to select both people. In the unlikely but possible case that both the Speaker and deputy speaker are absent, the House of Commons will temporarily appoint the *deputy chairperson of committees* from the government side of the House to the **Speaker's chair**.

The Clerk of the House

The House of Commons staff is headed by a permanent civil servant, the **Clerk of the House**, who advises the Speaker and Members of the House on parliamentary procedure. The Clerk sits at a table in front of the Speaker in the House of Commons. Some of the most important responsibilities of this officer are to keep the official record of the proceedings and to prepare Commons documents. Much like a deputy minister in charge of a government department, the Clerk supervises all the permanent staff of the House of Commons. As the chief parliamentary administrator, the Clerk prepares and delivers the daily order paper to the Speaker. The Clerk also provides the minister of justice with two copies of every bill tabled in the House.

Party Whips

Party whips are important in the organization and structure of the House of Commons.[6] Named after the "whippers" in the organization of the traditional English fox hunt who kept the hounds from straying, they are chosen in party caucus as special officers of their political parties. A whip seeks to assure that all party members are present for important votes. The authority of the whip is accepted

because MPs recognize that only by voting as a bloc can their party continue to be effective in the House of Commons, as government or opposition. To defy the whip by abstaining or even voting for the other side is seriously to challenge party discipline. Such actions may result in MPs losing the support and respect of their party colleagues. So, in addition to ensuring party discipline, the party whip must educate party members about the ramifications of party policies so that these are as palatable to as many members as possible. Whips are the party negotiators who decide among themselves what items on the agenda are subject to political compromise and how much debate will be expended on them.

Working alongside the whips are the *House leaders* of the various parties. The House leaders guide the flow of business through the House of Commons. On the government side, the House leader is a Cabinet member responsible for the organization of government business and, if possible, its quick passage through the House of Commons. Like the party whips, House leaders negotiate the apportionment of time to be spent on legislation and other matters of procedural business.

The Importance of Committees

The structure and functions of the House of Commons are also determined by its committee system. The basic challenge to the House of Commons is how to organize its 295 diverse members in order to get things done. One major response to the challenge since the mid-1960s is the specialization of parliamentary business in numerous legislative committees. Currently, there are 20 *standing committees* of the House of Commons, 14 standing committees in the Senate and standing

Table 7.4:
Standing committees of Parliament

House of Commons

- Agriculture and Agri-food
- Canadian Heritage
- Citizenship and Immigration
- Environment and Sustainable
  Development
- Finance
- Fisheries and Oceans
- Foreign Affairs
  and International Trade
- Government Operations
- Health
- Human Resources Development
- Human Rights and the Status
  of Disabled Persons
- Indian Affairs
  and Northern Development
- Industry
- Justice and Legal Affairs
- National Defence
  and Veterans' Affairs
- Natural Resources
- Procedure and House Affairs
- Sub-Committee on
  Private Members' Business
- Public Accounts
- Transport

Senate

- Aboriginal Peoples
- Agriculture and Forestry
- Banking, Trade and Commerce
- Internal Economy, Budgets
  and Administration
- Legal and Constitutional Affairs
- National Finance
- Energy, the Environment
  and Natural Resources
- Fisheries
- Foreign Affairs
- Privileges, Standing Rules and Orders
- Scrutiny of Regulations
- Selection
- Social Affairs, Science and Technology
- Transport and Communications

Standing Joint Committees

- Library of Parliament
- Official Languages
- Scrutiny of Regulations

Source: Committees Directorate, House of Commons and the Senate.

joint committees made up from members of the House and the Senate. The **Selection Committee** (sometimes called a "Striking Committee") decides on the membership of the standing committees. Each party caucus provides the Striking Committee with the names of qualified committee candidates.

This prevents the government from assigning the least experienced and least able opposition members to important standing committees (table 7.4).

Under the **Standing Orders** of the House of Commons, adopted in June 1978, these committees are permanent and are struck at the commencement of each session of Parliament to consider all subjects arising from the process of national lawmaking in Canada. Committee assignments are party-based and reflect the percentage of seats a party commands in the Commons. For example, if the government party won 60 percent of the seats in the House of Commons, it will occupy approximately the same proportion of positions on each committee. So if there are ten positions on a committee, the members of the governing party would occupy six. Committee power is more closely concentrated in the House when there is strong majority government. But opposition parties can be more influential in committees in a minority-government situation.

■ ■ **standing orders:** the rules and forms that regulate procedures in the House of Commons. ■ ■

A number of factors influence MPs' requests for committee assignments. One of these is the desire to be where the action is. They also want to serve on committees that handle the broadest central concerns of government – such as the Public Accounts Committee. Another major motive of House members in requesting committee assignments is being in a position to influence public policy. Some committees are attractive to members because they play important roles in the key areas of government decision-making, like taxing and spending, the economy, and social-welfare policy.

Making Laws   239 first   P. 248

However, the main function of the House of Commons is the passage of legislation. The legislative process converts a proposed bill into law. Bills may be proposed and introduced to the House of Commons as a private-member's bill or as a **government bill**. A private-member's bill can be introduced by any member of parliament on either the government or opposition side of the House. Usually, at the time they are introduced, these kinds of bills do not have the support of the government and rarely become law. Opposition members who introduce private-members' bills recognize these facts, using the opportunity to generate public opinion that will influence the direction of a particular government policy.

A government bill is a policy proposal or a **money bill** requiring legislation that is introduced in the House by a cabinet minister (figure 7.2). The minister responsible calls for the drafting of legislation by the Department of Justice. After the draft is approved by the same minister, it is presented to the Cabinet Committee on Legislation and House Planning. Once this committee has approved the draft bill, it is then signed by the prime minister and introduced in the House of Commons in its *first reading* by the minister responsible. During this stage, the title of the bill is read, followed by a short explanation of its contents. At the *second reading*, the bill is debated and a vote is taken on principle to approve or reject it in total. If it is "approved in principle," and it usually is, the bill is then considered by the appropriate standing committee, where it is given a clause-by-clause examination.

At the *committee stage,* the bill is debated and witnesses may be called to testify about their positions, pro or con. All standing committees are empowered to make amendments to the original draft. It should be noted that

Figure 7.2:
How a Canadian bill becomes a law

Royal Assent
After the bill has been passed by both Houses,
Members are summoned to the Senate Chamber,
where the bill is given Royal Assent and becomes law.

Senate
After the House passes the bill, it is sent to the Senate,
where it follows a similar legislative process.

Third Reading
Members debate and vote on the bill.

Report Stage
Members may move additional amendments at this stage.

Committee Stage
An appropriate committee examines the bill clause by clause
and submits it with amendments in a report to the House.

Second Reading
Members of Parliament debate the general principle of the bill.

First Reading
The bill is introduced, considered "read" for the first time, and printed.

money bills, unlike other bills, are not considered by standing committees; rather, they go before the **Committee of the Whole**. When this committee has completely examined the bill to its satisfaction, it reports the bill with any recommended amendments back to the House of Commons. In this *report stage*, the opposition will vigorously debate the bill and try to reintroduce the amendments it made at the committee stage. Any final changes the government wishes to make must also be made at this time, before the bill goes to its *third reading*. In almost all instances, a bill passes quickly through its third reading. However, if revisions made during the committee stage are unacceptable to the full House, the bill can be rejected. After a bill is finally passed through the House of Commons at this third reading, it is then introduced in the Senate, where it receives a *pro* *forma* repetition of the legislative process of the House. Once a bill is passed by both houses of Parliament, it is presented to the governor general who confers **Royal Assent** by signing it into law. **Proclamation**, which can be delayed, follows royal assent and a new Canadian law has finally been enacted.

The Senate

Anyone reading the Constitution Act, 1867, would have to conclude that the Senate and the House of Commons are about equal in power. But because the Senate is an appointed body, it has usually avoided the exercise of its constitutional powers in a manner that would challenge the popular legitimacy of the House of Commons.

Originally, the Fathers of Confederation expected the Senate to do two things: first, to play a legislative-review role by acting as a check against the majority in the elected House of Commons and, second, to represent the various regions of the country. The Senate has usually not been able to do either effectively. As a legislative-review body, the Senate lacks the authority to exercise its substantial powers because the public does not think it has the legitimacy to use them. In fact, the Cabinet has assumed the Senate's legitimate role as a forum for regional representation. So have first ministers' conferences, which give provincial governments a special voice to provide their own views on national issues and policies. This has been referred to as "executive federalism," the direct result of frequent federal/provincial negotiations for settling questions of regional concerns. Finally, political parties, especially their elected representatives, have displaced the role of the Senate, assuming the responsibility for the expression of regional viewpoints. Thus, regional representation at the national level is carried out by a variety of political institutions.

Nevertheless, the Senate remains an integral part of Canada's Parliament. All senators are formally summoned by the governor general, who appoints them on the advice of the prime minister. Presently, the Senate has 104 seats, allocated on the basis of four representative divisions: Ontario and Québec each have 24 seats; the three Maritime provinces share 24 seats (ten each for New Brunswick and Nova Scotia, and four for Prince Edward Island); the four Western provinces share 24 seats equally; Newfoundland has six seats; and the Yukon and Northwest Territories have one each.

Controversies sometime flare up about the conduct of the Senate, often resulting in calls for its abolition as a parliamentary institution in Canada. One such call came in May 1989, when the Senate's Liberal majority proposed an amendment to a supply bill authorizing the Mulroney government to borrow about $33 billion, even though the bill had been approved in the House of Commons. They also called upon the president of the Treasury Board and the minister of justice to justify the way the government had spent $7.5 billion by using **governor general's special warrants**. The issue was whether Parliament has control over Canada's finances. By stalling the bill, the

■ ■ **proclamation:** an important stage of the official lawmaking process in Canada involving the act of proclaiming, publishing, or declaring under the Great Seal a statute that thereby comes into force as law. ■ ■

Senate created a new round of demands for reform, even for outright abolition.

On paper, the Senate can amend or reject a bill passed by the House of Commons; this is as important a part of the lawmaking process as are royal assent and proclamation. From 1960-1991, 14 bills sent from the Commons to the Senate failed to receive royal assent. In 1988, former Liberal Leader John Turner directed the Liberal majority in the Senate to delay enabling legislation for the Canada-United States free trade agreement. Notwithstanding the fact that a federal election intervened, the Senate was exercising its right to delay a bill. Although the Senate powers of *delay*, *rejection*, and *amendment* have been but rarely exercised, the formal role of the Senate in the passage of legislation remains mandatory. Such a role was crucial to the government in 1991 when the Senate defeated the abortion bill with a stunning 43:43 vote (under Senate rules a tie means a defeat), leaving Canada without an abortion law.

Controversy also erupted in 1993 when the Senate voted itself a $6000 increase in the expense allowance of senators. The $6000 increase in the travel and accommodation allowance would have been added to the existing tax-free allowance – an increase of 58 percent in the aftermath of one of the worst recessions in Canadian economic history. When added to their salaries, the increase would have meant that some senators would have access to nearly $90,000 a year for a part-time job. After widespread negative public reaction, the senators reluctantly returned to the Red Chamber to rescind the expense increases they had given themselves.

■ ■ **governor general's special warrants:** extra-parliamentary executive borrowing privileges, authorized under Canada's Financial Administration Act and used only in emergencies for urgent and unforeseen government expenditures. ■ ■

Senate Reform

Much recent action and discussion about Senate reform has revolved around creating a permanent solution to the problem of inadequate institutional regional representation.[7]

Interest in changing the Senate is demonstrated by a wide range of publications and proposals. Senate reform was an important provision in the constitutional proposals made by Québec in its submission to the Constitutional Conference of 1968. The Government of Canada drafted white papers on Senate reform in 1969 and 1978. A Special Joint Committee of the Senate and the House of Commons on the Constitution published its report in 1972. But in 1978, the Supreme Court of Canada struck down an attempt by the Trudeau government to replace the Senate with a House of the Federation because the provinces had not given their consent. And in 1985, the Mulroney government moved to draft a constitutional amendment that would prevent the Senate, as presently constituted, from ever repeating its stalling action on important government business. This could prove to be a daunting task. Under the Constitution, the Senate's powers could be curtailed only with the consent of at least seven provinces, representing 50 percent of the Canadian population, and even after that, the Senate could itself delay changes in its powers for 180 days.

Reports on reforming the Senate were also prepared by the governments of British

Columbia (1978) and Alberta (1982 and 1985); the Ontario Advisory Committee on Confederation (1978); the Progressive Conservative Party of Canada (1978); the Canada West Foundation (1978 and 1981); the Canadian Bar Association (1978); the Pépin-Robarts Task Force on Canadian Unity (1979); La Fédération des francophones hors Québec (1979); the Goldenberg-Lamontagne report of 1980; and the Royal Commission on the Economic Union and Development Prospects for Canada (the Macdonald Commission, 1985). The future role of the Senate was also a major part of the deliberations of the Federal-Provincial Continuing Committee of Ministers on the Constitution from 1978 through to summer, 1980. In its "beige paper" entitled, "A New Canadian Federation," the Québec Liberal party recommended an intergovernmental council that would operate independently of Parliament but would perform some of the functions proposed for a reformed Senate.

In 1985, a Special Select Committee on Senate Reform, established by the Government of Alberta, recommended a *"Triple-E"* Senate: a Senate where members are directly *elected* based on *equal* representation from each province to a Senate with *effective* powers. Since 1985, important progress has been made toward Senate reform. In 1986, all the premiers agreed at the Annual Premiers' Conference in Edmonton that Senate reform is a priority for constitutional change. In the same year, the federal government pledged to address Senate reform in a new constitutional amendment. The 1987 Constitutional Accord contained a provision for Annual Conferences of First Ministers to address Senate reform. This was the first time that both the federal and provincial governments had agreed to concrete measures to reform the Senate. The Accord promised that Senate reform would be the next priority in building national reconciliation. The 1992 Charlottetown Accord would have changed the Senate by providing for equal representation for the provinces, with six elected senators each, regardless of population, and the Territories would have elected one senator each. The powers of the Senate would have been expanded to approve or reject government nominations for the governor of the Bank of Canada, the heads of institutions such as the CBC and federal boards and agencies. But the Senate's powers to defeat a government bill would have been reduced and refined.

The architects of a new Canadian Senate have many options from which to choose. They can reconstruct the second chamber in such a way that its present legislative-review and legislative-support functions are effectively enhanced by means of new methods of appointing or electing senators. To give senators more representative legitimacy in the eyes of Canadians, the federal government and the provincial governments could share a method of appointment. This would give people of all regions in the country a feeling of being effectively represented. Another recommended method of appointment would remove the federal government entirely from the process and give the power of appointment solely to the provinces. This would institutionalize provincial and regional input into the national legislative process. It would also give the provinces additional powers beyond those already delegated to them in the Constitution.

Another possible way of choosing senators

is by indirect election – a Senate elected by the provincial legislatures. Such is the practice for electing members to India's Rajya Sabha by the state legislative assemblies. In 1978, the federal government proposed a Senate selected by means of proportional indirect election. Under the terms of the proposal, the Senate would reflect the proportional popular results of political parties in the most recent federal election. This was criticized because it would not guarantee the representation of important regions in the country if political parties were unsuccessful in gaining seats nationally.

In the reports by the Fédération des francophones hors Québec (1979), the Canada West Foundation (1981), and the Macdonald Commission (1985), direct election of the Senate was proposed. In these and other reports it has been argued that direct election would give Canadians a feeling that the regions of the country have national as well as provincial representation. The Macdonald Commission advocated an elected Senate, based on proportional representation, with the power to hold up legislation for six months. An elected Senate would be a direct voice of the people from various regions, rather than of political parties or governments. In this regard, the Senate might also be designated to reflect the existence of certain minorities, especially Canada's aboriginal peoples.

There is no doubt that there are many ways to reform the Canadian Senate. What is certain is that the present means of legislative review and regional representation are inadequate and are perceived as such. Because of

■ ■ **floor leader:** a person who is in charge of getting a U.S. congressional bill passed, or in the case of the opposition, of getting it defeated. ■ ■

this, many Canadians continue to ask whether they should follow the example of other federations that assign a more functional use to the second chamber. In reviewing the performance of this legislative body, it is close to the truth to say that with the Senate as a functional legislature in Canada's Parliament there is much at issue and much at stake.

The United States Legislature

The United States has a bicameral national legislature called the Congress. Congress is divided into the *House of Representatives* and the *Senate*. Members of the House of Representatives are called representatives, also congressmen, congresswomen, or congresspersons. Members of the Senate are called senators. This structure was the result of a compromise that resolved a most important conflict of the Constitutional Convention (1787). The smallest populated states feared that representation by population would favour the largest populated states of the union. Therefore, they insisted that one House – the Senate – should represent each state equally and that the approval of both Houses should be required to pass a law.

The Senate has 100 members: two from each of the 50 states, elected for six-year terms. Approximately one-third of the senators are elected every two years. There are 435 members of the House of Representatives. This number, fixed by legislation, is divided among the fifty states in proportion to population. When states gain or lose population (taken by census every ten years) they also may gain or lose representatives. No matter how small the population of a state, it is entitled to at least one representative.

Despite the outward appearance of the separation of powers, the Congress of the United States *shares* its powers with the president and the Supreme Court.[8] Although the Constitution designates the Congress as the legislative branch, the president is very much a part of the lawmaking process. If the president opposes legislation passed by Congress, he can refuse to sign it and can return it to Congress, giving reasons for so doing. This is called a veto. The fate of such a bill would then be up to Congress. If, after the veto, Congress passes the bill by a two-thirds vote of each House, it overrides the veto and the bill becomes law without the signature of the president.

Legislative Leaders and Committees

As with all legislatures, Congress has its legislative leaders who organize the lawmaking process. Each House of Congress has two sets of leaders: those who achieve strong positions (mostly committee chairpersons) usually by virtue of their seniority, and those who are elected to the positions of congressional leadership.

The House of Representatives, controlled by the majority party, elects the *Speaker*. The Speaker is more than a party figure; this person presides over the House and is next in line of presidential succession after the vice-president. The minority party in the House has no similar office, otherwise, the leadership organizations of the two parties are similar. Each party has a **floor leader**, a whip, and a number of assistant whips in charge of

floor business. On the majority side of the House, the Speaker joins these officers, acting as party spokesmen, and representing House Democrats or Republicans to the president and the general public.

Party organization in the Senate takes a similar form. The U.S. vice-president is the presiding officer of the Senate. This person, not usually in attendance, has relatively little influence there except to cast the deciding vote in case of a tie or to issue a decision on a congressional ruling.

What role do party leaders play in the legislative process of Congress? The majority leadership in both Houses manages legislation after it comes out of committee. Majority leaders schedule and delegate the workload on a bill as it passes through each stage of legislation. They are at the centre of a network of information about legislation and must be consulted on every bill and kept informed on the progress of each. Although U.S. congressional leaders have a great deal of influence, they do not enjoy the same degree of influence over their fellow lawmakers as do their Canadian counterparts. They cannot tell their party members how to vote or expect them to follow orders. Party discipline is much weaker in the U.S. Congress. Party leaders cannot even control how much campaign assistance will go to individual candidates for the House and Senate. Because they only have marginal influence in keeping their party members in office, they exercise only marginal power over them in Congress.

The congressional committee system is by far the most important element in the legislative organization of Congress.[9] Members of the House and the Senate establish their reputations through the committee work

Table 7.5:
Standing committees of Congress

House of Representatives	Senate
■ Agriculture	■ Agriculture, Nutrition, and Forestry
■ Appropriations	■ Appropriations
■ Armed Services	■ Armed Services
■ Banking, Finance, and Urban Affairs	■ Banking, Housing, and Urban Affairs
■ Budget	■ Budget
■ District of Columbia	■ Commerce, Science, and Transportation
■ Education and Labor	■ Energy and Natural Resources
■ Energy and Commerce	■ Environment and Public Works
■ Foreign Affairs	■ Finance
■ Government Operations	■ Foreign Relations
■ House Administration	■ Government Affairs
■ Interior and Insular Affairs	■ Judiciary
■ Judiciary	■ Labor and Human Resources
■ Merchant Marine and Fisheries	■ Rules and Administration
■ Post Office and Civil Service	■ Small Business
■ Public Works and Transportation	■ Veterans' Affairs
■ Rules	
■ Science and Technology	
■ Small Business	
■ Standards of Official Conduct	
■ Veterans' Affairs	
■ Ways and Means	

Source: *Congressional Quarterly Weekly Report*, May 1, 1993, p.1.

they do. The Congress is much too large for all its members to make important public decisions collectively. No congressperson can possibly learn about every issue before the legislatures. Only through the committee system can the work of Congress get done. Each bill must go through the hands of at least one, and often more than one, committee in each House. The vast majority of bills flow through standing committees for their scrutiny and approval or disapproval. There are 16 standing committees in the Senate and 22 in the House (table 7.5).

These standing committees are divided into subcommittees that do specialized work within the overall jurisdiction of the full committees. The party composition of standing committees is roughly equivalent to the relative party strength in each House, and the chair of the committee and subcommittee is usually held by a *ranking member* of the majority party.

The U.S. Congress also conducts **select committees**. Ordinarily, select committees do not play a significant role in the process of passing a bill. But there are times when select committees capture a prominent role in the legislative process, as did the Senate select committee that investigated Watergate.

Finally, two other kinds of congressional committees deserve attention. **Joint committees** are those made up of an equal number of senators and representatives. The chairs of these committees alternate between the Houses from Congress to Congress. Joint committees rarely have anything to do with initiating legislation but do long-term studies on important questions like taxation. **Joint conference committees** are also composed of equal membership from both Houses and function to iron out any technical difficulties a bill encounters because of the procedural differences between the Houses, as well as trying to reconcile major policy differences in Congress.

Because of its size and political complexities, Congress could be viewed as a collection of committees that often meet solely to vote on the recommendations each committee has tabled. In any case, the committee system has earned a great deal of respect among U.S. legislators. Congresspersons will rely on expert opinion and intelligence-gathering before deciding the direction of their votes. For them the "committee" has done all the credible groundwork, held hearings, studied the issues, and consulted with experts and interested parties. Consequently, committee opinion is usually respected.

■ ■ **joint conference committees:** congressional committees composed of members of the U.S. House and Senate formed to resolve differences resulting from conflicting interpretations of the same bill. ■ ■

How Bills Are Passed

The U.S. legislative process follows an often slow and formidable path, although political will in the Congress can speed a bill through a labyrinth of hurdles (figure 7.3). A bill may be formally introduced by any member of either House. Sometimes a companion bill is introduced in the other House simultaneously in order to speed up the process of legislation. In addition, any number of members of Congress may *sponsor* a bill. Presidential bills are introduced by a member of the president's party who has seniority on the standing committee that will hold hearings on the bill.

When the bill is introduced on the floor, it is read and immediately assigned by the presiding officer to the appropriate standing committee handling such matters. The subcommittees of the parent committees are then assigned the job of investigating the purposes of the bill, determining its value, amending it in accordance with the wishes of the subcommittee, and then re-submitting it to the parent committee. Sometimes the full standing committee will specifically investigate certain provisions of the bill. This is generally followed by hearings of the parent committees and subcommittees. These hearings perform several broad functions. One is to assist congresspersons in collecting information and opinion from the interested parties. Within this process, special-interest groups will have their say. As the bill passes through the hands of these committees, it may come to bear only a slight resemblance to the original draft or even to the intent of it.

Figure 7.3:
How U.S. bills pass into law: the lawmaking process

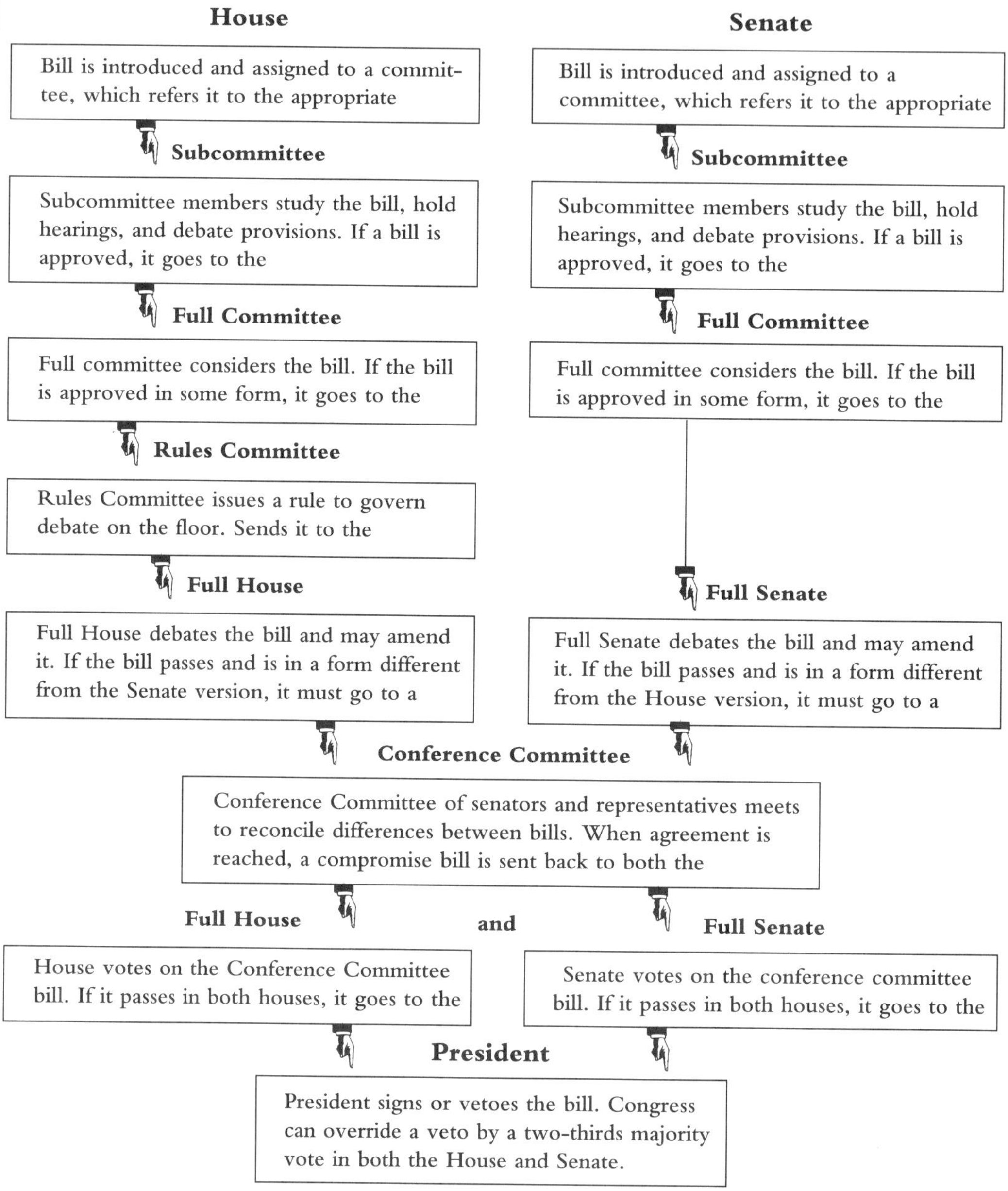

House	Senate

House

Bill is introduced and assigned to a committee, which refers it to the appropriate

Subcommittee

Subcommittee members study the bill, hold hearings, and debate provisions. If a bill is approved, it goes to the

Full Committee

Full committee considers the bill. If the bill is approved in some form, it goes to the

Rules Committee

Rules Committee issues a rule to govern debate on the floor. Sends it to the

Full House

Full House debates the bill and may amend it. If the bill passes and is in a form different from the Senate version, it must go to a

Senate

Bill is introduced and assigned to a committee, which refers it to the appropriate

Subcommittee

Subcommittee members study the bill, hold hearings, and debate provisions. If a bill is approved, it goes to the

Full Committee

Full committee considers the bill. If the bill is approved in some form, it goes to the

Full Senate

Full Senate debates the bill and may amend it. If the bill passes and is in a form different from the House version, it must go to a

Conference Committee

Conference Committee of senators and representatives meets to reconcile differences between bills. When agreement is reached, a compromise bill is sent back to both the

Full House   and   **Full Senate**

House votes on the Conference Committee bill. If it passes in both houses, it goes to the

Senate votes on the conference committee bill. If it passes in both houses, it goes to the

President

President signs or vetoes the bill. Congress can override a veto by a two-thirds majority vote in both the House and Senate.

Many riders or amendments may be added along the way. Once the House of Representatives committee reports a bill out by returning it to the legislature, it is scheduled by the Rules Committee for the second reading, debate, and voting on the floor of the House. If a bill survives the second reading, it is **engrossed** by printing the amendments in final form, and given a third reading. This reading is by title only, unless a member requests that the bill be read again in full. The Speaker asks for a vote after the title is read and the bill is either defeated or passed. As in Canada, the third reading is merely *pro forma*, because the sentiments of the House have been expressed in the Committee of the Whole, where the entire legislative body sits as one large committee.

All *revenue* bills are required by the Constitution to originate in the House of Representatives. Once passed in the House, they are taken up by the Senate. But all other bills may originate in either the House or the Senate. If one House passes the bill first, it then goes to the other House where it goes through the same process. Bills must eventually be passed in both Houses in exactly the same form before being sent to the president for signing. Even after a bill authorizing a new government program becomes law, the new program must still get an appropriation of money if it is actually to get underway. **Appropriations bills** go to the House and Senate appropriations committees. These committees regard themselves as having a special role to play in protecting taxpayers from unnecessary federal expenditures.

The primary concern of Congress is the thousands of bills and resolutions that are introduced each year. The number of bills and resolutions introduced in one Congress has been as high as 44,000, but a number between 15,000 and 20,000 is more usual. The odds are that over 90 percent of these legislative proposals will be killed or permitted to die in committee.

Although the U.S. Congress was born in an age of great legislative activity, much has changed in the last 200 years. Today, most observers agree that the branch of government first mentioned in the Constitution has been greatly surpassed in power by the executive branch. One reason frequently advanced for the decline in the power of Congress has been its inability to organize rapidly and legislate on the ever-changing social exigencies of American society.

Functions of Non-democratic Legislatures

Authoritarian Assemblies

At first glance, legislatures in authoritarian and totalitarian states resemble democratic lawmaking institutions. In most cases their members are elected, they elect or appoint presiding officers, they meet regularly, make speeches, vote on proposed legislation, and formally enact laws and constitutional amendments. But on closer examination, we see that the roles they play in their respective political systems are quite different from those of democratic legislatures.

In authoritarian states, the character of the policy-making process is strongly influenced by the concentration of power in the hands of the civilian political executive or the military.[10] The very personal way in which power is exercised means that the legislature has little actual autonomy and cannot play an independent role in the policy-making process. In all authoritarian states, the vital centre of governmental power is the executive itself; political parties, legislatures, and courts are usually not important challenges. Any institutional constraint on these powerful executives remains extremely weak. It was President Mobutu of Zaïre who completely sidestepped the legislature when he declared that even his speeches have the force of law. By means of presidential decrees and without any legislative consultation, Mobutu introduced sweeping institutional changes, subject to no legal or political challenges. In 1992, Mobutu suspended "until further notice" a national convention of delegates who met to establish a multi-party system in the National Legislative Council.

In many African states, legislatures are colonized by a single party or a dominant party under the influence of the military that tolerates only marginal opposition, if it tolerates any at all. In these authoritarian political systems, the legislature functions to uphold the government rule of the incumbent regime. As a result, the vitality of democratic accountability is virtually non-existent. The legislatures provide merely ceremonial and decorative functions. In some states, such as Kenya, the National Assembly provides an arena through which members can successfully represent the claims of their constituents to gain minor amenities such as a paved road or a new school. But legislators cannot effectively challenge the executive leadership in areas of general policy.

Constitutionally, the legislatures in most states are theoretically equal partners with the other political branches of government – the executive and the judiciary. However, in all authoritarian states, this equality is more fiction than fact. In states such as Guatemala and Honduras, the legislative body is always overshadowed by the president and does not even hold as much independence or influence as the judiciary.

There are many reasons for the predominance of authoritarian executives and the minor supportive role of their legislatures. One is that in many states the legislature is a hand-picked body of the executive. The 1974 Constitution of Zaïre, for example, gives the president the power to name the members to the leading organs of the state, such as the legislature and the Supreme Court. Often it is impossible for legislators to be elected or re-elected without the personal approval of the president. In Mexico's single-party dominant system, the president, who since 1929 has always been the nominee of the Partido Revolucionario Institucional (PRI), has such control over the electoral process that the party's candidate not only influences who the next presidential nominee will be, but has final approval over the party's slate of candidates to both Houses of Congress. And in Zambia under President Kuanda, all candidates for the National Assembly were required to be members of the United National Independence Party (UNIP) and had to be confirmed by the president. Even in states where the president does not personally endorse party candidates for the legislature, legislators often owe their election almost entirely to the influence of political executives and are, therefore, beholden to them.

Legislators in authoritarian systems are well aware that in a contest of power among the branches of government, the executive holds most of the trumps, especially the high ones, such as the support of the armed forces and the national police. In a showdown of political power, executives will even use these trumps against members of the legislature.[11]

Many other factors contribute to the inconsequential role of legislatures in authoritarian states. The widespread presence of illiteracy, poverty, and lack of political experience have contributed substantially to the weakness of legislatures. This is particularly true in states such as Niger, where the adult literacy rate is 4.7 percent and the per capita GNP is $480.00 U.S.[12] This legislature is virtually non-functional. Low levels of literacy, education, and information curtail the formation of a participant political culture. In states such as Peru and Ecuador, many people are denied the privilege of voting because of illiteracy. Even when suffrage is extended to a wider range of the population, the great majority of citizens in authoritarian states hardly know what is going on in government and are uninterested in the legislature's work, its problems, or its degree of independence. Conversely, the continuing tradition of strong executive leadership that can capture the emotions of the masses serves to relegate the functions of any representative bodies to a position of minor importance.

The net result is that legislatures in such systems tend to function as rubber stamps. In authoritarian states, open debate is mainly window-dressing for the sake of the international community. Usually the legislative order of business, even the outcome of the proceedings, is a foregone conclusion. Most of the important bills considered by the legislature have already been formulated or decreed by the executive. In the final analysis, the legislative process is exploited by dictators to whip legislators into line behind the policies they feel are in the national interest. Often the bureaucratic machinery of the state is well underway, implementing the policies even as they are being considered by the legislature.

Totalitarian Assemblies

Legislatures in totalitarian socialist states, modelled after democratic parliamentary assemblies, function quite differently. They work to legitimize the policies and rules of the executive levels of government, which in this case is the party leadership. For this reason, assemblies in these states have tended to remain subordinate to the Communist party. The impact of *democratization*, however, has altered the relationship between the party and the legislative branch of government. Some observers view the totalitarian model of government as transitional in all remaining communist regimes.[13]

All of the enduring communist states have unicameral legislatures. China is a unicameral state. According to the Chinese Constitution of 1982, "the highest organ of state power" resides in the National People's Congress (NPC) (figure 7.4). The NPC has over 3000 members and is the largest legislative assembly in the world. Its delegates are elected every five years but its awesome size prevents it from being an effective decision-making body. The meetings of the NPC are short and mostly ceremonial because its deputies ratify the major reports presented to them by the Chinese Communist Party.

The three levels of Chinese government include national, provincial, and county or

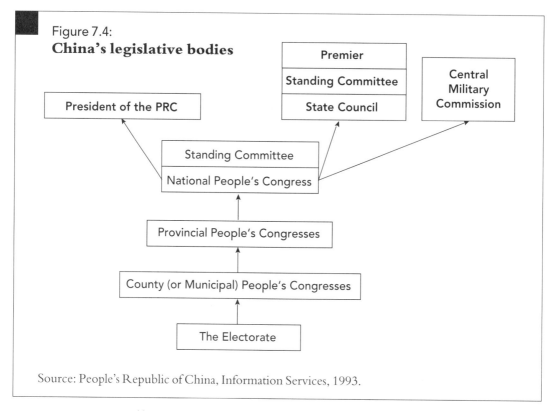

Figure 7.4:
China's legislative bodies

Source: People's Republic of China, Information Services, 1993.

municipal (figure 7.4).[14] Each level has a legislature called a "people's congress," defined constitutionally as the "local organ of state power." Like the NPC, these local congresses meet irregularly and briefly. The standing committees of the people's congresses have the role of supervising the government organizations and of keeping the goals of the party well entrenched in the administrative structure of government. Congresses at the national and provincial levels are indirectly elected for five-year terms by lower-level congresses. But congresses at the county, district, and municipal levels have three-year terms and are elected directly by the voters. The district and township congresses are directly elected and administer government programs at the grass-roots level.

The 1982 Constitution gave formal and legal approval to several new trends in Chinese politics. It increased the legislative powers of the congresses and clearly specified the roles of the party, state, and government in the political system. The effort to give the legislative structures of government a greater role in the political process indicates the willingness of the Chinese Communist Party to institutionalize the decision-making process.

Almost all contemporary political systems have legislatures in which individuals assemble either to make laws or formally enact laws proposed by the executive branch of government. A legislature's relationship to the political executive varies significantly from polity to polity. It is always affected by the degree of democratic, authoritarian, and totalitarian ideology practised by political leaders and accepted by the citizens. Other factors include the number and nature of the individual houses of the legislature, the power of committees, and the political customs and mores practised in a state.

Legislative power is seldom separate from executive power. However, how closely connected they are or what the relationship is between them depends on the state's constitution and the type of system is prescribes. Where legislatures merely function to formalize decisions made elsewhere about the laws that govern people, it is important to find out where laws are really being made and exactly what procedures are being followed. In some states, a great amount of effort is made to show that lawmaking is the job of the legislature, but in practice, that body has progressively surrendered a larger role in the exercise of lawmaking to the executive branch.

We have seen that the lawmaking function is usually assigned to representative legislatures, if not as an effective body than as a formal, symbolic one. In all probability, however, the power to make laws is not held exclusively by the legislature but is shared to a greater or lesser extent with other decision-makers outside that body.

References

1. Dell Gillette Hitchner and Carol Levine, *Comparative Government and Politics* (New York: Harper and Row, Publishers, 1981), 202.

2. Based on comparisons of legislatures described in Brian Hunter, ed., *Statesman's Year Book*, 1994-95 (London: Macmillan Press, 1994).

3. Hanna F. Pitkin, "The Concept of Representation," in Pitkin, ed., *Representation* (New York: Atherton Press, 1969), 16.

4. Paul Fox and Graham White, *Politics: Canada* 6th ed. (Toronto: McGraw-Hill Ryerson, 1987), 453-500.

5. Kenneth Kernaghan and David Siegel, *Public Administration in Canada* (Scarborough, ON: Nelson Canada, 1991), 563-610.

6. Martin Westmacott, "Whips and Party Cohesion," *Canadian Parliamentary Review* (Autumn 1983): 14-19.

7. Gordon Robertson, *A House Divided: Meech Lake, Senate Reform and the Canadian Union* (Halifax: Institute for Research on Public Policy, 1989); Roger Gibbins, *Senate Reform: Moving Toward the Slippery Slope* (Kingston, ON: Institute of Intergovernmental Relations, Queen's University, 1983), 1-50; and *Report of the Special Joint Committee of the Senate and the House of Commons on Senate Reform* (Ottawa: January 1984).

8. Karen O'Connor and Larry Sabato, *American Government: Roots and Reform* (New York: Macmillan, 1993), Ch. 6.

9. James Wilson, *American Government* (Lexington, MA: D.C. Heath and Company, 1992), Ch. 11; Richard Hall and Bernard Grofman, "The Committee Assignment Process and the Conditional Nature of Committee Bias," *APSR* (December 1990): 1149-1166.

10. Constantine Danopoulos, *From Military to Civilian Rule* (New York: Routledge, 1991), 200-288.

11. Robert Fatton Jr., *Predatory Rule: State and Civil Society in Africa* (Boulder, CO: Lynne Rienner Publishers, 1992), 60-185.

12. World Bank, *World Development Report, 1993* (New York: Oxford University Press, 1993).

13. Edward Gargan, *China's Fate: A People's Turbulent Struggle with Reform and Repression* (New York: Doubleday, 1991); Harvey Starr, "Democratic Dominoes: Diffusion approaches to the spread of democracy in the international system," *Journal of Conflict Resolution* (35): 356-381; David Held, "Democracy, the nation-state and the global system," *Economy and the State (*20) (1991): 138-172.

14. Lucian Pye, *China: An Introduction,* 4th ed. (New York: HarperCollins, 1991), 35-57.

Suggested Readings

Michael Atkinson, *Governing Canada Institutions and Public Policy* (Toronto: Harcourt Brace Jovanovich Canada, Inc., 1993).

Roger Davidson and Walter Oleszek, *Congress and Its Members* 3rd, ed., (Washington, D.C.: Congressional Quarterly Press, 1990).

Munroe Eagles et. al., *The Almanac of Canadian Politics* (Peterborough: Broadview Press, 1991).

Robert Fleming, *Canadian Legislatures 1992* (Agincourt, ON: Global Press, 1992).

House of Commons, Standing Orders of the House of Commons, May 1991.

Magnus Gunther and Conrad Winn, eds., *House of Commons Reform* (Ottawa: Parliamentary Internship Program, 1991).

Hung Yung Lee, *From Revolutionary Cadres to Party Technocrats in Socialist China* (Berkley: University of California Press, 1991).

P. G. Normandin, ed., *The Canadian Parliamentary Guide, 1990* (Toronto: INFO GLOBE, 1990).

David Olson and Michael Mezey, *Legislatures in the Policy Process* (New York: Oxford University Press, 1991).

Richard Sakwa, *Russian Politics and Society* (New York: Routledge, 1993).

Glossary

appointment: The formal and official designation of a person for a political or government office; the exercise of public power by authority of constitution, statute, or political convention.

appropriation bills (U.S.): A Congressional enactment to authorize government expenditures.

auditor general: The financial watchdog of Parliament, who performs an annual audit of the *Public Accounts*, prepares an annual report to Parliament on the government's financial management, and releases the report to the general public.

Clerk of the House: Advises the Speaker and members on parliamentary procedure and practice and sits at a table in front of the Speaker in the Chamber. The Clerk is the most senior executive officer of the Commons and is responsible for keeping official records of proceedings, preparing Commons documents, and supervising the procedural officers and clerks.

Committee of the Whole: The entire parliamentary body.

committee system: The complex and formal arrangement whereby a legislative body investigates matters deemed worthy of possible legislative action by the use of committees composed of legislators.

constituency: A legislative district or riding from which an individual or group of individuals is chosen to represent in a public fashion the interests of people, known as constituents.

constituent: A resident in a legislator's district or constituency.

engross: To make a formal transcript of the draft of a legal instrument, such as a bill or agreement.

executive prerogative: Usually refers to a special privilege, power, or immunity vested in an executive office or person who alone enjoys particular rights and capacities in contradistinction to others.

floor leader: A person who is in charge of getting a U.S. congressional bill passed, or in the case of opposition, of getting it defeated.

government bill: A bill approved by cabinet and introduced into the House of Commons by a minister.

governor general's special warrants: Extra-parliamentary executive borrowing privileges, authorized under Canada's Financial Administration Act and used only in emergencies for urgent and unforeseen government expenditures.

House Leaders: Members of the government or of the opposition who express and represent their party's priorities for arranging the business of the House of Commons.

indirect election: The process of electing individuals to a legislature using procedures that do not directly involve those who are represented, or by using electors who are not chosen by the people directly, as in the U.S. Electoral College.

initiative: An electoral process whereby designated percentages of the electorate may initiate legislative changes by filing formal petitions to be acted upon by the legislature or the total electorate in a general election or referendum.

interpellation: A procedural action by a legislative member to interrupt the order of the day by asking a minister or committee official to explain some matter belonging to his or her jurisdiction.

joint committee: A congressional committee struck on special subject-matter areas, made up of members of both Houses of the U.S. Congress.

joint conference committee: Congressional committees composed of members of the U.S. House and Senate to resolve differences resulting from conflicting interpretations of the same bill.

money bill: Financial bills that authorize taxation and appropriations or expenditures which must be introduced first into the House of Commons by a minister of the Crown.

non-partisan: Political conduct showing no preference for any government, political party, or ideological position.

petition: A method of placing a candidate's name on a primary or a general election ballot by submitting a specified number or percentage of voters' signatures to appropriate officials.

popular election: An election whereby the voters directly elect the candidates.

private-member's bill: A bill introduced by a member of parliament who is not a minister.

proclamation: An important stage of the official lawmaking process in Canada involving the act of proclaiming, publishing, or declaring under the Great Seal a statute that thereby comes into force as law.

public-opinion poll: A systematic and often scientific analysis of selected groups and individuals randomly chosen and queried on what they think about a particular issue, party, event, or person.

question period: An amount of time, approximately one hour, of most days that Parliament is in session, in which ministers answer questions raised by the opposition.

recall: A procedure enabling voters to remove an elected official from office before his or her term has expired.

referendum: An electoral process by which legislative or constitutional questions are referred to the total electorate.

representation by population: Representation within a legislative body based on the principle that each legislator represents approximately equal populations.

roll-call voting: A "yea or nay" vote in a legislative body where each member's vote is required to be recorded.

Royal Assent: The last stage through which a bill passes before becoming an act of parliament and a law of the land. Royal Assent is sometimes given personally by the governor general, but more often it is granted by a justice of the Supreme Court of Canada acting on the governor general's behalf.

select committee: A legislative committee of the U.S. Congress established for a limited period of time for a special purpose.

selection (or striking) committee: A selection committee that decides on the membership of all other committees.

Speaker's chair: The Speaker's chair of the Canadian House of Commons is a replica of the Speaker's chair in the Palace of Westminster that was destroyed during an air raid in 1941.

standing committee: A permanent or regular committee created by a legislative body to consider matters on which the legislature may act.

Standing Orders: The rules and forms that regulate procedures in the House of Commons.

subcommittee: A supplementary group of individuals appointed by the chairperson of a legislative committee to investigate legislative matters and report to the larger committee.

EIGHT

The Administration of Government

Revenue Canada workers at tax time

Chapter Objectives

After reading this chapter, you will be able to:

- appreciate the nature and widespread presence of bureaucracy and public administration

- describe the characteristics of public bureaucracy and relate them to Canadian government

- describe what governments do when they administer public policy

- explain the advantages and disadvantages of widespread government bureaucracies in modern political systems

- examine the role of bureaucracy in the emerging United States of Europe

- discuss the consequences of powerful public bureaucracies in a democratic system of government

- define the concept of administocracy

- explain how bureaucracy and bureaucrats can be controlled

- outline the instruments available in Canada for regulating the bureaucrats

- explain the relationship of ministers and deputy ministers

- compare public administration in Canada and the United States

The First Bureaucracies

Many traditional societies compiled and stored information on tilling, hunting, fishing, animal husbandry, and human population for the purposes of social **administration** and survival.[1] Egypt, China, and India produced highly developed bureaucratic mechanisms before Europe had emerged from barbarism. The so-called **bureaucratization** of human behaviour became evident in agriculture, commerce, fishing, justice, military and municipal affairs. Traditional modes of government based on ties among members of an extended kin group were no longer adequate for administering the affairs of societies whose populations sometimes numbered in the millions. Though rulers continued to rely on relatives to help them govern, they increasingly were forced to turn to others. Eventually, all the more successful rulers found it necessary to create new kinds of governmental structures that were not based on kinship alone. The casual and informal practices of traditional societies had proved inadequate.

For these early societies, the problems of administration multiplied, new kinds of governmental positions were created and a *governmental bureaucracy* began to take shape. In addition to the people who were responsible for administering the complex personal and family affairs of the rulers, there were *officials* scattered throughout the countryside to administer the affairs of the towns, villages, and districts of the governed communities. Each official had a staff of scribes and lesser officials to assist with compiling written records about the civic affairs of each community. Because of the political importance of their skills and the limited number of people who could write and keep records, most scribes were members of a special class of governors.

As traditional agrarian societies evolved into industrial economies, the range and diversity of government activities grew enormously. The original functions of government, to preserve law and order and defend the society from external threat, were compounded by demands from growing populations to provide many new government services: to educate, to regulate, to licence, to provide health care, to manage and referee the economy.

Especially in European states, the growth of government resulted from a greater interdependence of national populations. More and more people became engaged in specialized work, becoming dependent on the labour of others to survive and on the maintenance of a complex social system of exchange by which goods and services could be delivered to consumers. A disruption at any point in the system had serious consequences for almost everyone, and people generally supported the efforts of governments to prevent it.

Similarly, as societies became geared to a higher degree of interaction among members, dependable systems of transportation and communication were essential. The more populous urban communities required the organization of fire, police, health, and other government services. Private individuals and organizations were unable to assume these responsibilities; only governments commanded the resources, **expertise**, and authority to deal with such problems. Gradually, European states forged effective central governmental administrations to administer these tasks.

The full-blown model of the modern **administrative state** was Prussia. Under Frederick William I (1713-1740), a pattern for a professional administrative corps was organized, embracing many of the characteristics now generally recognized as normal adjuncts to the public service.[2] Frederick William I was the first to establish universities to train government bureaucrats. Recruitment and selection were by competitive examination after the completion of specialized training, and **career tenure** was the normal expectation. It was this well-organized and efficient government administration, as much as any other single factor, that enabled Prussia to emerge as the leader among the competing German princedoms that existed until 1870.

The Prussian model was copied by many other continental states, most notably by eighteenth-century France. Under the centralizing leadership of Napoleon, France developed a professionalized civil service, with a **hierarchical** structure of offices and officials – uniform throughout the country – that followed elaborate patterns of law and administered rules established by the executive, legislative, and judicial branches of government. The term "bureaucracy" is derived from the French *bureaux*, the desks of government officials that came to symbolize the authority and administration of the public service.

In Britain, the painful struggle for parliamentary supremacy was as much pursued to control the centralizing governing apparatus that successive kings and queens had developed as it was to control the monarchs themselves. Monarchs could rule only through their servants in the administrative structure: control of the one could not be asserted without control of the other.

The development of administrative government in both Canada and the United States owes much to Great Britain; thus, **public administration** in North America is more like that of our English cousins than like the continental model. In fact, the Canada of 1867, with its simple economy, sparse population, wealth of resources, and remoteness from the broils of the old world, needed but a minimum of government of any kind. The problem of administrative development in Canada and the United States was one of overcoming a tradition hostile to bureaucracy and deeply rooted in political cultures that stressed egalitarianism, equal opportunity, and a militant antigovernment approach to staffing the political system.

In the late nineteenth century, Canadians were not prepared to assign more than a rudimentary role to government involvement in their lives. There was no personal or corporate income tax, no family allowance, no Canada Pension Plan, and no medicare. CBC radio and television did not exist, nor did the Canada Council, Investment Canada, the Canadian International Development Agency (CIDA), or Atomic Energy Canada, Ltd. Government consisted of Parliament, a postal service, customs and immigration, a system of courts, and public works. The public service of the day was largely unprofessional by current standards, made up of people whose only expertise amounted to reading, writing, and perhaps some bookkeeping.

Until the early twentieth century, administrators were selected and obtained tenure as a consequence of partisan preference through an elaborate system of **patronage**: the characteristics of a professionalized bureaucratic service on the European model were conspicuously absent. During the 1920s, under Mackenzie King, the Canadian civil service was upgraded from an essentially clerical force into a highly qualified group of professional policy advisors. When R.B. Bennett became prime minister in 1930, he kept on most of the senior civil servants who were appointed by Mackenzie King, thus firmly establishing the tradition of a non-partisan civil service. Deputy ministers were and still are the most powerful civil servants in Ottawa. Today, more than 600,000 people work directly for the federal government, in its departments, crown corporations, agency corporations, and other federal bodies. The Canadian system, because of its federal structure, is much less centralized than the British or French systems. Never before have so many Canadians been so involved with bureaucracy or so affected by it. If provincial and municipal administrations are added to the federal total, government administration presently employs over 12 percent of Canada's total labour force.

Characteristics of Bureaucracy

The first systematic study of bureaucracy was conducted by German sociologist Max Weber (1864-1920). His classic studies formulated an ideal set of features for any public bureaucracy. However, no modern government administration is bureaucratic in the strict interpretations of his definitions. Weber himself always emphasized the exaggerations and simplifications of his model. Nevertheless, the constituent elements of his formulations are present in varying degrees in such diverse organizations as the Secretariat of the United Nations, the Vatican's *Curia* (which has handled the business of the world-wide Catholic Church over the past 1800 years), and Revenue Canada Taxation. Weber argued that every bureaucracy – whether its purpose is to run a day-care centre, a family business, or an army – will share five basic characteristics. These characteristics are discussed below and summarized in table 8.1.

1. Division of Labour

Specialized experts are employed in each position to perform specific tasks. The prime minister of Canada need not know how to use the computer used by Revenue Canada. A judge need not be able to hire public accountants. By working at a specific task, people are more likely to become highly skilled and to carry out a job with maximum efficiency. This emphasis on **specialization** is so basic a part of our lives that we may not realize that it is a fairly recent development in Western political cultures. Unfortunately, when government workers become specialized, they can develop blind spots and fail to notice obvious problems in the operations of the government body. Even worse, they may not care about what other government "specialists" are doing, even when they are close at hand.

2. Hierarchy of Authority

Bureaucracies follow the principle of hierarchy; that is, each position is under the supervision of a higher authority. The Canadian Armed Forces are ultimately responsible to the command of the minister of defence. Within the organization of the armed forces, generals outrank colonels, colonels outrank majors, majors outrank captains, and the hierarchy extends downward to sergeants and privates.

Table 8.1:
Characteristics of bureaucracy

Characteristic	Positive Consequences	Negative Consequences	
		For the Individual	For the Organization
Division of labour	Produces efficiency in large-scale organizations	Produces trained incapacity	Produces narrow perspectives
Hierarchy of authority	Clarifies who is in command	Deprives employees of a voice in decision-making	Permits concealment of mistakes
Rules and regulations	Let workers know what is expected of them	Stifle initiative and imagination	Lead to goal displacement
Impersonality	Reduces bias	Contributes to feelings of alienation	Discourages loyalty to the organization
Security	Discourages favouritism and reduces petty rivalries	Discourages ambition to improve oneself	Allows **Peter Principle** to operate

The close supervision often associated with hierarchical organizations can often lead to inflexible behaviour. While bureaucracies may not totally suppress individuality, they usually do not tolerate a great deal of flexibility among individuals.

3. Written Rules and Regulations

Rules and regulations, as we are aware, are an important characteristic of bureaucracies. Ideally, through such procedures a bureaucracy ensures uniform performance of every task. Through written rules and regulations, bureaucracies offer employees clear standards as to what is considered an adequate or exceptional performance. In addition, procedures provide a valuable sense of continuity in a bureaucracy. Government workers will come and go, but its structure and records give the organization a life of its own that outlives the services of any one bureaucrat. Of course, rules and regulations can overshadow the larger goals of an organization. If blindly applied, they can fail to achieve the objectives of the organization.

4. Impersonality

Max Weber wrote that in a bureaucracy, work is carried out *sine ira et studio* (without hatred or passion). Bureaucratic norms dictate that officials perform their duties without the personal consideration of people as individuals. This is intended to approximate equal treatment for each person; however, it also contributes to the often cold and uncaring tone associated with modern government organizations. We typically think of governments as being impersonal bureaucracies.

5. Security

With a government bureaucracy, hiring is based on technical qualifications rather than partisanship, and performance is measured against specific standards. This is intended, in part, to protect bureaucrats against arbitrary dismissal. Promotions are dictated by written personnel policies, and individuals have a right to appeal if they believe that particular rules have been violated. Such procedures give civil servants a sense of security and encourage loyalty to the organization. In Canada, for example, a bureaucrat goes through a process of promotion based on the merit principle laid out in the civil service acts of the federal government and the provinces, not because he or she did favours for a political party or the government. Above all, the bureaucracy is expected to value technical and professional competence, which is essential in the day-to-day functioning of a complex government.

Weber introduced the concept of bureaucracy but tended to emphasize its positive aspects. More recently, social scientists have described the negative consequences (or dysfunctions) of bureaucracy, both for the individual within the organization and for the bureaucracy itself.

Administrators and political scientists today feel that Weber's bureaucratic ideal has drawbacks in its application to modern democratic administrations, as well as to the authoritarian administrations it originally described. In the Weberian model, the bureaucracy is politically neutral, carrying out public policies regardless of which party or government faction is in power. But in all modern political systems, the process of decision-making is itself inexorably affected by those agencies of the state created to administer government programs and policies. The bureaucracies of modern democratic and non-democratic governments do more than merely implement decisions authorized by law or by executive fiat.

Today, a bureaucracy's functions include the provision of policy information and advice to elected officials — and therein lies a source of potent influence over the shaping of policy decisions. There are some who can persuasively argue that bureaucracies govern when no other branch of government is setting policy at all! In other words, public planning in many states reflects the power of the modern administrator over the elected or appointed representative. The permanent official, able to spend a career accumulating expertise in policy areas, has an enormous advantage over the nominally powerful politician and is not the captive of a stratified hierarchical government as described by Weber. Late twentieth-century bureaucracies are human institutions and are not as impersonal or predictable (nor are they as efficient) as the Weberian ideal described.

As well, in all modern political institutions, the administrative apparatus can be viewed as people performing the special functions of government. If the structural form represents the framework within and around which administrative activity is oriented, the lifeblood of the system is the people who staff the various departments and agencies and carry out the functions of government.

What Government Bureaucracies Do

We noted that modern states, regardless of their philosophical persuasion, require vast amounts of governing. All such national communities must perform a variety of administrative functions, which include implementing and formulating policy and regulations, performing services, and gathering information. The point is not how these functions are set – whether by elections, legislatures, and referenda, or by dictators and monolithic parties – but that however set, these functions must be implemented. And implementation requires bureaucracy, no more or less in the EU than in Canada.

Implementation of Policy

The primary function of all government administrations is the execution and enforcement of the laws and regulations passed by the executive and legislative branches of government and ruled on by the courts. In this regard, bureaucratic activity sometimes affects everybody, every day. In the process of implementing government policies, bureaucracies

assess our property values, issue our driver's licences, collect our taxes, pay our pensions, execute court orders, and send us our unemployment insurance cheques. Many people earn their living in bureaucratic jobs. Some of us may be arrested, prosecuted, and defended in court by officials who carry out laws and policies of government. Government bureaucracy determines whether we can build a house, add to the one we own, or pave our driveways. It follows us through life, recording our marriages, the births of our children, and finally our deaths.

Public administration can affect the quality of life of other people in the international community. In Ottawa, the Department of Foreign Affairs and International Trade administers Canada's foreign policies, not only through a world-wide network of embassies and consulates, but also through the international divisions of other domestic departments such as Agriculture, Communications, and Fisheries and Oceans. Its policies towards other states vis-à-vis trade, investment, and development assistance create jobs for Canadians, as well as provide benefits to the people of the states in which these policies apply.

The patterns of administration vary from state to state with respect to arrangements, structures, and techniques. In the Western world, two general patterns of administration have evolved: the *Anglo-American* type and the *continental European* type.

The Anglo-American pattern grew out of a basic distrust of centralized authority and encouraged the accountability of administrators through legislative and executive controls of their activities. Differences are also apparent among Anglo-American administrations. Unitary governments, like Great Britain's, exercise a great number of centralized administrative services, usually because their areas are relatively small. But the federal systems of larger states like Australia, Canada, the United States, and India have intermediate levels of administration under the separate jurisdictions of provinces and states. Because of their federal structures, the administrations of these states are much less centralized than the British and, to some extent, much more accountable.

> ■ ■ **red tape:** the phrase (derived from the red ribbons tied around official documents in the royal courts of Europe) that refers to the complex system of rules and procedures applied by bureaucratic organizations in their routine affairs. ■ ■

The continental type maintains a tradition established under the previous monarchical rule of administrative control from the centre. Local levels of administration are organized as appendages of the central government. In France, the ministries of the national government dominate local administration through *tutelle administrative* (administrative tutelage). One deviation from the continental model is Germany, where the *Länder* (states) conduct most administrative functions, enforce federal laws, and supply federal services. But the public funds allocated to these programs originate at the federal level.

Authoritative governments at various levels of economic development reflect an affinity to the continental European administrative model. For reasons associated with political control, their administrative structures appear to allow only very limited autonomy to local bureaucratic initiatives. The national administrative organizations of authoritarian states tend to be elitist, hierarchical, and departmentalized in the application of national policies. This is particularly true in many African and Latin American states. Authoritarian states in these regions of the world are characterized by centralized bureaucracies that include the usual ministries, departments, and bureaus organized under the direct control of the dictator. Because all these governments have embraced policies of development, decentralized agencies have been permitted to form, composed of independent and semi-independent organizations that are removed from executive control. These include credit banks, development corporations, national oil and mining companies, and regional development agencies.

Today, many authoritarian government administrations are a confusing jumble of "departments," "agencies," "sections," "offices," and "centres." Authoritarian executives have developed two control strategies over their administrations. The first is to staff as many key positions as possible with political followers, friends, and family, e.g., Saudi Arabia's ruling family. The second is to create a relationship of political and financial dependency upon the executive branch of government. The practices of patronage and other instances of corruption by dictators and bureaucrats build an especially loyal relationship between the executive and administrative branches of government.

Two major effects of the formal control systems characterized by executive decision-making procedures are **red tape** and corruption. It is frequently observed that officials at all levels of public administration delay decisions for weeks and sometimes years, and accept bribes for special favours or even for the routine performance of their regularly constituted duties.

Totalitarian states have created enormous administrative machines to achieve their ultimate goals of communism. Communist theorists regard the primary functions of the state apparatus to be the implementation of party discipline. Because of the enormity of these administrations, the management of totalitarian government has usually been inefficient and characterized by apathy, corruption, delay, and confusion. China, the biggest and oldest of the world's bureaucracies, is also a surviving communist administrative system. Not only does the bureaucracy in China implement the policies of government, but it is also charged with exercising political control through the rule of the Communist party. Under its constitution, China's state administrative apparatus is the guarantor of the official ideology and so constantly adjusts its actions to meet the dictates of communist theory.

Formulation of Policy

In modern democracies, the vast house of bureaucracy has come to have an immense impact on the creation of public policy. Today, public administrators have assumed the important task of initiating many policy proposals based on the changing needs of their departments and the people they serve. The fact that civil servants often *formulate* policy proposals that are then passed by a congress or parliament is a source of concern to the public and their elected officials, who worry that politicians may be colonized by administrators.[3] In a democracy, it is one thing for administrators to exert *influence* on the lawmaking process, but quite another for them to draft the laws. However, access to information, expertise, and the organizational wisdom of government departments make many administrators much more than just advisors to their political bosses. In Canada's Department of Foreign Affairs, for example, civil servants enjoy a virtual monopoly over information on foreign-policy matters. Senior civil servants take the lead in recommending changes to the minister in the complicated matrix of Canadian foreign policy. Because politicians rarely have alternative sources to use in analyzing the intricacies of Canada's external relations, they tend to accept the authority of bureaucratic policy.

Much of the legislation passed by democratic legislatures is broadly framed. This allows bureaucratic agencies a great deal of discretion in the implementation of programs and policies. Government departments and agencies need loosely outlined rules so that they are able to meet new situations as they arise. But often the details of a program are left to the discretion of administrators out of political necessity. The end result is that administrators have broad powers of interpretation to fill in the specific details of a policy. In this process they have much to say about how a policy is applied. When a bureaucracy fills in the details of a policy or program, its direction is generally consistent with administrative policy. It is, in fact, in the business of making policy.

The steady growth of public administration in all governments, both federal and unitary forms, has been one of the most distinctive trends during the twentieth century. As a result, the number of public servants has expanded dramatically in every state, constructing an elaborate administrative apparatus. The discretionary policy-making powers of public servants permit them to play a major role in the decision-making processes of modern governments. Over the years, students of public administration have written extensively about the implications of the growth of the administrative state and its effects on the relationship between bureaucracy and democracy. The exercise of decision-making powers by bureaucrats who are largely anonymous and indirectly accountable blurs the line between political and administrative authority. The public can justifiably ask whether the real powers of government are exercised by the politicians they elect or by the appointed administrators.

■ ■ **administocracy:** a type of government created when bureaucrats make decisions that permit them to simultaneously formulate and implement public policy. ■ ■

The Eurocrats

One of the best examples of a government bureaucracy that extensively formulates policies is the *European Commission*. The commission's chief role is to initiate and propose new policies and regulations for the European Union. By comparison to other democratic government bureaucracies, the European Commission overtly prepares and formulates legislation for approval by the Council of Ministers and the European Parliament.

At their massive headquarters in Brussels, the "Eurocrats" make policies on everything from the elasticity of athletic shorts to the digestive quality of zucchinis. They decide what regulations should be imposed on the items people manufacture and consume. So powerful are the Eurocrats in the New Europe that they can dismantle state-owned monopolies without the former approval of the member states. The commission also has the power to act on its own in the formulation of competition policy, farming, trade policy, and customs duties.

There are 16,000 European Commission bureaucrats, most of whom work at the International Congress Centre, the nerve centre of the New Europe. The Eurocrats are the elite, the clergy of the New Europe. At the Commission's present stage of political evolution, the Eurocrats are the self-appointed high priests of bureaucracy, accountable to no one but themselves. The supranational government developing in Europe is an excellent example of an **administocracy**; these are the people who are making the policies that will unite the 12 member states and permit the governance of this new political system.

Regulation

Many of us meet bureaucracy head-on when it applies the plethora of **regulations** that governments generate and update each year. Things seem to be done to us or for us according to stringent regulations that demand our acquiescence, and always the completion of forms. Encounters with bureaucracy are very often shaped by books of rules, manuals of procedure, and forms to fill out.

In Canada, numerous regulations flow from all the departments of the provincial and federal governments. Virtually every aspect of private, corporate, and governmental behaviour is regulated: airlines, atomic energy, customs and immigration, consumer and corporate affairs, labour, radio, television, and sports are some of the most visible areas of regulatory activity. The Economic Council of

Figure 8.1:
Regulating your hamburger

Bun – if enriched, must use enriched flour and must contain between .44 – .77 milligrams of thiamin; .27 – .48 milligrams of riboflavin; 3.5 – 6.4 milligrams of niacin; 2.9 – 4.3 milligrams of iron.

Pesticides – for most pesticides, not more than 0.1 parts per million in lettuce, tomatoes, pickles, onions, and meat.

Lettuce, tomatoes, pickles, onions – must be fresh, ripe, and have good colour.

Beef Patties – must be ground beef. If beef is mixed with cereal or pork it must be called a "Hamburg Patty."

Pepper – cannot include additives.

Salt – must be crystalline sodium chloride; must be iodized.

Ketchup – no flow requirements; must be made from tomatoes, vinegar, salt and seasonings.

Cheese – must contain no more than 39% moisture and not less than 31% milk fat; may contain salt, flavours, cultures, colour, woodsmoke and preservatives.

Fat – in Canada there are 3 grades of ground beef: Regular Ground must not contain more than 30% fat; Medium Ground must not contain more than 23% fat; and Lean Ground must not contain more than 17% fat.

Growth Promoters – use of growth-stimulating hormones must end well in advance of slaughter. Animal must go through withdrawal period to excrete drugs and medicines. Diethyl stilbestrol is banned in Canada.

Mayonnaise – must contain vegetable oil, whole eggs or yokes, vinegar or lemon juice.

Canada has reported that in recent decades the federal government passed more statutes regulating the economy than had been passed for the first hundred years since Confederation.[4] Along with the dramatic increase in the number of regulatory statutes has been the proliferation of regulatory agencies by which governments seek to influence, direct, and control economic and social behaviour. For example, in three areas of fundamental importance to government in Canada – telecommunications, transportation, and energy – regulatory agencies make decisions that have enormous impact on the allocation of Canadian resources, the organization of production and consumption, and on the distribution of monies. The Canadian Radio-television and Telecommunications Commission (CRTC), the Canadian Transport Commission (CTC), and the National Energy Board (NEB) actually make and interpret regulations in their respective fields that have the effect of law and directly affect citizens every day.

Regulating Your Hamburger

All levels of government in Canada have something to do with the regulation of the foods we eat. Something as simple as a hamburger cannot escape the regulatory scrutiny of governments. If the Canadian government did not regulate pesticides on crops, as the consumers who eat the crops, we would be in significant risk of serious illness. If governments did not inspect livestock to make sure they were free of diseases such as tuberculosis, the incidence of TB among Canadians would be much higher.

For most Canadians, the hamburger is a quick, inexpensive meal we eat fairly often, taking for granted that there are few complications in presenting this food in a market economy. But the hamburger is subject to hundreds of federal, provincial, and municipal regulations, many stemming from laws, ordinances, and precedent-setting court cases (figure 8.1). Health and Welfare Canada, Agriculture Canada, Consumer and Corporate Affairs Canada, all provincial departments of health and consumer affairs and municipal governments set the standards, legislate inspections, and administer the acts that apply to food. These rules touch on everything involved in meat production: grazing practices for cattle, conditions in slaughterhouses, and the methods used to process meat for sale to supermarkets, restaurants, and fast-food outlets.

There is an extensive relationship between regulative bureaucratic agencies and the individual in contemporary Canada. In periods of high unemployment, the application of regulations of the Unemployment Insurance Commission and provincial welfare agencies affect the quality of life for millions of people. In recent years, regulations in Canada have extended to include the prohibition of discrimination against minorities and women by employers, the control of pollution, and the commercial uses of metric and imperial weights and measures.

But Canada is not an exception. The regulative activities of modern bureaucracies have proliferated enormously all over the world in the last century. Industrialization and urbanization have produced problems in transportation, health, and public order in all countries. Growth in industry and technology has created problems of monopolies, industrial safety, the ethical application of modern technologies, and labour exploitation. At the same time, the growth of science and the widespread attitude that people should control their environment have led to the recognition that social control can only be achieved through administrative action. Political modernization is identified with the performance of regulatory activities.

Servicing

Many administrative agencies are created to provide government services of various kinds to individuals and groups in society. Environment Canada is one of the best examples of an important service agency administered by the federal government. Its inland and marine forecasts are vital to all modes of transportation, as well as to businesses, farming, and fishing. Canada's Department of Agriculture and its provincial counterparts conduct research on pest control, land management, livestock improvement, and the marketing and distribution of agricultural products. Canada Employment and Immigration runs an extensive job-finding service (Canada Job Strategy) in all Canadian towns and cities of a certain size. And the Department of National Health and Welfare funds and co-ordinates Canada's medicare program with the departments of health in the provinces.

Because the efforts made by governments in different administrative service areas use up a percentage of the GDP and are a reflection of their political values, they vary from one state to the next. In 1991, Israel spent 27 percent of its GDP on defence and only 4.5 percent on health and other welfare services, whereas Germany spent 3.5 percent of its GDP on defence and 24 percent on health and other welfare services.[5]

Education, social security, and health are administrative services provided by most governments, but they are affected by the level of national wealth or the general health of an economy. It is difficult for poor economies to allocate their financial resources to services like these when their budgets are limited. All the wealthier states can afford to choose how and for what purposes they will provide government services to their citizens.

Licensing

As an administrative function, licensing is both a means of control and a source of government revenue. It enables governments to set standards and qualifications on activities having public consequences. Driving a car, hunting, fishing, practising medicine or law, selling real estate, teaching in public school, and owning and operating a radio or television station are just some of the areas in which governments impose licensing requirements. In Canada and other federal states, most of these standards are set by the provinces; however, some licences are issued by the federal government. For example, the Canadian Radio-television and Telecommunications Commission, under the Broadcasting Act, is delegated with the responsibility to license all radio, television, and cable television companies operating in Canada. However, in unitary countries such as France, Great Britain, and Israel, the national government is the sole licensing authority.

In one sense, licensing involves the provision of a service, but in another sense it also involves a considerable amount of regulation. In the case of the CRTC, the agency was created in 1968 to protect the Canadian broadcasting system. Its objectives are to make sure that Canadians monitor the broadcasting system and to regulate programming to ensure that it is of high quality for public consumption. The main concern is Canadian content. Similarly, the regulatory functions of any agency are involved in the power to grant or withhold licences.

Gathering Information

All bureaucracies gather and store vast amounts of information from the outside world. In a government, the intake of information is a major function of public administration. Eventually, this information-gathering results in an output of policy or action by the political system. Governments want to know everything about you: who you are, when you were born, how much education you have, what your occupation is, when you died, and what caused your death. Governments gather information by means of administrative research, polls, public hearings, commissions, task forces, committees, and licensing.

In Canada, all government departments and administrative agencies generate and consume massive quantities of data about the private and corporate behaviour of Canadians, as well as about Canada's external relations with the international community. Health and Welfare Canada conducts research into the diseases that afflict Canadians. Consumer and Corporate Affairs co-ordinates information on businesses and corporations in Canada. And the Department of Foreign Affairs receives vital information from its embassies around the world.

Many departments of government, in order to carry out their programs, gather information on the private lives of individuals. The Department of Justice has, among other responsibilities, the role of gathering statistics on crime and subversion. Its files hold information on the most intimate aspects of the lives of certain citizens.

Most of the information collected by governments is not controversial. In Canada, the census gathers information about the population in order to help government make policy choices that fit the needs of the people. Canada's thirteenth census, taken in 1991, contains about 50 million pages of data on almost everything Canadians have or do. Canadians willingly told the 31,653 enumerators whether they were athletes (1.9 million said they were) and how many flush toilets they had (103,200 had none).

But there is always a potential danger in the collection of such data. Bureaucratic agencies know about our life histories, our financial affairs, our credit ratings, our reputations for loyalty, our politics, and our places of residence. Even without our knowledge, police investigations may detail and hold on file whatever stories a neighbour or even a stranger has told about us.

In these days of computerized data retrieval, this information can be pulled together and disseminated with frightening speed. Only such human factors as the goodwill and decent motives of most bureaucrats may save us from the worst invasions of our privacy. But people do lose jobs and suffer other hardships because of unsubstantiated rumours that are registered in government files. The private lives, opinions, and morals of individuals are becoming increasingly vulnerable to bureaucratic scrutiny. The sheer volume of personal information in data banks, both public and private, is a threat not only to our credit ratings but to our freedom to live as we choose.

In most states, the public has no right of access to the vast store of information in reports, records, files, and statistics gathered by governments through their administrative agencies. But a growing number of democratic states have decided that this practice is wrong and should be reversed: all unclassified administrative documents ought to be accessible to the public, except for information classified as secret by law. Usually called a freedom of information act, access act, or privacy act, this kind of constitutional and legislative provision is now operative in nine democratic states.

Sweden was the first state to grant the right of public access to government documents in its constitutional law, over 200 years ago. Other states have proclaimed access laws in more recent times: Australia (1982); Canada (Privacy Act, 1982, and Access to Information Act, 1983); Denmark (1970); Finland (1951); France (1978); the Netherlands (1978); Norway (1970); and the United States (1966, revised 1974). In Canada, two provinces, Nova Scotia (1977) and New Brunswick (1978), passed access to information legislation applicable to provincial administrative documents and government files. At the federal level, the Privacy Act gives citizens and residents access to information about them held by the government, protects their privacy by preventing others from gaining access to it, and gives them some control over its collection and use. The Access to Information Act gives the same people the right to examine or obtain copies of the records of a federal government institution, except in limited and specific circumstances. The Access Register and Access Request Forms are located in public libraries, government information offices, and in postal stations in rural areas.

Redistribution of Wealth and Income

Governments intervene in the social system for reasons other than efficiency and regulation. When governments administer what are called *redistributive policies*, it is, in effect, taking garments from wealthy tailors and giving them to those who have no clothes and nothing to trade. Policies of this sort redistribute the shares of the economic pie among certain individuals and groups in society. They are aimed at changing the existing patterns of wealth and income in the economy. In short, they aspire to widen the range of those who receive a share of the national wealth. They produce benefits to some segments of society at a cost to others. In the 1990s, the politics of redistributive public administration flow from broad budget decisions that may place the viability of social programs against the deficit and the debt.

In theory, the progressive income tax is itself a redistributive measure, because it is designed to take more tax money from the rich than the poor, and thus to reduce the traditional disparities of wealth and income across the population. In Canada, minimum-wage laws also have a redistributive effect, resulting in higher expenditures by employers on wages for unskilled workers. Welfare laws designed to help the needy are also redistributive. Each year the federal government transfers billions of dollars to the provinces as a national strategy to redistribute wealth and to standardize, as much as possible, the delivery of government services to Canadians.

Table 8.2:
Controls on bureaucratic behaviour

	Formal	Informal
E **X** **T** **E** **R** **N** **A** **L**	Political executives: (presidents, prime ministers, premiers, governors) Elected assemblies: (parliaments, congresses, city councils) Courts Ombudsman	Public opinion Media Pressure groups Electorate University public- administration programs
I **N** **T** **E** **R** **N** **A** **L**	Public hearings Inquiries Royal commissions Decentralization and deregulation	Professional standards Upgrading Accountability

Source: Adapted from Florence Heffron, *Organization Theory and Public Organizations: The Political Connection* (Englewood Cliffs, N.J.: Prentice-Hall, 1989); Kenneth Kernaghan and David Siegel, *Public Administration in Canada* (Scarborough, ON: Nelson Canada, 1991).

Controlling the Bureaucrats

Executive Controls

All states have developed a variety of formal and informal controls on bureaucratic behaviour (table 8.2). One of the obvious major government controls external to a state's administrative apparatus is the political executive. Prime ministers, presidents, and ministers formally control the bureaucracy through their powers of appointment and removal. They also have control of the public purse from which bureaucracies are funded and programs are planned. While it is true that political executives cannot get along without the services of bureaucracies, it is also true that bureaucrats are controlled by them in a variety of ways. The executive can tame an autonomous administration by threatening to reduce government spending and to cut back the size of the civil service. Where the political executive chooses to spend money among its administrative agencies, and how it supervises the public services, encourages bureaucrats to conform with the goals of the elected government.

Legislative Controls

Legislatures are another branch of government that can exercise significant external controls on a bureaucracy. Through questioning and criticism of the government, public administrators are held accountable to the ministers who run the departments. The public expects legislators – both the opposition and government backbenchers – to monitor official waste of public funds, and to deal with those who violate the law or violate citizens' rights in the conduct of their jobs. Legislative committees can scrutinize departmental administration and are empowered to investigate abuses of administrative authority. Public inquiries, auditors' reports, questions of parliamentarians, hearings, commissions and inquiries, and ultimately court decisions all have an effect on bureaucratic performance. These formal controls work to secure a responsive, effective, and honest civil service.

Legislatures can compel a bureaucracy to change administrative policy by creating a new law or revoking a department's or agency's powers. In all parliamentary systems of government, bureaucracies must defend their budgetary requests before an appropriate legislative committee or cabinet minister. In Canada, legislative committees have, among

■ ■ **auditor general:** a special parliamentary officer who performs an annual audit of the Public Accounts and prepares the annual Auditor's Report to Parliament. ■ ■

other functions, the power to scrutinize how government departments manage their budgets. The Public Accounts Committee and the Standing Joint Committee of the Senate and the House of Commons are chaired by a member of the opposition whose independence from Cabinet control forces a greater accountability in the administration of government departments.

In many states, especially the United States, the power of the purse is as much a legislative as an executive power. The mere threat of withholding funds can force an administrative change in policy. In Canada and Great Britain, individual members of parliament indirectly exercise restraints by becoming experts on particular subjects. An MP can ask a question of any minister concerning the administrative policies and practices of his or her ministry. Asking questions is the principal method by which backbenchers can review and criticize the action of the civil service. And in general, the committee system of parliament or congress supports the scrutinizing role of the legislature over the bureaucracy.

In Canada, another legislative control instrument that scrutinizes bureaucratic behaviour is the Office of the Auditor General and the provincial auditors in the provinces. The auditor general reports annually to Parliament on its verification of government's financial records and on whether departments have wisely spent the monies appropriated to them. The Auditor General operates independently of executive controls and the auditor general's Report keeps bureaucrats accountable to their departmental budgets.

In the United States, the General Accounting Office, the Congressional Research Service, the Office of Technology Assessment, and the Congressional Budget Office give Congress information about bureaucratic conduct independently from the executive branch of government.

Courts

Then there are the courts. They have the final authority to interpret the law and to rule on the proper administration and enforcement of laws in society. When private citizens or corporations feel that an administrative practice is unfair or that an administrator has stepped outside his or her jurisdiction, they can seek a legal remedy through the courts. In Canada, the courts can review administrative discretion when there have been breaches of human rights, when the constitution is violated by bureaucratic behaviour, and when there are errors of law made in the interpretation and implementation of public policy.

In 1991, the Supreme Court of Canada ruled that ministers cannot be held criminally responsible for what goes on in their departments unless they have special knowledge of an illegal act. But the court also noted that ministers cannot seek refuge behind an entourage of government lawyers when bureaucrats in their departments abuse their powers without their direct knowledge. Nor can they pretend to be blind ("willful blindness") to what their departments do when these actions are held judicially accountable.

In Canada and the United States, courts can initiate remedies of bureaucratic indiscretions that may take the form of writs instructing administrators to conduct themselves in appropriate ways. These may include a *writ of mandamus* (a court order requiring a public official to do his or her duty as the law dictates), a *writ of injunction* (a court order prohibiting an official or a private citizen from performing a particular action), or a court decision resulting in the payment of damages or the determination of responsibility for the abuse of administrative powers. A *writ of certiorari* is a superior court order that may be issued against bureaucracies when they violate the doctrine of fairness. *Habeas corpus* is a writ issued by a court requiring that a person who has been detained be brought before a court to determine whether the detention is legal. In administrative law, this writ is rarely used except in immigration cases involving orders of custody or deportation. *Quo warranto* is a court order inquiring whether an appointment to public office is legal. *Damages* are court remedies that require a certain amount of money be paid to compensate for an injury or wrong done to an individual by, in this case, a government bureaucracy. But courts are not always successful in keeping a close check on bureaucratic activities; they are primarily concerned with making and adjudicating laws, not watching over the administration of them.

Constitutional Protections

The Canadian Charter of Rights and Freedoms provides constitutional protections of administrative law. The conduct of bureaucrats is subject to the rigor of Charter rights guarantees and makes the public service subject to the scope of constitutional protections affecting an individual's human and civil rights. Many of the statutes and regulations that existed prior to 1982 now have been harmonized under the Charter.

In the United States, a basic principle of

the Constitution is limited government. There are certain things that bureaucrats cannot do and should not do under the U.S. Bill of Rights. Bureaucratic powers were very important to the founders of the American republic. They expected Congress to make policy and a representative president to administer it. The U.S. Constitution has very few provisions that describe administrative duties. But it does postulate a "government of laws." No one should stand above the law, especially in the administration of it.

The Office of Ombuds

Recognizing the limitations of legislative and judicial controls that leave the initiatives to elected officials or to the aggrieved, an increasing number of states have created a special office of *ombudsman* (parliamentary commissioner) to advocate, investigate, and publicly criticize on behalf of citizens who complain about unfair bureaucratic treatment. Sweden was the first country to create a *Justitieombudsman* (representative of justice) in 1809. The Swedish *Riksdag* (parliament) appoints the ombudsman, who is empowered to hear and investigate citizens' complaints of official **arbitrariness**, **negligence**, or **discrimination**. The ombuds has comprehensive jurisdiction, which includes the supervision of courts and the military.

The office of ombuds has been adopted in about 25 democratic states, including Canada, Denmark, Fiji, Finland, France, Great Britain, Israel, New Zealand, and Germany. Not all states have offices at the national level. Canada and the United States have no general ombuds at the federal level. However, both have ombuds at the provincial and state levels, respectively. In Canada, all provinces except

Prince Edward Island have ombudsmen to remedy complaints against provincial administrations. In the United States, only Alaska, Iowa, Hawaii, and Nebraska have ombuds officers, but the office has been established in a number of U.S. cities as well, including Atlanta and Seattle.

As an investigator and mediator appointed to protect the rights of individuals and groups in dealing with government, the ombudsman hears many complaints. When regular government agencies do not satisfactorily resolve problems, the ombudsman is asked to investigate grievances. In general, these involve a) claims for social assistance benefits or Workers' Compensation; b) property affected by work on highways; c) employment, or consumer services regulated by the province; c) difficulties in obtaining licenses or permits; and d) any other matter regulated by provincial or municipal laws. In Canada, provincial ombuds do not have the authority to investigate grievances arising from decisions of the Cabinet, the law courts or judges, the federal government, private companies, or individuals.

In April 1978, the Trudeau government introduced a bill to create a federal ombudsman, but it died on the order paper and the government was defeated in May 1979. The Clark government left it off their legislative agenda, and the new Trudeau government, elected in February 1980, did not revive the bill. The Mulroney governments (1984 and 1988) did not move on a bill for a general ombuds office to cover all aspects of federal administration. Though as a leadership candidate in 1993 Kim Campbell promised to establish such an office at the federal level, she did not follow through on this promise during her brief tenure as prime minister. Upon his election in November, 1993, Jean Chrétien failed to place the appointment of a federal ombuds on his immediate agenda.

However, it is important to note that Canada has created ombuds-like offices for special matters under federal jurisdiction. For example, there is a Commissioner of Official Languages who reviews complaints from members of the public who feel that they were unfairly treated in their own languages by federal agencies. There is a correctional investigator who receives complaints from inmates about injustices in the penal system. Under the Access to Information Act, the government has established the office of information commissioner to deal with complaints about the wrongful denial of access to information. And, under the Privacy Act, the government empowers a privacy commissioner to investigate complaints about personal information retained by government agencies and to make recommendations to the institution involved if there is a denial of access. But all of these offices are highly specialized and in no way perform the comprehensive functions of a general ombuds officer.

Among the extra-governmental forces and agencies that attempt to control bureaucracies are pressure groups and the mass media. Pressure groups attempt to reform the bureaucracy by using their own investigative staffs to challenge the efficacy of many types of social programs and to bring pressure to bear upon the government to change the programs. In Canada, the Canadian Federation of Independent Business (CFIB) has prompted many other organizations to use public opinion as a way to reform the tax-collection methods of Revenue Canada Taxation. In the United States, Ralph Nader has gained prominence in connection with administrative reform in both public and private-sector bureaucracies. The mass media provide still another avenue for curbing an unresponsive bureaucracy.

Bureaucratic accountability is also affected by internal controls, such as professional standards and upgrading, as well as advisory committees made up of people representing political parties and interest groups. The variety and kinds of controls vary from state to state. The term "administocracy" was coined by Guy S. Claire in the 1930s to refer to tensions between the ideals of popular sovereignty and the growth of an aristocracy of administrators within a democratic state.[6] In a democracy, people pay great attention to the values of elected officials, but very little to the values of the people who administer government programs. This is all the more important to recognize due to the fact that career civil servants are neither elected nor are they removable by the electoral process. But a multiplicity of formal and informal controls function to keep democratic bureaucracies accountable.

In totalitarian and authoritarian political systems, many of these controls are lacking or are so constrained as to be virtually useless. In dictatorial states, political executives and legislators are not often responsibly elected and courts do not function as an independent branch of government. The roles of the mass media and pressure groups are not those of an external conscience for the bureaucracy or a forum for public grievances. Instead, bureaucracies are affiliated with the goals of an elite-directed party and government apparatus. In the absence of an open and pluralistic political system, the effectiveness of all controls on bureaucracy are very limited.

Canada's Public Service

Broadly speaking, the Canadian bureaucracy consists of the personnel in federal government departments (e.g., the Department of Finance), federal government agencies (e.g., the Bank of Canada and the Canadian Wheat Board), central control agencies (e.g., the Treasury Board and the Privy Council Office), and crown corporations (e.g., Air Canada and the Canadian Broadcasting Corporation). The great bulk of federal government employees are recruited by the **Public Service Commission**, itself a central control agency that performs its wide staffing functions by means of competitive examinations and interviews in which merit is the determining factor. As an independent agency that serves Parliament, the Public Service Commission controls the forces of political and administrative patronage by implementing the merit principle in the operation of the federal bureaucracy. Legally, Canada's public employees are not appointed or removed from their positions for political reasons. Civil servants are directly responsible, through a clear chain of command, to their administrative superiors. It cannot be denied that political favouritism sometimes plays a part in the choice of job assignments and the speed or delay in promotions, even though in theory, the public service rules out politics. In 1988, a ruling by the federal Court of Appeal struck

■ ■ **merit principle:** the concept, employed by modern government bureaucracies, that hiring public servants should be based on entrance exams and promotion ratings to produce an administration of government by people with the proper qualifications, talents, and skills. ■ ■

down part of the law (the Public Service Employment Act) that restricted the political rights of federal public servants on the grounds that it infringed on their freedoms of expression and association.

The basic structural units of the Canadian federal government were reduced under Kim Campbell to 23 departments that exercise jurisdiction over national and international policies and programs.[7] The large reduction in the number of federal government departments was continued under Jean Chrétien. The amalgamation of the federal government into fewer departments has increased the responsibilities of ministers and deputy ministers.

Beginning with the federal administrative establishment, the key political actor is the cabinet minister, who functions as the formal department head and who is responsible for the administration of the government's policies through its public employees. The administrative efficacy of the minister in leading the department is often solely dependent upon the qualities of his or her personal leadership and aggressiveness.[8] But generally, the energies of a minister are focused and directed on the politics of cabinet decision-making. The minister tends not to tamper with administrative functions of the department itself. Instead, the minister must learn to deal with what Flora MacDonald called "the civil service policy" and adapt the political exigencies of Cabinet and constituency pressures to the routines of the department's administration.[9]

The DM

The person second in the line of authority within a department is the deputy minister (DM), who also is appointed by the prime minister. Unlike other civil servants, the deputy minister retains an administrative position "at the pleasure" of the government. He or she does not enjoy permanent tenure, and may be shuffled, demoted, or fired at the will of the prime minister. Although deputy ministers are held accountable for the policies they helped to devise and for the loyalties they may have demonstrated toward the government that appointed them, most of the time they seem to be able to overcome their associations with out-of-favour governments and are kept on by succeeding governments as experienced sources of advice. The two most important skills of a deputy minister – those of advising and departmental management – are indispensable to political ministers who need to take command of an administrative machine that was in operation long before they rose to power and that will function quite well after they have gone.[10]

In terms of the policy process itself, the deputy minister is a senior policy adviser not only to the minister, but to the entire government. The segmented process of federal decision-making requires deputy ministers to advise other ministers and deputy ministers in order to co-ordinate cabinet policies and programs. In particular, all deputy ministers must represent and co-ordinate their department's affairs with three central agencies: the Prime Minister's Office (PMO), the Privy Council Office (PCO), and the Treasury Board secretariat. Over many years of gaining administrative experience, the deputy minister builds an important network of personal and professional contacts that is invaluable to the operation of the government. As administrative head of a department, the deputy minister is like the managing executive of a large corporation. As an executor of political policies, the deputy minister is an interdepartmental diplomat, a policy co-ordinator, and a negotiator.

> ■ ■ **division of labour:** the separation of work into distinct parts, each of which is completed by an individual or group of individuals for the purposes of increasing production, efficiency, and specialization of expertise. ■ ■

The deputy minister is at the top of a hierarchical chain of command within the structure of the department. The people who work at subordinate levels are almost exclusively civil servants who stay on over the years, in contrast to the political executives above them, who come and go with each changing government or cabinet shuffle. All departments have certain characteristics that seem to be universal bureaucratic traits: (1) *specialization* or **division of labour**: individual jobs have specific tasks assigned to them irrespective of the individual who holds the job; (2) *Hierarchy* or *fixed lines of control*: each civil servant knows who the boss is, and whom, if anyone, he or she may supervise; and (3) *Incentives,* to attract people to work for the department and be loyal to its purposes. By far the most important incentive is the assurance that once someone has a job, he or she will keep it unless a gross transgression is committed by that person.

For John Tait, Deputy Minister of the Department of Justice, one of the most important skills of the DM is that of human resources manager. "Good government management requires communicating with people, meeting them and consulting with them on a frequent basis." Especially in a government department, people need to feel engaged in the decisions that affect them.

Deputy ministers advise their political bosses on policy matters, plan and control expenditures in the department, scrutinize the organization and structure of the department, and assume the wider responsibilities of co-ordinating departmental activities with those of other government departments. He or she must manage the personnel in the department, and when necessary, advise the executive government departments, the PMO, the PCO, and the Treasury Board about departmental needs and problems.

Quite understandably, deputy ministers who are the permanent heads of a department will have administrative interests that may be different from those of the minister and the prime minster they serve. Usually, deputy ministers are fiercely dedicated to the programs they administer. They expect that the minister who heads their department will take their advice and avoid the many transient political pressures that cause cabinet ministers to alter the administration of government programs. They want the minister to represent the interests of the department to the prime minister. As a result, the minister is somewhat at cross-purposes between the bureaucratic and political forces of government. This is augmented by the fact that ministers are responsible only for their part of government and thus lack the prime minister's need to balance a wider range of interests.

Ministers

Ministers are not totally without ways of dealing with centrifugal tendencies of the bureaucracy. Cabinet ministers are accompanied by an entourage of aides, executive assistants, and parliamentary secretaries who are directly responsible to them. Parliamentary secretaries are members of parliament who are designated by the minister to assist in the political operation of the department. In the last ten years, ministerial aides, executive assistants, and parliamentary secretaries have occupied an increasingly important place in the functioning of Cabinet. As the complexity and size of the bureaucracy increase the challenges to ministerial control, the staff acts as a buffer to the growing colonization of the political adminstration by the civil service.

One major function of the minister's staff is to protect and advance the political interests of the department and the Cabinet. This includes liaison with Parliament, press relations, control of the minister's schedule, travel, and relations with major interest groups and party figures. Ministers also have assistants to perform such inevitable but disagreeable tasks as refusing access, discharging employees and officials, and denying requests for special consideration. The parliamentary secretaries have some input into the development of new programs and legislation. They also serve to take the heat off the minister from time to time in the House of Commons by standing in to answer sensitive questions directed at the department from members of the opposition. Sometimes, as well, when the minister has accepted an engagement to speak in a politically hostile area of the country, the parliamentary secretary is sent instead to deflect the political flak away from the minister. Despite such stratagems, all cabinet ministers are aware of the many difficulties involved in gaining control of the very bureaucracy that is one of the bases of their power.

Crown Corporations

Crown corporations are another important aspect of public administration in Canada.[11] Since World War II, public enterprises have rapidly expanded in the Canadian economy. Crown corporations have been used to meet national or local needs in the interests of the public where private enterprise and investors have not been ready or willing to take the risk to promote economic growth. The development of a national or provincial infrastructure has been costly and risky, culminating in the incorporation of such public enterprises as the St. Lawrence Seaway Authority, Ports Canada, the CNR and Air Canada. **Private sector** corporate behaviour is profit-motivated; government-owned corporations consider factors such as unemployment, welfare, market failures, and national standards when operating in a community.

There are a number of different ways of defining crown corporations[12]: the characteristic of government ownership is considered to be the most important legal criterion for defining a crown corporation. However, there is some disagreement as to what amount of government ownership determines the status of a crown corporation.

Mixed enterprises are companies, such as the Canada Development Corporation and Telesat Canada, in which ownership is shared by the government (in the name of the Crown)

■ ■ **private sector:** in a mixed economy, that part of the economy not under governmental control, i.e., all private enterprise, private profit- and non-profit-making organizations and exchanges between individuals. ■ ■

with the private sector. *Joint enterprises* are public companies, such as the Newfoundland and Labrador Development Corporation, and the North Portage Development Corporation, in which ownership is shared between governments, usually a provincial government and the federal government.

From a functional perspective, crown corporations reflect common criteria, whether they are provincially, federally, or jointly owned: a) majority ownership is held by a government; b) there is an arm's-length management strategy, independent from government; c) corporate goods and services are directed at the private sector, not the government; and d) prices for goods and services provided by crown corporations must be fair and competitive.

Federal crown corporations are accountable to Parliament under the Financial Administration Act, known as the FAA (1952), as amended in 1984. This legislation applies only to corporations which are wholly government-owned, such as the Canada Development Investment Corporation and Via Rail Canada Inc. The FAA places crown corporations into three *schedules*, classified as *B, CI,* and *CII.* Under schedule B are crown corporations such as the Canadian Centre for Occupational Health and Safety, and the National Museums of Canada. Formerly categorized as departmental corporations, they perform a wide range of administrative, advisory, regulatory, and supervisory functions of a governmental nature. Schedule CI lists crown corporations such as Loto Canada Inc., the Export

Development Corporation, and the Federal Business Development Bank. These companies perform a variety of commercial, developmental, managerial, and service functions. They make up the majority of corporations listed under the act and experience varying degrees of ministerial direction. Schedule CII includes most companies formerly categorized as proprietary corporations, such as Teleglobe Canada, Petro-Canada, and Canada Ports Corporation. These corporations are often in direct competition with privately owned companies and are expected to operate as financially self-sustaining.

Under the 1984 amendments, some crown corporations were dropped from the listings of the FAA. The Canadian Broadcasting Corporation, the Canada Council, the Canadian Film Development Corporation, and the National Arts Centre perform special cultural functions and are distanced from the political controls applied to other corporations. Some crown corporations such as the Bank of Canada, the Canada Wheat Board, and the International Development and Research Centre have been established by special legislation. They perform many diverse functions that require independence from political and ministerial control. For example, the Bank of Canada sets the prime lending rate on Canadian currency in order to keep the interest rate differential between Canada and the United States from becoming too great or too small. In order for the Bank of Canada to manage and regulate Canadian monetary policy, it must remain free from direct political interference.

The governor of the Bank of Canada frequently finds himself at the centre of momentous struggles – involving the federal government, the provinces, and lenders and borrowers – over the bank's monetary policy on such questions as "tight money" or the most desirable political and economic means of combatting inflation or recession.

Crown corporations have a working arrangement with the Public Service Commission that allows them almost complete discretion in hiring and promotion at all levels, particularly at management levels. The labour standards of the public service commission are a model aimed at preventing arbitrary and unfair decisions and at equalizing promotion and pay policies among the various crown corporations.

By the 1990s, nearly half of all federal government employees, or about 250,000 Canadians, were working for both classified and unclassified crown corporations. An additional 300,000 people were employed by the federal departments of government such as National Revenue, Foreign Affairs, and Consumer and Corporate Affairs. When the nearly 85,000 members of the armed forces are taken into account, over 600,000 people are employed by the federal government. By any measure, the bureaucracy is overwhelmingly the largest part of the federal government. In effect, this makes Canada's public service its own constituency, with the federal bureaucracy acting as any other pressure group by prodding, probing, expanding, and consolidating its own position in Canada's political system. The federal bureaucracy has grown large enough to constitute a fourth branch of government. Neither the mass media, nor elected politicians, nor interest groups have the aggregate power of the federal bureaucracy.

A growing consensus among political

scientists points to the conclusion that Canadian society may be *ruled* by the politicians but it is *governed* by the bureaucrats. The bureaucracy makes thousands and thousands of interpretive decisions each day, thus having an enormous amount of supplementary lawmaking power after bills become laws. At the departmental level in Canada, the bureaucracy is a major initiator of public policy. Many of the proposals for new legislation come from senior civil servants who set the agenda of alternatives for the government out of view of the public. It is true that the crucial initiative for the most important new legislation comes from the Cabinet. But even here, the departmental civil servants provide much of the background and analysis, and they frequently draft the actual bill as well. Furthermore, they provide a significant share of the continuity and flow of information necessary to pass legislation.

The routine decisions of the Canadian government are a preserve of the federal bureaucracy. For example, the federal government is a very large buyer of goods and services. In some cases, it is the largest buyer, or the only one. The millions of decisions about what the government will or will not buy, or provide its money for, are made by career civil servants subject to very general supervision and guidelines. The collective impact of these decisions is the government's policy. Because the bureaucracy is so vast and complex, the sum of so many apparently small decisions has an impact rivalling that of the few obviously big ones. Canadians may be unwarranted in their easy use of the term "bureaucrat" as a purely negative stereotype. However, they are warranted in their desire to watch and evaluate the public service.

Public Administration in the United States

In the United States, the term "bureaucracy," in reference to the national government, is used loosely to designate a group of administrative organizations serving the president, the Congress, and the judiciary. Beginning with the federal administrative establishment, the primary units of the bureaucracy are the 14 departments — collectively the largest part — most of whose heads carry the title *secretary* and who make up most of the Cabinet. Also included are the *independent regulatory commissions*, the *government corporations*, the *unaffiliated agencies*, and a host of *boards* and *administrations*.

The oldest and largest administrative units are the departments, which employ over 1.5 million of the over three million civilian employees working for the federal government in the mid-1990s.[13] The secretaries are appointed by the president and approved by the Senate. Most of the departments have more than one *undersecretary* who function as the personal assistants to the secretary. Below the undersecretaries are the assistant secretaries, each of whom is responsible for a major division within the department. Each division is made up of bureaus. Each bureau is headed by a director or an administrator who functions as a bureau chief and manages the administrative programs of the departments.

Independent regulatory commissions are other major components of the federal bureaucracy. They are intended to make and administer regulatory policies in the public interest. The commissions, such as the Federal Trade Commission (FTC), the Civil Aeronautics Board (CAB), and the Federal Aviation

Agency (FAA) are independent in the sense that, unlike conventional departments, they are not in the chain of command leading to the president: the commissioners cannot be dismissed by the president at will. The commissions are quasi-legislative; they are empowered by Congress to make many supplementary laws of their own. They are also quasi-judicial, holding court-like hearings to make decisions affecting industry, commercial services, and private citizens. Most regulatory commissions deal with industries that are natural monopolies (such as electric power companies) or with business activities in which unrestrained competition damages the industry or the public interest.

Congress also uses the government-owned corporation to pursue specified government policies. These specially chartered corporations, such as the Federal Deposit Insurance Corporation (FDIC), the Tennessee Valley Authority (TVA), and the United States Postal Service (USPS), are created by the government to do a particular job. The FDIC is generally responsible for insuring the deposits of the banking public, and the TVA makes and sells electric power to the vast region in the Tennessee Valley; it operates in much the same way as any large business corporation.

A host of other unaffiliated agencies, boards, and administrations stand on their own, but are directly responsible to the president or Congress. Some of these agencies are very large, complex, and important. The Veterans Administration (VA) operates a national system of hospitals and administers veterans' programs employing nearly 200,000 people. It is larger than any other department except Defence. Other important unaffiliated bodies

are the National Aeronautics and Space Administration (NASA) and the Environmental Protection Agency (EPA). Such agencies are often established in order to pioneer a particular policy area, NASA being an obvious case in point with respect to space.

The origin of a *professional* civil service in the United States was a product of an act of political violence. In the latter part of the nineteenth century, the patronage system (in which federal jobs were given as rewards for service to one of the political parties) flourished. A new president could make patronage appointments to most of the administrative jobs in the federal government. "To the victor belong the spoils" was the caption of the **spoils system** in U.S. federal politics.[14] Incumbent office holders were simply turned out after a new president was inaugurated. In 1881, an angry, unsuccessful spoils seeker shot and killed President James Garfield. After a great deal of pressure from reform groups campaigning against the patronage system, Congress passed the Pendleton Act (1883), establishing the Civil Service Commission (now called the Office of Personnel Management); as a result, a *merit system* based on competitive examinations was created for hiring and promoting federal employees. Today, over 75 percent of all civil servants in the United States are under the central merit system administered by the Office of Personnel Management. Most of the remaining federal employees are recruited by the separate merit systems of individual agencies such as the Federal Bureau of Investigation (FBI). There are over 1000 jobs not covered by civil service regulation that go mainly to people within the president's party (a mini-spoils system). Many of these appointees are close friends and supporters of the president.

The Office of Personnel Management is the central employment agency for the national government. It advertises positions, receives applications and, most importantly, establishes, administers, and evaluates a system of competitive recruitment. When a government department or agency wants to hire someone, the Office of Personnel Management is notified. It then supplies the names of the three top achievers on the appropriate exam to the recruiting agency. The administrator must select one of the three successful candidates.

In Canada, the fusion of powers brings the federal bureaucracy under the direction of the political executive; in the United States, *both* the executive and legislative branches of government have the power to create their own separate bureaucracy under the Constitution. The bureaucracy serves both executive and lawmaking functions of the president and the Congress. However, as in Canada, the American federal bureaucracy is involved in every stage of the policy-making process. It drafts the bills that eventually become laws, administers the execution of them, and interprets the patterns of detailed applications that determine what those laws eventually mean in practice. The more routine a policy decision, the larger part the bureaucracy is likely to play in it.

The president and Congress play greater roles in what appear to be the major decisions. The only preventive controls available to deal with the bureaucracy belong to the president and the Congress. The checks-and-balance system is constantly brought into play by these two branches of government. Presidents must give the bureaucracy executive direction because they represent the entire country, and also must see to it that administrators follow that direction. The Congress, which represents the many regional interests of Americans, must be ever watchful of the bureaucracy, too. Through its powers of appropriation and investigation, the Congress checks possible abuses of bureaucratic authority from the perspective of constituents and constituencies.

However, the U.S. federal bureaucracy has evolved to become a power with an independent life of its own.[15] It is at least partially independent of the president, the Congress, and the courts. The federal bureaucracy is primarily directed by a relatively small group of experienced career executive administrators with permanent civil-service status, numbering about 5000. These people occupy the "super-grade" positions of the administration, and they remain in their positions despite changes in the White House or the Congress. Career executives are protected from the perils of partisan politics and are expected to serve the "national interest" even through changes in the political fortunes of the two major political parties. As in Canada, the bureaucracy must be viewed as the fourth branch of government.

Bureaucracy is a characteristic of almost all aspects of modern life, not simply the government. Government bureaucracies, like those of Canada and the United States, however, pose special problems because they compete with politicians for power and can ultimately govern us without our consent. The uses to which bureaucrats put their authority must, therefore, be monitored and evaluated by elected officials, and especially by the people themselves.

References

1. Stanley Udy, Jr., *Organization of Work: A Comparative Analysis of Production Among Non-industrial Peoples* (New Haven: HRAF Press, 1959), 10-35; Max Weber, *Economy and Society* (New York: Bedminster Press, 1968).

2. Donald Kagan, Steven Ozment et al., *The Western Heritage Since 1300* (New York: Macmillan Publishing Co., Inc., 1983), 550-553.

3. Joel Aberback and Robert Putman et al., *Bureaucrats and Politicians in Western Democracies* (Cambridge, MA: Harvard University Press, 1981); and Gabriel Almond and G. Bingham Powell, Jr., *Comparative Politics Today: A World View* (Boston: Little, Brown and Company, 1984), 109-112.

4. Economic Council of Canada, *Responsible Regulation* (Ottawa: Nov., 1979), 16; Hugh Segal, "The Accountability of Public Servants" *Policy Options,* Vol. 2, 5 (Nov. - Dec., 1981): 11-13.

5. United Nations, *Yearbook of National Account Statistics, 1993* (New York: United Nations, 1993).

6. Guy S. Claire, *Administocracy* (New York: Crowell-Collier and Macmillan, Inc., 1934).

7. The Prime Minister's Office, *Press Release* (Ottawa, June 25, 1993).

8. J. Johnson, "The Role of the Deputy Minister" in Kenneth Kernaghan, ed., *Public Administration in Canada: Selected Readings,* 5th ed. (Toronto: Methuen, 1985), 293-297.

9. Flora MacDonald, "Cutting Through the Chains," (*The Globe and Mail,* Nov. 7, 1980), 7.

10. Gordon Osbaldeston, *Keeping Deputy Ministers Accountable* (Scarborough, ON: McGraw-Hill Ryerson, 1989), Ch. 14.

11. Jeanne Kirk Laux and Maureen Appel Molot, *State Capitalism: Public Enterprise in Canada* (Ithaca, N.Y.: Cornell University Press, 1988); Economic Council of Canada, *Minding the Public's Business* (Ottawa: Supply and Services Canada, 1986).

12. Kenneth Kernaghan and David Siegel, *Public Administration in Canada* (Scarborough, ON: Nelson Canada, 1991), 198.

13. *Employment and Trends as of March 1992* (U. S. Office of Personnel Management, Federal Civilian Workforce Statistics), 10.

14. Milton Cummings and David Wise, *Democracy Under Pressure* (Fort Worth, TX: Harcourt Brace Jovanovich College Publishers, 1993), 430-433.

15. Paul Johnson et. al., *American Government,* 3rd ed., (Boston: Houghton Mifflin Company, 1994), 528-573.

Suggested Readings

Gregory Albo, David Langille and Leo Panitch, *A Different Kind of State? Popular Power and Democratic Administration* (Don Mills, ON: Oxford University Press, 1993).

George Berkley, *The Craft of Public Administration* (Madison, WI: Brown and Benchmark Publishers, 1993).

Stephen Brooks, *Public Policy in Canada* (Toronto: McClelland & Stewart, 1993).

Lief Carter, *Administrative Law and Politics* (New York: HarperCollins College Publishers, 1991).

Bruce Doern, *Canadian Public Policy* (Scarborough, ON: Nelson Canada, 1992).

William Coleman and Grace Skogstad, eds., *Policy Communities and Public Policy in Canada* (Mississauga, ON: Copp Clark Pitman, 1990).

Kenneth Kernaghan and David Siegal, *Political Administration in Canada: A Text* (Scarborough, ON: Nelson Canada, 1991).

Gordon Osbaldeston, *Keeping Deputy Ministers Accountable* (Toronto: McGraw-Hill Ryerson, 1990).

Leslie Pal, *Public Policy Analysis* (Scarborough, ON: Nelson Canada, 1992).

Paul Pross, *Group Politics and Public Policy* (Don Mills, ON: Oxford University Press Canada, 1992).

Glossary

administocracy: A type of government created when bureaucrats make decisions that permit them to simultaneously formulate and implement public policy.

administration: The ways in which the activities of an organization are managed in order to implement certain policies.

administrative state: The elements of government bureaucracy that respond to the needs and demands of political institutions, the national public, and other states.

arbitrary power: The exercise of authority by officials who use their authority for personal rather than institutional goals.

auditor general: A special parliamentary officer who performs an annual audit of the Public Accounts and prepares the annual Auditor's Report to Parliament.

bureaucratization: The tendency to organize human behaviour into formal organizations and structures for the purposes of efficiency and control.

career tenure: Job security that comes when a prescribed amount of time and certain qualifications have been met within a public administration.

controls: The techniques and strategies for regulating human behaviour in any society.

discrimination: The according of different treatment to persons, bodies, or groups without sufficient reason or legal authority for so doing.

division of labour: The separation of work into distinct parts, each of which is completed by an individual or group of individuals for the purposes of increasing production, efficiency, and specialization of expertise.

expertise: Expert or technical advice used by governments to help determine what policies to recommend and how to administer policies already formulated.

hierarchical: The term used to describe the relative positions of individuals or groups of individuals within a body or society and their relationship to power and control.

merit principle: The concept, employed by modern government bureaucracies, that hiring public servants should be based on entrance exams and promotion ratings to produce an administration of government by people with the proper qualifications, talents, and skills.

negligence: The omission of some action that a reasonable person, guided by ordinary considerations would do, or the doing of some act that would ordinarily not be done.

patronage: The practice of appointing political supporters to public office or to desirable positions on public boards, commissions, and committees.

Peter Principle: The idea named after and formulated by American executive Lawrence Peter that every employee tends to rise to his or her level of incompetence. For government organizations, the implication is that no one who is doing a job well is permitted to remain in that position, and that at a given moment, most jobs are occupied by incompetents.

private sector: In a mixed economy, that part of the economy not under governmental control, i.e., all private enterprise, private profit- and non-profit-making organizations and exchanges between individuals.

public administration: The term preferred by political scientists to describe the bureaucratic process – how governments conduct themselves, the norms and values of government officials, the organization and accountability of bureaucrats, their relationships with politicians and the public, and the systems they use to make and implement decisions.

Public Service Commission: In 1967, the Canadian Civil Service Commission became the Public Service Commission, a central agency that under the Public Service Employment Act is empowered to recruit potential employees for public service through competitive examinations and interviews.

red tape: The phrase (derived from the red ribbons tied around official documents in the royal courts of Europe) that refers to the complex system of rules and procedures applied by bureaucratic organizations in their routine affairs.

regulations: Rules that are usually written down in such documents as bylaws and operating manuals that define such diverse matters as decision-making authority, criteria for promotion, and the everyday operating procedures of an organization.

specialization: The apportionment of various tasks or procedures among individuals in an organization so as to maximize efficiency and decision-making facility.

spoils system (U.S.): The political advantage enjoyed by a victorious president who appoints his supporters and party members to most of the jobs in the federal bureaucracy.

NINE

Law and the Judiciary

The Canadian Supreme Court Bench

Chapter Objectives

After reading this chapter, you will be able to:

- distinguish the concepts of law and custom and put them in a Canadian context

- identify the four essential elements of law and consider their application in the laws we obey every day

- define positive law and give examples of it

- outline the sources of law in Canada and other states

- explain the origin and meaning of common law

- differentiate common law and civil law

- explain why Québec uses civil law codes in private law

- describe the unique character of other legal systems

- conceptualize what the judiciary is and distinguish between the legal and judicial systems

- explain Canada's court system

- outline the functions of the judicial system

- clearly portray the job of a Supreme Court justice

- compare the Canadian and U.S. judicial systems

Defining Law

Years ago a legal expert wrote: "Those of us who have learned humility have given up on defining law."[1] There are many definitions of law because there is no universal agreement about what law is and what it should do. Some definitions include the role played by administrators, journalists, legislators, and pressure groups in forming and changing law. In their definitions, Canadians place high value on the rule of law and the establishment of official legal services, such as the role of prosecutors, defence lawyers, and the judicial system. Most societies see law as a powerful means of maintaining social order.

One of the difficulties in arriving at a definition of law is that it pervades culture without any clear-cut limits. Law is not sharply separable from all other forms of human action. Moral and ethical principles are often the basis of law in society. But **custom** and **usage** may also gain legal importance if a people regard them as culturally significant. When it becomes necessary for a society to protect what it deems socially important, rules and regulations are established for that purpose. Laws codify certain norms, mores, and folkways present in every society. Norms tell us how we should and should not behave – how we should conduct ourselves in business, marriage, interpersonal relationships, etc. Folkways are informal customs and etiquette (such as apply to eating and dress) that do not require severe sanctions when they are violated. Mores are customs that a society considers to be right, obligatory, and even necessary for group survival. Because we con-

■ ■ **usage:** as it pertains to law, the manner of using, treating, handling, and resolving a legal matter in society. ■ ■

sider mores so important, they often form the basis of our laws, such as laws that deal with sexual assault, incest, murder, and child abuse. While most mores are supported by laws, laws may be enacted without the support from mores, norms, or folkways. Laws are the final social parameters that set down prescribed and **proscribed behaviour** in precise terms and usually include specific guidelines for the kind and length of punishment to be given to violators.

A *law* differs from a custom in the quality of its obligation. A person who violates a custom may be regarded as eccentric but cannot be legally punished for the infraction. For example, a person may not approve of the dress and mannerisms of a rock star but that person is not doing anything against the law. However, if someone rides a motorcycle beyond the prescribed speed limit or decides to undress in front of a police officer, that person may be liable to arrest. These distinctions sometimes appear arbitrary because some societies permit what others do not, and laws within a society may change over a period of time. For example, laws that govern abortion, death and dying, and certain kinds of human conduct such as the use of marijuana, are subject to change as political and legal systems reflect transformations in the social perceptions of these rules. But laws are customs that persons *must* abide by or be prepared to accept the consequences. This means that laws must somehow be enforced; they are enforced by a legitimate agency that is recognized as having the political and legal authority to do so.

According to E. Adamson Hoebel, "law is merely one aspect of our culture – the aspect which employs the force of organized society to regulate individual and group conduct and to prevent redress or punish deviations from prescribed social norms."[2] A number of leading legal experts have defined law in terms of the judicial process. American justice Oliver Wendell Holmes put it this way: "The prophecies of what the courts will do in fact, and nothing more pretentious, are what I mean by law."[3] B. N. Cardozo emphasized that law is a basis for *prediction* rather than a mere guess: "A principle or rule of conduct so established as to justify a prediction with reasonable certainty that it will be enforced by the courts if its authority is challenged is...a principle or rule of law."[4]

Taken together, these definitions contain the four essential elements of law as Canadians would understand it:

■ The first is a *normative* element – a standard or model of conduct that may improve human behaviour or achieve some collective good.

■ The second is *regularity* – that laws are made by a recognized political authority and are predictably and generally applied. The practical advantage of this element is that it emphasizes law as a "process," not just a series of particular commands. Law is a body of principles that is regularly enforceable on all persons and groups within a legal jurisdiction.

■ The third element is that the courts will objectively *apply* and *administer* the law. The task of a court in actual litigation is to determine the facts of a case, to declare the rule that is applicable, and then to make a specific order that is the result of the application of the law to those facts that are considered relevant.

■ Finally, for the law to have teeth, there must be legitimate *enforcement* by a recognized legal authority.

The lawmaking process and its enforcement by a system of courts is a primary means of peacefully resolving disputes in most societies. Modern industrialized states have formal institutions and offices, such as legislatures, the police, lawyers, courts, and penal systems to deal with conflicts that arise in society. All these institutions generally operate according to codified laws – a set of written or explicit rules stipulating what is permissible and what is not. Transgression of the law by people gives the state the right to take action against them. The state has a monopoly on the legitimate use of ultimate force in any society because it alone can coerce its subjects into compliance with its legislation, regulation, customs, and procedures. Sometimes the state will use deadly force – killing civilians in the name of the law. This may take the form of capital punishment, as in many states of the United States, but it can also result in prejudicial and racist conduct on the part of a state. In Canada, shootings of natives and people of colour by police have been linked to systemic racist policing policy.[5]

Sources of Law

The laws that human beings abide by are drawn from many sources.[6] Throughout history, legalists have struggled to distinguish the formal sources of law as derived from a deity, morality, nature, or human political and legal institutions. Ethical, moral, and natural principles have always been important guides to human behaviour, and many of these principles have been given legal sanction. But the principal source of legal practice within nation-states and for the international community has been **positive law**. Positive law is human-made law, derived from the will of the state. Its main sources are custom, legislation, statutes, treaties, and the decisions of courts.

Custom is a source of positive law because certain practices and usages are enforced by governments. For example, in many states, the custom that the chief wage-earners, usually men, continue to provide support to their spouses and children during and after divorce was legislated as law by governments. Custom provides the raw material from which many laws are enacted or adjudicated. **Judicial rulings** are another source of positive law because the decisions of judges add to the total body of law. Canadian judges not only adjudicate the law, they also interpret and thus in part, make it. Judicial interpretation is thus seen as a source of law in most states. Constitutional laws are primary laws that give legitimacy to all other lawmaking bodies in society, including legislatures, the division of legislative powers, and the rights and duties of governments and citizens. Legislation in the form of constitutional amendment, decrees, statutes, and treaties is another source of law. The sovereign authority of the state and its institutions are the sources of the validity of law in most legal systems. Many states regard law as valid because it is the expression of divine, moral, or natural justice, but in the modern world it is clear that legal validity of a system of law depends on its **enactment** and **enforcement**.

The dynamics of social, political, and technological change also contribute to the formation of new law. With respect to social change, new laws have been passed and old ones transformed, especially in regard to gender relations, work, age, sexual behaviour, and race. In Canada, laws now proscribe sexual harassment, smoking in certain areas, and discrimination on the basis of sexual preference. At the level of politics and ideology, fundamental changes in government can result in the generation of new regimes of law. Revolutionary governments, communist governments, fascist regimes, and fundamentalist Islamic regimes bring with them different approaches to the law. Finally, new technologies alter the ways we interact, often producing the need for laws to protect us from their use and abuse. The invention of computer crime, and of technologies to help people commit suicide signal areas for which new law is needed in society.

Law and Legal Systems

History reveals that every civilization has developed a recognizable legal system – a body of laws, rules, and regulations, enacted by a lawmaking authority that delegates judicial powers to special groups of people. Western civilization developed two complete and influential legal systems, one from English *common law* and one from Roman *civil law*.

English Common Law

Although the Romans had evolved a formidable legal system well over 1000 years before the appearance of what we now call "Anglo-American law," it collapsed in Great Britain when Rome was forced to relinquish her frontiers in the face of barbarian onslaughts. The complete withdrawal of Rome's military presence from England in A.D. 410 meant the eventual disappearance of Roman culture on the island. On the European continent, however, modern civil law systems are directly traceable to the Roman influence.

After Rome recalled her armies from Britain in the fifth century, waves of invaders crossed the English Channel for the next 500 years. Each of these groups of arriving Angles, Saxons, Jutes, and Danes brought their own rules for settling legal disputes. Over the centuries, they carved out petty kingdoms where legal customs became fixed. Even the final successful invasion of 1066, led by the Norman conqueror William, did not affect the customary legal practices of these little enclaves, although it transformed the political life of England.

It remained for Henry II (1154-1189) to implant the unique legal practices of common law. King Henry trained representatives called "justices" to travel throughout England and administer his land law (the basis of taxation and property rights), provide adjudication in cases of breaches of the "King's Peace" (criminal law), and supervise local officials. In this way, judicial administration was made the same in all parts of the country, and differing customs were united into a body of law "common" to the whole kingdom.

In time, these justices began keeping records of their decisions in legal disputes. Thus a body of **precedent** was built up. Jus-

> ■ ■ **equity:** the application of fairness when deciding general law, which provides remedies not always specified in the law. ■ ■

tices developed the practice of following the precedent, calling this practice **stare decisis** (*stare decisis et non quieta movere* – let the decision stand and do not change what has been settled), which added the element of predictability to regularity in the evolving legal system. By referring to past situations, they could make the same decisions in identical cases and arrive at judgements in legal disputes that were similar, but not the same. The system of relying on precedent made the law very conservative, but also elastic and flexible. In short, it fulfilled the minimum requirements of justice in that it was predictable, regular, and evenly applied.

Alongside laws administered by justices, the rules of **equity** developed. Since the king was believed to be the fountain of justice, the keepers of his conscience were empowered to dispense justice and fairness, or equity, in ruling on legal disputes. In deciding a case **ex aequo et bono** (out of justice and fairness), the justices were authorized by the king to apply equity by overruling other rules that stood in the way of a remedy. Thus, if someone maliciously killed a productive animal of a farmer, not only would the animal have to be replaced but compensation would have to be paid by the culprit for any losses the owner incurred while the matter was being remedied.

The practice of summoning a jury to assist in arriving at a ruling in criminal cases was also an English invention. Henry II recognized the potentialities of swearing 12 men from the local area and four from surrounding towns to inform justices of persons suspected of grave infractions against the King's Peace. The use of a jury in civil cases grew from

Henry's idea of using a group of neighbours to determine ownership and possession of disputed land. Once made available to the people, trial by jury established its superiority over trials by combat, ordeal (an experience designed to test one's character and endurance), and swearing oaths that had been practised in England for half a millennium.

Gradually, the consolidation of English law into a complete corpus by absorbing independent systems of law (commercial law, **admiralty law**, **probate law**, etc.) gave England a body of law common to all in the realm. A later strand in the development of English common law came from the statutes or legislation enacted by Parliament. By the nineteenth century, this acquired real significance, as the needs of Britain's urban industrial society required an extensive recasting of traditional common-law practices. Today in Canada, *stare decisis* is still followed in matters about which Parliament has not enacted legislation.

After the American Revolution, colonists at first reacted against the application of common law as a legacy from Great Britain. Some states even passed laws making it a criminal offence to cite English cases, and judges began to turn to French codified law as a substitute. But the years of British predominance and the lack of a codified system obliged reluctant states to accept the common-law system. Louisiana is the only one of the 50 states that does not have its legal system based entirely on common law.

Other states governed by common law are Australia, Canada (except Québec, which applies common law only in civil cases), Ireland, and New Zealand, to name only a few. Common law has been a major influence in the legal systems of India, Israel, Pakistan, the Scandinavian countries, and the newer states of Africa and Asia. In all of these countries, many acts of the national assembly have displaced much of the traditional character of common law. But still their judges and attorneys bring the heritage of a thousand years of British legal development to the bench and to the bar.

Roman Civil Law

The most impressive intellectual achievements of the Romans were in law, and the sharpest minds of the empire developed a comprehensive legal system. Roman law developed over many centuries, creating voluminous legal records of generations of lawyers and government officials. The emperor Justinian (527-565) attacked the problem of codifying the law in his *Digest*, *Corpus Juris*, and the *Code*. These extracts dealt with the basic problems of law and justice but they also included a restatement of Roman law and legal experience that provided Europe and other parts of the world with a rich legacy. Justinian's **Code** became an essential part of Western legal tradition and affected every Western European state, as well as many legal systems in the New World.[7]

After Rome collapsed, Justinian's Code was challenged by the more primitive Germanic legal system, canon law, and disparate commercial and maritime legal practices. But Roman law was rediscovered in the twelfth century, after which it gradually reasserted its influence through the teachings and practices of European jurists and professors of law.

Throughout the states of Europe, the tendency has been to **codify** law in the legal system. France's Napoleonic Code, beginning with the Civil Code of 1804, was the first great modern contribution to the civil-law system. It was widely copied, as in Belgium, Italy, the Netherlands, Portugal, Spain, and Latin American republics. The legal systems of Germany, Japan, and Turkey have also relied heavily upon a codified law. In the French and Swiss codes, as well as others, law is developed not by the courts through definition and interpretation, but rather by legislatures, ministries of justice, and academic institutions. Reason, logic, and legal expertise are accorded high value in the civil law system. The *letter* of the law rather than its *spirit* as derived by judicial interpretation and precedent, is the dynamic force behind legal systems based on civil law.

Québec's Civil Codes

When the Seven Years' War was ended with the Treaty of Paris of 1763, Québec was brought under British rule. The British government moved to guarantee the private law of French Canada under the French-Canadian civil law, which is based on the French civil code. As a result, today the civil law codes remain in force as the private law of Québec. In August 1866, Québec's private law was codified by legislative enactment as the *Civil Code of Lower Canada*. The only official revision of the code came in 1981, when it was proclaimed the *Civil Code of Québec*.

The private law of Québec deals mainly with persons, corporations, civil status, marriage, and with property, ownership, co-ownership, gifts, wills, trusts, contracts, loans, rentals, and pledges. Unlike the common law, civil law applies abstract principles or doctrines of law to the settlement of disputes. The facts of each dispute are analyzed on principle,

not through reference to prior judicial interpretations of the law. The civil law contains no formal notion of *stare decisis* or any other technique of binding case precedent. Instead, the writings of legal scholars and professors are given pre-eminent attention in the interpretation of civil law doctrines.

Today in Québec the widespread use of the case approach of common law in federal and public law has diluted the purity of the civil law. The Québec system is sometimes described as "mixed" or "hybrid" because of the powerful influences of the common law. It must be remembered that the Québec Civil Code predates the Constitution Act, 1867, and like the use of the French language, clearly illustrates the distinct character of Québec society in the legal and linguistic landscape of Canada.

Other Legal Systems

Islamic Legal Systems

The Islamic system of law governs over 750 million Muslims who live in many of the countries of Africa, Asia, and the Middle East.[8] Islamic law originated in the seventh century, based on rules regulating all areas of human conduct in traditional pastoral societies that possessed very few social and governmental institutions. Islam was the last of the three great world religions to emerge, and for many centuries it was more vigorous than either of its rivals – Christianity in the West and Buddhism in the East. Today it has the second-largest following of the world's religions.

The founder of Islam, Mohammed, left a collection of his revelations which became known as the Koran. These revelations are at once a religion, an ethic, and a legal system. The Koran forbids wine-drinking, usury, gambling, and bans certain foods, especially pork. There was also a rudimentary sacred code of law, the Shari'a, designed to check the selfishness and violence that had prevailed among the Arabs. Arbitration was advocated to take the place of the blood-feud, infanticide was condemned, and elaborate rules of inheritance safeguarded the rights of orphans and widows. Mohammed also made an effort to limit polygamy by ruling that no man might have more than four wives simultaneously. Divorce was still easy, but the divorced wife could not be sent away penniless. These and other provisions were enough to furnish a framework for a judicial system.

Because the Koran was immutable law, it proved incomplete as the Muslim states began to modernize, have more contact with the West, and establish sovereign national governments. In the nineteenth century, European legal codes were adopted to supplement Islamic law in Egypt and Turkey. In the twentieth century, Turkey abolished Islamic law altogether, as did Egypt as recently as 1956. However, in 1980, Egypt amended its constitution to make Islamic revelations the main source of its legislation. At present, twenty Muslim states combine some elements of Islamic law with European civil-law codes in commercial, criminal, and public law. These include Afghanistan, Iraq, Morocco, and Indonesia.

Some states, such as Bahrain, Saudi Arabia, and the United Arab Emirates, have attempted to retain the complete Islamic traditions as a consequence of renewed Islamic fundamentalism. Pakistan's Constitution of 1973 forbids the enactment of laws that are contrary to the injunctions of Islam. In that state, the traditional punishments of flogging, amputation, and stoning have been reinstituted as they were practised according to the Shari'a. Libya, under Colonel Mohammar Khadafy, followed a similar path. Finally, Iran, under the Ayatollah Khomeini, combined Islamic fundamentalism with fierce nationalism, generating a great deal of internal instability and spreading political tensions in the region. Strong reactions against secular law have also surfaced in Malaysia, Syria, and Turkey.

Communist Legal Systems

What distinguishes communist legal systems from those in the West is the effective control by a single agency, the Communist party. In all the remaining totalitarian socialist states, law enforcement and legal scholarship are controlled by the party. The party influences judicial practices through the doctrine of social legal consciousness, which requires that lawyers and judges be guided by party policy when deciding cases. The fate of a defendant is decided on the basis of the regime's ideology.

Under the principles of socialist legality, the range of activities defined as criminal is extensive. Crimes such as murder and theft are treated as in the West. But the severest punishments and broadest interpretations of the law are applied to crimes against the state, such as failure to meet production goals, inefficiency, and poor-quality production. Even harsher penalties are applied for political crimes, such as anti-state agitation, of which dissidents are frequently accused.

In all cases, the legal profession is controlled by the party. Judges are civil servants who are usually members of the Communist party. Rarely can they conduct their courts independent of party influence. Lawyers are also tied to the Communist party. At times they can exercise some independence in their defensive strategies but they are legally bound to uphold the interests of the state.

Most cases, civil and criminal, are heard in *people's courts*, although appeals can be made to higher courts. In some states, *comrades' courts,* staffed by volunteer citizens, hear cases. These courts hear a variety of cases, from those concerning petty theft and public drunkenness to violations of labour discipline. In China, people's courts and comrades' courts educate citizens in loyalty and compliance with party principles.

Combined Legal Systems

Many of the authoritarian states of Africa, Asia, and Latin America blend the customs, procedures, and codes found in other systems of jurisprudence into their own. Most of Africa was colonized by European powers that transplanted their legal traditions to each country. African legal systems reflect the civil-law codes of France, Germany, and the Netherlands, as well as British common-law practices, Islamic legal prescriptions, and customary tribal law. Particularly in states influenced by British jurisprudence, judges often exhibit remarkable dedication to the integrity of the legal process. In states such as Zaïre, Kenya, Tanzania, and even South Africa, judges have displayed great personal courage in pronouncing verdicts counter to the political sentiments of the authoritarian ruler.

The legal systems of Latin America are also good examples of a blend of many influences. By far the major influence on the legal systems of Latin America has been Roman

civil law. Bolivia adopted verbatim the French civil code. Argentina, Colombia, Ecuador, and Paraguay modelled their codes after the French, German, and Swiss codes. The civil law as practised by Spain and Portugal was transplanted to the New World by the conquistadors. By the time of the independence of most Latin American countries in the early nineteenth century, civil law had taken firm root. But while civil law has been a major influence, the legal systems of Latin America also strongly reflect the impact of English common law, especially the doctrine of *stare decisis* and the recognition of custom and usage as important sources of law. The constitutional law and practice of the United States has also had considerable influence in Latin America, especially in the federal republics of Argentina, Brazil, Mexico, and Venezuela.

Finally, in Southeast Asia, Western powers exerted considerable influence on the legal practices and institutions of the region. Many states refer to case precedents established under colonial rule. In the Philippines, courts cite legal precedents in the English and American courts, as well as legal decisions made before their independence.

The Judiciary

The administration of justice has been one of the most important functions of government since the dawn of recorded history. Courts first appeared in Egypt in 2900 B.C. At that time, Egyptian kings began to delegate a large part of their judicial powers to a chief judge who heard and ruled on cases at the royal residence. Somewhat later, between 1950 B.C. and 1700 B.C., courts in Mesopotamia applied the Code of Babylon and the Code of Hummurabi. The Hebrews, Hindus, Arabs, Chinese, Greeks, and Romans had elaborate court systems to administer justice as a function of government. In the New World, the Aztecs held courts and adjudicated market disputes in daily sessions. There were local courts, a court of appeal, and a supreme court; decisions were recorded by means of knots made of cords of various sizes and colours. They also had an elaborate judiciary.

The courts today do not have to draw pictures to portray concepts of justice or knot variegated cords to record judicial decisions, but the administration of justice still remains an important responsibility of the judiciary. Modern courts can be classified into two broad categories: courts of original jurisdiction and courts of appeal. A **court of first instance** hears prosecutions and actions in criminal and civil cases. A court of appeal hears a case and rules to confirm or reverse a decision made by a lower court. In some states, **appellate courts** review the decisions of lower courts to determine if judicial errors have been made and whether a uniform interpretation of law is occurring. Thus, courts of appellate jurisdiction serve as a check upon errors of law that arise in the course of trials in lower courts. They also serve to give a losing party another chance to win a case. In all states, the scope of appellate jurisdiction – that is, the type of cases and legal questions that may be appealed – is determined by rules of procedure established by the courts themselves or by a legislative body.

The Functions of the Judiciary

The primary purpose of courts everywhere is to independently uphold the constitution as the first law of the land. What distinguishes the courts in democratic states from courts in authoritarian and totalitarian states is the relative neutrality and impartiality of judges when their own government is on trial. The degree of independence of the court from the political and governmental system is an important measure of its ability to act in justice and fairness to the litigants. In every state, judges are government officials, the laws they apply are made by the government and, from time to time, the government may be one of the litigants. But, while politics can never be excluded from the appointment process of judicial officials, it is important to know to what extent a judicial system remains detached from the political system that appoints and funds it. *Judicial independence* protects the courts from outside interference and provides judges legal immunity from the consequences of their decisions. This principle of judicial independence is not a component of every judicial system, although most states outwardly proclaim it to be.

Adjudication

The judiciary differs from the executive and legislative branch of government by the way it conducts itself with respect to the lawmaking process. Courts are passive and do not initiate action; rather they wait until a case is brought before them. A case becomes an occasion for the courts to *adjudicate*, i.e., to settle disputes or to proclaim a general rule of law. The process of adjudication involves elaborate procedures for gathering evidence and establishing the facts in a case. Adjudication permits those actually affected by a law to bring forward the particulars of their case and to ask for a reasonable interpretation of the law in the light of the evidence revealed. In court, arguments focus on the neutral principles of justice. To win, it is necessary to show that a claim is just, or that an indictment or settlement is just.

A final commentary concerning adjudication relates to the effectiveness of the courts to generate social reform. It is sometimes argued that a single decisive ruling by the courts may initiate reform far quicker than years of lobbying and legislation. The 1954 landmark decision of the U.S. Supreme Court in *Brown v. Board of Education of Topeka*, which ruled that racial segregation in public schools is unconstitutional, led the way to the most extensive civil rights legislation in U.S. history. Judicial rulings enjoy a decisive authority and legitimacy not often accorded to the prescriptions of political institutions. Courts that interpret the law in a sense also create it.

Constitutional Interpretation

Probably the single greatest influence a court can have on the destiny of a particular nation-state is through **judicial review**. The practice, borrowed from the United States where it has worked so well, is used in some form by the courts in most states today. Judicial review means that some courts may declare unconstitutional an executive, legislative, or judicial act that is judged to be in violation of the spirit and letter of the Constitution. In the United States, any court may examine the **constitutionality** of an act when deciding a case before it. The United States Supreme Court enjoys full judicial review, empowering it to interpret what the clauses of the Constitution mean and to set aside acts of Congress or of state assemblies as unconstitutional.

In Canada, the practice of limited judicial review – so-called because it adjudicated only jurisdictional questions of the federal and provincial governments involving their powers as outlined in the 1867 Constitution – has changed significantly since the entrenchment of the Charter of Rights and Freedoms in 1982. The Supreme Court of Canada now is responsible for interpreting and enforcing the Canadian Constitution and the Charter of Rights and Freedoms. Prior to 1982, the role of the Supreme Court of Canada was limited to the application of law as defined by statute or legal precedent to cases brought before it. Since the proclamation of Canada's patriated constitution, all law, the legislatures, even the federal Parliament itself is *subordinate* to the Constitution. With that came a dramatic increase in the power of judicial review in Canada, giving the Supreme Court the ultimate responsibility for interpreting the Constitution and for striking down laws that are in conflict with it. Thus the adoption in 1982 of the entrenched Canadian Charter of Rights and Freedoms recast the Canadian judicial role to more closely resemble that of the United States.

In other states, the power of judicial review exists, but usually in a more limited form. Parliament in the British tradition best represents the national will; any law it passes should therefore be nullified or rescinded not by a court ruling, but only by another legislative act. The High Court of Australia may determine only which level of government is supreme with respect to the powers outlined

■ ■ **constitutionality:** the conformity of legislation, government conduct, and judicial decisions to the spirit and letter of the Constitution. ■ ■

in the constitution. Such federal parliamentary states are examples of limited judicial review because the supreme courts deal with the kinds of powers and jurisdictions that national and subnational governments may exercise.

In Latin America, about three-quarters of the states confer a limited power of review on the courts. In the remainder, the review function is shared between the congress and the courts, or is solely the responsibility of the congress. A unique form of judicial review is Mexico's **writ of amparo**. Any citizen may apply to one of the federal courts to redress a law or act of government that impairs the rights guaranteed to a citizen under the constitution. The writ applies to each case and does not declare as unconstitutional any act of the president or of congress. Rather, it provides a remedy for a violation of individual rights in the instance for which *amparo* is applied. But in the process, a judicial review of the articles in the constitution does take place because others could have their rights impaired by the same provision under similar circumstances.

Law Enforcement and Administration

Judicial institutions perform the important function of upholding the law in a society. The imposition of fines and other punishments is a credible component of law enforcement as administered by the courts. Courts enforce compulsory adjudication by the issuance of writs and orders. Court orders direct police officials to execute the law.

Courts authorize **warrants** of arrest, **summons** to appear in court, **subpoenas** to summon witnesses, **writs of mandamus** to order a party to perform an act required by law, **writs of habeas corpus** to remove the illegal restraint of personal liberty, **writs of prohibition** to stop a court or other government body from proceeding beyond its jurisdiction, and injunctions to order a stop on certain actions.

In civil-law states such as France, Italy, and Portugal, administrative courts issue writs and orders on the executive branch of government. In Greece and Japan, courts can interfere with executive actions if they clearly violate the constitution.

In many states, courts are assigned administrative responsibilities. In Canada and the United States, courts probate wills, manage estates of deceased persons, grant and revoke licences, grant admission to the bar and announce disbarment, administer bankruptcy proceedings, grant divorces, and naturalize aliens. In many states, when elections are disputed, courts conduct recounts to verify the results.

Canada's Judiciary

Federalism determines the structure of the Canadian judiciary. There are separate federal and provincial courts, with the *Supreme Court of Canada* being a general court of appeal – Canada's highest appeal court in all areas of law – as well as a court of first instance for certain types of cases. But the system of courts is essentially hierarchical and unified (figure 9.1).

Provincial Courts

The following levels of court are found in each province, although actual functions, structures, and nomenclature vary among the provinces.

Figure 9.1:
The Canadian judiciary

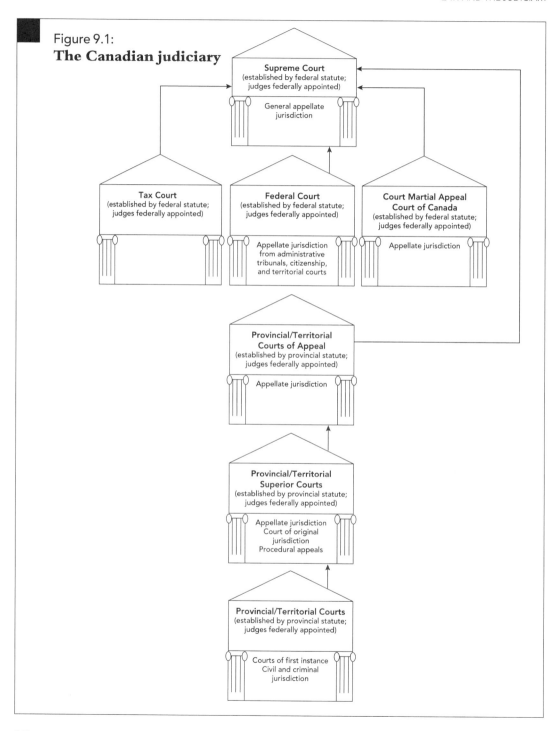

Within the hierarchy of the provincial judiciary are magistrates' courts, small claims courts, and family courts. These courts hear criminal offences, small claims, and juvenile litigation. They adjudicate **summary offences**, bail hearings, preliminary criminal hearings, offences under the Young Offenders Act, and civil cases. Federal as well as provincial law may be decided in civil or criminal matters in all courts. Jurisdictional limitations are established according to the types of proceedings, the value of claims, and the nature of offences. Each province exercises sole jurisdiction over the creation and staffing of these courts at this level. Consequently, the administration and procedure of provincial courts varies from province to province. But in all cases, judges are appointed by the lieutenant-governor-in-council and paid by provincial appropriation.

Finally, provincial *superior courts* or *supreme courts*, the Superior Court in Québec, or Courts of **Queen's Bench,** as in Alberta, Manitoba, New Brunswick, and Saskatchewan, are the high courts of justice established by provincial statute. Supreme courts hear appeals from lower courts within the province and exercise unlimited jurisdiction in civil and criminal matters. At the top there is a *superior appellate court*, ordinarily sitting with three judges, with the general jurisdiction to determine appeals from lower courts in the province. In some provinces there is one superior court divided into trial and appellate divisions. The appointment of all supreme court judges is by the federal government with remuneration set by federal statute. Supreme courts exercise *concurrent jurisdiction* with lower courts for most **indictable crimes** and *exclusive jurisdiction* concerning the most serious indictable crimes, such as murder. Apart from the processes of appointment and removal of judges and of establishing rules of criminal procedure, the provinces are given jurisdiction to administer justice in the province, which includes determining the number of judges, and the structure, organization, and administration of courts.

> ■ ■ **indictable crimes:** common-law offences or statutory offences that result in formal charges listing information on the crime, the number of counts charged, a record of the defendant's pleas, and other records related to the offence. ■ ■

Federal Courts

A federal court system, separate and independent of the provincial courts, has existed in Canada since 1875, with the creation of the **Exchequer** Court of Canada. Federal courts now consist of the Supreme Court of Canada, the Federal Court, the Tax Court, the Court Martial Appeal Court, and the territorial courts in the Northwest Territories and Yukon. The Federal Court, which replaced the Exchequer Court, was established by the Federal Court Act of 1970 with a trial division and an appeal division. It consists of 25 judges, with tenure until age 70, four of whom must come from Québec. Sometimes called the "Unknown Court," it is located in Ottawa, but both divisions will sit in other parts of the country when justified by demand and convenience. It rarely deals with high public-profile legislation.

The Federal Court exercises original jurisdiction in matters involving suits against the federal government, interprovincial and federal/provincial legal disputes, citizenship appeals, and matters formerly the original jurisdiction of the Exchequer Court, relating to the Excise Act, Customs Act, Income Tax Act, National Defence Act, Patent Act, and the Shipping Act. The principal areas of litigation are revenue and taxation; trademarks and patents; immigration and citizenship; maritime and aeronautical matters; customs and excise, aspects of banking law; penal and correctional service matters, food and drug control; administrative law, and supervision by review of various federal agencies and tribunals. The Federal Court serves to ease the load of appeals flowing to the Supreme Court, especially those of special national character, arising from federal boards, commissions, and tribunals.

■ ■ **supernumerary judges:** semi-retired judges who wish to continue judging on a part-time basis and who serve at various levels of the judiciary. ■ ■

Although the Federal Court rarely deals with high-profile cases, it has a very busy docket. In 1993, the number of cases disposed of by the Trial Division was 2347. In addition, during that year it resolved 6018 immigration cases.

The Federal Court also felt the impact of the Charter. Canadians are able to raise constitutional challenges to the enabling legislation of administrative boards and tribunals. Federal Court judges are sometimes called upon to determine if an administrative body has violated the Charter. The court deals with a wide range of Charter issues, including those of equality, life, liberty, and security of the person, and the freedoms of association, expression, conscience, and religion.

In 1983, Parliament instituted the Tax Court of Canada, with 15 judges to hear cases that arise from federal tax laws. This court has jurisdiction in matters arising from the Income Tax Act, Customs and Excise, the Unemployment Insurance Act, the Canada Pension Plan, Old Age Security, the War Veterans' Allowances Act, and the Civilian War Pensioners and Allowances Act. The court has 25 judges appointed at the discretion of the governor-general-in-Council, which in practice means the minister of justice and the prime minister. This court is also assisted by three **supernumerary judges**. These justices have been reappointed beyond their retirement age for a specific period on the recommendation of the chief judge or judicial council or have opted for semi-retirement prior to retirement age.

The Supreme Court of Canada

The Constitution Act, 1867, made no mention of a Supreme Court of Canada. The Fathers of Confederation granted statutory authority to Parliament which, after having bills to establish a final court withdrawn in 1869 and 1870, succeeded in passing the Supreme Court Act, 1875. The fact that this federal statute gave existence, jurisdiction, and composition to the Supreme Court generated concern over the years among constitutional, legal, and political experts that the highest courts in the country could be removed by ordinary legislation. Accordingly, in 1982, the Supreme Court of Canada was entrenched in the Constitution by Sections 41(d) and 42(1)(d) of the Constitution Act, 1982. And, the Meech Lake Accord (Constitution Amendment, 1987) would have legitimized the current composition of the court as consisting of a *chief justice* and eight *puisne* (junior-rank) judges, with at least three justices from Québec to ensure that some justices have a background in the distinctive civil-law tradition of that province. In addition, the appointment process would have been entrenched, for the first time giving provinces a constitutional voice in the selection of Supreme Court justices by filling vacancies from provincial lists of nominees.

The early Supreme Court had only six justices and its first sittings were held in the Railway Committee Room of the House of Commons: thereafter the court sat in the old Supreme Court Building at the foot of Parliament Hill until 1946, when it took possession of its present building. But until 1949, the **Judicial Committee of the Privy Council** in England was the highest court of final appeal for Canadian civil cases, as it was for criminal cases until 1931. In 1949, the Supreme Court assumed that role. It sits only in Ottawa. Since 1949, the composition of the court's bench has followed the pattern of appointing three justices from Ontario, three from Québec, two from the western provinces, and one from the Atlantic region. This pattern had only one temporary deviation between 1979 to 1982, when there were two from Ontario, and three from the West. All nine judges are appointed until age 75 by the governor-general-in-council.

Candidates must have at least ten years' experience in law practice. Normally, Supreme Court judges are selected from provincial courts of appeal; for example, Beverley McLachlin was appointed in March 1989 from the B.C. Supreme Court. But from time to time, practising lawyers are elevated directly to the high court, as exemplified by the appointment of John Sopinka in 1988,

■ PROFILE *OF A* SUPREME COURT JUSTICE

Madame Justice Claire L'Heureux-Dubé

Before they are appointed to the Supreme Court of Canada, justices have earned solid reputations in the legal profession. Such is the case of Madame Justice Claire L'Heureux-Dubé, who is the second woman to be appointed to Canada's highest court. After putting herself through law school and graduating cum laude from the Faculty of Law at Laval University, she was called to the Québec Bar and practised law in her native Québec City from 1952 to 1973, where she quickly earned a distinguished record as counsel and justice. In February, 1973, she was appointed to the Superior Court of Québec, and in 1979 to the Québec Court of Appeal, where she served as justice until her appointment to the Supreme Court of Canada in April, 1987.

Within a span of 40 years, Justice L'Heureux-Dubé enhanced her professional experience as Lecturer in Family Law in the Cours de formation professionelle du Barreau du Québec; was a counsellor of the Québec Bar, and delegate in its General who replaced Justice Willard Estey as one of Ontario's representatives on the bench. Judges are removable from the Supreme Court by the governor-general-in-council (on the advice of the Cabinet), which removal is accompanied by a joint address to the Senate and the House of Commons.

The chief justice presides over and directs the work of the court as its principal administrator. For this, the chief justice receives an annual salary of approximately $185,000. This position is one of great judicial influence rather than one of power. The chief justice has only one vote as do the other judges in deciding cases. The other eight puisne justices, whose annual salaries are about $160,000, unavoidably bring their own personal values and political philosophies to the bench. These men and women, ranging in age from their 50s to mid-70s, have usually left more lucrative careers in law and teaching to accept prestigious judicial appointments – initially to the supreme courts of their home provinces.

The Supreme Court, notorious for its lengthy deliberations, has the capacity to hear only about 100 cases of the several hundred filed each year. As one justice told an interviewer: "We're like an oversold airline; we have an airplane with 100 seats and 1000 passengers trying to get in." There are two classes of people who have the automatic right to appeal: those whose acquittal of a crime was reversed by a provincial appellate court on an appeal from the Crown and those whose conviction was upheld by an appellate court with one of the judges dissenting on a question of law. An appeal is accompanied by a lawyer's written arguments called **factums** which, together with the appeal books containing all of the trial transcripts and judgements

Council; was a five-year member of the Conseil consultatif de l'administration de la justice de la Province de Québec; spent three years in a judicial inquiry into certain matters relating to the Department of Manpower and Immigration in Montreal; accepted a three-year term as vice-president of the Canadian Consumers Council; spent four years as president of the Family Law Committee and of the Family Court Committee of the Québec Civil Code Revision Office; and devoted a year as vice-president of the Vanier Institute of the Family and chairman of the Editorial Board of the Canadian Bar Review.

Since the early 1980s, Justice L'Heureux-Dubé has been granted six honourary doctor of law degrees. She has published numerous professional articles in Canada and the United States. She has served as president of the International Commission of Jurists, and in1992 took on the position of vice president in order to continue her role there. In the same year, she was made a member of the International Academia of Comparative Law.

Throughout her busy legal career in Québec City, Madame Justice Claire L'Heureux-Dubé learned to work long hours, including nights and weekends, on matters of judicial importance. Likewise, on the High Court she begins most thought-filled weekdays in the same way – she gets up at six, often goes swimming at a downtown Ottawa hotel, eats breakfast, and reads the newspaper. By 8:00 a.m. she passes through the bronze doors in the entrance hall of the Supreme Court building, rides the elevator to the second floor, and enters the churchy atmosphere of her small book-lined chamber. There, she begins to read and answer correspondence, which might include memorandums to and from members of the court on current opinions circulated. She receives invitations of all kinds: requests to speak at lunches, dinners, and conferences. She is frequently asked to participate at seminars, from lower courts, frequently reach several thousand pages. One case involving Québec's Bill 101, which legislated French as the only official language in that province, contained 55 volumes of complex legal arguments.

In response to a 1987 report on the Supreme Court by the Canadian Bar Association, the court instituted reforms to streamline its operations for faster, more efficient, service. The court now limits most submissions to 40 pages and permits lawyers to beam their arguments to the Supreme Court's television screens via satellite (video-conferencing). The Supreme Court has adopted the latest technologies to deal with its ever-increasing workload. Several years ago, all of the court's record-keeping was computerized so that every document filed with the court can be tracked electronically. The court uses satellite-TV links for many of its routine hearings that are conducted to determine whether a full appeal will be heard. Such "applications for leave to appeal" do not require lawyers to come all the way to Ottawa for a 15-minute session with the judges. Most appeals are turned down. For example, in 1992, the Supreme Court refused to hear an appeal by a New Brunswick motorist who wanted a traffic ticket quashed because he was not given a choice of getting it in English or French.

In recent times, the Supreme Court has not hesitated to pass judgement on basic political and moral questions. For example, it ruled that TV cameras can be barred from federal and provincial legislatures because the assemblies of Canada have "inherent privileges" that are a cut above constitutional rights to a free media. It ruled that those found not guilty of a crime by reason of insanity cannot be automatically committed to a mental institution, and that

conventions, and annual meetings, all of which consume precious time in preparing speeches and fulfilling the protocol of a Supreme Court justice. All of these engagements must be organized around the schedule of the Supreme Court, which holds three sessions during the year and sits about 16 or 17 weeks from the end of September to the end of June.

Most of her office time is spent reading and writing. When she became a superior appellate court judge, she earned the reputation of being a good writer, an adventurous thinker, and a tireless reader. When Justice L'Heureux-Dubé arrives at her office, the factums for a case the court will hear are waiting on her desk. She must read these carefully because they contain the lawyers' presentations of the facts on which the legal contest is based as well as their refutations of the means of the adverse party. She must interpret these in conference with her colleagues. Thus, the job demands a cautious professional approach, tactfulness, diplomacy, and most of all, patience. Law clerks are assigned various tasks. Sometimes she will direct them in the research to be done, while in other circumstances she will request specific answers, and when the research is completed, the law clerks and the justice will have discussions about it. Often the clerks are recent law-school graduates recruited from all provinces who share the invaluable experience of working closely with federal judges.

The court usually convenes for a session from 10:30 a.m. to 12:30 p.m., which is followed by a one and a half hour lunch at the Court House. The afternoon session begins at 2:00 p.m. and continues to 4:30 p.m., when it is followed by a half hour Conference of the Court to discuss the cases of the day. The justices enter the court through a door directly behind a long elevated bench, wearing black silk gowns with white-collared vests. At the formal opening and closing of each session, they usually will wear their evidence obtained illegally by the police was admissible in court. It has also ruled that police cannot recruit informers to try to get a confession from an accused person. It upheld the decision that mandatory retirement is a legitimate infringement of the Charter of Rights because work benefits society as well as the majority of employees, and it concluded that the results of a polygraph (lie-detector) test have no place in the legal system.

Indeed, over the past two decades, Supreme Court judges have made important rulings on the guarantees of equality and individual freedom in Canadian society. And, since the Charter of Rights and Freedoms became law in 1982, the Supreme Court has decided over a hundred cases involving its provisions. Thus the court ruled that if police obtain authorization to bug private premises they also have the right to enter these premises secretly to plant the bug. In its ruling, the Supreme Court decided that even though Parliament does not say police can trespass, it undoubtedly meant to do so. Dismissing an appeal from Alberta's attorney general, a unanimous Supreme Court struck down the federal Lord's Day Act because it compelled all residents to observe the Christian Sabbath, thereby violating the right of individuals to determine their religious preferences. In a 5:0 decision, the court ruled that the provision banning the use of languages other than French on public signs (Bill 101) was invalid because it violated the Québec Charter of Rights. And in 1993, by a narrow margin of 5:4, the Supreme Court upheld the prohibition on assisted suicide in the Sue Rodriguez case, basing their decision on the interest of the Crown in protecting life.

bright scarlet robes trimmed with Canadian white mink, which they also wear at the opening of each new session of Parliament. The most junior justices sit on the far flanks and the others range closer to the chief justice, who occupies the centre position. A *quorum* consists of five members, but the full court of nine sits for most of the cases, unless illness prevents the attendance of all the justices.

One day a month (motion day) is devoted to motion hearings. Motion days start at 9:30 a.m., the Court convenes at 10:30 a.m. and sits until about 4:30 p.m., and there is a one and a half hour break for lunch. Court motions are requests by parties to have their cases heard by the Supreme Court. The Court receives 20 to 30 motions a day. Justice L'Heureux-Dubé, like her colleagues, must consider the merits of a request before giving an opinion. Each motion requires a judge to spend valuable time reading and doing research. Some motions are accepted, others are rejected. Those that are accepted have their day in the high court.

Unless by **special leave of the court,** the only people who may argue before it, apart from the litigants themselves, are lawyers

No other branch of government is more removed from public scrutiny. The public's only real influence on the high court comes indirectly from the power to elect governments which appoint the justices to the Supreme Court. Appointments to the Supreme Court have never been an election issue in Canada. These summit judicial appointments receive little public scrutiny. Almost the only thing to appear in the newspapers is the name of the appointee, a few sentences about the person, and all sorts of quotes from professors and lawyers affirming "this person has the best legal mind in Canada." Senior lawyers are reluctant to criticize such appointments because they may wish to maintain goodwill among the judicial community in case they have to appear before the Supreme Court.

In Parliament, the tradition is to praise. In general there is no wish among parliamentarians to cast Canada's top court into disrepute by questioning the appointment of a specific member. In addition, the Canadian legal establishment is very much opposed to public hearings or some sort of ratification by a parliamentary body as in the United States, where the Senate hears evidence and testimony on the competence and appropriateness of presidential nominees and ratifies or does not ratify the appointment. To some, the idea of introducing ratification hearings smacks of the Americanization of Canada's political and judicial cultures – an Americanization already seen in the more activist role of the court itself since the entrenchment of the Charter of Rights and Freedoms.[9]

Appointments follow strict protocol. The government decides from which region the appointee should come. As already noted, *by law,* three judges must come from Québec; but by tradition, the remaining positions are filled according to the pattern of three from Ontario, two from the West, and one from Atlantic Canada, which some feel represents an unfair distribution of high-court appointments. Ottawa asks the legal community to point out top candidates. Some applicants make the first contact, either by mentioning their interest to their province's chief justice or by writing directly to the federal justice minister or prime minister. Most Supreme Court members are appointed from appellate courts.

Professionally, the current justices of the Supreme Court of Canada have the collective

from any Canadian province or territory. When the arguments are being presented to the court, any justice may ask questions of the lawyers retained. Sometimes a decision will be rendered at the conclusion of the arguments, but usually decisions are reserved for further deliberation or to enable judges to write their reasons. Decisions are made by the majority and need not be unanimous; dissenting reasons are frequently given. On adjourning, the justices file out of the back door of the court to the conference room directly across the corridor. At this time, Justice L'Heureux-Dubé sits by a circular oak table and begins the ritual of discussing the case she has just heard. Each judge speaks to the points and issues raised in the case. The proceedings in this room are more confidential than federal cabinet meetings.

The decisions of the Court are published in the *Supreme Court Reports* and lodged in the *Registry*, managed by the *registrar*, who holds the status of deputy minister responsible for the administration of the Supreme Court. Justice Claire L'Heureux-Dubé and her colleagues perform an essential governmental task – the peaceful settlement of legal disputes at the highest judicial level.

reputation for intensity on the bench. They often work 80-hour weeks, including weekends, and at an average age of 65, make up one of the youngest benches in the history of the court. But as private citizens, they do what most people do: raise their families, participate in sports such as swimming, tennis, and fishing, and go through the daily routines of managing their personal affairs.

An unwritten rule of the court is that justices should lead restrained social lives, and close their lifestyles to public scrutiny so that their judicial impartiality is preserved for cases pending their decisions. Other restrictions af-

Figure 9.2:
The judiciary of the United States

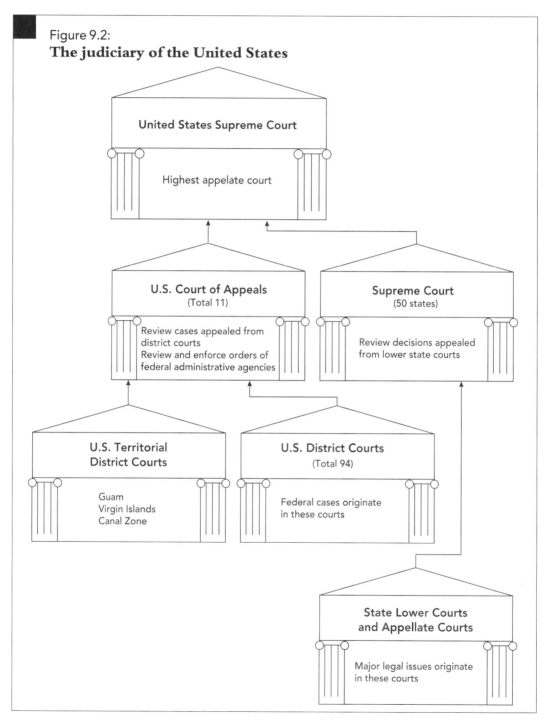

fect judges' lives as well. They may not hold any other remunerative positions with the federal or provincial governments, nor can they engage in business. They must live in the National Capital Region or within forty kilometres thereof. For reasons such as these, a judge's life is a complex one.

Ideally, the court should have a mix of talents, ages, ethnicity, and backgrounds – men and women, academics, practising lawyers, judges with trial- and appeal-court experience. The bench should also possess other important qualities essential to the operation of the most powerful court in Canada. This means appointing judges who are honest, unbiased, neither racist nor sexist, industrious, empathetic, intelligent, and knowledgeable of the law.[10] It is up to Canadians to demand that their judicial branch of government reflect the norms and values in their society. And it is up to Canadians to ask whether their best interests are served in a Supreme Court to which appointments are left to the backroom machinations of the prime minister.

As a result of these general attitudes and conduct, Canada's judicial institutions are perceived to be beyond the scope of political influence. A recent judgement of the Federal Court removed the disqualification of judges from voting in federal and provincial elections. Change is rarely sudden in the Supreme Court. Governments may come and go, and with them their national policies, but the judges, whatever their political leanings, seem to prize continuity and predictability.

The U.S. Judiciary

State Courts

The laws that prevail in the United States facilitate the peaceful remedy of personal and group conflicts in a system of courts. At the state level, the legal machinery is complicated because the court systems of the 50 states operate within a variety of organizational patterns of jurisdictional and appellate arrangements. This diversity reflects the decentralization of the U.S. legal system that has evolved in this large federal country[11] (figure 9.2).

At the lowest level are the local courts, whose jurisdiction is limited to minor civil and criminal matters. They are called *municipal courts* in 26 states and *county courts* in the remaining states. In addition, many cities have *magistrate* or *police courts* that deal with traffic violations and misdemeanors punishable by small fines or imprisonment for periods of up to six months. It is at this level that one finds the *rural justice courts*. These are staffed by justices of the peace, who are often untrained at law and largely uncontrolled. These courts had their origin in feudal England, where justices of the peace enforced the King's Peace.[12] Today in the United States, they are gradually disappearing and being replaced by special courts that deal solely with one kind of legal problem. Thus, many states have domestic relations courts, juvenile courts, and probate courts (to examine wills of deceased persons).

In all states, however, there is a distinction between the courts of general jurisdiction and those of special jurisdiction. The courts of general jurisdiction are responsible for major civil and criminal cases. These include trial courts, usually called *superior courts* or *circuit courts,* and *appellate courts* of various kinds. Every state has an appellate judicial structure that culminates in a supreme court.

State court judges are selected in a variety of ways. In general, most states elect their judges. Some states use executive appointment, subject to the approval of the state legislature. Four states use legislative election, an inheritance from the time of the American Revolution. A few states use non-partisan selection by special nominating commissions made up of lawyers, judges, and distinguished citizens.

Compared to the judicial machinery of the states, the federal court system is less complicated. There are specialized courts to deal with matters relating to customs and patents. But apart from these tribunals, U.S. federal courts are organized in a three-layered pyramid. Most cases that fall under United States law are settled in the 94 federal *district courts,* of which there is at least one in each state, in the District of Columbia, and in the Commonwealth of Puerto Rico. Their basic authority flows from Article III of the U.S. Constitution, which extends the "judicial power [to] all cases, in law and equity, arising under this Constitution, the laws of the United States, and treaties made...under their authority and to the controversies between citizens of different states." At the second layer of the pyramid, 11 *courts of appeal* (plus one in the District of Columbia) review the conclusions (decisions) of district courts.

The U.S. Supreme Court

At the apex of the pyramid, the highest federal court, the Supreme Court of the United States, hears cases from two separate avenues.[13] The Supreme Court hears cases on appeal from the circuit courts of appeal, and in special circumstances from the district courts. Because the court operates under a broad constitutional grant of power, it can take appeals from state judicial systems. But in matters of purely state law, the Supreme Court has no authority.

The Supreme Court is a single tribunal of nine judges who hand down full opinions in no more than 100 to 150 cases a year. The Supreme Court, however, disposes of over 3000 cases each year; in most instances this means that, after some examination, the court concludes that the appeal lacks merit.

All federal judges are appointed by the president, subject to the approval of the Senate. Senatorial approval means that senators, especially those from the state where a judge is selected, have a veto power over the president's choice. Consequently, the appointment of federal judges leads to complicated political bargaining among the Justice Department, the senators of the state concerned, and local party leaders.

Unlike in Canada where prime ministers show less concern for the political philosophies of potential Supreme Court candidates, U.S. presidents consider political philosophies very significant. When Ronald Reagan nominated Robert Bork in 1987 on his conservative judicial record, the Democrat-controlled Senate voted 58 to 42 to reject him. The next nominee, Justice Douglas Ginsburg, notwithstanding his conservative stripe, might well have won the approval of the Senate were it not for his admission to having smoked marijuana in his younger days. Finally, Reagan's third candidate, Judge Anthony Kennedy, met the approval of the Senate.

Former President Bush had the opportunity to alter the court's political complexion in June 1991 when liberal Justice Thurgood

Marshall, the only African-American justice in U.S. Supreme Court history, resigned. Bush nominated federal judge Clarence Thomas, a prominent African-American conservative, to replace Marshall. Thomas's nomination was bitterly attacked by those who wanted to return a more liberal candidate to the bench. They noted that Thomas opposed affirmative action, opposed abortion, and refused to discuss his views on many other issues. But the day before the Senate was to vote on his confirmation, opponents of his nomination revealed that a University of Oklahoma law professor, Anita Hill, had claimed that Thomas had sexually harassed her while she worked for him on the Equal Employment Opportunity Commission, and prior to that at the Department of Education.

■ ■ **gerontocracy:** a government or ruling body made up of the oldest people within the social and political system. ■ ■

The dramatic Senate hearings that were televised around the world addressed charges of sexual misconduct, racism, and perjury from the testimonies of Thomas and Hill. Thomas denied her allegations and charged the Senate with racial prejudice and what he called a "high-tech lynching." No definitive conclusions were ever reached regarding Hill's allegations. In the end, Thomas was confirmed by the Senate, allowing the president to further solidify the court's conservative majority.

President Clinton became the first Democrat since Lyndon Johnson to nominate a Supreme Court justice in 1993 when he chose Ruth Ginsberg, who had served on the court of appeals for the District of Columbia.

Judges serve for life, but can be removed for "cause" if, following a special trial, they are impeached by the House and convicted by the Senate. The Supreme Court is a **gerontocracy**. At present many of the justices are 75 or older. The inevitability of death or retirement on the high court can offer a historic opportunity to some presidents to fill several vacancies. Assuming that the appointees are relatively young, the president can set the course of the Supreme Court for decades.

Throughout much of its history, the U.S. Supreme Court has laid many legal cornerstones, some of which deserve special note. In the case of *Marbury v. Madison* (1803), Chief Justice Marshall managed to divert the attention of the contesting parties from their petty quarrel to what was the most significant element in the decision – the bold assertion that the Supreme Court, on the basis of its interpretation of the Constitution, was empowered to set limits to what Congress could prescribe. This case laid the cornerstone of judicial review by decisively establishing the Supreme Court's right to define the limits of government activity.

In another case that dramatized the clash of federal and state powers, *McCulloch v. Maryland* (1819), the Supreme Court firmly established itself as the interpreter of the Constitution, and justified the expansion of federal powers in the U.S. federal system. In the case of *Brown v. Board of Education of Topeka* (1954), the court ruled that in the field of public education, the doctrine of "separate but equal" has no place, and thus racial discrimination could no longer be regarded as consistent with the constitutional principle of equality before the law. In the case of *Roe v. Wade* (1973), the Supreme Court extended the right of privacy to cover a woman's right to terminate a pregnancy free from government-imposed constraint at the beginning of pregnancy. But the court also recognized that, toward the end of pregnancy, government interest in protecting the fetus's right to life normally will outweigh a woman's right to an abortion.

This bitterly controversial decision spawned two competing social movements that have sometimes violently confronted each other – the opponents of abortion, who want to amend the Constitution to permit states to forbid abortions, and the defenders of abortion, who want to use government money to pay for abortions for poor women. Neither movement has succeeded.

The U.S. Supreme Court is primarily a public tribunal. Almost all of its cases are of two general types. First, the court tests state actions against federal law, including the Constitution, laws, and treaties of the United States. Second, it interprets the meaning and decides the constitutionality of the work of Congress, the president, and the administrative agencies. Because of these functions, the Supreme Court is almost always controversial. It is the primary arbiter of political conflicts in legal dress and its decisions that interpret laws and, ultimately, the Constitution, are inescapably political, even though Americans generally regard it as an apolitical institution.

In its 200-year history, the United States Supreme Court has often aroused ambivalent emotions among the American people. Viewed as a largely politically neutral government body, the Supreme Court elicits more deference from Americans than does the office of the presidency. In recent years, especially, the Supreme Court has been regarded as the exemplar of democratic values, a role thrust upon it by the reluctance of other branches to act impartially on matters of political (or national) importance. But it has rarely stimulated a dispassionate response towards its judicial/political decisions and the reason is plain. The Supreme Court is a unique judicial tribunal; it addresses the conflicting forces that contend in U.S. society, with decisions that mix law and politics. By so doing, it contributes to the formation of national policy and influences the direction of political change.

References

1. B. N. Cardozo, *The Growth of the Law* (New Haven: Yale University Press, 1924), 3.

2. E. Adamson Hoebel, *The Law of Primitive Man* (New York: Atheneum Press, 1968), 4.

3. Quoted in H. A. L. Fisher, *The Collected Papers of Frederic William Maitland* (Buffalo, NY: W. S. Hein 1981), 173.

4. Jerome Frank, *Law and the Modern Mind* (New York: Coward -McCann, 1949), 46; Beryl Levy, *Cardozo and Frontiers of Legal Thinking* (Cleveland, OH: The Press of Case Western Reserve University, 1969), 31.

5. See C. Yerbury and C. Griffiths, "Minorities, Crime, and the Law" in M. Jackson and C. Griffiths, eds., *Canadian Criminology: Perspectives on Crime and Criminality* (Toronto: Harcourt Brace Jovanovich, 1991), 315-36; and M. McMahon and R. Ericson, "Reforming the Police and Policing Reform," in R. S. Ratner and J. L. McMullan, eds., *State Control: Criminal Justice Politics in Canada* (Vancouver: University of British Columbia Press, 1987), 38-68.

6. Richard Yates and Ruth Yates, *Canada's Legal Environment* (Scarborough, ON: Prentice-Hall Canada Inc., 1993), 56-82.

7. Donald Kagan et al., *The Western Heritage Since 1300* (New York: Macmillan Publishing Co., Inc., 1983), (I-23)-(I-41).

8. John Esposito, ed., *Islam and Development: Religion and Sociopolitical Change* (New York: Syracuse University Press, 1980), ix.

9. A. Wayne Mackay, "Judicial Free Speech and Accountability: Should Judges Be Seen But Not Heard?", *National Journal of Constitutional Law* (Vol.3, No.2, Oct., 1993), 159-242.

10. P. McCormick and I. Greene, *Judges and Judging: Inside the Judicial System* (Toronto: Lorimer, 1990), Ch. 4.

11. James Wilson, *American Government: Brief Version* (Lexington, MA: D.C. Heath and Company, 1994), 277-306.

12. Kermit Hall, ed., *Oxford Companion to the Supreme Court* (New York: Oxford University Press, 1992).

13. Ronald Pynn, *American Politics* (Madison, WI: Brown and Benchmark Publishers, 1993), 397-425.

Suggested Readings

David Barnum, *The Supreme Court in American Democracy* (New York: St. Martin's Press, 1992).

W. Bogart, *Courts and Country, The Limits of Litigation and the Social and Political Life of Canada* (Don Mills, ON: Oxford University Press, 1994).

Donald Barry, *Toward the Rule of Law in Russia?* (New York: M. E. Sharpe, 1992).

Stephen Burton, *Judging in Good Faith* (New York: Cambridge University Press, 1992).

T. R. van Geel, *Understanding Supreme Court Opinions* (New York: Longman, 1992).

Christopher Manfredi, *Judicial Power and the Charter* (Markham, ON: McClelland & Stewart, 1993).

Peter McCormick and Ian Greene, *Judges and Judging* (Toronto: James Lorimer & Co. Ltd., 1990).

David O'Brien, *Storm Centre: The Supreme Court in American Politics* (New York: W. W. Norton & Company, Inc., 1993).

Paul Wice, *Judges and Lawyers* (New York: Harper-Collins College Publishers, 1991).

Richard Yates and Ruth Yates, *Canada's Legal Environment* (Scarborough, ON: Prentice-Hall, Canada 1993).

Glossary

admiralty law: The law relating to ships, navigation, harbours, and mariners.

appellate courts: Courts that are empowered to hear appeals from lower courts.

code: Legislative enactment or a group of statutes and regulations brought together in a single body to provide more or less a complete set of rules on one or more fields of law.

codify: To arrange laws into a written systematic body, as opposed to unwritten mores, norms, and traditions.

constitutionality: The conformity of legislation, government conduct, and judicial decisions to the spirit and letter of the constitution.

court of first instance: A court before which an action is first brought for trial.

custom: A conventional or accepted practice that may be recognized as legitimate behaviour and is reinforced by the actions of legal and political institutions.

enactment: Laws that are formally made by parliamentary legislatures, for specific purposes, to regulate specific forms of behaviour, with punishments clearly stated and carried out by the state.

enforcement: The process of applying and administering the law, its regulations, penalties, and rewards.

equity: The application of fairness when deciding general law which provides remedies not always specified in the law.

ex aequo et bono: Literally means "in justice and fairness" and is used when a court is permitted to apply the doctrine of equity in the determination of a case.

Exchequer Court: This court evolved under English law to hear cases involving the monarch's accounts and royal revenues. The Exchequer Court of Canada was created in 1875, the same year as the foundation of the Supreme Court of Canada, for the better administration of the laws of Canada. The Court's jurisdiction was originally to hear matters pertaining to federal revenue law where the Crown was being sued. Over the years, more specialized areas of law were added, among them admiralty law, as well as patents, trademarks, and copyright. The Exchequer Court of Canada was replaced by the Federal Court in 1971.

factums: A legal memoir which contains the facts upon which a contest is based.

gerontocracy: A government or ruling body made up of the oldest people within the social and political system.

indictable crimes: Common-law offences or statutory offences that result in formal charges listing information on the crime, the number of counts charged, a record of the defendant's plea, and other records related to the offence.

judicial committee of the privy council: The Judicial Committee of the British Privy Council that acted as the court of final appeal for Canadians until 1949 when the Supreme Court of Canada was established as the final arbiter in Canadian jurisprudence.

judicial review: The power of a court, in the course of litigation, to declare the actions of other branches of government unconstitutional.

judicial ruling: The binding decision of a court on a matter before it.

law clerks: Recent graduates of law school who typically serve a justice for a period of time to do research, to summarize petitions, and to assist in writing and to critique drafts of opinions.

positive law: Human-made law actually and specifically enacted or adopted by a proper authority in order to govern a society or international community.

precedent: A common-law principle that recognizes the high persuasive authority of previous court decisions on cases of similar legal character.

probate law: The laws that affect the originality and validity of wills.

proscribed behaviour: Generally refers to human conduct that is forbidden.

Queen's Bench: The name for a court so-called during the reign of a queen.

special leave of the court: Permission obtained from a court to take some action which, without such permission, would not be allowable.

stare decisis: "Let the decision stand." The principle in the Anglo-American tradition of law by which a precedent or decision of one court binds courts lower in the judicial hierarchy.

subpoena: A written court order that requires witnesses to appear before a court and produce testimony.

summary offence: An offence under any enactment of a province.

summons: A written legal order issued by a judicial officer to a person who has had a formal legal complaint against him or her.

supernumerary judges: Semi-retired judges who wish to continue judging on a part-time basis and who serve at various levels of the judiciary.

usage: As it pertains to law, the manner of using, treating, handling and resolving a legal matter in society.

warrant: A judicial writ issued to an authorized legal official requiring the official to arrest a designated party, or search certain persons or premises, or seize property.

writ of amparo: A written legal order that grants a citizen judicial relief from the denial of personal rights that are guaranteed by the constitution.

writ of habeas corpus: A written judicial order demanding legal officials to immediately produce or release a prisoner and cite the reasons for his or her imprisonment.

writ of mandamus: A written judicial order that compels a party to perform a certain act required by law.

writ of prohibition: A written judicial order demanding that a specified action cease.

TEN

Constitutions and Constitutionalism

First Nations leaders at a constitutional conference

Chapter Objectives

After reading this chapter, you will be able to:

- define constitution and constitutionalism

- contrast the elements of a written and unwritten constitution

- apply these concepts to the character of Canada's Constitution

- outline the features of democratic constitutions and compare them

- trace the development of Canada's Constitution

- describe how the Constitution determined the framework of Canadian federalism

- understand the formulas for, and relate the challenges of changing Canada's Constitution

- define the Charter of Rights and Freedoms

- discuss the impact of the Charter on our Constitution

- review the development and content of the Meech Lake and Charlottetown Accords

- characterize the U.S. Constitution

- discuss why Canada and the United States – two democracies with intimate histories – could develop such different constitutional traditions

What is a Constitution?

The word "constitution" carries an ancient, broad usage and a modern, narrow usage. The Greek word for constitution, *politeia*, means basically any form of government or regime as it functions in its entirety. Plato's six governmental forms were thus constitutions. The Greek *politeia* was the spirit *(ethos)* that animated the institutions of a government. The ancient Greeks saw the constitution as a cultural phenomenon – a formal expression of the way people do politics and the appropriate public attitudes that support a particular form of government.[1] Thus, to them a constitution is a product of culture, what modern political scientists call a "political culture." Hence, aristocracy, monarchy, or democracy are embodiments of the attitudes, customs, usages, and values of a people – an ideal summation of their collective behaviour. In the ancient view, constitutions *evolve* as the political needs of people change in society.

Today, in most of the nation-states of the world, the word "constitution" is understood in a much narrower sense. The modern format for a constitution, as exemplified by many but not all democratic states, e.g., Great Britain, is that it be a written document adopted at a given point in time by a sovereign authority. The British Constitution is really made up of a series of documents, spanning centuries. It consists of scattered major acts of Parliament that time and custom have endowed with paramount authority. Many modern constitutions are merely show-

> ■ ■ **modus operandi:** In politics, usually a formal method of operating that includes all of the written and unwritten rules of procedures, traditions, and customs as they apply to a constitution. ■ ■

cases for the international community and provide some governments with a rhetorical opportunity to appear "democratic." The ancients stressed the *evolution* of a constitution; modern governments stress the authoritative **enactment** of a constitution as a single event. But most contemporary students of constitutional law recognize the **unwritten** as well as the **written** dimensions of modern constitutions. No constitution can be properly understood solely as a written document. Judicial interpretations as well as modern political customs, conventions, and usages modify and sometimes nullify the written assertions of all constitutions in operation today.

Some scholars avoid the distinction between the written and unwritten features of a constitution and focus on the *formal* and *effective* elements of constitutions.[2] The formal constitution is the sum of the original documents, statutes, charters, and other authoritative sources that explicitly outline the structures and goals of a government. The effective constitution is the actual **modus operandi** of a political system that includes customs and practices that have evolved according to the spirit of the constitution, but are not specifically mentioned in the constitution. For example, Canada's formal constitution does not mention the federal Cabinet, political parties, or the federal civil service. There is no mention that the prime minister and the Cabinet must always have the support of or even have seats in the House of Commons. Effectively, these important institutions of Canadian government have constitutional *legitimacy* by virtue of legislation, custom, and judicial interpretation. Similarly, according to its constitutional documents, Great Britain is a monarchy, but effectively, it is a parliamentary democracy. In the United States, members of the electoral college may elect any eligible person to the presidency. However, electors are effectively pledged to elect the same president selected by the American people in a national election.

For analytical purposes, political scientists define constitution in the widest possible context. As we shall use the term, a constitution is a body of formal and effective rules and practices, written and unwritten, according to which the people and the political institutions of a society are governed. This broad definition enables the political scientist to recognize the functional constitution operating in each political system. Because in most states many fundamental constitutional principles remain largely informal and unwritten, the political analyst must include the accumulated traditions, political mores, and practices of a people as constituent parts of all constitutions.

The Meaning of Constitutionalism

Constitutionalism may be thought of as the superego of a democratic constitution. It is to a constitution what character is to an individual. The essence of constitutionalism is its belief system, which asserts the need for formal limitations on political power: that is, that power is curtailed and procedures of government are defined in a constitution.

Historically, modern constitutionalism grew out of the abuses of autocratic government in Europe during the fifteenth and sixteenth centuries. Constitutionalism was the major accomplishment of individualism in its attack on absolute government in Europe. In its purest form, constitutionalism treats government as a necessary evil: humans accept limited government to escape the chaos of anarchy. The term and its related concepts revolve around the idea that **individual rights** should be protected by inclusion of those rights in a formal constitution.

At the turn of the century, constitutionalism almost disappeared from the standard vocabulary of students of politics, due to shifting academic fashions and a changing international system. The rapid growth in the number of nation-states adopting authoritarian regimes, as well as the emergence of totalitarian dictatorships after World War I, challenged the ideal of *limited government* protected by a constitution. Even among the democratic states, social, economic, political, and military exigencies encouraged the rapid expansion of government in all of the traditionally private preserves of society. The legal ability of governments to ignore constitutional standards became insurmountable, and it became common practice to simply change a constitution to meet the needs of autocratic executives.

Recent global concerns over the struggle for human rights and the almost universal phenomenon of violent political change have spurred a renewed academic interest in constitutionalism. John Rawls, the internationally respected Harvard professor of philosophy, devoted one-third of his *Theory of Justice* to the analysis of constitutionalism in his just society. His position is that a virtuous republic is a product of a virtuous people. Hence, constitutionalism is only as meaningful as the people want it to be. Constitutionalism is the will of the people regarding the just forms of a society's political, economic, and judicial institutions.

Modern constitutionalism has much to do with public attitudes, standards, and expectations. A constitution and its rules grow out of a belief system that people support and tend to confirm. In order to be effective, the constitutional rules that govern the political behaviour and institutions of a people must be venerated. Yet even if they are, when constitutions become political liabilities to autocratic rulers, they will simply replace them. For example, over 200 constitutions have been in force in the 20 Latin American republics in the period since their independence, between 1810 and 1830. No constitution now in force in any Latin American state dates from the independence of that state. The average number of constitutions for all of Latin America is about ten per state. Nearly half the constitutions currently in force were enacted since the 1960s. The reality of constitutionalism in Latin America is that many constitutional provisions are either ignored, *suspended*, or rewritten at the whim of the government in power. For the rest of the world, only a dozen constitutions are in effect from even the nineteenth century or earlier. Most of the constitutions in operation today were written and enacted following World War II.

Thus, in today's world, it would be accurate for us to conclude that there are two concepts of constitutionalism. One concept, that of *democratic constitutionalism*, is based on Western political traditions, and asserts that constitutions are created as the supreme law of the land. Their purpose is to guarantee that no public official should ever exercise unlimited authority or govern without accountability to the people. As an additional protection against autocratic rule, the individual is ensured certain **inalienable rights** and freedoms. The other concept, *authoritarian constitutionalism*, practised in non-democratic states, which are today the majority, no longer upholds these constitutional standards. Many of the constitutions of authoritarian and totalitarian states resemble political and ideological manifestos, in which platitudes are stated or combined with descriptions of "democratic" offices and agencies of government and parties.

It is important to note that because a constitution exists, there is no guarantee that it actually works. All independent nation-states, whether democratic or non-democratic, consider the **promulgation** of a constitution a legitimizing step towards attaining full recognition as a legal entity in the international system. In 1993, South Africans were provided with a new interim constitution designed to bring full democracy and a long list of fundamental rights to nearly 30 million blacks excluded from the governing system under apartheid. In an effort to show the world that South Africa was a democratic member of the international community, the interim constitution legitimizes a bicameral parliament, one house elected by proportional representation, the other by nine new provincial legislatures, and enables South

■ ■ **inalienable rights:** rights that cannot be transferred or removed by legislation or constitutional amendment. ■ ■

Africans to write a permanent constitution. The *practice* of constitutionalism that asserts the supremacy of the first law is the only measure we have of determining whether a nation-state has a working constitution. A democratic constitution is more than pieces of paper. It is a living thing that embodies much more than mere words can convey – it embodies intangibles that enable it to work and to survive. Moreover, it provides clues to the political values and beliefs that are dominant in a nation-state.

The Features of Democratic Constitutions

All democratic constitutions actually *restrict* government power. Those states, such as Canada and the United States, that limit the powers of government by a written constitution or by statutes and customs are called **constitutional regimes**. In order to evaluate the democratic character of a constitution, many political objectives, features, and procedures must be taken into account, including the extent to which the constitution (a) promotes the public good; (b) has procedures to make amendments; (c) places limitations on the various branches of government; and (d) enumerates individual rights and freedoms.

The Public Good
The Irish Constitution of 1937 provides that "the State shall endeavour to secure that private enterprise shall be so conducted as to ensure reasonable efficiency in the production and distribution of goods and as to protect the public against unjust exploitation"; the Japanese Constitution of 1947 includes the right of

"choice of spouse" and the right to "maintain the minimum standards of wholesome and cultural living"; the Italian Constitution of 1948 states that "the Republic favours through economic measures and other provisions the establishment of families and the fulfillment of their functions, with special regard to large families"; the Canada Act of 1982 affirms that "Parliament and the Government of Canada are committed to the principle of making equalization payments to ensure that provincial governments have sufficient revenues to provide reasonably comparable levels of public services at reasonably comparable levels of taxation." All of these are examples of constitutions in the Western democratic tradition that try to advance the welfare of all the people, rather than to increase the power of the state and government. Constitutions establish broad and *positive purposes* to enhance the public good and to achieve general public goals. They are not documents written primarily for governments; rather, they are *legal instruments* outlining the relationship of people to the governmental institutions of society. Constitutions establish the context within which people co-exist with government.

The concept of *majority rule* is the most widely applied principle to achieve the public good in all democratic constitutions. We see it at work in Canada's Constitution through the requirement that the most solemn constitutional questions be decided by "resolutions passed by a majority of members of the Senate and the House of Commons." Even though it is difficult for the political system of any society to define the public good, the notion of majority rule set in the Constitution serves as a guide and check on policy-makers. Therefore, the public good can only be derived from the principles and rules of the game laid down in a constitution. Insofar as this is the case, the criterion for measuring the success of any democratic constitution flows from the question: Do all individuals and groups in this society have an equal opportunity to benefit from the majority principle? Evaluating constitutions in terms of people is a relatively straightforward matter with regard to the public good: the constitution provides a framework within which the public good is attainable.

Amending Procedures

Most constitutions have certain procedures by which they can be formally amended. Constitutions vary with respect to flexibility and rigidity.[3] Only a few constitutions (e.g., those of Great Britain and New Zealand) are **flexible** to the extent that they can be amended by the same procedures used to pass ordinary laws. Many other constitutions are **rigid**, in the sense that they can be formally amended only by special procedures more complicated to enact than ordinary legislation.

Every special **amendment procedure** is intended to ensure that constitutional reform is the result of sober deliberation. Amendments to the constitutions of many European states, including Denmark, Ireland, and Switzerland, must be *approved by the electorate* in a referendum. In Belgium, the Netherlands, and Sweden, an amendment must be approved *by the national legislature*, which is subsequently dissolved; this is followed by a general election to return a new legislature, which then must pass the amendment in its identical form.

Almost all amendment formulas are in-

tended to prevent basic constitutional changes that are arbitrarily initiated by government. In the United States, amendments are proposed by a two-thirds majority of Congress but the powers of ratification are granted to the states, requiring the approval of three-quarters of the total number of states. In Canada, provincial legislatures must give their approval for amendments on the use of the English and French languages, the composition of the Supreme Court, and the alteration of provincial boundaries. And in Australia and Switzerland, a majority of national voters must also be accompanied by a majority of state and canton voters before the amendment is passed.

Finally, some amendment formulas are designed to protect the rights of linguistic, religious, and cultural minorities. For example, the Swiss Constitution stipulates that Switzerland is a trilingual country, where the French, German, and Italian languages have equal status under constitutional law. Our Constitution Act, 1982, specifies that "English and French are the official languages of Canada and have equality of status and equal rights and privileges as to their use in all institutions of the Parliament and Government of Canada."

Limitations on Government

Constitutions operating in the democratic model adhere to the fundamental principle that proclaims the supremacy of law, establishing limits on public officials in the exercise of their powers.[4] Limitations on government are established through a number of constitutional devices, including a blueprint of the formal structures of government, sometimes a system of checks and balances, judicial controls – and in federal states – the distribution of powers among the various levels of government. By limiting the powers of government, its institutions, and personnel, a democratic constitution prevents the accumulation of personal power within the political system and is an instrument for protecting the rights of individuals from arbitrary interference by officials.

Federal constitutions can significantly limit the accumulation and exercise of political power at one level of government. Federal states have more than one sphere of government: a national system for the entire country, and a subnational system of governments with specific powers over limited jurisdictions. In most federal systems, both levels of government can derive their legitimacy only from the powers enumerated in the Constitution and from the various judicial reviews and interpretations directed at resolving intergovernmental disputes. Federal constitutions vary considerably in their limitations of power among the different levels of government. In the United States, each state can legislate in any area not constitutionally reserved to the federal government or *to the people*. This strong national bias in the Constitution has given the federal government the power to expand its activities into the areas of state jurisdiction (state rights). The Australian form is similar. In Canada, on the other hand, powers are separately delegated to the federal government and the provinces, but Ottawa retains extensive residual powers. Areas of concurrent powers are specified in the Canadian Constitution. In the German Federal Republic, the Basic Law enumerates areas of exclusive federal jurisdiction and the concurrent powers exercised by the Federal and *Länd* governments.

Enumeration and Protection of Rights

Most constitutions, whether upheld by democratic or non-democratic regimes, establish and outline fundamental rights and freedoms for citizens. The extent to which these civil liberties are guaranteed depends on how dedicated a government and its people are to the principles of democratic constitutionalism. The safeguard of the rights of the individual has been the testimony of democratic constitutionalism since the American and French revolutions. But the performance of contemporary governments in these matters varies from one extreme to another. In states such as Australia, Austria, Belgium, Canada, Iceland, Sweden, and the United States, the protection of civil rights enjoys widespread constitutional and community support. However, in the most repressive regimes, those of Cuba, North Korea, Libya, and Vietnam, individual rights are flagrantly violated by government policy, notwithstanding the community will or constitutional guarantees that formally promise to protect them.

In spite of the entrenchment of rights of the individual in the majority of constitutions around the world, the power to violate enumerated freedoms exists in *all* states. In the late 1970s, Canada solemnly assured the United Nations that it was "unlikely" to use (nor has it ever used) its existing constitutional powers to execute children or pregnant women under military law. Among the many civil-rights issues confronting the United States, none is more troublesome than that of the place of African-Americans in American society. The freedoms of speech, religion, assembly, the press, and others have much less significance to African-Americans in the face of both obvious and subtle racial prejudice by whites. Even Great Britain stands condemned for torturing suspected terrorists in the interrogation centres of Northern Ireland.

These infringements of individual rights, which take place in the most democratic of states, necessarily pale before the extreme violations in some other states. Between 1966 and 1970, thousands of members of Biafra's Ibo tribe lost their constitutional rights in the Biafran Civil War, leading to the death and starvation of over two million people at the hands of the Nigerian government. The Ugandan constitution was rendered equally meaningless as the ruthless Idi Amin engaged in mass killings of over 300,000 people, and imprisoned and tortured thousands of others from 1971 to 1979.

In 1993, Somalia's Mohammed Farah Aidid initiated the most ruthless clan warfare in recent memory within his country, killing thousands even as U.N. peacekeepers sometimes watched helplessly. And Romania's dramatic revolution, which overthrew the tyranny of Nicolae Ceausescu stalled for a while after 1991. Former Ceausescu officials had crept back into power, committing atrocities against the powerless, including street people and the residents of state orphanages and mental hospitals.

At the heart of democratic constitutionalism is the right to personal liberty. In Canada's Charter of Rights and Freedoms, this guarantee appears as the "right to life, liberty and security of person and the right not to be deprived thereof except in accordance with the principles of fundamental justice."[5] But despite what a constitution says, infringements upon elementary rights are common even in the most democratic – as well as the non-democratic – states. In many Latin American states, the infringement upon fundamental rights is so customary that most incidents go virtually unnoticed. In India, millions of people born into the lowest caste are kept in a state of servility and poverty by the upper classes. In the Middle East, many Islamic governments are intolerant of religious freedom as an individual right.

Closely associated with individual liberty is *freedom of speech and the press*. All states limit this freedom to some extent. In Great Britain and Canada, **slander** and **libel** can only be committed against individuals, who then can seek legal redress.[6] However, in Italy, institutions such as the army, the police, and the church can regard statements made about them as slanderous and libelous, with due legal recourse. In Great Britain, an editor was convicted of blasphemous libel for publishing a poem depicting Christ as a homosexual.

Freedom of speech and the press exists in most states, at least according to their constitutions. In some, this freedom is quite genuine and comparable to that of the most democratic states. In many states, including Canada, various restrictions are imposed on the press, such as on the publication of evidence in a case before the courts, or on access to classified information. In Uruguay, all authors as well as their publishers are liable to severe penalties if their words are interpreted as abusive by the government. Colombia's constitution restricts newspapers from accepting outside grants from a foreign government or corporation, except with the permission of the government. In Chile under military rule, heavy restrictions on the freedom of the press were imposed by presidential decrees until 1993. Under Libya's sweeping press law, the government has virtual control over all news media in the country. In that state, the president is immune from criticism, and authors and publishers are censored. In Israel, the press enjoys a considerable latitude in its freedom to criticize, but the government regulates news when it perceives certain information to threaten national security.

There are numerous constitutional provisions and laws aimed at guaranteeing the *freedom of association and assembly*. But these and many other rights, which look so impressive on paper, are frequently limited with impunity, even in those nation-states that have a democratic commitment to free associations. Many governments retain the power to determine when a peaceful assembly becomes a threat to the order of the state. In some states the formation of communist and fascist parties is illegal. Italy's constitution prohibits the Fascist party but the government has tolerated the formation of neo-fascist groups. In Latin America, five states – Brazil, Chile, Guatemala, Haiti, and Uruguay – not only have made the Communist party illegal, but actively persecute party militants, sometimes with torture and harassment. In others, such as Argentina, the Dominican Republic, Panama, Ecuador, and Honduras, the Communist party is illegal but functions at a low level. During the McCarthy era in the United States, a number of legislative proposals were made to outlaw the Communist party but federal courts ruled against them, and today the party regularly competes in elections. Other democracies, such as Australia, Canada, India, Japan, and Scandinavian states, currently permit the Communist party to organize and run its candidates in any election.

A large number of authoritarian and totalitarian states permit only one party, making it illegal for opposition parties to participate in the electoral system. In totalitarian states, the party effectively controls the organization of groups such as labour unions, students, and women by extending auxiliary party organizations into all levels of society and mobilizing popular participation in them. Many people participate in such groups only because the organization has a monopoly on some activity they want to do, not because it can effectively influence party policies.

Compared with the highly combustible freedom of association, *freedom of religion*, which most constitutions profess, has been a sporadic issue that makes headlines from time to time. In the United States, laws restrict the Mormon practice of polygamy. And Canadian authorities have prosecuted the Sons of Freedom, a small but distinct sub-group of the Doukhobors, for acts of violence and public nudity. In totalitarian states, restrictions on religious minorities have been instituted when religious beliefs are perceived as a threat by the government.

The majority of modern constitutions mention the rights to *privacy and private property*. The constitutions of France, Germany, Italy, Japan, and Turkey, for example, entrench the right to own private property, provided that such ownership does not conflict

■ ■ **bill of rights:** usually comprises amendments to a constitution that place restrictions on the powers of the national government, and protect the rights and liberties of individuals. The first ten amendments to the U.S. Constitution, ratified in 1791, constitute its bill of rights. ■ ■

with the public interest. The U.S. **Bill of Rights**, adopted in 1791, is long on states' rights and property guarantees. But it took an extensive period of judicial interpretation to resolve the competing demands of property rights in this constitutionally egalitarian society. The U.S. Supreme Court has come a long way from its notorious **Dred Scott Decision,** in which it upheld the property rights of slave owners.

It is discouraging to many Canadians that the words "privacy" and "property rights" are not mentioned in either the Constitution Act, 1867, or the Constitution Act, 1982. It seems so basic – the inclusion of property rights in the Constitution – yet the proposed "enjoyment of property" has sparked controversy in the House of Commons and has been the subject of heated debate in provincial legislatures across the country. The proposition to protect property and privacy is opposed for various reasons by the governments of Alberta, Manitoba, Newfoundland, Prince Edward Island, Québec, Saskatchewan, the federal New Democratic Party, and the Canadian Civil Liberties Association.

The champions of a property-and-privacy amendment are the federal Progressive Conservative and Liberal parties, the governments of British Columbia and Ontario, the Canadian Bar Association, and the Canadian Real Estate Association. Nobody is opposed to the general principle that people should have the right to own their homes and farms. The concern is that, when interpreting a property-rights clause, the courts might place severe limitations on the legislative powers of governments to expropriate lands for public works, they might award in favour of native land claims, control land use and zoning, and

place restrictions on the uses of public property. Only time and jurisprudence will determine whether Canada's Charter of Rights and Freedoms is comparable or even superior to the U.S. Bill of Rights.

But even with embracing constitutional guarantees, all governments place some restrictions on the rights to privacy and private property. By means of taxation, expropriation, and policies on land use and land reforms, governments in every corner of the globe have the powers to restrict the right to private property.

Canada's Constitution

The Constitutional Framework

There have been two major influences on Canada's constitutional history. Like the British tradition of constitutionalism, more than one document has had constitutional significance in Canada. And like the American Constitution, the most substantive aspects of our constitution are written. In fact, much of what is described as the Constitution of Canada is found in a number of documents and practices. Thus, Canada's Constitution includes the Constitution Act, 1867; the Constitution Act, 1982; the Supreme Court Act, 1875; the Statute of Westminster, 1931, and the Letters Patent of 1947; the Emergencies Act, 1988 (which replaced the repealed War Measures Act, 1917); the federal acts that admitted new provinces since 1867, such as the Alberta and Saskatchewan Acts of 1905; and the various customs, conventions, judicial decisions, and statutes that are considered permanent components of Canada's political system. Some experts believe that we must also include certain pre-1867 instruments that

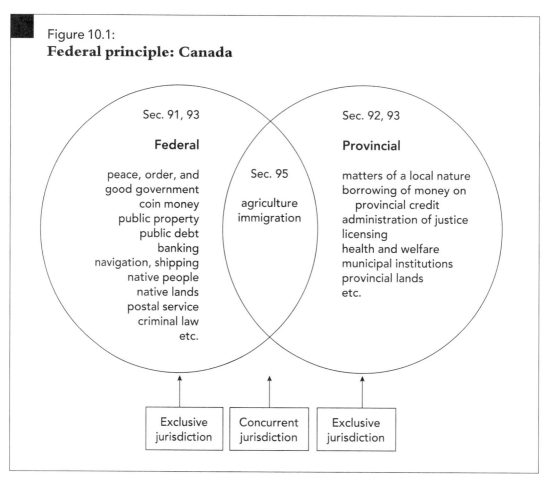

Figure 10.1:
Federal principle: Canada

Sec. 91, 93

Federal

peace, order, and
good government
coin money
public property
public debt
banking
navigation, shipping
native people
native lands
postal service
criminal law
etc.

Sec. 95

agriculture
immigration

Sec. 92, 93

Provincial

matters of a local nature
borrowing of money on
provincial credit
administration of justice
licensing
health and welfare
municipal institutions
provincial lands
etc.

| Exclusive jurisdiction | Concurrent jurisdiction | Exclusive jurisdiction |

retain their constitutional significance, such as the Royal Proclamation of 1763, the Québec Act, 1774, the Constitution Act of 1791, and the Union Act of 1840.[7] Some of the unwritten practices of constitutional consequence are Cabinet solidarity, the dominance of the political executive over the formal executive, the role of the prime minister and Cabinet in Parliament, and the function of political parties in the parliamentary system.

The *Constitution Act, 1867,* is the heart of the overall Canadian constitutional framework. Despite the political, social, and economic changes that have taken place in the country since the British North America Act was enacted in 1867, Canadians still legitimize their political decisions by rooting them in the constitutional authority of this document. Canadians harken back to the Constitution Act, 1867, as the preeminent source of all political and legal authority. Even though the original document is in part ambiguous and omits much (as already noted, it includes no reference to the Cabinet or political parties, for example), it has acquired encrustations of precedent and tradition. The Constitution Act, 1867, is the symbol of Canada's legal and political diversities. For Canadians it is their first and highest secular law, containing the important principles of federalism and parliamentary democracy.

The Constitution Act, 1867, made Canada the third state in history, after the United States and Switzerland, to adopt a federal system of government. As part of the basic constitutional outline, the division of powers between levels of government persists as a major part of the institutional setting of Canadian politics. This system of federalism – in which the provinces retain an allocation of powers, autonomy, and sovereignty, even while they are subordinate to the sovereignty of the central government – is one of the most distinctive features of the Canadian political system. The essential legal characteristic of Canadian federalism is that both the federal and provincial governments enjoy **exclusive** and **concurrent** powers derived directly from the Constitution.

The Constitution and Federalism

The principle of federalism is a major component of Canada's political culture. It is an extremely important aspect of the workaday world of Canadian political life. Without understanding Canada's federal system as outlined in the Constitution Act, 1867, it would be impossible to understand such factors as the distribution of popular support among the national political parties, voting behaviour in the House of Commons, the striking of a national budget, the pattern of policy outcomes, and the many other features of national politics. To a great extent, the provinces are the building blocks with which the national parties are constructed, and the operating agencies through which a large share of federal programs are carried out.

The Constitution Act, 1867, allocates and delineates the exclusive powers of the federal government under Section 91, and those of the provinces under Section 92 (see figure 10.1). Under Section 91, the federal government enjoys 29 classes of political functions in addition to jurisdiction over public property and public debt, banking, credit, navigation and shipping, native people and their lands, postal services, and the criminal law. To the provinces, Section 92 allocates exclusive powers stated as "generally all matters of a merely local or private Nature in the Province." These powers included the borrowing of money based on the credit of the province; the administration of justice and prisons in the province; and control of licensing to raise provincial revenues, health and welfare, municipal institutions, and provincial lands. Section 93 gives the provinces control over the education rights of religious minorities. But it also gives the federal Cabinet and Parliament the right to scrutinize provincial laws and to pass remedial legislation, should provincial action in the area of education run contrary to Section 93.

Federalism provided the provinces with an enormous number of opportunities for small victories in local affairs. But the intent of the Fathers of Confederation was that there indeed ought to be a central government with effective powers and institutions.[8] For them, nothing else would guarantee political unity, provide a stable monetary system, and allow for the development of the economic resources of the country. But the most distinguishing powers that established the dominance of the central government over the provinces were in the area of taxation. The federal government has almost unlimited taxation powers under Section 91(3). It can offer to dispense huge sums of money to the provinces provided they spend the money according to policies established by the federal government. Section 92(2) gives the provinces the power of direct taxation to raise revenues for their purposes. The superiority of the federal taxation power has enabled Ottawa to expand its sphere of activity into many areas of provincial jurisdiction, to the point at which most of the provinces have become dependent on the national treasury. In addition, the Constitution Act, 1867, granted the Parliament of Canada the power to make laws for "Peace, Order and Good Government." The courts have interpreted these words as granting **residual powers** to the federal government, so that when a particular matter cannot be distinguished from the specific categories of powers enumerated in the Constitution Act, 1867, it moves under the authority of Parliament. On the surface, residual powers that favour the federal government would seem to permit Ottawa the potential, at least, to govern Canada as if it were a unitary state. But this has not happened.

Despite these powers, however, Canadian federalism ought not to be seen solely in terms of the constitutional capacity of the federal government to colonize provincial jurisdictions. The Constitution Act, 1867, does not tell us how Canadian federalism has actually evolved or how it presently works. Indeed, much of the transformation of Canada's federal system points in the direction of

"... MY NAME IS BOB, AND I'M AN ASYMMETRICAL FEDERALIST ..."

increased power and prestige for the provincial governments.[9] Since 1867, the expansion of governments at all levels in Canada has been enormous. But because of the present-day importance of property and civil rights, health and welfare, and provincial ownership of natural resources, the provinces have gained striking powers in most of the important areas of public policy affecting all Canadians, even in external affairs.

Today, all areas of federal actions and policies must align themselves with the interests of the provinces. The vast size of Canada and the obvious geopolitical diversities that surface within the country enable the provinces to challenge and renegotiate federal powers. Socio-cultural diversities also exist to favour support for provincial autonomy, particularly in Québec. The growth of Québec nationalism and its example of constant resistance against federal incursions into provincial matters has affected the tone and solidarity of provincial politicians committed to local autonomy in many parts of the country.

Section 95 of the Constitution Act, 1867, refers to concurrent jurisdictions among the federal government and the provinces in the areas of *agriculture* and *immigration*. Here again, even though the Constitution gives supremacy to the Parliament of Canada, when conflicts arise on matters of concurrent jurisdiction, the federal government has been willing to negotiate its policies in these areas with the provinces.

In many other areas where exclusive federal jurisdiction is provided by the Constitution, the provinces have successfully challenged and subsumed the powers granted to Ottawa. In 1978, the Supreme Court ruled that the federal government had exclusive jurisdiction over cable television. But in the face of contravening provincial pressures, the government has been willing to bargain that jurisdiction with the provinces. In similar fashion, the provinces have gained special input into the formulation of foreign policy, particularly in the area of *trade*. The federal government has withdrawn its institutional involvement in municipal affairs by disbanding the Department of Urban Affairs in 1978, after heavy and persistent provincial resistance. And yielding to yet another provincial preserve, the federal government gave control of family allowances to the provinces and withdrew its direct involvement in post-secondary education.

Thus, with regard to federalism, the constitutional context of Canadian politics is complex. The Constitution Act, 1867, obviously leaves open the path of federal/provincial negotiation as a permissive political approach to the problem of constitutional jurisdictions. In this sense, the Constitution Act, 1867, does not close the question of divisional jurisdictions in Canada's federal system. It sets the context and establishes definite outer limits within which each level of government may choose to operate. A less formal way to put this is to say that the written constitution does not tell us how Canadian governments and politics actually work. But it is an important element in establishing the context – the political geography – within which politics and governments operate.

Backgrounder to the Constitution Act, 1982

Before presenting a detailed description of the complicated process of amending Canada's Constitution, it is important to consider the conventional relationship that existed between Canada and Great Britain on constitutional change from 1867 to 1982. For much of Canada's history as an independent nation-state, the Constitution Act, 1867, lacked an **amendment procedure** in Canada.[10] Until 1949, the British Parliament amended the Constitution on all substantive matters by request from Canada through a joint address to the House of Commons and the Senate. From 1949 to 1982, amendment of the Constitution Act, 1867, could be passed by Canada to increase the number of senators by two, one each from the Yukon and Northwest Territories. But Parliament still could not amend the Constitution on a wide range of matters, including provincial jurisdictions, the English and French languages, and provisions on the tenure of Parliament. In fact, Canada was the only democracy that could not reform its constitution in its entirety without the parliamentary approval of another state.

Three months after his return to the office of prime minister in February 1980, Pierre Elliot Trudeau pledged that his majority government would **patriate** the Constitution, giving it a Charter of Rights and Freedoms and an amendment formula. After a constitutional conference that ended in failure in September 1980, Trudeau moved unilaterally to patriate the Constitution. The Patriation Resolution introduced in Parliament in October 1980 came up against considerable resistance from the Conservatives as well as from the provincial governments. Only two provinces, Ontario and New Brunswick, supported it. This state of affairs culminated in a number of court battles to determine the le-

■ ■ **patriate:** to return a constitutional document to its home country, in this case, to Canada. ■ ■

gality of unilateral patriation. In February 1981, the Manitoba Court of Appeals, in a close decision of 3:2, ruled that the Patriation Resolution was legal. Two months later, the Newfoundland Court of Appeals ruled unanimously against unilateral patriation. And in April 1981, the Québec Court of Appeal ruled in favour of the federal proposal in a 4:1 decision. Finally, the Supreme Court heard arguments stemming from the Manitoba, Newfoundland, and Québec decisions, and rendered its judgement on the Constitution Act on September 28, 1981. In a 7:2 decision, the court ruled that the federal government had the legal right to ask the Parliament of the United Kingdom to amend the British North America (BNA) Act, and to implement a Charter of Rights and Freedoms, without the unanimous consent of the provinces.

In the ensuing weeks, the Trudeau government bargained intensely with the provinces and reached agreement with all except Québec on the final concessions of the Constitutional Accord. In December 1981, Parliament passed the Canada Act by a vote of 246:24 in the House and a vote of 59:23 in the Senate. In the same month, the Act was delivered to the British Parliament by the secretary to the governor general and Minister of Justice Jean Chrétien. The British Parliament finally approved the Canada Act in March 1982, and on April 17 of that year, the Queen proclaimed the Constitution Act, 1982, completing the process of patriation.

The Constitution Act, 1982, was Canada's manifestation of independence from Great Britain. The formal amendment process had finally severed the need for

Britain's legal imprimatur on Canada's first law of the land. It was the British Parliament's last bill that was binding on Canada. However, without Québec's official acceptance of the accord, Canada would remain constitutionally impaired.

Canada's Amendment Procedures

The procedures for amending the Constitution are listed in Part V, Sections 38-49 of the Canada Act, 1982. There are five methods applicable to the broad areas of constitutional reform, three requiring the approval of the House of Commons, the Senate, and the legislative assemblies of at least two-thirds (7) of the provinces that together make up at least 50 percent of the population of Canada. This is often referred to as the 7-50 formula.[11]

■ *Method 1*:

The amendment is proclaimed by the governor general for:

a. resolutions of the House of Commons and the Senate.

b. resolutions of the legislatures of at least two-thirds (seven) of the provinces that have, in the aggregate, according to the latest Census, at least 50 percent of the national population.

The first method is used when constitutional reform is required that alters provincial legislative powers, proportionate representation in the House of Commons and the Senate, Senate reform, the Supreme Court of Canada, the creation of new provinces, or the expansion of existing provincial boundaries. The so-called **opting-out formula** is applicable here: a province can dissent from an amendment by passing a resolution supported by a majority of its legislative members, with

the result that the amendment shall not apply in that province.

■ *Method 2*:

The amendment is proclaimed by the governor general for:

a. resolutions of the House of Commons and the Senate, and

b. resolutions of the legislative assembly of each province.

The second method is for the following matters: The Office of the Queen, the governor general and the lieutenant-governor of a province; the right of a province to a number of members in the House of Commons (not less than the number of senators to which the province is entitled), the use of the English or French language, the composition of the Supreme Court, and an amendment to the formal amendment procedures outlined in Part V.

■ *Method 3*:

The amendment is proclaimed by the governor general for any provision that applies to one or more, but not all provinces for:

a. resolutions of the House of Commons and the Senate;

b. resolutions of the legislature of each province to which the amendment applies.

The third method is applicable to amendments to alter boundaries *between* provinces and to the use of the English or French languages *within* a province, or any other issue affecting only one province.

■ *Method 4*:

Parliament may exclusively make laws amending the Constitution for matters pertaining to the executive and legislative branches of the federal government.

■ *Method 5:*

The legislature of each province may exclusively amend the constitution of the province.

Constitutional Rights and Freedoms

At the time of Confederation, Canadians felt secure in adopting the British guarantees of individual rights and freedoms embedded in the traditions of common law. The **Magna Carta** (1215), the Habeas Corpus Act (1679), and the Bill of Rights (1689) seemed quite enough to protect Canadians for most of the century after 1867.[12] In 1960, however, the Diefenbaker government was determined to reiterate legislatively these assumed guarantees by passing its Canadian Bill of Rights. This measure suffered from an inherent weakness: because it was a legislative rather than a constitutional enactment, it could be rescinded by a simple act of Parliament, or rights guaranteed in the legislated bill of rights could be denied by other legislation. This weakness was exemplified by the Drybones case, in which Joseph Drybones, a native, was convicted under the Indian Act of being intoxicated off the reserve, even though this provision of the Indian Act was in direct conflict with the Bill of Rights' guarantee of "equality before the law." But by entrenching these rights in a new constitution in 1982, Canadians could feel more secure in the knowledge that the rigid amendment formulas would work to prevent any rapid erosion of basic freedoms.

Thus, with the proclamation of the Canada Act, 1982, which contains the 34-clause Canadian Charter of Rights and Freedoms, two important guarantees were branded on Canada's political culture. One was **substantive rights** that specify a condition of freedom and advantage that can be enjoyed for its own sake. Another was the guarantee of **procedural rights**, which provided political and legal devices through which governments are controlled and the people protected from arbitrary action.

Clause 1 of the Canadian Charter states that rights are subject "to such reasonable limits prescribed by law as can be demonstrably justified in a free and democratic society." On the surface, at least, rights are guaranteed in the Constitution, but they are subject to overriding by Parliament and provincial legislatures. Enactment of the Charter has also placed the Supreme Court of Canada in the difficult position of arbitrating disputes to adjudicate on whether they are "reasonable" or have been "demonstrably justified."

Similarly, Clause 33 states that "Parliament or the Legislature of a province may expressly declare in an Act of Parliament or of the Legislature, as the case may be, that the act or provision thereof shall operate *notwithstanding...*this charter." In effect, the Constitution allows the enactment of bills that say they operate notwithstanding the Charter of Rights and Freedoms. In other words, laws that infringe on the most fundamental rights of individuals may be passed, even though they contravene the spirit and letter of the Charter. The danger in such clauses is that legislators can simply specify that their legislation is operative despite certain provisions in the Charter, as in the case of Québec's Bill 101, which attempted to legislate French as the only "official" language in that province.

There is not much more assurance for Canadians in either a legislated bill of rights or an enacted charter of rights if rights can be pre-empted by a "notwithstanding" clause. Only time and jurisprudence will tell whether Canada's Charter of Rights and Freedoms is superior to the Bill of Rights.

But the Canadian Charter does contain two major provisions that have received much praise from constitutional scholars. One is a clear statement of the *equality of men and women* (Clause 15 [1]). The second is Clause 15(2), an *affirmative-action* provision. It permits the adoption of laws, programs, and activities to advance the cause of groups that are disadvantaged because of race, national or ethnic origin, colour, religion, sex, age, and mental or physical disability. However, the rights outlined in Section 15 could not be applied for three years from the proclamation of the Canada Act, 1982. This was to give the provinces until April 17, 1985, to bring their existing legislation into line with the Charter's provisions, not to mention the approximately 1100 federal laws that conflict with Section 15.

All the other provisions in the Charter resemble those of most democratic constitutions in the world today. Like many other Western documents, the Charter affirms that "Canada is founded upon principles that recognize the supremacy of God and the rule of law." Under Sections 2 to 5, it lists the basic *civil and political liberties* to which Canadians are entitled. Sections 7 through 14 outline the legal rights of Canadian citizens, which fall in line with other democracies such as Germany, Great Britain, Sweden, and the United States.

The Meech Lake Accord, 1987

With the defeat of the *Parti Québécois* government by Robert Bourassa and his Liberal candidates in December 1985, the way was cleared for a new set of negotiations to gain Québec's official acceptance of the 1982 Constitutional amendment.[13] In May 1986, at Mont-Gabriel, the new Québec government laid out five conditions for its acceptance of the Constitution Act, 1982, in a manifesto entitled "Maîtriser l'avenir." They were:

1. Recognition of Québec as a distinct society
2. A larger provincial role in immigration
3. Provincial input into appointments to the Supreme Court of Canada
4. Limitations on federal spending power
5. A veto for Québec on constitutional amendments

On April 30, 1987, at the federal government's retreat at Meech Lake, Québec, Canada's First Ministers agreed in principle on Québec's five proposals. This was followed in June with an all-night negotiating session at the Langevin Block in Ottawa that resulted in the drafting of the 1987 Constitutional Accord.

The unanimous Accord reached at Meech Lake, by all First Ministers (the prime minister and all provincial premiers) was concluded after only one day of negotiations. The Accord was approved in Ottawa by all First Ministers on June 3, 1987. Its provisions were contained in a bill that would have been enacted as the Constitution Act, 1987; however, it failed to be ratified by resolutions of the legislatures of Manitoba and Newfoundland. The important provisions of the Accord were:

i) *The Distinctiveness of Québec*

The Constitution of Canada would have recognized that Québec constitutes within Canada a distinct society and that demographically, French-speaking Canadians are present throughout Canada, but are centred in Québec, and that English-speaking Canadians are present in Québec but are concentrated outside that province. The federal Parliament and the provincial legislatures are declared to have a role in preserving these characteristics. The significance of this provision in relation to other constitutional provisions, including the Canadian Charter of Rights and Freedoms, would not have been apparent until it was authoritatively interpreted in the courts and ultimately in the Supreme Court of Canada. The interpretation of the declaration of the "distinctiveness" of Québec was entirely open.

ii) *The Amendment Formula*

An agreement to meet Québec's demand for a direct veto power in the constitutional amending formula was achieved by accepting unanimity as the general amending formula. Certain amendments would have been achieved by the 7-50 formula – a resolution of Parliament with the support of seven provinces that have 50 percent of the population of all provinces. The formulas for amendments concerning fewer or particular provinces or exclusively federal matters would have remained. This change was of particular concern to Canada's two territories – the Yukon and the Northwest Territories – which are evolving toward provincial status. The unanimity requirement in the Meech Lake Accord would have made agreement on such a status much more difficult.

iii) *The Entrenchment of the Supreme Court of Canada and the Procedures for Appointment of Judges to the Court*

When it was first instituted in 1875, the Supreme Court of Canada was the product of ordinary federal legislation. The Meech Lake Accord would have entrenched the Court and the appointment procedures of its judges within the Constitution, thus protecting this government institution from legislative abolition.

iv) *Senate Reform*

The First Ministers responded to demands from the western provinces that the role and functions of the Senate be modernized, and that the method of selecting senators and determining their representation in the Senate needed to be reformed. Ottawa agreed to select senators from lists of nominees submitted by the provinces. All provinces would have had a veto on any future changes to the Senate. These contentious reforms required unanimity. A commitment was made to a constitutional conference on Senate reform within one year after the Accord's ratification.

Beyond these specific legal issues, the proposed amendment would have significantly altered the economic relationship between the federal and provincial governments. It would have required the federal government to provide "reasonable compensation" to a province that decided to establish a provincial social program in an area of exclusive provincial jurisdiction rather than to participate in national "shared cost" programs so long as the provincial program was compatible with the federal objectives. This provision had decentralizing and diversifying potential as an economic balance to the development of "national standards" through the Canadian Charter of Rights and Freedoms with respect to civil liberties.

The Meech Lake Accord needed ratification by all provincial legislatures by June 1990. Newfoundland initially approved the Accord, but later rejected it by a narrow margin of Members of the Legislative Assembly (MLAs). And in Manitoba, the image of MLA Elijah Harper – former Chief of the Cree Red Sucker Lake Band – holding his ceremonial eagle feather, stonewalled the vote and prevented the legislature from short-circuiting prescribed procedures to ratify the Accord before the June 23 deadline. His powerful actions brought aboriginal issues and rights back to the top of any future constitutional agenda.

After the defeat of the Meech Lake agreement, some nationalist forces in Québec developed much more militant proposals for constitutional change. The Québec Liberal Party's *Allaire Report* wanted extensive decentralization of powers to Québec, demanding exclusive control over 22 jurisdictions and recommending that the federal government act as a kind of clearinghouse for the provinces. The *Bélanger-Campeau Commission* made demands for major transfers of federal powers to Québec and recommended a referendum to decide between outright sovereignty and a renewed federalism that would respect Québec's rights to substantial new powers.

The federal government rebutted with the *Citizens' Forum on Canada's Future* (The Spicer Commission) which reported to Parliament and led to federal proposals for constitutional change. This so-called "Canada Round" of proposals greatly broadened the agenda again, adding issues concerning the Senate, economic union, and aboriginal rights to Québec's preoccupation with the division of powers and provincial autonomy. Subsequently, in the course of the public debate, a "social charter" would be added to the list of concerns for the next constitutional agenda. Parliament struck a *Special Joint Committee on a Renewed Canada* (the Beaudoin-Dobbie Committee), which moved the debate along with its reaction to the federal package. The report kept most of the broader federal agenda items alive, including Senate reform, economic union, aboriginal rights, Québec's distinctiveness, the division of powers, and a social charter.

The Charlottetown Accord, 1992

By 1992 another Accord was reached at the Charlottetown Constitutional Conference. In this constitutional agreement, the prime minister, ten provincial premiers, leaders of the territories and the Chief of the Assembly of First Nations developed a Consensus Report on the Constitution. This report marked the completion of a long process of constitutional negotiations, which included political representatives from the federal, provincial, and territorial governments. It also drew from numerous royal commissions and public meetings held over a two-year period.[14] The document that was reached produced an agreement to obtain Québec's official acceptance of all constitutional provisions, to include a Canada Clause in the Constitution, to amend the Constitution, to reform the Senate and modify the House of Commons, to entrench the Supreme Court, and to open the way for aboriginal peoples to exercise self-government.

The most important provisions of the Consensus Report were:

■ i) *Canada Clause*

The Accord would have added a new clause to Section 2 of the Constitution Act, 1867, that expresses fundamental Canadian values. The clause would guide the courts in future interpretations of the Constitution. Specific references in the clause would identify Canada's parliamentary democracy and federalism. Special mention would be made of aboriginal peoples and related rights and responsibilities. The clause would recognize Québec's distinctiveness and describe the linguistic duality of the province and the country. The Canada Clause would also focus on equality of race, ethnicity, and gender. The equality of the provinces, and the recognition of their diverse characteristics is also acknowledged in the Canada Clause.

■ ii) *Recognition of Québec's Distinctiveness*

The Accord recognized the assertion that the distinctive character of Québec's society has existed for more than 200 years, since 1774, when the *Québec Act* renamed the colony "Québec" and preserved its religion, language, seigneurial system, and the civil legal code. Under the Accord reached at Charlottetown, Québec's distinctive character was recognized through the French-speaking majority in the province, the unique culture within Québec's society, and the civil law tradition affecting its legal and judicial system.

■ iii) *The Charter of Rights and Freedoms*

The Accord would have strengthened some sections of the Charter to ensure aboriginal rights and protect native languages, cultures, traditions, and treaties. The Constitution would be amended to recognize the inherent right of aboriginal self-government.

■ iv) *Social and Economic Union*

A new provision would have been added to the Constitution describing the commitment of governments and legislatures within Canada's federal system to the principle of preserving and developing Canada's social and economic union. Such policies as universal health care, the network of social services and benefits, education, collective bargaining, and environmental integrity would have been entrenched in the Constitution.

■ v) *An Elected Senate*

The Constitution would be amended to elect senators directly for five-year terms by means of proportional representation instead of the plurality system used in the House of Commons.

■ vi) *House of Commons Reform*

Reforms would encourage aboriginal representation and facilitate the interaction of the Senate with the House of Commons.

■ vii) *Other Provisions*

Exclusive provincial jurisdiction would be assured and clarified in the areas of culture, forestry, and mining, but would permit the federal government through intergovernmental agreements to participate in the operation of these jurisdictions.

To build a national consensus for the Consensus Report, the federal government decided to hold a referendum. For the first time in their history, Canadians were asked to give their approval to a sweeping set of constitutional proposals in a national referendum.

The referendum was held on October 26, 1992, and attracted a large voter turn-out. The result was that 54 percent of Canada's voters rejected the Accord. Only Newfoundland, Prince Edward Island, New Brunswick, and the Northwest Territories gave significant margins to the "Yes" side of the referendum question.

The Constitution of the United States

The first organic "superlaw" of the United States was the **Articles of Confederation**. In 1777, these articles had been proposed to the states by the Continental Congress – the body of delegates representing the colonies that met to protest their treatment at the hands of the British and that eventually became the government of the United States. The proposed articles were finally ratified in 1781 and they provided for annual meetings of the states "in Congress assembled" to conduct the business of the United States, with each state entitled to one vote. Soon after, the Articles of Confederation were widely viewed as unsatisfactory because the government of the United States could not raise revenues on its own and the states were slow and often delinquent in submitting their appropriations to allow the "confederate" government to operate. The perceived powerlessness of the U.S. Congress led it to call for a constitutional convention that would create "a more perfect Union."

This constitutional convention met in Philadelphia in 1787 to produce a relatively short but eloquent document, whose chief draftsman was James Madison. When this document was finally ratified by enough states in 1788, it became the Constitution of the United States. This same basic document, amended only 26 times in 200 years, governs one of the most dynamic societies in the world today.[15]

The U.S. Constitution is clearly organized and provides a straightforward declaration of the supremacy of the rule of law, as well as an outline of the institutions of government. Structurally, the Constitution deals with the following: Article 1: the legislative powers of the U.S. government; Article 2: the powers of the executive; Article 3: judicial powers; Article 4: general provisions relating to the states; Article 5: the amendment formula; Article 6: the supremacy of federal law; and Article 7: **ratification** of constitutional amendments.

In all, four aspects of the American Constitution have contributed to its adaptability: (1) the amendment process; (2) broad grants of institutional power and authority; (3) the growth of extra-constitutional practices permitted by the silence of the Constitution on key matters; and (4) the judicial interpretation of constitutional generalities.

The Formal Amendment Procedures

The formal amendment of the U.S. Constitution has been infrequent, and some of the amendments have been used for minor changes in the functions of government. But most of the amendments have been significant adaptations of government to new social circumstances. The original Constitution did not include a bill of rights, so the founders promised to adopt amendments to provide such rights. The first ten amendments were proposed and ratified together, addressing vital issues of human rights. The famous "Civil War Amendments" (the thirteenth, fourteenth, and fifteenth) outlawed slavery, defined the privileges and immunities of citizenship, and provided the right to vote regardless of race, colour, or prior servitude. Other amendments have given new meaning to the Constitution and expanded some democratic rights, such as the direct election of senators, women's suffrage, repeal of the poll tax, and the lowering of the voting age to 18. One of the most consequential amendments, the sixteenth, ratified in 1913, authorized the taxation of income.

Amending the U.S. Constitution is not an easy process. The Constitution specifies *two* different tracks for its own amendment: the first is that amendments can be proposed by a two-thirds majority of both houses (357 of 535 members), and amendments are ratified when three-quarters of the states (38 of 50) approve them. The second (which has never been used) is by a national convention convened by Congress upon petition by two-thirds of the states. The same ratification process would apply to these proposals.

Broad Grants of Power and Authority

In some places, the U.S. Constitution seems to have been written with deliberate ambiguity. The founding fathers used ambiguity as a strategy for winning the approval of the diverse factions that disputed the document. The vague phraseology contributed to the flexibility and accommodation the document provided for later generations to interpret some sections as giving broad grants of power and authority to key institutions. For exam-

ple, the power of the Supreme Court to declare acts of Congress unconstitutional is neither explicitly stated nor denied in the Constitution. However, in 1803, the Supreme Court ruled that it did have the power of judicial review, an interpretation of the words in the Constitution that greatly enhances its political significance. The executive powers of the president are not distinctly spelled out in the Constitution, either. But the words "the President shall take care that the laws be faithfully executed" have justified the creation of a huge bureaucracy to administer and execute the laws of the land.

The Silence of the Constitution

Flexibility and adaptability also flow from what is not written in the U.S. Constitution. As with the Canadian Constitution, political parties are not mentioned in the original document and the party system is extra-constitutional. Every major elected official and most appointed ones take office under the banner of a political party. All of this takes place outside of the framework of the Constitution. Because of the absence of precise *terminology*, political institutions have been able to adapt to the requirements of twentieth-century politics. To say that a constitution is flexible is another way of saying that it does not provide ready-made answers for new political questions and social issues. The capacity of American politics to redefine its institutions has been facilitated by this silence in the Constitution.

Constitutional Generalities

The U.S. Constitution is a document of general formulations that have been amenable to modern interpretation.[16] In the modern

Figure 10.2:
Federal principle: United States

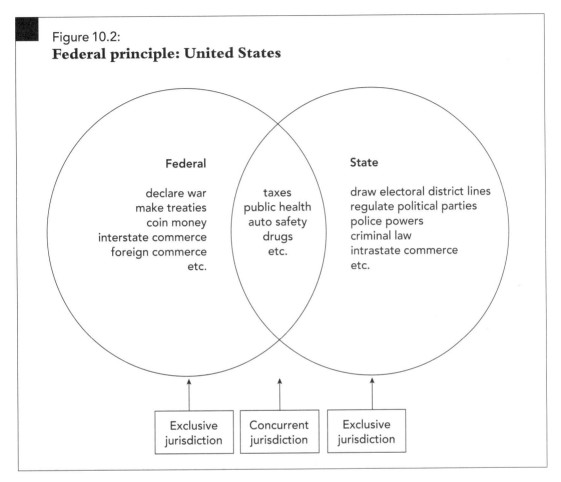

world of American politics, this means that old words have been given new meanings and old institutions have acquired new functions. The original words of the Constitution have acquired modern-day application. The framers of the U.S. Constitution opposed the manner in which colonial officials arbitrarily searched private residences. The Fourth Amendment, ratified in 1791, declared that "the right of the people to be secure in their persons, houses, papers, and effects, against unreasonable searches and seizures, shall not be violated." Today, despite a technology that permits electronic surveillance, wiretaps, hidden microphones, and telescopic cameras, the principle inherent in the Fourth Amendment is sustained. The old argument that places individual rights above the government's right to know has been given credence in the American legal system.

Similarly, the electoral college is an example of new functions being assigned to old institutions. As laid down in the Constitution, the electoral college was instituted as a method of using a small group of respected citizens to choose a president and vice-president. This small group of people comprising the electoral college was to be chosen by the state legislatures. The electoral college continues to play a major role in selecting the president, but it does so by performing a function not at all envisioned by the framers of the Constitution. It has become an institution of popular democratic control, but also grossly distorts the electoral percentages of a candidate's support. Because all of a state's electoral votes go to the winner of that state, it is possible for a candidate to be elected without winning a majority of the popular vote.

The Federal Principle

One of the primary objectives of the framers of the U.S. Constitution was to allocate powers between the national and state governments within a federal structure, which at the time was a radically new idea in its application on a continental scale. The basic constitutional outline permits the federal government and the government in each state to be separate in *scope* – in *what* areas of jurisdiction each may govern. But, the federal structure unites the national and state governments in *domain* – the people whom they govern. In other words, the federal government and the government in each state operate directly on the individual, within their respective spheres of power.[17] The so-called residual powers, not explicitly granted either to the federal government or to the states by the Constitution, are now held to belong to the federal government.

Under the Constitution, some powers are forbidden to the national government, while others are granted exclusively to it. Many powers are forbidden to the states, but several are shared by both the national and state governments (figure 10.2). The Constitution is rather hazy on state powers in that states can do what has not been specifically granted to the federal government or forbidden to the states. Since 1787, conflicts over what is exclusive and concurrent jurisdiction between the states and the federal government have often been adjudicated by the Supreme Court, sometimes ruling in favour of national institutions and sometimes ruling for the states. By means of Supreme Court decisions and federal and state legislation, the whole concept of federalism, as originally conceived by the framers of the Constitution, has been reinterpreted under the pressures of a changing society making new and different demands on government. In recent years, the federal government has placed itself in the position of providing funds for the development of state-oriented highway, school, and public-housing programs. Federal-guaranteed loans, **grants-in-aid** to states, and outright grants of money to federally designated areas have all brought the federal government more into the private lives of Americans than ever before. The powers of the national government have also increased significantly through congressional legislative enactments, but so have those of the states. State governments are doing more than ever before in the fields of health, education, welfare, housing, and highway construction. So while the government in Washington has grown, so have state governments.

However, the ultimate vehicle of control is money. Without federal aid, many states simply cannot carry out programs they urgently need. And with federal money comes federal control. The unlimited taxation powers of the federal government have made it predominant: it can offer to dispense huge sums of money to the states with the proviso that they will spend the money according to policies established by the federal government. The states do what the central government wants or they do not get the money.

As in Canada, federalism continues to be a dynamic political process. Like the Canadian provinces, the states are political entities to be reckoned with. Their governments have powerful governors, legislatures, and bureaucracies. They demand that federal programs serve state interests. In this regard, the U.S. Constitution has provided the legal and institutional framework for the resolution of conflicting political interests. The result is a continuing battle over legal authority, bureaucratic jurisdiction, and constitutional legitimacy.

The American Constitution was drafted by eighteenth-century men for an obscure and fragile eighteenth-century nation-state. Yet in spite of the enormous changes that have taken place in American society, the Constitution has been amended only intermittently. Thus, the American Constitution is an extraordinary achievement. For over two hundred years it has remained the vital foundation of American government and a model for many other political systems. The Constitution of the United States has also continued to evolve and change: first, it has been amended only 26 times and, second, the power of judicial review has imposed important changes on the meanings of the original document. Through the interpretations of the Supreme Court, the Constitution has been elaborated, enlarged, and updated to meet new conditions in a rapidly changing society.

Almost every state on earth has a consti-tution, but constitutions take different forms in different political systems. Some, like Canada's Constitution, consist of a series of documents, often spanning centuries. Many, like the United States Constitution, are single documents, usually that have been amended over the years. Canadian-style or American-style, a real constitution is more than just written platitudes.

Constitutions matter because of what they do (or do not do) and what they are or are not. First, a constitution outlines the organization of government. The outline may be long or short, detailed or sketchy, but a constitution answers key questions about the design of a government. Are executive functions performed by a monarch, prime minister, president, or a ruling *junta*? Who makes the laws? Still, a constitution will probably not answer all the structural questions about a political system. The Canadian Constitution leaves out a lot about the operation of Canada's governing system, especially the role of the prime minister, the Cabinet, and political parties. Yet a picture of Canadian politics without them would be woefully incomplete. Knowledge of a constitution may be a good place to start for a student of politics and government but it is rarely the finishing point.

Second, a constitution establishes and delimits governing jurisdictions. Governments exist to get things done, and under the idea of constitutionalism, governments need authority to act. Not all areas of jurisdiction are specific or clear. Thus a tug of war can take place between and among governments in a federal system, and questions of the role of government in the economy are always present in both unitary and federal systems of government. Jurisdictions imply limits on power.

This is the principle of constitutional government in Canada. Those who govern us are bound by us to the terms of a written charter. So a constitution can also be a mainstay of rights and freedoms. Inclusion of a specific right in a constitution by no means assures its protection. There must be institutions, such as courts and ombuds officials, with a commitment to the enforcement of those rights, along with a public willing to support them both. Otherwise a constitution amounts to little more than a showpiece. In authoritarian and totalitarian states, the rights, freedoms, and other constitutional guarantees are ignored by those in power.

Finally, a constitution is a symbol of unity and a repository of political values. With time, a constitution comes to be more than the sum of its parts. More than a document that organizes, authorizes, and limits, it becomes an object of national pride. However, in some states, the constitution can be divisive. Especially in federal states such as Canada, the need to address the special character of one or more subnational governments can erode the symbolic unity of the national constitution.

References

1. Mark Hagopian, *Regimes, Movements and Ideologies* (New York: Longman Inc., 1984), 38-39.

2. J.R. Pennock and David Smith, *Political Science* (London: Collier-Macmillan Limited, 1965), 241.

3. Robert Jackson and Doreen Jackson, *Contemporary Government and Politics* (Scarborough, ON: Prentice-Hall Canada, Inc.), 167-201.

4. Keith Banting and Richard Simeon, eds., *Redesigning the State: The Process of Constitutional Change in Industrialized Nations* (Toronto: University of Toronto Press, 1985), Ch. 1.

5. David McDonald, *Legal Rights in the Charter of Rights and Freedoms* (Toronto: The Carswell Company Limited, 1989), 219-220.

6. David Schneiderman, *Freedom of Expression and the Charter* (Toronto: Thomson Professional Publishing Company Limited, 1991), Intro.

7. Peter Hogg, *Constitutional Law of Canada* (Toronto: The Carswell Company Limited, 1992), 8-26.

8. Bayard Reesor, *The Canadian Constitution in Historical Perspective* (Scarborough, ON: Prentice-Hall Canada, Inc., 1992), 45-50.

9. Rand Dyck, *Provincial Politics in Canada* (Scarborough, ON: Prentice-Hall Canada, Inc., 1991), 1-29.

10. Garth Stevenson, "Federalism and Intergovernmental Relations," in Michael S. Whittington and Glen Williams, *Canadian Politics in the 1990s* (Scarborough, On: Nelson, 1990), 380-400.

11. Marc Kilgour, "A Formal Analysis of the Amending Formula of Canada's Constitution Act, 1982," *Canadian Journal of Political Science* XV1: 4 (December 1983): 772-777; and Neil Finkelstein and Brian Rogers, *Charter Issues in Civil Cases* (Toronto: The Carswell Company Limited, 1988), 3-73.

12. F.L. Morton, *Law, Politics and the Judicial Process in Canada* (Calgary, AB: University of Calgary Press, 1984), 2.

13. K. E. Swinton and C.J. Rogerson, *Competing Constitutional Visions* (Toronto: The Carswell Company Limited, 1988).

14. Patrick Monahan and Ken McRoberts, *The Charlottetown Accord* (Toronto: University of Toronto Press, 1993).

15. John Morre Jr. and Myron Roberts, *The Pursuit of Happiness: Government and Politics in America,* 5th ed. (New York: Macmillan Publishing Company, 1992), 47-79.

16. Neal Tannahill and Wendell Bedichek, *American Government* (New York: HarperCollins Publishers, 1991) 35-59.

17. Milton Cummings Jr. and David Wise, *Democracy Under Pressure* (Fort Worth, TX: Harcourt Brace Jovanovich College Publishers, 1993), 60-85.

Suggested Readings

Joel Bakan, and David Schneiderman *Social Justice and the Constitution* (Don Mills, ON: Oxford University Press, 1992).

Alan Cairns, *Charter Versus Federalism: The Dilemmas of Constitutional Reform* (Montreal: McGill–Queen's University Press, 1992).

William Conklin, *Images of a Constitution* (Toronto: University of Toronto Press, 1993).

Michael Foley, *The Silence of Constitutions: An Essay in Constitutional Interpretation* (New York: Routledge, 1990).

Alain Gagnon, *Québec: State and Society* 2nd ed (Scarborough, ON: Nelson Canada, 1993).

Andrew Heard, *Canadian Constitutional Conventions* (Don Mills, ON: Oxford University Press, 1991).

Rainer Knopff and F.L. Morton, *Charter Politics* (Scarborough, ON: Nelson Canada, 1992).

David Milne, *The Canadian Constitution* (Toronto: James Lorimer & Company, 1991).

David O'Brien, *Constitutional Law and Politics* (New York: W.W. Norton & Company, Inc., 1993).

Peter Russell, *Constitutional Odyssey* (Toronto: University of Toronto Press, 1993).

Glossary

amendment procedure: The formal and informal methods used to change a constitution.

Articles of Confederation (U.S.): The instrument of government that served as the basic document for the American states that had broken away from Great Britain between 1775 and 1781.

bill of rights: Usually comprises amendments to a constitution that place restrictions on the powers of the national government, and protect the rights and liberties of individuals. The first ten amendments to the U.S. Constitution, ratified in 1791, constitute its bill of rights.

concurrent powers: Powers that are shared by the various levels of government constitutionally designated to exercise certain jurisdiction.

constitutional regime: An elected government that operates according to principles of constitutionalism whereby it is limited in the exercise of its powers.

Dred Scott Decision (U.S.): The racist decision of the United States Supreme Court in 1857 that precipitated the Civil War because it held that descendants of African slavers were not included under the word "citizen" used in the Constitution and could claim none of the rights and privileges conferred on citizens.

enactment: The formal process of giving validity to a bill or constitutional amendment.

entrenched: To embody provisions within the protection of a constitution, subject to amendment procedures not affected by ordinary legislation.

exclusive powers: Those political entitlements that, under a constitution, may be exercised only by either the national government or the subnational governments.

flexible constitution: A constitution that is easily amended.

grants-in-aid (U.S.): Monetary grants made available by one government jurisdiction to another, usually on the basis of prescribed conditions designed to meet specific program objectives.

inalienable rights: Rights that cannot be transferred or removed by legislation or constitutional amendment.

individual rights: The capacity residing in an individual to exercise certain recognized privileges, free from interference by others, by groups, or by the state. These rights, such as the right to a fair trial, are usually protected by statute or constitutional law.

libel: To defame or injure a person's reputation by a published writing.

Magna Carta: An English constitutional document, signed in 1215, affirming that the power of the king was not absolute.

modus operandi: In politics, usually a formal method of operating that includes all of the written and unwritten rules of procedures, traditions, and customs as they apply to a constitution.

opting-out formula: The prerogative of a province to dissent from a constitutional amendment so that the amendment has no effect in that province.

patriate: To return a constitutional document to its home country, in this case, to Canada.

procedural rights: Certain rights, such as the right to a fair trial, which are protected by the strictest application of legal processes and procedures.

promulgation: The order that is given to cause a law to be executed and to make it public.

ratification: The validation, acceptance, or approval of an action of an official, agency of government, a treaty, or a constitution.

residual powers: Sometimes also called reserved powers, these are powers that are potentially broad in scope and may be constitutionally or judicially allocated to the national government or the subnational units.

resolutions: A formal statement by a convention or a legislature or some other body that declares or decides on a motion before it.

rigid constitution: A constitution that makes no allowances for amendments or that requires a procedure so difficult that it is almost impossible to add amendments.

slander: The speaking of base and defamatory words tending to prejudice another's reputation, office, trade, business, or means of livelihood.

substantive rights: Fundamental inalienable rights created and defined in a constitution.

suspended provision: A constitutional right that is temporarily stayed with the expectation that it will be resumed when certain conditions are met.

unwritten constitution: A constitution that consists primarily of custom, convention, or statute that is not written down in one comprehensive document.

written constitution: The fundamental law as it appears in one or more written documents.

ELEVEN

Political Parties and Pressure Groups

Chapter Objectives

After reading this chapter, you will be able to:

■ define political parties as they appear in different political systems

■ recount how political parties evolved

■ outline the types of political parties and classify different political parties under these prototypes

■ describe the functions of political parties and explain why our system of government depends on how they perform

■ list and describe the political party systems that develop in various states

■ explain how Canada's political party system developed and how it is sustained in our parliamentary system

■ reveal how parties can be organized and how this affects their performance

■ describe the evolution of primary political parties out of ideologies such as liberalism, conservatism, socialism, and communism

■ classify Canada's various political parties according to the ideologies they portray

■ distinguish political parties from pressure groups

■ explain how the different functions of parties and pressure groups affect the operation of the political system

■ classify pressure groups and evaluate their tactics

How Political Parties Evolved

In ancient Rome, representatives sought their re-election and the election of their friends by identifying with a prominent group.[1] Because Roman suffrage was very limited, there was little need for using a label to attract voters, nor were these groups organized as extra-parliamentary bodies with an ongoing bureaucracy that functioned between elections.

The genesis of modern political parties as institutions representing a multiplicity of socio-political factors is traceable to the growth of parliamentary governments during the eighteenth century in Europe and the United States. The first formal parties in England and the United States evolved from legislative factions that consisted of friendly groups of notables that were more like political clubs. To some degree they did organize for elections, maintaining an ongoing structure that worked systematically between elections. They formed electoral committees made up of prominent citizens who sponsored candidates by raising funds necessary for the election campaign. The historic roots of modern democratic parties are found in the struggle of fledgling legislative bodies that challenged the autocratic powers of a monarch or dictator. Initially, parties were divergent groups – almost totally without ideologies or programs – that formed within an expanding electorate, taking opposite sides in the battle to demand recognition of voting **franchise** and to dismantle property and class qualifications as requirements for political participation.

By the end of the nineteenth century, the growth of democracy and the rise of industrial societies spawned a new kind of political organization, the *mass political party*, which continues to serve as an institution designed to mobilize public participation on a grand scale in support of candidates and political programs. Today, in the majority of states where they are permitted to function, most political parties attempt to appeal to the widest possible interests in their respective societies. Almost all contemporary parties are mass parties. Wherever there are more candidates than offices, there is a process of competition and selection, and the candidates supported by these mass-appeal parties are usually the ones that survive.

However, a number of contemporary states do not permit political parties to function at all. Approximately 30 states have either declared parties illegal or have discouraged their formation through repression. In the 1990s, a group of states have outlawed political parties. These include Chad, Cyprus, Ghana, Liberia, Niger, North Yemen, Pakistan, Rwanda, and Uganda. In another group of states, political-party systems have simply not developed. These include such states as Andorra, Bahrain, Bhutan, Brunei, Jordan, Kuwait, Oman, Nepal, Qatar, Saudi Arabia, Swaziland, Tonga, and the United Arab Emirates. In many of these states, a surviving traditional kingship has prevented the evolution of a pluralistic and competitive political-party system. The concentration of political power clusters around the monarch by custom and tradition. Contemporary states without political parties are found chiefly in the Middle East, Southeast Asia, and sub-Saharan Africa.

> ■ ■ **franchise:** in the field of politics, a term meaning the right to vote. ■ ■

Not Weier in
north snal

What Is a Political Party?

One of the most general and flexible definitions of a political party was provided by a Bahamian party leader, Sir Randol Fawkes: "A political party consists of a group of persons united in opinion or action, more or less permanently organized, which attempts to bring about the election of its candidates to public offices and by this means to control or influence the actions and policy of government."[2] A political group can be defined in terms of the purpose for which it was organized, the size and character of its membership, its structure, and the functions it performs. American political scientist Leon Epstein points to the distinguishing characteristic of the party "label," because in his opinion size and membership are less significant components. He defines a party as "any group, however loosely organized, seeking to elect governmental office-holders under a given label."[3] The French scholar Maurice Duverger, in contrast to Epstein, focuses on "ideologies, social foundations, structure, organization, participation, strategy – all these aspects must be taken into account in making a complete analysis of any political party."[4]

These definitions make sense particularly when a political party is viewed from a behavioural perspective. In competitive party systems, all political parties have as their primary goal the conquest acquisition of *power* or at least some influence in the distribution of it. Political parties try to win seats at elections in order to take control of the offices of government. When this is not possible, they assume the strategy of an opposition to scrutinize

■ ■ **aggregating:** the group process of bringing together a range of demands and of building a coalition of support across many levels of society on some issue, e.g., tax reform or social-welfare programs. ■ ■

government action and to offer *alternatives* to the electorate. In most cases, political parties seek support from a broad social base so as to claim representation and legitimacy in articulating the interests of the people. They are particularly adept at **aggregating** as many interests as possible under a common organizational structure and some ideological identification, such as liberalism, conservatism, nationalism, socialism, or communism.

In authoritarian systems, one party or a small number of parties try to mobilize the backing of interest groups and voters. Where political competition is controlled or nonexistent, the aggregation of many interests still takes place within parties, but the groups that are aggregated (such as unions, business organizations, and consumers) are mobilized to accept the party platform whether they support it wholeheartedly or not. In totalitarian party systems, a single party controls group demands and tries to create a single world view among the various groups in society.

Types of Parties

Political parties can differ in several respects. A structural-functional definition and approach to parties sensitizes us to the fact that different structures may perform similar functions, and the same structures may perform different functions. Some parties, including the Liberal and Progressive Conservative parties in Canada and the Republican and Democratic parties in the United States, are basically of a **pragmatic/brokerage** type.[6] They are generally found in the well-developed party systems of the traditional democracies. The Australian Liberal party, the British Conservative party, and the Swedish Moderate Coalition party are other examples. These parties are mass-appeal parties with no strong ideological commitments and no well-defined or differentiated party programs. Some analysts refer to these characteristics facetiously as "tweedledum and tweedledee," suggesting that brokerage parties sacrifice identity for electoral "market" success. Their chief goal is to elect their candidates to public office and to attract special-interest groups, giving them preferential legislative treatment in exchange for electoral and financial support.

The fact that pragmatic parties can embrace the original ideas and platforms popularized by other parties, even though the same policies may have been previously attacked or ignored, indicates something important about them. On close examination, one observes that mass-appeal parties are **coalitions** of many dissimilar groups that, at times, seem only to share a common party label. Pragmatic parties are much more concerned with political success than with political philosophy, opting usually to put together a winning coalition of candidates rather than attempting to reconcile the **doctrinal** persuasion of the party label with the voters.

In contrast to the brokerage-type parties are the *ideological* parties, many of which were formed in the last century and the early part of the twentieth century.[7] Operating within democratic as well as non-democratic party systems, these parties are doctrinal in that they pursue a set of prescribed principles in a political system. Ideological parties based on socialism and communism are almost universal among those states that permit political parties. Under the socialist label, they appear in the Netherlands and Norway as labour parties. Those based on Marxist-Leninist ideologies operate in numerous states, including Britain, Canada, France, Mexico, and the United States. Some ideological parties are organized around religious doctrines, such as the Swiss Evangelical Party, Pakistan's Islamic party, and Israel's United Torah Front.

Since World War II, many doctrinal parties have become less ideological and more pragmatic. The communist parties of Vietnam and Cuba are good examples of this newer trend. The present Chinese Communist Party (CCP) moved sharply away from Maoism by stressing the importance of material economic considerations (as opposed to subjective human factors, under Mao) in development and the basic unity of Chinese society.

One type of ideological party that deserves special mention is the *indigenous* or *nation-building* party.[8] Indigenous parties gear their platforms to the political systems in which they are found. They build their ideologies from a multiplicity of political doctrines that are relevant to the national problems in their particular social and economic environment. Increasingly, they have come to represent the peasant or tribal masses, the new proletariat, and the middle sectors. Many indigenous parties adopt a platform of land reform, nationalization of industry, a full range of economic and social reforms, and an opposition to communism. In Latin America, the Peruvian Aprista Party, Venezuela's Acción Democrática, Costa Rica's Liberación Nacional, Puerto Rico's Popular Democratic Party, and Guatemala's Partido Revolucionario are indigenous parties with nation-building ideologies. In Africa, Botswana's Democratic party is a nation-building political party.

Another meaningful classification of ideological parties focuses on party objectives. *Revolutionary* parties are dedicated to the fundamental transformation of the political, economic, and social system in a society. The formation of revolutionary parties has been encouraged by population explosion, growing urbanization, the concentration of land ownership, rigid class structures, and the support of revolutionary movements by external powers in the developing states of the world. More direct and immediate factors contributing to the growth of revolutionary parties include the proven success of similar groups in other states. For example, following the ascendancy of Fidel Castro in his successful overthrow of the dictatorship of Fulgencio Batista in 1959, contentious *Fidelista* movements sprang up in many countries of Latin America, such as in Peru, Guatemala, Venezuela, Uruguay, Argentina, and Bolivia. Revolutionary parties tend to suppress competition and mobilize the population around the goals of the regime's leaders, rather than promote the participation and representation of various groups in society.

In contrast to pragmatic and ideological parties are *special-interest* parties. These parties organize around a particular issue or interest and usually attract the support of an intensely dedicated and well-organized segment of the electorate. By so doing, special-interest parties focus on a dominant issue that the major parties are unwilling to endorse and sometimes can take enough votes away from the larger parties to change the outcome of elections. In Canada, for example, the Reform

Party of Canada has as its special interest the need to reform Parliament, to reconstruct the federal system, to reduce the national debt, and to change the fundamental ways MPs represent their constituents. When special-interest parties form a government, they are hard-pressed to implement their political goals as soon as possible. If this is not done, political support may wane within the party as well as in the electorate. Sometimes a special-interest party becomes the Official Opposition, as when the Bloc Québécois (BQ) won the second largest number of seats in the 1993 Canadian federal election. In Canada's federal Parliament, the Bloc represents the interests of those who want a sovereign Québec. It wants to promote a radically different arrangement between Québec and "its Canadian partner."

Another special-interest party is Québec's Parti Québécois, a party that fights for independence within the confines of Québec's political and governmental system. In 1984, the Parti Québécois found itself in the throes of bitter crisis when former premier René Lévesque announced his decision to jettison the goal of independence, the very raison d'être of his party's existence for over 16 years. His statement triggered a series of backbench defections and ministerial resignations, including his own, that nearly tore the party apart. Under the leadership of Lévesque's successor, Pierre Marc Johnson, the PQ struggled with the policy of "national affirmation," which preached that Québec would somehow assert a separate identity within the Canadian federal system. While in opposition to the Liberals, the party gradually drifted into a kind of ideological wilderness, eroding its electoral base of support and bringing enormous internal party pressures on Johnson to resign. As soon as the PQ's new leader, Jacques Parizeau, took office in Montreal in April 1988, he reaffirmed the secessionist aspirations of the party, returning to its special-interest character, restoring sovereignty as the number-one goal of its followers, and gaining widespread popularity in the province.

In 1980, a new political party, the Greens, was created in Germany in response to the established parties' lack of action on environmental issues. To gain rapid electoral strength, the anti-NATO Greens allied themselves with other political groupings to form the Green Alternative List (GAL). This strategy led to their growing electoral success in six *Länd* legislatures.

Parties representing special interests have emerged in many states around the world. For example, the Green Party of Canada ran 68 candidates, and the Confederation of Regions Western Party ran 55 candidates in the 1988 federal election. The Netherlands Farmers' Party, the Finnish Centre Party, and the Australian National Country Party are other examples of special-interest parties. In some states, women's parties have joined in the political competition of the party system. Referring to themselves ideologically as the "third dimension," the Women's Alliance in Iceland rejected the pyramidal structure of other political parties. In Belgium, the Women's Unity Party was organized in 1972, and similar parties have formed in Canada, France, and Norway. The Feminist Party of Canada has not been electorally competitive in the provinces or at the national level and is said to be dormant.

The Function of Political Parties

Political parties are institutions in most states and as such are considered as primary political units. Parties vary a great deal in their structure, goals, and the actual functions they perform in the political system. They often differ in political ideology, in adherence to democratic and constitutional methods, in their legislative platforms, in the size of their membership, and in their socio-economic bases of support. They operate in political cultures with different traditions of **partisanship**, degrees of popular participation, and legal requirements regulating party competition. The Communist Party of China, the Progressive Conservative Party of Canada, and the Likud (consolidation) party of Israel all illustrate how parties differ in ideology, organization, and function.

Teaching Us About Politics and Government

All political parties are agents of political learning. They interpret political events, initiate new political philosophies or combine old ones to form new policies and platforms, and transmit political messages to the people through their candidates and the media.

In Canada, all political parties have a political socialization function in competition with other parties, groups, and the media. Canadian political parties are just one kind of institution among many that openly and legitimately transmit political information. The family, schools, neighbourhood and peer groups, churches, professional and work groups, trade unions, business associations, and especially the mass media also share in po-litical socialization. Some of the socializing activities of Canada's political parties take place in the riding associations and local clubs and societies affiliated with them. Riding as-sociations seek to recruit and initiate new members. They canvass voters, distribute lit-erature, and invite candidates to make speeches. At the leadership level of the parties, clubs, caucus meetings, and parliamentary committees are constantly training and indoc-trinating party members.

Choosing Our Leaders

Political parties also perform the function of choosing our leaders. Parties vary in their re-cruitment of members, candidates, and lead-ers. The techniques of recruitment include appointment, election, and **party conven-tions,** where political leadership is formally slated. In most party systems, the government party has access to a large number of patron-age appointments that enhance executive leadership.

In Canada, the recruitment function is di-rectly affected by the nominating functions of competing political parties. Political parties are the main vehicles for presenting and se-lecting Canada's representatives and their leaders. But people can enter the political sys-tem as *independents* without formal ties to any of the competing political parties. The success rate of independent candidates who run in many Canadian ridings is marginal. Even though political parties are *extra-constitutional* organizations in Canada's political system, there is no question that they give Canadians primary access to the parliamentary process.

Vocalizing Our Interests

Another important function of political parties is to convert opinions, attitudes, beliefs, and preferences into coherent demands on the po-litical system. Many interests requiring politi-cal expression exist in all societies. They can call for the legalization of abortion, legislation to institute capital punishment, the control of interest rates, the adjustment of tax laws to favour certain groups, or any interest that de-mands political representation and public visi-bility. Political parties vary in the intensity and extent to which they make and articulate the interests that are present in society. And the processes of *interest articulation* differ among the various political party systems.

In Canada, a wide range of social and economic interests are organized. Within a highly competitive political system, political parties seek to attract the support of many of these interest groups by articulating their de-mands as either government policies or as op-position strategies. But most of Canada's interest groups prefer to remain non-partisan, avoiding the politically hazardous tactic of af-filiating with one of the parties competing in the political system. To win the support of the various interests, political parties invite inter-est groups to make their claims and influence party policy through the activities of the rid-ing associations, annual party conferences, and in the party committees in Parliament.

In most non-democratic states, people have learned that they cannot effectively make demands on the government without fear of severe reprisals. In these states, interest-group activity and interest articulation exist, but only on a relatively small scale and under controlled circumstances – carried on at the local level and satisfied within those limits.

Bringing Many Interests Under One Group

Interest articulation is the expression of group demands by means of campaigns, the mass media, direct action, petition, lobbying, and the interpenetration of elites. Interest aggregation is the joining of interests in such a way that they are related to the selection of government and party leaders and to the making and administering of policy.

The aggregative function of Canadian parties cuts across a wide variety of organized economic interests and professional and non-professional groups. But interest groups are aware that the structure of government and the political party in power are the two political realities that can bring about the materialization of their demands. Thus, the Cabinet, which itself usually is a microcosmic representation of many organized interests, is the target of concentrated group pressures. Organizations such as the Canadian Chamber of Commerce, the Canadian Manufacturers' Association, the Canadian Federation of Agriculture, and the Canadian Labour Congress make annual submissions to the Cabinet. When government is unresponsive, they will usually turn to opposition parties to carry their banner. In all cases where parties wish to aggregate the interests of groups, a process of bargaining takes place in which inducements are offered to business and labour, specific industries and professions, and the various regions of the country.

Making and Implementing Policy

In democratic political systems, political parties may play a crucial role in making and implementing public policy. However, because of the competitive nature of democratic political systems, organizations other than political parties also shape the policy process. Besides political parties, interest groups and the civil service participate in policy-making. Sometimes the party system itself reduces the ability of political parties to formulate and implement policies in line with their ideology and their base of popular support. Especially in European democracies, where multi-party systems abound, few parties ever gain a majority in the legislature at either the national or local level. In these states, parties need to participate in coalitions in order to form governments; this procedure usually requires compromising certain policy positions.

In most political systems, political parties are limited in their policy-making roles by the agenda of the executive branch of government. Frequently there is a gap between a party's policy positions and its government programs and actions. As a general rule, party activists are more seriously committed to party philosophy and the ideology behind policies than are elected officeholders, especially those who hold executive positions. Executives have a broader constituency and must gain rapport not just with party ideologues but with a plurality of voters, who generally relate more to political action than to abstract ideology. But even when an ideological party forms a government, it must govern all the people and strive to serve the broad public interest. In most parties, candidates view success at the polls as the primary party objective, because without electoral victory the party cannot implement its programs. The overriding desire to win seats in a legislature or to form the political executive reduces ideological consistency. Despite this, political parties do influence policy by shaping legislators' voting behaviour and the attitudes of political leaders toward specific issues.

In democratic party systems, membership in a political party usually produces a high degree of cohesion when legislators vote on bills. Generally, **left-wing** parties demonstrate a stronger party cohesion in legislative voting than do **right-wing** parties, partly because they take their ideology more seriously. This has also been true in Canada, where the left-leaning New Democratic Party demonstrates stronger legislative and caucus loyalty than do the large Progressive Conservative and Liberal parties, in which political **factions** tend to form. In the United States, Republicans and Democrats reveal weaker legislative cohesion than do Canadian or European parties, mainly because the parliamentary system necessitates greater **party discipline** to sustain the government in office.

In Canada, the policy-making and implementing process is highly complex. It is true that parties do generate public policy and compete in its creation, but the conversion process from party platform to government policy can be slowed down by bureaucrats and parliamentary procedures. Opposition parties advance policies of job creation but quickly temper the implementation of these policies when they become governing parties. Upper-echelon civil servants (deputy ministers and assistant deputy ministers) greatly influence the adaptation of party policy to public policy.[9] Department officials reformulate the bulk of party policy within the administrative realities of budgets and implementation. Civil servants sensitize their political masters to the limited number of policy

■ ■ **faction:** a small, relatively homogeneous group of individuals within a larger organization such as a political party. ■ ■

alternatives available to a government in the face of fiscal and monetary restrictions. In addition, before any policy decision is implemented, many consultations must take place among cabinet ministers, advisory committees in Parliament, and provincial premiers.

Political-Party Systems

There are many ways to classify political parties. Numerous typologies have been designed; all are largely impressionistic, e.g., personalistic parties, revolutionary parties. Another type of classification involves the number of parties in the party system. In this typology, it is assumed that legislative representation is a reflection of real party influence in the national system, the only exceptions being those parties that are outlawed or denied representation, and those exceptional circumstances when parties decide not to participate for strategic reasons. It is important to note that legislative representation is not always a reflection of party popularity. Parties may be popular but may not win representation. In fact, representation is more than anything a reflection of the impact of an electoral system (i.e., single-member district or proportional representation) upon the success of parties.

In the case of most authoritarian states, no assumption should be made that legislative representation is an indication of power, for legislatures in non-democratic states are not usually powerful. Nevertheless, parties do compete for legislative representation, which is an important factor in determining a party's relationship with other parties, if not with the institutions of government. The classification of party systems adopted in this study distinguishes single-party systems from multi-party systems.

One-Party States

The term "party system" implies competition between two or more political parties. States without political parties or that have only one political party are therefore not systemic in terms of party competition. Prior to World War II, one-party systems appeared for the first time under communist and fascist regimes. They were unique because they outlawed all political competition and served as instruments of social control. They adhered to one all-encompassing orthodox ideology that outlined the conditions of political recruitment and determined the economic, military, and social strategies of the state.

Today, this type of party continues to flourish in non-democratic socialist states. In states such as China and Vietnam, the party has ceased to be a mere reflection of contemporary political values in the Western sense, and functions instead as a permanent institution for which the government serves as an administrative agency. In these states, the party has established itself as a sort of supragovernment, a supreme decision-making and policy-making authority. This peculiar and historically novel scheme has merited the label "party state."[10] It accords with the Marxist dictum that the state is a mere instrument of the ruling class.

Party-centred decision-making maintains the monolithic and monopolistic position of the party, claiming singular legitimacy and legality. In states where this exists, the party would have less social status, while the government, with its specialized functions, would be more subject to interest-group pressures and party influence. In these political systems it is imperative to keep authority within the party framework in order to maintain a coherent, organized elite group, bound by ideological purpose, to control and supervise the state and ensure the necessary unity of the political system. Sometimes very strong rulers such as Castro, Stalin, and Tito have taken decision-making entirely onto themselves, concentrating decision-making almost entirely in the personalistic style of their leadership.

Since World War II, single-party systems have spread to many developing states, creating a number of versions of one-party systems. Less ideologically orthodox and disciplined than in one-party socialist states, these parties do not penetrate or extensively control all levels of the social infrastructure. However, in the political realm, they monopolize the recruitment of political elites and permit no party competition. As in states where the official party aspires to communism, only one party is legal, yet in a few instances, one or more additional government parties may be authorized, provided they are regime-sponsored and operate within the strict guidelines established by the government.

Single-party systems differ as well in their internal organization, leadership, and their *degree* of authoritarianism. They are usually more elitist than mass parties, and more likely to attract personalistic leaders. Once in power, the governing party tends to surrender its policy-making and implementation functions to the state apparatus. Ideologically, these types of parties combine nationalism with an eclectic philosophy of modernization, mixing elements of traditional agrarian societies. They advance the need for dictatorship in order to overcome problems of corruption, disunity, or separatism, and counter them with enforced political integration, socialization, and repression.

Many one-party states are civilian regimes, most of which appear in Africa, the Caribbean, and the Middle East, such as Guinea-Bissau, Guyana, and South Yemen. African military regimes with one-party systems include Angola and Ethiopia. In Central and South America, they include Guatemala, Paraguay, and Peru. And in the Middle East and Asia, they appear in Algeria, Iraq, Libya, Syria, Afghanistan, Bangladesh, Myanmar (Burma), Indonesia, Taiwan, and South Korea.

Two-Party Competitive Systems

A two-party political system is one wherein political power and governmental offices tend to alternate between two major political parties. This does not preclude the presence of minor parties in electoral competition. In all political systems where it has evolved, the two-party system has never remained pure. Numerous minor parties have formed to challenge one or both of the dominant parties. And although these parties may disappear with time, their presence is seldom without influence. The chief function of minor parties in a two-party competitive system has been to bring new issues, or new ways of looking at old issues, to the political agenda. As they succeed in forcing new policies on the older, established parties, these minor parties tend to disappear. This is one of the ways in which the party system stays alive and remains responsive to changing conditions and issues.

Some analysts have attempted to quantify the system, not so much for precision as to locate the parameters in which two dominant political parties compete: for Ronald McDonald, a two-party competitive system reveals two dominant parties each receiving approximately 40 percent – and never more than 60 percent – of the total number of seats in the legislature.[11] The two-party competitive system exists only in some English-speaking democracies, and appears in some 20 states. The British party system is frequently cited as the classic example. Even so, more than a dozen minor parties also compete with the Conservative and Labour parties. The bipolar character of the British party system appears in other states that have at one time or another come under direct British influence, including the United States and the Commonwealth countries, such as Barbados, Jamaica, and Malta. In Ireland, the United Ireland party (*Fine Gael* – party of the Irish) and the Republican party (*Fianna Fáil*) have been the two dominant parties.

As for the United States, it is not difficult to imagine a multi-party system in a country so diverse. There could feasibly be a party of labour, of southern whites, of blacks or chicanos, of western agriculture, and so on. In fact, the contrast between the galaxy of American interest groups and the presence throughout their political history of only two major parties is striking, notwithstanding the fact that at different times the United States has had more than two parties competing in its federal election. The two-party competitive system has an extraordinary heritage: the Democrats descend from the party of Thomas Jefferson founded for the election of 1800, and the Republican party has its roots in the time of Abraham Lincoln.

Table 11.1:
Party standings in the Canadian House of Commons, 1900–1993

Date of Election	Liberal	Conservative Unionist*/	Progressive	CCF - NDP	Social Credit	Reform	BQ	Independent	Total seats
Nov 7, 1900	133	80							213
Nov 3, 1904	138	75						1	214
Oct 26, 1908	135	85						1	221
Sept 21, 1911	87	134						1	222
Dec 17, 1917	82	*153							235
Dec 6, 1921	116	50	64					5	235
Oct 29, 1925	99	116	24					6	245
Sept 14, 1926	128	91	20					6	245
July 28, 1930	91	137	12					5	245
Oct 14, 1935	173	40		7	17			8	245
Mar 26, 1940	181	40		8	10			6	245
June 11, 1945	125	67		28	13			12	245
June 27, 1949	193	41		13	10			5	262
Aug 10, 1953	171	51		23	15			5	265
June 10, 1957	105	112		25	19			4	265
Mar 31, 1958	49	208		8					265
June 18, 1962	100	116		19	30				265
Apr 8, 1963	129	95		17	24				265
Nov 8, 1965	131	97		21	5			2	265
June 25, 1968	155	72		22				1	264
Oct 30, 1972	109	107		31	15			2	264
July 8, 1974	141	95		16	11			1	264
May 22, 1979	114	136		26	6				282
Feb 18, 1980	147	103		32					282
Sept 14, 1984	40	211		30				1	282
Nov 21, 1988	83	169		43					295
Oct 25, 1993	177	2		9		52	54	1	295

*Unionist: The conscriptionist Conservative government of Robert Borden,
  formed from a coalition of English Liberals and Conservatives.

Source: Adapted from Paul Fox and Graham White, *Politics Canada,* 7th ed.
     (Toronto: McGraw-Hill Ryerson Ltd,. 1991), 342.

Table 11.2:
Non-registered minor parties, 1993

Party	Number of candidates 1993
Communist Party	7
Rhinoceros Party	0
Social Credit	10
Confederation of Regions Party	6
Canada Economic Community	30
Canada Party for Renewal	6
Freedom Party	0
Option Party	0
Parti Nationaliste du Québec	0
Reform of the Monetary Law	0

Source: Elections Canada, 1993

Three factors set the United States on the road to biparty politics. First, since the War of Independence, two main political groupings (initially known as the Federalists and the Jeffersonian Democrats) organized around conflicting economic interests and built coalitions of support within the country. Second, the adoption of the single-member legislative district electoral arrangement has worked to discourage lasting third-party movements, because only those parties that have a chance of attracting the most votes have the political momentum to continue functioning as independent groups.[12] Finally, a major institutional incentive for preserving the two-party system has been the presidency. Because only one party can win the presidency in any given election, there is little point in voting for the presidential candidate of a party that has no chance of winning.

Many Minor Parties

Canada's party system retains its biparty character in spite of the persistent representation of minor parties in the House of Commons over the past six decades (table 11.1).[13] It is still a fact that the Liberals and the Conservatives are the only two parties that have ever governed at the federal level. However, if we look at Canada's party system from the perspective of party competition, a multi-party system is discernible. For example, in the 1993 federal election, 14 *registered* parties competed for seats in the House of Commons but only five were successful at electing candidates. Another ten political parties failed to run the minimum of 50 candidates to meet the 1993 registration requirements (table

Table 11.3:
Registered minor parties in Canada: federal elections 1984, 1988, and 1993

Party	Number of candidates 1984	Number of candidates 1988	Number of candidates 1993
Rhinoceros Party	89	74	
Parti Nationaliste du Québec	75	0	
Libertarian Party	72	88	
Party for the Commonwealth of Canada	65	59	
The Green Party	60	68	79
Confederation of Regions Western Party	55	51	
Communist Party	52	52	
Social Credit	51	9	
The Reform Party	0	72	207
Christian Heritage Party (first election campaign, 1988)		63	59
Bloc Québécois			75
National Party of Canada			171
Abolitionist			80
Party of the Commonwealth			59
The Canada Party			56
Libertarian Party			52
Marxist-Leninist			51
Natural Law Party			231

Source: Elections Canada, 1993

11.2). The single-member-district (plurality) electoral system almost eliminates the representation of smaller parties in Canada's parliamentary institutions. In addition, in 1993, only two parties, the Liberals and the Progressive Conservatives, ran candidates in all 295 ridings. The NDP ran 294 candidates. Minor parties, also called "small" or "fringe" parties, run substantially fewer candidates and consequently reduce their chances of winning seats

373

(table 11.3).[14] With these parties the political message ranges from the extreme right to the extreme left to the just plain silly.

Many of the small parties are driven by a cause; for example, for the Libertarians, the goal is to dramatically cut the size of government, and to reduce taxes and social services. The Party for the Commonwealth of Canada follows the writings of the convicted American extremist, Linden Larouch, who forecasts global financial collapse. The Green Party of Canada is committed to cleaning up the environment and to making environmental concerns a mainstream issue in the Canadian political system. The Christian Heritage Party, which ran candidates for the first time in 1988, wants a return to Christian values, is opposed to abortion, is for capital punishment, wants to toughen immigration laws, and to balance the budget. The Reform party wants to reform Canada's political and governing systems, placing greater reliance on the private sector, to design a strategy to reduce the deficit and address the national debt, to abolish universality of government benefits, and to establish the equality of provinces within a reconstructed federal system. For the Confederation of Regions Western Party, one of the issues is language, to unite English-speaking people of Canada against government mandated bilingualism. The Communist Party of Canada called for curbing the power of big business as the real guarantee of independence for Canada.

For all these parties, the goal is to be taken seriously by targeting discontented voters. But with the Rhinoceros party, mania is the message, and their campaigns have been strictly for laughs. They parody big-party policies and mock the political process in

Canada. In 1980, the Rhinoceros party came close to getting elected in two Québec ridings, stood as Canada's fourth most popular party in 1984, called themselves "the fringe party to beat" in the 1988 election, but ran no candidates in 1993.

On the provincial level, one encounters a variety of party systems, not all of which are examples of the classic two-party type.[15] Nova Scotia, and Manitoba reveal interparty competition between, and the representation of, two parties. In Nova Scotia the electoral struggle is between the Liberals and the Conservatives, and in Manitoba, the Conservatives, Liberals and the NDP fight for the reins of government.

In Québec, three parties have governed the province in the post-war period, the Liberals, Parti Québécois, and Union Nationale. The case of the Parti Québécois served to illustrate how a provincial minor third party can stun itself, as well as the country, by springing to power, weathering political storms, and staging impressive recoveries. And in Ontario, prior to 1987, the Liberals had last won a provincial election in 1937; the Conservatives (the "Big Blue Machine") had governed continuously from 1943 to 1985. Until June 1985, when the Liberals, with assistance from the NDP, gained power on a vote of no confidence, Ontario was a singular provincial example of a one-party-dominant system. In its 1987 election, Ontario gave the Liberals a strong majority with 95 of the 130 seats, and realigned the province in the direction of three-party competition. And in 1990, the NDP formed a government for the first time in Ontario, taking 74 of the 130 seats. In 1987, in New Brunswick, a rejuvenated Liberal party under the stewardship of Frank

McKenna won all of the 58 seats in the provincial legislature, a first-time political occurrence in that province. But in 1991, the Liberal majority was reduced to 44, with opposition taking the remainder of the 58 seats: Confederation of Regions (CoR) 8; PC 5; and one independent.

On examination, Canadian politics deviates from a pure two-party model not only because of the presence of third parties, but because one party – the Liberal party – has dominated federal government in Canada throughout most of this century. Of the 28 federal governments since 1900, the Liberals formed 20. If we think that the two most successful parties should be roughly equal in the two-party system, that they should alternate frequently in power, and that almost every federal election is "up for grabs," the Canadian experience is not a strong example. Instead of being a relationship of two roughly equal competitors, the relationship between Canada's two government parties has been that of dominant to dominated. That is, one party has repeatedly formed a government, controlled the Senate, selected most of the Supreme Court justices, and elaborated public policy during its dominance, with relatively few interceptions of power by the other party.

Nevertheless, the two-party system as it persists in Canada has been extolled as a model of political stability. As in its British and American versions, the Canadian system has been characterized by continuity and compromise. The ideological distance between the two traditional parties is very slight, driving the party system toward moderation at the centre. However, a heightened ideological distance, detectable among the successful competing parties, especially Reform and the Bloc Québécois (BQ), means that there are disagreements on fundamentals; for example, on the role and nature of Parliament, and on the federal system. Historically, Canada's electoral system has favoured the larger parties, amplifying the proportion of seats they hold in the House of Commons compared to the proportion of popular votes that elected them.

A stable biparty system has emerged in various states. Even though proportional representation is the applied formula in its electoral system, Germany has produced a stable two-party system within a multi-party structure. Since 1961, two major parties – the Christian Democratic Union, with its Bavarian affiliate, the Christian Social Union (CDU/CSU), and the Social Democratic Party (SDP) – have accounted for over 75 percent of the popular vote. However, the largest of the other parties, the Free Democratic Party (FDP), has captured between 5 and 10 percent of the vote, and has often won enough seats to have a pivotal role in forming government coalitions. In Colombia, a biparty system between the Conservative and Liberal parties has existed for over 100 years, even though many minor parties have competed in the electoral system. But in Costa Rica, proportional representation tends to create a disproportionate influence of minor parties on the two major parties, the governing National Liberation party and the Social Christian Unity Party.

Multi-Party Systems

A multi-party system exists where three or more parties contest elections, gain representation, and form coalitions with the governing party. Such a system may include a variety of major parties as well as minor parties that vie for political power and government offices. It is often necessary for a coalition of interests to work together in order to carry out a program of government. The number of organized political parties varies among multi-party systems. In the 1992 Israeli elections, more than 25 parties competed. Spain has up to 55 organized parties running candidates when elections are held.

Many factors converge to generate a multi-party system. The adoption of proportional representation and the expansion of the suffrage usually encourage its development. A lack of political consensus also contributes to the formation of a multi-party system. The widespread presence of conflicting political values and philosophies usually fosters the emergence of opposing groups which seek to change the structure of institutions or the formal policy-making process itself. Socio-economic factors, such as ethnicity, language, or religion contribute to the development of a pluralistic system. In Belgium, for example, different parties represent the French-, Flemish-, and German-speaking people. And with regard to religious orientations, Christian Democratic parties appear in most western European states, as well as a large number in the Caribbean and Latin America. Some parties are also formed to represent the interests of special groups, such as labour and women. Multi-party systems basically reflect the ideological differences that evolve in a given society, as witnessed by the presence of anarchist groups, communist parties, nationalist parties, revolutionary parties, and socialist parties. These parties perceive concrete events in light of abstract ideas. Ideology is at a pre-

mium, while bargaining and compromise are rejected. This general situation is both the cause and effect of a pluralistic party system and, in contrast to two party systems, it runs counter to their basic dualist tendency.

Multi-party systems can be *one-party dominant*, and *multi-party competitive*. In a one-party-dominant system, a single party wins approximately 60 percent or more of the seats in a legislature and two or more other parties usually win less than 40 percent of the seats.[16] Mexico has been a good example of a state with a one-party-dominant multi-party system. The Partido Revolucionario Instituciónal (PRI) has never had one of its nominees for president or governor defeated since the party was founded in 1929. Only since the 1970s have other parties been able to win appreciable numbers of seats at municipal levels and in the lower house of Congress. Other examples of single-party dominance are India with its Indian National Congress Party, and the Bahamas with its Progressive Liberal Party.

In some multi-party systems, one party is sufficiently strong to dominate the others but the dominance of the system is much weaker than in the one-party-dominant multi-party system. There is a greater amount of challenge from opposition parties and a higher frequency of shifting of power among competing parties, as Japan's party system illustrates. When one party appears to dominate the system, incentives arise for opposition parties to form coalitions, either to minimize the strength of the government party or to form a government in order to prevent the dominant party from coming to power.

Sometimes, however, even though one party may dominate in terms of the attraction of popular votes, **coalition governments** are formed, often with great difficulty, and may vary in their composition from government to government. In the 1992 Israeli election, in order to form a government, the Labour party, with its 44 seats, constructed a successful coalition, after much persuasion, with the Meretz party, which had captured 12 seats, and the Shas party, which won six seats. In Israel, a party needs to win at least 62 seats or negotiate a coalition of at least 62 seats in order to form a government in a Knesset (parliament) of 120 members.

Multi-party-competitive systems can also demonstrate high fragmentation when no single party dominates the system. In this looser expression of party competition, no single party wins more than 40 percent of the legislative seats. As a general rule, parties enter and exit the electoral system with relative ease. Party formation and cohesion is often based on personalities, transient issues, or economic and political events that encourage ephemeral party organizations. Within these multi-party systems, coalitions are formed with ease. Opportunism, pragmatism, and mutual self-interest are the primary forces that encourage coalitions which, however, easily come apart, resulting in frequent general elections or in the interference and dominance of a strong overriding executive. Denmark, for example, with more than two dozen parties, has averaged one general election every two years since the 1960s. Other states with multi-party systems, such as Bolivia, the Dominican Republic, Ecuador, Finland, the Netherlands, Spain, Thailand, and Turkey, have experienced varying degrees of political instability.

The most extreme cases of fragmentation have been France and Italy. Because of the large number of weak parties in both states, most parties represent only a small segment of the electorate. Many parties simply cannot claim to represent the interests of the entire electorate.

In most multi-party systems, the maintenance of coalitions between elections is exceedingly difficult. "Gentlemen's agreements" based on ideology, personalism, friendship, money, and patronage are frequently offered to induce post-election allegiance. There is little doubt that parliamentary instability is often the by-product of intense ideological competition in multi-party systems. If political stability is defined in terms of the constitutional tenure of governments and their ability to predictably carry out their policies, then states in this category tend to demonstrate more frequent instability than one-party, bi-party, and dominant-multi-party systems. But among all systems, multi-party systems are neither the most stable nor the least.

Party Organization and Structure

Political parties represent three distinct groups: candidates and officeholders, citizens who are party members or identify with the party, and the *formal party organization*. These groups can range from a few legislators who co-ordinate strategies and policies under a shared party label, to a decentralized party structure open to anyone interested in becoming a candidate, to a highly centralized and almost closed party organization, characteristic of single-party state systems.

Political parties reflect essentially two organizational arrangements – *hierarchy* or *stratarchy*. Hierarchically organized parties are structured so that the distribution of power, privilege, and authority is systemic and unequal, with control of the party organization in the hands of a few people at the top. Robert Michels was the first student of organizational behaviour to note the *iron law of oligarchy* in party structures.[17] He observed that a full-time professional staff dominates the party organization and that the perspectives of the leader may not necessarily be those of the members. *Stratarchy* is characteristic of democratic political parties, in which power is shared by the leader with several layers of the party organization. In this kind of party organization, the leader needs grassroots support, the voluntary contribution of workers, especially the few who are dedicated to working for the party between elections. Leaders do not exercise punitive action against those in the party who might challenge the way things operate. Instead, the leader depends on the policy input and support of the membership below, while those who work within the party organization need the special stewardship skills of the national leader. In Canada, the Reform party reflects a stratarchy of party organization. At the same time, the Liberal and Progressive Conservative parties tend to exemplify hierarchically organized parties.

The organization of political parties usually reflects the organization of the state, i.e., unitary or federal. In most federal states, national parties are really confederations of subnational party organizations, held together by national committees. The extent to which the national party regards itself as "integrated" or "federated" with the subnational party organizations will vary from one electoral system to another. Factors that can determine the affilia-

tion of national and subnational party organizations include: the popularity and co-operation of the national and subnational party leaders; the criteria of party membership; the degree of personnel interaction between the national and subnational organizations; whether an integrated or separate fund-raising strategy is employed; the congruence of party policy and ideology; and the allegiance of voters within the federal system.

In the United States, there is generally little organizational connection between state and national party organizations. In a majority of states, party chairpersons are not frequently involved in national committee affairs. Of the two political parties, the Republicans at the state level tend to receive more staff assistance, financial help, research and polling data, and campaign instructions from the national party organization than do state Democrats from their national organization. But in both parties, the national organization tends not to intervene in state activities, unless asked. In Canada, the co-ordination of political strategies between the federal and provincial wings of the same party tends to vary from province to province, but in general the two can be characterized as independent. Parties of the same name may, from time to time, share workers and facilities, but generally tend to keep their distance at the highest levels of party organization. Inter-provincial party ties also tend to be weak among the traditional parties; however, the New Democratic Party maintains strong interprovincial ties and extensive organizational and financial linkages among its provincial parties, as well as among the provincial parties and the national party.

The organization of Canada's three parliamentary parties is quite similar. Each has a *parliamentary wing*, which consists of the leader and the party caucus, who are front-line in the legislative battles in the House of Commons and the Senate. There is also an *extra-parliamentary wing*, consisting of the national party headquarters, a national executive, and its committees, which are dominated as well by the party leader, whose image and performance affects the party organization at three levels. The first of these levels is the grassroots organization at the *constituency level*. From here, federal candidates are nominated, delegates to conventions are elected, volunteer personnel and members are recruited, and fund-raising campaigns are initiated. The *provincial level* is next on the pyramid of the national-party organization. At this level, the party faithful plan and co-ordinate the strategies that are employed at the constituency level. Members of the executive at this level are responsible for all the federal constituencies in the province. At the apex of the extra-parliamentary party organization is the *national level*.

The national association normally organizes a biennial convention to stimulate debate, consider new policy directions, and elect party officials.[19] Conventions are also the occasions for electing party leaders. Because the main impact of contemporary parties comes through elections, the party organization is an apparatus oriented towards the convention and the selection or retention of a national leader. The predictable occurrence of party conventions provides an opportunity for disgruntled party members to bring about change as well as for those who want to protect the status quo. In the final analysis, conventions are vehicles for important communication among competing political parties, their membership, and the independent voter.

Party Membership

From an organizational point of view, a political party in Canada is a small inner circle composed of officeholders, candidates, a professional staff, and the party faithful. But we often hear that someone is a "member" of the Liberal Party of Canada, or of the New Democratic Party. Yet generations of political scientists, lawyers, judges, and politicians have been unable to agree on exactly what it means to be a member of a party. Some see membership as party identification – a voter's sense of psychological attachment to a party, which goes beyond merely voting for the party. Although this concept is useful to social scientists, party identification has no legal significance. A second definition of membership has to do with the process of "joining" a political party by meeting a set of criteria such as registering, paying dues, doing committee work, etc. In some European states, people can "apply" for membership (as in Germany's Christian Democratic party and Socialist party), are accepted, pay dues, and carry a membership card. In the United States, legal membership in some states involves registration as a Democrat or a Republican. The main purpose of registration in these states is to prevent adherents of one party from voting in another party's primary. Some parties, such as the Communist party, have strict criteria that are meant to exclude people who do not meet their ideological standards.

In general, membership in a party involves engaging in its activities, with or without the process of formal admission procedures. A party consists of all those people who participate in any of the following activities: running for office under the party label, seeking nomination for candidacy, contributing money, working for a candidate, attending meetings, or voting as a delegate.

Party Finance

Party organizations, activities, and campaigns require huge amounts of money. Funds are needed to pay for office space or the purchase of land and building, staff salaries (administration and research), telephone bills, computers, postage, travel expenses, campaign literature, polling, and advertising in the mass media. In the 1990s, most political parties in democratic political systems must make strenuous and systematic efforts to broaden the base of their contributors. In most democratic states, there are four primary classes of contributors: individuals, corporations, interest groups (defined broadly to include trade unions and private organizations), and the public treasury. For political parties, the ability to attract money is related to the quality of candidates offered, especially the leader; the party organization between elections and the campaign organization during elections; performance in past elections and standing in the polls; the capacity to present issues and promises put forward by the leader and the candidates; and the ability to *win* elections.

Next to voting, financial contributions to political parties are the most common form of political activity. But it is difficult to generalize about money and political parties because governments have different rules and laws to regulate party financing and spending. However, the reasons for drafting legislation to regulate party financing tend to be similar

among governments. The first is public disclosure: the amount of money parties raise and spend is brought out in the open. Second, regulations place limitations on the amounts of money parties can spend on elections and other activities, thus reducing the influence of money on politicians. Third, regulation is designed to reduce the dependence of political parties on wealthy donors by partially subsidizing election costs with public funds. Fourth, parties are required by law to record their financial activities and to audit their books. And fifth, such legislation is meant to discourage the corruption of party fund-raising by means of internal and external auditing requirements.

In Canada, the Elections Expenses Act, 1974 (with its 1983 amendments), is the legal instrument that governs how political parties raise and spend their funds.[20] Prior to these dates, corporate donations were the source of most (75-90 percent) of the money raised by the Liberal and Progressive Conservative parties. The New Democratic Party drew most of its support from members, trade unions, and from grassroots fund-raising strategies. Since the passage of the Elections Expenses Act, all parties have gained greater access to individual contributions because tax credits for political donations are embodied in the legislation, (allowing 75 percent on contributions up to $100, 50 percent for amounts between $100 and $550, and 33.3 percent on amounts over $550). Just as important are the provisions for disclosure, requiring parties to file financial reports and to name contributors donating $100 or more. The legislation has reduced the financial burden of political parties by providing reimbursements of half of the permissible spending for candidates who win 15 percent of the total votes cast in their ridings.

The major effect of regulatory legislation on political party finance in Canada has been to facilitate a more equitable access to donors. Both the Liberal and Progressive Conservative parties have lessened their dependence on contributions from corporations since the mid-1970s from as much as 90 percent to 50 percent or less. Not surprisingly, the NDP raises very little money from corporations but relies heavily on individual and union donors. Contributions from individuals have grown substantially, but the higher costs of administering this kind of fund-raising campaign can override the benefits it appears to provide.

In order to avoid some of the spending restrictions in the legislation, all three parliamentary parties have increased expenditures outside of the designated campaign periods, when expenditures are limited only by a party's ability to raise money. The growth of non-election spending indicates a higher level of inter-party competition and reflects the importance party leaders assign to maintaining strong party organizations between elections.

Money is a frequently misunderstood aspect of politics. Without adequate financing, a political party's chances of success are seriously hampered. Money buys attention – not necessarily votes. Parties must be able to reach the electorate. This is done not only by door-to-door campaigning, but by the expensive process of media advertising, targeted mailings, and the use of trained public-relations specialists. But in the final analysis, if one party spends a large amount of money, what is important is how well it is spent and how expenditures compare with those of competing parties.

Primary Political Parties

Communist Parties

Among all ideological parties that have ever won power or that compete with other political parties in competitive party systems, communist parties are ideologically the most rigid and organizationally the most structured.[21] The principles of communism are drawn from the philosophies and practices of Karl Marx (1818-1883), his collaborator Frederick Engels (1820-1895), V.I. Lenin (1870-1924), Joseph Stalin (1879-1953), and Mao Tse Tung (1893-1976). No communist party is ideologically identical to any other, but in all communist parties the members are expected to master the principles of Marxism-Leninism as interpreted by national party elites. Thus, notwithstanding the post-World War II emergence of different national roads to communism, most communist ideologies accept Marx and Lenin as their philosophical forefathers. Regardless of which communist system one studies, for example the Chinese, Cuban, or Vietnamese, all political leaders use Marxism-Leninism to justify their public policies.

The Communist Party of Canada, formed in 1921, is also a Marxist-Leninist organization. Under the leadership of Tim Buck, the party adapted its strategies and tactics to the prevailing Soviet line. Like its counterpart in the United States, the Communist Party of Canada has played a minor role in the Canadian electoral system. In the 1984 and 1988 federal elections, the party unsuccessfully ran 52 candidates, attracting less than one percent of the electoral vote, but in 1993, it fielded only seven candidates. Because of its failure to run 50 candidates, the party, like all others in the same circumstance, has been "de-registered" in

1994 under the Canada Elections Act. Perhaps more important than its electoral presence is the party's involvement in the trade-union movement. But the party had only a marginal impact on Canada's political system. In 1994, the Communist Party of Canada sold off or gave away its few assets, paid its debts, and disbanded.

Today, communist parties in Italy, France, Finland, Ireland, Spain, and Portugal receive electoral support from manual workers and intellectuals because they advocate a command economy, that is, one planned extensively by the state. In Europe and some Asian states, communist parties want to take full command of the economy. There may be variations in application, particularly in China where peasants are the backbone of the Communist party. In Latin America, all political systems include communist parties that operate either openly when legal or clandestinely when outlawed. While communist parties are small, constituting only about one percent of the total population, they draw some support from urban wage earners, labourers, the lower-middle class, and students, but usually not from the peasantry. It is important to note that all governing communist parties have come to power at the national level by the violent overthrow of the previous regime or as a consequence of major international conflict. No communist government has ever been "democratically" elected. However, communist governments have been elected at the state level in India and frequently in many Italian cities, as well as at subnational levels in other states.

In communist states there is one governing party that usually excludes any other political groups from legitimately challenging its position. Some communist political systems have permitted "allied parties" that are subordinate to join with the governing communist party in a "national front." But no communist party-controlled political system lays claim to having achieved the goals of communism to date: the implementation of a communist society is a goal of the future.

The rigidity of communist ideology is fostered and protected by the way communist parties are structured. At the top of the organization is a small group of party officials called the *politburo* or *presidium* (as in Cuba). This inner circle of powerful decision-makers determines the direction of party doctrine and transmits its directives down through lower party levels and across to the state and governmental apparatus. The party secretariat maintains the purity of the ideological and policy decisions of the politburo by supervising lower party organizations and monitoring internal party loyalty and discipline. Below the central level of the party organization are the local-party and primary-party organizations that scrutinize the application of ideological goals. Communist parties also encourage the development of *cadres* − community leaders who agitate and mobilize public support for the party at the local levels. The Chinese have been particularly successful in organizing cadres for ideological purposes to "correct" the ideas of rebellious party members and intellectuals who deviate from the official party line.

Socialist Parties

In "communist" states, socialism is a historical phase that must be completed before communism emerges as the final political synthesis in human social development. According to its constitution, China is officially "a socialist state of the dictatorship of the proletariat led by the working class and based on the alliance of workers and peasants." But the socialist parties that have been formed in democratic states view socialism as the highest stage of political and economic development. They attract the greatest support in the democratic states of Europe: Austria, Belgium, France, the United Kingdom, the Republic of Ireland, Holland, Scandinavia, and Germany. They also enjoy extensive political support in Australia, Canada, New Zealand, and many of the states of Africa, Asia, and Latin America.

In contrast to the communist parties, the democratic-socialist parties seek to secure greater economic equality without the violent overthrow of the capitalist system. Political democracy is the primary goal of all democratic-socialist parties. When forming a government, alone or in coalition with other political parties, socialist parties generally enact or enhance comprehensive social-service programs: old-age pensions, family allowance, health care, income supplements, and unemployment compensation. They also believe that economic growth should be stimulated largely through government investment in a modified market economy made up of public and private enterprises. In this way, democratic-socialist parties work towards peacefully transforming capitalist-based economies in the Western economic tradition into a more egalitarian socialist mode of production.

All socialist parties adopt one of three approaches to the economic order: *corporate socialism*, *welfare-state socialism*, and *market socialism*. Parties that promote corporate socialism, such as the Partido Socialista de Ecuador (PSE), assume that experts and professionals – economists, engineers, managers, and scientists – can best plan the economy to serve the public good. They see the role of a socialist government as one of co-ordinating public and private corporations in order to achieve full employment, low inflation, and the provision of social programs for the disadvantaged. Welfare-state socialists, as in Canada, Sweden, and Germany, reject the state-planning corporate brand of socialism.

Government should act as a *referee* in the economy, balancing the goals of public and private enterprises in a mixed economy. Socialist parties that advocate market socialism, such as the Socialist Party of Peru and the Argentine Socialist Party, want an economy in which the government owns the means of production but yields control of production decisions to decentralized workers' councils. Workers decide on investment and production goals in the marketplace, and the role of the government is to rectify market inequalities.

Socialism in Canada

In Canada, democratic socialism maintains a low ideological profile.[22] When it first appeared in Canada, socialism was a movement that became a party. The Co-operative Commonwealth Federation (CCF) was formed in 1932, and in 1933 drafted its Regina Manifesto which declared the party's ideological positions founded on the principles of democratic socialism. Led by J.S. Woodsworth, the party attracted the support of farmers and workers, and members contested federal and provincial elections from 1935 until 1960, when it reconstituted itself. Its first major success was in Saskatchewan, where it took power in 1944. The following year, the party captured an impressive 28 seats in the federal election. Following World War II, economic prosperity and the tensions of the Cold War gradually eroded the pre-war electoral support for the party. The Winnipeg Declaration of 1956 indicated – by its support for a **mixed economy** made up of private and public corporate units – the party's abandonment of the dream of a North American socialist commonwealth.

The CCF attempted to broaden its popular support by adopting a new label and image. In 1961, after one year of calling itself the New Party, the New Democratic Party (NDP) was founded.[23] In order to expand its popularity, the NDP united with major labour unions in the Canadian Labour Congress, thus taking on a more industrial image and departing somewhat from its rural and agrarian base of support. In effect, the NDP took action to become a mass party in Canadian politics, presenting itself as a competitive alternative to the Liberals and Progressive Conservatives.

Ideologically, the NDP never fully embraced socialism. During the late 1960s and the early 1970s, a number of academics and intellectuals (the Waffle Movement) challenged the party leadership to abandon their pragmatic and centrist tendencies to return to fundamental socialist principles, with an emphasis on Canadian nationalism. The Waffle called for an independent socialist Canada based on a policy of nationalization of key industries and an expanded program of Canadian content in the media and educational

■ ■ **mixed economy:**
an economic system in which private ownership of the means of production is predominant, although government maintains a substantial role as a consumer, investor, and producer. ■ ■

institutions. The Waffle Movement was rejected in 1973. Other factions, such as the BC Socialist Fellowship, the Ontario Ginger Group, and the Left-Caucus, unsuccessfully attempted to move the party toward a firm commitment to socialism. Today, ideological moderation seems to prevail in the party. What might be described as a pragmatic left-of-centre platform characterizes the ideological focus of the NDP.

The party has been only marginally successful at the federal level. In the 1979, 1980, 1984, 1988, and 1993 federal elections, the NDP captured 26, 32, 30, 43, and 9 seats respectively. The party's caucus, following the 1993 election, constitutes only about two percent of the membership of the House of Commons, and has rarely exceeded 20 percent of the popular vote in federal elections. Provincially, the NDP has formed governments in Ontario, (1992), Manitoba (1981-1988), in British Columbia (1972-75, 1991-) and Saskatchewan (1944-64, 1971-81). In 1991 in the territories, the Yukon Party defeated the NDP government. No major inroads have been made by the party in the Atlantic provinces or Québec.

During its history, the CCF/NDP has had seven party leaders: J.S. Woodsworth, M.G. Coldwell, Hazen Argue, T.C. Douglas, David Lewis, Ed Broadbent, and Audrey MacLaughlin. The average tenure of the party's leader is eight years, compared with 12.8 years for Liberal leaders and 5.7 years for Conservative leaders. Ed Broadbent, who served as leader for over 14 years, led his party to its best showing in terms of seats and popular vote since 1961, but his campaign stumbled and stalled as the issue of free trade commanded the 1988 election. Broadbent and his party's organization entered a period of soul-searching to re-examine the direction the party should take, ultimately prompting Broadbent to step down as leader in 1989. Under MacLaughlin's leadership, the party's traditional union and intellectual support eroded substantially. The 1993 federal election battered and bruised the NDP across the political landscape, reducing its electoral support from 43 to 9, its lowest level since 1961, and causing it to lose its status as a recognized party in the House of Commons. The long journey back from the political wilderness began with calls for a new leader, a modernized platform, a revamped organization, and a party leadership convention in 1994.

Liberal Parties

The Industrial Revolution stimulated a demand to free the taxpayer from arbitrary government action. This demand for liberty and individual freedom of action came primarily from the rising industrial and trading class, and was directed against restrictions imposed by government (in legislation, common law, and judicial action) upon the freedoms of economic enterprise.

The origin of liberal political parties in the modern sense – those groups organized for the purpose of electioneering and controlling government through a representative assembly – lies in the chaotic years of European history between 1700 and 1800. In Great Britain, **Whigs** and **Tories** were the ancestors of the Liberals and Conservatives, the Democrats and Republicans of two centuries later.

Liberal parties were formed in many European political systems and those of the western hemisphere by the end of the nineteenth century. They reflected positive assumptions about human nature, asserting faith in the basic goodness and reasonableness of people, and in their perfectibility. Liberal parties promoted liberty itself, maximizing individual freedom and advocating laissez-faire attitudes to achieve the greatest social good.

The first liberal parties opposed any state intervention in the economy and emphasized free enterprise, individual initiative, and free trade. In the twentieth century, as governments had become more democratized, liberal parties shifted this position to a more optimistic role for the state in regulating, administering, and promoting society's affairs for the public good. Modern liberal parties advance economic and social reform through government regulation and stimulation of the economy, and through positive social-welfare programs. They stand firm on their support for political and legal equality, by which the laws and political freedoms of a society apply equally to all people. However, before the twentieth century, British liberals restricted suffrage to the propertied, taxpaying, and well-educated citizens. Today, Liberal parties uphold the right of all adults to vote and to run for public office. Such twentieth-century liberals as John Dewey and Frederick van Hayck bridged the old liberal values of trust in human nature and reason, a belief in the idea of progress, and compassion for the downtrodden to the modern liberal tenet of economic development through government intervention in the economy.

In the contemporary world of liberal political parties, it is possible to identify three ideological positions: *libertarianism*, *corporate liberalism*, and *reformist liberalism*. Libertarians, as found in the Libertarian Party of Canada, for example, adopt the classical laissez-faire position that accords people maximum individual liberty. They call for the resurrection of the "minimal state" in which government plays a passive role, operating only to protect individuals from force, fraud, and theft, to secure law and order, and to enforce binding contracts. Corporate liberals, such as the members of the Democratic party in the United States, recognize the importance of individual freedom but protect the role of large-scale institutions, such as government, business corporations, and trade unions, as important centres of decision-making. Social good results from the interplay of all of these individual and corporate forces. Reformist liberals, such as the Liberal Party of Canada and the Liberal Party of Australia, place the greatest stress on government intervention to encourage and protect the values of freedom and equality. From their perspective, the government should represent the interests of the disadvantaged: the unemployed, the disabled, low-income senior citizens, consumers, and minorities. The role of the government is to redistribute wealth, and to develop programs directed at those economically deprived through monetary and tax policies. Through such policies as medicare, public education, income maintenance, family allowance, and old-age pensions, the government can foster the freedom and equality of individuals in a social context.

The Liberal Party of Canada

In the election of 1874, Alexander Mackenzie led his **Grits** to electoral victory over the Mac-donald Tories with the support of rural and small-town Canadians, especially moderate reform groups in Ontario and anti-business, anti-clerical reform elements in Québec. The Liberals were defeated in 1878 and in the next three national elections primarily because a new flock of voters, brought into the electorate by the accession of Manitoba and British Columbia to the federation, had different economic and social demands from the rest of the country.

The Liberals worked vigorously to broaden their base of support, building on urban and rural grassroots strengths in most of the provinces. By the time they came to power under the leadership of Wilfrid Laurier in 1896, the Liberal party governed every province except Québec. The new western provinces of Alberta and Saskatchewan contributed to the tenure of Liberal success to 1911. However, the party suffered deep divisions over the issue of conscription for overseas service, splitting support from English-speaking and French-speaking party members in Québec and Ontario. Laurier retired, and at the leadership convention in 1919, the party chose William Lyon Mackenzie King as leader. By 1921, he led the party to form a minority Liberal government and was to serve as prime minister for over 21 years. King set the Liberal party on its pragmatic reformist path, constructing an industrial-relations and welfare-state platform. This thrust was to dramatically influence Canada's laws and practices governing health care, pensions, trade unions, the franchise, and taxation. King viewed the party primarily as a machine for winning elections and only secondarily as an instrument to advance the principles of liberalism.

His successor, Louis St. Laurent, strengthened the support of the party in Québec and Ontario and greatly expanded the industrial and economic base of the Canadian economy. Liberals had come to accept the role of government as a major actor in the Canadian economy, and under St. Laurent's stewardship, they projected the idea that their party was the governing party of Canada. St. Laurent retired in 1958 and was succeeded by Lester B. Pearson, who, during his tenure as prime minister, never commanded a Liberal majority in the House of Commons. As a result, he was not in a strong position to influence the direction of Liberal policies as a party leader. In a minority government situation, Pearson and his ministers did not venture to develop a system of policy priorities. His avoidance of political controversy and the reluctance to create and debate during his tenure as leader of the party weakened the ideological appeal of the Liberal party. Unable to win a majority of seats, Pearson gave way to new leadership.

His successor, Pierre Elliot Trudeau, was the first Liberal leader to assume that position with a previously articulated philosophy of policy-making. Trudeau introduced what he called "rational" liberalism, which meant creating and expanding the role of bureaucracy to develop rational policies and decisions in all areas of the economic and social environment. It also meant enlarging and strengthening the chief advisory bodies around the prime minister, namely, the Privy Council Office and the Prime Minister's Office. In the years during his tenure as leader of the Liberal

■ ■ **administrative state:** this term is used to describe a phenomenon of governance through which public policies and programs ostensibly created by elected politicians are, in fact, influenced by the decisions of bureaucrats who are the principal agents in the formulation and implementation of the public agenda. ■ ■

party, the size of Canada's public service grew enormously. Under successive Trudeau governments, Canada took on many of the characteristics of an **administrative state** by expanding the sphere of government into areas traditionally under private control; by increasing government involvement and regulation of the economy; and by increasing bureaucratic specialization and professionalization.[24] Under Trudeau's stewardship, the Liberals remained faithful to the party's traditional tenets such as the universality of social programs (keeping family allowances and old-age security payments free of "means tests" – tests to determine qualification), they also advanced Canadian economic and cultural nationalism, protected French-language rights, and mapped out the constitutional destiny of the country.

Liberal fortunes fluctuated under Trudeau's leadership. An astounding victory in 1968 was followed by near defeat in 1972 and the struggle to maintain a minority government in the House of Commons. The Liberals enjoyed another substantial victory in 1974 but suffered electoral defeat in 1979. Trudeau announced his resignation, but in December 1979, the controversial Conservative austerity budget introduced by John Crosbie was defeated. Trudeau was persuaded to stay on as party leader and subsequently led the Liberals to a majority victory in the 1980 election. During the last three years that Trudeau was prime minister, the Liberal party slipped to its lowest levels of popularity, stigmatized by budgets that failed to reduce unemployment, an uncontrollable deficit, and by a public increasingly cynical of its leader. Before his resignation, Trudeau had not prepared the party for his departure. Up to that time, federal Liberal governments had ruled for 62 years in the twentieth century. Party members had grown accustomed to winning elections in the face of dwindling popularity. Many believed that Trudeau's successor, whoever he or she might be, could – by tinkering with party reorganization, some policy renewal, and procedural reform – return the party to power.

Such was the bravura of the party elite at the Liberal leadership convention in June 1984 when John Turner was chosen as the Liberals' glittering political star. Turner, who had served in the Commons for 14 years, ten of them in the Cabinet, had broken with Trudeau in 1975 and brilliantly divorced himself from the legacy of a tarnished Liberal record. From a distance, the star glistened with looks, personality, and intelligence. But on the hustings, the sparkle was revealed as nervousness, and he appeared awkward and dull to the merciless eyes of the TV cameras. Turner served as prime minister for only 80 days – from June to September, 1984. In that brief period the public could not discern where he stood on the ideological spectrum. His uncertain ideological direction coupled with lack of leadership moxy led to the stunning electoral defeat that traumatized the Liberal party in every part of the country.

Turner and the remnants of his parliamentary caucus embarked upon a comprehensive reconstruction of Liberal policies and finances from the grass roots to the party elite. Turner's inability to unite the party around

him resulted largely from his controversial positions on issues such as the Meech Lake Accord and the free trade agreement. Turner's quick support of the Meech Lake Accord distanced him from many of the old-guard Liberals who agreed with Trudeau that the accord was seriously flawed. Lingering doubts about Turner's leadership skills persisted well into the 1988 election campaign and, in 1989, Mr. Turner resigned after much speculation.

His successor was Jean Chrétien, who won the Liberal leadership campaign in 1990. Chrétien had to overcome his widespread public image as a relic of past Liberal governments and their former policies. After running a strong campaign, Chrétien won the 1993 federal election by holding out the promise of a kinder, more prosperous Canada, more sensitive of the needs of unemployed Canadians, and less obsessive about the market-driven economics of the past Progressive Conservative governments. He talked about restoring integrity in government and injecting hope back into the economy.

To achieve his campaign promises, Chrétien advocated a two-year multi-billion-dollar program to be cost-shared with provinces and municipalities to rebuild roads, bridges, and transit systems with the goal of building and rebuilding Canadian infrastructures. He promised to make financing available to stimulate small businesses and to increase apprenticeship programs. Liberals pledged to support universal health care and to oppose user fees. The party sought to amend NAFTA, to increase trade with the Pacific Rim economies and to support the thrust of the GATT as the cornerstone of its overall trade policy. In deference to the policies advocated by the Reform party, Liberals proposed a greater role for MPs in preparing legislation and more influence of MPs on the spending decisions of government. In addition, the party would support more free votes (no imposition of the party position in the House of Commons) and would reform MPs' pensions so as to prevent "double dipping," the practice of benefiting from a number of government pension plans.

Meanwhile, beneath the struggle for a unified national Liberal party, provincial party machines began to show impressive successes. By the end of 1984, there were no Liberal governments in Canada. But in 1985, Liberal fortunes took a turn for the better in two important provinces. In Ontario, where the last Liberal government was a pre-World War II memory, the Liberal party came close to defeating the Conservatives in the 1985 provincial election. Not long after that, the Liberals and the NDP signed an agreement to topple the Conservative government and form a minority Liberal government for at least two years. In 1987, the Liberals won a resounding victory at the polls to form the first Liberal majority government in Ontario since 1937. However, the party was unable to sustain its momentum in order to prevent the NDP from forming a government in 1991. Another good turn for the Liberals came in Québec, with the return of Robert Bourassa and a strong Liberal government, reversing the barren trend of Liberal electoral failure on Canada's political landscape. The Bourassa Liberals were returned to power again in 1989. In 1994, Daniel Johnson replaced Bourassa as leader of the Québec Liberal party.

In Prince Edward Island, in March 1993, Catherine Callbeck continued the Liberal momentum started in 1989 by former premier Joe Ghiz by leading the Liberals to power again, winning 31 of 32 seats. In Manitoba, Paul Edwards increased the number of Liberals from one to seven in the 1990 election. In Nova Scotia, in 1993, the Liberals were led to a majority government by Dr. John Savage, whose victory ended 14 years of successive Conservative governments. In British Columbia, the Liberals have manoeuvred towards the political centre, given the polarized nature of BC politics. And, in Newfoundland, voters swept the Liberal party back into power under Clyde Wells in 1989, ending 17 years of political seclusion. In Alberta and Saskatchewan, party memberships have increased, generating better financial health for the party, and Liberal party prospects look more optimistic. The Liberals won 32 seats out of 83 in the 1993 provincial election. In Saskatchewan, the Liberals revitalized their provincial image by electing a new leader, Lynda Haverstock.

Small-l liberalism runs deep in the Canadian political psyche.[25] Its followers advocate government intervention to "help" protect individual freedom, but also to curb it. In practice, it is often difficult to accomplish the one without the other. The Liberal penchant for pragmatism over doctrinaire solutions has made philosophical liberalism an ambiguous yet popular creed. What is certain is that liberalism in the post-Trudeau era is still a powerful political force in Canada.

Conservative Parties

In the early nineteenth century, the first conservative parties were formed in many political systems in Europe and Latin America. The conservatives, having much to conserve, championed the vested interests of the landed aristocracy and the church. At first, conservative parties were almost exclusively preoccupied with the defence of the monarchy and hereditary ruling classes against the demands of popularly elected assemblies.[26] But conservative parties shared other, more formal, ideological positions, possessing both a political and a historical depth that liberals could not match.

Many of the theoretical political ideas of the early conservative parties were drawn from Edmund Burke (1729-1797), a brilliant Irishman who served as a member of the British House of Commons for 30 years and was widely recognized as a romantic writer and thinker.

Early conservative parties emphasized the existence of natural human distinctions in wealth, opportunity, ability, intelligence, and privilege in the economic order of society. Their chief concern was the defence of traditional wealth against the onslaught of the Industrial Revolution. Conservative parties were deeply committed to the concept of private property as the fundamental dynamic of the economic order. For them, the economy was the interaction of government, institutions, landed aristocracy, and different classes of people as they related to the pursuit and ownership of private property. These parties subscribed to the concept of a natural economic elite comprising those who held property and whose positions were protected by government. Property was the basis of the economic order for generations of citizens. Both time and survival were the principal tests for the endurance of conservative economic principles.

The first conservative parties tended to see social justice achieved in a society that permitted social, economic, and political inequality, if only because these were the characteristics of all societies throughout recorded history. But in Europe, conservatives defended their elite social status as *noblesse oblige* – the responsibility of the dominant classes for the welfare of the whole society. Conservatism had not been so presumptuous as to identify the well-being of all citizens with the conservative's own self-interest. But, from earlier times, upper classes believed they carried an obligation to those less fortunate.

Politically relevant conservative parties operating in Europe and North America have a classical liberal, not a Burkean, root. Many modern conservative parties advocate less government, and the laissez-faire values of classical liberalism. Some conservative parties continue to be pessimistic about human nature and dubious about the effectiveness of government expenditures for domestic welfare programs. They believe that people are better off when they are spared the restrictions of government power and regulation. They point to the decades of liberalism in the twentieth century, during which poverty has not been erased, social unrest has not been calmed, and wealth has not been effectively redistributed. Conservative parties rate the private sector of society much more highly than do Liberals and assert that social benefit will more likely come from the work of voluntary associations and private business than from government ventures. At a more abstract level, conservatives tend to resist fundamental changes in social or governmental arrangements, believing that meaningful improvement in the human condition will come only slowly and naturally, like evolution.

They believe that the future must be built on the past and, therefore, they believe in maintaining traditions.

In Canada, conservatives see the role of political parties as one of "conciliators," building coalitions of interests to achieve a national consensus, harmonizing regional conflicts, and strengthening the fabric of society within the traditional framework of government institutions.[27] They stress social and legal order based on fundamental principles of conservation and preservation to protect the national interest. The conservative penchant for order requires the presence of a strong and effective government but with a limited or restricted role so as not to undermine self-reliance and individual freedom. As a balance to highly centralized government authority, conservative party policies encourage the vitality of countervailing forces of power such as the provinces, trade unions, farm organizations, trade associations, and the media, to check the arbitrary tendencies of federal institutions.

As we can see, both the Liberal party and the Progressive Conservative party believe in protecting individual rights. Canadians are fundamentally pragmatic, regardless of their political persuasion. Both parties want to protect the liberties of the individual citizen. But they see the threats to individual liberties as coming from a different direction, and therefore they adopt different strategies aimed at what is essentially the same end.

Canadian Conservatives do not ask ultimate questions and hence do not expect final answers. But they remind people of the institutional prerequisites of social order. At the Conservative Party Leadership Convention held in Ottawa in June 1983, David Crombie

summed up his feelings on what it means to be a conservative: "I am a Tory. I glory in the individual. I cherish community. I seek liberty. I neither trim nor track to every social whim. I honour tradition and experience. I exalt faith, hope, and fairness. I want a peaceful, ordered, well-governed Canada. I am a Tory."[28]

It is important to point out that statements like this reflect the weak ideological character of Canadian politics. It is a vague statement which, if "tradition and experience" were removed, could have been uttered by a Canadian Liberal. Most Canadians have a very low level of ideological consciousness.[29] What is more, people who call themselves Conservatives often do not take the conservative position on specific issues, just as many self-declared Liberals stray from the liberal side of many issues. "Conservative" and "Liberal" are handy labels that many people apply when talking about politics. These terms are used far beyond our ability to define them. Even at the doctrinal level within a political party, Canadians do not have internally consistent, fully coherent political ideologies. Both for citizens in general and for the most involved and informed observers of Canadian politics, the terms "Conservative" and "Liberal" have always been a source of confusion. Upon close examination, we can see that conservative and liberal belief patterns overlap greatly in their basic values and each contains internal contradictions of its own.

The Progressive Conservative Party of Canada

In 1854, a coalition comprising business, professional, and church leaders in Ontario, and French Catholics and business elites in

Québec was constructed by John A. Macdonald to unite the British North American colonies into a single political unit. Under his leadership, this amorphous partnership of business and church elites was the genesis of the Conservative Party (first called the Liberal-Conservative Party). Macdonald, who became the first prime minister of the Dominion of Canada, won six out of eight federal elections held in the latter part of the nineteenth century. Canadian conservatism took shape as a powerful pragmatic political force, the result of a series of modernization measures that Macdonald called the "National Policy."[30] The chief component of the policy was the construction of the transcontinental railroad, completed in 1885. Other components included an industrialization plan nurtured by protective tariffs, primary resource development in the Maritimes and the West, and the encouragement of interprovincial trade.

At first, Macdonald succeeded in maintaining the tenuous coalition of political loyalties in Québec and Ontario. But in 1885, Macdonald's decision to execute Louis Riel, a francophone Catholic Métis who had led an armed rebellion in Saskatchewan, placed bitter strains on the Québec segment of the Conservative coalition. The support of the Conservatives in Québec was further eroded by the party's hedging on its commitment to provide financial support to Catholic schools. These issues, the death of Macdonald, and the desperate succession of new leaders between 1891 and 1896 (John Abbott, John Thompson, Mackenzie Bowell, and Charles Tupper) led to the rout of the Conservatives in 1896.

The party remained out of power until 1911, when its leader, Sir Robert Borden,

defeated the Liberal government of Wilfrid Laurier. Support for the Conservatives was drawn from an alliance of anti-American and protectionist forces in Ontario combined with isolationist Québec Conservatives who had come to an understanding with Borden that some from their ranks would be selected as cabinet ministers in the new government. This alliance disintegrated over the conscription crisis of 1917 that embittered many French- Canadians because of Borden's insistence on conscripting men for overseas service in World War I. It soon became apparent to Québecers that none of the French-Canadians in Borden's Cabinet had much influence over his decisions. The party subsequently lost its support base in Québec.

Arthur Meighen, Borden's successor as prime minister, carried on the legacy of Québec's abandonment. Like Borden, Meighen failed to understand the sentiments of French-Canadians. The Conservatives were quickly stigmatized as an English-speaking Protestant party by the Québec electorate, and Conservatives would not see a revival of French-Canadian support until John Diefenbaker's landslide victory in 1958. Lacking substantial support in Québec, the Conservatives were defeated in 1921, and except for a brief period between 1925 and 1926, they were to remain out of office until 1930. The party's new leader and prime minister, R.B. Bennett, like Arthur Meighen, did little to expand the support base of the Conservative party. He continued to antagonize Québec by failing to keep the lines of political communication open to that province, and divided his own party when, without consulting his cabinet colleagues, he brought forward his New Deal program, based on Roosevelt's American package. Under Bennett, these two weaknesses – the inability to nurture support in Québec and a proclivity to generate internal divisions and factionalism – became symptomatic of what was later called "the Tory syndrome."[31]

Bennett was soundly defeated in 1935 and three years later he turned over the leadership of the party to R.J. Manion and his successors. Arthur Meighen, John Bracken, and George Drew were unsuccessful in broadening the support-base of the party, especially in Québec, and could not defeat the Liberals in the period between 1940 and 1957. Credit for that accomplishment went to Drew's successor, John G. Diefenbaker.

In the election of 1957, Diefenbaker led the Progressive Conservatives to a minority-government victory. The following year, Diefenbaker led them to the greatest electoral victory in Canadian history. Perhaps the most ideological of any Canadian prime minister, Diefenbaker resuscitated conservatism in Canada and gave it a most discernible North American character. His "vision" of Canada, his devotion to the monarchy and the Commonwealth, his penchant for strong national government, the National Development Policy, the Bill of Rights, and his pro-Canadianism, all were hallmarks of Diefenbaker's Toryism. But by 1962, Diefenbaker's personal charisma and strong electoral support had suffered a sharp reversal. He antagonized his party colleagues in Québec by his reluctance to appoint them to important cabinet positions and by his indecisiveness in handling the **Munsinger scan-**

■ ■ **Munsinger scandal:** a political controversy during the Diefenbaker period that raised questions of national security resulting from an alleged affair between associate Minister of Defence Pierre Sevigny and East German prostitute Gerda Munsinger. ■ ■

dal. Also, internal divisions in both the Cabinet and the caucus grew out of Diefenbaker's demand for loyalty in the face of growing public discontent. The remarkable national coalition that he led in 1957 was no longer cohesive by 1963, and his government was defeated in the election of that year. It was not long before serious intraparty divisions surfaced over the quality of Diefenbaker's leadership, leading to his replacement by Robert Stanfield in 1967.

Stanfield took the reins of a deeply divided party that was unable to rally its forces to oust the Liberals in 1968, 1972, or 1974. His style of party leadership was much less exciting and more subdued than his predecessor's. But Stanfield held a deep regard for conservative ideology, espousing the honest ideals of national purpose, order, and a reverence for Canada's institutions and symbols. Stanfield lacked the popular appeal necessary to convert his political philosophy into electoral support, and he retired under pressure in 1976.

Of the 11 candidates at the hotly contested leadership convention in 1976, Joe Clark emerged the winner at age 36, with only four years of parliamentary experience under his belt. But nearly three years later, Clark's party managed only a narrow victory in the May 1979 election. Clark resisted ideological pigeonholing, preferring to be judged as a pragmatic Tory rather than as a party leader acting in accordance with preconceived conservative philosophy. Although his tenure as prime minister and party leader was short-lived, it is possible to discern both conservative and liberal tenets in Clark's political thinking. He held that "big government" was much more of a detriment to Canada than were "big business" and "big labour." Clark expressed confidence in the private sector to create jobs and to stimulate the recovery of the Canadian economy. But Clark's expressed desire to privatize Petro-Canada, to sell other crown corporations, to relocate the Canadian embassy in Israel, and his support of a tax policy governed by the principle of "short-term pain for long-term gain," generated serious doubts about the new Tory minority government. In December 1979, the Clark government's austerity budget, and his government, were defeated.

For the next three years, Clark struggled to maintain his leadership of the party.[32] In the eyes of many, his failed political record and weak public image continued to hurt the Conservative party. After two successive biennial meetings of the party in 1981 and 1983, at which about one-third of the delegates voted to call a leadership convention, Clark, recognizing the growing dissension, announced his resignation and at the same time declared his candidacy in the upcoming leadership race.

It was billed as the largest political convention in Canadian history. As many as one-third of the voting delegates were undecided when they arrived at the convention, which fielded eight candidates. Clark led the other candidates on the first three ballots, but on the fourth ballot he was defeated by Brian Mulroney.

From the outset of his successful leadership campaign, Mulroney's personality and style changed the image of the Progressive Conservative party. The party had selected its first leader from Québec since Sir John Abbott. But unlike other Conservative leaders, Mulroney promised to bring Québec in, not merely as a stronghold, but as an ongoing constituency of support for the Progressive Conservative party.

During the 1984 election campaign, Mulroney demonstrated to Québecers that he was as committed to furthering the lot of his native province as Pierre Trudeau had been. Mulroney's reputation as a competent conciliator, based on his career as a labour lawyer, boosted the stolid image of the party and had an enormous political pay-off in his bid for Québec's support. Because of his adept conciliatory skills, not only did legions of Lévesque supporters work for Mulroney but the former premier complimented him for choosing so many "authentic Québécois candidates." In the process of political conciliation within Québec, the Tories were able to crush the once-impregnable Liberal strong-hold, claiming 58 of the province's 75 seats in 1984, and 63 of its seats in 1988. Under Mulroney, the Conservatives penetrated every region of the province. This strong francophone presence in the party caucus did a great deal to mend the traditional English/French split within the party. Across the country, the same powerful tide of support permitted Mulroney to give his party a national constituency and a unified image.

Ideologically, Mulroney was a pragmatic centrist. He won the federal elections in 1984 and 1988 not only because he succeeded in uniting a fractious party, but because ideologically he surfed the crest of a conservative wave sweeping the country. When Mulroney first ran for the leadership of the party in 1976, some members of the party prematurely identified him as a **red Tory**. In seeking delegate support within the party, Mulroney moved pragmatically, opting for compromise over ideological combat. For the red Tory delegates, Mulroney vowed to keep Canada's extensive net of welfare programs intact. But for the majority of party delegates, he promised to revive Canada's sluggish economy by relying on the private sector, not on the government, to provide the economic stimulus for recovery.

Once in power, Mulroney entered the twilight zone of Canadian pragmatism, adopting a political strategy to solve Canada's problems that defies ideological identification. The massive federal deficit after the 1988 election left little room for the application of doctrinaire solutions. Mulroney saw the only way out as sustained economic growth: by creating new wealth, by unfettering the private sector in an atmosphere of deregulation, by federal/provincial co-operation and by generating jobs out of the newly implemented Free Trade Agreement. But the party's scandals and controversial policy decisions eroded Mulroney's influence almost everywhere in government, and in the public eye, weakening much of his conciliatory posture within the party.

Mulroney was determined to pass a Conservative government on to a new leader who could win a third consecutive term. Within weeks of his resignation on February 24, 1993, several strong candidates had declared their desire to lead the party. The Conservative leadership campaign generated compelling media coverage of the convention where two candidates seemed to dominate the events, Kim Campbell and Jean Charest. After a close and tough campaign, Campbell led the delegate support and held it into the convention, becoming the first woman leader of the Progressive Conservative party and Canada's first female prime minister.

As a political leader, Kim Campbell had politically desirable attributes: her intelligence, gender, age, and her region of representation – Western Canada. In her short tenure as prime minister, she adopted a smaller cabinet, initiated extensive government reorganization, and promised to develop a new politics in the governing of Canada. She attended the G-7 meeting in Toyko, playing her role carefully and taking full advantage of some excellent photo opportunities with U.S. president Clinton.

Campbell's policy package included a multi-billion-dollar program for job training and adjustment, but regarded the reduction of the federal deficit as the only sure method of creating long-term "economically meaningful" jobs. She promised to eliminate the deficit within a five-year period. She remained committed to the large transfer payments to the provinces but promised to seek cost-cutting efficiencies for programs such as medicare. In Campbell's view, the U.S.–Canada Free Trade Agreement, NAFTA and GATT were cornerstones. She promised to create advisory panels to develop trade strategies for both Latin America and the economies of the Pacific Rim. Campbell maintained that constitutional questions

> ■ ■ **red Tory:** a left-wing faction of the Progessive Conservative party of Canada that advocates economically egalitarian policies that one might expect to be more exclusively championed by Liberals or socialists. ■ ■

involving Québec must be resolved without opening full-scale constitutional negotiations, but her first priority would be to improve the economy.

However, Campbell ran into trouble early in the 1993 election campaign. She had made changes in the management of the PC Canada Fund, alienating some of the key fund-raisers for the party across the country. She distanced herself from Mulroney and his best campaign advisors, refused to reach out to Jean Charest and his Québec base, and headed into the election with only her personality as the party's major card. She was running neither on the Tory record, which many campaign advisors believed to be still saleable, nor on a distinctively new platform of her own.

Campbell's performance in the televised debates inspired derision and despair among many of the Progressive Conservative candidates. Then in the middle of the campaign, she made critical comments about Mulroney, Don Mazankowski, and Jean Charest in an interview, which led to serious tensions within the election team. By election day, party organizers were in despair. With the election lost, the party gave the awesome task of reconstruction to Jean Charest, one of only two Tory survivors in the House of Commons.

The Future of Political Parties

In the history of governmental experience, political parties are very young institutions. Those that appeared in the United States in the late 1790s are some of the oldest in the world. These parties were the offspring of egalitarianism – the institutional response to the idea of popular sovereignty and the belief that rank and file citizens should have final authority in the business of governing. Less than two hundred years later, political parties are found throughout the world. But parties did not evolve without ambivalent views of their role, function, and future within the confines of democratic and non-democratic political systems. In the eighteenth century, philosophers and politicians had doubts about a permanent role for political parties. Political theorist Henry St. John, Viscount Bolingbroke, saw parties as "a political evil."[33] They were regarded as divisive and elitist, representing special interests against national interests, and blocking the pursuit of the common good.

Prior to the nineteenth century, only one prominent theorist, Edmund Burke (1729-1797), the great philosopher and politician, defended the idea of political parties as essential instruments of representative government. Burke advanced the case for a mature party system long before one came into existence. Once established and organized, political parties would become the links between citizens and governmental institutions. Even in the United States, where they first matured, political parties were not well received. The American federalist, James Madison, did not envision a place for them in the constitutional order and criticized their factious effects on national unity. Thomas Jefferson held similar views even though he constructed one of the first permanently organized political parties, the Republican Party – later called the Democratic-Republicans, and eventually the Democratic Party.

Ambivalence about the complementarity of political parties and democratic goals continued in the early years of the twentieth century, when studies by professors Michels and Ostrogorski portrayed parties as manipulative and elitist.[34] This was followed by a swell of optimism in the mid-twentieth century that glorified the functions of parties and regarded them as the custodians of liberal democracy. But this optimism quickly waned in the latter years of the century. Some political scientists in Canada and the United States became increasingly skeptical about the assumed functions of political parties and noted the opportunistic tendencies of these institutions to be publicity-oriented rather than issue-oriented, to be poll-driven rather than representative, and to be fixated on leadership style, imagery, and "win-ability."

A growing body of professional opinion is concluding that the party system is less than adequate owing to a number of social, economic, and political factors. One is that the media have displaced the party as the means of communication between people and their government and as the institutions capable of reaching a large number of people quickly. Another factor has been the rise of a professional public (civil) service with its objective hiring standards and its criticisms of the old-style patronage system that contributed so much to the success of political parties in the past. As well, in democratic states since the 1950s, researchers have noted the steady weakening of party identification and the accompanying decline in the ranks of the party faithful. An additional factor frequently cited is that most democratic governments have legislated strict limitations on party fund-raising methods and spending practices. Finally, the effectiveness of interest groups to influence the direction of public policy on behalf of a cohesive body of opinionated citizens has challenged the existing party system by luring precious campaign resources and public support.

All of these factors may not lead to a demise of political parties as modern agents of democracy. The challenge to the traditional party system is not that the things parties do will not get done, but that they will be done differently and perhaps by different agents.[35] The gloomiest predictions are that political parties are outmoded institutions to be observed by analysts in a sort of death vigil. Others believe it is conceivable that parties will limp along for many more years. They see their continuing role as psychological reference points for many individuals, and as conventional instruments for selecting candidates in elections.

Parties may well persist as the most significant though not the only institutions through which political power is organized. Parties are not as strong as they once were but in view of many of the useful functions they continue to perform, it may be premature, if not unwarranted, to claim that they are doomed.

Pressure Groups

What Are Pressure and Interest Groups?

Political parties are not the only decisive forces in shaping policy outcomes. If we are to fully appreciate politics, we need to see the roles played by pressure groups as vehicles of public participation. In perhaps less obvious ways than political parties, pressure groups articulate the **interests** of people who want to influence decisions about public policy.[36] This kind of popular participation in the political process is less familiar and apparent – and certainly less official – than voting, but it is nonetheless just as real and important. When a group of neighbouring parents is galvanized by the need for a stop sign on the corner of their street and circulates a petition to present at City Hall, they are a pressure group taking political action. Moreover, their efforts to influence the municipal government are considerably more direct, and likely to be more effective in achieving their goal, than reliance on the electoral machinery would be. In fact, all the public can usually do to influence any government through their participation in political parties is to alter the tone and emphasis of general policies and programs.

During the past century, as societies have industrialized and modernized, the scope of group activity has widened and the quantity and variety of pressure groups has grown proportionately. In the 1990s, individuals the world over are more conscious of themselves as belonging to groups that have the potential of exercising political influence. To some degree, everyone can claim membership in a group based on culture, race, religion, age, or sex, or in a professional, occupational, or labour group. Even if one professes to no religion, one is part of a group of atheists or agnostics. If one disavows membership in a political party, one is a member of a group that thinks the same way. Group consciousness and the political patterns of group interaction then become important, perhaps even more important than the sets of common characteristics that bring people together in the first place.

Many social scientists analyze why people do what they do as members of groups. Political scientists are interested in those groups that

are organized to make their opinions known and to have an influence on the process of government. By definition, a *pressure group* or *interest group* is any collection of people organized to promote a goal they share or to resist some objective of government or of other groups that somehow relates to the political process. A women's club is not, therefore, a pressure group unless its membership decides, for example, to demand, among other possibilities, equal rights with men in such areas as property law, education, employment, and promotion. The Canadian Medical Association (CMA) is a pressure group by our definition even though its members are ostensibly organized for professional reasons. However, the association frequently concerns itself with public matters. The CMA was involved in the political process that led to the establishment of medicare, and continues to press for influence in administering such programs. In the United States, the National Rifle Association (NRA), a group of over one million members, seeks to advance the safe use of firearms and vehemently opposes gun-control legislation. Since 1968, it has been registered as a lobby, and it has operated as one of the most powerful and influential groups on the Washington scene, with an elaborate network of offices throughout the United States.

Most organizations that are national in scope have as a major objective the protection of a narrow cluster of interests or the advancement of a public interest they deem to be important.[37] Accordingly, they relate to the political process as they attempt to influence the passage or defeat of legislation before Parliament or provincial legislatures. Numerous pressure groups of this kind – business, labour, professions, trade, religious, and other types –

exist in order to promote their own objectives in the political process. Pressure groups constitute an *extra-institutional* aspect of politics. They are intimately related to the daily functioning of legislatures, executives, courts, and political parties. One cannot understand the dynamics of any democratic political system without understanding the deep involvement of pressure groups at all levels of society.

As a democratic state, Canada is an excellent society for the study of pressure-group activity.[38] Canada is a multi-group society, as manifested by its numerous associations, groups, institutions, and organizations that pressure governments for legislative and administrative concessions. Canadian society is so group-oriented that, in most cases, anyone who wants to have an impact on policy decisions must either become a part of the government apparatus itself or lend support to one or more groups trying to influence government in particular ways. Canadians are joiners; we belong to a variety of groups reflecting countless interests and political demands. The essential problem in Canada's highly competitive democratic system is to balance all these various group demands within an ordered, yet free, society.

Pressure-group activities do not flourish in non-democratic states. In authoritarian states the status of pressure groups varies widely, depending upon the prevailing political system and the level of economic and political development that has been achieved. In many Latin American dictatorships, peasants (who constitute the largest numbers of any group) are commonly the least organized and the least politically articulate, although in a number of Central American countries – including El Salvador, Honduras, and

Guatemala – peasants have organized in the face of heightened political and military repression. In all authoritarian states where they are permitted, most pressure groups exist defensively; that is, they do not try to influence government directly, but try to prevent the government from affecting their groups adversely.

In totalitarian states, the party does not allow the development of autonomous pressure groups. Formal organizations exist, such as labour unions, industrial and commercial associations, guilds and specialized societies, but they must affiliate with the party apparatus or they are regarded as dissidents or insurgents.

Types of Pressure Groups

Identifying the types of pressure groups in a society requires a knowledge of their ideologies and political structures. Most democratic states are pluralistic societies of great diversity, widespread heterogeneity, and a multiplicity of interests. Their political institutions are receptive to a variety of group demands. In non-democratic states, where the free expression of interests is closely monitored and controlled by a governing elite or a party apparatus, pressure-group formation may be difficult, or even considered officially subversive.

In democracies, political parties and pressure groups are relatively separate. In some countries, such as Britain and Canada, trade unions may support a particular political party but the party may act quite independently of trade-union pressure. Hundreds, sometimes thousands, of pressure groups with some stake in the political and economic system stand up and are heard. The great advances in industry, communications, science, and technology have brought more organized groups into the process of decision-making.

Gabriel Almond developed a classification of pressure groups that applies to both democratic and non-democratic societies. These are *anomic, non-associational, associational,* and *institutional* pressure groups.[39]

Anomic Groups

Anomic groups are spontaneous gatherings of people whose behaviour demonstrates public concern and a demand for political action. Such anomic groups (*anomie* means feeling separated from social norms) do not feel bound to any need of organizing beyond the immediate expression of frustration, disappointment, or anger about a government policy or lack of government response to a question of public policy. Without previous organization or planning, anomic pressure groups vent their emotions as the news of government action or inaction sweeps a community and triggers a public reaction. These groups rise as flashes of support or non-support and subside just as suddenly. In Canada, anti-abortion crusaders and right-to-lifers react strongly to Dr. Henry Morgentaler's arrests and acquittals. Well-organized and representative advocates on both sides of the issue have gained a great deal of public visibility, and as a result have attracted anomic support in those provinces where abortion clinics have been opened or were about to open. For these people, the opportunity to demonstrate their political positions on abortion to the provincial and federal governments may come only once and they may not attempt to extend their involvement any further. Their actions do not lead to violence, but there have been frequent incidents of civil disobedience.

In other political systems, anomic pressure-group behaviour occurs because parties, governments, and organized pressure groups have failed to provide adequate representation of the group members' interest. In the 1990s, in the Israeli-occupied Gaza Strip, the *intefadeh* (uprising) is classic anomic behaviour challenging the presence of Israeli soldiers and continuing notwithstanding the 1994 peace accord signed between Israel and the Palestine Liberation Organization (PLO). In 1992, many Russian cities experienced bread riots as the withdrawal of government subsidies in the new market economy meant that food shortages reached a peak. Some countries, including Iran, India, Italy, and the United States, have been marked by frequent incidents of such spontaneous group behaviour. The pressures of anomic political activity flow from its spontaneity and the ultimate threat that it could result in widespread anti-government behaviour.

Non-Associational Pressure Groups

Non-associational groups, like anomic groups, are not formally organized. But these groups are more aware of themselves as distinct from other groups because they possess a common activity, characteristic, or interest. Members of non-associational groups share a feeling of identification without the cohesive interplay of leadership and organization. Examples are the unorganized unemployed, prisoners and former inmates, members of reference groups in ethnic communities, such as Polish-Canadians, consumer groups such as vegetarians, and normative groups such as non-smokers and non-drinkers.

These groups can be important in politics. For example, an increasing number of governments at all levels in Canada have moved to protect the rights of non-smokers by means of legislation, municipal by-laws, and agency regulations. Their political influence is derived from their mere presence and from the widespread support for their pressure on government and in the general population. But also, non-associational groups that are poised in society as reference groups can be rapidly transformed into well-organized associational ones. Groups may organize around ethnic interests, such as the National Congress of Italian-Canadians Foundation and the Italian-American Foundation in the United States, or around a common interest, such as the Non-Smokers' Rights Association in Toronto.

Any group may be represented by a wide variety of associations, bureaus, unions, or other organizations. The potential supporters of an organized interest group are frequently dispersed throughout society, living in different areas and occupying different roles. The likelihood always exists that they will unite in a collective effort to place demands on government. Modern channels of communication can instantaneously unite a group that otherwise would remain non-associational. Non-smokers' rights groups recently have been organized in almost every city in Canada, yet, just a few years ago, the members of such groups were essentially people who were aware only that other non-smokers existed. They are now making their demands effectively because the channels of communication exist to project the health rights of the public as a political issue.

Associational Pressure Groups

Associational pressure groups include business, industrial, and trade associations, labour groups, agricultural groups, professional associations, and public-interest groups. These pressure groups represent the expressed interests of a particular group, maintain a full-time professional staff, and use effective procedures for formulating and processing interests and demands.

Despite their very real political interests, it is important to remember that most pressure groups do not exist exclusively for *political* purposes, and often have a minimal or non-existent political mandate. A labour union is not organized primarily to bring political pressure; neither is the Canadian Food Processors' Association, the Canadian Federation of Independent Business, or the Canadian Manufacturers' Association. The importance of political pressure to these groups does vary a great deal, but to all of them it is essentially a by-product of their central concerns, not their basic reason for being. Moreover, the first requirement for interest-group leaders is to keep their membership happy. A union leader who fails to produce a good contract may be defeated at the next election. An official of the Canadian Food Processors' Association who takes a public position that the members dislike may be silenced or dismissed. Similarly, the head of the Canadian Manufacturers' Association must be cautious when making public remarks because members will begin to drop out of the association if the public is offended by its leadership. It is only after the basic requirements of members' satisfaction have been met that group leaders can begin to effectively exercise political pressure.

In Canada and the United States, professional groups of teachers, lawyers, physicians, and others are as numerous as business, consumers', women's and senior citizens' groups;

they actively pressure governments in promoting their interests. In fact, the list of associational pressure groups grows longer and more varied each year, reflecting the pluralistic and open character of these societies. These numerous pressure groups are active participants in the political process and are instrumental in implementing changes of policy or initiating new ones. For example, the Canadian federal government sets numerous regulatory standards for the food industry under three important pieces of legislation: the Canadian Agricultural Products Act, the Food and Drug Act, and the Consumer Packaging and Labelling Act. Frequently these standards must be adapted to new products, equipment, and technology introduced by the food-processing industry. The Technical Committee of the Canadian Food Processors' Association educates as well as pressures the government to harmonize its regulations so that the industry functions in the public interest.

In other political systems, such as France, Italy, and the Latin American republics, associational pressure groups tend to be less likely to protect their narrower interests, which might include the rights of renters, taxpayers, bankers, and peasants. In many countries, associational pressure groups are not nationally organized and play only a limited role in national politics. They lack autonomy and independence because they are controlled by other groups, such as political parties or the church. For example, in France and Italy, many trade unions and peasant organizations are controlled by the Communist party or the Roman Catholic church. The subordination of these pressure groups to other organizations restrains their capacity to operate in the wider national interest.

Institutional Pressure Groups

Institutional pressure groups are well-established social structures such as bureaucracies, business firms, churches, and universities. These highly self-conscious groups can and do make a stream of specific demands on government.

Most people do not perceive the institutional character of businesses, even though they make up the largest number of institutions in our society. Business firms, acting independently or in concert, are probably the most important and active of all pressure groups operating for their economic interests in the body politic. Businesses tend to pressure all facets of the political system, sometimes concentrating on the regulatory agencies of government administration and at other times acting directly on the politicians who draft the laws that affect commercial practices. Businesses as institutional entities have a number of advantages in dealing with governments in Canada. First, they have a pre-existing organization. This is a ready-made instrument for providing and receiving information about public policy, and for creating wider networks of associations in pursuit of business goals. Second, business organizations, whether they are individual firms or large corporations, are more likely than individuals to have an ample supply of money. This enables businesses to purchase advertising and to retain professional lobbyists to press their interests on government. The business community generates the largest amount of money for lobbying tactics, as well as the largest number of active pressure groups operating on the federal, provincial, and municipal governments in Canada.

Pressure-Group Tactics

All pressure groups try to influence key decision-makers. Groups may use both formal (lobbying) and informal methods (demonstration) to articulate their interests to policy-makers. Pressure groups vary in the tactics they employ and in the ways they organize and direct their influence. The available avenues for expressing group demands in a society are important in determining the methods used by pressure groups and their range and effectiveness. Thus, the strategies and techniques used by pressure groups are determined by the character of the government they seek to influence, as well as by the nature of their goals and means.

Quite often in democratic states, pressure-group activity is conducted by **lobbying**. The term "lobbyist" developed in the United States from the practice of speaking to legislators in the lobby just outside the congressional chamber about pending matters. A regular occupant of the lobby whose function was to influence legislators came to be known as a lobbyist. Standard lobbying tactics, including appearances and testimony before legislative committees, are common practices in many political systems.[39] Pressure groups lobby to induce legislators to introduce, modify, pass, or kill legislation. Professional lobbyists are sometimes hired on a part-time or full-time basis by interest groups that are preoccupied with the professional representation of their membership's interests.

In Canada, the Lobbyists' Registration Act, proclaimed in 1989, requires lobbyists to register with the federal government so that there is public knowledge about who is trying to influence policy-makers. Under the act, individuals who for payment communicate with federal public office-holders for the purpose of influencing the development, introduction, passage, defeat, or amendment of legislation are considered to be lobbyists. Two types of lobbyists are recognized: professionals, who are in the business of lobbying for a client; and "others" who lobby on behalf of an employer. There is another group of lobbyists who do not have to register because they work on a voluntary basis, usually for a cause. The act requires lobbyists to register but does not attempt to regulate their activities. The registrar of lobbyists is appointed by the registrar general of Canada.

Most of the lobbyists who work to influence policy in Ottawa gained their professional credentials in private industry, inside government, or by espousing special-interest causes. Many lobbyists have worked closely with their governments and some are former politicians. Often, they are on a first-name basis with hundreds of politicians and reporters and are major spokespersons for the interests they represent. Hiring a lobbyist (sometimes a prestigious law firm, public-relations firm, or a legislative consultant) helps ensure that the group's interests are made known to the decision-makers in government in a professional manner, and – through a kind of watchdog function – that pending government action is brought to the attention of the group.

If the pressure group is large enough, its lobbying component may be quite sizable. Numerous organizations maintain offices in

> ■ ■ **lobbying:** any individual or group activities that seek to influence legislators and bureaucrats. Many states now require lobbyists to register and disclose their activities to the government and the public. ■ ■

the national capital and many of them employ more than a dozen people to co-ordinate the political relations of the group. The lobbying staff may include, in addition to a director and assistants, a number of liaison officers, researchers, copywriters, an editorial staff, and specialists with contacts in the various branches of government. The larger the interest represented, the more sophisticated its lobbying operation can be.

Influencing public officials in the lobbies of their workplace is still very much a part of pressure-group activity in Canada.[40] But pressure groups employ many means other than lobbying to aggregate citizen influence for the purpose of affecting public policy. In recent years, there have been significant changes in the tactics of Canadian pressure groups, some of which involve direct action. Practices can include demonstrations, organized boycotts and strikes, advertising, writing books, and staging various events to attract the attention of the media and to inform the general public. In 1993, environmental demonstrators blocked access to logging roads and chained themselves to trees in an attempt to draw attention to what they believed to be the indiscriminate cutting of old-growth forest in such areas as Clayoquot Sound, British Columbia. Pressure groups will sometimes penetrate political parties to get closer to the decision-makers. Associations of campers, conservationists, environmentalists, birdwatchers, and naturalists have used these methods, which have proved very successful in their communications with government agencies.

Mass demonstrations, providing information, and disseminating propaganda are becoming standard tactics for some pressure groups such as peace organizations. Another dramatic and direct action designed to put pressure on government was staged by Greenpeace protesters when, in an attempt to abort a scheduled military operation, they lofted balloons carrying nets into the flight path of cruise missiles. Changing circumstances, needs, and technology have encouraged an ever-increasing array of pressure groups to use demonstrations to articulate their demands and grievances and to pressure authorities into taking remedial action. With respect to the peace movement in Canada, it is increasingly evident that the public is taking notice.

Any survey of pressure-group tactics and techniques must also include illegitimate and coercive ones in which violence and terrorism are employed. No society has escaped the use of violence and vandalism by pressure groups. In Canada, violence has marked group struggles between labour and management since it became an independent nation-state. The consequences of continued physical violence are alarming but violence is, nevertheless, always a possibility with pressure-group activity. Terrorism has taken the form of deliberate assassination of diplomatic representatives, armed attacks on other groups or government officials, the provocation of bloodshed, and the threat of bombing. Terrorists are often successful in drawing world attention to their cause, but at the same time they can lose public support by their violent actions.

Here, of course, lies the great dilemma of direct action, and is the point around which debate on the propriety of some pressure-group activities revolves. Some would argue that violent protests are never appropriate in a democracy such as Canada, where other more peaceful channels exist. They point out that protest and violence are not always the same thing and that violence should not be tolerated as though it were an inalienable political right. But both are political acts, engaged in by individual citizens or groups who want to pressure the government to respond.

Usually, the squeakiest wheel gets the oil. But violent protests sometimes flash quickly and then fade, leaving behind only bad memories and a more defensive political system. Often, the most effective pressure activity is a well-organized assertive protest. An urban demonstration bordering on mayhem, a massive descent on Ottawa of the outraged unemployed, attempts by citizens to block the infiltration of pornographic materials – all such activities may cause government leaders to change their course sharply.

Pressure-group protests are likely to be particularly effective as signalling devices. The urgency demonstrated by the protest and the vast coverage it receives through the media make pressure groups powerful vehicles for indicating discontent to political leaders. They are also signalling devices to potential participants. Such overt and powerful manifestations of discontent may help to mobilize others to become more active.

As might be expected, the network of relationships that links pressure groups with government and the policy-making process generally is a highly complex one. The ballot box is by no means the only channel of access that people have to their government; the range of activity that falls under the heading of pressure-group politics supplements election politics in most democratic societies. Even a sampling of the avenues of access available to pressure groups confirms that, in their sheer number, not to mention flexibility, these groups rival political parties as guarantors of popular sovereignty. Sometimes the cabinet or the minister responsible can be more favourably persuaded by a pressure group than by the combined tactics of the parliamentary opposition.

The factors that most interest political scientists about political systems – equality, freedom, participation, revolution, security, and stability – are very much a consequence of the performance of political parties and pressure groups. When they fail to aggregate people and articulate people's needs, political systems can become unstable and may even fail. Unaccommodated interests rarely dissipate, and the means used by people to seek retribution are likely to grow more disruptive throughout the body politic.

References

1. Lily Ross Taylor, *Party Politics in the Age of Caesar* (Berkley: University of California Press, 1961), 6-23.

2. Sir Randol Fawkes, *The Faith That Moved the Mountain* (Nassau: Nassau Guardian, 1979), 211.

3. Leon Epstein, *Political Parties in Western Democracies* (New York: Frederick A. Praeger, Inc. 1967), 9.

4. Maurice Duverger, *Political Politics and Pressure Groups* (New York: Thomas Nelson and Sons Ltd,. 1972), 5.

6. Janine Brodie and Jane Jenson, "Piercing the Smoke-screen: Brokerage Parties and Class Politics" in Alain Gagnon and Brian Tanguay, eds., *Canadian Parties in Transition* (Scarborough, ON: Nelson Canada, 1989) 24-44.

7. Roy Macridis, *Modern Political Regimes, Patterns and Institutions* (Boston: Little, Brown & Co., 1986), 64-70.

8. Gabriel Almond and G. Bingham Powell, Jr., *Comparative Politics Today: A World View* (Glenview, IL: Scott, Foresman and Company, 1988), 82-88.

9. Kenneth Kernaghan and David Siegel, *Public Administration in Canada* (Scarborough, ON: Nelson Canada, 1991), 452-457.

10. Giovanni Sartori, *Parties and Party Systems: A Framework for Analysis* (London: Cambridge University Press 1976), 42-47.

11. Ronald McDonald and J. Mark Ruhl, *Party Politics and Elections in Latin America* (Boulder, CO: Westview Press, 1989), 20-35.

12. Steven Rosenstone et. al. *Third Parties in America* (Princeton, N.J.: Princeton University Press, 1984).

13. Janine Brodie and Jane Jenson, *Crisis, Challenge & Change: Party & Class in Canada* (Toronto: Methuen 1980), passim; Joseph Wearing, *Strained Relations: Canada's Parties and Voters* (Toronto: McClelland & Stewart, 1988).

14. See Alain Gagnon and Brian Tanguay "Minor Parties of Protest in Canada: Origins, Impact, and Prospects," in Alain Gagnon and Brian Tanguay, eds., *Canadian Parties in Transition* (Scarborough, ON: Nelson Canada, 1989), 220-248.

15. Rand Dyck, *Provincial Politics in Canada* (Scarborough, ON: Prentice-Hall Canada, 1991), 1-31, 626.

16. Ronald McDonald, *Party Systems and Elections in Latin America* (Boulder, CO: Westview Press, 1971), 17.

17. Robert Michels, *Political Parties* (New York: The Free Press, 1962).

18. Rand Dyck, "Relations Between Federal and Provincial Parties," in Alain Gagnon and Brian Tanguay, eds., *Canadian Parties in Transition* (Scarborough, ON: Nelson Canada, 1989), 186-219.

19. George Perlin and Hugh Thorburn, "The National Party Convention," in H.G. Thorburn, ed., *Party Politics in Canada,* 5th ed. (Scarborough, ON: Prentice-Hall Canada, 1985).

20. W.T. Stanbury, "Financing Federal Political Parties in Canada, 1974-1986," in Alain Gagnon and Brian Tanguay, *Canadian Parties in Transition* (Scarborough, ON: Nelson Canada, 1989), 354-383; *Report of the Chief Electoral Officer Respecting Election Expenses*, 1980, 1981, 1982, 1983, 1984, 1988, 1993.

21. Gabriel Almond and G. Bingham Powell, Jr., eds., *Comparative Politics Today: A World View* (Glenview IL: Scott, Foresman and Company, 1988), 392-95, 406-407.

22. Hugh Thorburn, ed., *Party Politics in Canada* (Scarborough: Prentice-Hall Canada Inc., 1991), 324-341.

23. W.D. Young, *The Anatomy of a Party: The National CCF 1932-61* (Toronto: University of Toronto Press, 1969); for a history beyond 1961, see: Desmond Morton, *The New Democrats 1961-1986: The Politics of Change* (Toronto: Copp Clark Pitman, 1988).

24. Christina McCall-Newman, *Grits: An Intimate Portrait of the Liberal Party* (Toronto: Macmillan Canada, 1982); R.W. Phidd, "The Administrative State and the Limits of Rationality," in Dwivedi, *The Administrative State*, 233-250.

25. Joseph Wearing, *The L-Shaped Party: The Liberal Party of Canada* (Toronto: McGraw-Hill Ryerson Ltd,. 1981).

26. N.K. O'Sullivan, *Conservatism* (New York: St. Martin's Press, 1976).

27. Robert Stanfield, "Conservative Principles and Philosophy," in Paul Fox, ed., *Politics Canada,* 7th ed. (Toronto: McGraw-Hill Ryerson Ltd., 1991), 297-300.

28. Quoted from the CBC program, "The House," aired June 11,1983.

29. William Christian and Colin Campbell, "Political Parties and Ideologies in Canada," in Alain Gagnon and Brian Tanguay, *Canadian Parties In Transition* (Scarborough, ON: Nelson Canada, 1989), 45-63.

30. Rod Preece, "The Political Wisdom of Sir John A. Macdonald," in *Canadian Journal of Political Science* vol.II, no.3 (Sept. 1984): 459-486.

31. George Perlin, *The Tory Syndrome: Leadership Politics in the Progressive Conservative Party* (Montreal: McGill-Queen's University Press, 1980).

32. Jeffrey Simpson, *The Conservative Interlude and the Liberal Restoration* (Toronto: Personal Library Publishers, 1980), 118.

33. Henry Saint-John Bolingbroke, "A Dissertation Upon Parties," in *The Works of Lord Bolingbroke,* Vol.2 (Philadelphia: Carey and Hart, 1841).

34. R. Michels, *Political Parties,* trans. by E. Paul and C. Paul (New York: Free Press, 1915); and M. Ostrogorski, *La democratie et les partis politiques*. Textes choisis par P. Rosanvallon (Paris: Seuil, 1902).

35. Stephen Frantzich, *Political Parties in the Technological Age* (Mississauga, ON: Copp Clark Pitman, 1989).

36. A.J. Cigler and B.A. Loomis, eds., *Interest Group Politics* (Washington, D.C.: CQ Press, 1991), 33-62; William Coleman and Grace Skogstad, eds., *Policy Communities and Public Policy in Canada* (Toronto: Copp Clark Pitman, 1990), Introduction.

37. Leslie Pal, *Interests of State* (Montreal: McGill-Queen's University Press, 1992). (See especially Ch.6.)

38. Paul Pross, ed., *Pressure Group Behaviour in Canadian Politics* (Toronto: McGraw-Hill, 1975); Hugh Thorburn, *Interest Groups in the Canadian Federal System,* Vol. 69, (Toronto: University of Toronto Press, 1986).

39. Gabriel Almond and G. Bingham Powell, Jr., eds., *Comparative Politics Today: A World View* (Glenview, IL: Scott, Foresman & Co., 1988), 62-68.

40. See Paul Pross, "Pressure Groups: Talking Chameleons," in Michael Whittington and Glen Williams, eds., *Canadian Politics in the 1990s,* (Scarborough, ON: Nelson Canada, 1990), 285-309; "The Persuaders" in *Maclean's* (Feb. 24, 1986).

Suggested Readings

Associations Canada: An Encyclopedic Directory (Mississauga ON: Canadian Almanac & Directory Publishing Co., 1991).

Herman Bakvis, *Canadian Political Parties: Leaders, Candidates and Organization* (Toronto: Dundurn Press, 1991).

Stephen Brooks and Andrew Stritch, *Business and Government in Canada* (Toronto: Prentice-Hall, 1991).

Paul Allen Beck and Frank Sorauf, *Party Politics in America,* 7th ed. (New York: HarperCollins College Publishers, 1992).

William Christian and Colin Campbell, *Political Parties and Ideologies in Canada,* 3rd ed., (Toronto:McGraw-Hill Ryerson, 1990).

William Coleman and Grace Skogstad, *Policy Communities and Public Policy in Canada* (Mississauga, ON: Copp Clark Pitman, 1990).

Murray Dobbin, *Preston Manning and the Reform Party* (Toronto: James Lorimer & Company Ltd., Publishers, 1991).

Carol Graham, *Peru's APRA: Parties, Politics and the Elusive Quest for Democratic Consolidation* (Boulder, CO: Lynne Rienner Publishers, 1992).

Michael Laver and Norman Schofield, *Multi-party Government: The Politics of Coalition in Europe* (Oxford: Oxford University Press, 1991).

Alan Whitehorn, *Canadian Socialism: Essays on the CCF-NDP* (Scarborough, ON: Oxford University Press, 1992).

Glossary

administrative state: These terms are used to describe a phenomenon of governance through which public policies and programs ostensibly created by elected politicians are, in fact, influenced by the decisions of bureaucrats who are the principal agents in the formulation and implementation of the public agenda.

aggregating: The group process of bringing together a range of demands and of building a coalition of support across many levels of society on some issue, e.g., tax reform or social-welfare programs.

coalition government: A government formed by several minority political parties which constitute the cabinet when no single political party can command a majority in the legislature.

conventions: An assembly of official delegates representing a political party in the discharge of some official duty, such as the choice of party candidates, the adoption of platform statements, or the selection of delegates to represent the party at a higher-level meeting.

doctrinal: A term generally used to denote any outlook or activity that is characterized by adherence to political, religious, or social ideals and practice.

faction: A small, relatively homogeneous group of individuals within a larger organization, such as a political party.

franchise: In the field of politics, a term meaning the right to vote.

Grits: An American slang term referring to the stuff a person is made of. It was used to label members of the Reform party in Canada in the 1840s, and because of the merger of that party with the Liberal party, it is frequently used to describe contemporary Liberals.

interests: The desires, values, or objectives held in common by any number of individuals and groups.

left wing: The political designation of persons, parties, or groups supporting liberal or radical economic and political programs within a social system.

lobbying: Any individual or group activities that seek to influence legislators and bureaucrats. Many states now require lobbyists to register and disclose their activities to the government and the public.

mixed economy: Economic systems in which private ownership of the means of production is predominant, although government maintains a substantial role as a consumer, investor, and producer.

Munsinger scandal: A political controversy during the Diefenbaker period that raised questions of national security resulting from an alleged affair between associate Minister of Defence Pierre Sevigny and East German prostitute Gerda Munsinger.

partisanship: The degree of loyalty members of a political party or government display towards one another.

party coalitions: A temporary alliance of political parties united for some specific purpose.

party discipline: Refers to the ways that members of a political party relate to its leadership, platform, voting strategy, and parliamentary procedures.

proletariat: In Marxist theory, the proletariat are those belonging to the industrial working class who do not own the means of production and who are solely dependent for their livelihoods on their ability to sell their labour to the bourgeoisie.

red Tory: A left-wing faction of the Progressive Conservative party of Canada that advocates economically egalitarian policies that one might expect to be more exclusively championed by Liberals or socialists.

right wing: The political term used to indicate persons, parties, or groups supporting conservative or reactionary economic and political programs.

Tories: A word derived from the Irish *toraighe*, which referred to a group that terrorized English settlers in Ireland. Gradually the term was used in reference to the English Conservative party that was committed to free trade, a market economy, democracy, and human rights.

Whigs: A term used in reference to Scottish rebels in the 1670s and, later, to the English Liberal political faction that sought to transfer power from the monarch to Parliament. Eventually the term applied to the British Liberal party.

TWELVE

Elections and Electoral Systems

Eighty-nine year-old Nellie Zimema votes in South Africa's first all-race elections

Chapter Objectives

After reading this chapter, you will be able to:

- define psephology

- differentiate the concepts of voluntary and compulsory voting and suffrage

- describe what an electoral system is and how it can affect the results of elections

- list what the major electoral systems are and understand how they work

- discuss the advantages and disadvantages of proportional representation and simple plurality systems

- apply this knowledge to Canadian elections at the federal and provincial levels

- recount the results of the Canadian federal election of 1993

- discuss the strategies used by the various political parties in the 1993 Canadian federal election

- explain the role of primaries as used in the United States

- compare the role of national conventions in Canada and in the United States

- review the results of the 1992 U.S. presidential election

Voting

Elections are one of humankind's oldest social institutions. Anthropologists have traced the practice to ancient Sumeria of nearly 6000 years ago, when people living along the Tigris and Euphrates rivers elected leaders to bring them through emergencies and natural disasters.[1] Elections first took a formal central role in politics much later, during the fifth and sixth centuries B.C., in the Greek city-states of the eastern Mediterranean. The Greeks elected people in popular assemblies to fill offices of political authority. They voted sometimes by a show of hands, sometimes with written **ballots** in the form of pebbles (psephite). Hence, the modern term *psephology* – the study of voting, elections, and electoral systems.

Today, elections may or may not be conducted democratically, but even the most authoritarian and totalitarian states are hardpressed to stage them. Although the frequency of elections varies among political systems, states that do not hold elections are the exception to the rule. In the modern world, elections are omnipresent political practices, even among the most repressive regimes. Many authoritarian as well as democratic states make voting obligatory: Belgium pioneered **compulsory voting** in 1893, followed by the Netherlands in 1917, and Australia in 1924. Other states that have adopted compulsory voting are Argentina, Brazil, Italy, Liechtenstein, Nauru, Paraguay, Peru, and Spain. In Italy, voting is not "legally" compulsory but is regarded by the state as a civic duty; failure to vote is recorded for five years on an elector's identity card. Italy also provides its citizens with free rail transportation home to vote. Some states, such as Uruguay, have compulsory voting laws but do not enforce them. Even though voting is one of the simplest political activities, the percentage of electoral turnout varies from state to state (table 12.1).

In most states today, the electorate is 21 years of age or over, an age qualification that usually permits the majority of citizens to vote. Table 12.1 illustrates a wide range in the percentage of voter turnout among the states selected: between 41 and 99 percent. In many states, the high proportion of eligible nonvoters is a persistent concern to government leaders because, despite the simplicity of the voting process, the implications of the vote are profound.

When people withdraw from an election or feel no political anchorage in the system, the resulting voter apathy can lead to political discontent. Studies cannot really pinpoint all the causes of non-voting, but indifference is certainly among the most influential. The groups usually cited as apathetic and alienated are women, the young, the uneducated, the poor, and those generally disenfranchised from the political system.[2] In Canada, where voter turnout is relatively high in comparison to other democratic states, political alienation expressed as non-voting is often related to a region's economic weakness. In such an area, many non-voters feel that one government is as helpless as another to make any difference

■ ■ **compulsory voting:** electoral participation by qualified voters that is required by law as used in Australia, Belgium, the Netherlands, Austria, Brazil, Italy, and other states. ■ ■

Table 12. 1:
Voter turnout in national elections, selected states

State	Compulsory Voting	Average turnout since 1945
Australia	yes	95.1
Belgium	yes	92.5
Canada	no	76.7
Denmark	no	85.5
France	no	78.7
Israel	no	81.1
Italy	yes	92.4
Japan	no	73.0
Luxembourg	yes	91.0
Nigeria	no	41.0
United Kingdom	no	77.3
United States	no	47.4

Source: For comparative data since 1945 see: *Keesing's Record of World Events*, 1979-1993, and United Nations, *Demographic Yearbook* (New York: UN, 1993).

in reversing economic insecurities. Many non-voting Canadians feel alienated even while possessing an advanced education, working in a high-status occupation, and enjoying a comfortable income.[3]

In the advanced industrialized nation-states, non-voting is often the result of other factors related to the complications of living in a highly mobile society. Common reasons given by eligible non-voters for failing to go to the polls include a recent change of job or residence, not knowing where the polling places are, conflicting hours of work and family obligations, or sickness and disability.

In totalitarian states such as China and Vietnam, where voter turnout at national elections has traditionally been expected and "directed," non-voting is penalized with fines, the publication of names at places of employment or recreation, and even the exclusion of public-service benefits. In such states, elections are considered to be a mechanism for demonstrating citizen support of the political system, as well as support for the slate of leaders running for government and party positions. At Beijing's Square of Heavenly Peace in May 1989, students and workers led a massive protest. Along with their demands for reform, they demanded democratization, and that the forces of pluralism be allowed to organize into political groups competitive with the Chinese Communist party.

Suffrage

Most states, whether democratic or non-democratic, apply the principle of **universal suffrage**, whereby every *qualified* person in the community, rather than everybody who happens to be in the community on election day, has the right to vote. The history of suffrage has been similar in many states: gradually, restrictions to voting have been removed with respect to property requirements, sex, and race. As a result, ever-larger proportions of the population have been included in the **electorate**. In the first Canadian election in 1867, only about one in every thirty adults was eligible to vote. Women were the largest single ineligible group. Through succeeding decades, restrictions on suffrage were removed one by one. Women gained the right to vote in 1918; in 1960, legislation amended the Canada Elections Act and the Indian Act to grant federal voting rights to native Canadians.

All political systems have established certain suffrage qualifications for people who want to vote. One is *citizenship*. Most states permit only native-born and naturalized citizens to vote. People with dual citizenship or multiple citizenship are usually allowed to vote in the country where they have taken up permanent residence and have demonstrated some loyalty toward the political system in which they wish to participate. Several Latin American states permit foreigners to vote in municipal elections after a five-year period of residence. Venezuela has permitted foreigners to vote in a number of its presidential elections.

■ ■ **returning officer:** In Canada, a person from each riding appointed by order-in-council to supervise the conduct of the election after writs of election are issued by the chief electoral officer. ■ ■

A certain minimum *age* is another requirement in all states extending the right or privilege of voting in governmental elections. The most common age limit is 21 years, but many states have lower limits. The Cuban Constitution permits persons aged 16 or older to vote for municipal councils, which are the only popularly elected bodies. Eighteen years of age is the limit in Canada, Great Britain, Israel, the United States, and Uruguay. Some Latin American states that use 21 as the voting age for most people will allow married persons to vote at age 18. Denmark has the highest limit at age 25. And Italy permits persons who are 21 and over to elect deputies to the Chamber of Deputies, but permits only citizens over 25 to vote for senators. Another important qualification for voting in elections is *registration*. Most states compile voters' lists against which the names of people asking for ballots can be verified. There are basically two registration systems practiced by states: one places the responsibility of registration on the voter; the other uses state-appointed officials to enrol eligible voters. In the United States, each voter must take the initiative by going to a registration office and applying.

In Canada, the preparation of voters' lists is the responsibility of the **chief electoral officer**, an independent civil servant chosen by the House of Commons to administer the Canada Elections Act, and who issues writs of election to the **returning officer** in each **riding**.[4] These officials direct the preparation of voters' lists by supervising enumerators who canvass door to door, beginning 49 days before the election. Finally, *literacy* continues to be a requirement in some states. Literacy requirements can disenfranchise many persons. Brazil and Ecuador disenfranchise large numbers of illiterate Indians and peasants by literacy testing.

Besides these four qualifications, many states exclude certain people for various reasons. In many states, electoral laws exclude people in prisons, jails, mental institutions, judges, and the chief electoral officer. In Canada, a judgement of the Federal Court in 1988 reversed the disqualification of federal judges from voting. In the same year, the Federal Court struck down as unconstitutional the section of the Canada Elections Act that denied the vote to the mentally ill. But returning officers are permitted to vote *only* in the case of a tie vote in a riding. One Canadian inmate challenged the Canadian Elections Act on the grounds that the Charter of Rights and Freedoms gives every citizen – including prisoners – the right to vote. However, the Supreme Court of Canada turned down the prisoner's appeal of a ruling of the federal appeal court which had denied the inmate the right to vote in the 1984 federal elections because he was a prisoner.

> ■ ■ **homeostasis:** the tendency in a social or political system to stabilize by means of self adjustments (such as elections) that counter or compensate for disruptive and destabilizing influences. ■ ■

Functions of Elections

Elections in Democracies

Elections perform a variety of political and social functions in all states. In democratic electoral systems, elections are the primary mechanisms for *recruiting* political leaders and representatives. As the special democratic events that link the institutions of govern-

ment with people who aspire to a political career, elections are the vehicle of **political succession**, a peaceful process that transfers power from one set of political leaders to another. Therefore, elections have a **homeostatic** function in a political system; they provide a process for orderly political change while preserving the basic continuity of political and governmental institutions.

Another function of elections is to **aggregate** individual choices into a *collective decision*. In all societies there is a continuous, often intense, political struggle to influence what collective goods will be provided, who will mostly pay for them, and who will benefit from them. In democracies, elections determine which majority will command the reins of power to authoritatively allocate these collective goods. And, because no society stands still, new social challenges constantly provoke the need for the widest possible consensus on social problems. On the public agenda today are the issues of abortion, crime, drug abuse, defence, environmental protection, unemployment, and many others. Elections not only provide the channel for expressing new social concerns about these issues, but are also an outlet for shifting public sentiment. Elections enable societies to capture changing public attitudes and to respond collectively to social exigencies.

Still another function of elections is *political socialization*. Elections provide one of the few opportunities in most societies for all citizens to learn about the issues and personalities in the political system. The 1993 federal election provided an opportunity for Canadians to learn about the North American Free Trade Agreement (NAFTA) and its potential impact on the economy. Thousands of copies of the agreement were sent to individuals, MP constituency offices, radio and TV stations, libraries, and universities for distribution and discussion. While it is true that elections offer citizens only the minimum amount of voting participation, with some impact on policy-making, they are an important means of political education for both the people and their representatives.

Election campaigns, usually of two or more months' duration, offer politicians an opportunity – and an obligation – to educate the public and to justify their political views. It becomes increasingly important to the citizenry, which has access to both domestic and international sources of information, to learn about and judge the quality of a regime's activities at home and abroad. Elections are one of the few genuine learning experiences that people, as a community, go through together.

In Canada, almost everyone develops partisan attachments based on ethnicity, religion, socio-economic status, ideology, and general social issues. The public is continuously exposed to political information conveyed by newspapers, television, and radio during the election campaign, usually followed by a substantial amount of media analysis after the election is over.[5] In most states, this constitutes a total-immersion political learning experience for the citizenry. The learning process provided by elections may also include the reinforcement of positive attitudes toward authority and political obligation. In most authoritarian and totalitarian political systems, voting plays an important role in political socialization, serving as the symbolic input of citizen support for the undisputed authority and legitimacy of the party and the government.

Finally, elections can foster a sense of *personal efficacy*, a feeling of psychological satisfaction derived from the belief that the political system is affected by and must respond to the aggregate results of voting behaviour. For those who vote in elections, personal efficacy means a perception that no matter how insignificant a single vote is, it may actually be part of a groundswell of messages to political leaders or aspiring political recruits. Much national research has shown that political participation is closely related to feelings of personal efficacy.[6]

Elections in Dictatorships

In many authoritarian states, elections are confused, hectic, and often negative learning experiences for citizens. In these kinds of political systems, the coup d'état is still a widespread method of governmental change. Elections are held as undesirable events that further accelerate the possibility of political violence and corruption. This was dramatized during the elections held in Panama after former president General Manuel Antonio Noriega was removed from power. At a rally of opposition parties protesting the widespread exercise of electoral larceny in Panama, Noriega's Defence Forces appeared on the scene with clubs and metal pipes slashing and striking anyone in their way. The ordered brutality was political revenge on people who had supported opposition candidates before the election was annulled by the government. People are exposed to electoral manipulation and fraud, obscurantist campaigning, military intervention, proliferating candidacies, and last-minute political fiascos. They learn that personalism is rampant and that candidates try to magnify their own personal popularity and appeal by viciously attacking their political rivals, by slanderous name-calling, or by identifying them as puppets of Marxists and communists.

In many Latin American states, people are exposed to flagrant corruption of the electoral process.[7] The media are particularly vulnerable to official interference because they are subsidized by the government. In Mexico, it is not uncommon for the government to forgive loans to newspapers if the editorials appearing around election time are favourable. From 1964, when the military came to power in Brazil, until 1985, when it withdrew from politics, censorship was institutionalized and was particularly restrictive against the press and popular candidates when elections were held. In Paraguay, the 1988 landslide victory of General Alfredo Stroessner was achieved through widespread fraud, as witnessed by the absence of opposition ballots at polling stations, a lack of closed booths to protect secret balloting, voting by underaged voters, and ballot-box stuffing. The following year, during a coup, Stroessner was forced into exile for reasons of massive government corruption. Under his successor, General Andrés Rodríguez, the leader of the coup, election irregularities at the national and municipal levels continued to be engineered by the Colorado Party, which has been in power since 1947.

In many authoritarian states, registration procedures are used to manipulate the electoral process and to discourage all but the

■ ■ **enfranchisement:**
The extension of the right to vote to certain groups and categories of individuals formerly excluded by law or procedure. ■ ■

most dedicated voters. Poor people, who are less interested in politics to begin with because they have so many other immediate problems to worry about, must face the costs of needed documents and photographs. In nation-states with large peasant populations, the long journey from the countryside to urban polling stations is a strong deterrent to voting. In addition, there are also the well-known practices of buying votes, threatening voters, and fraudulently tallying the votes cast.

Nevertheless, millions of people in authoritarian states turn out at the polls whenever elections are held. This occurs, at least in part, because they need to keep a job, to maintain the support of a superior, or to avoid fines imposed in states with compulsory voting regulations. In these political systems, people are voting in ever-increasing numbers despite what they have learned about fraudulent electoral practices. The almost universal **enfranchisement** of women and increasing urbanization have contributed to greater electoral participation all over the world. Urban dwellers are more easily reached by competitive political parties; voting is physically easier in cities than in the countryside and the election experience itself socializes and politicizes more people now than ever before. Whenever elections are called in the authoritarian regimes of Africa, Asia, and Latin America, people have increasingly shown considerable sagacity in casting their votes.

Major Electoral Systems

An electoral system consists of all the customs, laws, procedures, and institutions used to elect representatives in a political system. A comprehensive description of an electoral system would include the customs and practices of campaigning and voting, the rules regulating the behaviour and funding of candidates, the methods of calculating and representing the popular vote, and the institutions (political parties, conventions, electoral colleges, and government agencies) that administer, recruit, and compete when elections are held.[8]

Most states have evolved an electoral system of their own to choose a government and its representatives. The size of the electoral district, the number of political parties that compete, and the timing of elections are all variables affecting the performance of any electoral system. For purposes of analysis and classification, political scientists divide electoral systems into two main types: **majority systems** and systems of **proportional-representation** (PR). Majority systems are designed to produce either a simple **plurality** or an **absolute majority** for one candidate representing a single constituency. Where more than one candidate is elected from multi-member constituencies, the candidates with the largest pluralities are declared elected. Majority systems appear as single-member constituencies, multi-member constituencies, and constituencies using **preferential** and **run-off ballots**.

Proportional representation (PR) systems are designed to give the minority political viewpoints a share of the seats in the legislature based on their proportion of the popular vote. PR systems appear in constituencies using party-list systems and the single-transferable vote.

Majority Systems

The Single-Member Constituency

The single-member district/simple plurality electoral system is the easiest to understand and the most widely utilized among the democratic nation-states of the world. It is used extensively in a diminishing number of states, including Canada, France, Great Britain, India, and the United States. In 1994, Italy partially adopted the simple-plurality electoral system for 75 percent of the seats in the Chamber of Deputies. The remaining 25 percent of the seats were filled using PR. This was done in an effort to reduce the number of parties that compete and to produce a strong national government capable of handling widespread corruption.

The single-member district is based on a geopolitical principle that divides a state or its subnational units into relatively equal constituencies, with one representative elected from each district. The candidate who gains a plurality of popular votes wins the election. This winner-take-all system usually means that the candidate who wins a plurality of support does not necessarily command the majority of votes cast in the constituency. In fact, a minority win always occurs in a single-member district when a candidate merely wins more votes than his or her opponents and does not get more than 50 percent of the total. For example, in the Toronto riding of Beaches-Woodbine, in the 1993 Canadian federal election, the Liberal party candidate won 17,639 votes, the NDP candidate attracted 8037 votes, the Reform party candidate got

6844, the Progressive Conservative candidate earned 4316 votes, and other candidates took 6470 votes. Thus the winner, Liberal Maria Minna, with her 17,639 votes, had a grand total of 25,667 votes against her. When this kind of situation is repeated in riding after riding, the net effect is to over-represent the winning party in the House of Commons and under-represent the losing parties.

When the Liberals under Jean Chrétien won the federal election in 1993, they polled 41.23 percent of the popular vote but won 60 percent of the seats in the House of Commons. The Progressive Conservatives under Kim Campbell polled 16.04 percent of the popular vote but won less than one percent of the places in the Commons. The Bloc Québécois won 13.52 percent of the popular vote and holds about 18 percent of the seats in the House. The New Democratic party under Audrey McLaughlin polled 6.87 percent of the popular vote and won only three percent of the seats in the House. But the Reform party won 18.69 percent of the popular vote and took about the same percentage of the Commons seats.

In Canada, the single-member constituency rarely produces a government that has the support of the majority of Canadians.[9] Even with what has been billed as the return of a credible majority in the House of Commons after the 1993 election, the Liberals still have the support of less than half of the voters, and when the percentage of votes given to opposition and other parties is taken together, over 50 percent of the electorate voted against the government. Because plurality is the rule of success in single-member constituencies, only on rare occasions will a majority of popular support be achieved.[10]

Multi-member Constituencies

Another type of constituency used in majority electoral systems is the multi-member district. In these circumstances, two or more representatives are elected from the same riding. The multi-member constituency is used to elect members to Turkey's National Assembly, as well as to a number of subnational and local legislatures in Canada, Great Britain, and the United States. Most people are unaware of the fact that U.S. senators represent multi-member districts – two senators are elected from each state. Because one-third of the Senate is elected every two years, U.S. citizens rarely have the opportunity to vote for two senators simultaneously. This produces the popular misconception that senators are elected from single-member constituencies.

In Canada, many of the provinces that had multi-member constituencies have abolished them. For example, the following provinces – Newfoundland in 1972, Nova Scotia in 1981, Saskatchewan in 1965, and Manitoba in 1958 – all abolished multi-member districts. But in Prince Edward Island, all the 16 constituencies are multi-member, each electing two members to the provincial Legislative Assembly. In British Columbia, seven constituencies in the Vancouver area are multi-member ridings; all the rest in that province are single-member constituencies. In multi-member constituencies, the electorate is permitted to vote for as many candidates as there are posts to be filled. As in the single-member district, the candidates with the highest pluralities are declared elected.

Preferential and Run-Off Ballots

Some states – concerned that the plurality principle rarely achieves an absolute majority of support for successful election candidates – use a number of ballot techniques to guarantee that every elected representative wins with the approval of more than half the electorate. One of these techniques is the *preferential ballot*, which is currently used to elect representatives to the Australian House of Representatives and to four of its eight states and territories. On a preferential ballot, the voter *ranks* the candidates in order of preference, by placing numbers rather than Xs beside their names. If a candidate obtains a majority of first-choice votes on the first count, he or she is declared elected. If no candidate gains a majority on the first count, the candidate with the fewest first-choice preferences is dropped and his or her ballots are redistributed based on the second-choice preferences on each. This time-consuming process is continued until an absolute majority of support is obtained by a candidate. He or she is then declared elected.

Another technique is to use a *run-off,* or second, ballot in order to facilitate an absolute majority victory for successful candidates. In France, for example, unless candidates for legislative and executive posts receive a majority on the first ballot, they compete in run-off elections that continue until a candidate polls a majority.

Ten southern U.S. states also hold run-off elections between the two top candidates when no candidate in the first primary gains a majority vote. In these states, where the Democratic party tends to be dominant, winning the primary is tantamount to winning the general election. The run-off election guarantees that the candidate who wins the primary will have the majority support of the voters, rather than determining a victory by a mere plurality when three or more candidates are contesting an election.

Proportional Systems

In the 1993 federal election, about 59 percent of the votes cast by Canadians were against the Liberal Party. However, not all of these votes went unrepresented or under-represented. After all, the Reform party gained 18.69 percent of the popular vote and won 52 seats in the House of Commons; The Bloc Québécois won 13.52 percent of the popular vote in Canada (52 percent in Québec) but won 54 of the seats; the New Democratic party polled just over 6.87 percent of the popular vote and won only nine seats; and the Progressive Conservatives attracted 16.04 percent of the popular vote, gaining only two seats. But on closer examination, we must conclude that the electoral system Canadians use to choose their parliamentary leaders usually under-represents their votes when they vote against the winning party. Many other political parties competed in the 1993 election. These included the Abolitionist Party, Christian Heritage party, the Canada Party, the Green Party, Libertarians, Marxist-Leninists, the National Party, and the Natural Law Party, which together attracted nearly four percent of the popular vote but won no seats in the House of Commons.

With a system of proportional representation, the votes that would remain under-represented or wasted in other electoral systems are given legislative representation in proportion to the total popular vote.[11] Hypothetically, had the principle of proportional representation been employed in Canada's federal election of 1993, the Liberals would have won only 120 instead of 177 seats; the Bloc Québécois would have earned 40 seats instead of 54; Reform would have received 54 instead of 52 seats; the NDP would have 18 seats instead of nine, and the Progressive Conservatives would have won 47 seats instead of a mere two. In a proportional system, the other parties would have held about 12 seats in the House of Commons with only four percent of the popular vote.

Proportional representation is an attempt to give legislative expression to the dispersion of votes (majority and minority) as they accrue in a democratic electoral system.[12] The proponents of PR believe that a truly *democratic* assembly should reflect voter preferences in a polity as accurately as possible. PR is designed to accurately represent the electoral results of political parties according to their relative strengths in the electorate.

Many states employ a system of proportional representation: Denmark, the Republic of Ireland, Germany (for half the seats in the Bundestag), Israel, and Sweden. Basically, these states allot seats in their legislatures in direct proportion to the distribution of votes. In fact, it can be argued that all PR systems now operative in modern democracies are variations of two basic types, the **party-list system** and the **single-transferable-vote system**.

Party-list Systems

Party-list systems operate on the principle that all qualifying political parties are awarded seats in the legislature in proportion to the percentage of popular votes they attract in an election. Party lists are prepared by the leaders or executive committees of various parties and submitted to the electorate in multi-member constituencies. Though the size of

the constituencies and the methods of counting and distributing seats vary from one state to another, three distinct variations of the party-list system are detectable.

One variation gives the voter no choice among the candidates once the list is prepared. Israel is the best example of this take-it-or-leave-it party-list system. There is only one multi-member constituency in Israel – the entire country, which elects 120 members to the unicameral Knesset (parliament). All contending political parties must get 750 signatures from eligible voters before they can submit their lists of up to 120 candidates. Once the list has been made, no independent candidates are able to get on the ballot, as they can in some other states, including Denmark and Finland. Even the order in which the candidates appear on the list cannot be changed. At the polling station, the voter selects the ballot – and the list – of his or her party as is, and deposits it in the ballot box. Each party is entitled to a number of seats in the Knesset according to its percentage of the total popular vote. In Israel's system it is the *party*, rather than individual candidates, that is the primary attraction of voter support. The voter knows what the ideological position of each party is and that only the most experienced and influential candidates of those on the party list will occupy the seats the party is awarded on the basis of proportional representation.

Another variation of the party-list system involves giving the voter some choice among the party's candidates. The voter may decide not to alter the party list and to vote for it in its entirety, or may move preferred candidates to the top of the party list. When a majority of voters indicate preferences for certain can-

Table 12.2:
Four-member constituency, 20,000 votes cast
Hare quota: 5000

Party	Votes	Quota	Seats	Remainder	Seats	Total Seats
A	8200	5000	1	3200	1	2
B	6100	5000	1	1100	0	1
C	3000	—	0	3000	1	1
D	2700	—	0	2700	0	0
Total	20,000		2		2	4

didates other than those originally listed by the party, the seats won by the party are allocated in accordance with popular preference. Belgium, Denmark, and the Netherlands permit voters to indicate their preferences, but for only one candidate; Norway and Sweden permit voters to choose up to four candidates.

The final variation in the party-list system gives voters complete freedom to choose among candidates running in a multi-member constituency. The voter has as many votes as there are seats to be filled in the constituency. He or she may choose to expend those votes on one particular candidate, or to place one vote with each of several candidates. The voter may also vote for candidates from different party lists. When the votes are totalled, each party is allocated seats in proportion to the total votes for all lists. This system is used in Switzerland and Finland.

The Single-Transferable Vote

The single-transferable vote is a system of balloting that combines the principle that voters should have maximum choice of the candidates with a formula that guarantees all votes will be used to select representatives. Voters in multi-member constituencies indicate their preferences by writing numbers in the boxes beside the names of the candidates. A quota is established for each constituency to determine the minimum number of votes a candidate must have to be declared elected. The *Droop quota* is often employed. This quota (Q) is derived by dividing the total number of votes cast (V) by the number of seats to be filled (S) plus one, and adding one to the result:

$$Q = \frac{V}{S+1} + 1$$

Thus, in a three-member constituency with 100,000 votes cast, the quota would be 25,001. Initially, the ballots are sorted according to the first choices among voters. If no candidate obtains enough first-place votes to meet the quota, the candidate with the fewest first-place votes is eliminated. His or her ballots are then *transferred* to the candidates who received the largest number of first-, second-, and third-choice votes, but who may not have had enough votes to satisfy the quota. Eventually, the quota is satisfied by the single transfer of votes from eliminated candidates. This system is used in the Australian Senate, in Northern Ireland in the Senate of Ulster, the Republic of Ireland, Malta, and other states.

Another commonly used quota is the Hare quota, named after Thomas Hare, a Victorian lawyer and associate of John Stuart Mill. This quota (Q) is derived by simply dividing the total number of votes cast (V) by the number of seats to be filled (S):

$$Q = \frac{V}{S}$$

Seats are allocated on the basis of a system that uses the largest remainder from the votes that are cast for a party. For example, in a four-member constituency where 20,000 votes have been cast, the quota would be 5000 (table 12.2). Only two of the four parties (A&B) succeeded in surpassing the quota of 5000, thus each are directly entitled to receive one seat. But under the largest-remainder system, the third seat also goes to party A and the fourth seat to party C.

A nineteenth-century Belgian lawyer, Victor D'Hondt, devised a system that divides each party's votes by successive divisors, and then allocates the seats in descending order of quotients (table 12.3). The first seat will go to party A, the second to party B, the third to party A, and the fourth to party B.

Canada's Electoral Process

After the governor general dissolves a parliament on the request of the prime minister, the machinery for administering a federal election

in Canada is put in motion. The Cabinet (governor-in-council) instructs the chief electoral officer to issue writs of election to the returning officer in every federal riding in Canada. Returning officers are responsible for preparing voters' lists, for appointing deputy returning officers to the subdivisions in every riding, for receiving the nominations of the candidates, and for authorizing the printing of ballots.

The preparation of voters' lists is conducted by enumerators under the supervision of the returning officers. In urban centres, two enumerators, one from each of the two parties that in the last election obtained the first- and second-highest pluralities in the constituency, go from door to door to register voters. Only one enumerator is required to compile lists in each rural riding. The final revision of voters' lists should be completed 12 days before the election.

The returning officer also designates the location of polling stations in each riding. At these stations, a deputy returning officer and a poll clerk watch over the polling process under the scrutiny of two agents (scrutineers) representing each candidate. The voter is given a ballot on which are printed the names of the candidates, two identical detachable serial numbers on the back, and the initials of the deputy returning officer (see sample ballot). For purposes of verification, the deputy returning officer tears off the identical serial number.

After the voter has taken the ballot to a voting booth and marked an "X" beside the name of the preferred candidate, he or she folds the ballot paper so that the initials and the remaining serial number on the back can be read without unfolding it. The ballot is

Table 12.3:
Four-member constituency, 20,000 votes cast
Division by D'Hondt divisors

Party	Votes	Divisor:1	Divisor:2	Divisor:3	Total seats
A	8200	8200(1)	4100(3)	2733	2
B	6100	6100(2)	3050(4)	2033	2
C	3000	3000	1500	1000	0
D	2700	2700	1350	900	0
Total	20,000				4

then handed back to the deputy returning officer who confirms, by verifying the initials and the remaining serial number, that it is the same ballot paper given to the voter. If it is the same, the deputy returning officer then detaches the remaining serial number and deposits the ballot in the box. When the polls are closed, the ballots are counted by each returning officer in front of a poll clerk and party scrutineers. The ballots are locked in the ballot box and given to the returning officer who issues a declaration of election in favour of the winner. If there is a tie, the returning officer may cast the deciding vote in favour of one of the candidates.

All candidates for election to the House

Sample ballot

J030608152343JG

DOE, Jane
•••Indépendant/Independent•••

DOE, William
Appartenance politique/Political Affiliation

BERRY, Liba
•••Indépendant/Independent•••

UNTEL, Paul
Appartenance politique/Political Affiliation

Table 12.4:
Comparative cost of national elections per eligible voter – selected states

State	cost per elector
Canada	$9.06
Republic of Ireland	4.10
Israel	5.13
Germany	4.02
United Kingdom	0.63
United States	
Congressional	1.95
Presidential	2.10

Source: American Institute for Public Policy Research; and *Elections Canada* (Ottawa: Elections Canada, 1993), data for the 1993 federal election.

of Commons must be Canadian citizens, 18 years of age or over. In order to file nomination papers, a candidate must be endorsed by 100 other electors (50 signatures suffice in certain sparsely populated electoral districts) and must provide a $1,000 deposit to the returning officer for the constituency. The deposit is refunded if expense returns are filed within the prescribed time limit and if the candidate obtains at least 15% of the votes cast in the electoral district. Otherwise the deposit is forfeited to the Crown.

General elections appear to be expensive political theatre in Canada. The chief electoral officer's requirements for staff and supplies amounted to an estimated $138,000,303 for the 1993 election. In addition, an estimated $22 million was set aside to reimburse some candidates and political parties for ex-

penses, bringing the total estimated cost to $160,000,303. About one-third of these expenses are for the preparation, enumeration, revision, and printing of lists and notices. About 30 percent of the cost of the election is spent on the operation of polling stations and the printing of ballots. Then there are the fees and allowances paid to returning officers and election clerks. Added to these are headquarters' expenses, cost of postage, wages, and extra staff, and special voting for the armed forces and the public-service electors (such as embassy staffs) overseas.

The final report of the Royal Commission on Electoral Reform and Party Financing was published in 1992 and contained many important recommendations on improving the operation of Canada's electoral system.[13] The implementation of some of these recommendations increased the general cost of staging the federal election of 1993. For example, the institution of the *special ballot* was introduced to replace **proxy voting** and voting in the office of the returning officer. The special ballot serves electors in the Canadian Forces, electors and their spouses and dependents who are absent from Canada, federal or provincial public-service electors posted outside Canada, electors posted to an international organization, inmates serving sentences of less than two years, and electors residing in Canada who are unable to vote in their own electoral district.

Do Canadian elections really cost too much? We can compare the cost of Canada's federal elections to the cost of national elections held in other electoral systems (table 12.4). Actually, compared with the United States, the Republic of Ireland, Israel, and Germany, the cost of a Canadian federal election to each elector is quite high.

Canada's electoral system is necessarily one of the most expansive in the world and carries a relatively high per-voter cost as a result. However, there is always the possibility of improving a system that works well most of the time. Some electoral-system shortcomings due to human error are unavoidable, but others are correctable.

Canada's Election '93

Campaign '93

Years from now when people think back to the election of 1993, the memories they conjure up will be both comic and tragic. There will be the light moments: Jean Chrétien lugging beer cartons to demonstrate his virility, Audrey McLaughlin arm-wrestling with Paul (the Butcher) Vachon, Kim Campbell revving up a tractor, Lucien Bouchard taking the Oath of Allegiance, Preston Manning speaking French, and the Natural Law Party espousing the benefits of yogic flying.

But other images will also be remembered, ones in which incompetence, desperation, arrogance and fear-mongering all blended into the mix. All remember the negative Progressive Conservative campaign ad that visually focused on Jean Chrétien's physical disability. Then there were those PC candidates who began to use the media to attack their leader and to publicly concede defeat before the election. The Liberals tripped, as well. In Westmount, Québec, Jean Chrétien attended a cocktail party attracting party contributions of $1000-a-head from the corporate elite in exchange for privileged access to the future prime minister. The NDP were red-faced, as well, when it was revealed that one campaign video that criticized the government for exporting jobs to the United States was *made* in the United States. Preston Manning's Reform party strategists scrambled to control the damage inflicted as the result of racist remarks made by the Reform candidate running in York Centre.

The Debates

Even the two television debates of the 1993 campaign were short on discussion of issues but long on finger-pointing and strident voices. The quality of dialogue during the debates left much to be desired. Now a standard feature of federal and provincial elections, debates receive mixed reviews by analysts and have mixed effects on the electorate.[14]

Preston Manning could not lose in such an agitated public-speaking climate. All he had to do was show up, ask a few rhetorical questions, look like a reasonable human being, and his right-of-centre Reform agenda would benefit. All he had to do was not be extreme. Throughout the debates, he conducted himself calmly and rationally while others let their debating skills dissolve into a mess of angry accusations and recriminations.

Kim Campbell was criticized by all the other party leaders. She fought back gamely and was able to land a few blows against Bloc Québécois leader Lucien Bouchard and Liberal leader Jean Chrétien. She showed that she could manage in French, sometimes substituting an English word for what she wanted to say. But her efforts during the debates did little to stem the flow of voters from the Progressive Conservatives in Québec and throughout the country.

Lucien Bouchard and his sovereignists came under fire from all federalist leaders. The issues of Canadian unity raised tempers and exposed the anger of a past and future Parliament severely divided. Bouchard was able to score points in Québec by arguing that the federal government, federal taxes, and the federal deficit were to blame for Québec's current economic problems. Bouchard demanded to know why Québec should continue to operate under such a system of government. Such intense accusations were fired at Kim Campbell and Jean Chrétien with equal vehemence.

Jean Chrétien defended his federalist positions as consistent with being a Québecer and a Canadian. Mr. Chrétien listed poignantly the reasons he was as good a Québecer as Mr.

■ ■ **spin doctors:** loyal party supporters whose role it is to "spin" positive opinions about their leaders and policies to other party members and the media, and to create negative opinions about their political enemies. ■ ■

Bouchard. Of all the leaders, Chrétien lost the least during the debates. He showed Québecers that he has no horns, he refused to get into the Campbell-Bouchard bickering, and he kept repeating his basic campaign propositions: job creation and injecting hope into a beleaguered Canadian economy.

Probably the person who most surprised Canadians in the debates was New Democratic party leader Audrey McLaughlin who, in calm and very respectable French, kept repeating her party's basic messages on job creation and social programs. Of the two women on the stage during the debates, McLaughlin appeared the more open and approachable. But her performance was not strong enough to help save her party from the severe electoral thrashing soon to be exercised at the polls.

The Hustings

Election '93 focused clearly on many issues: free trade with the United States and Mexico, jobs and the state of the economy, and the image, win-ability and governing competence of party leaders. But, as in other recent federal elections, "leadership image" was one of the most important short-term factors contributing to voter preference and defection. On the **hustings**, most party leaders tried to put forward newer, more refined, images of their leadership styles.

In recent years in Canada, electoral campaigning has become an increasingly sophisticated art. Politicians enhance their fortunes by engaging **spin doctors**, and by using consultants, "photo-ops," computer-generated mailings and carefully crafted image-making exercises that rely on tracking polls and interviews with focus groups. Party campaign strategists spend millions to shoot TV commercials, hire marketing gurus, and conduct exhaustive coaching sessions for leaders' debates.

It has become axiomatic that within the first two weeks of a federal election campaign electoral trends are already beginning to jell. But when a campaign is beset by blunders, bad ads, voter skepticism, and the confusion of a five-way political race, a large portion of the electorate remains undecided and unwilling to commit until they enter the poll booth. With 14 political parties in the election arena – five of these as major competitors – voters were faced with many choices, the permutations and combinations of which were difficult to predict. Widespread voter hostility to the Progressive Conservatives could have dissipated votes everywhere. NDP supporters could have voted for Liberals because they would be a lesser evil than the Reform party. Québec federalists could have jumped to the Liberals to stave off the Bloc. And when the Liberals appeared to be heading for a majority, Prairie voters could have turned to Reform to counter the rise of the Bloc.

The Progressive Conservatives

Never in Canada's electoral history has a governing party been as completely humiliated and overwhelmed in a federal election campaign as were the Progressive Conservatives in 1993. Neither of Canada's two founding parties ever hit such a low as did the Progressive Conservatives in terms of the seats and the share of the popular vote lost. It was billed as "the Conservative collapse" because a party

that had reached such heights in the 1984 and 1988 elections was reduced to a rump of merely two members of parliament.

The campaign started on a high note as Kim Campbell became the first female Canadian prime minister, taking the reins of her political party with a promise to institute a new politics in Canada. Her tenure lasted for 123 days – the first 76 were diamonds, the last 47 were stone. Her initial freshness appeared a heaven-sent opportunity for the Conservatives to help Canadians bury their anger toward Brian Mulroney. On the eve of the election call, the polls showed Canadians felt Campbell ranked far ahead of Liberal leader Jean Chrétien in leadership ability. Nearly six in ten Canadians were willing to consider Kim Campbell and her candidates when the prime minister called the election, but much of that goodwill evaporated once the campaign began. The entire campaign was built around her, with the caption "The Kim Campbell Team!" printed on the placards, pamphlets, and billboards of Progressive Conservative candidates.

But having put all their eggs in her basket for the election campaign, the Conservatives saw their fortunes splatter every time she tripped. Her first major slip began on the very day the election was called, when in a general comment, she seemed to predict that Canadians would have to suffer double-digit unemployment until the turn of the century. Before she called the election, her quick rebuttals in the House of Commons and to the media were one of her biggest assets. Her candor and her diamond-hard quips helped her to fame. Visions of Pierre Trudeau's star-like campaign danced in the heads of Tory campaign organizers. They saw her as another charismatic winner, like Trudeau, a political intellectual, but one who could pull the country together in difficult times and bring a new style of leadership to government.

But the same frankness that first grabbed the attention of Canadians was a liability for Campbell in the campaign. Her fumbling performances soon could not be recovered, even though she was working 15-hour days. She repeatedly warned that Canadians would have to suffer cuts to their social programs, and rarely addressed the problem of unemployment, except as a by-product of high deficits and the national debt. In response to repeated questions from the media on what she might do about unemployment and Canada's social safety-net, she said that elections were not the time and that they were the worst possible time to debate very serious issues.

The Liberals

Jean Chrétien spent three years preparing for the 1993 election campaign. When the ballots were counted, he had won the keys to the Prime Minister's Office and a comfortable majority. All through the campaign, Québec was his Achilles' heel. The reality of forming a majority government without substantial representation in Québec was a major concern. By election day in Québec, the separatist Bloc Québécois was leading with 52 percent of the popular vote, although the Liberals moved into second place with 30 percent. Notwithstanding the powerful showing of the Bloc during the campaign, the Liberals were still

able to win 19 of the province's 75 seats.

The intent of Liberal strategists throughout the campaign was not to look cocky while carrying a decidedly strong lead in the polls. From the beginning of the campaign, other parties tried to peg Chrétien as "yesterday's man," as unable to understand the problems of contemporary Canada. He spent more than 16 years in the Cabinet, serving as minister of revenue, Indian affairs, Industry, finance, justice, energy, external affairs, and as president of the Treasury Board. Strategists had to show that the man who faithfully served and identified with the policies of Prime Ministers Lester Pearson, Pierre Trudeau, and John Turner could be a government leader for the 1990s.

Thus, Jean Chrétien had to perform well enough to overcome his image, within Québec especially, of being a political relic of past Liberal governments. During the campaign, he emphasized "the little guy from Shawinigan" image, one reinforced by his appearance in denim shirts with the sleeves rolled up, working on a strategy to create jobs. He maintained a hectic pace but avoided confrontations with the media and hostile voters. Instead, he urged voters to reject the surging regional parties in Québec and in the western provinces and asked Canadians to hand him a majority to deal with the country's future.

Campaign strategists took a risk by unveiling their platform the first week of the election race. The gamble paid off because the plan targeted the issues – jobs and the failure of the Progressive Conservative agenda – that were paramount in the minds of many Canadians. Once the campaign got under way, the Liberal machine purred like a precision timepiece. That enabled Chrétien to so-

lidify his reputation as the "Teflon man," his gaffes overlooked or forgotten because, unlike those of the Campbell campaign, the mistakes were the exception, not the rule. Campbell's error-prone performance and the public squabbling among candidates served the Liberal campaign well. These cracks in the Progressive Conservative support structure provided the Liberals with their best opportunity in a decade to capture the reins of power in Ottawa.

Against the backdrop of continuing economic hardship and Conservative disarray, the Liberals' economic program and a new posture on the economy helped Chrétien and his candidates take a commanding lead at the polls. They forged the idea that the Liberals had changed. No longer the party of spenders, Liberal strategists tried to imbue the notion in the electorate that they could govern responsibly but with a sensitivity to human suffering in hard times.

The Bloc Québécois

All through the 1993 federal election campaign, Canadians felt that Québec would shatter political tradition with a strong showing of the Bloc Québécois (BQ). Ignoring the long-standing rule of voting with the party perceived to be the likely winners, Québecers sent 54 sovereignist Bloc Québécois MPs to Ottawa. And for the first time in history, sovereignists made up the majority of Québec's 75 MPs. Through much of the campaign, Lucien Bouchard's political team appeared unstoppable – moving unobstructed toward a big victory. But very few people predicted that the Bloc would form the Official Opposition.

Many people underestimated the lingering anger in Québec over the failure of the

Meech Lake constitutional accord, Québecers' distrust of traditional political parties, and the persuasive power of Québec nationalism. The campaign in Québec gave voters the chance to show they did not accept the repackaged image of the Liberal party and the intense cynicism of Jean Chrétien's position that Québec would be doomed under a sovereignist plan. Even last-minute warnings against voting for the Bloc from newspaper editorials in *Le Nouvelliste* in Trois Rivières, *La Tribune* in Sherbrooke, and *La Presse* in Montreal, and from former Prime Minister Pierre Trudeau and Premier Robert Bourassa were too little, too late, to stop the flood of voter support for the Bloc.

Part of the strategy of the Bloc was to show that it was not a one-issue party. Lucien Bouchard promised throughout the campaign to fight for the rights of French-speaking Canadians who live outside Québec. Although the Bloc ran no candidates outside Québec, campaign strategists were always aware of the possibility that the party might become the Official Opposition. On the campaign trail, the party vowed not to ignore the rest of Canada. The party pledged to fight for all Canadians against injustice.

The Bloc upheld its intent to defend Québec's interests first and foremost, but when these interests also coincided with the concerns of all Canadians, the party would fight for them in the House of Commons. The Bloc shelved the nationalist rhetoric that sold sovereignty in the 1960s in favour of speeches about job creation and effective monetary policy. Bouchard blamed the federal status quo for Québec's economic woes and those of all of Canada. The party campaigned to fight any attempt to cut the deficit by dismantling the social safety-net, and came up with policies on international affairs. At the same time, the party attacked federalism and promised to demand a bigger share of the federal pie for Québec, which, in its view, has been shortchanged in the federal system.

The Reform Party

In some parts of the country, Preston Manning and his party represented the revolt against the status quo. Reform, which started as a Western protest movement led by disgruntled Tories and Social Credit supporters, grew on a wave of middle-class anger and despair over the federal government's obsession with Québec, its inability to control the national public debt, and its implementation of the goods and services tax. In appealing to the general anger sweeping the land, Reform tapped into the resentment of many Canadians over Canada's welfare-state policies, the unease about how immigration was changing the face of Canada, and the growing fear of crime.

Preston Manning asked voters to "stick it to 'em" in the polling booth. "Stick it to 'em" was a revolt against the status quo. It was a call of protest. The Reform strategy was to try to present the party as the constructive alternative. Manning pledged to reform Parliament, balance the budget, to bring in tough new "law and order" measures, and to act as an English-Canadian neutralizer against those Québec sovereignists collecting federal paycheques in Parliament.

Prior to the election call, the Reform party was mired in single-digit support in the public-opinion polls. But as soon as the election was called, support for the Reform party began to increase quickly. Constituency phones began to ring with calls from people who wanted to help. The trickle of donations became a flood. Reform's backing more than doubled in less than two months.

The Reform party campaign placed its fundamental political strategy before Canadians. It pledged to erase the age-old definition of Canada as a compact of "two founding peoples," the English and the French. Reform stated emphatically its opposition to any special status for Québec, constitutional or otherwise. Instead, the party promised to make all provinces equal and give them control over most linguistic and cultural matters. It promised to rescind the Official Languages Act and put an end to federally supported French-immersion schools. Reform sees itself as a federalist party negotiating for change with a federalist government, which in its view is much better than a separatist party dealing with a federalist government.

The New Democrats

All through the 1993 election campaign, the NDP braced itself for a dignified defeat at the polls. Unable to attract the large undecided and anti-government vote, the NDP slipped into Canada's political wilderness, running a campaign that produced the worst results since the party was created in 1961.

NDP strategists did not latch on to a campaign theme, and seemed to slash away at clusters of issues without any particular focus. The campaign vacillated everywhere – on Senate reform, on tax reform, on NAFTA, on the economy, the deficit and debt, medicare, leadership, and other issues. The campaign seemed to carry no clear message nor could it identify its real political enemy. To many in the public, it seemed to target everything political that moved in the electoral ring. Free

trade and Senate reform never became an issue in the NDP's campaign. As a result, they were seen to be grasping at straws.

The ads prepared by NDP strategists were calculated to shock and forcibly seize the attention of Canadians. But they produced quite the opposite effect to the party's dispirited election campaign. The ads portrayed the anger of citizens over Senate patronage appointments, lost jobs, and gutted social programs. But the images the ads created formed a stark and curious contrast to the benevolent personal style of leader Audrey McLaughlin, who tried to build her political reputation as that of an anti-politician in Ottawa.

McLaughlin made a serious tactical error during the campaign when she predicted a Liberal majority government. The move was designed to convince Canadians that they no longer needed to worry about a Progressive Conservative resurrection, and could vote NDP to counterbalance Jean Chrétien's anticipated victory. This logic appeared to be born of desperation as the polls revealed that a serious tumble was in store for the party.

Throughout the campaign, McLaughlin tried to dissociate herself from the unpopular actions of the NDP governments of Ontario, Saskatchewan, and British Columbia – including the controversial Social Contract. But the party that was once viewed as the alternative to the establishment was now perceived to be the establishment. In Campaign '93, the Reform party replaced the NDP as the political outsider.

During the campaign, McLaughlin occasionally faced the criticism that she and her party stood shoulder to shoulder with Brian Mulroney in promoting the Charlottetown Accord. It came as a surprise to party insiders

Table 12.5:
Election results by province: 1984, 1988, and 1993

Province	1984			1988			1993					
	PC	L	NDP	PC	L	NDP	PC	L	NDP	BQ	R	I
Nfld	4	3	0	2	5	0	0	7	0	0	0	0
PEI	3	1	0	0	4	0	0	4	0	0	0	0
NS	9	2	0	5	6	0	0	11	0	0	0	0
NB	9	1	0	5	5	0	1	9	0	0	0	0
Qué	58	17	0	63	12	0	1	19	0	54	0	1
Ont	67	14	13	46	43	10	0	98	0	0	1	0
Man	9	1	4	7	5	2	0	13	0	0	1	0
Sask	9	0	5	4	0	10	0	5	5	0	4	0
Alta	21	0	0	25	0	1	0	4	0	0	22	0
BC	19	1	8	12	1	19	0	6	2	0	24	0
Yukon	1	0	0	0	0	1	0	0	1	0	0	0
NWT	2	0	0	0	2	0	0	2	0	0	0	0
	(282)			(295)			(295)					

PC:	Progressive Conservatives	BQ:	Bloc Québécois
L:	Liberals	R:	Reform
NDP:	New Democratic Party	I:	Independent

Source: Elections Canada, *Results by Provinces, 1984, 1988, 1993*
(Ottawa: Elections Canada 1993).

that the constitutional referendum would produce such public anger and long memories of every politician who promoted it.

The Results

At the dissolution of Parliament in September 1993, the Progressive Conservatives held 157 seats in the House of Commons while the Liberals, as the Official Opposition, held 80. The NDP had 44 MPs, the Bloc had eight, and Reform had just one representative. There were two independents and three vacancies.

When the election was over on the night of October 25, nine years of Progressive Conservative government had ended and the Liberals led by Jean Chrétien were swept into power with a respectable majority.

The Liberal sweep began immediately after the polls closed in Atlantic Canada. The swing to the party continued into Central Canada and in part to the Prairies. Québec deprived Chrétien of the national presence he wanted. The sovereignist BQ captured more than two-thirds of Québec's 75 seats. Not only would they inhabit much of Québec's political landscape but they would gain a foremost presence in Ottawa as the Official Opposition. The dramatic Conservative decline in Québec followed Ms. Campbell's lackluster performance in the debates, and those who had supported the Tories in 1984 and 1988 were divided almost equally between the Bloc and the Liberals. But Ontario, the largest electoral prize, gave all but one seat to the Liberals. The party did well in Manitoba and Saskatchewan and made some gains in Alberta, although the Reform party clearly held the lead there (table 12.5).

The results showed beyond any doubt that Kim Campbell led the Progressive Conservative party to its most disastrous defeat of any prime minister in Canadian history by the loss of all but a humiliating two seats in the House of Commons. The old coalitions in Québec and the western provinces that had so successfully elected Progressive Conservative governments in the past could not hold together in the face of the Reform Party and the Bloc Québécois.

With the election of 54 Bloc Québécois members, the true face of Canada is reflected in the House of Commons. The Bloc Québécois pledged to go to Ottawa to get the most for Québec out of the federal system, while promising to fight for Québec's independence from that system.

A protest vote by millions of Canadians alienated from traditional politics provided the Reform Party with the large contingent of 52 MPs in Parliament. The historic success of Reform guaranteed them formal recognition in the House of Commons as well as the financial benefits and increased exposure of a political party that won nearly 20 percent of the electoral vote.

The 1993 election drastically reduced the NDP's presence in the House of Commons from 43 seats to just nine. A party is required to have a dozen seats in order to keep all the financial and parliamentary privileges awarded to official parties in the House of Commons. The lack of official party status is just one of the many problems that confronts the NDP caucus. The party suffered a drastic loss of financial resources and staff workers. It has fewer opportunities to ask questions in the House of Commons. And the question of leadership is placed high on the agenda.

Women and Elections

Women made an historic breakthrough in the 1993 federal election, winning substantially more seats than in any previous election. But women still hold less than 20 percent of the seats in the House of Commons. The result falls short of the 30 percent "critical mass" feminists have been hoping to achieve.[15] The critical mass refers to the point at which the number of women representatives begins to have a significant influence on the operation of Parliament by placing issues of special interest to women high on the political and government agenda.

One of the most notable outcomes of the elections in 1984, 1988, and 1993 was the breakthrough of women into the area of federal politics. In 1984, 29 women won seats in the House of Commons – about double the number of the previous Parliament – and an

Table 12.6:
Percentage of women in the single or lower chamber of national legislatures, selected states

State	% of Women
Albania	22.5
Austria	12.0
Bangladesh	9.1
Canada	18.0
Denmark	29.0
Germany	18.2
Lebanon	0
U.S.	6.0

Source: Inter-Parliamentary Union, Geneva, Switzerland, 1992; and Elections Canada, 1993.

unprecedented six women were appointed to Mulroney's first cabinet. In 1988, 39 women were elected but the number of women in the Cabinet remained at six. Kim Campbell's government had five women, including herself, in a much-reduced federal cabinet of 25 during her 123 days as prime minister. Of the 2155 candidates running in the 1993 election, 475 were women, of whom 53 were elected. In an even smaller political executive than Campbell's, Jean Chrétien appointed 22 ministers to his first cabinet, four of whom were women. In some ways, these appointments may have shattered the myths of political prejudice once and for all, although compared with other states, Canada's showing is a respectable one in terms of the percentage of women in its lower house (table 12.6). The social and psychological barriers that have impeded women from their rightful representation in Canada's male-dominated federal institutions are crumbling. But the fact remains that women, who constitute 51 percent of the population, hold only about 18 percent of the seats in the House of Commons.

In the 1980s, women's issues attained public visibility to a much greater degree than at any previous time in Canada's electoral history. Since the early 1970s, the executive of the National Action Committee on the Status of Women has challenged federal party leaders to debate women's issues, and all have felt compelled to say yes. This, too, was a turning point – the recognition of women's equality in Canada's political system.

In 1984, one indicator of the ascendancy of women into the hitherto male preserve of national politics was more women in cabinet, constituting an unprecedented 15 percent of the political executive. But no further increases took place after the 1988 election. For the first time in the history of the Canadian political executive, there is at least one woman on every cabinet committee, putting women firmly in the inner circles of government power, notwithstanding the under-representation of women at every level of Canadian politics.

The 1993 election demonstrated that the contemporary Canadian electorate is beginning to love its daughters as much as its sons. But as Canadian women look ahead only a few years to the next century, they wonder whether the promises to deal with violence against women, to legislate equal pay for equal work, and to work toward the elimination of all discriminatory federal legislation against women will happen in the twentieth century. Where this agenda will lead, no one can say precisely − except that it will entail much more than a simple re-definition of political equality. Indeed, political equality is still a long-term goal.

Elections in the United States

As in Canada, elections to public office are dramatic events in American political life. With the possible exceptions of assassination and public scandal, they command more attention from more people than any other political phenomena. Thousands of candidates take part in the numerous elections that characterize the American political scene.

The excitement of elections and electioneering is not limited to campaigns for the presidency. All members of the U.S. House of Representatives and about one-third of the senators are up for re-election every two years. Many state and local officials are elected

in the meantime. In addition, there are many referenda held on school taxes, bond issues, state constitutional amendments, and other municipal questions.

Elections in the United States are complicated events. Candidates and their supporters expend a lot of energy and money on a wide range of campaign activities. Presidential campaigns can begin a few months after a presidential election.[16] Many aspiring candidates manoeuvre and posture to test the political waters before they declare their intentions to stand for party nominations. These nominations are won only after arduous and expensive presidential primary campaigns, during which candidates try to lure delegates.

Throughout the campaign period, speeches are made, issues are debated, images are projected, personalities are revealed, and voters finally choose their government decision-makers. The electoral process is, therefore, critical for the recruitment of candidates and for the operation of the political system. Even though elections by no means determine what the U.S. government does, they can have enormous impact upon public policy. In November 1992, Americans again elected a new president, one who promised revolutionary changes to the U.S. economy and the reconstruction of the health-care system.

One very important aspect of U.S. elections is that they occur regularly; federal elections take place on the exact dates specified in the Constitution, regardless of convenience or partisan advantage. They have never been postponed. State and local elections, though governed by different constitutional calendars, also are held regularly, as are primary elections held by states to nominate candidates. The regularity of elections guarantees that public office-holders are accountable to their constituents.

These elections in the U.S. are structured in another important way. Most election activities – filing for candidacy, selection of nominees, raising and spending money, and a host of campaign activities – are shaped and regulated by law. Many of these laws are state regulations; they vary somewhat from one state to another. The patterns that emerge provide a basis for the study of U.S. electioneering practices.

Primaries

In the early years of the American republic, party nominees were chosen by the **caucus**, an informal meeting of leaders who selected a candidate to carry the party banner in the election. Presidential candidates were selected by caucuses of party senators and congresspersons. As the electorate expanded, so did the complexity of party organizations at the grass-roots level. The method of caucus selection gradually became inadequate and **party conventions**, made up of delegates elected by local party organizations, were established to choose party nominees for president, vice-president, and other elective offices. The conventions greatly democratized the nominating process, but **party bosses** tended to control the conventions, especially between 1850 and 1900. Conventions of this period often were rigged and dominated by certain party factions. The reformers of the progressive era at the turn of the century demanded that nominations be made directly by the people, not by politicians or party organizers.

■ ■ **party boss:** a person who heads a political machine and who manipulates political power in a particular area (state, county, city), especially through the use and control of patronage. ■ ■

The mechanism for these nominations was the *direct primary*. The primary, taken from the Latin word for first, is the first election taking place within the party. Primary elections are the means of involving party followers in the nominating process. They are followed by a general election, during which competition transpires between parties. Some primaries, held in about 40 states, are *closed*, requiring voters to declare in advance that they are registered members of a particular party. Other primaries are *open*, and do not force partisan declarations; people can decide when they enter the voting booth on election day in which party's primary they will participate. Voters are given each party's primary ballot; they vote on one. Idaho, Michigan, Minnesota, Montana, North Dakota, Utah, Vermont, and Wisconsin have open primaries. Some states have a *run-off primary*, in which, if no candidate gets a majority of the primary votes, there is a run-off between the two candidates with the most votes. Two states, Alaska and Washington, provide a variant of the open primary called a *blanket primary* which permits a voter to mark a ballot that lists the candidates for nomination of all the parties. Thus, in this kind of primary, the voter can help select the Democratic party candidate for one office and the Republican party (the GOP – Grand Old Party) candidate for another.

The South was the first region of the United States to institute the direct primary; however, its purpose was to prevent a coalition of poor blacks and poor whites from presenting their candidates for public office. By appealing to racism, dominant economic groups aligned with rural whites to sustain one-party domination in the region. In contrast, the political structure of the urban northeast was characterized by sharp competition between parties.

The primary system has greatly influenced the structure of party competition and the outcome of presidential elections in the United States.[17] When they were first used in many states, it was widely believed that primaries would be a more democratic way to nominate candidates, involving many more people than the handful who participate in conventions or caucuses. Later, primary elections were formed to involve party followers in the nomination process. Reformers felt that a larger dose of democracy would bring about mass political participation of truly representative character. Today, the voters in primary elections are far from a simple cross-section of the population. Usually older, wealthier, and better educated, they tend to be more politically aware and ideologically conscious than people who vote only in general elections. Therefore, primaries retain an elitist character and, as such, defy the democratic assumptions of most Americans.

■ ■ **demagogue:** a person who takes political advantage of social and political unrest through the use of highly emotional and prejudiced appeals to the general population or a particular segment of the general population. ■ ■

The primary system today is confusing because each state has its own rules for presidential primaries. The variations are considerable and can have extraordinary consequences for the fortunes of presidential candidates. In Texas, a voter must vote for local delegates once on Saturday morning and once more in the evening to have the vote count. Because of the many issues in each state, candidates find it difficult to enunciate national policies. In New England, candidates usually must talk about the price of heating oil or the fishery. In New York, candidates must cultivate the support of Jews, African-Americans, and Italians in their concentrated urban constituencies, to the exclusion of other groups such as farmers. In Texas and California, they court Hispanic voters and those involved in the oil industry. In the farm and industrial states, candidates must woo farmers whose needs conflict with those of steelworkers in Ohio and Pennsylvania.

Many candidates say off the record that the direct-primary nominating system is too important to be left to disparate state practices, and that Congress should step in to standardize the system across the country by law. Unquestionably, the primary permits voter participation in the selection of candidates. It permits unknowns to compete for office, and it gives candidates opposed to the party leadership a chance to win. The primary also places great emphasis on image and personality and enhances the power of money and the media. In these ways, it has contributed both to democracy and to **demagogy** in American party politics.

National Conventions

Conventions are the next step in the process of selecting a presidential candidate. But unlike in Canada, where conventions actually choose the party's candidate, most conventions in the U.S. tend to ratify the choice of the candidate who has succeeded in gaining the most committed delegates during the primaries. Even before the convention meets, the leading candidate usually has enough delegate votes to remove any doubt about the outcome.

Delegates to the presidential nominating convention are selected in a variety of ways. In some states, delegates are bound to the candidate winning the primary election, while in other states delegates can exercise their discretion about voting at the national convention for the winner of the state primary. In yet other states, delegates are selected by state party committees. Because not all of the 50 states hold primaries, these states send delegates to the convention who have been selected by party committees and caucuses. The results of these primaries does not tell us who will win the convention. Consider the caucuses held in Iowa in early February of a presidential-election year. Anyone who does badly in Iowa is at a disadvantage because of the predictive analyses provided by the media. Few would argue that making sense of the bewildering array of primaries and caucuses to determine candidates for presidential conventions is easy.

Conventions perform other important functions in addition to the glamorous selection of a presidential candidate. They are the supreme governing body of their respective parties. They formulate rules for the party and write the platform. All of this is done in less than a week by several thousand people, most of whom do not know one another, and in all likelihood will never meet again.

For the first day or two, the convention is concerned primarily with the work of the Committee on Credentials and the Platform Committee. The Committee on Credentials works out conflicts that arise between rival groups of delegates from the same state or when rival groups are pledged to different candidates. The Platform Committee works hard to placate all factions in the party and attempts to put together a statement of national party policies.

Conventions are also forums for keynote speakers. These orations are stylized political spectacles in which the speaker points to his or her party's achievements, views with alarm the sinister plans of the rival party, and attempts to excite the delegates to a state of high emotion.

When all the candidates have been nominated, balloting begins. The roll of the states is called and the world watches to see where the delegates' support will go. Party politicians prefer to decide the contest on the first ballot, thereby minimizing the danger of exposing party divisions and reducing the risk of the convention choosing a **dark horse** nominee. The candidate who begins slipping is usually deserted like a sinking ship. At a crucial time, a switch in an important state can start a domino effect. California is always an important state to watch because it combines the advantages of having many votes and is called to the roll near the top of the alphabet. As soon as the nominee has received enough votes to win, it is customary for rivals to move that the nomination be unanimous.

The nomination for the vice-presidency is usually an anticlimax because it is left to the determination of the party leaders. The considerations marking the choice are the per-

■ ■ **dark horse:** an unexpected compromise candidate who is nominated for office by a political party after a series of deadlocks over more conspicuous contenders. ■ ■

sonal preferences of the presidential candidates, the number of political IOUs resulting from the campaign, and the observance of the political maxim to "balance the ticket." Eight times in American history a vice-president has become president because of the death of his predecessor and once because of a presidential resignation.

After the excitement of the nominating process, candidates have about six weeks to get their second wind before beginning the dash to the election finish line. By the end of September, the campaign is in full swing, and the candidates spend 15 to 20 hours a day making speeches, shaking hands, travelling, and meeting with the media.

Elections are won and lost by a combination of long-term forces such as party identification, and short-term forces such as the issues and the personal appeal of the candidates. The mass media have become a crucial factor in influencing major shifts in electoral support toward candidates. Party identification seems to have lost much of its power. Even though the characteristics of people identifying themselves as strong Democrats and strong Republicans have remained stable since the early 1950s, Americans are voting in more widely diverse ways. It is not uncommon, for example, for a party's candidate for president to receive 30 or 40 percent more or fewer votes than the same party's candidate for governor or senator. At the **gubernatorial** level, Republicans are in the minority; Democratic governors presently control most of the statehouses.

Many politicians and journalists think that public issues in a political campaign are not important. Instead they stress candidate image, party loyalty, and get-out-and-vote drives. Other scholars and politicians concede the potency of all of these factors but nevertheless argue that in recent years, more and more people have come to base their choices on the closeness of fit between their own issue positions and the candidates' stand on policy. Increasingly, the American electorate is judging candidates in terms of the policies for which they stand.

The other side of the coin is exhibited by repeated findings that many voters do not have opinions – or have only weak and unstable opinions – about most issues. Voters are often ignorant of the candidates' positions or of the issues, and vote solely on candidate image. Some American voters misperceive where the candidates stand. Many will decide to support a favourite candidate because they mistakenly think that he or she agrees with their policy preferences. At the same time, these voters dismiss other presidential candidates by imagining that the candidates disagree with them even when they do not. Some voters even change their minds on issues so as to be consistent with the candidate they prefer.

U.S. Election '92

Republican Decline

As George Bush's first term in office came to an end, the Reagan coalition that was so successful during the 1980s had begun to unravel. The two main ingredients in the electoral appeal of Reaganism were prosperity at home and strength abroad. Reagan and Bush had promised Americans that by freeing the energies of the market, Republicans could deliver a new generation of prosperity to America. But just as important, Reagan and Bush promised to keep America powerful.

They asserted that only Republicans could be trusted to sustain the global power of the United States in the face of the "evil empire" controlled by the Soviet Union. Reagan's strategy of military build-up and economic stimulation seemed to fulfill both these pledges.

But by 1992, domestic and global circumstances for the United States had changed dramatically. First, the economy became ensnared in one of the longest economic downturns in recent decades. Second, the Soviet Union had collapsed, ending the Cold War, its "evil empire," and the threat of an all-out nuclear war between superpowers.

During Bush's presidency, all the indicators of economic performance told the same story: unemployment, declining manufacturing and retail sales, dwindling corporate profitability, continuing penetration of American markets by foreign firms and the loss of American jobs to foreigners, a sharp drop in real estate prices, followed by a wave of bank collapses and large numbers of business failures.

The inadequate performance of the U.S. economy during his term in office eroded Bush's popularity and divided the Republican coalition. But by 1992, widespread hardship in the U.S. economy was dividing the business community, as well. Some business sectors, especially "big business" and the multinationals, continued to support the Republican party because it advocated laissez-faire economics. The largest U.S. companies liked the Republican policies of free trade and unrestricted competition. These policies enabled them to expand their manufacturing base in foreign economies where labour and production costs are much lower than in the

United States. Big firms favoured the North American Free Trade Agreement (NAFTA) because it would allow them to move much of their production to Mexico and significantly reduce their costs. However, small- and medium-sized companies felt they could not as easily move to Mexico or elsewhere to gain the benefits of free trade and low labour costs. As a result, they were reluctant to support Bush's free-trade initiatives.

The severe economic downturn in the U.S. economy in the early 1990s also eroded blue-collar support for the Republican coalition. These voters traditionally had supported the Democratic party since Roosevelt's New Deal in the 1930s on the basis of that party's pro-labour stance. In the 1980s, a major purpose of the Republican "social agenda" – opposition to abortion, support for prayer in the public schools, and unabashed patriotism, was to lure blue-collar voters from the Democratic camp by persuading them to regard themselves as right-to-lifers and patriots instead of workers.

By the time of the presidential election in 1992, however, the political attraction of the social agenda had declined. Faced with widespread lay-offs in many of their industries, blue-collar voters could no longer afford the luxury of focusing on issues other than their economic interests. The issues of prayer, abortion, and patriotism lost their political potency and were abandoned. This explains why George Bush's approval rating – a remarkable 91 percent following the Persian Gulf war – dropped as much as 50 points in less than a year as bread-and-butter issues replaced citizens' pride in American military prowess. During the Republican decade, millions of working-class voters became unemployed or were forced to find lower-paying jobs. These disillusioned voters gradually deserted the Republican camp.

Even though the broad base of support for the Republican social agenda shrivelled, the moral fervour of the groups most fiercely committed to those issues increased. When right-to-life forces launched protests and sought to block the doors of abortion clinics across the country, President Bush had no choice but to strongly endorse the activities of these loyal Republicans. Unfortunately, however, Bush's support of these groups hurt his standing among other suburban Republicans. The traditional suburban upper-middle-class Republican constituency had never been enthusiastic about the social agenda or about the sorts of people it had brought into the party.

All through his presidency, Bush's popular base of support on the right was weaker than Reagan's. In this regard he may have felt obliged to do more to satisfy anti-abortion groups and other social conservatives. A pattern of conservative Supreme Court appointments and legislative initiatives may have pleased social conservatives, but it offended many upper-income suburban Republicans who had been the party's backbone. As the 1992 campaign got underway, Bush suffered a considerable loss of support from this income group that was only aggravated by the prominent role assigned to social conservatives at the 1992 Republican convention. The poor economy was the main cause of the erosion of Republican support among middle-class urban and suburban voters. This explains why these same groups that had been enthusiastic supporters of Reaganism in the early 1980s had broken away from the GOP by the early 1990s.

Soviet disintegration may have symbolized a victory for Republican foreign policy, but paradoxically, it had a negative impact on the Republican domestic political strategy. When the Soviet Union finally collapsed, the reasons for sustaining high levels of military spending disappeared, as did much of the justification for focusing on international rather than domestic problems and priorities. Industries and workers that had benefited from Republican military spending now began to look to the Democrats, whose call for massive investment in the U.S. economic infrastructure held out the promise of a new array of government contracts to replace those lost by the ending of the Cold War.

President Bush found himself increasingly dependent on a core Republican constituency of hard-line social and political conservatives. But political conservatives had been furious with Bush since 1991 when, in order to reach a budget agreement with congressional Democrats, he broke his "read my lips" promise never to raise taxes. Bush angered these conservatives even further when he signed the 1991 Civil Rights Act and the Americans with Disabilities Act.

Bush knew that in order to have any chance of re-election he must not lose his support on the political right. For this reason, he gave conservatives, including his nemesis from the presidential primaries, Patrick Buchanan, a prominent role in the 1992 Republican national convention, according their views a significant place in the Republican platform, and he emphasized "family values" in his presidential campaign. Unfortunately, Bush's efforts to accommodate the right led to unease among moderate Republicans, whose support for the president was already tottering under the pressure of economic hardship and world events.

The Rise of the Democrats

The fractured Republican coalition gave the Democrats their best chance in two decades to regain the White House. First, however, it was necessary to put their own party's house in order. Since the early 1970s, Democratic candidates had been hindered by the American public's perception that they were too liberal on issues of welfare and race.

But by 1992, the Democrats were able to successfully handle both these challenges. Since Richard Nixon's landslide victory over George McGovern, moderate Democrats had been contending that the party should occupy the centre of the political spectrum if it hoped to be successful again in national elections. The major organizational vehicle for the centrists was the Democratic Leadership Council (DLC). During the Reagan and Bush years, the DLC organized networks of state and local party officials and tried to develop political themes that would generate more party unity and that would appeal to American voters.

In the early 1990s, the DLC and its moderate allies dominated the Democratic party's presidential nominating processes as well as the Democratic National Convention. Bill Clinton and Senator Al Gore were founding members of the DLC. It was not surprising that the party chose them as its presidential and vice-presidential candidates. Sensing the power of American conservatism, the Democratic platform adopted at the party's national convention was widely perceived to be the most conservative in decades, stressing individualism and private enterprise while implicitly criticizing welfare programs.

Democrats hoped that the Clinton/Gore ticket would appeal directly to the southern white voters who once had been Democratic faithfuls but who had made the Deep South a Republican stronghold during the Reagan years. Clinton assured white conservatives in both the North and South that, unlike previous Democratic candidates, he would not cater to or indulge African-American voters. In this regard, Clinton was careful to elude public association with Jesse Jackson, the most prominent African-American Democrat.

By carefully positioning himself at the centre, Clinton was the first Democratic presidential candidate in two decades who was neither hounded by an excessively liberal image nor plagued by the party's racial divisions. With Democratic strategists believing they had stabilized the party's traditional southern, African-American, and blue-collar base, Clinton and his supporters tried to enlarge the Democratic coalition into core Republican electoral territory – business and the middle class.

Clinton's campaign called for the development of a "national economic strategy."[18] One major element of this strategy was to support free trade with the proviso that Americans would act against economies guilty of unfair trade practices, poor labour policies, or deficient environmental programs. A second element was to support scientific research and development with strong government backing for new technologies and industries. A third element was an economic strategy to retrain workers, preparing them for jobs in the new, high-technology industries of the future. Fourth, the strategy called for massive federal spending to rebuild America's industrial infrastructure. Finally, the Democrats promised to increase funding for education, health care, and other social services – to be paid for by tax increases on the wealthy.

As they entered the presidential campaign, the Democrats redefined social spending as an economic resource rather than a liability. No longer was social spending simply a transfer of public money to the poor. Rather, it was now to be seen as an investment in national resources needed to improve the competitive position of the U.S. economy in the world.

Campaign '92

In an environment of continuing economic recession and Republican disarray, the Clinton/Gore ticket took a commanding lead in the polls after the Democratic National Convention in August 1992. Bush fell back upon the theme of "family values" and attacks upon Clinton's character in his attempt to catch up in the polls. For three months Americans were captivated by the often bitter campaigning, the renewed candidacy of billionaire populist Ross Perot, and the presidential and vice-presidential debates that led to the crucial vote on November 3.

While the Democratic candidates focused on America's economic distress, forcefully reminding voters of the need for programs and policies targeted at improving the economy, Bush and Quayle, for their part, had considerable difficulty articulating a positive message. Clinton and Gore focused on jobs and the economy, Bush and Quayle preferred to talk about personalities and the perceived character flaws of Bill Clinton.

The peculiar candidacy of billionaire Ross Perot complicated the presidential campaign.

In the spring of 1992, Perot announced his intention to campaign as an independent presidential candidate if his name were placed on the ballot in every state. At first, Perot's blunt, no-nonsense, can-do style generated momentous excitement among voters who were tired of mainstream politicians. Perot made very effective use of television talk-show and call-in programs such as "Larry King Live" to present himself as an ordinary American tired of self-indulgent politicians who could not solve many of the problems they created. The Perot candidacy became a force to contend with, and by mid-June both major-party candidates began to assess the potential damage he could inflict on their campaigns.

But on the last day of the Democratic National Convention, Perot surprised his supporters by withdrawing from the race. Perot never fully explained his decision, though many analysts believed he had grown irritated with constant media scrutiny of his private life. He had won the support of many disaffected Republicans who could not yet bring themselves to back a Democrat. But many of these voters were now ready to take the plunge and give their support to Clinton.

However, to the surprise of many, Perot re-entered the race in the fall, claiming to be acting at the behest of the American people. At first, political observers greeted Perot's return with suspicion, believing that he could no longer have much impact on the presidential election after his initial withdrawal. But Perot soon re-established himself as a formidable presidential competitor, performing extremely well in the three presidential debates and again impressing voters as a plain-spoken man of action. The more money Perot spent, an estimated $60 million of his own funds, the higher his standing in the polls rose, and observers once again began to wonder how much the billionaire could affect the outcome of the election.

The Perot election balloon, however, could gain only so much altitude by late October. On November 3, Perot captured nearly 19 percent of the popular vote. This was the best showing for an independent presidential bid since Theodore Roosevelt's Bull Moose candidacy in 1912. Perot, however, carried no states and appeared to draw support away from Clinton and Bush in roughly equal percentages. Thus, despite its sound and fury, the Perot campaign ultimately had little effect upon the outcome of the election.

How the Democrats Won

After the gruelling campaign, the result was almost an anti-climax. The Clinton/Gore ticket earned a comfortable victory, winning 43 percent of the popular vote and 370 out of 538 electoral votes. Bush and Quayle received 38 percent of the popular vote and only 168 electoral votes. The economic recession, the end of the Cold War, and a more centrist Democratic party platform combined to oust the Republicans from the White House for the first time in 12 years.

In the immediate aftermath of the election, exit-polls confirmed that the single issue with the largest impact upon the election's outcome was the economy.[19] Nearly half of the voters surveyed cited jobs and the economy as their central concerns, and these voters supported the Democrats by a 2:1 margin. Among voters who felt that their own economic prospects were worsening, Clinton won by a 5:1 margin.

In contrast, Bush led Clinton by a 2:1 margin among voters citing the Republican theme of "family values" as an important issue. However, this major Republican focus was of concern to only one voter in seven. The once-powerful Republican tax issue had thoroughly lost its credibility in the face of Bush's failure to adhere to his own pledge never to raise taxes. Only one voter in seven cited taxes as an important issue. Twenty percent of those surveyed said that Bush's failure to keep his promise on taxes was "very important."

At the same time, the Democrats' racial strategy was successful. They had opted to ignore African-Americans and to court conservative whites, calculating that against the backdrop of economic hard times, African-Americans would have no choice but to support the Clinton ticket. This calculation proved to be correct. Conservative white voters in the North and South responded positively to Clinton's well-publicized conflicts with Jesse Jackson and other Clinton gestures designed to distance him from African-Americans.

After 12 years, the political coalition formed by Ronald Reagan in 1980 had been shattered. The Republicans' strongholds in the South and West had been breached. Many of the so-called blue-collar "Reagan Democrats," lured to the GOP by social, patriotic, foreign policy, and racial issues, had returned to the Democratic fold. Even the southern Bible belt – the prime target for the GOP's family values campaign – was attracted to a Democratic ticket featuring two southern Baptists. At the same time, the GOP's core upper-middle-class and business constituency could muster little enthusiasm for a Republican administration that had failed to hold the line on taxes and had allowed the economy to deteriorate while devoting its energy and attention to abortion and other social issues. As a result, Clinton outpolled Bush even in the GOP's traditional suburban strongholds. Indeed, according to the *New York Times* exit polls, among voters earning more than $75,000 a year, normally the country's most solid Republican group, Bush support fell from 62 percent in 1988 to 48 percent in 1992. Thus, on November 3, 1992, Americans elected a new president. For them, it was time for a change.

Congressional Elections

Neither the Democrats nor the Republicans were completely happy with the results of the 1992 congressional contest. In the Senate, the party balance remained basically unchanged. Prior to the election, the Democrats had held 57 seats and the Republicans 43. After the 1992 contest, the Democrats continued to hold 57 seats while the Republicans controlled 42. In the House of Representatives, the Republicans gained ten seats, giving the Democrats a 259:176 margin.

Some Democrats were disappointed that Clinton's victory in the presidential election did not bring Democratic gains in Congress. It remains to be seen if Clinton's victory was a **realigning election**. In their euphoria following Clinton's victory, however, most Democrats predicted that the new Congress would work effectively with the Clinton administration. For their part, Republicans were sorry that the public's alarm over congressional scandals and Americans' mood to punish **incumbents** did not result in more Republican congressional victories. However, Republican congres-

sional leaders breathed a sigh of relief that the collapse of the Bush campaign had not undermined their own positions.

However partisan it might be, the new Congress reflected a number of the changes manifesting themselves in American society during the past decade. Most striking was the comparatively large number of women elected to the House and even to the Senate. Women had been mobilized for political action in the wake of the Clarence Thomas confirmation hearings. Now, 47 women had won election to the House of Representatives (compared to 28 in the previous House), and four women had won election to the Senate, creating a total of six women in the upper chamber. One of these women, Carol Moseley Braun (D-Ill.), became the first African-American woman ever elected to serve in the Senate. Two women now represented California: Dianne Feinstein and Barbara Boxer.

African-American and Hispanic-American representation in Congress also increased in 1992; the former rose from 25 to 37 and the latter from 11 in the old House to 18 in the new one. Four Asian-Americans also were elected to the House. One, Jay C. Kim, former Republican mayor of Diamond Bar, California, became the first Korean-American elected to Congress. Increased minority-voter registration coupled with the redrawing of congressional district boundaries to enhance African-American and Hispanic-American representation had achieved their purpose.

When it was all over, Americans had elected 11 new senators and 110 new House members in 1992. This was the largest group of congressional freshmen elected to Congress since 1948, larger even than the group of

447

newcomers brought in by Lyndon Johnson's landslide victory in 1964, or by the post-Watergate election in 1974. However, this huge freshman class could not be said to signal a clear or consistent message from the electorate.

The American electoral process had fulfilled its basic function of giving the citizens a periodic opportunity to review and change the performance of political leaders. However, there is little indication that even presidential elections are important enough to many Americans to increase voter participation much above 50 percent. Recent presidential elections have not involved rivetting issues that inspire voter turnout or divide Americans into rival political camps. As in Canada, leadership seems to dominate the decision of the American voter. The Democratic and Republican parties still play an important role, even though voters are increasingly likely to make independent judgements about the leadership qualities of presidential candidates. The parties are also still a major force in local, state, and congressional races. Thus, from the standpoint of encouraging executive responsiveness to the people, the American political party system appears to function adequately.

References

1. T.H. Jacobson, "Primitive Democracy in Ancient Mesopotamia," *Journal of New Eastern Studies* 11 (1943): 159-172.

2. R.J. Dalton, *Citizen Participation in Western Democracies* (London: Chatham House Publishing, 1988); Richard Leonard and Richard Natkiel, *World Atlas of Elections: Voting Patterns in 39 Democracies* (Ann Arbor, MI: The University of Michigan Press, 1986); G. Bingham Powell, "American Voter Turnout in Comparative Perspective," *American Political Science Review* 80 (March 1986): 17-44.

3. Joseph Wearing, *The Ballot and its Message: Voting in Canada* (Toronto: Copp Clark Pitman, 1991), 223-236.

4. Paul Fox, ed., "Electing a Canadian Government," *Politics: Canada,* 5th ed. (Toronto: McGraw-Hill Ryerson Ltd., 1982), 368.

5. F. Fletcher and D. Taras, "Images and Issues: The Mass Media and Politics in Canada," in Michael Whittington and Glen Williams, *Canadian Politics in the 1990s* (Scarborough, ON: Nelson Canada, 1990), 221-246; Gerald Caplan, Michael Kirby, and Hugh Segal, *Election: The Issues, the Strategies, the Aftermath* (Scarborough, ON: Prentice-Hall Canada, 1989).

6. Sidney Verba et al., *Participation and Political Equality: A Seven-Nation Comparison* (New York: Cambridge University Press, 1978); and Samual Barnes et al., *Political Action: Mass Participation in Five Western Democracies* (Beverly Hills, CA: Sage Publications, 1979); and Jon Pammett, "Elections," in M. Whittington and G. Williams, *Canadian Politics in the 1990s* (Scarborough, ON: Nelson Canada, 1990), 268-84.

7. Ronald McDonald and Mark Ruhl, *Party Politics and Elections in Latin America* (Boulder, CO: Westview Press, 1989); and Howard Wiarda and Harvey Kline, *Latin American Politics and Development* (Boulder, CO: Westview Press, 1989).

8. Richard Rose, *International Almanac of Electoral History* (Washington, D.C.: Congressional Quarterly, Inc., 1991).

9. J.P. Johnston and H.E. Pasis, eds., *Representation and Electoral Systems: Canadian Perspectives* (Scarborough, ON: Prentice-Hall Canada, 1990).

10. William Irvine, "The Electoral System: The Laws of Political Science as Applied to the 1988 Federal Election" in Hugh Thorburn, ed., *Party Politics in Canada,* 6th ed. (Scarborough, ON: Prentice-Hall Canada, 1991), 87-93.

11. See Paul Fox, "Should Canada Adopt Proportional Representation?" in Paul Fox and Graham White, *Politics: Canada,* 7th ed. (Toronto: McGraw-Hill Ryerson Limited, 1991), 343-350.

12. Alan R. Ball, *Modern Politics and Government,* 4th ed. (London: Macmillan Education Ltd., 1988), 90-93.

13. Royal Commission on Electoral Reform and Party Financing, *Report,* 4 Vols. (Ottawa: The Canada Communication Group – Publishing, 1992).

14. Lawrence Leduc and Richard Price, "Campaign Debates and Party Leader Images: The 'Encounter 88 Case,' " (Victoria, B.C.: Canadian Political Science Association, 1990); David Lanoue "Debates that Mattered: Voters' Reaction to the 1984 Canadian Leadership Debates," *Canadian Journal of Political Science* (March, 1991): 51-65; Lawrence LeDuc and Richard Price, "Great Debates: The Televised Leadership Debates of 1979," *Canadian Journal of Political Science* (March, 1985): 135-153.

15. Janine Brodie, *Women and Politics in Canada* (Toronto: McGraw-Hill Ryerson Limited, 1985); Nancy Adamson et al., *Feminist Organizing For Change* (Toronto: Oxford University Press, 1988), 3-26.

16. James Wilson, *American Government,* 5th ed. (Lexington, MA: D.C. Heath and Company, 1992), 171-182.

17. Stephen Wayne, *The Road to the White House 1992* (New York: St Martin's Press, 1992), 1-15.

18. Bill Clinton and Al Gore, *Putting People First: How We Can Change America* (New York: Times Books, 1992).

19. Thomas Edsall and E. J. Dionne, Jr., "Younger, Lower-Income Voters Spurn GOP," *Washington Post*, Nov., 1992.

Suggested Readings

Elections Canada. *Towards the 35th General Election: Report of the Chief Electoral Officer of Canada* (Ottawa: Chief Electoral Officer of Canada, 1994).

Keith Archer, *Political Choices and Electoral Consequences* (Montreal: McGill-Queen's University Press, 1990).

Herbert Asher, *Presidential Elections and American Politics* (New York: Wadsworth, 1992).

Tom Brook, *Getting Elected in Canada* (Stratford, ON: Mercury Press, 1991).

Frank Conley, *General Elections Today* (Manchester: Manchester University Press, 1990).

Murray Dobbin, *Preston Manning and the Reform Party* (Toronto: James Lorimer & Company Ltd. Publishers, 1992).

Mark Franklin, Tom Mackie, and Henry Valen, *Electoral Change* (New York: Cambridge University Press, 1992).

Benjamin Ginsberg, *Do Elections Matter?* (New York: M.E. Sharpe, 1991).

Paul John and Harvey Pasis, *Representation and Electoral Systems* (Scarborough, ON: Prentice-Hall Canada, 1990).

Andrew Reeve and Alan Ware, *Electoral Systems: A Comparative and Theoretical Introduction* (New York: Routledge, 1991).

Glossary

absolute majority: A number of votes equal to more than 50 percent of the eligible votes cast.

aggregate: The process by which two or more individuals or groups combine their demands to seek a common political objective.

ballot: Derived from the term "ballotta," a round bullet, this word eventually came to mean a voice or a lot used in the act of voting, usually in secret, by written or printed tickets or slips of paper.

caucus: A closed meeting of the members of a political party, either to select a candidate for office or to discuss a legislative position.

chief electoral officer: In Canada, an independent official who is responsible to the House of Commons and sets the election machinery in motion.

compulsory voting: Electoral participation by qualified voters that is required by law as used in Australia, Belgium, the Netherlands, Austria, Brazil, Italy, and other states.

dark horse: An unexpected compromise candidate who is nominated for office by a political party after a series of deadlocks over more conspicuous contenders.

demagogue: A person who takes political advantage of social and political unrest through the use of highly emotional and prejudiced appeals to the general population or a particular segment of the general population.

electorate: All persons taken as a group who have qualifications to vote in an election.

enfranchisement: The extension of the right to vote to certain groups and categories of individuals formerly excluded by law or procedure.

gubernatorial: Of or relating to the office of governor, whose functions include the management of state governments in the United States and other nation-states.

homeostasis: A biological term meaning the internal equilibrium of an organism. In a political context, homeostasis is the tendency in a social or political system to stabilize by means of self-adjustments (such as elections) that counter or compensate for disruptive and destabilizing influences.

hustings: Any place where political campaign speeches are made.

incumbent: The person currently in office.

majority system: An electoral system requiring either a plurality or an absolute majority to elect representatives to an organization or political institution.

party boss: A person who heads a political machine and who manipulates political power in a particular area (state, county, city), especially through the use and control of patronage.

party convention: A special meeting held by a political party to select its leadership candidates, write a platform, choose a national or provincial committee, and otherwise conduct party business.

party-list system: A method of electing representatives to multi-member constituencies. Political parties prepare lists of their candidates from which electors may choose, or they must vote for the list in its entirety as prepared by the party.

plurality: The number of votes secured by a candidate that is more than the number obtained by any rival candidates for office and may be less than a majority of total votes cast.

political succession: The transfer of leadership and the exercise of power from one person or group of persons to another by violent or nonviolent means.

preferential ballot: An electoral form that permits the voter to mark the candidates in the order of his or her preference by placing numbers rather than Xs beside candidates' names.

proportional representation: A multi-member electoral system in which each qualified party wins seats in a legislature in proportion to its total popular vote.

proxy voting: Allows a person in the same category to vote for another elector who is unable because of their occupations, such as students, fishers, prospectors, topographers, mariners, and air crews. In Canada, the proxy ballot was replaced by the special ballot in 1993.

realigning election: Amid widespread social change caused by past economic dislocations and a lack of response by the majority party, the minority party seizes upon the new issues, as millions of voters transfer their support and demand fundamental policy changes in government.

returning officer: In Canada, a person from each riding appointed by order in council to supervise the conduct of the election after writs of election are issued by the chief electoral officer.

riding: A legislative constituency from which an individual is elected with the charge to act on behalf of the people residing within the constituency.

run-off ballot: A final election to break a tie or to force a majority of support for one candidate.

single-transferable-vote system: A system of selecting representatives for a multi-member constituency whereby once a candidate receives a certain number of votes determined by a quota to get elected, any additional votes are transferred to other candidates that may require more votes to fill the quota.

spin doctors: Loyal party supporters whose role it is to "spin" positive opinions about their leaders and policies to other party members and the media, and to create negative opinions about their political enemies.

universal suffrage: The right of all qualified voters to participate in the electoral process of a political system through the use of the vote.

THIRTEEN

The International System

Canadian peacekeepers with the UN forces in Bosnia

Chapter Objectives

After reading this chapter, you will be able to:

■ define international system and understand the scope of the international community

■ identify the components of the international system and discuss how they are interrelated

■ classify international organizations by purpose and function

■ recount the development of the United Nations and outline what each of the major organs does

■ describe the role and purpose of other international organizations, such as NATO, the GATT, and the Organization of American States

■ define and describe the role of multinational corporations and non-governmental organizations in the development of the international system

■ explain the presence and operation of trans-national groups on the dynamics of the international system

■ discuss the directions towards which the international community appears to be moving

■ describe Canada's role in global affairs

■ identify the advantages and disadvantages of the North American Free Trade Agreement (NAFTA)

What is the International System?

Think of the world as an economic and political community made up of state and non-state actors.[1] Today, this global community is complexly interdependent. The actions of one actor on any number of participants can touch and affect the lives of people anywhere. By the 1990s, Canada was supporting nearly 5000 development projects in over 100 countries. In the last decade of the twentieth century, fewer than 500 multinational corporations (MNCs) control over 30 percent of the financial resources of the planet. In Lockerbie, Scotland, Pan American Flight 103 is blown out of the sky by a terrorist's bomb. In Canada, an organization called *MATCH* International supports projects that help women in the developing world obtain better health care, refuge from violence, child care options, occupational training, and employment. In 1989, a United Nations-sponsored treaty to control the proliferating trade in hazardous waste is unanimously approved by 116 states, including Canada. Peter Lown and Yevgeny Chazov, co-founders of International Physicians for the Prevention of Nuclear War, are two individuals who have affected the international system by their will and energies to work for peace.

The above examples serve to identify the six types of actors in the contemporary global system: states, international organizations, multinational corporations, non-governmental organizations, trans-national groups, and individuals.

Until the twentieth century, students of comparative international politics assumed that the state was the core unit of the international system and that knowledge of interstate relations was all that was necessary to understand and explain events in the global political system. Most present-day students of global politics still recognize the importance of a state-centric perspective in world affairs, but they are also aware that the global political system consists of many other autonomous actors interacting in patterned ways to influence the character of the system.[2] While still accepting the principal role played by states, it is no longer possible to ignore the presence of non-state actors and the challenges they make to the dominance of states in the global system. There is a growing recognition that the vast majority of states are no longer able to cope with the new global problems emerging from development, the environment, food, space, and technology. Governments are aware that they cannot solve the world's problems alone and recognize the need for international co-operation.

Nation-States

The predominant actors of the international system are sovereign and independent states. On close examination, the international system reflects their behaviour and decisions. Nation-states create the rules of the system: they trade with, aid, and invest in one another; they form international organizations; they host multinational corporations; they exchange diplomats; their citizens interact with foreign nationals; they sign treaties and they go to war. They also set the tone and establish the character of relations within the international system. They can engage in relations of consensus, relations of overt manipulation, or relations of coercion.

In the latter part of the twentieth century, the viability of the nation-state has been challenged by many factors. The destructive power of contemporary weapons, the interdependence of the global economy, the international character of environmental pollution and energy conservation, the internationalization of the mass media – all these challenge the capacity of individual sovereign states to survive as independent autonomous members in the international system.

These global challenges now affect the laws and customs of the world community, and may lead to the creation of new international instruments for the resolution of international conflict. The nation-state, as it first evolved, was a response to challenges that were beyond the problem-solving capacity of small principalities and kingdoms. The present character of human problems on the global scale is likely to produce an increase in the building of new regional and global international institutions. The state is not likely to wither away in the face of these challenges, but it may have to surrender more of its autonomous decision-making capacities to supranational institutions.

The 12-member *European Union* (EU) is a regional approach to trade and political and economic integration. With a 567-member European Parliament, a system of courts, a Common Agricultural Policy (CAP), and a European Monetary System (ESM), the EU is committed to completing the integration of goods and services. Other such supranational efforts have begun in Central and South America, as well as in the Caribbean. Likewise, the proliferation of multinational corporations, such as Exxon Corporation, International Telephone and Telegraph (ITT), and International Business Machines (IBM), has created new international approaches to trade, the flow of capital and labour across national boundaries, and the planning of production for the global marketplace. Many of these massive corporations, with their equally enormous assets, escape national regulation simply because their decision-making centres are beyond the reach of individual states.

The predominance of the state is also threatened internally by decentralizing tendencies. As large centralized bureaucracies, modern states are domestically pressured to respond to the special needs of certain regions and groups. The internal adjustments required to accommodate these kinds of pressures have strengthened the functions of subnational and regional governments. The efficient management of national resources, the response to language, religious, and minority rights have all weakened the traditional sovereign preserves of national governments and their state bureaucracies. In order for people to accomplish their purposes, they have had to form even larger political and economic associations. The modern nation-state as we know it, with its strong tendency toward autonomy and independence, is required to accommodate these new forces of international co-operation.

International Organizations

International organizations are unique constructs within the world community. They are formed solely on the consent of states, groups

Table 13.1:
Principal multi-purpose IGOs

Name	Date Formed	Membership 1993
Organization of American States (OAS)	1948	35
Organization of African Unity (OAU)	1963	51
Commonwealth	1926	60
Council of Europe	1949	26
Organization of Central American States (ODECA)	1952	5
Andean Group	1969	5
Association of Southeast Asian Nations (ASEAN)	1967	5
League of Arab States	1945	21

Source: Brian Hunter, ed., *The Stateman's Yearbook*, 1993-94
(London: The Macmillan Press Ltd., 1993).

of non-governmental organizations (NGOs), and the private associations of individuals with trans-national goals. Once formed, international organizations take on a life of their own, establishing a global presence greater than the sum of their parts. They perform a multiplicity of functions that give the international system rules, structures, and interdependence. These functions involve **collective security**, conferences, global and regional research, cultural ties, diplomacy, international administration, international economic co-operation, international law, international social co-operation, international trade, the peaceful settlement of disputes, scientific exchanges, world business, world communications, and world travel. All international organizations establish permanent organizations staffed by international civil servants whose ideas and attitudes transcend national interests. The frequent interactions of these people gradually build attitudes and customs that foster an ideology of internationalism.

International Governmental Organizations (IGOs)

International governmental organizations are voluntary associations of two or more sovereign states that meet regularly and have full-time staffs. IGOs may be described according to their size of membership or the scope of their goals. Only one organization, the United Nations, approaches global membership, with over 180 member states. Regional organizations, such as the Organization of American States (OAS), the Organization of African Unity (OAU), and the Association of Southeast Asian Nations (ASEAN), are multi-

Table 13.2:
Principal functional-regional IGOs

Name	Date Formed	Membership
Benelux Economic Union (Benelux)	1948	3
European Coal and Steel Community (ECSC)	1952	12
European Union (EU)	1967	12
European Free Trade Association (EFTA)	1960	7
European Atomic Energy Community (Euratum)	1958	12
Organization for Economic Co-operation and Development (OECD)	1961	24
Latin American Integration Association	1981	11
Southern Cone Common Market	199	14
Central American Common Market (CACM)	1961	5
Arab Common Market	1965	21
Council for Technical Co-operation in South and Southeast Asia (Colombo Plan)	1950	26
Caribbean Community (CARICOM)	1973	13
Inter-American Development Bank (IDB)	1959	43
African Development Bank (AFDB)	1964	47
Asian Development Bank (ASDB)	1966	42
Central American Bank of Economic Integration (CBEI)	1961	5
European Investment Bank (EIB)	1958	12
Organization of Petroleum Exporting Countries (OPEC)	1960	13

purpose IGOs that have limited memberships based on the geographical proximity of states sharing common interests (table 13.1).

Many IGOs are formed as voluntary associations of independent states from various regions of the world that have some common purpose for co-operating with one another.

For example, the 60 members of the Commonwealth of Nations are drawn from Africa, Asia, Europe, Oceania, and the Western hemisphere. These states were once part of the British Empire and freely co-operate and assist one another without formal agreements. Another example is the Organization of Petro-

Table 13.3:
Principal collective-security IGOs

Name	Date Formed	Membership
North Atlantic Treaty Organization (NATO)	1949	16
Australia, New Zealand, United States Security Treaty Organization (ANZUS)	1952	3
Western European Union (WEU)	1954	9

Source: Brian Hunter, ed., *The Statesman's Yearbook*, 1992-93
(London: The Macmillan Press Ltd., 1993)

leum Exporting Countries (OPEC), which is a functional IGO consisting of a group of thirteen oil-exporting countries that formed an intergovernmental **cartel** to regulate the production, distribution, and pricing of oil (table 13.2). A number of IGOs have a security orientation and collectively form a military alliance system for defence (table 13.3).

At the turn of the century, less than ten IGOs existed. By World War I there were 50 IGOs. The rapid expansion of IGOs has taken place in the post-World War II era: from 1945 to the present, the number of IGOs grew from 90 to over 400.[3] This represents the birth of an enormous number of international organizations in a very brief period, historically speaking. The international system has become highly interactive and bureaucratized. What Marshall McLuhan described as the "global village" is under construction at the international level.

Why IGOs Multiply

There are several reasons for the continuous proliferation of international bodies at this time in human history. One is the realization in the minds of most national policy-makers that no state acting alone can prevent war and that a world composed of autonomous and nationalistic actors greatly enhances the possibility of violent conflict. The mass destructive powers of modern conventional and nuclear weapons have made war between any two states a global concern. No longer is it possible to isolate the destructive effects of contemporary warfare from all of humankind or from all living things on this planet.

Many of the IGOs created since World War II address themselves to the issues of war and peace – applying their skills of negotiation and communication rather than the destructive technologies of war. One of the most recent international creations is the Gulf Co-operation Council, established in March 1991 by the Declaration of Damascus, which committed Bahrain, Kuwait, Oman, Qatar, Saudi Arabia, the United Arab Emirates, Egypt, and Syria to form a regional peace-keeping force and an aid fund to promote development among member states.

Another reason for the rapid growth of IGOs has been the great advances made in the technology of human communication. Instantaneous global telecommunications informs and alerts people about events in every corner of the world. Today, governments have immediate access to one another. The ability of diplomats and policy-makers to travel long distances in short periods of time has been an impetus for governments to participate in international organizations and to co-operate on solutions to international problems.

Other reasons for the increasing number of IGOs as actors in the international arena have been global problems of poverty, starvation, underdevelopment, and disease. Governments have involved themselves in controlling these problems on a co-operative global level through the vehicles of international organizations. While humanitarianism may appear to be the main thrust behind the inclinations of governments to use international instruments to attack these problems, many governments are also motivated by practical expediency, as when developed economies apply their aid programs to developing economies so as to create new markets for their manufacturing and service sectors.

The United Nations System

Yet another factor contributing to the widespread recognition that multinational organizations are needed to address complex human problems is the expansion of the international civil service. By the 1990s, over 60,000 people world-wide were employed on a full-time basis by IGOs. They administer the resolutions and international policies of global and regional institutions. International civil servants tackle the world's pressing problems with solutions that rise above the national perspective. They are much less inclined to accept the narrow nationalistic approaches to international difficulties than are bureaucrats of autonomous governments.

The United Nations

The United Nations (UN) is the world's first IGO ever to gain the membership of over 90 percent of the states in the international community.[4] Membership is open to all independent nation-states upon recommendation of the Security Council. By 1993, there were 166 member states with most new members entering as former republics of the Soviet Union. It is the most representative intergovernmental forum ever organized by humankind. No other public institution in history has been mandated to accumulate and correlate information about every kind of global concern. The United Nations and its related agencies gather data on the frequency of international co-operation and conflict; on human rights; on variations in the key indicators of the international economic system – trade, investment, and development assistance; on world population trends; on the global demography of disease; on the global ecology; and on food, energy, and development. In short, the world is a United Nations' study.

The United Nations owns 20 acres of land donated by John Rockefeller for use as international territory. As an organization, the United Nations makes its own rules, has its own flag, and operates its own police force. It also owns a multilingual radio station, a post office, and a stamp mint. It uses six official languages: Arabic, Chinese, English, French, Russian, and Spanish. The United Nations is not a *supranational organization*, nor is it a **world government**. There are no citizens, taxes, or a regular army. It is the voluntary association of sovereign independent states for the purpose of dialogue to keep peace in the world. It serves as the only IGO capable of global decision-making. Through its organizations, it attempts to foster peaceful relations among states and to promote economic equality and human rights for all people.

■ ■ **world government:** the age-old concept of a global set of governing institutions that would make laws binding on all national and international actors which would surrender many of their sovereign rights to a supra-national authority. ■ ■

Prime Minister Mackenzie King signed the United Nations Charter on June 26, 1945. Even before the charter was drafted, Canada played an important role in the formulation of the United Nations system. Canada participated in the Dumbarton Oaks conferences in 1944 and at the United Nations Conference on International Organizations in 1945 at San Francisco. Canada also participated in the establishment of the principal organs of the United Nations. Presently, Canada contributes nearly $25 million to the general operation fund of the United Nations (not including its financial commitments to UN peacekeeping and specialized agencies).

The Security Council

Of these agencies, the *Security Council* has the primary responsibility, under the charter, for the maintenance of international peace and security. In general, the council is charged with implementing the **peaceful settlement of disputes** and may consider any action viewed by its members as a threat to peace, a breach of peace, or an act of aggression subject to investigation. After investigating a dispute, the council is empowered to make recommendations for the peaceful resolution of conflict. At the 2,693d session of the Security Council in 1990, Resolution 678 authorized member states to use armed force against Saddam Hussein unless he withdrew his occupying troops from Kuwait, legitimizing Operation Sandstorm in the Gulf War. In 1992, the Security Council sent peacekeeping forces to Cambodia and the former Yugoslavia to try to bring internal wars in those areas to an end. And in 1994, in an attempt to put an end to ethnic violence and genocide, the Security Council approved the movement of French troops into western Rwanda; the U.S. was also granted the right to invade Haiti with the goal of reinstating its democratically-elected president, Jean-Bertrand Aristide.

The Security Council consists of five permanent members (China,[5] France, Great Britain, Russia, and the United States) and ten non-permanent members elected by the General Assembly for two-year terms. Each of the five permanent members can veto an action deliberated by the council. In order for the council to take an action against a violator of the charter, the five permanent members must be in agreement on that action. In addition, a minimum of four non-permanent members must concur with the same action. Since 1945, Canada has been on the Security Council four times for two-year periods in 1948-1949, 1958-1959, 1967-1968, and 1977-1978. In 1988, Canada was once again elected to the council for a fifth time, after

Figure 13.1:
Flow chart of the United Nations

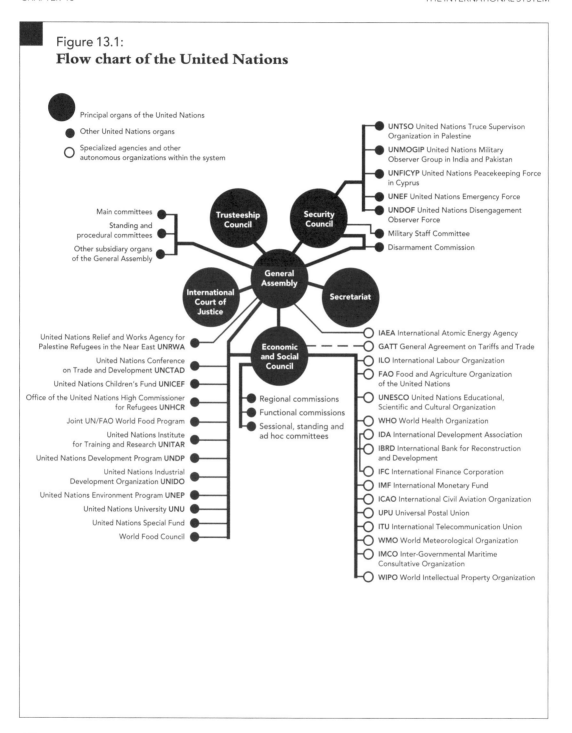

Principal organs of the United Nations

Other United Nations organs

Specialized agencies and other autonomous organizations within the system

Main committees

Standing and procedural committees

Other subsidiary organs of the General Assembly

Trusteeship Council

Security Council

UNTSO United Nations Truce Supervison Organization in Palestine

UNMOGIP United Nations Military Observer Group in India and Pakistan

UNFICYP United Nations Peacekeeping Force in Cyprus

UNEF United Nations Emergency Force

UNDOF United Nations Disengagement Observer Force

Military Staff Committee

Disarmament Commission

General Assembly

International Court of Justice

Secretariat

United Nations Relief and Works Agency for Palestine Refugees in the Near East **UNRWA**

United Nations Conference on Trade and Development **UNCTAD**

United Nations Children's Fund **UNICEF**

Office of the United Nations High Commissioner for Refugees **UNHCR**

Joint UN/FAO World Food Program

United Nations Institute for Training and Research **UNITAR**

United Nations Development Program **UNDP**

United Nations Industrial Development Organization **UNIDO**

United Nations Environment Program **UNEP**

United Nations University **UNU**

United Nations Special Fund

World Food Council

Economic and Social Council

Regional commissions

Functional commissions

Sessional, standing and ad hoc committees

IAEA International Atomic Energy Agency

GATT General Agreement on Tariffs and Trade

ILO International Labour Organization

FAO Food and Agriculture Organization of the United Nations

UNESCO United Nations Educational, Scientific and Cultural Organization

WHO World Health Organization

IDA International Development Association

IBRD International Bank for Reconstruction and Development

IFC International Finance Corporation

IMF International Monetary Fund

ICAO International Civil Aviation Organization

UPU Universal Postal Union

ITU International Telecommunication Union

WMO World Meteorological Organization

IMCO Inter-Governmental Maritime Consultative Organization

WIPO World Intellectual Property Organization

having vigorously campaigned on its general role in the United Nations and on its four decades of peacekeeping.

The General Assembly

The second principal organ of the United Nations is the *General Assembly*. This is the only body of the United Nations in which all member states are represented. Each of the 180 members has one vote. The General Assembly may discuss any question that falls within the scope of the United Nations Charter or that relates to the powers and functions of any other organ of the world forum. It may make recommendations to member states, as well as to the Security Council. In 1989, for the first time, the assembly moved to Geneva for a few days during its regular session. It did so to hear the chairman of the Palestine Liberation Organization (PLO), Yasser Arafat, after the United States refused to grant him an entry visa.

Decisions of the assembly have no binding legal force on governments, but they do have a **quasi-legal** character because these decisions carry the weight of international opinion as expressed by the members. Three instruments are used by the General Assembly to formulate a consensus of world opinion.

The first is a General Assembly *declaration*: a broad statement of general principal on an important global concern. The Universal Declaration of Human Rights passed in 1948, and the Declaration of the Establishment of a New International Economic Order (NIEO) in 1974 are examples of such an instrument generating world expectations. A General Assembly *resolution* is another quasi-legal in-

■ ■ **quasi-legal:** this term is used when people in positions of public and/or legislative authority use their discretion to investigate the facts or draw conclusions from facts in their official capacity. ■ ■

strument of world opinion. Resolutions recommend that member states follow a particular policy action. For example, in the 1980s and early 1990s the General Assembly passed numerous resolutions; these included resolutions to implement the UN plan for the independence of Namibia (1989), to acknowledge the proclamation of the Palestinian state (1989), and to implement a global effort to protect the biosphere (1992). In the first 40 years of assembly business, it has adopted countless resolutions and declarations, thereby establishing the norms of international conduct. For example, during that time, the assembly has passed nearly 70 resolutions on the subject of disarmament and proclaimed the 1990s as the Third Disarmament Decade.

Finally, a General Assembly *convention* is a legally binding instrument because it is a treaty requiring the ratification of signatory states – states that are then bound by its terms. There are two types of conventions: multilateral treaties passed by the General Assembly and ratified by member states, and a United Nations treaty with a state, as when Egypt in 1956 signed a treaty with the world body to allow multinational peacekeeping forces to enter Egyptian territory.

The assembly has also assumed the power to conciliate international disputes and to make recommendations for collective measures against an aggressor. The **Uniting for Peace Resolution** of 1950 gives the assembly a back-up role to the Security Council when that body is prevented from taking action by a veto of a permanent member. A series of stalemates in the Security Council led to special

Table 13.4:
Secretaries general of the United Nations, 1946–1994

Secretary General		years served
1st	Trygve Lie (Norway)	1946–53
2nd	Dag Hammarskjold (Sweden)	1953–61
3rd	U Thant (Burma)	1961–71
4th	Kurt Waldheim (Austria)	1972–81
5th	Javier Perez de Cuéllar (Peru)	1982–91
6th	Boutros Boutros Ghali (Egypt)	1991–

emergency sessions of the General Assembly to deal with Afghanistan (1980), Palestine (1980 and 1982), Namibia (1981), the Occupied Arab Territories (1982), and *apartheid* in South Africa (1989).

The 1950 resolution gives the General Assembly a critical role in peacekeeping when the Security Council is unable to fulfill its responsibility to maintain peace and security. Peacekeeping is not mentioned in the charter, but the organization has developed this method of dealing with conflict. Canada is the only state in the world that has participated in some way in *every* peacekeeping operation of the United Nations system. Canada has participated in such operations in the Middle East, India/Pakistan, West New Guinea, West Iran, Yemen, the Congo, Cyprus, and with the UN peacekeeping forces in Somalia and the new independent states of the former Yugoslavia. Canada also participated in non-UN peacekeeping activities in Indochina and Nigeria. Canada's major participation in peacekeeping began with the establishment of the United Nations Emergency Force (UNEF), which was established

after the Suez crisis in 1956. By 1993, Canada had contributed personnel to 17 peacekeeping missions since 1945, with its most recent commitments to Afghanistan, Iran/Iraq, in the former Yugoslavia, and in Somalia.

The Secretariat
The third major organ of the United Nations is the *Secretariat*. This is a body of international civil servants numbering over 20,000 people, one-third of whom work at United Nations headquarters in New York. The rest are dispersed in the Geneva office, as well as in the regional commissions operating in over 130 states. The Secretariat organizes conferences such as the United Nation Convention against Illicit Traffic in Narcotic Drugs and Psychotropic Substances (1988), collects and publishes data on world cultural, economic, and social trends, administers United Nations peacekeeping actions, and performs administrative, budgetary, and housekeeping functions. The Secretariat is headed by a secretary general (table 13.4), who is appointed by the General Assembly following a nomination by the Security Council.

The job of the secretary general is a complicated one that verges on the impossible. The secretary presides over a budget of just over $2 billion; is the chief administrator for the United Nations and for all its specialized agencies; and is also accredited as a diplomat plenipotentiary (possessing full powers) to the world, meaning that the secretary is expected to bring parties in dispute to a peaceful settlement by means of the mediating and conciliating instruments at the disposal of the United Nations. The secretary general is held responsible for the professional actions of thousands of international civil servants and must work to keep their loyalties in the face of mounting criticism that the United Nations is an ineffective IGO. The personality and political style of the secretary general are crucial to the success of the United Nations as a credible world forum.

The Economic and Social Council

The fourth principal organ of the UN is the *Economic and Social Council* (ECOSOC). It was established at the insistence of the developing states that participated in the drafting of the United Nations Charter in San Francisco. They justifiably saw the Security Council as dominated by the great post-war powers and considered the General Assembly too unwieldy to promote the welfare of the smaller powers. The present-day importance of ECOSOC is seen by the dramatic enlargement of that body from the original 18 members in 1946, to 27 after 1965, to 54 members after the charter amendment of 1971. All members are elected by a two-thirds vote of the General Assembly for three-year terms, 18 are elected each year. Canada was elected to a term on ECOSOC from 1987 until December 31, 1989.

ECOSOC conducts research on economic, educational, social and cultural problems: it drafts conventions that, when adopted by the General Assembly and ratified by member states, become international law. It co-ordinates the activities of 13 United Nation agencies. To assist in its operations, the council established six functional commissions (Human Rights, Narcotic Drugs, Population, Statistics, Status of Women, and Social Development). The council also administers five regional economic commissions: Economic Commission for Africa (ECA), Economic Commission for Europe (ECE), Economic Commission for Latin America (ECLA), Economic Commission for Asia and the Pacific (ECAP), and the Economic Commission for Western Asia (ECWA).

Of the principal organs of the United Nations, ECOSOC is the one most linked with all levels of the international community. It is authorized to advise and co-ordinate international programs with private organizations, generally referred to as non-governmental organizations (NGOs). By the 1990s, 700 or 20 percent of the NGOs operating in the United Nations member-countries were listed on the ECOSOC roster, sending observers to its meetings, submitting written and oral statements to the council's commissions, and influencing the direction of its programs around the world.

Finally, an appreciation of the importance and complexity of ECOSOC's global influence is seen in its consultative role to a number of other United Nations bodies offering programs in the economic and social fields. These bodies include: (1) the United Nations Development Program (UNDP); (2) the United Nations Children's Fund (UNICEF); (3) the

United Nations High Commissioner for Refugees (UNHCR); (4) the United Nations Conference on Trade and Development (UNCTAD); (5) the World Food Program (WFP); and (6) the United Nations University (UNU), which began operations in 1975 at its headquarters in Tokyo.

The Trusteeship Council

Another of the six principal organs is the United Nations *Trusteeship Council*. This body is also charged with the international supervision of trust territories. The membership of the council is composed of all trust-administering states, non-administering permanent members of the Security Council, and elective members drawn from the General Assembly. After World War II, the non-self-governing territories of the former League of Nations became trust territories. The Trusteeship Council has worked to prepare these territories for eventual independence, to hear petitions from trust-territory representatives, and to send visiting missions from time to time for on-the-spot supervision. For example, the trust territory of British Togoland merged with Ghana in 1957, Tanganyika became Tanzania in 1961, and New Guinea became Papua New Guinea in 1975. By 1982, ten of the 11 United Nations trust territories administered since 1946 had gained independence or had united with a neighboring nation-state. The only remaining territory is the Republic of Belau (Palau), administered by the United States, which defends its territory and provides financial support in its efforts to become independent.

The International Court of Justice

The sixth organ of the United Nations is the *International Court of Justice* (ICJ). The functions of this court are discussed in Chapter 14 (International Law). The ICJ was founded in 1945 as the judicial arm of the United Nations to rule on disputes arising between states and to advise the UN on matters of international law. The ICJ has judged cases whose issues have ranged from fisheries to border disputes to nuclear testing. However, the ICJ has been the least productive organ of the United Nations: in four decades of existence, it has reviewed only about 60 cases (excluding advisory opinions), most of them concerning minor disputes, such as establishing boundaries or determining fishing rights. Less than a third of the members of the United Nations have accepted the compulsory jurisdiction of the court, demonstrating a lack of confidence on the part of most states in conflict to seek a legal remedy from such a highly visible and respected body. A number of cases are dropped from the ICJ by the parties, some are settled out of court; the rest are removed because one party refuses to accept the ICJ's jurisdiction in the dispute.

During the 1980s, the United Nations experienced a decline in prestige and influence in world affairs. Perhaps unfairly, the world had expected too much from the resources it was providing to the UN. It blamed the United Nations for its failure to force South Africa to disgorge Namibia, to get the Cubans out of Angola, to get the Vietnamese out of Kampuchea, and for its own financial crisis as a global institution. But these assessments were unrealistic. The United Nations could never accomplish these goals without a collective change of attitude among its members, especially among the five permanent members of the Security Council.

An extraordinary outburst of common sense among the so-called "gang of five" – the permanent members of the Security Council – led to a great improvement in the international climate by the early 1990s. A number of actions reflected the new maturity among members of the Security Council, and led to international **détente** among members of the General Assembly. Increasingly, states in conflict have come to recognize that when they want the violence to stop, they go to the United Nations.

As an international organization, the United Nations is more than the sum of its parts. Since its conception during World War II, the United Nations has come to be regarded as an autonomous international actor. Its members speak and react to a common theme as if the UN were an independent entity, expressing itself authoritatively through its various organizations. No one of its members has the capacity – nor even the will – to eradicate world problems, but as a global forum, each is made aware of the need to do so. It is an effort on the part of the community of states to concur on norms of international conduct, to outlaw war, and to reduce conflictive behaviour. It provides for the peaceful settlement of international disputes, the regulation of armaments, the supervision of trust territories, and the co-operation of members in dealing with global economic and social problems. It is a human institution, reflecting the successes and failures of the humans who embody it.

So much has been expected of the United Nations. Many of these expectations were spawned in 1945: to beat swords into plowshares, to change the ways its members behave, and to make the lions lie with the lambs so there would be no more war. But in many ways, things are much the same as they were before; the new world order looks a lot like the old world order. Soldiers cross national borders killing enemy soldiers, civil wars abound, women are raped, and children are dying of starvation.

In response to these continuing human tragedies, the United Nations must reinvent itself every day. It has to learn how to move boldly and at the same time cautiously across the uncertain frontiers of the new world order.[6] There are bound to be disappointing moments along the way in a world of risks and opportunities. Yet every day the members of the United Nations have another chance to create the world of their charter: a world of justice, human rights, peace and security, and a better life for all. It's a tall order. Many have said the United Nations is fragile, but it has proven remarkably durable. Unlike its predecessor, the League of Nations, the United Nations is an international organization that almost no state has left.

> ■ ■ **détente:** a diplomatic term indicating a situation of lessened tension in relations between nation-states that is manifested by increased communication, negotiation and trade. ■ ■

Other International Organizations

The United Nations is the singular example of a broad-purpose world organization. All other IGOs neither approach global membership nor take the world perspective of the United Nations. Public international organizations with varying degrees of integration exist for the purposes of collective security, economic advancement, and multi-purpose regional alliances. The United Nations Charter supports the formation of regional IGOs as complementary institutions to the goals of the UN world organization, provided their actions are consistent with the charter (Articles 52-54). Examples of IGOs are the North Atlantic Treaty Organization (NATO), and the Organization of American States (OAS).

■ ■ **signatories:** under international law this usually refers to the party or parties signing a treaty. ■ ■

NATO

Since 1949, the North Atlantic Treaty Organization has functioned as a collective-security alliance of Western states against the perceived threat of communist aggression in the North Atlantic area.[7] NATO's 16 members – Belgium, Britain, Canada, Denmark, France, Greece, Iceland, Italy, Luxembourg, the Netherlands, Norway, Portugal, Spain (since 1982), Turkey, the United States, and Germany – form the largest and most highly organized international defence system in the world. Hungary received associate status to the alliance in 1991.

In 1994, NATO launched its "partnership for peace" program, which invites former members of the Warsaw Pact and the former Soviet republics to take part in a wide range of military co-operation arrangements. These arrangements do not necessarily imply full NATO membership or security guarantees. Russia joined the partnership, and other East-European states have expressed their intentions to join. Those states participating in the "partnership for peace" will take part in joint training and planning, and will possibly participate with NATO states in peacekeeping missions under the authority of the UN.

All the **signatories** of the North Atlantic Treaty agree that "an armed attack against one or more of the parties to the treaty in Europe or North America shall be considered an attack against them all." This collective-security provision legally requires member states to honour their commitments to take military action if aggression occurs against the **alliance**.

Collective security is supported by an extensive network of political and military structures designed to co-ordinate communications and decisions among members. The supreme governing organ of NATO is the *North Atlantic Council*, chaired by the secretary general of NATO in Brussels. The council consists of ministers of foreign affairs or defence and an ambassador from each of the NATO members. It meets at the ministerial level at least twice a year and at the ambassadorial level on a weekly basis. Its discussions and decisions flow from political/military matters, as well as from the financial and scientific aspects of defence planning.

In 1966, France decided to pull its armed forces out of the integrated military organization of NATO, but retained its political seat on the North Atlantic Council. Because of France's withdrawal, the other NATO states created a new committee, the *Defence Planning Committee* to determine military policy. The council and the Defence Planning Committee are chaired by the secretary general.

In over 40 years of existence, NATO has undergone stresses and strains in addition to a continuing consensus of support from its members. From time to time, European members have pushed to gain more control of the command structures of NATO, owing to the primacy of the United States and the often difficult defence relationships that member states have with this nuclear superpower.

In the past, a number of members have asserted their independence: the French withdrawal in 1966, for example. Canada reduced its NATO forces in Europe from 10,000 to 5000 in the early 1970s, but by 1990 had increased the number to 7500, and Greece withdrew its forces from NATO after Turkey's invasion of Cyprus in 1974, resuming full participation in 1980.

When the Warsaw Pact ceased to exist in 1991, NATO initiated a major review of its strategies on **nuclear deterrence**. Budget pressures and a changed geopolitical climate in Europe lessened the urgency to maintain such a formidable nuclear fortress in the area. By the fall of 1991, NATO announced that all tactical nuclear weapons fired by artillery or short-range rockets would be removed from Europe. Russia and France announced a temporary ban on all nuclear testing and called on other European states to make the ban lasting.

Reduction of the risk of nuclear war in Europe through arms control and confidence building has led to a major reassessment of NATO strategy and of NATO's relation to other international organizations associated with European security. In 1990, NATO's London Declaration made it clear that changed circumstances existed in Europe, permitting a major restructuring of military force commitments. In effect, the transformed environment in the international system with regard to superpower arms' competition had made reduced reliance on nuclear weapons possible. Europe could take greater control of its

own security needs in the 1990s by enhancing the European Union's defence functions; in such circumstances, NATO's role would have to change. But NATO displayed its special peacemaking role to United Nations peacekeeping forces in 1994 when it attacked Serb ground forces in Bosnia. The attack came when the Serbs continued to fire into the Muslim enclaves of Sarajevo and Gorazde after a cease-fire was declared earlier that year.

Despite a disparity of opinion on its role, NATO still enjoys widespread support in Europe, as well as in North America, as an IGO essential for the collective security of its membership and as a deterrent to possible Soviet aggression. Most Europeans, Americans, and Canadians agree on the need to participate in such an organization to protect the security of the North Atlantic community and to balance competitive military forces in Europe.

The General Agreement On Tariffs And Trade (GATT)

After World War II, a substantial number of the world's industrialized economies, spearheaded by Canada, the United States, and some West European nation-states, pushed to liberalize international trade among themselves. They considered the **protectionism** of the 1930s a significant factor in the rise of fascism, and as a major cause of the Second World War. Discussions on world trade policy began in 1943 among the Allies, leading to the implementation of a new international trading order under a treaty called the *General Agreement on Tariffs and Trade* (GATT) in 1947. The GATT treaty established an international organization to promote freer world trade and located its headquarters in Geneva, Switzerland.[8] Reflecting the liberal consensus in the post-war period, the GATT was based on free trade and non-discriminatory policies. The signatories of the GATT agreed to the **most-favoured-nation** principle, meaning that any favourable condition or privilege on trade given to one economy would automatically be extended to others.

In 1948, the GATT was institutionalized as an IGO, with a secretariat, a director general, and an administration to handle the work related to trade negotiations. By the early 1950s, the GATT had become the central international organization in the non-communist world committed to implementing a world trading regime, dedicated to the removal of trade barriers among members.

GATT's principal functions are dispute settlement and conference diplomacy. GATT uses panels of experts to handle complaints about violations of its trade rules that cannot be resolved through more routine consultation procedures. Conference diplomacy is the instrument used to organize *rounds* of multilateral trade negotiations that look for ways to cut trade barriers and liberalize international trade. The high point of trade co-operation in the GATT was the *Kennedy Round* of negotiations (named after U.S. President Kennedy) from 1963 to 1967, which culminated in the removal of many tariffs that had become serious obstacles to trade among the major trading economies.

Despite the success of the Kennedy Round, protectionism continued to flourish and still does in the world economy. The European Community (EC) – now called the European Union (EU) – and Japan placed re-

■ ■ **north-south axis:** the growing tension between the few economically developed economies of the North and the many deprived economies of the South. ■ ■

strictions on imports of agricultural products, cars, trucks, and other vehicles, electronics, and textiles. From 1967 onward, pressures for trade protectionism and discrimination increased in North America, Europe, and Japan. Canada and the United States demanded changes in the European and Japanese trade restrictions. By 1973 it was becoming clear that a *new international economic order* was emerging.

In September 1973, representatives of the 100 member states of GATT met in Tokyo to negotiate that new trade order. The *Tokyo Round* in the GATT ended in 1979, resulting in some reduction of tariff and non-tariff barriers. These trade talks continued in the 1980s into the 1990s as the *Uruguay Round,* which introduced the concept of a **North-South** dialogue, and negotiated many technical barriers to trade. When the most recent GATT round was launched in Punta del Esté, Uruguay, all members knew what was at issue. Either the GATT would dramatically expand its reach, or it would very probably fade into irrelevance.

The Uruguay Round opened in 1986 with an agenda that was complex and ambitious. There were fifteen negotiating committees with 108 states participating. They tackled the unfinished business of the Tokyo Round and brought in a new set of issues to resolve. The most important new issues included in the Uruguay Round were services, a vast sector embracing banking, insurance, telecommunications, construction, aviation, shipping, tourism, advertising, consultancy, and broadcasting. Other areas included the trade in intellectual property rights (TRIPs) and the trade in investment measures (TRIMs). TRIPs involves efforts to tighten the rules that protect patents, licences, trademarks, and copyrights against piracy. TRIMs addresses the taxation of investment portfolios and other fiscal and monetary instruments.

In 1994, after seven years of often bitter trade negotiations, more than 100 states signed the Uruguay Round accords of the GATT in Marrakech, Morocco. These signatories agreed to transform the small GATT secretariat into a trade watchdog with teeth called the World Trade Organization. The WTO will monitor the reduction of tariffs on a comprehensive list of trade items to an average of 40 percent. They will keep a close watch on any national laws that discriminate against goods.

The tortuous progress made at the Uruguay Round dramatized the enormous difficulties in liberalizing trade on a global scale for the benefit of developed and developing economies. Especially challenging has been the emergence since World War II of giant regional and bilateral trade blocs, such as the EU, an Asian group with Japan at the centre, and an expanding North American free-trade zone among Canada, Mexico, the United States. For strong supporters of GATT, the worry is that such powerful blocs, by leading a *balkanization* (or breakdown) of the global trading system, will eventually render GATT obsolete.

Seven Rounds of GATT negotiations since World War II have cut tariffs worldwide from 40 percent to just five percent in the 1990s. Nevertheless, in place of tariffs, member states have found newer, less overt ways to block trade under euphemisms such as "voluntary export restraints" and "orderly marketing arrangements." Many member states continue to subsidize agriculture, exempting farm trade from international trade law. Other economic sectors continue to be nurtured by the older instincts of protecting national economies from global influences and competition. But most of the world's trading economies are likely to continue to maintain a major stake in GATT if only because GATT is the only global rules-based regime for trade.

The Organization of American States (OAS)

In many respects, the OAS is the classic example of the type of multi-purpose regional organization endorsed by the Charter of the United Nations. The OAS is the most important IGO within the *inter-American system*. This hemispheric system now incorporates over 100 permanent and ad hoc bodies, which include committees, institutes, academies, congresses, conventions, courts, economic associations, and treaties. In effect, a system of international relationships has developed since the early nineteenth century based on the regular interaction and interdependence of the states of the Western hemisphere. What is noteworthy is that all these organizations set the Western hemisphere apart from the rest of the world as a regional international system.

The leading formal decision-making institution in this inter-American system is the OAS, established by the Ninth International Conference of American states at Bogota, Colombia, in 1948. Today the headquarters of the OAS are in Washington, D.C., where 35 regional states in the Americas meet to discuss regional economic, political, and military matters. Despite many invitations since the nineteenth century – the most recent from Colombia in 1984 – Canada did not join the OAS until 1989, and now participates as a full member of the inter-American system.[9] In 1991 the OAS achieved full regional membership of the 35 sovereign American states.

The largest decision-making body of the OAS is the *General Assembly*. It sits annually as a general conference of all members and has jurisdiction to consider any regional problem that a majority of its members wish to debate. The Permanent Council carries out directives of the assembly and performs pacific settlement functions when disputes among members are considered by the OAS. Two other bodies, the Inter-American Economic and Social Council and the Inter-American Council for Education, Science, and Culture sponsor conferences, draft treaties, and co-ordinate inter-American programs. When regional international disputes arise, the Meeting of Consultation of Ministers of Foreign Affairs is summoned at the request of a majority of members. The Inter-American Judicial Committee is a judicial advisory body of the OAS and promotes the codification and development of international law in the western hemisphere. In addition, special agencies, such as the Inter-American Development Bank (IDB), the Pan-American Institute of Geography and History (PAIGH), and the Inter-American Institute of Agricultural Science (IAIAS) – Canada participates as a full member in all three – function autonomously in support of general OAS objectives. The General Secretariat of the OAS, headed by a secretary-general, employs nearly 1400 staff workers and is the administrative arm of the OAS.

While the OAS functions as a general regional multi-purpose IGO, it also operates as a collective-security defence organization. All signatories to the charter of the OAS are automatically parties to the Inter-American Treaty of Reciprocal Assistance of 1947 (Rio Pact). This pact was originally drafted to deal with the threat of communism in the western hemisphere. The collective-security provisions of the treaty have been invoked on a number of occasions since it was adopted at Bogota in 1948: the Cuban Missile Crisis (1961-62), and the intervention of an OAS peace force in the Dominican Republic in 1965. The United States has played a dominant role in the application of this treaty because most Latin American governments depend on its superior military capacity to meet perceived threats of aggression.

In the area of the peaceful settlement of disputes, the OAS has played an important role, with the Permanent Council, the Meeting of Consultation of Ministers of Foreign Affairs, and the Inter-American Peace Commission serving as instruments through which **mediation** and **conciliation** have been attempted. Among the disputes considered by the OAS were those between Costa Rica and Nicaragua (1948-49, 1955-56, 1959); Honduras and Nicaragua (1957); Venezuela and the Dominican Republic (1960-61); Venezuela and Cuba (1963-64, 1967); the Dominican Republic and Haiti (1950, 1963-65); and Panama and the United States (1964 and 1989). The OAS was instrumental in resolving the "soccer war" between El Salvador and Honduras in 1969-70, and in 1980 a peace treaty between these states was deposited with the OAS. Argentina and Chile requested that the **Holy See** (a permanent observer of the OAS) mediate their disputes over the future of various island territories and maritime areas. And in 1981, the **good offices** of the OAS were used to restore peaceful relations between Ecuador and Peru. In 1982, the OAS adopted resolutions in support of Argentina during the Argentine-British war over the Falkland Islands. Latin American states upheld the provision of the Rio Pact "that an armed attack by any state against an American state shall be considered as an attack against all the American States." But the United States supported great Britain during the dispute and persuaded the Latin American members of the OAS to express mild denunciations of British military action in the General Assembly.

The OAS has served as a hemispheric instrument of economic and cultural co-operation. Through its various inter-American agencies, it has played a role in conducting research on economic and social problems, making recommendations directly to member governments, such as for the **Contadora Peace Initiative**. It has supported the work of the United Nations Economic Commission for Latin America (ECLA) and encouraged the founding of the Latin American Free Trade Association (LAFTA), the Central American Common Market (CACM), the Andean Group, and the Inter-American Development Bank (IDB).

There is no question that the overpowering presence of the United States, with its enduring and obvious effects on Latin American states, has generated a great deal of disillusionment among the other members of the OAS. The United States has used the OAS to provide a **multilateral** legitimacy to the implementation of its foreign policy goals in the western hemisphere. The United States has succeeded in converting its **unilateral** actions to the status of regional international "peacekeeping," often without consulting the OAS. The movement for an effective OAS was temporarily set back, for example, by the unilateral U.S. military intervention in Panama in 1989, but that event was transcended by an evolving consensus that hemispheric relations are best approached within established institutions of the inter-American system.

Multinational Corporations

Since World War II, multinational corporations (MNCs) have become major international actors.[10] More than any other actors in the international community, MNCs have transformed the global economy through their increased influence on four resources in the world economic system: capital, financing, marketing, and the technology of production and distribution. As corporations with a world focus, MNCs are the first institutions in human history, with the exception of the Vatican, dedicated to central planning on a global basis. According to Richard Barnett and Ronald Müller, "The rise of the planetary enterprise is producing an organizational revolution as profound in its implications for modern man as the Industrial Revolution and the rise of the nation-state itself."[11]

Multinational corporations are international actors because they conduct business activities and own assets beyond the jurisdiction of one state. They have political as well as economic impact on the international system because they move and control goods, services, money, personnel, and technology across national boundaries. As actors in the international economy, MNCs have tremendous bargaining powers with governments and international organizations. In the 1980s,

Table 13.5:

The 100 principal economic actors in the world, comparing MNC sales with the GNP of nation-states, 1993 (in billions of U.S. dollars)

1.	United States	$5678	51.	Israel	$47
2.	Japan	3389	52.	The Philippines	45
3.	Russia	2500	53.	Pakistan	43
4.	Germany	1504	54.	Malaysia	43
5.	France	874	55.	Colombia	43
6.	United Kingdom	858	56.	Venezuela	42
7.	Italy	844	57.	New Zealand	40
8.	Canada	517	58.	Ireland	39
9.	Spain	491	59.	*Du Pont*	38
10.	China	413	60.	*Texaco*	37
11.	Brazil	297	61.	Egypt	37
12.	South Korea	270	62.	*Chevron*	37
13.	Australia	254	63.	Iraq	35
14.	India	254	64.	Singapore	35
15.	Mexico	238	65.	Chile	32
16.	The Netherlands	222	66.	North Korea	30
17.	Taiwan	180	67.	*Chrysler*	29
18.	Austria	163	68.	*Boeing*	29
19.	Poland	159	69.	*Proctor & Gamble*	27
20.	Belgium	145	70.	United Arab Emirates	27
21.	East Germany	138	71.	Nigeria	27
22.	Sweden	138	72.	*Amoco*	26
23.	Switzerland	126	73.	Morocco	25
24.	*General Motors*	124	74.	Libya	24
25.	The Czech Republic	120	75.	*Shell Oil*	22
26.	The former Yugoslavia	120	76.	*United Technologies*	21
27.	Turkey	119	77.	Cuba	21
28.	*Exxon*	103	78.	Bangladesh	20
29.	South Africa	102	79.	Syria	20
30.	Indonesia	94	80.	Kuwait	20
31.	*Ford Motor*	89	81.	*Pepsico*	20
32.	Argentina	83	82.	*Eastman Kodak*	20
33.	Iran	80	83.	*Conagra*	20
34.	Saudi Arabia	79	84.	*Dow Chemical*	19
35.	Thailand	79	85.	Peru	19
36.	Denmark	78	86.	*McDonnell Douglas*	19
37.	Finland	77	87.	*Xerox*	18
38.	Greece	77	88.	*Atlantic Richfield*	18
39.	Norway	74	89.	*USX*	17
40.	Romania	70	90.	Myanmar (Burma)	17
41.	*IBM*	65	91.	Vietnam	15
42.	Hong Kong	64	92.	*RJR Nabisco Holdings*	15
43.	Hungary	61	93.	*Hewlett-Packard*	15
44.	*General Electric*	60	94.	*Tenneco*	14
45.	Portugal	58	95.	*Digital Equipment*	14
46.	*Mobil*	57	96.	*Minnesota Mining & Mfg.*	13
47.	Algeria	54	97.	*Westinghouse Electric*	13
48.	*Phillip Morris*	48	98.	*International Paper*	13
49.	Ukraine	48	99.	*Phillips Petroleum*	13
50.	Bulgaria	47	100.	*Sara Lee*	12

Source: International Monetary Fund (IMF), *International Financial Statistics* (Washington, D.C., 1993); *World Statistics in Brief* (New York: UN Publications, 1993); *Fortune* Magazine, (August, 1993).

evidence surfaced to show how one multinational corporation (ITT) undermined the economy of Chile in the early 1970s – it encouraged credit and loan terminations, caused fuel and weapons shipment delays, organized copper boycotts, intervened in the internal political affairs of the Chilean government, and sponsored a global propaganda effort to topple President Salvadore Allende. Actions such as these demonstrate the power of global corporations to change the international political system. The power of international companies is measured by their world-wide financial flexibility and influence, whereas the power of nation-states and their governments is essentially limited to that exercised within their territorial jurisdictions.

If we think of these two types of international actors (MNCs and nation-states) as economic units competing for dominance in a global economic system, we may make some interesting observations (table 13.5.) The annual sales of MNCs are comparable to the gross national product of national economies. General Motors, for example, is bigger than the combined GNPs of Israel, New Zealand, and Venezuela; Ford is bigger than South Africa.

By the 1990s, the world's 500 largest MNCs controlled over $5 trillion in assets, produced nearly $200 billion of the world's gross economic product and employed over 26 million people. Forty of the world's 100 principal economic actors were MNCs, and out of 185 nation-states, over 100 states had less economic strength than did these 40 global enterprises. Today over 7500 MNCs control and operate more than 27,000 subsidiaries that employ three percent of the world's labour force. Even socialist states host MNCs or one of their subsidiaries.

Because of their enormous sales figures and profits, MNCs collectively aggregate large amounts of international currencies and are in the position to influence exchange rates. By the mid-1970s, MNCs controlled more than twice the total of all international reserves held by all central banks and international monetary institutions. By the 1990s, MNCs accounted for about a quarter of the activity in the world's market economies and a staggering 80–90 percent of the exports in developed economies such as Britain, Canada, and the United States. One scholar has estimated that by the year 2000, MNCs will produce over half of the world's gross economic product.[12] Another analyst forecasts that before the turn of this century, fewer than 300 global corporations will control 80 percent of all productive assets of the world.[13]

The economic power of MNCs often translates into political and social power. Politically, MNCs promise investment, jobs, higher living standards, and the introduction of technology to assist developing countries to modernize and industrialize. In return, they demand political stability and concessions on taxation and government regulations. When national interest and corporate interest conflict, MNCs challenge the political decisions of governments from every possible vantage point.

In the social sphere, the global marketing strategies of MNCs serve to homogenize consumer tastes the world over. Because MNCs have created the "global shopping centre," there is a resulting tendency for people all over the world to adopt the same tastes and the same consumption habits. The proliferation of communications satellites has made global advertising a reality, with the result that world enterprises can now suggest new needs to new consumers anywhere and reinforce old needs for existing consumers in established markets. The rise of the global corporation has launched an important integrating force within the international community. As agents of political, social, and economic change, MNCs are creating a world society that transcends geography, race, and nationalism. Once considered economic outcasts, MNCs are now viewed increasingly as harbingers of economic growth around the world. The debate between the critics and supporters of MNCs rages on, but both groups agree that global corporations have entered the world arena as permanent and powerful actors in a competitive international system.

Non-Governmental Organizations (NGOs)

We have identified the three dominant classes of actors in the contemporary international system: states, international organizations, and multinational corporations. But there are other actors, not always recognized by states and IGOs, that stimulate international co-operation on all levels of human interaction. **Non-governmental organizations** are specialized organizations that work to develop national interest and involvement in world affairs. These types of international organizations are created from every conceivable field of human endeavour, from agriculture to science and technology. By organizing workshops, seminars, and conferences, and by publishing information on various aspects of their activities, these organizations have cre-

ated a social basis for international relations.

NGOs perform an educative function in the countries where they operate: they contribute to the gathering and dissemination of information about international problems. At the same time, they generate an internal domestic interest in world affairs. In the process of mobilizing public and private support for global concerns, NGOs create a flow of ideas, materials, and people across national boundaries. Many organizations make contributions in the forms of money, food, clothing, books, equipment, and expertise to promote co-operation and development in the international system.

By the 1990s, there were nearly 5000 NGOs of diverse size, composition, and purpose functioning in the world. This number could double by the year 2000. Many of these organizations have high visibility and are widely known in all countries: for example, the International Olympic Commission, the International Red Cross, and the International Chamber of Commerce. But others are not so prominent, such as the International Council for Philosophy and Humanistic Studies or the Council for International Organizations of Medical Sciences. In Canada, nearly 200 NGOs encourage and provide domestic links with all world areas. Organizations such as World Vision Canada, Plan International Canada, and the Salvation Army are among them.

Some NGOs are organized as professional associations that seek to protect the interests of their members but exercise an important role in the international community. For example, the Association of Canadian Medical Colleges (ACMC), with headquarters in Ottawa, has international affiliations with the Pan-American Federation of Associations of Medical Schools and with the Pan-American Health Organization. The International Federation of Airline Pilots' Association, with headquarters in Montreal, represents the interests of pilots in over 50 countries and functions to gain international agreements on the intricate patterns of interactions in the area of world air transport.

Still other NGOs undertake humanitarian efforts. In the field of human rights, Amnesty International is one of the best known. Its Canadian office (in Ottawa) has been operating since 1973. Founded in England in 1961, it has devoted its major efforts in over 160 nation-states toward the protection of prisoners of conscience, and collects information on the incidence of torture, arbitrary arrest, and capital punishment around the world. For example, in 1983, an Amnesty International mission visited Canada to investigate allegations that prisoners at Archambault Prison in Québec had been subjected to torture and ill treatment following a prison riot in July 1982. The allegations, supported by the sworn statements of 17 prisoners, referred to beatings, spraying tear gas into prisoners' mouths, keeping inmates naked for weeks, depriving them of sleep, and adulterating food. Amnesty International found reasonable grounds to believe that cruel and inhuman treatment had occurred and asserted Canada had an international obligation under the United Nations Declaration on Torture to undertake a full, impartial inquiry.

Trans-National Groups and Movements

Religious movements, trans-national political organizations, and terrorist groups must also be included in a composite of the contemporary international system. In this century, trans-national actors have added a new dimension of complexity to that system because they participate in a web of global interactions that affect the behaviour of governments, international organizations, individuals, and corporations. They can play a major role in international relations.

Organized Religion

Perhaps the most apparent example of an organized religion that has taken a leading role in world affairs is the Catholic church. The Vatican is the government of the church and represents the pope's authority. Pope John Paul II is the religious leader of one-sixth of the world's population and is the world's most visible moral leader. He is the only world leader ever to draw five million people to see him at one place (Mexico City, 1984).

The pope and the church he leads play a unique role in the contemporary international arena. Peace has been a recurrent papal theme: in 1982, the pope visited both Argentina and Great Britain in an attempt to help end the Falkland Islands War. He also visited strife-torn Central America and Ireland, bringing with him the moral and political pressures of a neutral Vatican to settle disputes peacefully. Another enduring papal theme is human rights. In the last decade, the pope's message of human rights as an international concern was taken to South Africa, Indonesia, Nicaragua, and Canada.

In Canada, this most-travelled pope in church history and the first pope ever to kiss Canadian soil added many politically charged statements to what he called his "essentially pastoral" visit. At Flat Rock, Newfoundland, the pope raised a storm of controversy when he spoke against the pursuit of profits by the few at the expense of the workers and supported the co-operative ownership of the fishery. In Edmonton, John Paul II assailed the neglect of the poor economies by the rich economies. He challenged political leaders the world over on the issues of the arms race, human-rights infringement, ethnic and minority rights, economic deprivation, and exploitation. He condemned the "imperialists" who monopolize economic and political powers at the expense of the poor economies of the Third World and called on Canada to take the lead in sharing its affluence in the North-South context. He issued a firm appeal for publicly funded religious education – an issue that is much more inflammatory in the United States and Latin America than in Canada. The pope's visit was no less controversial in Canada than in the numerous other countries he had visited. Women's groups expressed their anger at his lack of flexibility regarding the role of women in a patriarchal church. Proponents of the issues surrounding abortion and birth control continue to press the Vatican to modernize church doctrine.

As his Canadian visit demonstrated, the pope takes his role as a world diplomat and political leader very seriously. John Paul II placed himself and his church in the position of being a primary mediator for what he sees as a "troubled planet"; he uses his role as a world leader to influence international affairs in both the wealthy northern states and the developing states. He has used direct diplomatic intervention under specified conditions. He approved the Church's role in mediating the Beagle Channel dispute be-

tween Chile and Argentina. He intervened with George Bush and Saddam Hussein on the eve of the Gulf War, to plead against the use of force. He attempted Vatican mediation in Lebanon and the former Yugoslavia without much success. But the pope forges an active pontificate role in re-shaping the European international system in the post-Cold War era.

International Political Movements

Many political groups and movements transcend national boundaries, appeal to an international clientele, and thus influence the global political system. Anarchism, communism, and socialism are international movements that have influenced most national political systems. In the latter part of the nineteenth and early twentieth centuries, communist internationals (Cominterns) were established to bring world communists together in the goal of uniting workers and destroying capitalism. Today, the communists in states where they are still organized disagree on many fundamental issues but share the goal of building an international camaraderie.

In Latin America, *aprista*-type parties share the international goals of **aprismo**, which include land reform, nationalization of key industries, the solidarity of oppressed classes, the political representation of Indians, peasants, students, and intellectuals, and opposition to communism. Leaders of *aprista* parties are known to one another and agree on general principles of political, economic, and social change in Latin America. This international dimension of *aprismo* makes it a significant regional trans-national political movement.

All ideologically kindred parties and

movements of this kind seek to build systematic links in the international community. The founding session of a worldwide organization of conservative parties took place in London in 1983: the International Democratic Union has 20 members, including the Progressive Conservative Party of Canada. The Socialist International is a similar organization of 49 full members, including Canada's New Democratic Party. For liberal parties, there is the Liberal International with 31 members, which met in Ottawa in September 1987 to consider a range of global issues for which consensus could be achieved.

Terrorists

Finally, terrorists are also actors in the international system. In a world in which many different groups and organizations are prepared to use violence to achieve political ends, terrorism almost eludes definition. Diverse groups – armies, insurgents, mercenaries, freedom fighters, religious and national liberation movements, and even individuals – are frequently identified with terrorism as users of violence and psychological weapons in international affairs.

The use of the label "terrorists" seems to be a matter of one's perception of the objectives of political violence. For the Nicaraguans, the U.S.-backed *Contras* engaged in acts of terrorism against Nicaraguan peasants and their government, while to the American administration, the *Contras* were freedom fighters attempting to overthrow an undesirable government by conducting their military operations from bases on the Honduran border. The Palestine Liberation Organization (PLO) is differentially perceived as a national liberation movement, a state, and a terrorist group.

The U.S. condemns the Democratic Revolutionary Front and the Farabundo Marti National Liberation Front of El Salvador as guerrillas using terrorist tactics against the government, but hailed the anti-communist guerrillas in Afghanistan as "freedom fighters."

State terrorism consists of the use or the threat of violence by governments against their own populations as instruments of political and social control. Almost always, state terrorism has international consequences due to the mass exodus of refugees or the intervention of other governments, as with Nazi Germany in the 1940s and Cambodia in the 1970s. Amnesty International reports that in the 1980s no fewer than 98 states practised torture on suspected dissidents. In some of these nation-states, such as Syria and Uganda, tens of thousands of civilians have been massacred by their government's use of military forces.

Revolutionary terrorism is seen as the actions of extreme social and political movements that resort to violence across national boundaries to achieve their goals. Revolutionary terrorism tends to attract much more international attention because it targets prominent citizens, airlines, airports, embassies, and is usually reported globally in the media.

Terrorist organizations exist all over the world and today number about 3000. Among the most prominent and active terrorist groups are Italy's Red Brigade, which kidnapped and killed Italian prime minister Aldo Moro in 1980; the Red Army Faction, which bombed the Munich Oktoberfest in 1980; the Islamic Jihad Organization, which destroyed the American Embassy in Beirut in 1983;

Uruguay's Tupamaro; the Cuban exiles' Omega 7; the Fatah in the Middle East; the Bader-Meinhof group in Germany; the Basque separatists in Spain; and the Provisional Wing of the Irish Republican Army, (which has a history of terrorism dating back to the nineteenth century). The most enduring terrorist organizations tend to have religious, ethnic, and nationalist aspirations. The Bosnians and Croatians in the former Yugoslavia, the Basques in Spain, and the Kurds in Iraq and Iran have organized as ethnic extremist groups. The growing power of Islamic fundamentalism is reflected in the presence of Hezbollah (Party of God), and a multitude of Shi'ite Muslim movements in such states as Lebanon and Kuwait.

The activities of organizations such as these have international consequences and challenge the stability of the global community. Intimidation and random violence are unique features of these non-state actors: assassination, abduction, hijackings, hostage-taking, and murder seriously defy the structures and routine interactions of international relations. Some Western governments have responded to the threat of terrorism by training anti-terrorist combat units. The **Canadian Security Intelligence Service (CSIS)** and the emergency response teams of the Royal Canadian Mounted Police (RCMP), Great Britain's Special Air Services, Israel's 269 Headquarters Reconnaissance Regiment, the U.S. Delta Team, and Germany's Group Nine are examples of counter-terrorist and intelligence-gathering groups.

The use of terrorism typically reflects the desire of some groups to change the rules and structures of international politics. Violent tactics are used by groups who feel that they have little to lose from chaotic upheaval and whose expectations of the international system cannot be achieved by legitimate means. But just as significant are the probabilities that terrorist tactics will be successful. One study showed that terrorists are aware they have a 100-percent chance of getting worldwide attention; that there is a 77-percent chance of getting away with the act, an 86-percent chance of a safe exit if no one is hurt; and that there is a 40-percent chance of getting some demands met and a 26-percent chance of having all demands met.[14]

With reality outdoing fiction, the media has come to play an important role for terrorist groups the world over. In international political society, the media provides terrorists with instant public access and an escape from anonymity. The impact of terrorism on world affairs is measured by column inches and screen time. Pope John Paul II, the first pope since John XXIII to add the media to his divine ministry, also stumbled onto the other side of world exposure when, in front of the cameras, he became the object of an assassination attempt by a young Turkish far-rightist, Mehmet Ali Agca. The whole incident was steeped in the world of the media, not only for the victim, but equally for the aggressor and his international conspirators. What better opportunity for a terrorist contemplating notoriety! Indeed, in 1980, an ailing Marshall McLuhan was summoned by Italian authorities to unravel the troubled dialectic between the media and terrorism. He summed it up in one succinct comment: "Without the media there would be no terrorism."

Individuals as International Actors

The role that private individuals play in the international system often goes unnoticed because the actions and achievements of people are identified with the nation-states and organizations to which they are attached. But individuals have an impact on international affairs and examples abound.

American industrialist Andrew Carnegie willed $10 million U.S. for the abolition of war between civilized states. Swedish soldier Count Gustaf von Rosan created the Biafran Air Force during the Nigerian civil war. Argentine revolutionary Ché Guevara attempted to start a series of revolutions in Latin America. Bishop Desmond Tutu, who won the Nobel Peace Prize in 1984 for his unifying role in the campaign to peacefully resolve the problem of apartheid in South Africa, travelled extensively, calling for support to work against the South African government. American actor Ed Asner, star of television's "Lou Grant," raised over $1 million U.S. for medical aid, food, and clothing to be sent to the people of El Salvador to oppose the U.S. military assistance for the Salvadorian government. In 1985, Live Aid, the near-global musical extravaganza that raised over $60 million U.S. for African famine relief, was the brainchild and organizational achievement of one man, rock star Bob Geldof. In Canada, Terry Fox received over $25 million from all over the world in his unique fight against cancer. Another Canadian, Steve Fonyo, took up the same challenge and successfully completed Terry Fox's dream of running across Canada, attracting financial support from people and governments in Canada and around the world. And Vancouver wheelchair athlete Rick Hansen completed a 40,000-kilometre world tour to raise money for spinal research in the international community.

Each day millions of individual actors in the roles of tourists travel to foreign places, bringing with them money that translates into local jobs and industries. On a global basis the impact of tourism is considerable, not only in dollar terms but also in terms of the trans-national perceptions and interactions that take place. The cumulative effect of individuals who decide to emigrate to other countries is also a significant influence on the international system.

Large migrations of people to the great industrial countries are still occurring in the latter part of the twentieth century: Pakistanis and West Indians to Great Britain and Canada, North Africans and blacks to France, Turks, Kurds, Bosnians and Croatians to Germany and other European countries, Mexicans and Central Americans to the United States, Greeks to Australia, and Polynesians to other parts of the Pacific. At the individual as well as the social level, these population shifts may pose insoluble political problems for the host state, confounding classical "democratic" institutions like universal suffrage, equal education, and social-welfare programs. But also, these relocations make the world a more integrated community.

Individuals in their private capacity, as artists, businesspersons, journalists, professionals, and writers, are independent actors able to behave autonomously in the global arena. In recent years, individuals – in addition to states and international organizations[15] – have been given some recognition internationally as subjects of world law under certain circumstances. In short, individuals are an integral part of the contemporary international community. They are not, therefore, merely cogs in the large bureaucratic machinery of states and international organizations, because they have a capacity, through their actions, of influencing the character of world affairs.

The Future of the International System

In the twentieth century, the international system has undergone enormous transformation. Many new actors have entered the world arena, each with different capabilities, values, and goals. Most of these new actors, unlimited by the present territorial divisions of the world, are raising demands that challenge the very principle of centralized state power. Modern states are increasingly drained of their power and sovereignty. All are subject to the laws of the world market: the tyranny of market prices and interest rates; the difficulties of providing work, food, housing, and security to more and more people; the problems of the global physical environment.

New National Awakenings

These weaknesses of states are also sharpened by geographical disparities and internal divisions. Most of the newer states are quite artificial political creations, such as the states around the Sahara or the scattered islands of the Caribbean, South Pacific, and the Indian Ocean, where a multitude of "statelets" find it nearly impossible to manage their own social and economic space or to function as autonomous members of international society. Many peoples who are denied an identity by existing states (Inuit, Lapps, Samoyeds, and North, Central, and South American aboriginals) are laying claim to historical rights of place that antedate present territorial divi-

sions. They are demanding self-government, the return of their land, and are resisting forcible assimilation.

Other nations locked within the confines of modern communist nation-states broke out violently. In the 1990s, four of the previous republics of the former Yugoslavia – Slovenia, Croatia, Bosnia-Hertzegovina, and Macedonia – launched civil wars, each seeking international recognition of their contemporary independence as nation-states. However, their ability as new independent states to build their war-torn economies is extremely hampered in an era of European economic integration and the construction of a supranational government.

These new awakenings have coincided with the rise since the 1960s of radical movements in the West (feminism, ecology, counter-cultures, anti-militarism). These trans-state socio-cultural currents are increasing resistance to the dominance of territorial structures and the state-centric principle. From a broad perspective, these contemporary forces seriously challenge the idea of a single model of modern state development and suggest that many different future paths are possible.

Creating Regional Actors

Several other categories of actors have recognized the vulnerability of states in their present form of organization. Global corporations market an ideology that justifies their world management role and their executives make the same basic claim: nationalism and territoriality are passé. To these corporations the world is an integrated marketplace that is hindered by the economic nationalism and protectionism of the state. The secretariats of intergovernmental organizations argue that autonomous governments must transfer more sovereignty to supranational organizations if regional and global problems are to be successfully resolved. Similarly, non-governmental organizations advance the principles of international co-operation and development as an alternative to national self-sufficiency.

In the contemporary international system, only a few states are in a position to control their own destinies. The seven most industrialized economies – Britain, Canada, France, Italy, Japan, Germany, and the United States are able – albeit under greater limitations than ever before – to convert their national wealth and economic growth into independent international behaviour in matters of aid, investment, and trade. But for the majority of the other states of the world, independence is both a political and legal fiction. They see their destinies as tied to the advanced capitalist and socialist economies, which for reasons of protectionism are increasingly centralizing the global economic system to their advantage.

Economic Integration

In the wider context of international relations, which involve the fullest expression of trans-national human interaction (such as business, cultural, and scientific exchanges, tourism, and technological advancement), there is a growing tendency among people and their governments to seek a regional approach to problem-solving. Latin America and the Caribbean provide rich examples of the movement towards a regional system of international co-operation and integration.

■ ■ **common market:** an economic association of states that moves them several steps closer to economic integration. ■ ■

In 1960, the Latin American Free Trade Association (renamed the Latin American Integration Association in 1981) was established in response to the European Common Market to reduce tariffs among member states until a regional **free-trade zone** could be reached. That same year, the Central American Common Market (CACM) was founded to promote regional economic development in Central America through a **customs union** and industrial integration. In 1969, a six-member-nation economic group created a subregional market, known as the *Grupo Andino* (Andean Group), to eliminate all trade barriers, establish a common external tariff on imports, and develop a mechanism to co-ordinate investment as a **common market**. This Andean common market supports the ideas of regional co-operation, central planning, and directed economies for achieving economic integration in the Andean region. In 1992, the Andean Group created a free-trade zone among member states. The Caribbean Free Trade Association (CARIFTA) spawned the creation of the Caribbean Community and Common Market (CARICOM), which in 1973 established a regional organization designed to achieve a higher level of economic and political integration among Caribbean countries, based on the European Union model. The Latin American Economic System (SELA), established in 1975, is a regional organization similar in its purposes, tactics, and goals to the Organization of Petroleum Exporting Countries (OPEC). Because it is an effort on the part of many Latin American states to develop an advantageous regional strategy for producing, selling, and pricing primary products, SELA was formed to assist in getting materials such as bauxite, chrome, coffee, nickel, and sugar on the world market. And in 1991, Argentina, Paraguay and Uruguay founded the Southern Cone Common Market (Mercosur), culminating in a common market in 1995.

Canada and the United States entered a free trade arrangement in the late 1980s and moved to expand their regional association to include Mexico in a North American Free Trade Agreement. When all these organizations are seen in the context of the entire inter-American system, a pattern of regional international integration is observable as an evolutionary approach to the building of political and economic communities in the Americas beyond the state.

This pattern occurs elsewhere, too. The prolific growth of limited-member organizations since World War II has been a global phenomenon and stems from the new emphasis being placed on regional integration as a means of achieving national objectives. For the foreseeable future, the world appears to be moving in this direction.

The Shifting Balance of Power

On the level of intergovernmental relations, contemporary observers of international politics detect other changes in the character of the global community. Since World War II, the proliferation of state and non-state actors has altered the structure of the international system and the distribution of power within it. The analysis of the **balance of power** within the global state system is defined by the number of major actors, or *poles,* in that system. The term "pole" is used to refer to a "great power," usually measured in terms of military and economic strength. The disintegration of the Soviet Union into 21 competitive nation-states dramatically changed the global balance of power, setting in motion new alliances and a new world configuration of states.

Analysts have described the variations of the balance of power in the global state system as *unipolar, bipolar, multipolar,* and *multibloc* or *oligopolar.* At one hypothetical extreme, this configuration of power could be that of a world government, meaning this system would be unipolar. But there is only a very slight probability of a global governmental system being realized. Just as improbable is another unipolar variation in which one superpower acquires world **hegemony**. A bipolar balance-of-power system is one in which two superpowers dominate rival military, political, economic, and ideological camps; e.g., in the Cold War era of the United States and the former Soviet Union. In a bipolar system, international tensions and conflicts are intensified because each of the protagonists perceives any gain of power for the other as a loss of its own power and takes action to prevent this imbalance.

The growing significance of a united Europe in contemporary international politics could lead to a renewed bipolar political structure, where two poles – not necessarily equal in power – manoeuvre and shift their alliances in order to avoid isolation. In a tripolar

■ ■ **hegemony:** the domination of one state over another state, region, or the world by means of superior military capability, economic productivity, and foreign policy. ■ ■

structure, the international system is much less rigid and much more flexible and political: each of the three poles tries to prevent the emergence of a dominant coalition of the other two poles. Détente and rapprochement (reconciliation) are sought by the three competing powers, thus contributing to a more stable international political system based on superpower alliances and diplomatic compromise. A multipolar system exists when more than three powers function as major competing actors in the international system.

The more actors, the more complex and flexible is the balance-of-power system. In addition to the United States and Europe, the present balance-of-power system must also include China, Brazil, India, and Japan as significant players in the contemporary game of international politics. The multipolar bloc model goes one step further and portrays the international system as divided into many spheres of influence, with many actors. It views the world as a composite of large, autonomous, integrating regions, such as North America, Central America, South America, Western Europe, Eastern Europe, the Middle East, and the various regions of Asia and Africa.

These emerging regional units may be the forces that will replace states as the primary actors in global affairs. Increasingly, political scientists have challenged the credibility of a model that does not include all the actors in the system. In short, the conditions that might have facilitated the view that states are the only poles of power in the contemporary world of international relations have changed dramatically. The state as a pole of power will probably remain a central characteristic of the international community in the future, but its

pre-eminence has eroded and will, in all probability, continue to lessen as other actors gain power and influence. From the perspective of the 1990s, MNCs, IGOs, trans-national groups and organizations, and supranational organizations are all ascendant international powers.

Two of the most tangible elements of power – economic and military capacity – are now exercised by other actors in competition with states. MNCs, trans-national groups, individuals, and some IGOs and NGOs have access to great wealth that challenges both the viability and solvency of states. The world is no longer made up simply of rich states and poor states; rather, it is composed of strong actors and weak actors. A similar situation exists with respect to military capacity. Conventional and nuclear technologies are no longer possessed solely by the states. The recent proliferation and subsequent diffusion of nuclear arms have irreversibly altered the post-1945 nuclear balance. As we approach the twenty-first century, more and more states will come to possess nuclear weapons – and we can expect that other actors will, as well.

All these factors lead us to conclude that the future international system may be described in terms of emerging poles of power. Instead, it may be more accurate to analyze the system as a multi-level network of contending actors, each with a certain degree of power and influence, each with a capability to contribute to the system's stability or instability. At present, the international system seems to be made up of numerous national actors. Closer examination reveals that every one of its working parts, including each of us as individuals, is interdependently connected to all the other working parts. It is, to put it one way, the only truly closed political system any of us know about. And to put it another way, it is the ultimate human organization. As evolutionary time is measured, the system appeared only moments ago and has a lot of growing up to do. At present, despite its "youth," the international system is still the brightest spot on the horizon.

Canada in the International System

A decade ago, historian John Holmes remarked that "Canada is an inescapably international country."[16] From the geographical perspective, Canada appears to be locked into the western hemisphere as a North American country. But while it is true that Canada is geopolitically consigned to interact with the United States, the network of Canada's international relations was never historically contained in a geographically delimited hemisphere. Historian Andrew Burghardt says that "because of the continued predominance of the North Atlantic in world commerce, because of the early development of the Maritimes and Québec, because of ethnic ties, because of the broad St. Lawrence gateway and the extension of landmass eastward towards Europe, Canada has been heavily oriented toward the North Atlantic."[17]

All these factors encouraged Canada's political and economic ties with Great Britain, the states of continental Europe, and the Commonwealth. Historically, the Commonwealth tie expanded Canada's international relations with Asia, Africa, the Caribbean, and Europe. These linkages introduced Canada to a network of global bilateral and multilateral

interactions that earned Canada the widespread reputation of a good world citizen. As historian Barbara Ward observed, Canada was the "first international nation."[18]

Today, Canada continues to advance foreign policies with a global focus. Perhaps the most revealing component of Canada's reputation as an important international actor is its support and involvement in international organizations. In this regard, Canada's active participation in the creation of the United Nations, the Commonwealth, NATO, NORAD, the OAS, *L'Agence culturelle et technique de la langue français* (*L'Agence*), the General Agreement of Tariffs and Trade (GATT), the International Monetary Fund (IMF), and the Organization for Economic Co-operation and Development (OECD) is an insight into the enormous scope of Canada's global presence. Internationalist engagement marked by a commitment to international institutions has continued under successive Canadian governments since 1945. By 1990, the number of international institutions of which Canada was a member grew to over 250. The number of national economies with which Canada traded continued to expand, as did the number of Canadian representative missions abroad. In 1945, Canada had diplomatic missions in 22 states; by the 1990s, this number had grown to over 160, of which 89 were embassies.

Canada's openness to the world community is driven by its need to trade. Judged as a percentage of gross national product, Canada is the world's largest international trader. In the 1990s, 33 percent of its GNP is aggregated in trade, compared with 25 percent for Germany and the United Kingdom, 20 percent for France and the United States, and (surprisingly) only 15 percent for Japan. Approximately four-fifths of Canada's world trade is with the United States. The economic exchange between these two states is the largest bilateral trade relationship in the world, and was so even before the implementation of the Free Trade Agreement in 1989.

The global recession of the late 1980s shook the stability of Canada's international trade performance. In an economically depressed world, many governments introduced measures to protect their nascent or ailing domestic industries against foreign imports. At the same time, they have aggressively marketed their exports, competing for the same trade partners as Canada. This competitive climate in the international economy is further complicated by other interrelated economic problems threatening the viability of trade: high levels of inflation, high unemployment, high interest rates, sagging investments, and almost universal **balance-of-payments** deficits.

> ■ ■ **balance of payments:**
> a statistical record of all
> economic transactions that
> have taken place during a
> given time period between
> a state's residents and the
> rest of the world. ■ ■

The combined impact of these complex economic forces has stimulated Canada's international instinct. At the annual GATT meetings, Canada actively supports resolutions to *liberalize* international trade and encourages the reduction of protectionist measures. At the regular meetings of the International Monetary Fund (IMF) and the International Bank for Reconstruction and Development (**World Bank**), Canada has supported the provision of credits, loans, and subsidies to international importers in the developing countries. At the June 1988 economic summit in Toronto, Canada played a major role in the agreement to reduce the debt burden of the world's poorest economies, particularly in sub-Saharan Africa.

It remains Canada's view that *multilateral efforts* can be of major importance in addressing national problems and in resolving many international challenges of global significance – for example, the creation of a New International Economic Order (NIEO), international environmental issues, the food crisis, and human rights. Since the 1970s, Canada has urged other developed states to accept basic changes recommended by the less developed countries (LDCs) in the international economic system. As a proponent of NIEO, Canada has advocated the stabilization of international commodity markets, the expansion of development loans and assistance through the international banking system, and the preferential treatment of Third World products in international trade. One major component of NIEO to which Canada maintains a strong commitment is North-South dialogue. Canada was a principal contributor to a Common Fund for Commodities to assist developing economies adversely affected by volatile price fluctuations in the international marketplace. The dependence of the developing economies of the South on volatile commodity markets is an ever-increasing complaint.

At Cancun, Mexico in 1981, 22 states – including the world's richest and poorest – met to search for a solution to the North-South economic-disparities gap. Delegates from Canada and most of the other delegates attending were united in the need to move towards NIEO to address global problems in aid, trade, food, energy, and international debt resulting from the growing inequalities between the North and South. At the time, the Canadian government promised to increase its aid program to 0.5 percent of GNP, although it has failed to do so. This falls well below Lester Pearson's suggestion in the 1960s that Canada and other developed economies should donate one percent of their GNP as foreign aid. Though this target was later lowered to 0.7 percent, among the OECD member states only four (Denmark, Norway, Sweden, and the Netherlands) have given more than 0.7 percent of their respective GNP to assist developing economies. In 1992, Canada's strict austerity budget slashed its development assistance programs once again, making it very unlikely that Canada's long-overdue goal of 0.5 percent of GNP will be reached in the first half of the 1990s.

The most compelling arguments at the Cancun Conference for narrowing the gap between the North and the South were directed at financing the *international debt*. Developing states feed their people, fuel their economies, and compete in the world-trade markets by means of loans and long-term repayment schedules negotiated with international lending institutions, such as the World Bank and the IMF. The IMF is usually the last resort for financially strapped developing economies. In 1982, the World Bank and the IMF met in Toronto. Canada played a major role in the establishment of a special soft-loan fund for the International Development Association, an affiliate of the World Bank. At the 1988 economic summit, Canada proposed that debtor states should repay their debts based on different combinations of terms, partial write-offs and soft-loan provi-

sions. In the spirit of the new economic order, soft loans feature a low cost (no interest, except for a small annual service charge), a long repayment schedule (usually 50 years), and a slow amortization rate (usually a ten-year period of grace, followed by one percent of the loan repayable annually for the next ten years and three percent repayable annually for the following 30 years).

On *international environmental issues*, Canada was a major player in the negotiations that led to the signing of the United Nations Convention on the Law of the Sea in 1982. Canada, as the largest coastal state in the world, was successful in obtaining recognition of the need to manage offshore living and non-living resources, as well as obtaining the provision of international legal measures to prevent marine pollution, particularly in arctic waters. The creation of an International Seabed Authority to protect the resources of the deep seabed from indiscriminate exploitation and pollution was spearheaded by Canada.

In pursuit of its environmental objectives, Canada took part in many international meetings in the 1980s, particularly those sponsored by the United Nations Environment Program (UNEP). Canada was instrumental in the establishment of *EarthWatch*, UNEP's key program which keeps an eye on all corners of the planet day and night. UNEP's observations are passed on to governments, scientists, and industrialists in all regions. The Canadian delegation initiated work on a convention for the protection of the stratospheric ozone layer; the convention was signed by 45 states in March 1985. Canada also ratified a United Nations Convention on Long-Range Transboundary Air Pollution (LRTAP), which recognizes acid rain as a major international environmental problem. And in 1989, Canada was one of 25 states to sign the Convention on Air Pollution limiting the emission of carbon dioxide gases. Canada also contributed to the establishment of the World Atmospheric Trust Fund. At the Earth Summit in Rio de Janeiro in 1992, Canada signed an "ecopact" on the preservation of biological diversity. The biodiversity treaty recognized the relationship between poverty and the degradation of the environment and the need to protect endangered species and the areas they inhabit by providing financial relief to developing economies. The United Nations Conference of Environment and Development (UNCED), which drafted the accord, heard 100 of the world's leaders speak to the issues of poverty and the global ecology.

In 1984, the food crisis in Africa focused international attention on the spectre of a global food shortage. By 1990, the situation had actually worsened, even though the cameras of journalists were not sending back images of Africa's starving populations to the extent they had been in the mid-1980s. The food situation in Africa is a regional manifestation of a worldwide problem of massive food shortages and the need for thousands of tonnes of food aid and millions of dollars in development assistance. Emergency relief from Canada has been crucial in averting mass starvation not only in Africa, but in Asia, Latin America, and the Caribbean. Many people in disaster-stricken areas of the world would not have survived if Canadian grain had not been provided. Through food aid and funding for longer-term development projects that lead to the production of food, the Canadian International Development Agency (CIDA) administers food aid and other forms of development assistance using three main channels: government-to-government aid; multilateral aid, in which Canada supports the efforts of international organizations; and aid to Canadian non-governmental organizations that work through their affiliates in the receiving state. Canada endorsed the 1987 Beijing Declaration which reaffirmed the international commitment to eradicate hunger and malnutrition by a world food strategy.

In the field of human rights, Canada has ratified all relevant international conventions: the International Covenant on Economic, Social and Cultural Rights (1976), the International Covenant on Civil and Political Rights and its Optional Protocol (1976), and the Helsinki Agreement of 1975. In January 1982, the International Convention on the Elimination of All Forms of Discrimination Against Women came into force. Canada was instrumental in drafting and supporting this convention and is a member of the committee that monitors the implementation of its provisions. Because of strong domestic pressures to speak out on human rights violations in Poland, El Salvador, Guatemala, South Africa, and Afghanistan, Canada was a member of a working group that drafted the Convention against Torture and Other Cruel, Inhuman or Degrading Treatment or Punishment, which entered into force on June 26, 1987. One of the provisions of the convention is that a torturer may be prosecuted in any state, regardless of his or her nationality, the nationality of the victim or the place where the torture occurred. Canada also initiated the United Nations Working Group on Enforced or Involuntary Disappearances, which in urgent cases, authorizes the chairman of the group to make immediate contact with the government concerned.

Given Canada's vested interest in an *orderly international system*, its government has no option but to continue on the path of vigorous international engagement. Few states are as sensitive as Canada is to the trends in the international system, the linkages among NGOs, the business manoeuvres of MNCs, the growth of IGOs, and the general condition of the international economy. Most of the domestic sources of Canadian foreign policy are clearly oriented toward the international system.

Canada, the U.S., and Mexico in the International Context

The Free Trade Agreement

The complexity and constancy of Canada's relations with the United States are unique in international relations.[19] No other two states in the world share the intimacy of an undefended border 30,000 kilometres long that is crossed by over 85 million people each year and over which $200 billion in international trade is exchanged annually. This two-way trade exceeds two-way trade between the U.S. and Japan and between the U.S. and any four of its European trading partners combined. Just one province – Ontario – buys more from the United States than Japan, the UK, France, or Germany.

Given the increasing intimacy of these economies, neither of the national governments on either side of the 49th parallel takes this sort of trading relationship for granted.

Trade between Canada and the United States translates into about 1.3 million jobs in each economy. Prior to the implementation of the Canada-United States Free Trade Agreement (FTA) in 1989, both economies had already enjoyed a very large measure of free trade. Successive rounds of multilateral trade negotiations under GATT had eliminated tariffs on about 75 percent of goods and services flowing both ways across the border.

A great deal of this success had resulted from separate trade agreements involving agriculture, the fishery, and manufacturing. The historic Canada-U.S. Automotive Agreement of 1965 brought tremendous economic benefits in increased production and employment in both countries. Since the implementation of the Auto Pact, two-way trade in automotive products skyrocketed from less than a billion dollars annually to nearly $30 billion by the 1990s.

At the Québec Summit in March 1985, Prime Minister Mulroney and U.S. president Reagan committed themselves to reduce and eliminate the existing barriers on the roughly 25 percent of trade that remained subject to tariffs. The gruelling negotiations that followed led to the signing of an historic 1407-page accord, the Canada-United States Free Trade Agreement, implemented January 1, 1989. This bilateral treaty will eliminate all trade barriers (i.e., tariffs, duties, fees, quotas, or trade restrictions) between the two economies by 1999, thereby initiating the largest free-trade zone in the world.

The North American Free Trade Agreement

In 1992, Canada, the United States, and Mexico signed the North American Free Trade

Agreement. The NAFTA supplants the Canada-U.S. Free Trade Agreement, and creates the largest free-trade zone in the world, affecting about 360 million people, and leading to an economic output exceeding $7 trillion.

Not only are very different economies melding their industries and services but the political systems differ fundamentally as well. Unlike Canada and the United States, there is very little tradition of liberal democracy in Mexico. Mexico has been dominated by strong autocratic leaders who have been supported by a handful of wealthy families. For over 60 years, Mexico has been governed by one political party, the Institutional Revolutionary Party (PRI), whose presidential candidate has, to date, always won the presidency for each six-year term.

The trilateral negotiations that culminated in signing NAFTA at San Antonio presented 2000 pages of detailed trade conditions. Over 20,000 products are governed by this international treaty. Under the agreement, most tariff and **non-tariff barriers** would be eliminated over a 15-year period. Many rules and regulations require "domestic content" in order for products to be made within NAFTA. The treaty removes many restrictions on cross-border investments and other financial transactions. Advertising, banking, and insurance will flow much more freely. Commercial transportation will be much less impeded at the border points. Any trade disputes among the parties will be settled by an international commission with representation from all three signatories. There are provisions for other states in Central and South America, and the Caribbean to eventually join NAFTA, potentially creating a regional economic association analogous to the EU.

Canada and the United States already conduct the largest commercial bilateral trade relationship in the world, totalling about $200 billion annually. Historically, Canada's trade with Mexico has been much less, not exceeding one percent of Canadian imports and two percent of Canadian exports. At the time NAFTA was signed, only three percent of Mexico's exports went to Canada, and one percent of Canada's imports came from Mexico. Whether the overall economies of each state will be strengthened or weakened is very controversial.

Trade restrictions by each state are permissible under certain conditions according to the terms of the agreement: when there are critical domestic shortages of food or other essential products; when domestic cuts are required to prevent diminishing natural resources; to stabilize lower domestic prices on a commodity; and to secure other products in short supply.

MIKE CONSTABLE

491

Rightly or wrongly, government negotiators in the three economies saw that unhindered access to each market, including goods
or services purchased by the U.S., Canadian,
and Mexican governments, would permit
each economy to expand by attaining increases in productivity, generating more domestic employment, enhancing efficiency
through sharper competition, and by undertaking greater research and development at
the corporate level.[20] Consumers would gain
from lower prices resulting from the removal
of trade barriers, and governments would reap
the harvest of taxes from augmented growth.

The NAFTA includes almost all means of
production and services in the markets of
Canada, Mexico, and the United States. New
international rules and regulations will apply
to many sectors in addition to business and
manufacturing: agriculture, energy, financial
services, government procurement, investment, and services. In some sectors, exports
will grow disproportionately higher in one
state over the others, generating the need or
the incentive to specialize in the production
of certain goods and services. And even
though a balance is anticipated, many of the
necessary adjustments will be painful and will
be felt in all three economies.

Canada and the United States are two of
the world's largest net exporters of food. Yet
because of the complementary character of
agriculture in each country, trade in farm
products had remained at less than five percent of total bilateral trade. Under NAFTA,
some barriers to agricultural trade will disappear, stimulating a larger percentage of exchange over a ten-year period. This will
inevitably trigger the need to reform North
American farm policies so that Canada, Mexico,

and the United States will remain competitive
in the global market for agricultural products.[21]

The NAFTA assures that Canada will be the
largest supplier of energy to the United States.
By 1987, Canada had already achieved that
status due to its oil exports. In addition to petroleum products, Canada exports electricity,
natural gas, and uranium. Prior to the NAFTA
quotas, taxes and price restrictions were used
to control the flow of energy trade and to protect the domestic market and producers. The
NAFTA gives North American consumers access to energy supplies regulated essentially by
market forces rather than by government-imposed restrictions. Major obstacles to New
England's demands for hydroelectric power
from Québec will diminish under the FTA.
All barriers to the export of Canadian uranium
are being lifted, eliminating a source of bilateral friction in the nuclear-power industry.

Economic nationalism usually shows its
possessive character around financial institutions through the imposition of massive federal regulations and public policy restrictions.
The NAFTA attempts to give greater freedom
to banks, security and trust companies, and
other lending institutions to penetrate the financial markets of the three member states.

Trade liberalization will also affect government contracts. Cross-border bidding on
government business will expand trade
opportunities for suppliers on goods and services subject to competitive tender. Potential
suppliers in all three economies are entitled to
equal information about government business, as well as fair and non-discriminatory
consideration under the provisions of NAFTA.
Certain restrictions will remain: the provisions of NAFTA do not apply to state, local or

provincial governments or to departments of government that fall into the category of national security, such as some business under the Department of Defence in Canada and Pentagon purchases in the United States.

Environmental Protection

Beyond NAFTA, *environmental protection* has appeared over recent years as a major question of international concern between Canada and the United States. Acid rain is at the forefront of the issues of bilateral concern between the two states. Scientists have provided much evidence to show that acid rain is formed from emissions of sulphur dioxide and oxides of nitrogen that mix in the atmosphere, producing acids that eventually fall to earth in rain, dew, snow, and dust.[22] Acid rain causes annual damages in excess of $250 million to Canadians; environmental groups such as the Canadian Coalition Against Acid Rain say it threatens fishing, tourism, and farming in many parts of Canada and the United States. Two major sources of the problem are auto emissions and pollution from smelters. With time, legislated emission controls, and designated public monies on both sides of the border, acid rain may be a treatable problem.

Previous U.S. administrations have consistently opposed undertaking a costly clean-up program until more is known about the causes and effects of acid rain. But the Bush administration promised to take immediate action on the problem. In 1989, President Bush announced his intention to cut U.S. sulphur dioxide and nitrogen oxide emissions by one-half by the mid-1990s. The Mulroney government accepted the U.S. contention that Canada trailed the United States in cutting emissions and made a commitment to cut

Canadian emissions of sulfur dioxide and nitrogen oxides by 2.3 million tonnes by 1994. And in 1991, Canada and the United States signed an acid rain accord binding their commitments to curb emissions that cause acid rain.

Canada's federal plan aims at adopting and enforcing auto-emissions standards and providing government assistance to attack the smelter problem. Canadians and many Americans living in the northeastern states believe that enough is now known to move bilaterally against acid rain even as further research is conducted. The U.S. has indicated its willingness to reverse its position of cautious action as Canada demonstrates substantial progress in cutting emissions that cause acid rain.

Resource Management and Development

Both states place *resource management and development* high on their agendas. Fresh water, taken for granted by North Americans as an inexhaustible and free natural endowment, is now considered a long-range resource issue on the continent. Given the growing awareness of the effects of acid rain, the quality of both surface water and ground water is already a great concern in some places. But quantity of supply is also a resource-management concern because of the rising demand that is anticipated over the next decades. For that reason, it requires a different kind of bilateral response than acid rain now seems to be receiving. Although water seems to be plentiful in North America, drinkable water is in much shorter supply. The long-range supply of water is not only threatened by increased consumption but also by pollution and spoilage. Other resources, such as nickel and zinc, as well as such energy resources as oil and natural gas, are all in finite supply and eventually will be exhausted. Long-term planning is recognized by both governments as essential to their national interest.

North American Defence

Defence is another cornerstone of Canada-U.S. relations. Since the 1930s, Canadians have been aware that Canada is strategically one with the United States. After World War II, it became increasingly evident that Canada had a major military role to play in the defence of the North American continent. Thus it was natural for Canada to enter into the North American Air Defence (NORAD) agreement with the United States in 1958. Cross-border collaboration between Canadian and American military forces intensified with the installations of the Distant Early Warning (DEW) system. For nearly three decades, the DEW line served as Canada's main contribution to hemispheric defence and entwined Canadian military commitment with American strategic theory and practice. Recognition of Canada's strategic bond to the military security of the United States was demonstrated in the agreement that gave the U.S. permission to conduct cruise-missiles tests on Canadian territory. But this was just the beginning of a much more concrete contribution to continental defence.

By the 1980s, hostile intercontinental bombers armed with nuclear cruise missiles could fly over the polar cap in the Canadian high arctic, slip through radar gaps over Labrador, and skirt detection by the DEW-line installations. That possibility is the main reason that Canada and the United States agreed in 1985 to a massive overhaul of the NORAD system. The newer system put an end to most of the radar stations at the southern arc of the Arctic Circle and replaced them with a series of detection and warning stations around the North American continent capable of tracking aircraft and cruise missiles penetrating the northern hemisphere. Unlike the old DEW-line system, which was controlled by the U.S. Air Force, the North Warning System is Canadian-controlled, giving Canada sovereign decision-making authority over its use and development.

Finally, the high degree of interdependence between the two economies has raised concerns over questions of *national identity* and *cultural diversity*. Canadians may not be the most nationalistic people in the world but they are the most identity-conscious. The preoccupation with national identity is intimately tied to Canada's relations with the United States. Unlike most other bilateral relationships in the world, Canadian interaction with the United States goes well beyond government-to-government dealings between Ottawa and Washington or between the individual provinces and states. Indeed, Canada's intimacy with the United States goes beyond history and geography. The contacts at every level, between businesses, individuals and families, and between academic and other institutions constitute a unique and permanent socio-cultural relationship that defies definition. There have been mutual benefits and difficulties because of these ties. The states share two of the highest standards of living in the world, a rapid rate of industrial and technological development, and a dynamic daily exchange of communications, ideas, and people.

This close interaction, however, has also created some serious anxieties and problems in many sectors, especially concerning national identity and cultural diversity. For English-speaking Canadians, this concern is derived from the overwhelming influence of American culture on Canada; for French-speaking Canadians, it results from living among 260 million American and Canadian anglophones. In both cases, there is a genuine fear of cultural and political assimilation, which has led to the development of public policies explicitly designed to protect and nurture indigenous cultural activities.

References

1. For comprehensive analyses of the "actors" in the international system, see Gordon Schloming, *Power and Principle in International Affairs* (New York: Harcourt Brace Publishers, 1991), 393-515.

2. Joel Krieger, ed., *The Oxford Companion to the Politics of the World* (New York: Oxford University Press, 1993), passim.

3. John Rourke, *International Politics on the World Stage* (Guilford, CT.: The Dushkin Publishing Group, Inc., 1993), 60-61.

4. *Basic Facts About the United Nations* (New York: United Nations, 1988).

5. Until October 25, 1971, the Chinese seat on the Security Council was occupied by the Republic of China (Taiwan). After that date, the Chinese seat was occupied by the People's Republic of China.

6. Peter Fromuth, ed., *A Successor Vision: The United Nations of Tomorrow* (Lanham, MD.: University Press of America, 1988).

7. Adrian Hyde-Price, *European Security Beyond the Cold War: Four Scenarios for the Year 2010* (Beverly Hills, CA: Sage Publications, 1991); Randolph Siverson and Harvey Starr, *The Diffusion of War: A Study of Opportunity and Willingness* (Ann Arbor, MI.: University of Michigan Press, 1991).

8. C. Raghaven, "Recolonization: GATT in its historical context" in *The Ecologist* (20), 1990, 205-207; Edward Goldsmith, "The Uruguay Round: Gunboat diplomacy by another name," in *The Ecologist* (20), (1990), 202-204.

9. James J. Guy, "Canada Joins the OAS: A New Dynamic in the IAS," in *Inter-American Review of Bibliography* (Vol.XXXIX, No.4, 1989): 500-510.

10. Bruce Russett and Harvey Starr, *World Politics: The Menu for Choice* (New York: W.H. Freeman and Company, 1992), 429-435.

11. Richard Barnett and Ronald Müller, *Global Reach – The Power of the Multinational Corporations* (New York: Simon & Schuster, 1974), 15.

12. G. Modelski, ed., *Transnational Corporations and the World Order: Readings in International Political Economy* (San Francisco: W.H. Freeman, 1979), 241.

13. Howard Perlmutter, "Super-giant firms in the future," in *Wharton Quarterly* (Winter 1968); Jane Spero, *The Politics of International Economic Relations* (New York: St. Martin's Press, 1985).

14. Brian Jenkins, Janera Johnson, and David Ronfeldt, "Numbered lives: Some statistical observations from 75 international hostage episodes," in *Conflict*, (Vol. 1, 1978).

15. Robert Isaak, *Individuals and World Politics* (North-Scituate, MA: Dixbury Press 1975); Hugh Kindred et. al., *International Law: Chiefly as Interpreted and Applied in Canada* (Toronto: Emond Montgomery Publications, 1987), 122-30.

16. John Holmes, *Canada: A Middle-Aged Power* (Toronto: McClelland and Stewart Ltd., 1976), 66.

17. Andrew Burghardt, "Canada and the World," in John Warkentin, ed., *Canada: A Geographical Interpretation* (Toronto: Methuen Publications, 1968), 571.

18. Barbara Ward, "The First International Nation" in William Kilbourne, ed., *Canada: A Guide to the Peaceful Kingdom* (Toronto: Macmillan, 1970), 45-48.

19. Norman Hillmer, *Partners Nevertheless* (Toronto: Copp Clark Pitman Ltd., 1989).

20. Denis Stairs and Gilbert Winham, eds., *The Politics of Canada's Economic Relationship with the United States* (Toronto: University of Toronto Press, 1985).

21. Duncan Cameron and Mel Watkins, *Canada Under Free Trade* (Toronto: James Lorimer & Company Ltd., Publishers, 1993); Robert Chodos et. al., *Canada and the Global Economy* (Toronto: James Lorimer & Company Ltd., Publishers, 1993).

22. Don Munton and John Kirton, *Canadian Foreign Policy* (Scarborough, ON.: Prentice-Hall Canada, Inc., 1992), 367-381.

Suggested Readings

Duncan Cameron et al., *Canada Under Free Trade* (James Lorimer & Company Ltd., Publishers, 1992).

Werner Feld, *The Future of European Security* (Boulder, CO.: Lynne Rienner Publishers, 1993).

Alexander George, *Western State Terrorism* (New York: Routledge, 1991).

Daniel Papp, *Contemporary International Relations: Frameworks for Understanding* (New York: Macmillan Publishing Company, 1991).

Hoyt Purvis, *Interdependence: An Introduction to International Relations* (Fort Worth, TX.: Harcourt Brace Jovanovich College Publishers, 1992).

K.P. Saksena, *Reforming the United Nations* (Newbury Park, CA: SAGE Publications, Inc., 1993).

John Stoessinger, *Why Nations Go to War* (New York: St. Martin's Press, 1993).

Adam Watson, *The Evolution of International Society* (New York: Routledge, 1992).

Burleigh Wilkins, *Terrorism and Collective Responsibility* (New York: Routledge, 1992).

Wayne McWilliams and Harry Piotrowski, *The World Since 1945: A History of International Relations* (Boulder, CO.: Lynne Rienner Publishers, 1993).

Glossary

L'agence culturelle et technique de la langue français (Agency for Cultural and Technical Co-operation): An international association of French-language nation-states concerned with cultural and technical co-operation.

alliance: Normally an alliance is a bilateral or multilateral treaty that stresses co-operation wherein the member states are expected to come to the aid of the collectivity. Alliances can also be based on a common strategy on the part of states to have access to desirable economic and political resources.

aprismo: The democratic revolutionary movement spawned by the American Popular Revolutionary Alliance (APRA), founded by Victor Haya de la Torre of Peru, which came to be the prototype for other revolutionary parties of the democratic left in the Latin American region.

balance of payments: A statistical record of all economic transactions that have taken place during a given time period between a state's residents and the rest of the world.

balance of power: A concept used to denote several types of interstate relations in the context of shifting alliances and alignments.

Canadian Security Intelligence Service (CSIS): A special intelligence agency of the Canadian government that came into being in July 1984, with a legal mandate to place under surveillance anyone suspected of terrorism, espionage, sabotage, and foreign-influenced threats to national security of domestic subversion.

cartel: An international agreement among producers of a commodity that attempts to control the production and pricing of that commodity.

collective security: A concept that provides for a global or regional defence system based on the agreement of members to take collective action against an aggressive and belligerent state or group of states.

common market: An economic association of states that moves them several steps closer to economic integration. In addition to free trade among members and a common external tariff, common markets either eliminate or substantially reduce restrictions on the movements of labour and capital among member states. They may even co-ordinate fiscal, monetary, and exchange-rate policies.

conciliation: A procedure to peacefully settle disputes in which representatives of a group of impartial nation-states establish the facts and base recommendations on them to the disputants.

conflict: In the international system, it is a type of interstate interaction, characterized by antagonistic encounters or collisions of interests, ideas, policies, programs, and persons or other entities, sometimes involving the use of armed force.

Contadora Peace Initiative: A proposal produced by the so-called Contadora states - Colombia, Panama, Mexico and Venezuela, calling for a regional non-aggressive treaty to end hostilities among Central American states and requiring the support of the United States.

customs union: Eliminates tariffs among members but goes beyond the free trade area by erecting a common external tariff against imports from the outside world.

détente: A diplomatic term indicating a situation of lessened tension in relations between two or more nation-states that is manifested by increased communication, negotiation and trade.

deterrence: A political and military strategy based on the theory that the best way to prevent war and aggression is to build up such a massive and threatening arsenal of weapons that no other nation-state would risk an attack.

foreign policy: A policy that, like domestic policy, involves choice-taking, but involves choices about relations with other nations-states, international organizations, and the rest of the world.

free-trade zone: Eliminates tariffs among member states, but each member is permitted to set its own external tariffs on imports.

General Agreement on Tariffs and Trade (GATT): An international organization formed at Geneva in 1947 that promotes trade among members and provides a forum for negotiating the reduction of tariffs, quotas, and other trade barriers.

good offices: As viewed from the perspective of international law this is an instrument used for the peaceful settlement of disputes by which a state not party to a dispute offers the perceived neutrality of its territory and official resources to parties in conflict so as to facilitate a negotiated settlement.

hegemony: The domination of one state over another state, region, or the world by means of superior military capability, economic productivity, and foreign policy.

Holy See: This refers to the office or jurisdiction of the pope.

Inter-American system: The network of international relations among the nation-states of the western hemisphere based on American international law, international institutions, commitments, and agreements through which regional co-operation and integration are achieved.

Inter-American Treaty of Reciprocal Assistance: A permanent collective-security agreement, establishing a defence zone from the North to the South Pole, that provides for military assistance among signatories in case of an armed attack within the zone or any form of aggression against a signatory from outside the zone.

International Monetary Fund (IMF): A specialized agency of the United Nations, established in 1944, to promote exchange-rate stability and provide monetary services to help its more than 130 members overcome short-term disequilibria in the balance of payments.

mediation: A procedure to peacefully settle disputes, whereby an impartial third party assists the disputants to resolve a conflict by offering its good offices, recommendations, and diplomatic skills to reconcile opposing claims.

most-favoured-nation principle: A provision inserted in a trade agreement that extends tariff concessions to all other states participating in the reciprocal system, thereby favouring them in terms of economic benefits.

multilateral: A course of action taken by three or more states to foster co-operation in trade, collective security, or any economic, political, or military endeavour established by treaty, convention, or other international instruments.

Non-Governmental Organizations (NGOs): Private international organizations that serve to co-ordinate national and international groups, especially in economic, social, cultural, humanitarian, and technical fields.

non-tariff barriers (NTBs): Non-monetary restrictions on trade, such as quotas, technical restrictions, quarantines, and inspection procedures.

North/South axis: The growing tension between the few economically developed economies of the North and the many deprived economies of the South.

nuclear deterrence: The theory that if enough nuclear weapons are stockpiled by the government of one or more nation-states, other nuclear-weapons states would refrain from using them as a deterrent.

observer status: A formal arrangement between an international organization and a non-member state, allowing it to observe its decision-making councils without voting privileges.

Organization for Economic Co-operation and Development (OECD): A regional international economic organization established in 1961 to study and promote economic growth and free trade among its 24 members.

peaceful settlement of disputes: The resolution of international disputes, using legal and political procedural techniques such as arbitration, adjudication, diplomatic negotiation, good offices, inquiry, mediation, and conciliation.

plenipotentiary: Usually refers to the use of all available powers and resources in negotiation and diplomatic relations between and among states.

protectionism: The theory and practice of using government regulation to control, limit, or terminate the volume of imports entering a state.

quasi-legal: This term is used when people in positions of public and/or legislative authority use their discretion to investigate the facts or draw conclusions from facts in their official capacity.

signatory: Under international law, this term usually refers to the party or parties signing a treaty.

state terrorism: Acts of terrorism carried out directly by, or encouraged and funded by, an established government.

supranational organization: An international organization to which members surrender some sovereignty or jurisdiction to a higher authority in order to achieve a degree of political and economic integration.

third option: One of three policy options considered by the Trudeau government in its foreign policy review that entailed decreasing reliance on trade with the United States by reconstructing the economy and diversifying Canada's economic interaction with the rest of the world in order to achieve greater economic and political independence.

unilateral: An independent action or policy taken by a state from its own resources to advance its national interest.

Uniting for Peace Resolution: A resolution that authorizes the General Assembly to take collective action against aggression when the Security Council is paralyzed from ordering action by a permanent member's veto.

World Bank: With its headquarters in Washington, D.C., the World Bank, formally the International Bank for Reconstruction and Development (IBRD), is the largest single lending institution in the international community, instituted to encourage development and investment between the advanced industrial economies and the less-developed economies.

world government: The age-old concept of a global set of governing institutions that would make laws binding on all national and international actors which would surrender many of their sovereign rights to a supranational authority.

FOURTEEN

International Law

The captain of a U.S. scallop-dragger gestures angrily following his
April, 1994 arrest by Canadian Coast Guard officials for overfishing.

Chapter Objectives

After reading this chapter, you will be able to:

- reflect on the development of international law

- understand how law works in the international system

- define international law

- compare the character of international law with the various qualities of national law

- consider how binding laws can be made in the absence of an international legislature, or a world executive governing body

- identify what global instruments make international law

- describe how international organizations make international law

- understand the nature of compliance and deviance in the global community

- describe the role of the International Court of Justice in resolving global and international disputes

- comment on the role of national courts for adjudicating and creating international law

- consider the directions international law is likely to take in the future

Law and Order in the International Community

In the 444 days preceding January 20, 1981, the world witnessed one of the most blatant violations of international law that could be committed by a state. Under the new regime headed by the militant religious leader the Ayatollah Khomeini, Iran held 52 Americans hostage in Tehran in order to extract concessions from the U.S. government and to expose the corruption of the ousted Shah. The prolonged incident sent shock waves through the diplomatic corps of the entire international community as the principle of diplomatic immunity, which protects diplomatic personnel from seizure and punishment, was ignored by the Khomeini regime. For Canadians, events in Iran held a special significance because Ambassador Ken Taylor arranged the chilling escape of six American diplomats during the hostage crisis, making him the international hero of the diplomatic world.

In its unprecedented violation of a fundamental rule of international law, Iran did not legally answer for its conduct. And, in all probability, it may never have to. This incident is a vivid illustration of the dilemma of international law in an increasingly violent and potentially explosive international society. In 1989, the same leader, the Ayatollah Khomeini, pronounced the death sentence on author Salman Rushdie, a British citizen, thereby committing yet another fundamental breach of international law. Other than political, economic, and military sanctions, there are no **compulsory enforcement** instruments for bringing a recalcitrant government to justice in the international system: there is no international legislature for making laws; there is no regular international police force to counteract illegal behaviour; and there is no **compulsory adjudication** to force a violator to appear in court and respect the law.

It would appear that international law is a powerless deterrent against **deviant behaviour** in the international community. But this is a misconception. In reality, most states do not violate international law. **Compliance** with the laws of the international community is often greater than the degree of compliance and enforcement found in centralized national legal systems, where institutions to legislate and enforce laws are present and developed.[1] In the United States, for example, only three murders out of ten result in a conviction; and of all serious crimes reported (except murder), only 19 percent of the cases result in arrests, less than ten percent of those arrested are convicted, and only 2.5 percent of those convicted spend time in a correctional institution. In Great Britain, some 59 percent of all serious crimes known to the police do not result in convictions. In Canada, police do not gain convictions on 63 percent of most reported offences and are able only to record as few as one out of every 23 crimes committed. Yet these three legal systems are among the most highly developed in the world.

Compliance with international law tends to be greater than **municipal law** because states comply out of national interest. States are themselves the architects of systems of law and order in international affairs and so are willing to tolerate constraints on their own behaviour in the absence of strong legislative and enforcement mechanisms. In addition, in the international community (which is composed of only about 200 members), there are enormous pressures on governments to comply with the expected rules of behaviour. By means of legal challenges, diplomatic manoeuvres, and political jabs, violators are made to face the judgements of their peers.

When a state violates international law, it is almost always detected by other states, which may take extra-legal as well as legal measures against the perpetrator. For example, the international community expressed strong disapproval on learning that the United States was responsible for illegally mining Nicaragua's harbours in February and March 1984. The mining stopped in April of that year after the Sandinista government introduced a resolution before the United Nations Security Council in New York City calling for an immediate halt to such practices. Even though the U.S. vetoed the resolution, it had suffered a severe blow to its legal credibility in Central America. A long-time champion of the rule of law, the U.S. was seen to be breaking it. While the deterrent effect of law is less formal and less institutionalized in the international system, most states have learned that their compliance with it avoids chaos in the complex world of international commerce, travel, and politics.

What Is International Law?

International law has been defined as "a *system* of law containing *principles*, *customs*, *standards* and *rules* by which relations among states and other international *persons* are governed."[2] As with most definitions, key terms demand

elaboration. International law is *systematic* because it endeavours to establish persisting patterns of legal relationships among all members of the international community, which are interdependent and need a peaceful and orderly environment to survive. The systematic nature of international law results from its universal design, intended to invite compliance from all members of the international community. The **legitimacy** of international law is based on the consent of states to regard its authority as binding on their behaviour. Because of this need for consent, the probability of compliance increases significantly when a great number of states accept a rule of conduct. Thus, a multilateral treaty **ratified** by 150 states has greater legitimacy than one that only 25 states have ratified.

International law is made up of generally accepted *principles of law* governing the conduct of states. **Principles** are fundamental rules of conduct that guide the legal behaviour of states. One such principle is the **ius cogens** (law of pre-emptory norms), whereby a treaty becomes void if it is contrary to norms recognized by the international community as a whole.[3] For example, a treaty signed and ratified by some states to exterminate a racial or ethnic group runs contrary to general principles of international law and thus is void. Another accepted principle is the legal equality of independent states. This principle is generally recognized and upheld as international law. For example, Bolivia's vote in the General Assembly of the United Nations carries the same legal weight as Canada's, despite the differences in the size and wealth of the two states.

Customs form a substantial body of international law. In a landmark case of international law – *The Paquette Habana* v. *The Lola* (1900) – U.S. Supreme Court Justice Horace Gray defined custom as "ancient usage ripening into law." The incorporation of customs into **codified law** has occurred frequently in the twentieth century. Customs that are widely practised as binding on states still continue to surface, as with international behaviour on diplomacy and in space. For example, a growing number of states are placing restrictions on some of the codified rules regarding diplomatic immunities (see Chapter 15). And space is being researched and tested for the use of defensive and offensive military technology, despite the presence of treaties and conventions that have previously designated space a non-military area of scientific research.

> ■ ■ **codified law:** the process of collecting and arranging the laws of a state into a code, i.e., into a complete system of positive law, scientifically ordered, and promulgated by legislative or executive authority. ■ ■

Standards of conduct refer to the generally accepted procedures by which states reach agreements and apply solutions to resolve conflicts. Rather than resort to the use of force to settle disputes, states are expected to negotiate, **adjudicate**, and **arbitrate** when conflicts arise. States are obliged to employ peaceful instruments and skills in their relations with the other members of the international community.

Until the twentieth century, only states were considered as "persons," i.e., entities with rights and obligations under international law. Today, these legal rights are extended to international organizations and individuals. For example, diplomatic immunities are enjoyed by international organizations such as the United Nations and the Organization of American States, and are protected by international convention. These or-ganizations have rights and duties similar to those of states, and their general conduct is accountable under international law. Under international law, individuals can gain the status of legal "persons" only in a limited set of circumstances. Because most individuals possess a **nationality**, their own states either act as agents to protect them or to prosecute them for behaviour that has international consequences.

When individuals become refugees, or **stateless**, international law directs a limited measure of legal "personality" to them. The basis for the legal protection of refugees was established during the Convention Relating to the Status of Refugees in 1951. This convention determined the rights of refugees to work, to education, to social welfare, to religious freedom, and to legal processes. Article 15 of the Universal Declaration of Human Rights (1948) laid down standards for dealing with stateless persons. International law encourages states to adopt a flexible approach to the conferment of nationality on stateless persons and to provide them with proper identity documents to enable their legal admission to other states.

Finally, international law is a very special kind of law because of its consensual nature.[4] It is intimately tied to the presence of the decentralized international system that emerged in Europe in the sixteenth and seventeenth centuries. Since the Treaty of Westphalia in 1648, most states that comprise this decentralized international community have shown a willingness to abide by the law of the majority and have developed habits of compliance with international norms. This international system has been successful in developing an identifiable process for creating legally binding *rules* of conduct, even in the absence of a complete set of formal institutional lawmaking machinery. The sources of this process of law are officially recognized by the states of the world and have been documented as Article 38 of the Statute of the International Court of Justice, which is attached to the United Nations Charter.

Sources of International Law

The international legal system consists of a substantial body of law derived from five sources: (1) widely recognized and practised customs of states; (2) international treaties and conventions signed and ratified by states; (3) general principles of law recognized by states; (4) judicial decisions of national and international courts and tribunals; and (5) writings and teachings of qualified legal experts. These are fundamentally democratic instruments that help create and collect the legitimate laws of the international system.[5]

Some scholars have noted that the acts of international organizations, particularly the United Nations and its specialized agencies, also develop international law.[6] Each of these six sources has contributed to international legal development by recognizing the historical compliance of states and international organizations with the rules of international conduct and by establishing new laws (figure 14.1).

Ultimately, however, states themselves are the principle source of international law.

They hold the power of consent to the norms and customs that have evolved over a long period of time and they ultimately become parties to the treaties that bind them to the codified laws of international behaviour.

Custom

With the emergence of modern European states in the mid-seventeenth century, the vast majority of transactions among independent political units were governed by customs. This body of observable usages and practices in international conduct became widely accepted by states as obligatory and **binding** as law. Habitual, constant, and uniform conduct evolved in many areas of international behaviour. Rules of conduct in times of war, standard practices of navigation and maritime safety, diplomatic immunity, the observance of treaties, and the jurisdictions of states are examples of law built on the actual practices of states. Customs were transformed into legal rules because states recognized the expediency of order in a largely decentralized and lawless international community. The technical name for this psychological motivation to respect custom as law is **opinio iuris sive necessitatis** (*opinio iuris,* for short), which, literally translated, means "legal attitudes are necessary," meaning legal forms of conduct are necessary if chaos is to be avoided.

Until the twentieth century, custom formed the bulk of international law among states. Major and minor inconsistencies in state practices created difficulties in the interpretation and compliance with customary international law.[7] For example, in the sixteenth and seventeenth centuries, states began to make conflicting claims about their jurisdictions within the territorial sea. Many states

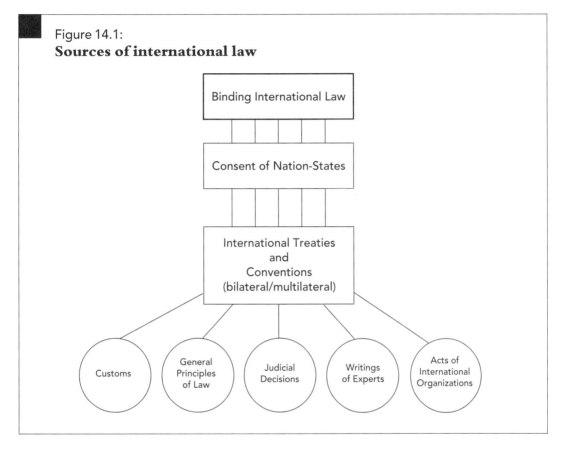

Figure 14.1:
Sources of international law

adopted the custom of regarding their territorial boundaries as including sea up to three miles from the shore – the range of a cannonball fired from the low-water mark on shore. Many states accepted this "cannon-shot" rule, but Scandinavian states claimed four miles of territorial sea and Spain and Portugal claimed six. In the twentieth century, the practice of codifying international law has done much to clarify these types of inconsistencies in the practices of states. The Third United Nations Conference on the Law of the Sea (adopted on April 30, 1982) went a long way toward codifying these kinds of ambiguous practices of states. Article 3 of the convention reads "every state has the right to establish the breadth of its territorial sea up to a limit not exceeding twelve nautical miles." When the convention is finally ratified by the required number of states (in this case 60, out of which 37 had ratified by 1990), it will have transformed hundreds of years of conflicting customs on maritime jurisdiction into an intelligible body of codified legal prescriptions.

Today, customary law continues to form an important part of international law, but treaties have displaced custom as its major source.[8] In a rapidly changing and more highly integrated international community, custom has come to be regarded as a scattered and imprecise source for determining rules of conduct. The younger states in the global community in Asia, Africa, Latin America, and the Caribbean demand more exacting instruments to consolidate and create law. The confusion in locating the existence of customary law, and determining the consent toward it, has increasingly motivated states to negotiate lawmaking treaties.

International Conventions

Conventions are sometimes called treaties, covenants, accords, pacts, charters, declarations, statutes, or protocols.[9] Regardless of the name, all conventions are international law and have a binding effect on the parties who consent to them, based on the legal principle **pacta sunt servanda** (pacts are binding).

By definition, conventions are formal international agreements between two or more states. When they are entered into by only two states, the treaty is bilateral; when many states sign and ratify a treaty, it is said to be multilateral. As sources of international law, multilateral treaties perform two important functions: (1) the codification of existing rules of customary international law (e.g., the Vienna Convention on Succession of States in Respect of Treaties, 1978), and (2) the creation of new international law (Outer Space Treaty, 1967).

Such treaties have global significance and are widely viewed as making world law because of their general and universal effect. Some international law experts have even identified multilateral conventions with the legislation of laws in municipal legal systems. One noteworthy exception in this analogy is that conventions legally apply only to those states that consent to their provisions. Yet even under circumstances where a state does not ratify a treaty because it objects to some of its provisions, there are extra-legal pressures on non-consenting states to comply at least with the spirit of a lawmaking treaty, if not with the letter of that treaty's law.

The U.S. decision not to sign the 1982 Law of the Sea (LOS) convention does not exempt that state from respecting most of the internationally agreed-upon provisions involving the laws of navigation, fishing rights, conservation, the continental shelf, and the proclaimed establishment off U.S. shores of a 200-mile Exclusive Economic Zone (EEZ) that is compatible with many of the provisions of the convention. Because 130 states adopted the LOS convention, the U.S. is sensitive to the near-global consensus on this regime of maritime law and recognizes the rights of other states in the waters off its coasts, as outlined in the convention. To behave otherwise would run contrary to the general will of the international community and ultimately would have negative consequences for U.S. national interests.

Article 102 of the United Nations Charter requires that all treaties be registered with the Secretariat of the United Nations so that they are known to the world. This requirement adds another important dimension of legitimacy to all treaties, bilateral as well as multilateral. Open publication of treaties is not only intended to discourage the practice of secret conventions, but to demonstrate the levels of consensus achieved concerning international norms and expectations. Lawmaking treaties are barometers of world opinion. To resist compliance with the expected behaviour of states is to run against the common will of the international community.

The continuing development of international law has been greatly enhanced since 1947, when the General Assembly of the United Nations created the International Law Commission (ILC). The ILC is charged with the tasks of studying, recommending, and codifying international law. Its numerous international law experts – who represent most of the world's legal systems – research and codify customary law in the area of recognition, state succession, diplomatic immunities, state jurisdictional immunities, law of the sea, nationality, statelessness, and arbitral procedures. They consolidate their legal research and prepare drafts that are reported to the General Assembly, which has often convened international conferences to adopt lawmaking treaties. The ILC did the preparatory work for a convention on diplomatic relations at Vienna in 1961; a convention on consular relations at Vienna in 1963; a convention on the law of treaties at Vienna in 1969; the convention on state succession at Vienna in 1978, and on the law of the sea at Geneva in 1958, and the United Nations in 1982.

The writing of draft articles of agreement by the ILC has been instrumental in summarizing international laws that have evolved over a period of 2500 years. By gradually displacing the uncertainties of disparate customs practised by states, lawmaking treaties have injected a high degree of precision in the application of international law. Indeed, the twentieth century will be remembered by students of international behaviour as a period when detailed written codes of conduct agreed to by a majority of states added much to the binding authority and competence of international law.

General Principles of Law

In cases where treaty law and customary law do not provide guidance in international disputes, the Statute of the International Court of Justice (ICJ) points to "the general principles of law recognized by civilized nations."[10] To avoid the possibility of a case remaining undecided and to ensure that justice is done when other sources of law provide no assistance, states in conflict will sometimes invoke generally recognized principles of national and international law to settle disputes.

Some of these general principles of international law revolve around the concepts of sovereignty, legal equality of states, territorial integrity, and non-interference in the internal affairs of other states. They have also been drawn from principles of justice derived from *natural law*.[11] The essence of law itself is discovered from the meticulous organization of the universe, which demonstrates that order (in this case, legal order) is required if the human race is to survive. Thus, as a general principle, prescriptions for human behaviour are necessary if order is to be maintained among interacting states. The concept that each side in a dispute is entitled to a fair hearing and that judicial decisions should be made *ex aequo et bono* (out of justice and fairness) when no exacting codes of law are applicable are examples of general principles of law applied in international tribunals.

The practice of incorporating international law into domestic municipal legal systems is another general principle linking national and international law. Canada, the United States, Belgium, France, and Switzerland, to name but a few, have practised the adoption, incorporation, and harmonization of international law with domestic lawmaking processes. This has important legal consequences for nationals of one state contesting an international dispute in another domestic legal system. In the case *The Paquette Habana* v. *The Lola*, Supreme Court of the United States (1900), the court reasoned that "international law is part of our law and must be ascertained and administered by courts of justice of appropriate jurisdictions." In *West Rand Central Gold Mining Co., Ltd.,* v. *The King*, King's Bench Division, Great Britain (1905), the court ruled that "it is true that whatever has received the common consent of civilized nations must have received the consent of Great Britain, and that to which the latter has assented...could properly be called international law."

In Canada, over 20 percent of the Revised Statutes of Canada incorporate the rules of international customary and treaty law.[12] But Canadian courts have not ruled consistently on the relationship of international law to domestic law. In some early cases, such as *The Ship "North"* v. *The King* (1906), it appeared that Canada was following court practices in the United Kingdom to take "judicial notice" of the rules of international law and to interpret the rules of domestic law in a manner compatible with them. In 1943, however, in two cases (*Reference re Power of Municipalities to Levy Rates on Foreign Legations and High Comm'rs Residences* and *Reference re Exemption of U.S. Forces from Canadian Criminal Law*), a number of justices of the Supreme Court argued that even customary international law is part of Canadian law only if those customs are formally "incorporated" by Parliament or given judicial notice. In another case, *République Democratique du Congo* v. *Venne* (1971), the Supreme Court clearly supported the principle that customary international law is part of Canadian law. Similarly, in 1969, the Québec Court of Appeal, in *Penthouse Studios Inc.* v. *Government of Venezuela*, recognized that even the changing character of custom is enforced in Canada.

There is no question that different systems of national law try to conform to general principles of law as derived directly from the international community or from within themselves. The problems of seeking and interpreting general principles of law result from the isolated traditions of law throughout the world. The Anglo-American system, the **Napoleonic Code**, the Islamic system, and the system of law most communist states follow are based on different philosophical and cultural premises. But the disparity of fundamental legal systems does not take away the political need to foster legal uniformity. There exists a tacit understanding in the world community that international order is safeguarded by specific rules of common acceptance. The Statute of the International Court of Justice has recognized the imperative character of these rules as a primary source on international law. And among states, we can detect a conscious subordination of state activity to the general welfare of the international community.

■ ■ **Napoleonic code:** the code of law promulgated in 1804, when Napoleon became emperor, which embodies the civil law of France. ■ ■

Judicial Decisions

Judicial decisions are cited in Article 38(1)(d) of the statute "as subsidiary means for the determination of rules of law." The problem international law presents is twofold: in the absence of formal lawmaking institutions, it is always necessary first to establish agreement as to the very idea of international law itself. This problem is significant for judicial decisions because they are viewed primarily as an indirect and subsidiary source of international law.

But upon close examination, the value of domestic and international court decisions as sources of international law can be discovered. If a court in a domestic legal system or an international tribunal interprets a contentious question of international law, its judicial opinion includes the rationale for the decision, the **ratio decidendi**. It indicates what the rule is held to mean at the time the decision is drafted. This provides the international community with a ruling on international law, a kind of precedent, to which analogous cases may conform. Even though in international law there is no doctrine of *stare decisis et non quieta movere* (to stand by decisions and not to change what has been settled) to affirm the obligatory character of previous decisions as precedents, most court systems take **judicial notice** of them and usually take them into account. In time, as precedents are rendered by a series of similar judicial decisions, a body of legal opinions is formed. As early as 1815, Chief Justice John Marshall of the Supreme Court of the United States ruled in the case of *Thirty Hogsheads of Sugar* v. *Boyle* that "the decisions of the Courts of every country show how the law of nations, in the given case, is understood in that country, and will be considered in adopting the rule which is to prevail in this." In the

> ■ ■ **judicial notice:** the act by which a court in conducting a trial, or framing its decision, will of its own motion, and without the production of evidence, recognize the existence and truth of certain facts that have a bearing on the matter before it. ■ ■

Barcelona Traction case, the ICJ made reference to the rulings on nationality in an earlier case (the *Nottebohm* case) in order to distinguish the nationality of a Canadian company that was controlled by Belgian shareholders and that incurred injuries inflicted by Spain.[13]

The ICJ has not only taken judicial notice of previous cases in affirming the existence of customary and codified law but has, in some cases, created new law. In the *Reparation for Injuries Suffered in the Service of the United Nations* case (1949), the court certified the legal personality of the United Nations and affirmed the capacity of that international organization to assert claims against other entities in the international system for injuries suffered by its agents. Similarly, in the *Anglo-Norwegian Fisheries* case (1951), the ICJ stated new criteria for the delimitation of base lines from which to determine the width of the territorial sea. These criteria were adopted by the Geneva Convention on the Territorial Sea and Contiguous Zone (1958) and included in the Law of the Sea Convention in 1982.

There is no question that international law is both summarized and created by judicial decisions rendered by domestic and international tribunals. The dramatic legal battle in 1984/85 between Ariel Sharon, a prominent Israeli politician, and *Time* magazine, a multinational corporation, in a Manhattan federal court, had international legal consequences. At issue in the $50 million lawsuit was the international reputation of an Israeli citizen who was directly linked to the vengeful massacre by Lebanese Christians of as many as 800

Palestinians in two Beirut refugee camps in a seven-page cover story of *Time* headlined "The verdict is guilty." As a result of the news story, Mr. Sharon was forced to resign as Israel's defence minister, and subsequently claimed that his worldwide reputation was destroyed. The three rulings of the U.S. federal court – two in favour of Sharon – decided the *Time* article was false; one vindicated *Time* of malice to libel Sharon and affirmed a growing tendency in the present century to recognize that individuals and companies have some degree of international legal personality.[14] Individuals and corporations have not only acquired rights and duties under special treaties, but have also had specific rights and duties identified by domestic courts, as in the case of Ariel Sharon and *Time* magazine.

Each decision carries its own prestige, which, when combined with the traditional and legal authority of the courts in question, creates a subsidiary but nonetheless important source of international law. The framework of national judicial power often extends far beyond the limited binding application of judicial decisions to the contesting parties in a legal dispute. In effect, all judicial decisions of international consequence contribute to the substance of international law, providing trans-national and cross-cultural norms in the international community.

Writings of Learned Experts

In addition to being a legal system, international law is also a formal academic field of study, drawing expertise from the disciplines of history, law, philosophy, and political science. The academic study of international law developed concurrently with the modern nation-state system in the sixteenth and seventeenth centuries. Learned writers, or "publicists," as they were once called, began to analyze and interpret the evolution of international law.

Hugo Grotius (1583-1645), widely acclaimed as the founder of international law, published his *De jure belli ac pacis libri tris* (*Three Books on the Law of War and Peace*) in 1625. It was the first modern study of the law of states. Other noteworthy publicists to follow Grotius were Richard Zouche (1590-1660), Samuel Pufendorf (1632-1694), Emmerich de Vattel (1714-1769), and John Austin (1790-1859). In 1790, Jeremy Bentham invented the term "international law" to designate what had previously been called "the law of nations" (**jus gentium**, *droit des gens*) in his book, *An Introduction to the Principles of Morals and Legislation*, which was published in 1789.

In more recent times, names such as Hans Kelsen, Josef Kunz, James Brierly, Richard Falk, and Michael Akehurst come to mind as modern legal publicists. Contemporary writers conduct comparative research into the behavioural aspects of international law. They plot trends in the legal expectations of states and monitor the international system for new sources of law in codified form, for any legal or academic reference is a major unofficial contribution to the body of scholarly materials on international law. Today, almost every state has a pool of international legal experts who publish work on a regular basis. These publications have created a vast and instructive body of opinion and analysis for use by justices who deliberate upon international cases.

Acts of International Institutions

The Statute of the International Court of Justice does not list the acts of international organizations as a source of international law. However, a growing number of scholars now detect a substantial body of international law directly emerging from the work of numerous international institutions.[15] Most international organizations are institutional forums in which legal norms are debated and generated by member states. Many of these organizations pass resolutions and declarations that carry quasi-legal authority and promote world law (table 14.1). It is true that these resolutions and declarations are not as binding as are ratified treaties. But they do represent a consensus of membership expectations on important matters of international behaviour. In the **inter-American system**, resolutions and declarations adopted at conferences are regarded as binding by Latin American states and thus create legal obligations among them. For example, the Charter of Bogota, proclaimed at the Ninth Inter-American Conference in 1948, established the Organization of American States (OAS), which creates an obligation for all signatory states to use peaceful settlement procedures, including diplomacy, good offices, mediation, investigation, conciliation, arbitration, and adjudication.

In the General Assembly of the United Nations, resolutions are not necessarily binding on member states, but often they call for the creation of an international conference to draft a multilateral treaty that would bind signatories. The consensus expressed through resolutions and declarations in the United Nations can lead to the creation of a new rule in conventional law or may reflect the presence of a new principle of international custom. For example, in 1963, the General Assembly passed its Declaration of Legal Principles Governing Activities in Outer Space based on a unanimous proclamation that "international law, including the Charter of the United Nations, applies to outer space...and that 'outer space' and celestial bodies are free for exploration and use by all States in conformity with international law, and are not subject to national exploitation." Later, in 1966, these principles were embodied in the Outer Space Treaty, which came into force in 1967.

Another international organization that has played a pioneering role in creating new international law has been the International Labor Organization (ILO). Since its establishment in 1919, it has built a body of law known as the International Labor Code. In the 1990s, the code consists of the work of nearly 160 conventions that have dealt with a wide range of ratified recommendations in the area of workers' rights, wages, insurance benefits, and the protection of women, young people, miners, and sailors. In a similar way, the World Health Organization (WHO) created the Code of International Health Regulations, adopted in 1969, to establish legal controls on hundreds of drugs used throughout the world.

One other specialized agency of the United Nations, the International Civil Aviation Organization (ICAO), headquartered in Montreal, has been one of the most active bodies in the development of international law in the area of air transportation. The ICAO has established regulations governing information standards, facilities, and services

> **Table 14.1:**
> ## Major international organizations and agencies promoting world law
>
> Amnesty International (London)
> European Commission of Human Rights (Strasbourg, France)
> European Court of Human Rights (Strasbourg)
> The Institute for World Order, Inc. (New York)
> Inter-American Council of Jurists (Juridical Committee) Rio de Janeiro
> Inter-American Commission on Human Rights (Washington)
> International Chamber of Commerce (Paris)
> International Commission of Jurists (Geneva)
> International Court of Justice (The Hague)
> International Labor Organization (Geneva)
> Organization of African Unity (Addis Abba, Ethiopia)
> Organization of American States (Washington)
> United Nations Commission on Human Rights (Geneva)
> United Nations Commission on International Trade Law (Vienna)
> United Nations Economic and Social Council (New York)
> United Nations Educational, Scientific and Cultural Organization (Paris)
> United Nations General Assembly (New York)
> World Federalists Association (Washington)
> World Health Organization (WHO) (Geneva)
> The World Peace Through Law Centre (Geneva)

in world air transportation. For example, as a result of deep concerns expressed by the International Federation of Airline Pilots Associations (IFALPA) over the downing by a Soviet military jet of a Korean passenger plane that had "strayed" into Soviet territory on September 1, 1983, the ICAO passed a resolution deploring the incident and calling for a clearer set of standards to regulate the identification of all aircraft in the future.

The International Court of Justice

The International Court of Justice, sometimes called the World Court, is one of the six principal organs of the United Nations, with headquarters at The Hague, Netherlands. The court comprises 15 judges serving nine-year terms who are elected by a concurrent vote of the General Assembly and the Security Council. In order to provide fair representation, no two judges of the same

Figure 14.2:
Disputed fishing grounds (Canada/United States) adjudicated by the ICJ

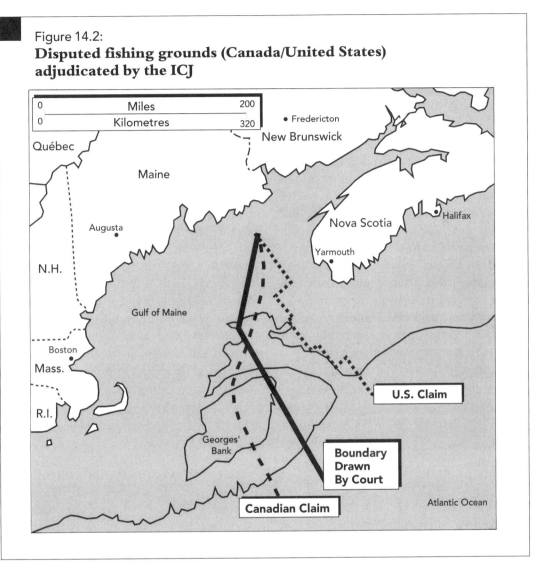

nationality may sit on the bench at the same time. And if parties to the dispute do not have national judges elected at the time the case is heard, they may appoint their own judge with full voting rights. Cases are decided by majority vote, and in the event of a tie, the president of the court casts the deciding vote.

According to ICJ statute, only states are entitled to appear as litigants before the court. When contesting states permit the court to make a judgement in a case, that judgement binds the parties. For this reason, many states have been reluctant to register their legal complaints with the court. And sometimes states that do submit cases to the court simply ignore the decision. Several states, including such outstanding international citizens as Iceland, India, and France, have refused to submit to the panel's rulings. For example, in 1984, the United States terminated its agreement to submit to the compulsory jurisdiction of the ICJ because the court found for Nicaragua, rejecting U.S. arguments that Nicaragua's charges against the U.S. were merely political. Nicaragua argued that U.S. support for the *Contra* rebels and the mining of Nicaraguan harbours by the U.S. constituted violations of international law. In 1980, Iran also ignored a judgement from the court to pay reparations to the U.S. for seizing its embassy in Tehran.

Because the ICJ lacks compulsory adjudication, whereby states would be compelled to appear before the world tribunal to defend their actions, the court can only hear those cases that states choose to bring before it. To strengthen the position of the court in this regard, Article 36 of the statute provides the *Optional Clause*. Under this clause, states agree in advance to accept the compulsory adjudication of the court involving questions of treaty interpretation, international law, breaches of international obligations, and reparations.

Canada and the United States accepted the compulsory adjudication of the court to settle a question of jurisdiction on the North American east coast. In 1984, the World Court ruled on a boundary dispute that had been raging for seven years between Canada and the United States over the rich resources and fishing grounds on the Georges' Bank off the coasts of Maine, Massachusetts, and Nova Scotia. The disputed jurisdictions resulted when both states extended their territorial limits 200 nautical miles to sea. In its decision,

the ICJ dismissed the arguments of both states, and developed its own criteria for drawing a new boundary line between Massachusetts and Nova Scotia, asserting that Canada and the United States had based some of their claims on false premises. The decision was binding in accordance with a 1981 Canada-U.S. agreement that registered the dispute with the ICJ and accepted its jurisdiction to rule on the Georges' Bank with no appeal.

The court's ruling was unexpected by both parties and, in effect, created new law that will likely affect five other maritime disputes in which Canada is involved – three with the United States, one with France over St. Pierre and Miquelon, and one with Greenland. Canada had proposed a line based on the principle of **equidistance** and disregarded the existence of Cape Cod and Nantucket Island, arguing that they constituted unusual geographic protrusions of the U.S. coastline. Washington claimed all of the Georges' Bank with a proposed line that came as close to Yarmouth, Nova Scotia, as 25 nautical miles.

The World Court awarded Canada one-sixth of the bank – only half the territory it claimed – but unexpectedly, Ottawa got the northeast edge, where there are concentrations of scallop beds, vital to Nova Scotia's $60-million-a-year scallop industry. The area awarded to the United States amounts to five-sixths of the Georges' Bank, over which Washington had claimed total jurisdiction (figure 14.2). Despite the dislocation and economic hardship generated by the decision on people in the fishing industries of both states, the court's ruling was accepted as international law.

Of the 160 states that are parties to the

Statute of the International Court of Justice, only 47 adhere to the Optional Clause, most with **reservations** that have the effect of rendering its acceptance meaningless. Since its creation in 1946, the court has rendered judgements in less than 100 cases. Thirteen cases have been removed without judgement because the defendant states refused to submit to the court's jurisdiction or because the plaintiffs removed the case to settle out of court. Besides hearing and deciding on this small number of cases since 1946, the ICJ has been utilized for only 17 advisory opinions, most of which were requested by the United Nations General Assembly.

As witnessed by the declining docket of cases since the 1950s, states are reluctant to submit to the jurisdiction of the World Court. There are several reasons why states appear to distrust the court as a legal instrument for resolving conflict:

■ Powerful states tend to avoid the embarrassment of a legal judgement on their behaviour. They are unwilling to entrust matters of national importance to a non-national legal body with high international visibility.

■ States are more inclined to resort to political instruments such as negotiation, conciliation, and mediation to arrive at the peaceful settlement of disputes.

■ Many states sense that the application of international norms to their disputes is alien to the legal principles in their domestic systems; consequently, they distrust the judicial process of the World Court.

For reasons such as these, the court has not **remedied** major international disputes. In their long-running boundary dispute over the waters surrounding the tiny French islands of St. Pierre and Miquelon, both Canada and France avoided the use of the ICJ in 1988, opting instead to have a mediator help settle their differences over fishing quotas while negotiators continued to seek agreement on geographical boundaries (France claimed 320-kilometre territorial waters and Canada recognized only a 19-kilometre boundary). Mediation, rather than adjudication, was more acceptable to authorities in both countries, even after the arrest by Canada of 17 French fishermen and four politicians for illegally fishing in Canadian waters and the French retaliation shortly thereafter, in which a Newfoundland trawler was seized for fishing in the disputed waters off St. Pierre and Miquelon. However, in 1989, Canada and France agreed to resolve their 12-year territorial dispute by sending it to binding international arbitration. The international tribunal is composed of five judges – one each from Canada, France, Uruguay, Italy, and the United States. In 1992, the **International Court of Arbitration** gave France exclusive economic jurisdiction over a sea corridor of 10.5 nautical miles running south of St. Pierre and Miquelon for a distance of 200 miles. However, the corridor juts deeply into Canadian waters, where many fish stocks – including endangered species of cod – swim freely, and through scallop beds that traditionally have been fished by Newfoundlanders. The ruling forced France and Canada to open new negotiations on the management of these important fish stocks.

Since 1945, international bodies other than the ICJ have been used to address serious international questions – parties to crises in Korea, the Congo, Palestine, Suez, Cyprus,

Zimbabwe, and Afghanistan did not request ICJ judgements. Political and military power have been the primary methods employed by states in major conflicts such as those of Vietnam, Biafra, the Cuban missile crisis, Northern Ireland, and the Middle East. Generally, international confidence in the court is weak and this diminishes the legitimacy of the highest tribunal in the world. But the ending of the Cold War in the early 1990s reduced the tendency of states to regard disputes as matters of polarized ideology. This may foster a new effort to build up the role of the court as part of a movement toward international co-operation. Among developing states there is a willingness to submit issues to the ICJ and to abide by its decisions. In 1991, Guinea-Bissau and Senegal submitted their disputes to the ICJ, permitting them to be settled by the court rather than by the use of force. But until more states are willing to place justice above politics and national interest, the court will remain basically an advisory legal institution of the United Nations.

Acts of the International Law Commission

The work of the International Law Commission (ILC) is a principal instrument for codifying and developing international law. The procedures the ILC employs clarify and standardize existing international law, as well as help to draft the results of research for consideration as new law. The commission uses the following steps to execute its mandate in all areas of codifying modern international law:

■ Researches and selects a relevant topic

■ Submits this topic to the General Assembly for approval

■ Appoints a commission *rapporteur* as liaison with the General Assembly

■ Reports preliminary drafts to the General Assembly

■ Meets to discuss and revise the submission

■ Receives feedback from governments

■ Incorporates suggestions into the draft

■ Submits the revised draft to the General Assembly

The General Assembly then decides whether to convene an international conference to consider the commission's draft. If a conference is held, the participating delegates may make further revisions before the document is prepared for consenting governments to sign. Then follows the slow process of state ratifications before the new convention comes to force. By way of example, these procedures were used by the commission in drafting the Convention on the Reduction of Statelessness (1961) and the Convention on Liability for Damage Caused by Objects Launched into Outer Space (1971).

In spite of what appear to be enormous obstacles, the track record of the ILC is impressive. Most of the multilateral treaties signed and ratified since 1950 have been drafted by the ILC. Its main achievements are in the codification of international customary law; but because of its direct link to world legal opinion, it has great potential to make major breakthroughs in the creation of new laws. The codification and accompanying globalization of international law – a phenomenon witnessed only in the twentieth century – has provided more opportunities and incentives for states to resolve international conflict peacefully rather than violently.

International law continues to evolve as we enter the challenges of a new century. Notwithstanding its many imperfections, the international legal system has come a long way in the twentieth century. No legal system, regardless of its enforcement capabilities, can completely deter violations of the law. International law **proscribes** genocide, yet acts of genocide were witnessed on a regular basis in Rwanda, Somalia, and Bosnia in 1993-94. Idi Amin of Uganda and Pol Pot of Kampuchea both ignored that proscription, killing thousands of their own citizens. Despite the unanimous condemnation of Iran by the General Assembly and the International Court of Justice in 1980, Iran's behaviour toward the United States' diplomats was not remedied. International norms were again disregarded in 1979 when the Soviet Union invaded Afghanistan, and in the same year, when China invaded Vietnam, in 1982 when Israel invaded Lebanon, in 1983 when the United States invaded Grenada, and in 1984 when Vietnam again invaded Cambodia (now Kampuchea). Yet in all these cases of invasion, it is important to note that the protagonist states attempted to justify their actions in terms of international legal standards. For example, both the Soviet and the American invasions were defended as military actions in response to legitimate invitations to rescue deteriorating political systems. In another example, Argentina sought to legitimize its capture of the Falkland Islands in 1982 in accordance with the United Nations Charter.

States believe it is of paramount impor-

■ ■ **proscribe:** when a legislative body or court order forbids a particular activity. ■ ■

tance that they not appear to be in violation of international law so that they can appeal to international morality and world public opinion in support of their actions. Every world leader is aware that the international system is a fish bowl into which all states can look to observe and judge the behaviour of their legal peers.

In past centuries, international law merely served as a normative constraint on the exercise of certain types of power practised by states. But in the twentieth century, there exists the largest number of legally binding bilateral and multilateral treaties governing the behaviour of states in human history. We also see more international organizations dedicated to the promotion and codification of world law than in any previous period. Today, a comprehensive set of binding rules, rights, obligations, and principles has immediate global impact upon the national interest of states. Most states of the world deliberately weigh every action they take in an attempt to comply with the general principles of international law and with the provisions of the treaties to which they are parties. In the sphere of international relations, it is no longer possible for states to view themselves as the highest authorities, absolutely free from restraint. As in all major legal systems, states as subjects are free to determine their own interests but they must do so in conformity with community law. Throughout this century, the organization of states into large and small groups, pursuing common goals, has generated the creation of a formidable legal regime, clearly recognizable by the international community as a coherent and effective legal order.

The Future of International Law

The future effectiveness of international law depends on the willingness of national governments and their legal systems to comply with and enforce international norms. The most significant challenges to international law concern the use of force, intervention, and peace-keeping. Throughout this century especially, an enormous body of treaty law has been proclaimed in the international community. Customary laws regarding retaliation and international intervention are evolving in areas such as Bosnia-Herzegovina and other Balkan trouble-spots, Kuwait, Haiti, and Somalia. With the passing of the Cold War, the forces of European nationalism violently erupted into civil war, at times compelling the United Nations to resort to legally dubious force and intervention to maintain security.

Paradoxically, the protection of human rights depends to some extent on high-level international security, sometimes requiring international interference with a state's domestic policies. The danger is always that powerful governments acting alone will intervene to enforce their own visions of democracy and human rights. The interventions by the United States in Nicaragua, Grenada, and Panama are cases in point. Clearly, international law should not be based on the principle that any state possessing sufficient military power may intervene in the affairs of another in accord with its own definition of human rights. Such a principle violates the very foundations of a multilateral and consensual international legal order.

Can international law meet the challenges in this rapidly changing decade? Part of the drama of the next century will depend on how well states can abide by contemporary international norms and can create new ones to cope with this rapidly changing global area. This century has confirmed that international law does exist, and, though recent increases in multilateral co-operation hold promise for an expanded role for international law, the shape, power, and influence of that law in the coming decade is a matter of speculation.

References

1. Richard Falk, *Revitalizing International Law* (Ames, IA: Iowa State University Press, 1989); and Richard Falk, *Explorations at the Edge of Time: The Prospects for World Order* (Philadelphia: Temple University Press, 1992).

2. Hugh Kindred et al., *International Law Chiefly as Interpreted and Applied in Canada,* 4th ed., (Toronto: Emond Montgomery Publications, 1987), 1-10.

3. Chrostos Rozakis, *The Concept of Ius Cogens in the Law of Treaties* (Amsterdam: North-Holland Publishing Company, 1976), 1-10.

4. Lung-chu Chen, *An Introduction to Contemporary International Law: A Policy-Oriented Perspective* (New Haven, CT: Yale University Press, 1989), Ch.1.

5. Thomas Franck, *The Power of Legitimacy Among Nations* (New York: Oxford University Press, 1990); Thomas Franck, "The emerging right to democratic governance," *The American Journal of International law*, 86, (1992): 46-91.

6. Peter Toma and Robert Gorman, *International Relations: Understanding Global Issues* (Pacific Grove, CA: Brooks-Cole Publishing Company, 1991), Ch.10.

7. Hidemi Suganami, *The Domestic Analogy and World Order Proposals* (New York: Cambridge University Press, 1989).

8. Gerhard von Glahn, *Law Among Nations,* 6th ed. (New York: Maxwell Macmillan, 1992), 17.

9. *Ibid.,* p 13.

10. Nagendra Singh, *The Role and Record of the International Court of Justice* (Dordrecht, the Netherlands: Martinus Nijhoff, 1989).

11. Wolfgang Friedmann, "The Uses of 'General Principles' in the Development of International Law," *American Journal of International Law,* 57 (1963): 279-299; and Josef L. Kunz, "Natural Law Thinking in the Modern Science of International Law," *American Journal of International Law* 55 (1961): 951-958.

12. S.A. Williams and A.L. de Mestral, *Introduction to International Law,* (Toronto: Butterworths, 1979), 27.

13. See *Barcelona Traction* case, International Court of Justice Reports (1970), 3, 42.

14. Michael Akehurst, "Custom as a Source of International Law," *The British Yearbook of International Law #7* (1974-75): 71-74.

15. M.S. McDougal, and M. Reisman, eds., *International Law in Contemporary Perspective* (Mineola, N.Y.: Foundation Press, 1981); and Robert Turner, "International Law, the Use of Force, and Reciprocity: A Comment on Professor Higgins' Overview," *The Atlantic Community Quarterly* 25: 160-174.

Suggested Readings

Robert Bledsoe and Boleslaw Boczek, *The International Law Dictionary* (Santa Barbara, CA: ABC-CLIO, 1991).

David Forsythe, *The Politics of International Law: U.S. Foreign Policy Reconsidered* (Boulder, CO: Lynne Rienner Publishers, 1990).

Gerhard von Glahn, *Law Among Nations* (New York: Macmillan Publishing Company, 1992).

Louis Henkin, *The Age of Rights* (New York: Columbia University Press, 1990).

Walter Jones, *The Logic of International Relations* (New York: HarperCollins College Publishers, 1991).

William Kaplan and Donald McRae, *Law, Policy, and International Justice* (Montreal: McGill-Queen's University Press, 1993).

Christopher Maule and Fen Osler Hampson, *A New World Order? Canada Among Nations, 1992-93* (Ottawa: Carleton University Press, 1992).

Wayne McWilliams and Harry Piotrowski, *The World Since 1945: A History of International Relations* (Boulder, CO: Lynne Rienner Publishers, 1993).

Peter Rowe, *The Gulf War and International Law* (New York: Routledge, 1993).

Paul Stephan III and Boris Klimenko, *International Law and International Security* (New York: M.E. Sharpe, 1991).

Janna Thompson, *Justice and World Order* (New York: Routledge, 1992).

Glossary

adjudication: Under international law, this is a legal technique for settling disputes peacefully which involves submitting them to an established national or international court.

arbitrate: An old pacific practice recognized by international law that permits parties to a dispute to agree on what issues need to be resolved, which judges will deliberate under the rules of international law, and prior agreement that the decision rendered will be binding.

binding: To bring or place under definite duties or legal obligation, particularly by treaty, convention, or custom, which can affect states in a constraining or compulsory manner.

codified law: The process of collecting and arranging the laws of a state into a code, i.e., into a complete system of positive law, scientifically ordered, and promulgated by legislative or executive authority.

compliance: Conduct that demonstrates an acceptance of legal authority, and a willingness to conform to the rules, regulations, and laws of international relations.

compulsory adjudication: The judicial process to compel the attendance in court of a legal person (state) wanted there as a witness or otherwise.

compulsory enforcement: The establishment of the necessary bureaucratic and military machinery to provide and administer the sanctions required to implement international law.

deviant behaviour: In the international community, deviance can be defined as behaviour that is contrary to the standards of customary and legal conduct (which are widely accepted as contributing to the stability of the system in inter-state relations).

equidistance: Boundaries for lakes, oceans, rivers, and straits based on the principle that the line is drawn down the geographical centre, giving each side equal and equally usable portions.

inter-American system: All the regional institutions, organizations and structures created by the Pan-American movement in the western hemisphere. The Organization of American States (OAS) is the largest of these.

International Court of Arbitration: Created at the Hague Conference of 1899 as the Permanent Court of Arbitration at the Hague, this international court institutionalizes and implements the procedures that have evolved on the arbitration of disputes.

ius cogens: The law of unnatural norms, which holds that a treaty is void if, at the time of its conclusion, it conflicts with a pre-emptory norm of general international law.

judicial notice: The act by which a court in conducting a trial, or framing its decision, will of its own motion, and without the production of evidence, recognize the existence and truth of certain facts that have a bearing on the matter before it.

jus gentium: The body of Roman law and equity that applied to all foreigners resident in the Roman Empire. The law was based on relations between foreigners and Roman citizens and reflected the common ideas of justice found in the laws and customs of the various peoples of the Empire.

legitimacy: The perception held by a majority of people that the exercise of power and the system of law are based on "rightful" authority and should be respected and obeyed.

municipal law: The technical term used by international lawyers to refer to the national or domestic law of a state.

Napoleonic Code: The code of law promulgated in 1804, when Napoleon became emperor, which embodies the civil law of France.

nationality: That quality or character that arises from the fact of a person's belonging to a particular nation or state, by birth or naturalization.

opinio iuris sive necessitates: Means "legal attitudes are necessary" and asserts that legal forms of conduct are required by international law.

pacta sunt servanda: Means "pacts are binding" and is the basic postulate on which the whole structure of positive international law is founded.

principles: A comprehensive rule or doctrine that furnishes a clear basis or origin for others unless contradicted by a proposition which is still clearer.

proscribe: When a legislative body or court order forbids a particular activity.

ratify: The procedures used by states to approve and sanction treaties, conventions, and other instruments of international law requiring formal legal adoption by sovereign governments or international organizations.

ratio decidendi: Literally, "the reason for the decision"; in cases of international consequences, court rulings contribute to the general principles of international law.

remedy: The means by which a legal right is enforced or a violation of a right is prevented under international and municipal law.

reservation: A clause in a treaty or other instrument of international relations whereby a signatory retains a right or exception to one or a number of provisions comprising the agreement.

statelessness: The condition of an individual who has lost the legal claim to nationality and who no longer has the protection of any state.

FIFTEEN

Diplomacy

Chapter Objectives

After reading this chapter, you will be able to:

■ appreciate the special privileges of the diplomatic profession

■ recount the development of diplomacy and place it in the context of world law and international relations

■ define diplomatic immunity and understand why it remains a significant aspect of modern negotiation

■ outline the procedures states use to exchange ambassadors and other diplomatic personnel

■ describe the modern international environment of diplomacy

■ outline the factors that most influence twentieth-century diplomacy and describe their influence on Canada

■ describe the job of Canada's ambassador to the United Nations

■ describe the job of Canada's ambassador to the United States

■ distinguish the functions of diplomats from those of consuls

■ comment on the future of diplomacy in the modern world of telecommunications and computer technologies

A Privileged Profession

One British expert on diplomacy, Sir Harold Nicholson, guessed that the first diplomat was probably a beleaguered primitive who, after licking the wounds suffered from battling the neighbours, decided to negotiate a truce with these enemies. Since the Stone Age, the world's diplomats have been motivated by the same instinct – negotiate and mediate. In ancient China, Egypt, and India, heralds, envoys, and orators engaged in forms of diplomatic behaviour. They conveyed messages and warnings, defended causes, and delivered gifts to distant places.

From the beginning, these negotiators demanded immunity from harm, having taken the risk that their presence before the enemy could result in their own demise. Because these first diplomats were foreigners, they were considered by their hosts to be impure. They submitted to rituals of purification to assure their doubtful hosts that they could be trusted and were worthy of credibility. Once the message was delivered and accepted, the earliest envoys left to report the sentiments of their hosts to their superiors. But there were no embassies or standard diplomatic practices accepted by the governments of ancient peoples. There was simply the recognized need to contact and communicate with both friends and enemies in order to thrive. In the words of Abba Eban, Israel's distinguished statesman, "It can certainly be said of diplomacy, as of few other human occupations, that mankind has never been able to live without it."[1]

Although all civilizations have conducted diplomatic activities, modern diplomacy is generally regarded to have been influenced primarily by ancient Greece. The Greeks made passports, called *diplomas,* from double metal plates folded and sewn together. Diplomas granted the bearer travel privileges and special treatment when presented to officials in foreign places. The Greeks called their messengers *angelos*, or angels, and accorded them the patronage of Zeus, the father of the gods, and Hermes, the messenger and herald of the gods, who was, as well, the god of cunning ruses and pretences.

The Greeks chose exceptional people to represent them in foreign places. Their envoys were the finest orators, well versed in the knowledge of theatre, the arts, literature, philosophy, and the general principles of law. They were drawn from the highest levels of polite society, and were usually from an aristocratic background. Because the *polis* was a republic, controlled by an assembly, envoys were appointed with popular approval to negotiate the affairs of state with other city-states, as well as with foreign places such as Sparta and Rome.

The Greeks believed that envoys had the power to negotiate on equal terms with one another and that they should possess immunity from local customs and hostilities.[2] They believed that envoys enjoyed the immunities of the gods to protect them from the harmful impact of human disputes. But they also developed the secular political practice of respecting the dignity and integrity of visiting envoys and expecting reciprocal treatment for their own diplomatic representatives when travelling abroad.

For example, the Greeks advanced the idea that an ambassador represented the person of the sovereign, and was entitled to the same respect that the sovereign would receive if he or she were personally present. Because sovereigns were so sensitive to embarrassment when visiting foreign places, the practice of according diplomatic representatives the highest courtesy – that of personal **inviolability** – developed. If a diplomatic delegation was in the unfortunate circumstance of being in a place where war was declared, its members would be accorded **safe conduct** from hostilities, as when Sparta voted for war against Athens while the Athenian delegation was present negotiating a trade treaty. Gradually, the Greeks elaborated a system of constant diplomatic relations based upon accepted practices of diplomatic privilege and immunities. They established an institutional style of diplomacy that spread far beyond the Aegean corner of the Mediterranean Sea. Greek diplomatic practices influenced and shaped the diplomacy of the high Middle Ages, when the newly formed state system adopted them as customary international law. They recognized **neutrality**, used **arbitration**, and empowered their envoys to further commercial relations with foreign governments.

Unlike the Greeks, the Romans had very little respect for the principle of equality in negotiation. The goals of the Roman Empire were not usually open to compromise. Roman ambassadors, called *nuntii,* travelled abroad as quasi-governors who treated their foreign colleagues more like colonists than equal negotiators. However, the Romans, with their penchant for laws, stressed the importance of binding contracts, and elevated

> ■ ■ **inviolability:** the universally recognized principle that diplomatic agents and their property should be protected from harm by the host nation. ■ ■

them to the sanctity of treaties.

Because of the dominance of the empire, the Romans were highly selective of the foreign envoys they received. When a representative from a foreign land came to Rome, authorities kept the envoy outside the city gates until diplomatic credentials were carefully scrutinized and the diplomatic status of the traveller was verified. Nowadays, this humiliating system of inspecting emissaries has been replaced and refined by the practice of requesting **agrément** (agreement): that is, the sending state does not announce the appointment of its ambassador until the receiving state signifies its acceptance of the individual chosen. This procedure is called **agréation**.

In the early Middle Ages after Rome's collapse, Byzantium rose as a world power. Chicanery, sharp dealing, and suspicion characterized Byzantine diplomacy. The Byzantines used diplomacy to weaken their adversaries by fomenting rivalry among them. Envoys acted as a **fifth column** in the lands to which they were sent, engaging in **sabotage** and using bribery and flattery to buy support. The Byzantines used their envoys to spy wherever they were sent, a practice not uncommon today in many capitals of the world. History confirms that Byzantine practices had a corrupting influence on the evolution of diplomacy.

What we would recognize as modern diplomacy – that is, an independent profession with qualified practitioners and resident missions – originated in Italy in the fourteenth and fifteenth centuries. At that time, diplomats no longer worked solely as messengers of their prince. Medieval ambassadors functioned as permanent representatives of the state, gathering information, advising, and negotiating on behalf of the home government. The profession and practice of diplomacy was seen as an ongoing process rather than an expedience. Permanent diplomatic missions improved opportunities to sign treaties and facilitated the organization of summit meetings as a diplomatic practice. Of course, treachery, deceit, and intrigue continued to characterize medieval diplomacy. In France, Louis XI advised his ambassadors: "If they lie to you, see to it you lie much more than them." In England, foreign diplomats were so distrusted that members of parliament would be deprived of their seats in the House of Commons if found talking with them.[3]

One crude expediency of diplomacy during the medieval period was best summed up by Niccolo Machiavelli in *The Discourses*: "For where the very safety of the country depends on the resolution to be taken, no consideration of justice or injustice, humanity or cruelty, nor of glory or of shame should be allowed to prevail, but putting all other considerations aside, the only question should be what will save the power and the liberty of the country."[4] But the practice of extreme self-interest in a world of competing sovereignties was itself a restraining force. Diplomats quickly learned that corruption and deceit were condoned but impractical because negotiations could not be conducted in good faith. Pragmatism and reason dictated honesty in diplomatic affairs. Intelligent diplomats recoiled from deception in the same way that politicians eschewed unpopularity.

Despite the amoral character of diplomacy during this period, diplomats made valuable contributions to their profession, some of which have survived to the present time. The first resident embassy was opened at Genoa in 1455. Permanent embassies soon became acknowledged as inviolable sanctuaries for the records and files of diplomats and they became the depositories for treaties and for diplomatic reports. Custom dictated that the *host state* respect the sovereign integrity of the embassy. As permanent embassies began to replace travelling diplomatic missions, the practice of stealing or confiscating diplomatic records from envoys grew less and less acceptable. Italian diplomats were the first to write periodic summaries of events taking place in the states to which they were accredited. They expected these reports to remain confidential within the security of their embassy.

The methods and procedures of Italian diplomacy spread throughout Europe, first to France, then through the Hapsburgs (the Austrian family that ruled the Holy Roman Empire in the seventeenth century) to the rest of the continent. The growing diplomatic community viewed its members as trustees of interstate relations. Privileges and immunities belonged to them as a special class of negotiators, not as individuals.

By the seventeenth century, the professional status of diplomacy was well established. In 1626 under Louis XIII, Cardinal Richelieu opened the first ministry of external affairs to exercise French diplomatic leadership in European affairs through one government agency. Richelieu insisted that honouring treaties was an ethical as well as a pragmatic responsibility. Under his influence, the French recognized diplomacy as a permanent part of state policy. French became the leading language in diplomatic communication, with most of its nomenclature still in use today.

The Peace of Westphalia (1648) generated 12 of the first independent states in Europe. Gradually a complex code of diplomatic procedures grew out of the international relations among these states. Nevertheless, conflicts arose regarding different interpretations of diplomatic rules and customs. As the number of sovereign states increased, it became necessary to standardize the practices of international diplomacy.

At the Congress of Vienna (1815) and Aix-la-Chapelle (1818), attending states ratified a **règlement** governing diplomatic titles and order of rank: (1) ambassador extraordinary and plenipotentiary, and from the Vatican, papal legate and nuncio; (2) envoy extraordinary, minister plenipotentiary, and from the Vatican, papal internuncio, (3) minister resident; and (4) chargé d'affaires, and chargé d'affaires ad interim. The Congress of Vienna determined that the rank of *ambassador* is the highest that a diplomat can hold. From this time on, ambassadors or ministers were recognized internationally as chiefs of diplomatic missions. Official diplomatic quarters were designated an **embassy** when headed by an ambassador, and a **legation** when headed by a minister. The Congress was the first multinational statement on the rules of diplomacy that codified the status and functions of diplomats. It gave diplomacy an international stamp of approval as a profession distinct from that of a statesman and legitimized the widely accepted immunities enjoyed by diplomats in the European world of politics.

The years between 1825 and 1914 were marked by relative peace and stability in international affairs. The six great empires of Europe – Austria-Hungary, Czarist Russia, Ottoman Turkey, Germany, Britain, and France – entered a period of diplomatic grace. This concept of Europe gave diplomats a sense of achievement and elevated their profession to a distinguished and specialized vocation. A dozen European states, together with the United States, formed an intimate and cohesive diplomatic community, the **corps diplomatique**. Diplomats associated as a small privileged group, insisting on immunities, practising discretion and avoiding the brush-fires of domestic politics.

Twentieth-Century Diplomacy

Many New States

Four factors have influenced the character of diplomacy in this century. The first is the proliferation of new states, each sending and receiving diplomats and struggling for a place in the international arena. At the turn of the century there were fewer than 1000 embassies and legations in the world; now there are well over 4000, generated by an expanded pool of nearly 200 states. As well, states that have never had diplomatic ties or, for various reasons denied one another diplomatic representation are now opening diplomatic missions. For example, in 1993, after 2000 years of religious conflict and rivalry, the Vatican and Israel opened diplomatic missions. These circumstances have greatly expanded the size of the diplomatic corps and complicated the process of negotiation. Diplomats of old were not encumbered by the entourage of specialized personnel that today constitute a formidable bureaucracy within an embassy.

Experts from every field of government are now attached to embassy staffs in most states, and modern negotiation has become a complex process of internal consultation, whereby diplomats rely on technical expertise before a decision can be made or a report submitted. For example, in addition to an ambassador, the Canadian embassy in Washington has 75 full-time diplomatic officers and representatives, apart from the other embassy staff members. These include ministers resident, minister/counsellors, commercial counsellors, general counsellors, first secretaries, second and third secretaries, and attachés. One of the jobs of the ambassador is to co-ordinate the work of all these people so that they can represent the policies of the Canadian government.

The Media

A second factor that has had a far-reaching effect on the world's diplomatic system is the ever-present and intrusive *communications media*. In all democratic states, the media have claimed the right to inform the public about all levels of government decision-making, and large press contingents, armed with batteries of microphones and television cameras, intent on discovering and revealing what is going on, descend on diplomatic meetings. This makes political compromise very difficult, and diplomats regard the media as an intrusion into the delicate balance of the negotiating process.

Those with a professional commitment to diplomacy say that press surveillance inhibits the strategy of the negotiator.[5] Secrecy provides negotiators with opportunities for making concessions without the fear of creating unnecessary anxiety in the public domain.

In 1979, Israeli foreign minister Moshe Dayan, after travelling in disguise, met with Egyptian authorities in Morocco to lay the groundwork for negotiations at Camp David. President Carter insured the seclusion of the negotiating parties by withholding invitations to the media. If he had not, public indignation in Egypt and Israel at what was being compromised may have scuttled the agreement. And, for obvious reasons, at the London Summit Conference in June 1984, the G-7 leaders refused to publicly discuss the agreement they had reached for dealing with the problem of international terrorism.

But states also use the media for their own diplomatic purposes, e.g., planting stories and carrying on negotiations through the media. In modern diplomacy, the presence of the media is not entirely unwelcome. During the Gulf War in 1990-91, one of the most dubious manipulations of the media was witnessed when the teenaged daughter of Kuwait's ambassador to the United States appeared on worldwide TV to report with great emotion that she was a witness to Iraqi soldiers taking Kuwaiti babies from their incubators and leaving them on the floor of a hospital to die. The stories were not true but were very successful in strengthening support for the coalition forces in the Persian Gulf.

International Negotiation

The third major influence on the modern diplomatic world has been multilateral conference diplomacy, in which negotiations take place among many states simultaneously.[6] Until the latter part of the nineteenth century, most diplomatic communications were bilateral. Whenever multilateral conferences were held, they tended to conclude peace treaties to terminate major European wars. But by the turn of the century, governments had started to send diplomats to multilateral conferences dealing with such subjects as agriculture, codification of international law, liquor traffic, navigation, tariffs, and weights and measures. Diplomats were expected not only to represent the interests of their own states, but also to contribute to the formation of international law. Under the League of Nations, ongoing conference machinery was established that gave international diplomacy a new institutionalized framework.

After World War II, the United Nations and its specialized agencies provided a permanent forum for multilateral diplomacy. Since that time, the advances in communications technology, the speed of travel, and the widespread recognition that world issues are everyone's problems, have made multilateral diplomacy a powerful lawmaking tool. Thousands of conferences have been hosted by the United Nations and other international organizations such as the Organization of American States (OAS) and the Organization of African Unity (OAU).

In the first decades of this century, Canada attended an average of one multilateral conference a year. Today, Canada participates daily in global and regional conferencing, as an ever-increasing portion of diplomatic communications is conducted through multilateral organizations. This in no way reduces the importance of bilateral relations between states, but it does tend to complicate the control of diplomatic news and activities for the ambassador and staff. Keeping abreast of diplomatic relations within the framework of international organizations is a complex and monumental task. Each year, the UN spends over $40 million U.S. printing millions of pages of reports on its diplomatic activities. Press releases alone to delegations run up to 10,000 pages a year. In addition to the rushed routine of embassy business, today's diplomat is expected to be aware of the complicated trends in multilateral diplomacy.

Inside the United Nations and other international organizations, diplomats are given the opportunity to communicate with representatives of states with whom they may not share bilateral diplomatic exchanges. A lot of bilateral negotiations occur within the walls of these organizations, providing an atmosphere as private and secret as that afforded by traditional diplomacy. But the multilateral diplomat is a new breed, a product of twentieth-century internationalism. He or she is not only representing the narrow interests of a state, but also participating as an architect of a much wider community, concerned with the global issues of population, malnutrition, nuclear proliferation, and world peace.

Canada's UN Ambassador

Much of Canada's multilateral diplomacy is conducted through its ambassador to the United Nations. In January of 1992, Louise Frechette, a career diplomat, became the first woman to inherit the prolix title Ambassador Extraordinary and Plenipotentiary and Permanent Representative of Canada to the United Nations, replacing Yves Fortier, who served in that capacity for four years. Ambassador Frechette is also the first foreign-service officer to be appointed to Canada's most prestigious foreign diplomatic post.

A native of Montreal, the trilingual (Eng-

Ambassador Frechette's program for the day of April 20, 1994.

8:45 a.m.   Various telephone calls

9:00 a.m.   Political Section Meeting
– Conference Room

9:30 a.m.   Meeting with Jeff Clarke
(PMO) re: PM's visit –
Ambassador's Office

10:00 a.m.   Consultations on UNICEF
chaired by Ambassador –
UN Conference Room 5

10:30 a.m.   General Assembly Statement
on Haiti, Ambassador is 3rd
Speaker – UN Conference
Room 2

Ambassador Frechette presents her credentials
to UN Secretary General Boutros Boutros-Ghali

11:30 a.m.   Meeting with Ambassador and delegates from "Voice of Women
in Canada" – Large Conference Room – (Mission)

13:15 p.m.   Luncheon with Venezuelan Ambassador – 16 East 81st Street

15:00 p.m.   UNICEF Meeting continues – UN Conference Room 5

20:00 p.m.   Dinner hosted by Poland's Ambassador to the UN – Mission of Poland

lish, French, and Spanish) Frechette began her diplomatic career with the Department of External Affairs in the early 1970s, working in Europe and drafting a trade policy for Canada in Geneva. She was an advisor to the Canadian Delegation to the United Nations in 1972. She became Canada's youngest female ambassador when she accepted a diplomatic posting to Buenos Aires, Argentina, in 1985. She then served as assistant deputy minister for international economic and trade policy, helping to develop a strategy for Canada's assistance to the transformed states of former Soviet Union and Eastern Europe. She also served as assistant deputy minister for Latin America and the Caribbean, where she was a key advisor in Canada's decision to join the Organization of American States.

Louise Frechette assumed her position at a time of unparalleled opportunities for Canadian diplomacy at the United Nations. She can apply her numerous talents to the task of propelling Canadian foreign policy to new heights in the UN system, where Canada enjoys a superb reputation. At the same time, the United Nations itself has regained credence among world leaders and global popular opinion. The UN post is considered paramount for Canada for a number of reasons, including the fact that Canada is a major financial contributor. As well, Canada is a major participant in United Nations peacekeeping operations. Increasingly, international issues are being successfully addressed by the UN system, and sovereign states have reached a mature realization of the crucial role for this global multilateral organization. This situation notwithstanding, Frechette, like her predecessors, joins an international organization facing severe financial and personnel problems. Under its complex systems of accounting, the UN is always on the verge of bankruptcy. She must negotiate Canada's world view in an international organization that has difficulty paying its electric bill.

From her office on the United Nations Plaza, Louise Frechette has almost instant access to diplomats representing nearly 170 nation-states. Because there are so many diplomats in one place, constantly passing one another in the corridors and lounges, eating and drinking together, and meeting in the debating chambers of the UN, important contacts can be made between an ambassador and other individuals and groups. The UN provides Canada's ambassador with a mixture of open conference diplomacy and secret talks and negotiations. It gives Louise Frechette near-global coverage from a single office.

A UN ambassador follows a crowded schedule. The range of Ambassador Frechette's work is no less comprehensive than that of a diplomat accredited to a traditional embassy. Frechette must conduct representation involving a heavy diplomatic itinerary; communicating her government's views to the councils of the United Nations, as well as to individual governments; reporting; public relations; and gathering information, analyzing it, and recommending policy options.

Summit Diplomacy

The fourth development of major significance in modern international politics is **summit diplomacy**, a phrase coined by Winston Churchill. Occasionally, summit meetings of great historic value took place before the twentieth century, such as the Congress of Vienna (1815) and the Congress of Berlin (1878). But diplomatic mythology has always held as undesirable the direct communication between heads of state. Today, in the Age of Summitry, many observers are critical of diplomacy at the highest levels because political executives are not often trained in the skills of negotiation. Diplomats advise that compromise is difficult when the prestige of the negotiating parties is at stake. The main argument against summiteering is that face-to-face meetings among leaders are much too dramatic and politically charged to provide a rational environment for delicate negotiations. Former U.S. Secretary of State Dean Rusk warned that "summit diplomacy is to be approached with the wariness with which a prudent physician prescribes a habit-forming drug...the experienced diplomat will usually counsel against the direct confrontation of those with final authority."[7]

It has been conceded by students of international relations that summit diplomacy has no greater possibility of success than do the traditional avenues of diplomatic communication. For example, in Vienna in 1961, a summit meeting took place between Nikita Krushchev and John Kennedy that ended in failure and increased world tensions until 1963. The two leaders met face-to-face to discuss the arms race, but each returned home determined to accelerate military build-ups. Nearly 25 years later, similarly dramatic diplomatic encounters took place at the Reagan-Gorbachev summit in Geneva in November 1985, in Reykjavik in 1987, and with Western world leaders at Toronto in 1988. Gorbachev's meeting with President Reagan and

President-elect Bush in New York in 1988 was widely reported as a confidence-building measure to facilitate long-term détente on matters related to disarmament.[8]

But the idea that only heads of state can settle intractable disputes or negotiate complicated international instruments is not supported by the evidence, although there have been some notable successes for summitry. One of the most successful in terms of positive international relations was the so-called Shamrock Summit between Reagan and Mulroney at Québec City in March 1985. Both leaders inaugurated the institution of annual summit meetings. The idea was to bring regular top-level management to Canada-U.S. affairs. The first working session between President Bush and Brian Mulroney in 1989 departed from the ceremonial trappings of the Reagan era and gave way to informality and a pragmatic approach to the issues without a highly scripted agenda. The visits to China of U.S. presidents Nixon in 1972 and Reagan in 1984 established a U.S.-Chinese **rapprochement** that was possible only because of contacts at the highest levels of power. The Camp David accords of 1979 showed how the intimacy of secluded summitry could successfully accomplish in just a few days what lower levels of negotiation had failed to do after years of effort.

The spectacular increase in the frequency of summit meetings indicates the new importance political leaders attach to them. In these times of instant communications and rapid travel, many leaders have discovered the political advantages of world exposure, and their efforts are directed toward maintaining direct contact with one another, thereby bypassing traditional diplomatic machinery. At the *Fran-cophonie* summit held in Paris in 1991, where the leaders of 44 states signed a Declaration of Human Rights and Democratization, Mulroney's presentation of Canada's human-rights policy enabled him to provide leadership in the promotion of human rights in Africa.

In spite of the growing cynicism concerning summitry by the global *corps diplomatique*, the increase in personal diplomacy by heads of state is a fact of life in the modern world of negotiation. Any analytical definition of diplomacy today must include the whole process of policy-making by heads of government, as well as through normal diplomatic channels. Summitry has permanently invaded the domain of diplomacy.

The Protocol of Modern Diplomacy

Today diplomatic relations between states are conducted according to an extensive code of behaviour embodied in the 1961 Vienna Convention on Diplomatic Relations.[9] The convention was a major international effort to codify international law in the area of diplomatic privileges and immunities. The Vienna conference was attended by 81 states that drafted a comprehensive agreement covering diplomatic activities; it had come into force by 1964. The conference was called because of the length of time over which customs and rules had been accumulating, and because of the changing circumstances in which these rules were applied. It was time to reach an agreement on the differing interests and interpretations of the rules by various countries. At Vienna, the attending states set forth the rules of diplomatic practice to conform to

Figure 15.1:
Letter of credence

In the Name and on Behalf of	Aux Nom, Lieu et Place de

Elizabeth II

by the Grace of God of the United Kingdom, Canada and Her other Realms and Territories Queen, Head of the Commonwealth, Defender of the Faith	par la grâce de Dieu, Reine du Royaume-Uni, du Canada et de ses autres royaumes et territoires, Chef du Commonwealth, Défenseur de la Foi

Ramon Hnatyshyn

Governor General and Commander in Chief of Canada	Gouverneur général et Commandant en chef du Canada

Your Excellency,

Wishing to promote the relations of friendship and good understanding which happily exist between our two countries, I have decided to accredit to You

in the character of Ambassador Extraordinary and Plenipotentiary of Canada.

The Experience which I have had of his talents and zeal assures Me that the selection I have made will be perfectly agreeable to You, and that he will discharge his important duties in such a manner as to merit Your approbation and esteem.

I, therefore, request that You will give entire credence to all that he shall say to You in My name, more especially when he shall convey to You the assurances of the lively interest which I take in everything that affects the welfare and prosperity of Your country.

Given at My Government House,

Your Good Friend,

Excellence,

Désireux de poursuivre les relations d'amitié et de bonne entente qui existent entre nos deux pays, J'ai décidé d'accréditer auprès de Vous

en qualité d'Ambassadeur Extraordinaire et Plénipotentiaire du Canada.

La connaissance que J'ai de ses talents et de son dévouement Me sont autant de garanties que Mon choix Vous sera agréable et qu'il s'acquittera de ses hautes fonctions de façon à mériter Votre estime et Votre bienveillance.

Je Vous prie donc de bien vouloir lui accorder entière créance en tout ce qu'il Vous transmettra de Ma part, surtout lorsqu'il Vous renouvellera l'assurance du vif intérêt que Je porte à tout ce qui concerne le bonheur et la prospérité de Votre pays.

En Mon Hôtel du Gouvernement,

Votre Grand Ami,

contemporary conditions and standards of diplomacy. The heads of diplomatic missions were divided into three general categories. The first two categories are ambassadors and ministers, respectively. These diplomats are **accredited** to the head of the host state. The third category comprises chargés d'affaires. These lower-ranking diplomats are accredited to the foreign minister of the host state.

The Appointment of an Ambassador

Before an ambassador is appointed to a post, the sending state seeks the approval or *agrément* of the receiving state. Approval is usually granted when the discretionary authority of the receiving state determines a diplomat is **persona grata** (a person in good grace). A receiving state may also declare a diplomat of another state to be **persona non grata** when that diplomat is found to be unacceptable after an initial investigation, or when a diplomat engages in criminal or antisocial behaviour or meddles in the internal affairs of the host state. But such a practice is exceptional and contrary to the spirit of international relations. This reciprocal procedure of confidential application and acceptance is an important instrument of **protocol** that builds trust and confidence in interstate relations. In the mid-1980s, one Canadian ambassadorial appointee was not accepted by Portugal because its government believed that the appointment of former Liberal cabinet minister Bryce Mackasey was made solely on the basis of patronage and would soon be reversed by a newly elected Conservative government.

Once *agréation* is reached, an ambassador is given credentials to present to the head of state. In Commonwealth states where the sovereign is the head of more than one state (e.g., the Queen for Canada, New Zealand, and Australia), ambassadors are provided with a letter of introduction from prime minister to prime minister. In accordance with diplomatic protocol, a *letter of credence* (figure 15.1) is provided for the exchange of ambassadors outside the Commonwealth.

On arrival, an ambassador will inform the minister of foreign affairs or secretary of state that he or she is ready to assume the duties of the embassy. In a letter referred to as the *copie d'usage*, the ambassador indicates a willingness to present the letters of credence to the head of state and includes the predecessor's *letter of recall* that terminated the mission. Once a diplomat presents credentials to the head of state, he or she is considered officially to represent the sending state.

Sometimes the ambassador and members of the diplomatic staff are assigned to more than one state. For example, Canada's ambassador to Costa Rica and his or her staff are also accredited to Honduras, Nicaragua, and Panama. No state maintains a diplomatic mission in every capital of the world. For economic reasons, most states are selective, balancing national interests against the costs involved in maintaining a permanent presence in a country. Canada has embassies and **High Commissions** in 110 capitals, but conducts diplomatic relations with over 180 states. In effect, Canada has virtually doubled its diplomatic presence in the world by accrediting many of its heads of missions as non-resident or visiting diplomats to other states.

Multi-accreditation or plural representation, and as it is sometimes called in Canada "concurrent accreditation," can cause difficulties between states. Those states in which the ambassador does not reside may feel that the *sending state* considers them inferior to states where embassies are permanently established.[10] Problems arise when two or more states covered by the same ambassador engage in hostilities or break diplomatic relations. Parties in dispute will usually doubt the objectivity of the multi-accredited ambassador. These situations are potentially embarrassing both for the ambassador and for the states involved.

Privileges, Exemptions, and Immunities

It is a well-established and widely accepted rule of international law that all categories of diplomatic personnel are *immune* from the civil jurisdiction of the courts of the host state.[11] This has never meant that **diplomatic immunity** should give diplomats a licence to violate the laws of the state to which they are accredited. Although every state's diplomatic corps can report cases of envoys who conspire to break local laws, the majority of the world's diplomats readily comply with these laws. Most governments are aware that lawbreaking foreign diplomats who try to escape local jurisdictions can be dealt with through political channels. Generally speaking, governments rarely, if ever, institute criminal suits against diplomats. In cases of flagrant criminal activity by a foreign diplomat, the host state will declare the individual *persona non grata*.

Sometimes diplomats are expelled from their posts, or embassies are closed because of sudden strains between governments.[12] Such was the case when Canada closed its embassy in Baghdad, upon the outbreak of the Persian

> ■ ■ **recall:** to summon a diplomat back to the sending state. ■ ■

Gulf war in 1991. Another diplomatic practice used when tension develops between states is **recall**. In 1989, Canada recalled its chargé d'affairs from Tehran to express outrage at the Ayatollah Khomeini's death threats against Salman Rushdie, author of *The Satanic Verses*. Similarly, Britain recalled its entire embassy staff and simultaneously expelled the Iranian chargé d'affaires because of the death threat to at least one of its citizens, Mr. Rushdie.

Once relations have improved, most states will restore their diplomatic ties with another state. In 1992, Mexico restored diplomatic relations with the Vatican that had been severed for 125 years. During that time, Mexico had expropriated church property, expelled foreign priests, and forbade local priests to wear their clerical garbs in public, all because in the early 19th century, two Spanish priests were excommunicated and executed for leading a violent independence movement from Spain.

Not all states recognize immunities and privileges as an absolute right. In April 1984, for example, the British embassy in Tripoli was surrounded by Libyan militia units, which prevented the diplomatic staff from leaving. Libyan officials indicated that the units would remain at the embassy until Libyan detainees held by British police for killing a police officer and wounding demonstrators, had been freed. The restrictions imposed on the British embassy staff limiting their freedom of movement were finally lifted after negotiations between the British foreign office and the Libyan government.

The United States also makes exceptions to the convention of inviolability of a diplomat when an envoy's conduct threatens the safety and security of the republic. In such cases, a diplomat will be restrained, although in time, he or she will normally be sent home. In 1982, U.S. law permitted the State Department to establish the Office of Foreign Missions to give the government more control over foreign diplomats. The law permits the United States to retaliate against diplomats from governments that mistreat U.S. envoys or whose diplomats habitually violate U.S. laws. In taking off its diplomatic gloves, the U.S. is now empowered to disconnect telephones in Washington embassies, to hold up shipments of goods, and to refuse to allow foreign diplomats to buy property. The Office of Foreign Missions levies income taxes on the diplomats of states that tax the incomes of U.S. emissaries overseas. Diplomats are now required to get red, white, and blue licence plates for their automobiles, as well as titles (proof of ownership) and liability insurance. Canada follows its policy of reciprocity in diplomatic affairs, which applies or denies privileges and immunities when they are reciprocated in the sending state.

All of these actions reflect changes in the official attitudes of some states toward traditional diplomatic privileges and immunities. Even though most states adhere to diplomatic protocol as codified by the Vienna Convention, many governments are legislating limitations on diplomatic privileges and immunities. With regard to criminal behaviour, it remains to be seen whether any state would honour the diplomatic immunity of an envoy who sought the audience of the head of state, then, as a premeditated act, performed an assassination.

One of the most impressive statements on the question of national security and diplomatic immunity was made by Justice Bissonette of Canada in the widely publicized case of *Rose* v. *The King*.[13] Justice Bissonette reasoned that diplomatic immunity is relative, not absolute, and that if a diplomat commits a crime against the security of a state, he or she renounces the privilege of inviolability. Even though the *Rose* case occurred long before the Vienna Convention, it is certainly possible that Justice Bissonette's legal arguments could be again cited in today's courts.

In 1977, Canada proclaimed the *Diplomatic and Consular Privileges and Immunities Act*. This act enabled Canada to ratify the 1961 Vienna Convention while imposing several limitations on its application within Canada. Section 2(4) permits the secretary of state for foreign affairs to withdraw privileges and immunities from foreign diplomats if those privileges are not properly accorded to Canadian diplomats in their state. And, under Section 5, when a question arises as to whether a person is entitled to diplomatic immunities, the matter is decided by the secretary of state for foreign affairs.

Diplomats enjoy personal inviolability as well as inviolability of premises and property. Full diplomatic privileges and immunities apply to diplomats and members of their families and staff, in all official as well as in most private activities, provided they are not nationals or classed as permanent residents of the state to which the diplomat is accredited.

The Vienna Convention asserts that diplomats and those properly associated with the mission are immune from civil and administrative jurisdictions of the host state. In most circumstances, a diplomat can sue but cannot be sued. However, if legal proceedings are initiated by a diplomat, he or she is subject to counterclaims. Under the convention, a diplomat is subject to legal action on private immovable property and on any commercial transactions undertaken outside of official diplomatic functions.

All property held on behalf of the sending state for the purpose of the mission is inviolable. The host state is obligated to protect the persons and property of a diplomatic mission and is not permitted to seize, search, or confiscate documents wherever they may be. Because the premises of the mission and the private residences of the head of the mission and staff are inviolable, they may not be entered by agents of the host state without special permission from the sending state. The **diplomatic bag** may not be opened or detained whether it is carried by an envoy, a diplomatic courier, or a designated national official who is making a special journey to the sending state. Diplomats and their families are also exempt from the inspection of personal luggage.

In addition to inviolability, diplomats enjoy a wide range of exemptions from national, regional, and municipal taxes. Except for services such as electricity, gas, refuse collection, water, and sewage, the premises of diplomatic missions are tax exempt. Any articles that are imported for the official use of the mission are also exempt from customs and excise duties, provided they are not sold or otherwise disposed of for profit in the host state.

Consular Diplomacy

Like diplomats, **consuls** are specialized agents of one state in another state. Unlike diplo-
mats, however, consuls do not conduct political relations or negotiations between states. They are not accredited by one head of state to another to represent the person of the sovereign in a foreign state. The consul represents the sending state in a different way from diplomats. Consuls are concerned with assisting nationals of their state and furthering the commercial, economic, cultural, and scientific relations between the sending state and the host state. They issue passports, visas, and appropriate travel and judicial documents to nationals. Consuls safeguard the interests of their nationals as individuals and corporations in a foreign state, particularly by acting as notary, civil registrar, and administrative agent for the sending state. They also exercise certain rights of supervision and inspection over crews of vessels having the nationality of the sending state.

Unlike embassies, consulates are not necessarily located in the capital city of the host state. They are usually opened in cities and towns that have special commercial significance to the sending state. In the U.S., Canada has consular posts in fourteen cities,[14] and each consulate provides consular services to a designated territory that includes a number of U.S. states. For example, the Canadian consulate in Boston services a territory that includes the states of Maine, Massachusetts, New Hampshire, Rhode Island, and Vermont. Canada's consular posts in the United States are operated by approximately 750 people; about 300 are from Canada, and the rest are hired locally.

Consular officers are appointed by their governments through diplomatic channels in the host state. They are given a commission (figure 15.2), which is a written document

Figure 15.2

Canada

Elizabeth the Second, by the Grace of God of the United Kingdom, Canada and Her other Realms and Territories QUEEN, Head of the Commonwealth, Defender of the Faith

TO ALL WHOM these Presents shall come,

GREETING:

WHEREAS We have thought it necessary for encouraging Canadian citizens trading to the Republic of the Ivory Coast to appoint a Consul of Canada at Abidjan with jurisdiction in the Republic of the Ivory Coast to take care of Canadian citizens and to aid and assist them in all their lawful and mercantile concerns.

NOW KNOW YE THAT reposing special trust and confidence in the discretion and faithfulness of Our Trusty and Well-beloved

We did, on the   day of   in the year of Our Lord one thousand nine hundred and eighty-five and in the thirty-fourth year of Our Reign, constitute and appoint,

CONSUL OF CANADA AT ABIDJAN

with jurisdiction as aforesaid, thereby giving and granting unto him full power and authority by all lawful means to aid and protect those Canadian citizens who may trade or visit or reside within his Consular District, and to hold the said office during Our Pleasure with all rights, privileges and immunities thereunto appertaining.

AND We do hereby strictly enjoin and require all Canadian citizens to take due notice of this Our Commission and yield obedience thereto.

IN TESTIMONY WHEREOF there is affixed hereunto the Seal of the Registrar General of Canada.

WITNESS:

BY COMMAND,

DEPUTY REGISTRAR
GENERAL OF CANADA

Elizabeth Deux, par la grâce de Dieu, REINE du Royaume-Uni, du Canada et de ses autres royaumes et territoires, Chef du Commonwealth, Défenseur de la Foi.

À TOUS CEUX qui les présentes verront,

SALUT:

ATTENDU QUE Nous avons jugé nécessaire, en vue d'encourager les citoyens canadiens qui se livrent au commerce avec la République de Côte d'Ivoire de nommer un consul du Canada à Abidjan ayant juridiction en République de Côte d'Ivoire pour s'occuper des citoyens canadiens et pour les aider et les assister dans toutes leurs entreprises légitimes et commerciales.

SACHEZ MAINTENANT QUE, en raison de la confiance particulière que Nous mettons dans la discrétion et la loyauté de Notre Féal et Bien-aimé

Nous avons, le   jour de   en l'an de grâce mil neuf cent quatre-vingt-cinq, le trente-quatrième de Notre règne, constitué et nommé,

CONSUL DU CANADA À ABIDJAN

ayant juridiction comme il est dit plus haut et lui donnant et lui conférant par ces présentes pleins pouvoirs et autorité pour aider et protéger par tous moyens légitimes les citoyens canadiens autorisés à se livrer au commerce dans les limites de sa circonscription consulaire ou à la visiter ou y résider, et pour remplir la dite charge pendant Notre bon plaisir avec tous les droits, privilèges et immunités qui s'y rattachent.

ET par ces présentes Nous enjoignons et prescrivons strictement à tous les citoyens canadiens de tenir dûment compte de Notre présente Commission et de s'y conformer.

EN FOI DE QUOI les présentes ont été revêtues du sceau du Registraire général du Canada.

TÉMOIN:

PAR ORDRE,

SOUS-REGISTRAIRE
GÉNÉRAL DU CANADA

DEPUTY ATTORNEY   SOUS-PROCUREUR
GENERAL OF CANADA   GÉNÉRAL DU CANADA

What missions do:

- contact relatives or friends at home to transfer emergency funds
- help you replace a stolen or lost passport
- notify and provide information to next of kin about accidents or deaths
- direct you to information about local laws and customs
- inform relatives or friends if you are arrested, and try to ensure that your hearing and imprisonment conform to the standards of the foreign state
- provide a list of local doctors and lawyers, or
- help you during emergencies, such as natural disasters and civil disturbances

What missions cannot do:

- pay your hospital, medical, legal, hotel, or transportation bills
- make travel arrangements, provide services, cash cheques, or provide loans
- provide legal advice, investigate thefts or losses, post bail, or pay fines
- find you a job or get you a work permit or a driver's licence
- intervene in the law enforcement or judicial processes of a foreign state, or
- provide postal services or hold your personal items for safekeeping

showing the consul's name, rank (e.g., consul general, consul, or vice-consul), the consular district, and the post. The host government issues an **exequatur** that approves and authorizes the appointment. The exequatur entitles the consul to certain privileges and immunities in respect of acts performed in the exercise of consular duties.

Originally, Britain provided Canadians with consular service. In the late nineteenth century, Canada appointed its own trade commissioners to secure Canadian commercial interests abroad, while the British maintained responsibility for consular work. Canada opened its first diplomatic mission in Washington, D.C., in February, 1927. During World War II, the Canadian foreign service was expanded and Canada established its first consulate in Godthaab, Greenland, in 1940. Today, Canada has 105 consular missions abroad, whose responsibilities include immigration, commercial and public affairs, and trade.

These missions are a busy and vital component of Canada's international presence. They include embassies, high commissions, consulates general and consulates, and they provide services to Canadians who travel to or reside in other countries. At certain locations, emergency consular assistance is available. Crises such as the events in Kuwait in 1991 are still rare, but they are an indication of the risks a person takes when travelling abroad.

The Vienna Convention on Consular Relations, 1963, codified most of the pre-existing rules of customary international law regarding consular immunities. Under the convention, the privileges and immunities enjoyed by a consular officer are similar to those enjoyed by members of a diplomatic staff. They apply, however, to a lesser degree. The host state is obliged to protect the consular officers, but personal inviolability and immunity from jurisdiction apply only to acts performed in the exercise of consular functions. A consul must respond to civil actions by third parties for damages arising from acts of personal negligence. Consuls must appear before proper authorities if criminal charges are brought against them. If found guilty of criminal acts, consuls are liable to imprisonment in the host state. In the event that a consular agent is charged with a "grave crime," the Vienna Convention states that a consul may even be detained pending trial. In Canada, the Diplomatic and Consular Privileges and Immunities Act of 1977 provides that a "grave crime" is any offence that is specified by an Act of Parliament for which an offender may be sentenced to imprisonment for five or more years.

In the Canadian case, *Maluquer* v. *The King*, it was ruled that a foreign consul is not entitled to the same degree of immunity enjoyed by a person who occupies a diplomatic position. When acting as a private person, a consul has the same legal rights as any other resident alien. This restrictive theory applied by Canadian courts in cases involving consular immunity has been widely shared throughout the international system. The Canadian position was clarified further in the Act of 1977, which firmly distinguishes the application of civil and criminal jurisdictions on diplomats and consular officers.

In spite of conventional and judicial restrictions of consular immunities, all governments want to ensure the effective fulfillment of consular functions.[15] Thus, consulates, their archives, and their documents are inviolable and may not be entered by local authorities without the permission of the head of the consular post. The consular premises, including the residence of the head of the post, are tax exempt. All career income is tax exempt to consuls and so are fees for consular services that generate income for the consulate. All consular personnel are exempt from local regulations concerning residence permits and the registration and employment of aliens.

The host state is obligated to give consuls access to nationals who are arrested or detained. Consuls also have the right of access to information in cases of death, guardianship, shipwrecks, and aircraft accidents. Finally, consuls have the right to communicate with appropriate authorities in the host state in order to perform official duties.

Profile of an Ambassador

In the complicated world of international relations, today's ambassador needs to possess the specialized talents of many professionals: the survival instinct of a business person, the organizational abilities of an administrator, the charm of an actor, and the intellectual curiosity and objectivity of a social scientist.

Foreign services in all states, therefore, seek to recruit people of unique character and high training. There is no question that the *corps diplomatique* has traditionally been elite. But today it is an elite not of breeding, but of talent. The academic qualifications of most diplomats are very high. Almost invariably they are university educated, holding professional degrees to the level of Ph.D. By the 1990s, for example, 80 percent of Canadian diplomats had two degrees or more. They have had extensive experience in government, usually in the public service, and have made a career of climbing to the rank of ambassador. Many diplomats are multilingual: Europeans excel in this qualification because of the geographical proximity of people speaking many different languages. Canada is officially bilingual and many of its foreign representatives are as well. Education and language skills are, to a great extent, personal achievements. But most of the formal training a diplomat receives is usually provided by the diplomatic corps of the sending state.

The formal procedure and protocols of diplomatic practice are a product of training, both at the home office and on the job. Yet all the formal training a diplomat receives cannot compensate for the innate qualities of character – moral integrity, flexibility, loyalty, courage, and political sense – required for the job. Most diplomatic observers seem to agree that the personal attributes of the envoy, rather than his or her formal qualifications, have a decisive influence on the outcome of diplomacy. The intellectual context in which an envoy is trained is often not relevant to many of the issues conducted among governments. J.W. Burton has observed that "languages and history are no longer sufficient as equipment [for diplomats]."[16]

Today's practitioners require, in addition to these traditional skills, knowledge of the latest technologies of peace and war. They must be aware that their negotiations transcend the interests of the governments they represent and that nuclear-age decision-mak-

ing has global consequences. Above all, ambassadors need to have what Sir Harold Nicholson called "the main formative influence in diplomatic theory...common sense."[17] In diplomacy, common sense is as much a skill as it is a gift. While such a quality may only on rare occasions change history, it is a vital ingredient in the daily operation of any embassy, whether in London, England, or Kuala Lumpur, Malaysia.

The art of negotiation requires a person who is an empathetic communicator – one who listens and understands. After all, the purpose of diplomacy is communication; everything connected with diplomacy – representation, protocol, procedures – is designed to facilitate communication with people. Diplomats have to be observant, pragmatic, and intuitive with the people they meet. Diplomats will make accommodations not because they are impressed with political rhetoric and argumentation, but because they believe that making a concession will be more useful or less harmful than refusing it. Thus, the strategy of diplomats is not so much to be eloquent in defence of their government's interests as it is to provide convincing incentives that rivals will perceive as concessions in their self-interest. In effect, the force of logic is more desirable than the logic of force in the negotiating process.

In addition to negotiating with the host state and handling sensitive or secret material, an ambassador takes responsibility for a large operating staff that depends on his or her leadership. This amounts to maintaining a complicated network of people above and beyond the important political relations with the officials of the host country. Every embassy maintains a mission staff made up of accountants, translators, chauffeurs, secretaries, cipher clerks, radio operators, gardeners, and hospitality personnel. Today's ambassadors are no longer considered too high up the ladder to get involved in the organization of a smoothly running embassy. Indeed, those with large staffs of diplomats, experts, and locally employed workers now have to fulfil a managerial role in addition to their negotiating functions.

In spite of the glamour the public is anxious to attach to diplomacy, in reality it is a profession much like other professions. It is filled with routine and protocol, and meeting people is the essence of the diplomat's craft. This usually means attending luncheons, receptions, giving speeches, hosting guests, giving interviews, and being present at celebrations of the host state's national holidays.

What an Ambassador Does

Almost everything an ambassador does is related to representation. Even going to a party or a dinner is really going to work. Entertaining (or representation) by diplomats is important because (1) social functions convey a positive image for the country concerned; (2) entertainment provides an opportunity for obtaining information; and (3) while entertaining, important contacts are made. Of a total annual operating budget of $12 million, the Canadian embassy in Washington spends just over $400,000 on representation.

The ambassador and his or her spouse attend approximately 200 social functions and host over 150 events a year, both at the embassy and at their residence. These functions include breakfast briefings, meetings, lunches, receptions, dinners and tea or drinks with

■ PROFILE
CANADA'S AMBASSADOR TO THE UNITED STATES
Raymond Chrétien

Raymond Chrétien was born in Shawinigan, Québec, and attended university at the Séminaire de Joliette and Laval University. In 1966 he was admitted to the Québec Bar. Later that year he joined the legal bureau in the Department of External Affairs (now called the Department of Foreign Affairs and International Trade). Over the next 12 years, he had assignments in Ottawa with the Privy Council Office, the Treasury Board and the Canadian International Development Agency. Outside Canada he served at Canada's Permanent Mission to the United Nations in New York and the embassies in Beirut and Paris.

In 1978, Mr. Chrétien was named Canada's ambassador to Zaïre. He returned to Ottawa in 1981 where he was policy director for Industry, Investments and Competition. He also served as assistant undersecretary, Manufacturing, Technology and Transportation, and inspector general in the Department of External Affairs. In groups that are invited to the residence. This is an important part of the information-gathering function of the diplomatic mission. Social gatherings provide an atmosphere that projects friendship and good public relations. They are opportunities for nation-states to give their best representation in a relaxed setting. But we should not assume that vital information concerning the affairs of state is a direct result of hosts pouring alcoholic beverages into their guests. Most of the information upon which an embassy will act comes from open sources and conventional channels. Formal meetings, conversations, newspapers, and public statements by governing officials all form the main sources of information needed to make or adjust foreign policy.

Usually the functional division of the mission provides the organizational framework for the acquisition of information. At Canada's new embassy in Washington, the political section (headed by a minister who answers to the ambassador) attempts to acquire information on subjects relating to the political trends and foreign-policy positions of the United States. The economic and commercial sections, each headed by a minister (also answerable to the ambassador), seek to gain information that might be of interest to Canadian government officials concerned with trade and economic policy. The Canadian embassy also has attachés concerned with military, scientific, cultural, and agricultural matters that affect both states.

The role of the ambassador is crucial in the process of receiving and transmitting information. It is the ambassador who usually reports to Ottawa any changes that may affect Canada's relations with the United States. Because there is an endless flow of potentially

1985, he was appointed Canada's ambassador to Mexico. Upon his completion of his assignment in Mexico, he was named to the position of associate undersecretary for external affairs, the second highest role in the department. Mr. Chrétien served as Canada's ambassador to Belgium and Luxembourg from 1991 to 1994. In January 1994, he became Canada's eighteenth ambassador to the United States.

The following is the schedule of a typical day in Ambassador Chrétien's professional life.

Tuesday April 19, 1994

Ambassador Chrétien

8:30   Ambassador arrives at the Embassy. Review of press reports and departmental communications with Executive Assistant

9:00   Ambassador returns phone calls

9:30   Meeting with the Executive Committee – Ambassador's Boardroom

11:00   Briefing for a meeting with Congressman Sam Gibbons (D–Fla.) – Rayburn House Office Building

12:30   Lunch hosted by Ambassador Chrétien with:

Karlyn Bowman,
American Enterprise Institute

David Gergen, Counsellor, the White House

Norman Ornstein,
American Enterprise Institute

Tom Mann, Director,
Government Studies, Brookings Institute

Edward Rollins, Political Consultant

Michael Kergin, Minister and Deputy Head of Mission, Canadian Embassy

Robert Wright, Minister, Canadian Embassy

significant information, what the ambassador chooses to send the Department of Foreign Affairs and the other departments of government is important. His or her ability to give priority to certain trends and events and to press diplomatic views to Ottawa determines whether the Cabinet can adjust its policies to meet new conditions in the United States.

At the same time, the ambassador must be aware of the long-term changes taking place in the country to which he or she is accredited. Ambassador Chrétien has to identify those significant political and constitutional changes in the United States that have taken place over the past ten years and that have far-reaching implications for Canadian interests. For example, the system of checks and balances in the U.S. among the three branches of government has become increasingly complicated. There is usually a strong spirit of congressional independence from the presidency, demonstrated by the much greater involvement of the legislative branch of government in foreign affairs. The U.S. Congress is much more inclined to assert its prerogatives and less willing to follow the lead of the White House. At the same time, Congress has become less cohesive and unified through the proliferation of committees and subcommittees, which are particularly receptive to professional lobbyists.

The Canadian ambassador to the United States no longer deals primarily with officials of the State Department. In the 1990s, an ambassador and his or her staff must deal with a myriad of politically active individuals and groups that now have a dramatic effect on the political landscape in the United States. Washington is populated by an army of lawyers, public-relations experts, political-ac-

14:30 Briefing with Minister Counsellor of Trade Policy and Trade Relations Section, for the meeting with Mickey Kantor, U.S. Trade Representative

15:30 Meeting with Mickey Kantor, U.S. Trade Representative – 600-17th Street, N.W. Washington

16:30 Meeting with Senator George Mitchell (D–ME) – Senate Majority Leader – Russell Senate Office Building, Room 176; M. Kergin to accompany

Ambassador and Mrs. Chrétien

18:30 Opening of the Exhibition "Yousuf Karsh – Selected Portraits"
• Receiving line
• Cocktails and viewing of exhibition

20:00 Dinner hosted by Ambassador and Mrs. Chrétien in honour of Mr. and Mrs. Yousuf Karsh

tion committees, pressure groups, political strategists, tacticians, and fund-raisers. Then there is the Congress, with over 20,000 staff members working on politics and substance.

In addition to the traditional departments of government, the Canadian embassy staff must negotiate with many of the independent federal regulatory agencies and commissions established by Congress, such as the Federal Aviation Agency and the Federal Maritime Commission. Added to this is the complication of monitoring the tactics of over 15,000 lobbyists who may, at any time, pressure executive and congressional staff members and officials on matters related to Canadian interests.[18] These can range from acid rain to special problems arising out of health care, free trade, or, as in 1994, the potentially damaging situation created when Canada arrested two American captains and seized their vessels for alleged illegal scallop-fishing off the Grand Banks. The impact of special-interest groups can have a damaging effect on trade and employment for both economies.

The separation of powers in the U.S. makes negotiating an especially complicated process. The executive branch of government may enthusiastically agree to a set of concessions in a negotiation, but the Senate, responding to an effective lobby, may not ratify the agreement or may add unanticipated provisions to it.

On matters of trade, the ambassador actively lobbies for Canadian interests. Trade between Canada and the United States creates enormous benefits for both states. On an annual basis, Canadians and Americans exchange about $200 billion U.S. worth of goods and services.

One important role for the ambassador is to promote the most positive environment possible for free trade. This brings the ambassador into frequent contact with U.S. trade representatives and the secretary of commerce. The ambassador also co-ordinates regular and continuing contact between Canadian cabinet ministers and their counterparts in Washington.

Much of the success behind Canada-U.S. agreements can be attributed to the behind-the-scenes efforts of the ambassador and his staff. In this connection, an important aspect of the ambassador's job in Washington is that of sensitizing Congress to the effect of trade actions on Canada. Canadian negotiators learned long ago that in Congress, when the interests of a foreign state are up against the constituency imperatives of a domestic group, the foreign state, even if it is the closest ally of the United States, is at a disadvantage. Even if

the targets of U.S. restrictions are Japan and Europe, and Canadian trade is not even at issue, Canada's economy is easily sideswiped by actions aimed at others. When this happens, the ambassador will attempt to inform members of Congress and their committees that trade restrictions hurt both economies.

In addition to representing Canadian interests in the American political system, the embassy staff also administer routine claims from Canadians who are visiting or who are involved in business in the United States. Such visitors can number in the thousands annually. In the ambassador's office alone, the embassy processes approximately 200 pieces of mail a week, of which about 75 percent require some form of follow-up. The Canadian embassy acts as a broker for its citizens, administering travel and business matters requiring official representation. The mission is required to protect those nationals who may have legal difficulties and to assist in ensuring fair treatment by the laws of the host state. An arrest or an affront to a Canadian in the United States may put strains on embassy officials who desire to settle these matters in good faith; the embassy staff never knows what political factors might be involved in a given incident. Many times they are faced with decisions that can have enormous consequences. The staff must walk a difficult line between maintaining good relations with the host state and protecting the interests of Canadians.

An important factor in routine interactions is the degree of friendship or hostility that exists between states. Canada and the United States enjoy a historic friendship and maintain a large number of regular interactions, especially in the areas of tourism and business. Geographic location is another very important factor. A common border and common bodies of water between the United States and Canada create many situations that must be handled routinely. Heavy mutual trading also creates frequent and varied interactions. This results in numerous administrative problems for the embassy, because so many Canadians have a huge stake in the economic policies of the United States.

No matter how varied the duties of an embassy might be, the prime concern of an ambassador is to keep international relations as routine and as friendly as possible. Whether executed by lower-level administrative officials or conducted by ranking diplomats at the foreign-policy level, the many areas of collaboration between states must be kept viable by diplomatic means. The Canadian embassy in Washington must see that the large volume of transactions across the Canadian-U.S. border is facilitated by minimizing potential conflict between the two governments.

Canada has never been complacent in its lopsided relationship with its powerful and affluent neighbor to the south. It has always feared that the United States could single-handedly crush its interests without taking notice. For that reason, the Canadian government has assigned the largest single concentration of diplomatic talent it has to Washington to make sure the United States does take notice. In addition, its $90 million investment in new embassy facilities demonstrates the importance Ottawa attaches to its diplomatic operation in Washington.

In the Ottawa headquarters of the Department of Foreign Affairs, the United States rates a branch of its own, headed by an assistant deputy ministry. The U.S. branch within Foreign Affairs includes six divisions: general relations (political and legal matters); trade and economic relations; trans-boundary matters (environment, transport, and energy); marketing; trade and investment; and programs. All these institutional representations reflect the large volume of international transactions that take place between Canada and the United States.

Diplomacy is the centerpiece of relations between and among states. It is by means of diplomacy that human problems arising in the international system are resolved. The work of a diplomat is frequently overlooked because much of it is routine and lacks the glamour of executive and legislative decision-making. But diplomacy and its high priests, the diplomats, will always be needed if states want to carry on a continuous dialogue on an inter-personal level. In a world in which people still engage in personalized politics despite encroaching technologies, diplomacy via human contact is still very relevant.

References

1. Abba Eban, *The New Diplomacy: International Affairs in the Modern Age* (New York: Random House, 1983), 332; see also Karl Deutsch, *The Analysis of International Relations* (Englewood Cliffs, N.J.: Prentice Hall, 1988), 172-181.

2. Frank Adcock, *Diplomacy in Ancient Greece* (New York: St. Martin's Press, 1975), 139-140.

3. Quoted in Charles Mayer, *Diplomat* (New York: Harper and Brothers Publishers, 1959), 43.

4. Quoted from Max Lerner, ed., *The Prince and The Discourses* (New York: Modern Library, 1940), 60.

5. See William Zartman, ed., *The Negotiation Process: Theories and Applications* (Newbury Park, CA: Sage, 1988).

6. John Rourke, *International Politics on the World Stage* (Guilford, CT: The Dushkin Publishing Group, 1993), 286-287.

7. Dean Rusk, "American Foreign Policy in the Eighties" (Washington, D.C.: LTV Washington Seminar, 1980).

8. Ronald Reagan, *An American Life* (New York: Simon & Schuster, 1990), 72.

9. Peter Toma and Robert Gorman, *International Relations* (Pacific Cove, CA: Brooks/Cole Publishing Company, 1991), 289.

10. Robert Hopkins Miller et al., *Inside an Embassy: The Political Role of Diplomats Abroad* (Washington, D.C.: Congressional Quarterly Press, 1992).

11. Grant McClanahan, *Diplomatic Immunity: Principles, Practices and Problems* (New York: St. Martin's Press, 1989).

12. Hans Tuch, *Communicating with the World* (New York: St. Martin's Press, 1990).

13. *Rose v. The King* (1946), 88 C.C.C. 114 (Que. C.A.).

14. Atlanta, Boston, Buffalo, Chicago, Cleveland, Dallas, Detroit, Los Angeles, Minneapolis, New Orleans, New York, Philadelphia, San Francisco, Seattle, Washington, D.C.

15. Martin Herz, *The Consular Dimension of Diplomacy* (Washington, D.C.: Institute for the Study of Diplomacy, Georgetown University, 1983).

16. J. W. Burton, *System, States, Diplomacy and Rules* (New York: Cambridge University Press, 1963), 208.

17. Sir Harold Nicholson, *Diplomacy,* 4th ed. (New York: Oxford University Press, 1988), 23.

18. Jeffrey Birnbaum, *The Lobbyists* (New York: Times Books, 1992).

Suggested Readings

Arthur Andrew, *The Rise and Fall of a Middle Power: Canadian Diplomacy from King to Mulroney* (Toronto: James Lorimer & Company Ltd., Publishers, 1993).

Hans Binnendijk and Mary Locke, *The Diplomatic Record, 1991-1992* (Georgetown University: Institute for the Study of Diplomacy, Washington, D.C., 1992).

Gordon Craig and Alexander George, *Force and Statecraft: Diplomatic Problems of our Time* (New York: Oxford University Press, 1990).

Allan Gotlieb, *I'll be with you in a minute, Mr. Ambassador* (Toronto: University of Toronto Press, 1991).

Marin Herz, *215 Days in the Life of an American Ambassador* (Georgetown University: Institute for the Study of Diplomacy, Washington D.C., 1990).

Cameron R. Hume, *The United Nations, Iran, and Iraq: How Peacemaking Changed* (Bloomington, IN: Indiana University Press, 1994).

Grant McClanahan, *Diplomatic Immunity* (London: C. Hurst & Co., 1990).

David Newsom, ed., *Diplomacy Under a Foreign Flag: When Nations Break Relations* (New York: St. Martin's Press, 1990).

Hans Tuchs, *Communicating with the World* (New York: St. Martin's Press, 1990).

Adam Watson, *Diplomacy: The Dialogue Between States* (New York: Routledge, 1992).

Glossary

accredited: An official acknowledgement of an envoy or diplomat who possesses the formal credentials of a representative having the general authority to act on behalf of a foreign sovereign.

agréation: The formal procedures used by states to exchange ambassadors.

agrément: An official gesture of response by a government of the acceptability of a foreign diplomat who has been proposed by the sending state.

arbitration: A legal technique for settling disputes which involves agreement between or among the parties as to what issues will be resolved, what procedures will be followed, who will judge the dispute, and that the decision reached will be binding.

consul: A foreign service official appointed to represent various minor diplomats, commercial, and service functions on behalf of a state.

corps diplomatique: The full diplomatic contingent of a state. Sometimes the term is used to refer to all diplomats in the community of diplomats around the world.

diplomatic bag: A sealed pouch or valise, clearly marked and identified as diplomatic property, that contains official records and documents for communication between an embassy and the sending state.

diplomatic immunity: Exemptions applied to diplomatic representatives of one country that protect them from certain internal civil and criminal jurisdictions of the country to which the representatives are accredited.

embassy: A diplomatic establishment located in a foreign state headed by an ambassador.

exequatur: Many states, although not required by international law to receive foreign consuls, issue a document called an exequatur, authorizing the consul to exercise a professional jurisdiction within the territory of the receiving state, with all the privileges and immunities customarily granted to such officers.

fifth column: A subversive strategy to weaken a government by infiltrating its organization in order to cause division, dissent, and disorder.

High Commission: A diplomatic mission of a state that is a member of the Commonwealth.

inviolability: The universally recognized principle that diplomatic agents and their property should be protected from harm by the host nation.

legation: A diplomatic mission that is run without someone at the rank of ambassador.

neutrality: The status recognized by international law whereby a state takes no part in war and enjoys certain rights and exercises certain obligations within the international community.

persona grata: An expression used to indicate that a particular diplomatic agent is acceptable to the host state as an official representative of a foreign state.

persona non grata: The expression used when a particular diplomatic representative appointed abroad is found to be unacceptable by the host state.

protocol: A document or practice serving as the preliminary to, or opening of, any diplomatic transaction.

rapprochement: The re-establishment of normal diplomatic and commercial relations between rival states after a period of estrangement.

recall: To summon a diplomat back to the sending state.

règlement: An agreement to establish rules, regulations, controls, and conditions to govern the conduct of officials under special circumstances.

sabotage: Originally referred to the practice (during the early stages of the Industrial Revolution) of workers placing their shoes (*sabots*) into machinery so as to bring production to a halt, but in diplomacy, the term refers to the willful obstruction and interference with normal diplomatic processes with the aim to inconvenience or discourage normal relations.

safe conduct: A guarantee or security granted by a sovereign to an envoy or stranger of safe travel in and out of the state.

summit diplomacy: The conduct of diplomacy by heads of state or governments instead of at the ambassadorial or ministerial level.

SIXTEEN

Toward the Next Millennium: The Challenges

Deforestation has worldwide social, political, and health repercussions.

Chapter Objectives

After reading this chapter, you will be able to:

- incorporate information from previous chapters into a general discussion of world problems

- understand Canada's role as an active participant in global politics

- discuss the contours of a new world order

- identify the challenges facing us in the last decade of the twentieth century

- understand peacekeeping and discuss issues arising from it

- clarify major global issues, such as arms control, arms proliferation, the population explosion, global problems of the environment, and AIDS

- feel confident about taking upper-level courses in political science

Defining the New World Order

As the coalition forces trained their high-tech sights on Iraq in 1990, the phrase "New World Order" became part of our political vocabularies, and was to be repeated many times in the wake of world developments of the early 1990s. Some understand the term as a utopian vision – a political illusion promoted by those seeking a more peaceful international community. Others argue that because of the dramatic events of the past few years, including the dismemberment of the Soviet Union, the dismantling of the Berlin Wall, the emergence of a more united Europe, and the ascendency of China, a new constellation of international alliances and structures of power has produced a New World Order that is both perceivable and definable.

In 1992, the keepers of the Doomsday Clock reset its hands, telling the world that it was safer from nuclear war at that time than at any time since World War II. The clock, which always appears on the cover of *The Bulletin of Atomic Scientists,* has been set backward or forward in relation to midnight, or "doomsday," nearly fifty times since 1945. But the end of the Cold War did not bring about the era of universal peace, harmony, tranquility, and safety that many had expected. Instead it has ushered in a period of great uncertainty.

In Eastern Europe and some of the areas of the former Soviet Union, as well as in other areas throughout the world, ancient religious, ethnic, and nationalist tensions have erupted violently and are threatening to spread. In addition, disputes over declining resources, especially water and national fisheries, the state of the global environment, the growth of world population, hunger, and the AIDS epidemic are now everyday threats to the economic, social, and political stability of the international community.

There is a new and heightened international interest writ large in the subject of security. This follows a growing realization that democracy, sustainable development, and global security are intertwined, and spawns new searches for a more satisfactory order in global affairs.

What are the components of this New World Order, and to what extent will they help us meet the challenges of peace, arms control, population growth, hunger, AIDS and environmental damage? The New World Order may not be much better than the Old World Order, but those who see it on the horizon believe that it will emerge from a convergence of events occurring at the end of the twentieth century.[1]

The first of these events is the emergence of a *global village*. The nation-states of the world are now so closely enmeshed, with such a density of economic and political transactions that, for example, the ways in which human beings in the Middle East behave have immediate consequences on humans living in Canada, Finland, or Aruba, and vice-versa. Global issues have converged in at least three areas – economic well-being, peace and security, and the challenge of the environment – thus providing an impetus to press toward international co-operation for the sake of pre-serving humanity.

A second component of the New World Order is the assumption of *peace through democracy*. This view assumes that there is a democratic revolution sweeping the world and that democracies will not attack each other. Both the "global village" and the "peace through democracy" views rest on the central belief that the New World Order will see a decline in the use of force between and among states.

The concept of *collective security* is the third component of the New World Order. Here the prominence of the United Nations in the role of peacekeeping and the fact that the Security Council is functioning according to its original mandate under the Charter fosters the belief that a global collective security system is possible. With ever-increasing expectations, the nation-states of the world are looking to the United Nations to supply solutions to challenges to peace.

The New World Order has one other important dimension, *Pax Americana* – an American perspective on what peace is. The post-Cold War world saw a dramatic shift in the international balance of power, resembling a **unipolar system** of global politics. The awesome military power of the United States enabled its strategists to deploy American armed forces anywhere in the world. This means that the United States is in a strong position to define the "ground rules" for the implementation of peace and to impose many of its ideological views on the international community. For some, this means that a world in which America pursues its good intentions abroad is a world also committed to American national interest and ideology. In 1993, American troops waded ashore in So-

malia to feed the hungry: soon after, their gunships hovered over Mogadishu firing rockets into crowded streets and knots of demonstrators. Famine relief had turned into counterinsurgency.

The Challenge of Peace

Philosopher George Santayana warned us of the dangers of not remembering the past. It is perhaps even more dangerous to remember the past incorrectly. Throughout all history, every major military technology invented – including nuclear weapons – has been used in wars among groups and states. In the 1990s, the danger of nuclear war is part of a much older problem: humans will use violence to settle disputes among themselves. Long before the existence of nuclear arsenals, societies could and did destroy one another.

In today's world, many states possess the military capability to destroy one another. Nuclear-armed missiles and bombers can withstand an enemy's attack and retaliate with devastating force – destroying, for all practical purposes, the attacker's economy, industrial base, and population, not to mention those of neighbouring states. The long-range effects on the ecology of the planet are inestimable. In this nuclear age, ultimate strategic capabilities tend to cancel one another out, making the risks of global devastation unacceptable. It is ironic that the historic race to build the most destructive weapons should now lead government leaders to consider an option that was available to them from the dawn of human history: peace. As Thomas Paine said, "Peace, which costs nothing, is attended with infinitely more advantage than any victory with all its expense."[2]

The term "peace" is often given a multiplicity of meanings. Some define peace narrowly as the absence of war. But to the majority of people in the world, peace is more than the mere absence of war. The word has positive connotations, implying rights to pursue human happiness through economic, social, and political opportunity. Religious and political thinking reinforce this positive view. Peace and goodwill are definitely linked to our conception of what is morally right and politically desirable. Peace is associated with trust, mutual respect, and with living free from the reality of war. On the international level, peace means the free collaboration and interaction of nation-states. At a personal level, peace is a state of mind.

The relative character of this highly prized human goal is subject to differing and at times contradictory interpretations between and among governments. Peace, like wealth or well-being, is a highly charged ideological concept. For some socialist states, peace is possible only after communism has triumphed over capitalism.

It is not difficult to infer that differing ideological perspectives of peace have generated barriers of distrust among states. The world of interstate relations is viewed by many leaders as essentially predatory and anarchic. Upon this ideological presumption, states spend significant resources on arms in order to engage in or deter aggression, and thus to achieve greater security. In these circumstances, peace is equated with military preparedness, deterrence, and arms competition. Here the concept of **strategic superiority** plays a major role in announcing to the rest of the world that the military arsenal a state possesses is formidable and destructive.

As we approach the year 2000, the challenge to peace focuses upon the widespread possession and proliferation of weapons. After the atomic bomb was invented, the choices available to humankind became narrow and ominous. The subsequent development of **thermonuclear** weapons and sophisticated delivery systems of great range and accuracy severely limited these choices. Of course, the dismantling of these weapons is an option, by far the most attractive, but it is the least likely one. Nuclear weapons can be dismantled, but they cannot be disinvented. In a world of profoundly divergent ideological focus, the level of trust necessary for complete nuclear **disarmament** is simply non-existent. The immediate problem is to use all available political and legal instruments to ensure that nuclear weapons are not used, and to survive international conflict engaging **conventional weapons** as best we can. But although nuclear

557

weapons are widely viewed as presenting the gravest threat to world peace, in fact the greatest threat arises from conventional weapons.

Today's conventional weapons approach the destructive scale of nuclear weapons without the residual radioactive effects. Recent wars in the Middle East and in the South Atlantic bear this out. Even at the level of small-group terrorism, modern conventional technology has severe destructive potential.

Peacekeeping

With ever-increasing hopes and expectations, governments are looking to international organizations to supply solutions to the challenge of peace. In the area of **peacekeeping,** the United Nations has responded frequently.[3] Since 1988, the UN has conducted more peacekeeping missions than it did in its first 38 years of operation. Military men and women from over 100 states have worn the Blue Beret and the Blue Helmet in the service of peace, security, and stability. By 1993 there had been more than 50,000 on duty in 13 missions. Peacekeepers have monitored and enforced cease-fires, verified security agreements, ensured the delivery of humanitarian aid, provided basic government structures and services, and assisted governments in the transition from a colonial to a modern form.

Peacekeeping can be defined as actions designed to enhance international peace, security, and stability that are authorized by competent national and international organizations and which are undertaken co-operatively by military and humanitarian organizations, civilian police, and other interested agencies and groups. The words "peacekeeping" and "peacemaking" are not mentioned in the United Nations Charter. The general subject comes under the "Peaceful Settlement of Disputes" and "Action with Respect to Threats to the Peace, Breaches of the Peace, and Acts of Aggression" clauses of the Charter. The UN Military Observer Group, established by the Security Council in April 1948 to supervise the cease-fire between India and Pakistan, is generally regarded as the first UN peacekeeping mission, although the word "peacekeeping" only came into use in 1956, at the time of the Suez crisis.

Bearing in mind the above definition, it is evident that the face of peacekeeping has changed. The great divide that once existed between military and humanitarian aid has been bridged. The peacekeeping umbrella is ever expanding to encompass non-traditional activities; for example, the use of a civilian police force such as the RCMP, and experts in the operations of elections, such as officials of Elections Canada. It also involves peacemaking, which entails the use of force by an international organization sanctioned by the United Nations to restore peace in areas designated as "safe" under the terms of a cease-fire by parties in military conflict.

When a nation-state considers its potential contribution to a peacekeeping mission, it decides on the percentage of each ingredient – personnel, financing, material and equipment, research, education and training – to be included. Each of these must be considered against the backdrop of command, control, and communications. This involves the need for a central authority that has the ability to

■ ■ **conventional weapons:** all weapons excluding nuclear, biological, and chemical weapons. ■ ■

define and oversee the entire peacekeeping operation.

Canada has always played a prominent role in peacekeeping. Since 1948, Canada has enjoyed a positive international peacekeeping reputation. Almost 100,000 men and women of the Canadian Armed Forces and thousands of Canadian civilians have taken part in peacekeeping missions – more than from any other nation-state. Canada has contributed personnel, material, and resources to every UN peacekeeping endeavour – no other state has matched that record. The negative consequences have been that some Canadian peacekeepers, and people under the charge of Canadians, have lost their lives during these operations. In 1993, seven Canadian peacekeepers were charged with the death of a Somali civilian who had been in their custody. The circumstances leading to the death have left a permanent blemish on Canada's excellent record in peacekeeping.

Canada has developed a New Peacekeeping Partnership, which is composed of the military, the Department of Foreign Affairs, the Canadian International Development Agency (CIDA), humanitarian aid agencies, several non-governmental organizations, public administrators in Elections Canada, civilian police agencies, and concerned citizens. The members of this partnership want to create the widest, most inclusive response possible to the challenges and opportunities of the post-Cold War era.

Throughout the years, most military and civilian peacekeeping ground forces have been very successful. Even when they have been unable to carry out their mandates, the United Nations Security Council has insisted that they remain in place and function as best they can. The United Nations has been extremely reluctant to wind down a mission where there is a possibility that it could serve a useful purpose in the future.

It is no longer desirable among members of the United Nations for only a small group of states to be the peacekeepers of the world. The number of missions has increased at such a rate as to require the widest possible participation by the greatest number of states. It is thus in the interest of those states with the most knowledge to pass it on to other states willing to participate in peacekeeping activities.

Peace Activism

Worldwide, the theory of deterrence, adopted by military strategists in the 1950s, is being challenged by the peace movement. Peace activists are found in every country of the world and they advocate plans for nuclear and conventional-arms control ranging from **unilateral disarmament** to freezes, bans, and moratoriums. The idea that adding more weapons to existing arsenals will deter aggression is under fire in many states. The notion of **nuclear freeze** calls for an immediate halt to the development, production, transfer, and deployment of nuclear weapons. But while the idea is almost universally popular, there is disagreement as to whether the freeze should be "unilateral" or "mutual and verifiable."

Britain's Campaign for Nuclear Disarmament (CND) calls on all states possessing nuclear weapons to dismantle their nuclear arsenals. The CND is anti-military, anti-American, and anti-NATO. In Canada, groups such as the Canadian Peace Congress and Project Ploughshares want Canada to be a **nuclear-weapon-free zone** (**NWFZ**). This includes opting out of the North Warning System for continental defence and refusing to permit U.S. Trident submarines from entering Canadian waters. The agenda of some peace activists also calls on Canada to leave NATO and proclaim its neutrality in international affairs. The Toronto Disarmament Network (TDN), formed in 1981, represents over 60 peace groups that maintain a network of organization and communication with other disarmament groups around the world. Besides this group, nearly 1000 peace groups are operating in Canada.

In much the same spirit, peace activists in Europe have rallied against the presence of nuclear weapons on their continent. The European Nuclear Disarmament group (END) is organized to persuade nuclear-weapons states to renounce the possession and use of their arsenals. They call for a zone free of nuclear weapons from Portugal to Poland. In Belarus, Kazakhstan, Russia, and Ukraine, peace advocates are calling for a NWFZ in Central and Eastern Europe.

Another zone proposal is the "**zone of peace**" (ZOP). The concept goes much further than the NWFZ. The ZOP is a regional approach to general disarmament and is not merely a ban on one particular type of dangerous weapon. States that would compose the zone would agree to resolve their disputes peacefully, without resorting to **biological** (bacteriological), **chemical**, conventional, or nuclear arms. The ZOP is also envisioned as a zone for regional economic and social co-operation. The concept was endorsed by the UN General Assembly in 1978, but rejected by the then superpowers because it would deprive them of their military bases, present in virtually every region of the world. One option is for the Arctic to be declared a zone of peace. But Canada has not been proactive on the idea because of its treaty obligations in NORAD. The concept of the ZOP may be more acceptable now that the Cold War has ended and the extreme rivalry of the superpowers has temporarily subsided.

Because millions of people from every continent have been involved in the peace movement, the organizations dedicated to peace activism have created a global network to pressure national governments to reduce their arsenals. But disarmament must be linked with mutual security. The final document of the first United Nations Special Session on Disarmament in 1978 stressed that "genuine and lasting peace can only be created through the effective implementation of the security system provided for in the Charter of the United Nations": other suitable institutions – such as the International Court of Justice and regional intergovernmental bodies – exist, but they are underused. States in conflict all too often resort to power politics.

Perhaps humankind's best chance at peace – or at least of preservation – is never to become complacent. The contagious nature of conflict forces us to rule out complacency. During the Gulf War, the world was shocked to learn about how close Iraq had come to acquiring a nuclear and chemical weapons arsenal, one which, if mounted on *Scud* missiles, could be extremely destructive against Israel, Egypt, Saudi Arabia, and other Gulf states. So long as political disputes continue to be resolved by military means, there is grave danger that some small spark – some little war far from our homes – could detonate the nuclear and chemical arsenals.

Peace is not simply something that follows

war, although historically peace has been successfully imposed by stronger military and political powers.[4] It is a human relationship towards which people must choose to work. It first requires the political will to eliminate the root causes of conflict. This involves trust, the opening of all possible lines of international communication, and the strengthening and reform of international institutions. It requires an increase in economic and social interaction: people doing business with one another and meeting one another through a vast network of social exchanges involving the arts, the sciences, sports, and tourism. Prime Minister David Oduber of Aruba sees the work of peace as a natural by-product of people doing business with one another. At the level of international organization, each block will have to recognize and respect the security of others. In the process, a gradual and balanced reduction of conventional and nuclear weapons can be obtained. But just as arms control is essential, so is it necessary to address the global problems of population and hunger before a lasting peace can be achieved. These are some of the immediate challenges.

The Challenge of Arms Control

Since the turn of the century, numerous international efforts have been made to control the deadly game of the arms race. Weapons of every possible kind were developed or acquired by most states in the international community. Even before the first atomic bomb was tested, other weapons of mass destruction (chemical and biological) were being stockpiled for military use. As early as 1915, chemical weapons had made their appearance on the battlefields of Europe – and Canadians were among the first casualties. By the end of World War I, 1,300,000 people had become victims of chemical warfare.

The Hague International Peace conferences of 1899 and 1907 were the first proposals for international arms control standards (table 16.1). The Geneva Protocol of 1925 (signed and ratified by 111 states) prohibits the use of asphyxiating, poisonous, or other gases and analogous liquids in warfare between states party to the agreement. But the protocol did not prohibit the development, production, and stockpiling of such weapons. By 1990, nearly 20 states possessed chemical weapons. In March 1988, one of those states – Iraq – unleashed mustard and cyanide gas on its own Kurdish civilians in Halabja.

During the 1950s and 1960s, progress in the negotiating rounds at the United Nations was very slow because there was no agreement on whether weapons of mass destruction should be considered separately. Yet at the same time, the world was witnessing new generations of more sophisticated and deadly weapons being developed at an unprecedented pace. However, in 1971, Canada and a small group of other states revised a proposal made at the Conference of the Committee on Disarmament (CCD). It became the Convention on the Prohibition of the Development, Production, and Stockpiling of Bacteriological (Biological) and Toxin Weapons and on their Destruction, and was adopted by the General Assembly in 1972, entering into force in 1975. Under the provisions of this convention, the parties renounce the development, use, and transfer of these weapons and undertake to destroy them within nine

Table 16.1:
Conventions on arms control: 1925-1993

Convention	Description	Date signed	Number of signatories
Geneva Protocol	Bans the use of gas or bacteriological weapons	1925	111
Antarctic Treaty	Internationalizes and demilitarizes Antarctica	1959	33
Partial Test Ban	Bans nuclear tests in the atmosphere, in outer space, or underwater	1963	116
Outer Space Treaty	Internationalizes and demilitarizes outer space, the moon, and other celestial bodies	1967	89
Latin American Nuclear Free Zone	Bans nuclear weapons in Latin America	1967	23
Non-Proliferation Treaty	Bans selling, giving, or receiving nuclear weapons, nuclear materials, or nuclear technology for other than peaceful purposes	1968	136
Seabed Arms Control	Bans nuclear weapons in or under the seabed	1971	78
Biological Weapons Convention	Bans the production and possession of bacteriological and other toxic weapons	1972	107
Strategic Arms Limitations Talks (SALT I)	Limited the number and types of U.S. and USSR strategic weapons (expired 1977)	1972	2
Anti-Ballistic Missile (ABM) Treaty	U.S. and USSR agreed to limit anti-ballistic missile sites and to undertake no further ABM development	1972	2
Threshold Test Ban	Limits underground tests to 150 kilotons for U.S. and USSR (not ratified but its provisions are observed)	1974	2

months of ratification. A Review Conference was held in Geneva in 1980, at which most states expressed satisfaction that the convention was comprehensive enough to encompass recent technological developments for these kinds of weapons.

In 1985, the General Assembly, on recommendations by the Ad Hoc Committee on Chemical Weapons, called for the speediest conclusion of a convention banning chemical weapons and providing for their destruction. Since that time, every superpower summit placed the issue of chemical weapons on its agenda. In 1989, representatives from 149 states met in Paris and reaffirmed the spirit of the Geneva Protocol and pledged to move the international community towards a treaty to ban the use of all chemical weapons. Finally, in 1990, a Chemical Weapons Accord was signed by the United States and the former Soviet Union.

The acronym SALT represents the first round of Strategic Arms Limitations Talks between the United States and the former Soviet Union over a two-and-a-half-year period from 1970 to 1972.[5] The SALT I Anti-Ballistic Missile (ABM) Treaty prohibited the United States and the former Soviet Union from con-

Convention	Description	Date signed	Number of signatories
Environmental Modification Treaty	Bans environmental modification as a form of warfare	1977	51
SALT II	Limits the number and types of U.S. and USSR strategic weapons (not ratified but its provisions are observed)	1979	2
The Moon Treaty	Bans placing nuclear weapons on or in orbit of the moon	1979	54
Physical Protection of Nuclear Material	Provides protection standards on materials during shipment and for recovering lost/stolen materials	1980	34
South Pacific Nuclear-Free Zone	Bans making and acquiring nuclear weapons in the South Pacific region	1985	9
Intermediate Range-Nuclear Forces (INF)	Eliminates all U.S. and USSR missiles of intermediate range (500 km –5000 km)	1987	2
Chemical Weapons Accord	Pledges the U.S. and USSR to drastic cuts in their chemical stockpiles	1990	2
Strategic Arms Reduction Treaty (START I)	First treaty to reduce arsenals of weapons by committing the U.S. and former republics of the USSR to reductions of strategic nuclear weapons	1991	5
START II	Reduces U.S. and Russian strategic nuclear forces	1993	2
Chemical Weapons Convention	Bans the possession of chemical weapons after 2005	1993	130

Source: *SIPRI Yearbook 1993* (Oxford, UK: Oxford University Press, 1993).

structing ABM defence systems at more than two sites. Both parties further agreed to freeze the number of offensive ballistic missile launches at their existing levels until 1977. The SALT II ABM Protocol, signed in Moscow in 1979, further limited the superpowers to one defensive site and committed both parties to limit the number of warheads they carry. SALT II was never ratified by the U.S. Senate, even though both Jimmy Carter and Ronald Reagan were committed to arms limitations.

The acronym START was coined by the Reagan administration in 1980 to begin a new round of nuclear-arms negotiations as distinguished from SALT I and SALT II. The Strategic Arms Reduction Talks brought the Americans and Soviets to the bargaining table in Geneva in 1982. These talks involved not only weapons deployed by the superpowers, but also the intermediate nuclear forces (INF) in Europe. After six years of intensive negotiations, the United States and the Soviet Union signed the Intermediate-Range Nuclear Forces treaty in 1987, eliminating an entire class of nuclear weapons from Europe and from the rest of the world. In 1991, after nine years of sporadic negotiations, START was finally signed in Moscow by Presidents

Gorbachev and Bush. Even though the treaty generated a reduction in the numbers of strategic nuclear arsenals, both states retained a massive nuclear capability. In the case of the former Soviet Union, most of these weapons are now located in Belarus, Kazakhstan, Russia, and Ukraine.

The major offensive weapons subject to ongoing negotiations are the **intercontinental ballistic missiles (ICBMs)**, bombers, and submarine-launched missiles, all of which are deadly accurate and capable of rendering nuclear devastation on an unimaginable scale. If negotiations on these weapons fail, the incomprehensible and unacceptable spectre of nuclear war looms over all humankind. Every word exchanged behind the closed doors of disarmament negotiations has a direct impact on every citizen of this planet.

The United States and the states that once comprised the Soviet Union have stockpiles of a variety of nuclear weapons, and nearly all of them were deployed on the European continent. Throughout the 1960s and 1970s, Europe became a nuclear fortress with British, French, and U.S. weapons assigned to NATO states aimed at missile installations in what is now Russia and the Central and East-European states.

The arms-control negotiations that began in Geneva in 1982 and that led to START may take years to reach a conclusion owing to the enormous number of strategic weapons that have been accumulated since the 1970s and 1980s.[5] The signing of START is a positive sign that some states are willing to reduce the numbers of weapons they hold. START I was signed in Moscow in July 1991. When the Soviet Union unravelled, the fate of this treaty was unclear. Belarus, Kazakhstan, Rus-

sia, and Ukraine all held large numbers of the former Soviet arsenal. A protocol to the original treaty was agreed upon, making the newly independent states equal partners with the United States. START I was finally concluded in Lisbon, Portugal, in May 1992. Under the terms of the treaty, the parties agreed to destroy nuclear weapons to a base number of 6000 strategic devices and to limit delivery systems to 1600 each. In January, 1993, Russia and the United States agreed to cut their nuclear weapons to 3500 for the United States and about 3000 for Russia. Both states agreed to eliminate all MIRVs (multiple independently targetable re-entry vehicles); i.e., MX and Minuteman missiles for the United States, and SS-18, SS-19 and SS-24 missiles for Russia. But the spread of nuclear and conventional military technologies to a growing number of states will make it impossible for the relative few that possess these weapons to reduce them to zero.

Compliance

Even though states are willing to sign arms-control agreements, they are not necessarily going to observe all of the provisions these treaties contain. The effective **verification** of the parties that sign such agreements is a fundamental process of arms control. Verification is an agreed-upon set of procedures whereby the parties to an arms-control agreement inspect the compliance of other parties to the terms of the treaty. Most states advocate on-site inspections, but there are states that have resisted such instruments for verifying the compliance to an arms-control treaty. The uses of sophisticated telemetric technologies employable at the highest altitudes or in space enable some states to verify the conduct of

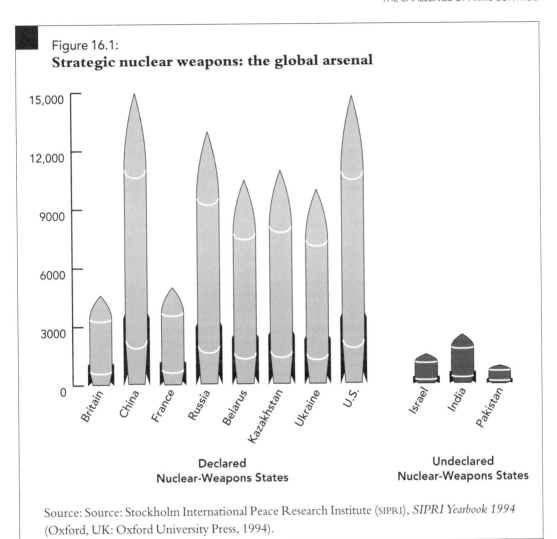

Figure 16.1:
Strategic nuclear weapons: the global arsenal

Declared Nuclear-Weapons States

Undeclared Nuclear-Weapons States

Source: Source: Stockholm International Peace Research Institute (SIPRI), *SIPRI Yearbook 1994* (Oxford, UK: Oxford University Press, 1994).

other states without their agreement to on-site inspections. *Intelligence* is another national instrument employed by states seeking to keep informed about the weapons capabilities of other parties to arms-control agreements. Thus when a verifiable agreement is in place, there are a number of alternative checks on the conduct of signing states.

Strategic Weapons

The field of nuclear-arms control has accumulated more than its share of acronyms, but the most notorious one is MAD (**mutually assured destruction**). Simply put, the doctrine of mutually assured destruction holds that neither side will launch a nuclear attack so long as it knows that the other side will be able to retaliate with an equally devastating nuclear blow. MAD is the fundamental dynamic behind the concept of modern deterrence. But not all **strategic nuclear weapons** provide the same deterrent value. For example, large land-based missiles and strategic bombers are not by themselves the best deterrent because the missiles are in fixed silos that could be destroyed in a first strike, and the bombers take hours to reach their targets. In contrast, nuclear submarines are a very credible deterrent because they are harder to detect and to destroy at sea. Thus, they are usually not vulnerable to a first strike.

In the 1970s, the Americans and the Soviets developed MIRV technology. Each MIRV missile can be armed with more than one warhead, each independently targetable. For example, all U.S. submarine-based missiles and the MX (experimental missile) carry 8-10 nuclear warheads; the giant Russian-made SS-18 missile is normally equipped to carry 10 warheads, but is capable of carrying up to 30. This multiple-warhead technology makes arms control very complicated. Now warheads have to be counted, too. By 1990, the United States could explode over 14,000 strategic nuclear weapons. When **tactical nuclear weapons** are added to strategic ones, the total combined global arsenal equals about 90,000 nuclear weapons.

The Challenge of Weapons Proliferation

Nuclear Weapons

As far back as the mid-1940s, when the first development of nuclear weapons was in process under the **Manhattan Project**, U.S. scientists were arguing for the non-prolifera-

tion of nuclear-weapons technology. By the early 1950s, the U.S., UK, France, USSR, and China had begun to build and expand their nuclear programs almost solely to amass weapons, and designed and operated nuclear facilities for that purpose. In the 1980s, Argentina, Brazil, India, Israel, North Korea, South Korea, Pakistan, South Africa, and Taiwan all developed the capacity to assemble and stockpile nuclear weapons. These 15 states are the principal nuclear-weapons powers in the 1990s. However, estimates range from a low of 15 states to as many as 20 that may have nuclear weapons by the turn of the century (table 16.2).

States desire to acquire nuclear weapons for many complex military and political reasons. Among the most obvious reasons are international prestige and enhanced military power. But the possession of nuclear weapons is also viewed as the *ultimate* deterrence against external aggression. However, the danger of nuclear proliferation is that the option of nuclear weapons available to a wide dispersion of political decision-makers increases both the possibility and probability of their deployment. As nuclear weapons spread, there is intense pressure on many governments to develop these weapons because others have done or may do so.

The first efforts to contain nuclear proliferation concentrated on regulating the peaceful uses of nuclear power. By 1945, Canada, the U.S., and the UK had signed the Agreed Declaration on Atomic Energy, which resolved that nuclear proliferation was a threat to world peace. The following year at the United Nations Atomic Energy Commission, the U.S. proposed that an international atomic-energy agency be established to regulate and

Table 16.2:
Nuclear candidates with demonstrated capabilities

Argentina:

Has the capacity to enrich uranium and is working towards the construction of its first nuclear weapon sometime in the 1990s.

Brazil:

Like Argentina, Brazil is very close to constructing its own nuclear arsenal. It possesses all of the necessary expertise and ingredients to assemble nuclear weapons.

Iran:

An ambitious nuclear strategy was initiated under the Shah. In 1981, the Khomeini regime renewed Iran's interests in developing its nuclear facilities. It is difficult to get reliable sources within Iran to confirm the progress of its nuclear-weapon capacity. But Iran will need more time to build its own bomb.

Iraq:

Israel bombed Iraq's nuclear facilities in the early 1980s, thereby delaying the progress of Iraq's nuclear capacity. The Gulf War further retarded Iraq's capabilities to assemble a nuclear arsenal. But Iraq has substantial quantities of uranium, and it is just a matter of time before it produces its first nuclear weapon, quite possibly by the mid-nineties.

South Korea:

This state has had a thriving nuclear-energy program since the 1970s and is capable of developing its own nuclear weapons when the U.S. withdraws its military presence and guarantees.

Taiwan:

Taiwan developed an ambitious nuclear-energy program in the early 1970s and will soon possess a complete domestic nuclear-fuel cycle.

Source: Stockholm International Peace Research Institute (SIPRI), *SIPRI Yearbook 1994* (Oxford, UK: Oxford University Press, 1994).

Table 16.3:
Non-signatories to the Non-Proliferation Treaty (NPT)

Albania	Chile	Israel	Tanzania
Algeria	Cuba	Kampuchea	Uganda
Angola	Guinea	Mozambique	Vietnam
Argentina	Guatemala	North Korea★	Zambia
Brazil	Guyana	Pakistan	
Burma	India	South Africa	

★North Korea signed the NPT but later withdrew.

Source: Joseph Pilat & Robert Pendley, eds., *Beyond 1995: The Future of the NPT Regime* (New York: Plenum Press, 1990); Bjørn Møller, *Common Security and Non-offensive Defense: A Neorealist Perspective* (Boulder, CO: Lynne Rienner, 1992); and interviews with officials at Foreign Affairs and International Trade Canada, Feb., 1993.

control all aspects of the uses of nuclear energy. One of the first resolutions of the United Nations created the Atomic Energy Commission (AEC) with Canada, China, France, Great Britain, the U.S., and the USSR as members. The AEC was finally dismantled in 1955 because of disagreements among members as to how to control the spread of nuclear weapons.

In 1957, a separate organization under the aegis of the United Nations, the International Atomic Energy Agency (IAEA), was founded with headquarters in Vienna. The major aim of IAEA is to prevent the diversion of atomic materials to military uses and to disseminate information on the peaceful applications of nuclear technology. Canada was the first state in the world to renounce the possession and spread of nuclear weapons, and has been represented on the board of IAEA since it was founded. *Safeguards* are applied by requiring

member states to design their nuclear facilities according to international standards, to keep detailed records of nuclear operations, and to submit reports to IAEA. *Inspections* are conducted on-site to verify that states are not diverting peaceful nuclear-energy facilities or materials to build nuclear weapons. Still, highly enriched weapons-grade uranium manages to slip by the eyes and ears of the IAEA. These undetected diversions of nuclear materials are a major contributing factor to proliferation. By the 1990s, 525 facilities around the world were producing nuclear materials. This growing number of nuclear-production facilities has made the monitoring of nuclear proliferation a difficult and complicated task.

To aid in this task, the United Nations drafted the Non-Proliferation Treaty (NPT), which entered into force in 1970 and is due for renewal in 1995. About 140 states adhere to the provisions of the NPT. They agree not to transfer nuclear weapons or assist non-nuclear-weapon states to manufacture them. And non-nuclear-weapon states agree to abide by IAEA safeguards on the peaceful application of nuclear technology.

But many states have not signed the NPT, or, as in the case of North Korea, have signed but then withdrawn from the treaty, primarily because they see its provisions as discriminatory between states that have already manufactured nuclear devices and those that have not (table 16.3). They point out that nuclear-weapon states can keep, and even increase their arsenals, while non-nuclear states are under no obligation to submit to IAEA safeguards and inspections, non-nuclear-weapon states must do so on signing the NPT. In 1991, China and France, which were long opposed to signing the NPT, finally pledged their support to the treaty. However, in October 1993, China breached the spirit of that agreement by conducting a nuclear test. The test alarmed the international community and led to renewed pressure for a comprehensive worldwide ban of all nuclear tests.

Despite the fact that a majority of states are parties to the NPT, the number of nuclear weapons continue to grow and concentrate among the nuclear-weapon states. Many non-nuclear-weapons states assert that those states that have already stockpiled nuclear weapons have not lived up to their obligations to stop testing and spreading nuclear-weapons technology and ultimately to negotiate towards general and complete disarmament.

Because of the shortcomings of the IAEA and the NPT, some states adopted their own controls to nuclear proliferation. After India exploded its nuclear device in 1974, approximately 15 states, including Canada, formed a nuclear-suppliers cartel named the "London Club." In 1977, the London Club drafted voluntary export guidelines, designed to ensure that the export of nuclear material be safeguarded. A so-called "trigger list" was made of all sensitive nuclear materials, the export of which require special safeguards. Canada's policy terminates the sale of nuclear materials and equipment to any state that does not apply these safeguards in all its facilities. The United States has developed a similar policy under its Nuclear Non-Proliferation Act. And in Latin America, the Treaty of Tlateloco, signed in 1967, prohibits the acquisition or production of nuclear weapons anywhere in Central and South America. This treaty effectively makes Latin America a nuclear-free zone.

But perhaps the most controversial unilateral action to control nuclear proliferation was initiated in 1981 when Israel bombed a nuclear reactor under construction in Iraq. Israel argued that its attack was a pre-emptive strike against Iraq to prevent its developing nuclear weapons. Iraq countered by charging that such an act was extreme, given that the reactor was being constructed according to IAEA standards and Iraq was a signatory of the NPT. During the Gulf War, coalition forces did extensive damage to the efforts Iraq had made to reconstruct its facilities after Israel's attack in the 1980s.

Conventional and Other Weapons

One of the short-lived myths of the post-Cold War period is that the world would be a safer place. Events have challenged this dangerous assumption almost every week.

Though the risk of superpower conflict has largely dissipated, for millions of Rwandans, Bosnians, Somalis, and others, the world has never been less safe. They are the victims of the so-called conventional wars, fought with conventional weapons – bombs, rifles, tanks and mortars.

So while it is true that the world is still ultimately threatened by nuclear military technology, it is no less threatened by the advances that have been made in conventional-weapons technology since World War II.[6] Our concern about nuclear weapons has diverted our attention from the proliferation of conventional weapons, particularly in the less-developed states. However, with the exception of the few atomic weapons used against Japan in the mid–1940s, all wars in this century have been fought with conventional weapons supplied by the major industrial powers. Since the end of World War II, more than 40 million people, nearly all of them in the developing states, have died as a result of limited wars that have swept the planet. None were killed by nuclear bombs; they were killed by conventional weapons.

Conventional weapons have evolved to become highly destructive, even though these kind of weapons are still regarded as "limited" because no residual destruction follows their use, as is the case with nuclear weapons. Advances in the technology of conventional delivery systems, and the accuracy and the destructive power of conventional weapons would make an all-out war using these weapons catastrophic.

Chemical and Biological Weapons

Chemical and biological warfare has been waged sporadically over the centuries. The Athenians poisoned the water supplies of their enemies in 600 B.C. And in the fourteenth century the Tartars used biological warfare against their enemies. Historically, the prevailing belief about using such weapons was that they violate the most fundamental principles of warfare, namely, **military necessity** and chivalry. Chemical weapons do not only kill, they also maim and cause untold human and animal suffering. All this became quite evident in March 1988, as television cameras scanned the results of Iraq's use of mustard and cyanide gases on its own Kurdish citizens in the town of Halabja. It became vividly apparent that these weapons contravene the age-old principle of military necessity by killing and maiming civilians as well as soldiers. And just as horrendous, biological weapons can cause disease in humans, plants, and animals.

During this century, the horror of chemical warfare was first experienced at Ypres in Belgium in 1915, when German forces released chlorine gas on thousands of Allied troops. The Allies retaliated with similar gas attacks against the Germans, and in 1917 the Germans again used chemicals against the Allies, this time in the form of mustard gas. The world reacted strongly against the use of such weapons by the adoption of the Geneva Protocol, 1925, which forbids the use of chemical and biological weapons. But states were still allowed to produce and stockpile these weapons. Partly for this reason, the U.S. did not ratify the protocol until 1975.

During the 1970s, there were initiatives in the international community to further control the production and distribution of biological and chemical weapons. The 1972 United Nations Biological Weapons Convention prohibited the manufacture and stockpiling of biological and toxin weapons, at first by over 100 states. But the growing threat of the rapid spread of these two categories of deadly weapons led to increased conferencing on the subject. In 1989, a Conference on the Prohibition of Chemical Weapons was held in Paris. Over 100 states agreed not to use, produce, or stockpile such weapons, and also agreed to drafting a treaty to ban the possession of chemical weapons after 2005. In January 1993, a chemical-weapons treaty (effective January 15, 1995) was drafted under the auspices of the United Nations Conference on Disarmament held in Geneva, Switzerland.

■ ■ **military necessity:** an ancient principle of war asserting that only military targets, armed forces, and weapons should be destroyed in combat, and that civilians are non-combatants. ■ ■

The Sale of Arms

Ironically, the conventional weapons that killed so many millions after World War II were almost all manufactured by the five permanent members of the United Nations Security Council, the body mandated to prevent the scourges of another world war. It has always been easy to purchase weapons of great destruction in the name of national security. In the two decades leading up to the Gulf War, Iraq spent nearly $90 billion buying arms. Vietnam, in the same period, spent $50 billion, India, $30 billion, Angola, $15 billion, and the United States, nearly $5 trillion.

Despite the global economic recession, the trade in arms has remained buoyant.[7] This trade is dominated by the United States, which is the major supplier of all arms exports in Asia, Africa, and Latin America. Russia retains second position of arms sales globally. These sales have become an important source of hard currency for the beleaguered Russian economy. France is the third-largest arms-exporting state in the world, accounting for 11 percent of the market. France's conventional arms sales are targeted at states that want to avoid dealing with the superpowers. Mirage fighter bombers, Etendard naval fighters, and Exocet air-to-ship missiles are good examples of French conventional weapons being sold abroad. Approximately 60 percent of France's military sales go to the Middle East. Behind France are the United Kingdom, Israel, Germany, China, and Italy, each of which have a share of the global arms market. Other states have established indigenous arms facilities for the production of conventional weapons and equipment; these include Brazil, India, Iran, Jordan, Libya, Singapore, South Africa, South Korea, and Taiwan.

In 1993, world military expenditures exceeded $1.5 trillion. About 80 percent of world military expenditures purchase conventional weapons and equipment. In the past decade, developing states have contributed significantly to the rapid expansion of these purchases. Poor states, such as Ethiopia and Somalia, spend a greater proportion of their GDP than do much wealthier ones such as Canada, Norway, Finland, and the Netherlands. In Pakistan, a nation-state of 120 million people, the government allocates nearly 40 percent of its budget to the military. This trend of increased military spending by less-developed states led the United Nations to focus on global military expenditures. Since the United Nations was formed, the General

Assembly has on many occasions considered the reduction of military expenditures as a approach to disarmament.

In 1978, the United Nations held a Special Session on Disarmament (UNSSOD I). The final document became the basis of the first international arms-control agreement negotiated through a special United Nations conference. The Convention on Prohibitions or Restrictions on the Use of Certain Conventional Weapons Which May be Deemed to Be Excessively Injurious or to Have Indiscriminate Effects, along with three protocols, was opened for signature in 1981. Nearly 60 states have signed the convention; it promises to be a major contribution to the international law of peace. A second Special Session on Disarmament (UNSSOD II) was held in 1982 to continue the development of international law in this area, but a consensus was not achieved on most agenda items and a multilateral convention was not forthcoming.

Canada contributed to the agendas of both UNSSOD I and UNSSOD II, promoting the theme of limiting and reducing conventional weapons under the aegis of the United Nations. Canada controls the export of conventional weapons by the Export and Import Permit Act, which regulates the sale of military materials abroad. The departments of National Defence and Foreign Affairs approve all military sales outside Canada. Nearly 80 percent of Canada's military exports go to the United States and the NATO alliance. Notwithstanding its international efforts to control the conventional arms race, Canada tripled its defence budget in the 1980s. Only severe budget cutbacks caused successive governments to reduce Canada's conventional arsenal in the early 1990s.

The available quantitative evidence on the historical predictors of war challenges the widespread assumption among many world leaders that military might prevents war and military weakness invites aggression.[8] Some studies now conclude that when disputes are accompanied by arms competition, they are more likely to escalate into war than disputes that transpire in the absence of arms competition. The present proliferation of arms is as unprecedented in magnitude as would be the war resulting from it.

The emerging strategic environment of the 1990s and beyond not only promises to be dangerous but will also be very expensive. In states caught in the upward spiral of arms competition, the dollars they spend on defence provide far fewer returns in the form of job creation and general economic advantage than if the same dollars were spent on the production of civilian goods. Increased defence spending creates inflation because huge payrolls and expensive weapons inject more money into the economy without necessarily increasing the supply of consumer goods. Arms control or reduction does carry an economically beneficial payload, sometimes called the "peace dividend." Will this realization act as a deterrent or will it be an irrelevant consideration to national leaders caught in the web of building their national militaries or selling weapons to states demanding them?

Terrorism

Terrorism has become a major challenge to peace in the international community. Terrorists conduct a very special kind of human aggression by engaging in psychological warfare against their enemies. Terrorist acts can be state-sponsored or *state terrorism*, whereby governments organize and conduct the violence. Or they can be group-sponsored, whereby aggrieved groups use stealth and technology to strike selected targets without warning. State terrorism consists of government repression of domestic or external opposition, and sometimes selective illegal violence directed at individuals or groups perceived as threats to the state. Sometimes acts of state-sponsored terrorism are actions by a government that provide the incentive and assistance to non-state terrorists in other countries. Usually, non-state terrorism is the weapon of groups that represent a cause rather than a government.

The proliferation of arms is not only a threat to global security because so many nation-states are in the marketplace, but also because groups and certain states committed to the use of violence and terrorism acquire destructive arsenals to use them without warning in the international community. Very small transnational groups that are well armed can have an enormous impact on world affairs.

Conventional arms have been the weapons of choice for most terrorist groups and state terrorist activities. Advances in the technologies of small explosives have greatly advantaged terrorists around the world. The 1993 attack on the New York Trade Center demonstrated just how effective terrorist strategies can be in a major North America city. But chemical and biological weapons are much more insidious, because they are relatively easy to produce and the materials for them are more accessible and less expensive than many conventional or most nuclear weapons. Advanced biotechnology enables the manufacture of new weapons containing deadly viruses and toxins that can be easily harnessed and delivered by terrorists.

The *miniaturization* of nuclear weapons makes their acquisition more likely for transnational groups as well as for states that do not have the capacity to manufacture them. Present trends point to the acquisition of nuclear weapons by international actors that may be more inclined to resort to nuclear weapons to meet their goals. Conflicts that are currently limited to the use of conventional weapons could more easily involve the use of nuclear weapons, should they be in the possession of non-state actors.

These developments are a growing threat to peace and complicate international attempts to contain the spread of weapons among states, groups, and individuals. Considering the terrible effects that will result from the proliferation of these kinds of weapons, the world is seriously challenged in its efforts to keep them from becoming the arsenals of states, groups, and individuals.

Peace in Space

Since the launching of the first human-made satellites, the exploration of space ceased to be a dream and became a challenge.[9] Yet space has also been assigned a strategic importance by a growing number of states. With the challenge came the desired opportunity to infinitely expand human knowledge. But the conquest of this new frontier was accompanied by the danger that it would one day become an extension of territorial and military conflict. By the 1990s, approximately 100 military satellites each year were deployed above the earth. Early-warning satellites and other electronic intelligence satellites comprise the greater number of these, making it virtually impossible for any state to now conceal its military operations.

Although it has yet to materialize, the Strategic Defense Initiative (SDI) announced by former U.S. president Reagan moved the world into a new era of military competition in space. SDI, or "Star Wars," aspired to replace the principle of Mutual Assured Destruction (MAD) with a theory of assured defence by using space to build a high-tech shield designed to detect, track, and intercept missile attacks launched on the ground by enemy states. While SDI is not a reality, the concept is conceivable and therefore probable eventually as a military strategy for space. But space provides the world with many opportunities for non-military use.

Canada has been involved in outer space for over thirty years, since the launching of the *Alouette I* satellite in 1962. A Canadian Policy for Space was adopted in 1974, which states that Canadian space technology will be used for peaceful purposes. The development of CANADARM, which was used on the U.S. Space Shuttle and in the Canadian Astronaut Program, has captured much public attention.

The peaceful benefits of space exploration involve communications, remote sensing, industry science, and interplanetary travel. The International Telecommunications Satellite Organization (INTELSAT) was created in 1964 to rapidly transfer information related to news, sports, and cultural events. In 1975, only Canada, the Soviet Union, and the United States had communications satellite systems. By 1990, INTELSAT, with its 15 systems, had over 100 member states including Canada, and formed the nucleus of the global space-based telecommunications system. Canada owns and operates four INTELSAT earth stations

and has played a vital role in the international use of space for communications purposes. In 1969, TELESAT Canada was created to operate Canada's domestic satellite communications system, the backbone of which is the ANIK series.

Another non-military opportunity in space is remote sensing. In 1972, the United Nations Committee on the Peaceful Uses of Outer Space (COPUOS) gave global approval to the remote observation of the earth's surface, its weather patterns, environmental depletions and other phenomena by means of air-borne and space-borne platforms. Remote-sensing satellites scan the topography of the planet to gather precise data that is then shared by all states and international organizations. Two of the more commonly known uses of remote sensing are weather forecasting (to gather data on hurricanes, tornadoes, and other severe storms), and crop assessment (to gather data on crops, forests, grasslands, deserts, and fisheries). Canada uses information provided by the U.S. LANDSAT satellites for resource management – to measure forest and crop inventories and to study ice-flow patterns. The SARSAT search and rescue program, created by Canada, France, and the United States locates airplanes and ocean vessels in distress.

Commercial satellites provide enormous opportunities for industrial development and experimentation. Weightlessness and airlessness in space make possible the production of certain goods that are not efficiently manufactured on earth. For example, the manufacture of homogeneous crystals, so important to the electronics industry, is much more efficiently carried out in the conditions present in space. New or better drugs can also be manufactured in the weightless environment of space. Almost every field of human enterprise could benefit from space exploration.

The growth in the deployment of space-based technologies spawned the development of international law regarding the sovereign and military uses of outer space. There is still no internationally agreed-upon boundary between national air space and outer space. Scientists of the Committee on Space Research (COSPAR) have recommended the lower boundary of outer space be established at an altitude of 100 kilometres. This is the altitude at which satellites can orbit freely beyond the earth's gravitational pull. Many states, including Canada, believe it is important to reach agreement on a space boundary because of the legal and practical risks in the application of a growing regime of space law.

In 1963, the Partial Test Ban Treaty (PTBT) prohibited the explosion of nuclear weapons above the atmosphere. In 1967, COPUOS drafted the Outer Space Treaty, prohibiting the extension of sovereignty beyond national air space. Signatories to this treaty agree not to send into orbit weapons of mass destruction, to install such weapons on celestial bodies, or to establish military bases in space. The ABM Treaty (1972) between the United States and the Soviet Union also related to space by prohibiting each party from developing, testing, and deploying ABM systems that are air-based and space-based. Another agreement that governs the activities of states on the moon and other celestial bodies is the Moon Treaty (1979), which prohibits placing nuclear weapons on or around the moon.

The challenges of space are many and they are perceived in various ways by various governments. To a few, space is the logical arena for the projection of political and military power. To others, space is yet another opportunity for international co-operation and exploration, where scientific benefits can be derived from exchanges of information, joint efforts on the problems of space research, and the pooling of financial, human, and material resources.

The Challenge of Population

In eighteenth-century Europe, the world's first great demographic transformation began, raising the earth's total human population from about 800 million in 1750 to 3 billion in 1960 (figure 16.2).[10] Today, with nearly six billion people populating the earth, human beings number more than any other type of vertebrate, having recently pulled ahead of rats. At the present rate of annual growth of 1.7 percent, there will be one square foot of earth surface for every human being in 700 years. And in 1200 years, the human population will outweigh the earth. On the surface, the reasons for these significant population increases appear generally positive: the fall in the **death rate** has increased **life expectancy** to an unprecedented level; most infectious diseases are now medically controllable; and the level of education has risen substantially.

However, a second great demographic transformation has been underway since World War II in the developing states, and it threatens to undermine the apparent progress of the past 200 years. Population growth in the developing world is far greater than in the developed countries; the rate is often more

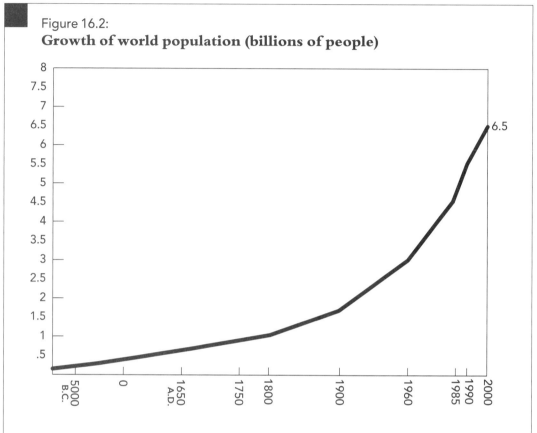

Figure 16.2:
Growth of world population (billions of people)

Source: Frederick Pearson and J. Martin Rochester, *International Relations: The Global Condition in the Late Twentieth Century* (New York: McGraw-Hill, 1992), 57.

than three percent a year (doubling in about 20 years), as compared to a rate of just over one percent (doubling in about 70 years). At current rates, world population growth approaches nearly 100 million per year (figure 16.3). Between 1990 and 2000, about 90 percent of the global population increase will occur in the developing countries. Of the 6.5 billion people expected to be living on the planet in the year 2000, five billion will live in developing countries. The best current estimates also suggest that the population of

developing countries will likely double in the next century and thereafter remain stable.

In the industrialized states of Europe and in Australia, Canada, Japan, and the U.S., low **mortality rates** have been accompanied by low **fertility rates**. A similar situation is also developing in states such as Argentina, Hong Kong, Taiwan, and Singapore, where economic development has reached a fairly high level. However, in most of the developing states of Africa, Asia, and Latin America, this demographic transition has not proceeded far.

Figure 16.3:

Where the human race is growing (billions of people): Developed regions and developing regions

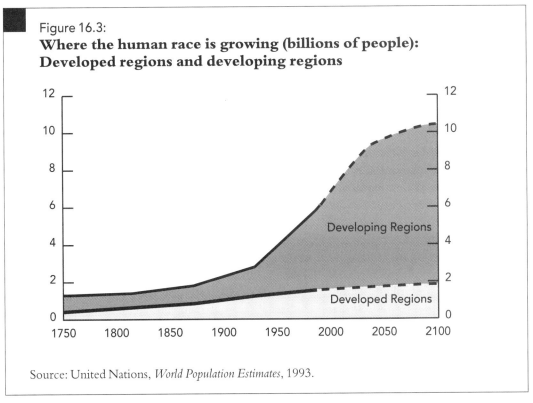

Source: United Nations, *World Population Estimates*, 1993.

The death rate has been falling rapidly over the past 40 years, but the fertility rate only began to decrease in the 1980s. It is because of this disparity in these rates that the population in developing countries is still growing rapidly. It remains to be seen how closely the course of demographic transition in the developing world will resemble that of the developed nation-states.

We know that demographic processes have a built-in momentum that takes years to stabilize. At present, the total population of developing states, taken as a group, is about 3.5 billion. By 2025, this will have risen to over eight billion and to ten billion by 2100. A century from now, the world's population will be more than 11 billion. If, at that time, a world population conference is held, representatives of attending states will be discussing the "population explosion" with deep concern. Over the coming decades, the consequences of population growth will challenge the pace of national economic development and the political stability of the developing regions. In these states, rapid population growth will worsen employment opportunities, exacerbate urban growth, put pressure on food supplies, widen the gap between the rich and poor, and foster non-democratic regimes.

In the years between 1980 and 2000 alone, the total number of working-age people in developing economies will have increased by 1150 million.[11] Only under the most optimal growth conditions in modern-sector labour-intensive economies will these people be able to secure employment. In most developing economies in the 1990s, there are intensive pressures to create jobs in the public sector. In these states, government itself is the major employer. In Kenya, for example, the public sector accounts for two-thirds of the growth in new jobs. The most tangible effects of this trend will be inflation and economic stagnation unless jobs can also be created at the same pace in the agricultural, manufacturing, and service sectors of developing economies.

Complicating the challenge of unemployment in developing regions is the problem that future population increases will take place in cities. The United Nations forecasts that in the decade 1990–2000, the global urban population will grow by 662 million while the rural population will grow by 219 million people.[12] The number of Third-World cities with populations of over ten million will grow from three to 21 by the turn of the century. By the year 2000, Mexico City (31 million) will have more people than Canada; São Paulo (26 million), Shanghai (23 million), and Bombay and Jakarta (with 17 million each) will experience unacceptable levels of congestion and municipal dysfunction. Housing, sewage, garbage collection, and the maintenance of the physical urban infrastructure will all suffer the consequences of overpopulation.

High population growth rates threaten the basic social and economic organization of developing nation-states. Excessive demands are placed on credit, financial, and marketing systems; food production is not sufficient to maintain per capita consumption; illiteracy, malnutrition, and disease diminish the performance of the education and health systems. In the face of such enormous pressures created by demographic expansion, developing states move to strengthen their administrative control over the population. All problems related to rapid population growth tend to be viewed by governments as threats to social stability and political order. In such cases, an authoritarian response to people by government is almost inevitable. Since 1970 in China, for example, the government has instituted a comprehensive birth-control policy involving forced sterilization, abortion, penalties, and fines to reach the goal of one-child families and **zero population growth (ZPG)**.

A growing number of states – Bangladesh, India, Kenya, Nigeria, Pakistan, and Zaïre – have moved towards a more pervasive regulation of social life, particularly with respect to birth control. Some states, such as China and Cuba, restrict movement from rural to urban areas so as to control rapid population growth in certain areas of the country. And restraints on reproductive freedom may become more common where governments, through incapacity or lack of awareness, allow demographic pressures to build to extremes. Sheer numbers can overwhelm national borders and administrative capacities. Some governments have adopted measures aimed at promoting greater social responsibility in the reproductive decisions made by families without using coercion to intrude into the decisions themselves. Such measures are aimed at reducing fertility, and are reflected in policies to expand basic family

■ ■ **zero population growth:** a population with a growth rate of zero because births plus immigration equal deaths plus emigration. ■ ■

education, to encourage small families, to ensure a more equitable distribution of income, and above all, to raise the status of women socially, economically, and politically. Brazil, Sri Lanka, South Korea, and Taiwan currently follow policy prescriptions along such lines.

The Problem of Small Population

While it is true that uncontrolled population growth can and does perpetuate poverty in a nation-state or region, it is also true that a small population can keep an economy poor.[13] A small population can compound and exacerbate national economic and social difficulties. Today, there are about 120 states with populations under 15 million, about one-half of these with populations under eight million. Most states with fewer than eight million people are found in Africa (29 states) and in the Americas (17 states).

States with small populations face higher costs to administer social-development programs because their tax revenues are small. Their markets are not big enough to attract labour-intensive or capital-intensive industries, resulting in a low levels of domestic competition, a tendency to form monopolies, and generally sluggish economic growth. As a result, the economies of nation-states with small populations can suffer from poor standards of performance, low productivity, and technological obsolescence. These states also reflect low levels of education and employment skills.

Global Population
from the National Perspective

For the majority of independent states, including Canada, the increasing number of people in the world is a distant problem.

Unless a state with a small population has high density (such as El Salvador or Taiwan), its rate of population growth tends not to concern its government. Low-population states point to the small number of major offenders that are responsible for the alarming post-World War II global population explosion. They cite China, India, Indonesia, and Pakistan as accounting for over 50 percent of the total world population increases. The obvious conclusion from their national perspective is for the world to pressure the few states with large populations to stabilize global population growth.

Few governments are willing or prepared to give serious consideration to an institutional approach to population control. Canada, for example, offers its population a Child Tax Benefit Program and tax policies that encourage families to grow. While the U.S. government promotes family planning, the Canadian government has not taken a position on this issue and financially supports fertility. Japan was the first state to pass fertility laws: abortion was legalized and the population's fertility rate fell dramatically. Taiwan began one of the world's most successful contraceptive programs in 1964, reducing its fertility rate from 5.4 in 1963 to 3.5 in 1990. But these are among the few exceptions. Throughout the international system, most states administer laws drafted to increase fertility, not to reduce it.

National and global institutions are at odds concerning their perception of the world's population problem. Nationalists argue that population growth is a sovereign preserve in the national interest. Global institutions point to the insidious nature of national population growth and call for international co-operation to control it. The challenge for all states lies in the recognition that the space and resources of this planet are limited. Governments must reject the idea that the quantity of human beings is of value apart from the quality of their lives.

Part of the remedy is to stop thinking of population as only a *national* problem. The world is much greater than the sum of its national parts. For the time being, a major international effort will be required to build a controllable balance between population, food production, and resource consumption. In order to prevent the disastrous consequences of global overpopulation, governments and the international organizations representing them will have to co-ordinate massive educational and informational programs designed to balance population growth with the ecological resources of the earth. Otherwise, the widening gap between resource sufficiency and resource scarcity will become unmanageable.

The Challenge of Hunger

More People Than Food

Nearly 200 years ago, Thomas Malthus alarmed the world by pointing out that the global population increase would press more and more insistently on the global food supply.[14] If unchecked, a **geometric progression** of world population growth would result in widespread misery and starvation. Until recent times, the Malthusian prediction was widely discredited. But Malthus's theory may have been more premature than erroneous.

During the nineteenth and the early part of the twentieth centuries, with the opening up of new land and the introduction of better agricultural methods, rates of food production increased more than the **arithmetic progression** predicted by Malthus. We now realize, however, that this growth will not continue indefinitely, and world population will soon outstrip global food production. At present, if all of the food produced was divided equally among the world's people, no one would die of starvation. But according to the Club of Rome's "Project on the Predicament of Mankind," by the year 2010, if the global food supply is divided equally among seven billion people, we will all gradually die of starvation. In the 1990s, the prevailing distribution system is partly responsible for hunger and starvation.[15] Even if the states of the world perfect their distribution systems, the growth of global population at current rates will severely strain the means of subsistence for all of humankind by the early twenty-first century.

There are some who say that the situation will take care of itself, through industrialization and the opening of new lands to cultivation, or that science will find a way out by improving food-production techniques, exploiting new sources of food resources (such as the oceans), and reducing food losses due to spoilage. But too little is happening too late. Quite simply, there is not enough capital, skill, or time available to change the traditional habits and attitudes among the bulk of the world's people. Population is already catching up with and outstripping increases in food production. The fact is that an annual increase of nearly 100 million mouths to feed requires more food than can possibly be produced year after year.

The growth of population has reached such dimensions and speed that it cannot help winning in a straight race against production. The situation is worsened by the fact that food production is competing at a serious disadvantage. According to the latest estimates of the World Health Organization (WHO), at least two-thirds of the world's people are undernourished. Before food production can overtake the *increase* in human numbers, it must catch up to minimum nutrition levels in order to correct this deficiency.

There are also intervening variables: land-tenure systems, which determine how land in a particular economy is organized, distributed, and owned, leave large tracts of unproductive land in the hands of a few; there is a high proportion of non-productive persons in the agricultural sector; production is impeded by the high cost of fertilizer and agricultural technology; and adverse weather conditions can result in drought and famine. Global food problems will continue to stem primarily from the production and distribution of food. But both these elements will also continue to be affected by climatic conditions, technology, farm-management practices, and government policies. Improving the global diet will be a complex and demanding challenge.

Since the early 1980s, the worst drought of the century has devastated sub-Saharan Africa. According to the United Nations, 24 African nation-states, with a population totalling 175 million, are in the grip of food shortages and mass starvation. In Mozambique, for example, famine is believed to have killed over 400,000 people from 1984 to 1990 alone, while another four million of its 13

■ ■ **geometric progression:** a geometric progression is one in which each term is derived by multiplying the preceding term by a given number called a common ratio (r). Thus if r is 2, the progression would appear as 2, 4, 8, 16, 32, 64, etc. ■ ■

million suffer from malnutrition. In Ethiopia, the famine went unnoticed until the fall of 1984, when news of drought awakened the world to the long-standing food crisis on the African continent. Not until television carried the ghastly images of the pain and suffering of Ethiopian families into our homes did the world take notice. Ethiopia got most of the attention because of the sheer scale of its famine, which continues to directly threaten seven million people, and which has turned the country's north into a dust-blown wasteland. Although successive years of drought were blamed for an ecological disaster unique in this century, other factors are involved. In Ethiopia, as in much of Africa, **deforestation** and overuse of land destroyed vast tracts even before the rain stopped. Undernourished, the land simply could not withstand the crisis or feed an ever-growing population. The spreading drought is simply the latest event in a tragedy many years in the making.

In Ethiopia and the Sudan, observers began using the term "mega-famine," predicting deaths by the hundreds of thousands. Aid-giving states had ignored the warning. At first, only a few states, such as Canada and the United States, provided extra aid when famine struck in full force in late fall, 1984. Tens of thousands would die in extreme misery before television cameras moved the world's conscience and an international relief effort was mobilized – one so hastily organized and so late that relief barely manages to keep pace with starvation. In many areas, the attempt to move food to the stricken has been hampered in turn by the structural weaknesses of so many African countries: the lack of roads, limited transport, and the chronic shortage of trained personnel. But the most outstanding weakness lies in the African governments themselves, which have in large part failed to develop agriculture properly, neglecting the countryside in favour of big projects and pampered cities.

In one sense, at least, the famine of the 1980s may have been a turning point. So enormous was the disaster that its bitter lessons alerted the aid-granting states of the world. African governments have finally started giving emergency priority to expanding food production and to saving the land. And aid agencies have begun to drive home the message that horrors like the famine in Ethiopia will be repeated unless long-term development becomes a world priority.

For many governments, there is the grim realization that Africa's crisis will not fade. There is no way to avoid an expensive prolonged commitment in aid. Ultimately, Africa could feed itself, but the time left to correct its wasted ecology is running short. At its current growth rate of 3.2 percent a year, sub-Saharan Africa's population will double in the next 12 years. If present trends continue, Africa, which already receives 60 percent of the world's food aid, will be able to feed less than half its population by the turn of the century. In the mid-1990s, Ethiopia, Somalia, and the Sudan are a startling vision of what lies ahead in Africa unless the process of desertification – currently creating new desert in its southward march of 10 kilometres per year – is halted. Each famine is worse than the last. Vast populations are being displaced. Their search for food becomes steadily more desperate.

Apart from the human tragedies of war, disaster, and famine, the number of people on this planet will somehow have to adjust to the resources available for supporting them. The question is: by what means? Starvation is one means well underway. Rational directive behaviour is another. Production techniques, of course, can be improved; the yield per acre can be increased; unused land in Asia, Africa, Latin America, and on tropical islands can be developed; arid and semi-arid regions can be made productive once the technology for converting sea water to fresh is economically feasible; and the seas can be farmed. But even if high-efficiency production techniques were presently available, at current rates of reproduction, human societies will still outgrow food supplies early in the twenty-first century.

Human beings do not grow and produce food in relation to population growth. Food production is essentially a response to a monied-market mechanism that returns profit. If you took a starving African child out of the desert and placed him or her in a well-stocked Canadian supermarket, the child would still die from starvation. Why? Because the child would not get past the cash register. All national economies, whether of capitalist or socialist organization, produce food in response to domestic and international market demands that are usually accompanied by some kind of economic reward. Otherwise, food supply is redirected to more profitable markets, or the industries die and production ceases.

The vital need, therefore, is for an integrated approach to economic, social, and technological policies with a long-term perspective and global outlook. We must learn how to apply humanitarian considerations to economic criteria in order to create long-term social benefits in place of short-term economic ones. Many believe that world hunger can be averted by combining competitive business practices with scientific and technological innovation. Although at present, total food production is not lower than that required for today's world population, national distribution systems and market mechanisms do not ensure that the world's needy receive the minimum necessary nourishment. Improved agriculture, through science and technology, cannot provide for a doubled world population unless there are fundamental changes in all economic and social systems and in international political thinking.

The problem of food production and distribution has not been addressed on a global scale. More than a decade could elapse before the results of any international reforms become fully evident. But extensive planning based on a future world outlook is essential if hunger is to be controlled. It is not difficult to predict with certainty what single desirable future we want. It is one that provides every human being with the basic dignity of enough to eat. Without a global food policy, we will reaffirm our sad destiny that derives its real and devastating failure from the lack of political, economic, and managerial insight.

Our future, if we choose to follow the same amorphous path of the past, will see much of the population of the world increasingly debilitated, diseased, aberrant, and violent. People will not curtail their birth rate sufficiently to bring population into balance with supportive resources, and per capita food production will begin to drop. As agriculture

falters, states like Canada and the United States will have to apply **triage** in their food diplomacy; there also will be the delicate question of how much international dole Americans and Canadians will be willing to fund. Beyond that, farming will be carried out only to the extent of supplying those who can afford to buy food. The world's labour force, increasingly malnourished and ailing, will become less productive, the **green revolution** will falter, and the effective commercial demand for food will drop. Under these circumstances, the great food exporters will be unable to provide the massive aid necessary to avert widespread famine.

The Challenge of AIDS

The AIDS Epidemic

Acquired immune deficiency syndrome (AIDS) was first identified as such in 1981, even though some medical scientists had tracked the syndrome under different names since the 1940s.[16] Its likely cause is the human immuno-deficiency virus (HIV), which damages the body's immune system by selectively infecting certain cells called T-cells. Wherever on earth a patient becomes ill, AIDS follows a similar course: the deficiency in the body's normal defences leaves the individual vulnerable to repeated viral, bacterial, and parasitical infection, which could ordinarily be controlled or eliminated. Those who succumb to AIDS-related illnesses worldwide typically die from rare forms of pneumonia and cancer.

AIDS is transmitted from person to person (figure 16.4). The HIV virus is fragile, easily killed by bleach, alcohol, detergent, heat, or drying. It is thus transmitted only through the intimate exchange of blood fluids, specifically

Figure.16.4:

How humans get AIDS:
Proportion of infections by mode of transmission

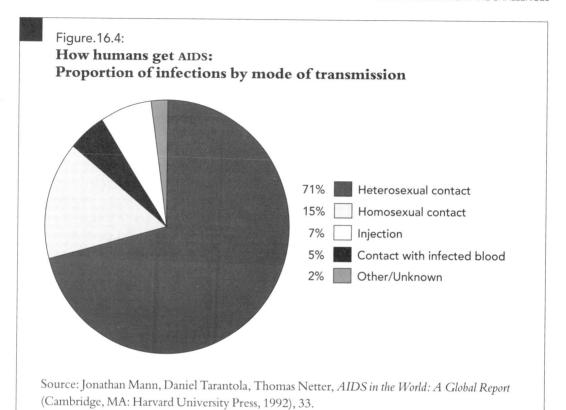

71%	Heterosexual contact
15%	Homosexual contact
7%	Injection
5%	Contact with infected blood
2%	Other/Unknown

Source: Jonathan Mann, Daniel Tarantola, Thomas Netter, *AIDS in the World: A Global Report* (Cambridge, MA: Harvard University Press, 1992), 33.

through blood transfusions, open sores, shared IV needles, and semen (sexual contact). High rates of AIDS are identified in various parts of the world among those who re-use hypodermic needles, drug abusers, and, in both heterosexual and homosexual groups, those who do not practise safe sex.[17]

As has been typical historically in cases of threatening epidemics, the world's reaction to AIDS and those infected, or even at risk, has not been generally characterized by either reason or empathy. The response of the international system has been deficient and disorganized. The efforts of the international community to deal with the spread of the HIV virus have been unco-ordinated at best.

Many governments are not informed and many express a distrust of experts in this area. Almost everywhere, people who have been identified as AIDS patients have been evicted, fired from their jobs, or quarantined by officials. National AIDS strategies are too narrowly implemented as strictly government programs, when the resources of many governments, non-governmental organizations, international organizations, and the private sector should be pooled in dealing with the crisis. Since the virus was first disclosed as a potential global threat in the early 1980s, the world has spent about $85 million per year on the issue. A global total of about $850 million had been spent between 1981 and 1991.

Table 16.4:
World HIV infections in adults and children by geographic area of affinity (GAA) as of January 1, 1992

GAA	Total no. of infections (millions)	% of global estimates for the year 2000		
		total HIV infections	low (millions)	high
North America	1.18	9.2	1.8	8.1
Europe	0.73	5.7	1.2	2.4
Oceania	0.03	0.2	0.22	0.45
Latin America & Caribbean	1.04	8.1	1.6	8.5
Sub-Saharan Africa	8.77	68.0	20.7	33.6
Caribbean	0.33	2.6	0.53	6.9
Southeast Mediterranean	0.04	0.3	0.89	3.5
Northeast Asia	0.04	0.3	0.6	0.48
Southeast Asia	0.70	5.4	11.2	45.0
Total	12.89	100.0	38.1	108.7

Source: Jonathan Mann, Daniel Tarantola, Thomas Netter, *AIDS in the World: A Global Report* (Cambridge MA: Harvard University Press, 1992).

The Global Pandemic

AIDS is a challenge to humanity in the 1990s because it is everywhere. It is a *pandemic*, occurring in all inhabited continents. Every nation-state has now officially reported cases of both carriers and fatalities. The virus infection appears globally. Everywhere in the world, HIV spreads through the same basic and narrow routes of transmission – by means of unsafe sexual activity, through blood or blood products, and from mother to fetus or infant. It is a virus that affects people directly, individually, and collectively. No insects, food, or water supply transmit the virus to humanity.

As of January 1, 1992, an estimated 11.8 million adults and 1.1 million children – a total of 12.9 million people worldwide – had been infected with HIV (table 16.4). The figures show that the pandemic is geographically diverse. Two-thirds of the infections are in sub-Saharan Africa, which contains only 8.8 percent of the world's population. Nearly 40 percent of the 11.8 million infected adults are women, representing 40 percent of the global total. In 1980, an estimated 80 percent of those infected with HIV were men.

By mid-1994, over four million people had developed AIDS and some 17 million had contracted the virus that likely causes it. By the year 2000, about six million people will be sick

Table 16.5:
Surveillance update: AIDS in Canada, geographic distribution

Province*	Male	Female	Total (%)	Known Deaths
British Columbia	1663	42	1705 (18)	1204
Alberta	567	28	595 (6)	219
Saskatchewan	67	7	74 (1)	51
Manitoba	111	3	114 (1)	83
Ontario	3787	159	3946 (41)	3183
Québec	2524	282	2806 (30)	1617
New Brunswick	67	8	75 (1)	35
Nova Scotia	129	12	141 (1)	100
P.E.I.	7	1	8 (<1)	7
Newfoundland	33	5	38 (<1)	31
N.W.T	6	1	7 (<1)	3
Yukon	2	0	2 (<1)	1
TOTAL	8963	548	9511 (100)	6534

*Cases are attributed to the province where onset of illness occurred.

< = fewer than

Source: AIDS Information Office, Regional Municipality of Ottawa-Carleton, April 1994.

with the virus and 30 million more will be infected. In some parts of Africa, a third of the population is infected by the AIDS virus.

AIDS in Canada

Since 1984, thousands of Canadians have died from AIDS. At least one million have been infected with the HIV virus (table 16.5). The economic and social cost of the AIDS epidemic in Canada are large, but not as great as in many other parts of the world. In Brazil and Haiti, hundreds of thousands of HIV-infected people are unaware that they are carriers and continue to spread the virus to the general population without much government con-

cern. As many as half of the residents of major cities in Africa, for example, have been infected with the virus. AIDS is a worldwide problem and one that is not about to disappear with national government strategies only.

Although initially the outbreak of AIDS was concentrated in major cities, among intravenous drug users and gay men, that pattern has been changing. As the epidemic matures, Canada's smallest cities are seeing an increase in cases. According to the World Health Organization, the transmission of AIDS will, by the year 2000, be primarily through heterosexual activity in most industrial countries.

Medically, there have been some successes.

After all, no one had heard of AIDS when doctors started describing the syndrome in 1981. Since then, researchers have learned how the AIDS virus infects cells and destroys the immune system. During the 1980s, a diagnostic test was developed, safer blood supplies were made available, and some treatments were introduced – notably the drugs AZT and pentamidine, which have prolonged AIDS patients' lives.

The initial response of the medical communities and governments in many states to the problem of AIDS was not only slow but was also political: gay men and Haitians were the two high-risk groups that were first targeted, but these are not people who generate rapid and favourable government response in the form of research and treatment funds. Some people even asserted that this disease was a punishment by God for immoral behaviour.

Outraged at the slowness and apparent hostility of provincial governments, the gay and lesbian community began to mobilize politically. Rallies, news conferences, and a strategy for inducing wider societal concern about the disease, as well as support for programs to find a cure, were launched. By the mid-1980s, a concerted effort was made to demonstrate that AIDS was a threat to all Canadians, not just to the high-risk groups. This became dramatically clear in 1985, when AIDS-contaminated blood was identified as the source of a number of infections of persons who fell outside the high-risk groups.

By the 1990s, AIDS had been taken up as a cause by celebrities in many countries. A huge quilt embroidered with the names of AIDS victims was assembled and displayed in many cities throughout Canada. Massive demonstrations were organized in Ottawa and elsewhere. The media lent its support to the pressure for AIDS research and treatment, while public-service television ads depicted white, middle-class, non-gay men and women with AIDS (the lowest-risk group). After much prodding, the government began to provide core funding for AIDS research, treatment, and education programs.

By 1990, some public-health experts began to lament that money for AIDS was now so abundant that it was threatening the funding of research and treatment for other major health problems that kill many more people, including cancer, heart disease, and Alzheimer's disease.

Meanwhile, statistics indicated that AIDS was still most likely to be a major problem for intravenous drug users, persons who engage in anal sex, and people linked to these two groups: for example, prostitutes who use intravenous drugs can spread it to their clients who spread it to other women; bisexual men can pass it on to other men and women; and pregnant women with AIDS can infect their unborn children. Particularly disturbing was the discovery in 1990 that many younger gay men (over 45 percent in one study) were engaged in unsafe sex – anal intercourse without condoms. Moreover, AIDS was also showing up in adolescents, drug users not using intravenous drugs (but using crack cocaine and alcohol), and women. Surgical workers and other medical professionals exposed to blood or blood products were also shown to be at increased risk. Even dentists began to wear surgical gloves, as did law-enforcement persons exposed to contaminated needles or to bleeding crime victims or criminals.

Studies to check the effectiveness of programs to reduce infection rates, such as providing free needles to intravenous drug users (who often share contaminated needles), or bleach to disinfect needles, were conducted with private funds because federal law prohibited the use of money for these purposes.

In the struggle to raise the visibility of AIDS issues on the political agenda in Canada, group activism has also played a very significant role. AIDS advocacy groups, such as the Canada AIDS Network, the AIDS Committee of Toronto (ACT), the Black Coalition for AIDS Prevention, and AIDS Vancouver have increased their protests, using marches and gatherings as a way of drawing attention to the killer virus. Other groups have bypassed the very slow government procedures for testing and licensing new drugs and, on their own, are testing drugs and medication that can help reduce the symptoms or prolong the lives of AIDS sufferers.

Public policy on AIDS in Canada is affected by a variety of complicating factors, including federalism, our parliamentary system of government, and the public-private split in our political system as to who is responsible for our AIDS programs. As is usually the case with complex public issues, there is conflict about how important the issue is relative to other issues – a question of obvious importance in the case of AIDS, because some groups in Canada fear in tight times that spending more money on AIDS will reduce spending on research linked to other health problems.

Whatever the level of effort nationally, no single government initiative is going to solve the AIDS crisis. It will require a concerted international effort to conduct research on the demography and physiological conduct of the virus, to co-ordinate programs of prevention, and to build multilateral strategies to halt the spread of the pandemic.

The Global Environment

Pollution and Development

In the latter part of the twentieth century, humanity is learning that the pollution and destruction of the global environment has consequences second only perhaps to nuclear war. Since the eighteenth century, the idea of progress led us to the dangerous conclusion that industrialization and technological change resulted in manageable environmental consequences. Industrialization has been taken as licence to pollute air and water with impunity. Most national economies are in the business of doing just that every day, under the guise of legitimate governmental policies encouraging industries to produce what other countries import, in order to increase national employment and strengthen national currencies. We think that technology can liberate us from disease, hunger, ignorance, and premature death. We may recognize that modernization has advanced us but we do not see that the advances are often at incalculable environmental costs.

Global issues of the environment have only recently become a concern to the public, as people and their governments begin to measure the deadly onslaught of despoliation within their legal jurisdictions.[18] Almost every state, regardless of wealth or ideology, now faces environmental problems at least as severe as the next. Underdeveloped states almost always trade off **ecological** sensitivity for economic growth, allowing foreign governments and multinationals to pour chemicals onto their coasts, and into their lakes, rivers, and soil. In Canada and the United States, high levels of toxic waste are steadily discharged into the oceans, creating hazardously high concentrations of arsenic, cadmium, copper, lead, mercury, nickel, polychlorinated biphenyls (PCBs), and zinc in the delicate salt-water ecology. Plant and animal life absorb the toxins and die, or share these insidious contaminants with their human predators. Chronic land-based pollution – chemical spillage, sewage, and garbage – mix with the agricultural run-off of fertilizers and pesticides to generate an anti-ecology, an independent toxic system that robs the environment of its benign life-sustaining forces.

Russia ranks among the worst offenders in this regard. But one tragedy of international dimensions, first reported by Swedish authorities, was the explosion of a nuclear reactor at Chernobyl in the former Soviet Union that contaminated a vast area on the European continent. Years later, livestock in Northern Europe still could not be slaughtered for food because of high radiation levels in the animals.

Nothing has come to symbolize the vulnerability of the environment to the selfish national goals of an industrialized civilization more than the massive ocean-going oil tankers constantly criss-crossing the high seas. Many supertankers can carry over 300,000 tons of cargo, and bigger ones are planned. When a supertanker cracks up and spills its oil into the ocean, fisheries and beaches are despoiled. Thousands of species are threatened and the world's delicate ecological balance is imperiled. The *Exxon Valdez* spill was the largest in U.S. history (over ten million gallons) covering 1000 square miles and damaging the fragile ecology of Alaska well into the twenty-first century. The 1991 Gulf War in the Middle East also resulted in tremendous environmental damage on land and in the ocean waters in the Persian Gulf and Gulf of Oman when massive oil-well fires, caused by Iraq's deliberate ignition of Kuwaiti wells, burned in the desert for months .

Changing the Earth's Ecology

During the summer of 1988, hundreds of climatologists, lawyers, biologists, engineers, and atmospheric chemists from six continents convened in Toronto to address an emergency – radical changes in the global atmosphere. This World Conference on the Changing Atmosphere focused on two phenomena: the destruction of the ozone layer, and global warming. In both cases, Conference participants called for individual, national, and international actions, which are needed soon, as we enter another century of industrial productivity.

Serious ozone depletion has occurred in the Antarctic: a hole of equal size around the North Pole would cover all of Canada. In reality, the ozone layer is very thin – about as thick as a pane of glass encircling the earth. Since the dawn of civilization, this rarified protective layer of gas has prevented animal and plant life from frying in the direct rays of the sun. Scientists point to the chlorine that originates from the breakdown of **chlorofluorocarbons (CFCs)** as a major contributor to the problem. These human-made chemicals, which are very useful (in aerosol cans, heat pumps, refrigerators, freezers, and air conditioners) and which are rather benign at sea level, break down in the atmosphere into chlorine, which combines with and destroys ozone. Canada contributes two percent of the global CFC problem. If all states

■ ■ **chlorofluorocarbons:** chemical emissions that have a negative impact on the levels of ozone (O_3) in the ozone layer, a thin protective layer of gas in the atmosphere. ■ ■

589

legislated a stop to the production of CFCs today, it would take about 100 years for them to be cleansed out of the atmospheric system. In 1988, the Montreal Protocol established a schedule for the gradual banning of CFCs. Assuming all signatories ratify the treaty, the hole over the Antarctic will not disappear until the early part of the twenty-second century.

Ozone damage prompted Environment Canada to provide the public with daily reports, beginning in 1992, on the cancer-causing rays that now reach the earth's surface in increased amounts. The ultraviolet (UV) radiation report informs Canadians whether reduced levels of ozone produce a higher risk of dangerous radiation exposure. Canadians can then decide whether to take precautions such as wearing a hat, applying sunscreen, or using sunglasses to protect themselves from the dangers of ultraviolet rays. Canada is one of a growing number of states that now provide their citizens with regular UV reports.

Another form of dramatic environmental change, called *global warming,* is also occurring at a rapid pace. This process is caused in part by large atmospheric accumulations of carbon dioxide from fossil-fuel burning and emissions of methane from agricultural and industrial practices. Scientists predict that the earth is rushing towards an historically unprecedented average global warming of up to 4.5 degrees Celsius within the next 50 years. Over the past 150 years, 1987 was the warmest year globally, and the four hottest years in the last 130 years have occurred since 1980. In 1992, 148 states agreed to a pact to fight the rising world temperatures that many scientists have warned threaten to change the earth's climate in very destructive ways. Possible effects include rising ocean levels, which could cause flooding in some areas and may dry other areas of the globe to desert. The treaty was signed at the Earth Summit in Rio de Janeiro in June 1992. The United Nations conference on Environment and Development which met at Rio de Janeiro reaffirmed the Declaration of the United Nations Conference on the Human Environment in 1972. At the 1992 conference, wealthy states agreed to give financial and technological help to developing ones. The conference was designed to mitigate the so-called **greenhouse effect** in which certain gases trap the world's heat.

Many states have become concerned about **acid rain,** which results from conditions that also contribute to the greenhouse effect.[19] About 150,000 Canadian lakes have already been seriously damaged by acid rain, and another 15,000 are considered dead. On the pH scale, the measure of acidity for which seven is neutral, some Canadian lakes consistently measure five (vinegar measures three). In 1990, Canada and the United States signed the Clean Air Act, committing their industries to reducing sulphur dioxide and nitrogen oxide emissions by the year 2000.

One of the solutions to the problem of acid rain is for states to plant trees. Trees absorb environmental impurities and convert them to oxygen. However, the twentieth century has witnessed extensive deforestation on most continents. Much of North America has suffered from deforestation as human habitat encroached and continues to encroach upon natural areas. In the tropics, especially in Brazil and Indonesia, enormous areas of forest are being cleared for commercial farming, hydroelectric dams, and industrial development. The usual method is burning, which generates more carbon and kills the very trees that help keep the carbon dioxide in balance. By 1993, Brazil had lost forest of an area larger than Denmark, Belgium, Switzerland, and Austria combined.

Deforestation usually occurs when people want to use land to live on or to use for agriculture. As a result, not only are trees felled by the millions, but the biological heritage these trees support is also destroyed. All of the animals that come to rely upon trees for their survival become threatened and eventually endangered. By 1993, Canada listed 211 species of plants and animals as endangered. Included for the first time were well-known mammals, such as the polar and grizzly bears. Other additions were birds, reptiles and amphibians, as well as fish and certain types of caribou.

The changing atmospheric phenomena of warming and ozone depletion from human-made chlorofluorocarbons and other gases has dangerous consequences for agriculture. The major world food crops, wheat, rice, corn, and soybeans in particular, are quite sensitive to ultraviolet radiation. These crops will respond to the damage with reduced yields worldwide. In southern parts of Canada, scientists have measured a three to four percent decrease in ozone levels. At a 10 or 15 percent ozone depletion level, food production in Canada, as well as worldwide, would be significantly reduced.

In 1988, the World Congress on Climate and Development met in Hamburg, Germany, and called upon all states, led by the industrial states to take unilateral action to reduce carbon dioxide emissions by 30 percent by the year 2000 and 50 percent by 2015. Environmentalists and scientists urged state participants to reduce their use of fossil fuels, their rates of deforestation, and to commence reforestation as soon as possible.

Solutions to global warming and ozone depletion are fundamentally political and international.[20] The idea that a remarkable technological fix is waiting in the wings is unrealistic. In an era of tight global connection, problems of peace, arms control, hunger, population growth, AIDS, and environmental deterioration do not merely require domestic response: the international face of these problems requires solutions beyond national jurisdiction to the level of a global will. But in the final analysis, we are individually and socially equipped to solve the problems we have brought upon ourselves. Hunger, overpopulation, and war are not extra-human forces acting upon us. They are engineered by our attitudes, ignorance, and actions. Our greatest threat is the way we think. As cartoonist Walt Kelly's Pogo observed, "We have met the ENEMY...an' HE IS US."

References

1. Charles Doran, *Systems in Crisis: New Imperatives of High Politics at the Century's End* (New York: Cambridge University Press, 1991); Janice Stein, "Why it's still the old world order," in *Foreign Service Journal* (July, 1991), 16-19; Robert Tucker and David Henrickson, *The Imperial Temptation: The New World Order and America's Purpose* (New York: Council on Foreign Relations, 1992).

2. Thomas Paine, *Rights of Man*, ed., Henry Collins (Middlesex, England: Penguin Books, 1969), 238.

3. *The Blue Helmets: A Review of United Nations Peacekeeping* (1990); John Tessitore and Susan Woolfson, eds., *A Global Agenda: Issues Before the 47th General Assembly of the United Nations* (Lantham, MD: University Press of America, 1992).

4. Michael Cromartie, ed., *Peace betrayed? Essays on Pacifism and Politics* (Washington, D.C.: Ethics and Public Policy Center, 1991).

5. Sir Michael Quinlan, "Nuclear weapons and the abolition of war," in *International Affairs* (67: 1991), 293-301.

6. Ethan B. Kapstein, ed., *Global Arms Production: Policy Dilemmas for the 1990s*, (Lantham, MD: University Press of America, 1992); Richard Wiggers, "Conventional Weapons" in *Briefing Paper* 21 (Ottawa: United Nations Association, Oct. 1986), 1-6.

7. Michael Klare, "Deadly convergence: The arms trade, nuclear/chemical/missile proliferation, and regional conflict in the 1990s" in Michael Klare and Daniel Thomas eds., *World Security: Trends and Challenges at Century's End* (New York: St. Martin's Press, 1991), 170-196.

8. Michael Wallace, "Armaments and Escalation: Two Competing Hypotheses," in *International Studies Quarterly 26* (March 1982): 32-56; Michael Wallace, "Arms races and escalation: Some new evidence," in *Journal of Conflict Resolution* (March 1979): 3-16; and Ofer Zur,"The psychohistory of warfare: The co-evolution of culture, psyche, and enemy," in *Journal of Peace Research* 24, (1987), 125-134.

9. Nandasiri Jasentuliyana, ed., *Maintaining Outer Space for Peaceful Purposes: Proceedings of a Symposium Held in The Hague* (Tokyo, Japan: United Nations University Press, 1984).

10. Ansley Coale, "The History of the Human Population," in *Scientific American 231* (Sept. 1974): 41-51.

11. Robert McNamara, "Time Bomb or Myth: The Population Problem," *Foreign Affairs 62* (Summer 1984): 1107-1131; Lester Brown, "Analysing the demographic trap," in Lester Brown et al. *State of the World 1987* (New York: W. W. Norton, 1987), 21-37.

12. For a comprehensive picture see John Rourke, *International Politics on the World Stage* (Guilford, CT: The Dushkin Publishing Group, Inc., 1993), 237-239, 555-558.

13. Allen Crosbie Walsh, "Special Problems in the Population Geography of Small Populations," in John Clarke, ed., *Geography and Population: Approaches and Applications* (Oxford: Pergamon Press, 1984), 69-76; L.A. Kosinski and John Webb, eds., *Population at Microscale* (New Zealand: New Zealand Geographical Society, 1976), 79-92.

14. Thomas Malthus was a British professor of political economy whose major work, *An Essay on the Principle of Population* (1978), had a major impact on the social sciences and contributed to the development of the discipline of demography.

15. United Nations, *Yearbook, 1990* (New York:Food and Agriculture Organization , 1991).

16. W.F. Batchelor, "AIDS 1988: The science and limits of science," in *American Psychologist* (45), 853-858.

17. Jonathan Mann, Daniel Tarantola, and Thomas Netter, eds., *AIDS in the World* (Cambridge, MA: Harvard University Press, 1992), Preface; A.M. Brandt, AIDS in historical perspective: "Four lessons from the history of sexually transmitted diseases," in *American Journal of Public Health* (78), 367-371.

18. Jessica Mathews, "The Environment and International Security," in Michael Klare and Daniel Thomas, eds., *World Security: Trends & Challenges at the Century's End* (New York: St. Martin's Press, 1991), 362-380; World Bank. *World Development Report 1992: Development and the Environment* (New York: Oxford University Press, 1992).

19. Alan Durning, "Enough is enough: Assessing global consumption," in Robert Jackson, ed., *Global Issues 92/93* (Guilford, CT: The Dushkin Publishing Group, 1992), 17-20.

20. William Rees, "The ecology of sustainable development," in *The Ecologist* (20), 18-23.

Suggested Readings

Virginia Berridge and Philip Strong, *AIDS and Contemporary History* (New York: Cambridge University Press, 1993).

Robert Boardman, *Canadian Environmental Policy Ecosystems, Politics and Process* (Don Mills, ON.: Oxford University Press, 1992).

April Carter, *Peace Movements* (New York: Longman Publishing, 1992).

Howard Fast, *War and Peace Observations On Our Times* (New York: M.E. Sharpe, 1992).

Harold James and Marla Stone, *When the Wall Came Down* (New York: Routledge, 1992).

Charles Kegley, Jr., and Eugene Wittkopf, *World Politics: Trends and Transformations* (New York: St. Martin's Press, 1993).

Christopher Maule and Fen Hampson, *A New World Order? Canada Among Nations 1992-93* (Don Mills, ON: Oxford University Press, 1992).

Bennett Ramberg, *Arms Control Without Negotiation: From the Cold War to the New World Order* (Boulder, CO: Lynne Rienner Publishers, 1993).

Timothy O'Riordan and Albert Weale, *The New Politics of Pollution* (Manchester, England: Manchester University Press, 1991).

John Stroessinger, *Why Nations Go to War* (New York: St. Martin's Press, 1993).

Glossary

acid rain: Rainfall contaminated by high levels of sulphur dioxide (SO_2), usually emitted from the burning of fossil fuels and industrial processes.

arithmetic progression: A sequence in which each term is derived from the preceding one by adding a given number called the common difference (d). Thus if d is 2, the progression would appear as 2, 4, 6, 8, 10, 12, etc.

biological weapons: Toxic substances that create diseases and epidemics when released against enemy troops or populations.

chemical weapons: Gases, herbicides, and other substances that can kill or paralyze enemy troops or populations.

chlorofluorocarbons (CFCs): Chemical emissions that have a negative impact on the levels of ozone (O_3) in the ozone layer, a thin protective layer of gas in the atmosphere.

conventional weapons: All weapons excluding nuclear, biological, and chemical weapons.

death rate: The number of deaths in any given year divided by the mid-year population and multiplied by 1000.

deforestation: Loss of forests due to harvesting, expanding farm and urban acreage, soil erosion, acid rain, and other deleterious impacts.

disarmament: The decision by one or more states to destroy weapons in their possession and not to build or acquire others.

ecology: A term coined in the nineteenth century that refers to the relationship of living things to one another and to their natural environment.

fertility rate: The annual number of births among women in a given age group divided by the number of women in that age group. Ordinarily, age groups of five years are used.

geometric progression: A geometric progression is one in which each term is derived by multiplying the preceding term by a given number called a common ratio (r). Thus if r is 2, the progression would appear as 2, 4, 8, 16, 32, 64, etc.

green revolution: A term coined in 1968 by William Guad, administrator in the U.S. Agency for International Development (AID), to describe the introduction and rapid worldwide adoption of high-yielding wheats and rices.

greenhouse effect: A global warming effect caused by an accumulated presence of carbon dioxide in the atmosphere that blocks the radiation of heat reflecting from the earth into space.

intercontinental ballistic missiles (ICBMs): Electronically guided land-based weapons that can deliver their nuclear payloads at distances of over 3000 miles.

life expectancy: The average number of years a person is expected to live from birth.

Manhattan Project: The U.S. government-sponsored research project that produced the first atomic weapon.

military necessity: An ancient principle of war asserting that only military targets, armed forces, and weapons should be destroyed in combat and that civilians are non-combatants.

mortality rate: The proportion of deaths occurring in a given population.

mutually-assured destruction (MAD): A strategic doctrine of deterrence under which each adversary preserves the capability to absorb a first nuclear strike by the other and to retaliate with devastating nuclear force, inflicting unacceptable damage on the attacker.

nuclear freeze: Measures taken unilaterally or multilaterally among states to stop the production and spread of nuclear weapons.

nuclear proliferation: The acquisition of nuclear weapons by nation-states that formerly did not have them.

nuclear-weapon-free zone (NWFZ): Any state, region, or zone designated as an area free of nuclear weapons as is Antarctica, the seabed, Latin America, and outer space.

peacekeeping: The use of military means by an international organization, such as the United Nations, which involves sending a neutral collective contingent to prevent fight-ing, usually by acting as a buffer between and among combatants.

strategic nuclear weapons: Large-scale, long-range nuclear weapons delivered by ICBMs and bombers that give a state a particular advantage in relations with other states.

strategic superiority: A temporary military advantage of one state or a group of states arising from the credible enhancement of their offensive and defensive capabilities.

tactical nuclear weapons: Small-scale, short-range nuclear devices for use in the battlefield.

thermonuclear: A term used to indicate the great destructive potential of nuclear weapons to unleash high volumes of measurable energy and heat when detonated.

triage: The sorting out and classification of casualties of war or other disasters, to determine priority of need and proper place of treatment.

unilateral disarmament: A strategy of disarmament advocates aimed at bypassing deadlock in multilateral disarmament negotiations by undertaking one-sided initiatives to reduce the number and level of arms.

unipolar system: A balance of power alignment that appears from time to time in the international system whereby one nation-state is perceived to possess the most significant power variables and is in a position to exercise that power in its own national interests.

verification: An agreed-upon process for determining compliance of all parties to the terms and provisions of an arms-control agreement.

zero population growth (ZPG): A population with a growth rate of zero because births plus immigration equal deaths plus emigration.

zone of peace (ZOP): Any country, region, or zone designated as an area free of any arms, conventional or nuclear.

Appendix A

Canadian Charter of Rights and Freedoms

Whereas Canada is founded upon principles that recognize the supremacy of God and the rule of law:

Guarantee of Rights and Freedoms
1. The Canadian Charter of Rights and Freedoms guarantees the rights and freedoms set out in it subject only to such reasonable limits prescribed by law as can be demonstrably justified in a free and democratic society.

Fundamental Freedoms
2. Everyone has the following fundamental freedoms:
(a) freedom of conscience and religion;
(b) freedom of thought, belief, opinion, and expression, including freedom of the press and other media of communication;
(c) freedom of peaceful assembly; and
(d) freedom of association

Democratic Rights
3. Every citizen of Canada has the right to vote in an election of members of the House of Commons or of a legislative assembly and to be qualified for membership therein.
4. (1) No House of Commons and no legislative assembly shall continue for longer than five years from the date fixed for the return of the writs at a general election of its members.
(2) In time of real or apprehended war, invasion or insurrection, a House of Commons may be continued by Parliament and a legislative assembly may be continued by the legislature beyond five years if such continuation is not opposed by the votes of more than one third of the members of the House of Commons or the legislative assembly, as the case may be.
5. There shall be a sitting of Parliament and of each legislature at least once every twelve months.

Mobility Rights
6. (1) Every citizen of Canada has the right to enter, remain in and leave Canada.
(2) Every citizen of Canada and every person who has the status of a permanent resident of Canada has the right
(a) to move to and take up residence in any province; and
(b) to pursue the gaining of a livelihood in any province.
(3) The rights specified in subsection (2) are subject to
(a) any laws or practices of general application in force in a province other than those that discriminate among persons primarily on the basis of province of present or previous residence; and
(b) any laws providing for reasonable residency requirements as a qualification for the receipt of publicly provided social services.
(4) Subsections (2) and (3) do not preclude any law, program or activity that has as its object the amelioration in a province of conditions of individuals in that province who are socially or economically disadvantaged if the rate of employment in that province is below the rate of employment in Canada.

Legal Rights
7. Everyone has the right to life, liberty and security of the person and the right not to be deprived thereof except in accordance with the principles of fundamental justice.
8. Everyone has the right to be secure against unreasonable search or seizure.
9. Everyone has the right not to be arbitrarily

detained or imprisoned.

10. Everyone has the right on arrest or detention
(a) to be informed promptly of the reasons therefor;
(b) to retain and instruct counsel without delay and to be informed of that right; and
(c) to have the validity of the detention determined by way of *habeas corpus* and to be released if the detention is not lawful.

11. Any person charged with an offence has the right
(a) to be informed without unreasonable delay of the specific offence;
(b) to be tried within a reasonable time;
(c) not to be compelled to be a witness in proceedings against that person in respect of the offence;
(d) to be presumed innocent until proven guilty according to law in a fair and public hearing by an independent and impartial tribunal;
(e) not to be denied reasonable bail without just cause;
(f) except in the case of an offence under military law tried before a military tribunal, to the benefit of trial by jury where the maximum punishment for the offence is imprisonment for five years or a more severe punishment;
(g) not to be found guilty on account of any act or omission unless, at the time of the act or omission, it constituted an offence under Canadian or international law or was criminal according to the general principles of law recognized by the community of nations;
(h) if finally acquitted of the offence, not to be tried for it again and, if finally found guilty and punished for the offence, not to be tried or punished for it again; and
(i) if found guilty of the offence and if the punishment for the offence has been varied between the time of commission and the time of sentencing, to the benefit of the lesser punishment.

12. Everyone has the right not to be subjected to any cruel and unusual treatment or punishment.

13. A witness who testifies in any proceedings has the right not to have any incriminating evidence so given used to incriminate that witness in any other proceedings, except in a prosecution for perjury or for the giving of contradictory evidence.

14. A party or witness in any proceedings who does not understand or speak the language in which the proceedings are conducted or who is deaf has the right to the assistance of an interpreter.

Equality Rights

15. (1) Every individual is equal before and under the law and has the right to the equal protection and equal benefit of the law without discrimination and, in particular, without discrimination based on race, national or ethnic origin, colour, religion, sex, age or mental or physical disability.
(2) Subsection (1) does not preclude any law, program or activity that has as its object the amelioration of conditions of disadvantaged individuals or groups including those that are disadvantaged because of race, national or ethnic origin, colour, religion, sex, age or mental or physical disability.

Official Languages of Canada

16. (1) English and French are the official languages of Canada and have equality of status and equal rights and privileges as to their use in all institutions of the Parliament and government of Canada.
(2) English and French are the official languages of New Brunswick and have equality of status and equal rights and privileges as to their use in all institutions of the legislature and government of New Brunswick.
(3) Nothing in this Charter limits the authority of Parliament or a legislature to advance the equality of status or use of English and French.

17. (1) Everyone has the right to use English or French in any debates and other proceedings of Parliament.

(2) Everyone has the right to use English or French in any debates and other proceedings of the legislature of New Brunswick.

18. (1) The statutes, records and journals of Parliament shall be printed and published in English and French and both language versions are equally authoritative.

(2) The statutes, records and journals of the legislature of New Brunswick shall be printed and published in English and French and both language versions are equally authoritative.

19. (1) Either English or French may be used by any person in, or in any pleading in or process issuing from, any court established by parliament.

(2) Either English or French may be used by any person in, or in any pleading in or process issuing from, any court of New Brunswick.

20. (1) Any member of the public in Canada has the right to communicate with, and to receive available services from, any head or central office of an institution of the Parliament or government of Canada in English or French, and has the same right with respect to any other office of any such institution where

(a) there is a significant demand for communications with and services from that office in such language; or

(b) due to the nature of the office, it is reasonable that communications with and services from that office be available in both English and French.

(2) Any member of the public in New Brunswick has the right to communicate with, and to receive available services from, any office of an institution of the legislature or government of New Brunswick in English or French.

21. Nothing in sections 16 to 20 abrogates or derogates from any right, privilege or obligation with respect to the English and French languages, or either of them, that exists or is continued by virtue of any other provision of the Constitution of Canada.

22. Nothing in sections 16 to 20 abrogates or derogates from any legal or customary right or privilege acquired or enjoyed either before or after the coming into force of this Charter with respect to any language that is not English or French.

Minority Language Education Rights

23. (1) Citizens of Canada

(a) whose first language learned and still understood is that of the English or French linguistic minority population of the province in which they reside, or

(b) who have received their primary school instruction in Canada in English or French and reside in a province where the language in which they received that instruction is the language of the English or French linguistic minority population of the province, have the right to have their children receive primary and secondary school instruction in that language in that province.

(2) Citizens of Canada of whom any child has received or is receiving primary or secondary school instruction in English or French in Canada, have the right to have all their children receive primary and secondary school education in the same language.

(3) The right of citizens of Canada under subsections (1) and (2) to have their children receive primary and secondary school instruction in the language of the English or French linguistic minority population of a province

(a) applies wherever in the province the number of children of citizens who have such a right is sufficient to warrant the provision to them out of public funds of minority language instruction; and

(b) includes, where the number of those children so warrants, the right to have them receive that instruction in minority language educational facilities provided out of public funds.

Enforcement

24. (1) Anyone whose rights or freedoms, as guaranteed by this Charter, have been infringed

or denied may apply to a court of competent jurisdiction to obtain such remedy as the court considers appropriate and just in the circumstances.

(2) Where, in proceedings under subsection (1), a court concludes that evidence was obtained in a manner that infringed or denied any rights or freedoms guaranteed by this Charter, the evidence shall be excluded if it is established that, having regard to all the circumstances, the admission of it in the proceedings would bring the administrations of justice into disrepute.

General

25. The guarantee in this Charter of certain rights and freedoms shall not be construed so as to abrogate or derogate from any aboriginal, treaty or other rights or freedoms that pertain to the aboriginal peoples of Canada including (a) any rights or freedoms that have been recognized by the Royal Proclamation of October 7, 1763; and (b) any rights or freedoms that may be acquired by the aboriginal peoples of Canada by way of land claims settlement.

26. The guarantee in this Charter of certain rights and freedoms shall not be construed as denying the existence of any other rights or freedoms that exist in Canada.

27. This Charter shall be interpreted in a manner consistent with the preservation and enhancement of the multicultural heritage of Canadians.

28. Notwithstanding anything in this Charter, the rights and freedoms referred to in it are guaranteed equally to male and female persons.

29. Nothing in this Charter abrogates or derogates from any rights or privileges guaranteed by or under the Constitution of Canada in respect of denominational, separate or dissentient schools.

30. A reference in this Charter to a province or to the legislative assembly or legislature of a province shall be deemed to include a reference to the Yukon Territory and the Northwest Territories, or to the appropriate legislative authority thereof, as the case may be.

31. Nothing in this Charter extends the legislative powers of any body or authority.

Application of Charter

32. (1) This Charter applies

(a) to the Parliament and government of Canada in respect of all matters within the authority of Parliament including all matters relating to the Yukon Territory and Northwest Territories; and

(b) to the legislature and government of each province in respect of all matters within the authority of the legislature of each province.

(2) Notwithstanding subsection (1), section 15 shall not have effect until three years after this section comes into force.

33. (1) Parliament or the legislature of a province may expressly declare in an Act of Parliament or of the legislature, as the case may be, that the Act or a provision thereof shall operate notwithstanding a provision included in section 2 or sections 7 to 15 of this Charter.

(2) An Act or a provision of an Act in respect of which a declaration made under this sections is in effect shall have such operations as it would have but for the provision of this Charter referred to in the declaration.

(3) A declaration made under subsection (1) shall cease to have effect five years after it comes into force or on such earlier date as may be specified in the declaration.

(4) Parliament or the legislature of a province may re-enact a declaration made under subsection (1).

(5) Subsection (3) applies in respect of a reenactment made under subsection (4).

34. This Part may be cited as the *Canadian Charter of Rights and Freedoms*.

Appendix B

The Work of a Political Scientist

For the political scientist who conducts basic political research in addition to teaching, the goals are to describe, explain, prescribe and forecast political behaviour and political ideas. These goals form the foundations of political enterprise. Ideally, political scientists want to gather enough information to construct *theories* and *models* about political behaviour. Theories enable us to understand complex political behaviours that would otherwise appear to be unconnected. Models are ideal constructs against which researchers can measure how things actually occur to understand how they might be improved. In the process of doing political research, the political scientist uses his or her skills of *intuition*, *common sense,* and the rigorous *scientific method*.

Describing What Happens

The first task in political science is to "get the facts"– to collect relevant information. Descriptions in political science are statements about the behaviour of people and institutions and the conditions under which this behaviour occurs. Describing political events objectively is not as simple as one might think because it requires us to be definite about what we actually see and not what we want or expect to see.

Description is an important learning skill that reduces uncertainty by giving form and character to an event or situation. The researcher must recognize that a situation or event is knowable to the extent that it can be described. Description is a way of reaching out for more information by applying conceptual labels to phenomena, thereby organizing our view of the political world. The process of describing a political event will encourage the researcher to develop mental images or word pictures of a situation, enabling him or her to convert observation into communication.

At the practical level, the scholarly description of political phenomena forces us to ask, "What am I looking at?" Often, the political observer will have no anticipated hypothesis. So asking "what" is very appropriate. Thus, the political scientist's first task is simply to observe the event as it evolves in order to discover what is happening. Once observation is complete, the researcher tries to communicate what has been seen. The traditional approach is to examine other expert evaluations, primary documents, and news reports, and to assemble these findings into a new framework. Scientific method involves a different approach – one that attempts to transform descriptions into *data*. Data are reports of observations as they occur without analysis or interpretation. Data-making procedures refer to the process of identifying in order to co-ordinate hypotheses. In either approach, once observations have been made, the result is called a descriptive study, one that describes *what* happened (in contrast to an explanatory study that specifies *why* it happened).

Explaining What Happens

An orderly understanding of the world of politics proceeds logically from descriptive questions of "what" to explanatory questions of "why." Those who conduct political research want to make sense out of described facts by considering their consequences. Explanation can be conducted on two levels, subjective explanation and scientific explanation.

Subjective explanation involves the use of intuition and common sense to explain an event.

A description of facts is explained through the personal talents and informed judgement of the observer, who applies his or her reasoning faculties to the task at hand. The process of reasoning can be either *inductive* or *deductive*. The inductive reasoning process uses particular events as a starting point and draws general conclusions from them, i.e., individual cases are the basis for constructing generalizations that explain a class of situations or events. By contrast, deductive reasoning begins with a general premise and moves to particular conclusions. If a logical connection can be made between the premise and the conclusions, the latter may be considered as a valid explanation of the event.

In the case of *scientific explanation,* the analyst may use deduction to construct hypotheses based on what is presumed true; the inductive method is then used to verify the hypothesis. No conclusions are accepted until they stand up to the rigours of testing.

Though description must stick to perceivable information, explanation deliberately goes beyond what can be perceived to try to uncover a principle or process or some political relationship that might exist. Inferences and speculations are extremely useful when it comes to looking for explanations.

Prescribing What Happens

Researchers will almost certainly make prescriptive comments without realizing their analytical value in political analysis. Prescription is a function of political inquiry, enabling students of politics to make normative judgements about political goals. The word prescribe means "to lay down as a rule or direction to be followed." For example, prescriptions can be made to evaluate whether family-allowance payments in Canada would be more effective as a selectively targeted program of social assistance; or, if native Canadians are to control their national destiny, should non-native control of reserves be removed so that teaching, policing, and general federal services (e.g., postal) can come under the direct jurisdiction of native Canadians across Canada? These are just two of an infinite number of politically relevant questions that may be considered by students who see the need for policy reform and are willing to conduct research into existing problems to prescribe changes in social direction.

Students need to be made aware of the efficacy of prescriptive research at the grass-roots level. Governments are not always aware of the real needs within each community in Canada. Social scientists, like political scientists and research-oriented social workers, are much closer to local problems and are able to call for government assistance to help resolve social injustices. For example, in Canada, the widespread establishment of "transition houses" to provide shelter and counselling services to battered women and children is a classic example of grass-roots reform initiated by research at the community level. Until the 1980s, domestic violence was largely ignored by governments at all levels. But because of the persistent efforts of Canadian social scientists, social workers, and community leaders, all levels of government in Canada have provided funds for these types of crisis centres. Now in the 1990s, almost every community in Canada has one.

Much of what constitutes political research is not different from the basic kinds of practical thinking and reasoning people use every day in their lives. We observe, organize, classify, and reflect upon daily problems so that we can make decisions and act on them. What distinguishes political research from the resolution of everyday practical problems is the careful use of systematic approaches in political inquiry. Political scientists always proceed tentatively, fully aware that political analysis requires a cautious examination of facts, because hastily drawn conclusions may be proved wrong with further investigation.

Forecasting What Might Happen

A forecast is a statement of the likelihood that a certain event will occur, or that a given relationship will be found. Some political forecasts are based on applying information about the past to future situations or on the belief that a prediction is possible through a rigorous analysis of the present. For many political scientists, predictions are based on an understanding of how events are related.

An inference made to explain political information is really only a hunch until it is tested by predicting that some event will happen if the hunch is true. Whenever we have a hunch about anything we expect that a certain event will result, given certain conditions. An investigator's hunch that candidate A is likely to win a riding may be based on previous patterns of voter behaviour that provide strong indications they will occur again. Forecasting political outcomes is founded on observing actual conditions. Once basic political relationships are understood, many events can be inferred with some certainty.

Ways of Knowing About Politics

Political science is not only what political scientists *do*, but *how* they choose to do it. That is why methods are so important when conducting political research. In a broad sense, methods condition our responses to questions. In a narrow sense, they are the procedures and tools used to answer them. The ways we gather information and solve problems determine the conclusions we draw and the range of actions available to reach those conclusions. There are a few innate skills that almost everyone possesses, namely that of intuition and common sense, which help us learn about the outside world. Together they provide the basis for engaging in a science of political knowledge.

Intuition

Intuition is a way of knowing based on feelings and hunches. For many social scientists, intuition often provides insights and understanding that other ways of knowing do not. Indeed, all political systems have information that is technologically and scientifically inaccessible. We must use our innate skills to get at this kind of information. To the political scientist, facts are not always trustworthy, often requiring the application of intuitive judgement. Policy questions relating to ethics, fairness, and justice readily lend themselves to intuitive knowledge because in most cases, it is difficult, if not impossible, to quantify these matters.

We all use intuition when making political judgements. We feel that a particular leadership candidate will not be good for the country or that the adoption of a certain policy will assist in economic recovery. Although intuition is seen as a non-scientific way of knowing, it has become a widely practiced technique for political forecasting. Even when conducting scientific inquiry, intuition may aid the researcher in developing hypotheses, generating data, and evaluating results. Often intuitive connections can give students clues that lead to accurate, testable knowledge.

Common Sense

Common sense is another useful tool of political inquiry for both the student and the professional practitioner. The Latin phrase *sensus communis* means the common application of all the senses to make sound judgements independent of any specialized knowledge. Common sense is the pursuit of knowledge based on experience and observation. What we have experienced in the past may provide us with valuable insights into political and social behaviour.

Common sense is the application of previous experience to a current problem – and it often includes the use of intuition as well as the knowledge we gain from experts. Common sense is what is always applied when uncertainty results from inadequate data or imprecise measurement. In such cases, common sense proves to be more reliable than incomplete scientific knowledge.

Every day, journalists and political scientists apply common sense to questions of value judgements and standards of public conduct. Normative questions often resist the tests of science because they cannot be proved either true or false.

For these circumstances, common sense is an important skill for prescribing solutions. Here the practitioner suggests what *ought* to be done in order to perfect or ameliorate a political problem. Without common sense, it is unlikely that political scientists could identify an expected relationship between political events or forecast developments in the political arena.

Science

Generally, students are curious about why we call this discipline "political science." One can answer by pointing out that one way of knowing about politics that is distinguishable from all others is the scientific method. This method as applied to politics is the most conservative approach to knowledge because all information is doubted by the scientist until it has been proved reliable by standardized methods of inquiry. Students of politics have a particularly difficult task because political behaviour constantly changes. The popularity of a political party will vary from month to month and may be affected by a wide range of events, from an offensive statement by a member, to the selection of a new leader. In this regard, the political "scientists" will make statements that are always either probable or tentative in nature. In fact, no scientific statement can be considered firm or absolute until it has been tested and verified by voters using similar tests.

This does not mean that social scientists are not sure of anything. But it does tell us that those who apply science to politics acknowledge that (a) there is a body of political knowledge that is attainable and understandable, and (b) there are verifiable methods of accurately assessing this knowledge. However, the research social scientist does not stop here. In order to discover regular relationships among political phenomena, the political "scientist" also assumes the following:

■ Nothing in politics "just happens," it can be explained if research is conducted.

■ Observation and classification of information leads to the discovery of patterns and regularities.

■ Being objective about what is observed means letting the facts fall where they may without incorporating the researcher's personal expectations.

■ Using systematic and standardized approaches will usually produce verifiable political knowledge.

At the outset, it is important to tell students that political science, as a science, is a young discipline. It has not been able to produce laws or principles of political behaviour; it has developed only what are called *pre-theories*.

Political science has advanced many pre-theories that achieve the middle range of theory building, but no convincing general theories. To date, pre-theories from political science research tell us which of the factors in a given situation are significant; they provide us with frameworks for classifying and interpreting what we observe, and for ascribing meaning to it.

Science is unique among the ways of knowing because it has succeeded in constructing theories in many fields of human knowledge. A *scientific theory* is a set of concepts and presuppositions that is used to explain and predict phenomena with certainty. Theories may be thought of as sets of hypotheses that have been proved to be interrelated and always connected. In time, scientists no longer actively question the validity of theories, but regard them as "laws" and principles." Thus, laws are well-established theories whose truths are taken to be self-evident. Students should know that because of the difficulties of measuring human behaviour, political theories are ordinarily expressed only in terms of hypotheses rather than as invariant laws.

Figure B.1 demonstrates the process of theory building. The first level of the paradigm refers to all political phenomena as they occur. It is the world of politics as it happens, a world of seemingly disorganized, disparate events that unfold each day. From out of this apparently formless political world, a political analyst may decide to investigate elections and the factors that affect voting behaviour.

This selection moves the researcher to the second level of the paradigm, where a systematic approach to the research target can be applied. Observations of elections lead the analyst to note that people behave differently, and that these differences may be viewed as whole classes of similar events. By organizing and classifying these events, the researcher begins to detect regularities that appear to relate significantly to voting behaviour. At this point – the third level of the paradigm – the analyst considers which variables might be significant. A *variable* is any characteristic of an object having two or more values that may vary over time. Some variables have only two values (dichotomous): For example, the characteristic "gender" has two values: male and female. But "political participation" is a characteristic that is multi-valued, i.e., "interest," "involvement," "political information," and "party identification" all *co-vary,* or change together. For research purposes, variables are usually classified as two types: the *dependent vari-*

able, which is what you want to explain (in this case "voting behaviour"), and the *independent variables,* those that explain the dependent variable because they are assumed to have a particular effect on it. For example, the researcher finds that age, education, income, occupation, religion, location, and gender are all independent variables that have an effect on voting behaviour. The researcher may also discover that other independent variables, such as the type of electoral system, number of political parties, issues, leadership, and the media, have a special relationship to voting behaviour in any particular country or region.

The next step involves the formulation and testing of *hypotheses.* It is here that variables are linked in order to determine causation or correlations. A hypothesis is a guess at the interrelationship of variables, and generalizations are statements that express that interrelationship. In this example, the political researcher wants to know to what degree the independent variables are causing the dependent one: how age, education, income, etc., co-vary in some regular way with voting behaviour. The task is to discover with some certainty whether, for example, voting behaviour varies with income.

At the next stage, political researchers attempt to confirm or reject their hypothesis by applying appropriate testing procedures to the propositions. Testing involves the use of standard measuring instruments to determine the acceptability of information. Once testing is complete, the researcher is prepared to offer a generalization that explains the dependent variable. For example, in federal or provincial elections in Canada, many people vote consistently *against* a government rather than *for* it. When many generalizations are interrelated and proved over time, they elevate scientific inquiry to the final level, that of theories as laws.

In spite of its shortcomings with respect to the fluctuating nature of human political behaviour,

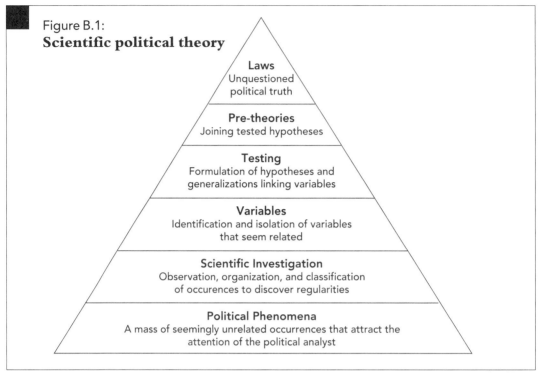

Figure B.1:
Scientific political theory

Laws
Unquestioned
political truth

Pre-theories
Joining tested hypotheses

Testing
Formulation of hypotheses and
generalizations linking variables

Variables
Identification and isolation of variables
that seem related

Scientific Investigation
Observation, organization, and classification
of occurences to discover regularities

Political Phenomena
A mass of seemingly unrelated occurrences that attract the
attention of the political analyst

the scientific method of inquiry will always be used for political research. Governments have increasingly employed it to determine policy, and social scientists are committed to its use for its objective qualities.

The Process of Political Research

Stages

Every research project – regardless of the problem being studied or whether it is scientific or non-scientific – requires five basic stages of development:

1. Identification and selection of the problem
2. Planning and research design
3. Gathering information and data
4. Analyzing information and data
5. Interpretation of research findings

These stages are interdependent and form a circular process (figure B.2). It is obvious why stage 5 is inextricably linked to stage 1: if the research cannot explain or resolve the original problem, it will be necessary to re-state the project. At each level in the construction of scientific political theory (figure B.1), the political scientist engages in these fundamental techniques of research. But in studies where the scientific method is not used, the interpretation of research findings is based on the experience and good judgement of the researcher. Even without the possibility of scientifically verifiable tests, the researcher must move systematically through each stage of political research. By examining each stage, the relationships in figure B.2 will have a more practical meaning.

Choosing a Research Problem

In selecting a research project or accepting a commission to do one, the political scientist must judge the relevance of the topic. Regardless of the topic is selected, a series of questions needs to be asked:

- What do we want/need to know?
- Why do we need to know it?
- Where can we find the information?
- How can we obtain it?
- What information sources already exist at the municipal, provincial, and federal levels?
- How can we most advantageously analyze and present the information?
- How will the information obtained be used?
- What will the information cost?
- How long will the project take to complete?

Answering these questions enables the researcher to focus on the overall objectives of the project and to determine its feasibility and relevance. The next stage is to consider the methods by which the information can be obtained practically and economically.

Observation

Once a political problem is selected, the researcher begins the process of observation. The purpose of observation is to gather as much information as possible about the topic by direct contact with the events and people being studied. Sometimes a researcher simply watches what is going on without getting involved in the political event. The researcher does not intervene in the production of new information and plays the passive role of an observer. This is sometimes referred to as *detached observation*. *Participant observation* refers to situations in which an observer joins in the events and interactions to be studied.

In the initial stages of research, observation can be carried out by simply watching, listening, and interviewing. But the most common mode of observation practiced by social scientists is *content analysis*. Here, the investigator researches a topic by systematically examining documents such as books, newspapers, magazines, government publications, and radio and television programs. The exercise of content analysis is important for beginning students because they explore the current literature for a particular quality or feature that can be classified or categorized. First used during the Second World War to decode propaganda messages, content analysis is a valuable laboratory tool for examining official policy statements and speeches.

Like all methods of observation, content analysis is evaluated on a subjective basis, so the type of document selected for a particular study may not be the only approach to the variable under study. But it is important to remember that scientific research to collect and analyze new data is not always possible, and content analysis allows the researcher to analyze many research topics by observing information already collected and compiled.

Research Design

Once an investigator is satisfied that enough observation data has been gathered, he or she should then proceed to organize it. At this stage, whether generating new data or engaging in traditional normative analysis, it is necessary to develop an outline or plan of the project. In designing any research project, one needs to create an explicit outline using headings and subheadings. The outline is a guide to the research, showing the steps that must be followed, from the introduction of the topic, to the body of the research, and finally to the summary and conclusion of the results. Writing down the steps and procedures to be followed can serve as a checklist for frequent reference.

The research design will also determine whether the problem selected is amenable to study. Is it possible for the researcher to go beyond observation? What are the empirical dimensions of the research? Is it necessary to

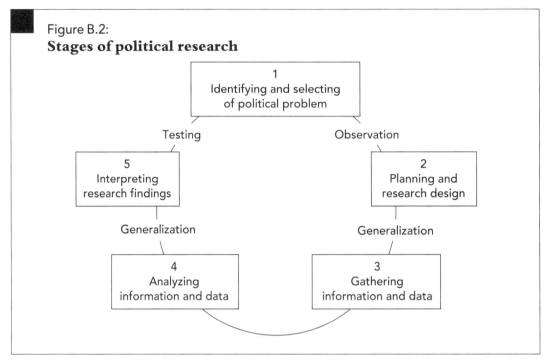

Figure B.2:
Stages of political research

generate new data or can we synthesize information already in existence? Are there normative questions involved? Is it possible to prescribe a solution from what we know? Thus, the overall plan of the research project amounts to a statement of intent, preparing the outline, determining the use of data, and showing the method of analysis.

But the research design may also be thought of as a program that guides the researcher through the process of collecting, analyzing, and interpreting information. It may be necessary to change parts of the design as the research is conducted, but usually the general framework remains intact. The research design is a constant reference point for the researcher throughout the course of study. It is a model of proof that permits the investigator to draw inferences about the causal relations of the variables to be considered. No student of political science can overlook this stage of the process of research. It is the most important exercise in advanced research methods.

Collection and Classification of Information

A great deal of the researcher's time is spent collecting, interpreting, and classifying facts, statistics and other forms of information that provide the raw material for analysis. The first encounter with information occurs by simply observing what interests you. But at some point in the process of collecting information, it will be necessary to begin the orderly arrangement of data in categories and classes. Usually this is done according to perceived similarities or differences in the various objects of inquiry.

All social scientists use concepts to classify information. Students should think of a *concept* as a unit of meaning. It is the way our mind organizes different stimuli into a single group or class. A concept can be likened to a box with a label on it, a box in which a range of experience can be classified so that a glance at a particular person or event recalls the pertinent label and gives meaning to a person or event perceived. Hence, a concept is a convenient way to summarize and categorize an array of detail. The concept *nation*, for example, subsumes Ukrainians, Poles, Iroquois and many other peoples. Note that concepts do not exist in the external world. There is no such thing as a nation that exists separate from Ukrainians and Poles, or some specific instance of the concept. The significance of the concept *nation* stems from its ability to transfer information in the form of images about experiences in the empirical world.

For purposes of research, concepts help us construct assumptions about the relationship of variables. A concept such as social class or income may be connected to other concepts such as political participation. Since the smallest unit of theory is the concept, the addition of a number of concepts may lead to the construction of a system of interrelated assumptions about which hypotheses can be tested. The process of building concepts (conceptualization) links observation to explanation and prediction.

Sometimes it is possible to gather information from data that has already been collected. In Canada, political scientists frequently use information from public records such as newspapers, legal documents, minutes of committee meetings, court records, voter registration lists, and annual reports of private and public corporations. A very important source of data for political scientists is the national census, which is taken every five years, in years ending in 1 and 6. Statistics Canada summarizes and publishes data collected by the Government of Canada each year. There is also the *Canada Year Book*, which summarizes social and political data and is widely used by social scientists. Each provincial government publishes its own reports and statistics, usually on an annual basis.

Ways of Gathering Information

When there are no available sources of political information, the political scientist is confronted with the problem of producing data. The researcher can solve this problem by using any one, or a combination, of the three primary methods of survey research: the face-to-face interview, the mail questionnaire, and the telephone survey. Survey research as a method of compiling information is not a recent enterprise.

The commercial polling firms started by George Gallup and Louis Harris developed and refined the most modern methods of survey research presently practised. These commercial polls have proved to be an invaluable source of data for secondary analysis and their techniques have been adapted to private research in the social sciences. More recently, with the advent of microcomputers and word processing technology, the scientific refinement of survey research has spread to universities, where social scientists can conduct survey analysis on every imaginable topic.

The Personal Interview

Most studies show that the face-to-face interview gives the researcher an 80–85% chance of getting the information wanted from a respondent. This means that if one is determined to generate one's own data, the personal interview is a highly dependable method of gathering information. One can observe as well as control the situation to guarantee the flow of pertinent information. The interviewer is able to clarify any confusing questions and note the reactions of the respondent. This is a great advantage when conducting research.

Political scientists use two types of interviews. *Structural interviews* are those in which the questions, their wording, and their sequence are predetermined so that each respondent is exposed to an identical experience. The *unstructured* or *nondirective* interview allows the interviewer and the respondent to discuss the replies openly. No fixed set of questions is employed and they are not necessarily asked in a specific order. The interviewer may probe or pursue an interesting line of thought that may not have been anticipated when the study was first initiated.

With either the structured or unstructured interview, a political scientist can poll any level of political inquiry, such as public confidence in government, differences among election candidates, or attitudes of political alienation held by the unemployed. Each of the two types of interviews offers both advantages and limitations to the interviewer. If the research objective is to measure actual differences of political opinion among respondents, then the structural interview is the better choice. But if the purpose of the research is to discover what opinions or events are significant to the respondent, then the unstructured interview should be used.

The success of all interviews is determined by the appropriate wording of the questions. Questions should be designed to motivate the respondent so that the information necessary for formulating hypotheses is obtained. Since words are usually subject to different interpretations, careful attention should be paid to constructing clear and concise questions. The cardinal rules should be that the wording of the question is understandable by a respondent with an eighth-grade education.

In most cases, the researcher will choose to ask either *open-ended* or *fixed-alternative* questions. Open-ended questions are unrestricted in that they are not followed by any degrees of choice or predetermined replies. For example, the question. "Do you favour increasing or decreasing Canada's development assistance to Third World states?" is an open-ended question that does not force the respondent to follow preconceived answers. The respondent is free to express his or her own thoughts using individual style and language. In a fixed-alternative question, the respondent is given a set of answers from which to choose the reply that most closely reflects his or her own views. A fixed-al-

ternative question on affirmative action would appear as follows:

In a case where a man or a woman can do a job equally well, I'd pick the woman for the job.

- ❑ Strongly agree   ❑ Disagree
- ❑ Agree   ❑ Strongly disagree
- ❑ Undecided

In any interview, the sequence of questions is important. Two types of questions frequently used by social scientists engaged in survey research are the *funnel sequence* and the *inverted funnel sequence*. In the funnel sequence, each question relates to a previous one and successive questions tend to get narrower in scope. The following questions demonstrate the funnel sequence of questioning:

(1) What do you think are some of the most important political problems facing Canada today? (2) Of the problems you have just mentioned, which do you think is the most important one? (3) Where have you obtained most of the information about this problem? (4) Do you have any political science training?

In the inverted funnel sequence, the questions are still all related, but the interviewer first asks the narrower questions then proceeds to more generalized ones. It is sometimes better to begin with narrower questions because they are easier to answer than the more generalized ones. In addition, the respondent may feel more relaxed with questions that, at the outset, allow simple or concise responses.

The Mail Questionnaire

In survey research, the mail questionnaire is a more economical way to gather information. You can mail a questionnaire, but you cannot mail an interviewer. There is no need to train interviewers to get the job done. The costs incurred are in planning, sampling, duplicating, providing stamped self-addressed envelopes, and mailing. All the researcher worries about is the response rate. To what extent will the mail questionnaire yield the results that are almost guaranteed by the personal interview? Some studies show that the expected response to the mail questionnaire will range from 20 to 40 percent. The response rate for a personal interview approaches 100 percent; so, after weighing lower costs and simplicity against the risks of lower response, the interviewer must decide which survey method is most suitable.

Usually the mail questionnaire is used when the questions require some careful thought and consideration. If a question is embarrassing to the respondent, a response is more likely to be given on a private questionnaire than in an interview. Other questions may require the respondent to consult private documents or to confer with other people, all of which takes time and is more suited to the format of a mail questionnaire.

The design of the questions is paramount and must be carefully prepared, especially since the questionnaire cannot control the response in the way an interviewer can. Many researchers find that leading questions or statements help to clarify the meaning of words and the direction of the inquiry. For example, a researcher who wants to gather data on attitudes of political alienation and powerlessness might construct leading statements such as the following to measure the responses according to a scale of intensity.

1. Sometimes I have the feeling that politicians are using me.
❑ Strongly agree ❑ Disagree
❑ Agree ❑ Strongly disagree
❑ Undecided

2. I don't feel that the government cares very much about what people like me say.
❑ Strongly agree ❑ Disagree
❑ Agree ❑ Strongly disagree
❑ Undecided

3. It doesn't matter which party is in power, big interests get better treatment from the government than ordinary people like me do.
❑ Strongly agree ❑ Disagree
❑ Agree ❑ Strongly disagree
❑ Undecided

4. Generally speaking, governments have lost touch with the problems that most people have to face.
❑ Strongly agree ❑ Disagree
❑ Agree ❑ Strongly disagree
❑ Undecided

5. More and more, I feel that the federal government has lost control over what's happening in the country today.
❑ Strongly agree ❑ Disagree
❑ Agree ❑ Strongly disagree
❑ Undecided

These statements will clearly lead a person to respond after some thought and private consideration. Let us score the responses in the following way: Strongly agree = 4; Agree = 3; Uncertain = 2; Disagree = 1; and Strongly disagree = 0.

If a respondent answers "Strongly agree" to all five statements, a total score of 20 would indicate a high degree of alienation. A respondent who answers "Strongly disagree" to all five will have a total score of 0, indicating no feelings of alienation. In reality, most people will score between these two extremes, and the researcher will have to define the degree of alienation in relation to the scoring system.

The researcher who uses the mail questionnaire is aware that if the printed instructions are confusing, the findings will be adversely affected. Moreover, the replies are final and there is no immediate opportunity to probe unusual answers nor to appraise the non-verbal behaviour of the respondents. There is no way of knowing for sure whether the person sampled actually completed the questionnaire or whether assistance was provided by others. The risks of conducting research by mailed questionnaires must be considered before the decision is made to gather important research data in this manner.

Telephone Surveys

Telephone surveys provide another impersonal method of collecting research data. Like other survey methods, the telephone survey has advantages and disadvantages. It is often a convenient, inexpensive, and rapid way to contact people for information. The telephone is a particularly good tool for reaction interviews before and after an important piece of legislation is passed. Radio and television research frequently relies upon the telephone survey for information on the impact of certain programs, including political broadcasts and debates. This research method provides a high degree of immediacy on issues and personalities affecting a given community. For the political scientist, the instantaneous nature of the telephone survey is valuable for testing political attitudes before an issue has been analyzed by the media. In addition, there is a much greater chance of contacting people directly involved in, or responsible for, an event at the time it is happening than by using the personal interview or the questionnaire.

However, the researcher who uses the telephone interview is usually faced with a sampling problem. Some households do not have telephones and many people have unlisted numbers. Often the researcher must continue to select random phone numbers until the sample is complete because people are out of town, refuse the interview, or have unlisted telephone service. Also, because some people cannot afford to have phones, the sample that can be reached by telephone may under-represent the disadvantaged and over-represent the affluent. Although the number of households without phones is decreasing each year, the researcher must be aware of the potential bias the sample might have if the telephone survey is adopted as a normal way of gathering data.

Sampling

Ideally, social scientists would like to learn as much about an entire population as possible before they formulate generalizations and make predictions about behaviour. Rarely is it possible to study every unit of analysis in a population. For example, it would be impossible for a political scientist to contact all 18 million Canadians who make up the electorate in order to determine how they will vote in a national election. But with a sample of 2000, properly selected, a researcher can learn about as much of the political intentions of the entire electorate as if each person had been personally interviewed. Sampling makes it possible to get information about a large population from observations of only a randomly selected part of that population.

A "population" may be defined as all of the units from which a researcher selects a limited sample of information in order to make general scientific statements. A research population may consist of all native people in a given community, e.g., from 415 on Cape Breton Island to 425,000 in all of Canada. It is not possible, or economically practical, to survey 425,000 people or perhaps even as few as 415 people, but the researcher can still have confidence in the findings by using a *representative random sample* of either population. A representative sample is a sub-part or subset of units that contains the same characteristics as the entire population under study. Random sampling means that each unit of the population has an equal chance of being selected by the researcher. If a researcher conducting a political survey wanted to cut corners by also interviewing the brothers and sisters of people randomly selected, the sample would be contaminated because these people had been included for convenience and were not randomly chosen.

Sometimes the unique characteristics of a population demand that the researcher use a *stratified sample*. For example, it is possible to draw a random sample of Canadians without selecting a representative French-speaking component in the survey. Because approximately 28 percent of Canada's population is French-speaking, the researcher would stratify the selection process so that 28 percent of those randomly selected would speak French. In this way, stratified sampling is a method of obtaining a greater degree of representativeness from special populations and of decreasing the probability of sample error. The number of units chosen for the sub-part must be proportional to the total number in each stratum of the population. Because the ethnic composition of Canadian society is 44.7 percent Anglos, 28.6 percent French, and 26.7 percent other groups, a researcher should stratify the sample in the same proportions.

Usually random samples can provide very accurate estimates on the population they select. When they fail, it is because the sample was not really randomly selected or because the sample was drawn too early in relation to the event. Gallup-type polls have tended to error in forecasting election results by prematurely taking a sample. This was particularly true in the 1948 U.S. presidential election and for the British elections of 1951, 1970, and 1974. In Canada, Gallup forecasts failed for this reason in predicting the Diefenbaker victory of 1957, the return of the Liberals to power in the 1980 federal elections, and the extent to which the Progressive Conservatives would lose seats in the 1993 federal elections. At the provincial levels in Canada, Gallup-type polls have been much less successful in predicting election results. But as a general rule, the successes of the Gallup and Harris polls have far outnumbered their failures.

The widespread use of the microcomputer has allowed a growing number of individual Canadian scholars to enter the polling field. Personal computers are excellent data-processing tools for survey research. The individual researcher can use one to store lists of names, addresses, and phone numbers of people to be interviewed. The computer can also be used to assign random numbers or to randomly select units of analysis for survey purposes. Using a computer, the political scientist can present, interpret, and analyze vast amounts of survey materials to a degree that would otherwise only be possible within the confines of a well-staffed corporate organization.

Suggested Readings

Robert Campbell and Leslie Pal, *The Real Worlds of Canadian Politics* (Orchard Park, NY: Broadview Press, 1994).

Maria Carland and Daniel Spatz Jr., *Careers in International Affairs* (Washington, D.C.: Georgetown University, Institute for the Study of Diplomacy, 1991).

Mary H. Curzon, ed., *Careers and the Study of Political Science: A Guide for Undergraduates*, 5th ed. (Washington, D.C.: American Political Science Association, 1991).

Chava Frankford-Nachimias and David Nachimias, *Research Methods in Social Sciences* (New York: St. Martin's Press, 1992).

Robert Heineman, et. al., *The World of the Policy Analyst* (Chatham, NJ: Chatham House Publishers, 1990).

Index

(t) = table, **(f)** = figure

Palestine Liberation Organization (PLO), 400, 463, 479

Pan-American Institute of Geography and History (PAIGH), 472

Parliamentary government: and accountability, 174, 175-176, 211, 238-239; authorization in, 238; British prototype, 231; Budget Speech, 175; components of, **170(f)**, 171; and evolution of political parties, 361; fusion of powers, 171, 172, 206, 208, 239, 240, 293; general audit function, 174-175, 177, 240; head of government, 171, 208, 210-212; head of state, 171, 208; members of parliament, 171, 177, 237, 242; opposition, 172-174, 175, 244, 364; parliamentary executive, 171-172, 208, 239; Question Period, 175, 241; parliamentary secretaries, 288; residual power of, 32; responsibility in, 238, 239; Speech from the Throne, 174, 203, 209, 215; shadow cabinet, 173

Partial Test Ban Treaty (PTBT) (1963), 575

Parti Québécois (PQ), 117, 118, 364, **471(t)**, 374

Party for the Commonwealth of Canada, **373(t)**, 374

Peace: activism, 559-561; challenge of, 556-561; defined, 557; through democracy, 556; and disarmament, 559-560; groups, 559-560; and individual responsibility, 561; and nuclear-weapon-free zone, 559-560; socialist view, 557; in space, 573-575; and supranational government, 178; zone of, 560. See also Arms control; Disarmament; Nuclear war

Peace of Westphalia (1648), 131, 132, 540

Peacekeeping: Cdn., 154, 207, 461, 464, 559; international, 152, 463-464, 558-559. See also United Nations

Pearson, Lester B., 387, 488

Persian Gulf war, 136, 152, 221, 461, 531, 538, 560, 569, 590

Plan International Canada, 476

Plato, 55, 56, 161, 164

Political awareness, stages of development: adolescents, 34, 36, 39; adults, 34, 36-37; children, 34, 35-36, 39

Political corruption, 11, 59, 87, 202, 203, 241-243, 273-274, 417-418, 528, 529

Political culture: as attitudes, 9, 11; as beliefs, 9, **9(f)**, 11; as customs, 8-9; differing, 10, 11; defined, 8-13, 166; elements of, 8-10; as expectations, 9; ideologies in, 84; qualities of, 10-11, 168; as skills, 10; as traditions, 9; as values, 9, 11

Political demonstrations, 403-405, 414

Political opinion. See Public opinion

Political parties: *aprista* parties, 478; authoritarian systems, 186, 222, 362; competition among, 41, 361, 362, 369, 370, 372-373; conservative, 389-391; defined, 362; and finance, 380-381; functions of, 365-368; future of, 396-397; historic roots of, 361; identification toward, 36, 379; ideological, 84, 363, 367, 376, 478-479; indigenous, 363-364; interest aggregation, 367; and interest articulation, 366-367; and leadership recruitment, 366; left-wing, 368; liberal; 385-386; and legislative representation, 368; minor (Cdn.), list of, **373(t)**; number of (global), 368; membership in, 368, 279-380; as opposition, 362; organization and structure of, 377-381; and party-list system, 422-423; and policy, 367-368, 369; right-wing, 368; and political socialization, 40-41, 365-366; pragmatic/brokerage, 362-363; revolutionary, 364; socialist, 382-383; special- interest, 364; in totalitarian systems, 224-225; types of, 362-365. See also Names of specific parties; Names of specific ideologies

Political party systems: classification of, 368-377; multi-party competitive, 367, 375-377; one-party dominant, 258, 376; one-party states, 362, 369-370; two-party competitive, 370

Political science: as academic discipline, 69-70; in the Age of Reason, 60-61; and allied fields of study, 71-76; and anthropology, 72, 75; in authoritarian systems, 77; and behaviouralism, 64-66, 76, 166; in Canada, 67-71; defined, 53, 60; in democratic states, 76; and economics, 71, 72, 75; in the Enlighten-ment, 61-62; evolution of, 55-62; and geography (discipline), 72-73; Greek contribution to, 55-57, 66; and history, 71, 73; journals and scholarly works, 62, 63, 69, 76; in the international system, 76-77; in the Middle Ages, 57-58; and philosophy (discipline), 71, 73-74; and post-behaviouralism, 66-67, 76; and psychology (discipline), 74, 75, 166; during the Reformation, 59-60; during the Renaissance, 58-59; Roman contribution to, 57; and social work, 75; and sociology, 71, 74-75, 166; and statistics (discipline), 75-76; subject areas (academic), 71; in totalitarian states, 77; traditionalism in, 63-64, 76; in the U.S., 62-67

Political socialization: of adolescents, 34, 36, 39; of adults, 34, 36-37, 74; agents of, 37-41, **38(f)**; in authoritarian systems, 201; and behavior, 34, 37, 74; as brainwashing, 37; of children, 45, 35-36, 39, 74, 201; defined, 34; and elections, 416-417; and the family, 39, 85; goals of, 35; and governments, 40; and interest groups, 41; and mass media, 40; and peer groups, 39-40; and political opinions, 36, 37, 38, 39; and political parties, 36, 40-41; and schools, 39; and self-definition, 35; in totalitarian systems, 34

Political sociology, 75